Research Methods
for Business Students

Research Methods for Business Students

Dr Mark NK Saunders
Dr Philip Lewis
Dr Adrian Thornhill

PITMAN
PUBLISHING

London · Hong Kong · Johannesburg · Melbourne · Singapore · Washington DC

PITMAN PUBLISHING
128 Long Acre, London WC2E 9AN
Tel: +44 (0)171 447 2000
Fax: +44 (0)171 240 5771

A Division of Pearson Professional Limited

First published in Great Britain in 1997

ISBN 0 273 62017 7

British Library Cataloguing in Publication Data
A CIP catalogue record for this book can be obtained from the British Library.

10 9 8 7 6 5 4 3 2

Typeset by M Rules
Printed and bound in Great Britain by Clays Ltd, St Ives plc

The Publishers' policy is to use paper manufactured from substantable forests.

CONTENTS

PREFACE

The idea for this book grew from our own experiences of undertaking and teaching business and management research. Over the past six years we have undertaken research together, taught research methods as a team and been involved in joint project supervisions at both undergraduate and postgraduate levels. These experiences have helped to develop our knowledge, understanding and skills as researchers and, in particular, our awareness of the realities of undertaking research. They have also provided numerous insights into the needs and wants of student researchers.

In our teaching and supervision we have used a number of research methods textbooks. However, none of these have fully met our students' needs or our needs as tutors. This was sometimes because of their focus on either quantitative or qualitative research, or due to relatively brief discussions in relation to particular aspects such as reviewing the literature or writing the project report. In addition, our students felt that there was sometimes a tendency to present research as a straightforward, unproblematic affair, rather than the messy process which they experienced.

Few of the textbooks we encountered made use of either case studies or examples to overcome the problems and pitfalls that are part of the process. Our students commented that few included activities which they could undertake to practise their skills and test their understanding. Clear guidelines to make the process as straightforward as possible were also rarely provided. Similarly, the application of appropriate information technology was rarely considered as an integral part of the text. Where this was considered the discussion was often software specific, rather than discussing general principles that would enable the researcher to utilise information technology most effectively. As such, we felt that the undergraduate and postgraduate student researcher was left unprepared for the realities of research.

When faced with these reservations about the suitability of existing textbooks for our purposes, we responded to the challenge set by our students. This book is that response! The book could not, however, have been written without considerable help from our students, friends, colleagues and families. They have contributed through their encouragement and ideas. Many of these ideas are reflected in the cases and worked examples used in the book, for which they kindly gave their permission.

We would like to thank our students, in particular the 1994–5 and 1995–6 cohorts of students on the management Master's research methods course, for their advice and constructive criticism on all of the chapters. Our colleagues at Cheltenham & Gloucester College of Higher Education also deserve thanks for their interest and assistance in reviewing parts of this book; in particular Lynnette Bailey, Barry Baker, Tony Beasley, Fiona Campbell, Jacquelyn Collinson, Valerie Cowley, Huw Davies, Sue Davis, David Dawson,

Brian Eaton, Andrew Gibbons, Andy Guppy (now at Liverpool John Moores University), Martin Jenkins, Jim Keane, Alison McGregor, Mike Millmore, Sheila Ryan, John Wilkin and Christine Williams.

Our thanks are also due to our head of department Paul Taylor for his support, and to our commissioning editor Kara Regan for her constructive comments and never-ending enthusiasm throughout the entire process.

Finally, our thanks to Jane, Jenny, Jan, Jemma, Benjamin, Andrew and Katie for putting up with the long hours when we were slaves to our wordprocessors. We hope you will find that it was worth the effort.

MNKS
PL
AT

September 1996

CONTRIBUTORS

Authors

Philip Lewis, BA, MSc, PG Dip M, MIPD, Cert Ed, PhD, is a Principal Lecturer in Human Resource Management (HRM) in the Department of Business and Finance at Cheltenham & Gloucester College of Higher Education. He teaches HRM to postgraduate, undergraduate and professional courses and is course leader for the MA in Management of Human Resources. His main research interest is in reward management. He has published articles on reward management, training and employee participation. Prior to working in higher education Philip was a training adviser with the Distributive Industry Training Board.

Mark NK Saunders, BA, MSc, PGCE, PhD, is a Senior Lecturer in Research Methods and Human Resource Management in the Department of Business and Finance at Cheltenham & Gloucester College of Higher Education. Prior to joining the College he was the Principal Research Officer for Hereford and Worcester Social Services. Mark is Research Co-ordinator for the Department of Business and Finance. He teaches research methods and quantitative methods to postgraduate, undergraduate and professional students, as well as supervising research degrees. He is co-author of a book on business statistics and has published on research methods, employee recruitment and mobility, and redundancy management. He has also undertaken consultancy in both the public and private sectors.

Adrian Thornhill, BA, PGCE, PhD, Grad IPD, is a Senior Lecturer in Human Resource Management (HRM) in the Department of Business and Finance at Cheltenham & Gloucester College of Higher Education. He teaches HRM to postgraduate, undergraduate and professional courses and is involved in research degree supervision. He also teaches research methods. Adrian's main research interest is related to managing organisational downsizing and redundancy, on which he has co-written a book. He has published articles on redundancy management, training and employee involvement. He has undertaken consultancy in both public and private sectors.

Contributors

Lynnette Bailey is a Subject Librarian with responsibility for Education at Cheltenham & Gloucester College of Higher Education.

Tony Beasley is a Lecturer in Accountancy in the Department of Business and Finance at Cheltenham & Gloucester College of Higher Education.

Fiona Campbell is a Postgraduate Research Student in the Department of Business and Finance at Cheltenham & Gloucester College of Higher Education.

Valerie Cowley is a Senior Lecturer in Public Relations and Marketing in the Department of Business and Finance at Cheltenham & Gloucester College of Higher Education.

Huw Davies is a Senior Lecturer in Operations Management in the Department of Business and Finance at Cheltenham & Gloucester College of Higher Education.

David Dawson is a Postgraduate Research Student in the Department of Business and Finance at Cheltenham & Gloucester College of Higher Education.

Andy Guppy is the Reader in Applied Psychology in the Centre for Applied Psychology at Liverpool John Moores University. He was formerly the Reader in Organisational Behaviour in the Department of Business and Finance at Cheltenham & Gloucester College of Higher Education.

Martin Jenkins is a Senior Subject Librarian with responsibility for Business and Management at Cheltenham & Gloucester College of Higher Education.

Jim Keane is a Senior Lecturer in Financial Services in the Department of Business and Finance at Cheltenham & Gloucester College of Higher Education.

Alison McGregor is a Lecturer in Ethics and Financial Services in the Department of Business and Finance at Cheltenham & Gloucester College of Higher Education.

John Wilkin is a Postgraduate Research Student in the Department of Education at Cheltenham & Gloucester College of Higher Education.

Christine Williams is a Principal Lecturer in Marketing and Operations Management in the Department of Business and Finance at Cheltenham & Gloucester College of Higher Education.

CHAPTER 1

Introduction

1.1 THE AIMS OF THIS BOOK

This book is designed to help you undertake a research project, whether you are an under-graduate or postgraduate student of business and management, or a manager. It provides a clear guide on how to undertake research as well as highlighting the realities of under-taking research, including the more common pitfalls. The book is written as an introductory text to provide you with a guide to the research process and with the neces-sary knowledge and skills to undertake a piece of research, from thinking of a suitable topic to writing your project report. As such, you will find it useful as a manual or handbook on how to tackle your research project.

After reading the book you will have been introduced to and explored a range of strate-gies and techniques with which you could tackle your research project. Equally important, you will know that there is no one best method for undertaking all research. You will be able to make an informed choice about the strategies and methods that are most suitable to your own research project, and be able to justify this choice. In reading the book you will have been introduced to the more frequently used techniques for analysing different types of data, have had a chance to practise them, and have been enabled to make a rea-soned choice regarding which to use. When selecting and using these techniques you will be aware of the contribution that the appropriate use of information technology can make to your research.

1.2 THE PURPOSE OF BUSINESS AND MANAGEMENT RESEARCH

People undertake research in order to find things out in a systematic way, thereby increas-ing their knowledge (Jankowicz, 1995). It therefore follows that business and management research involves undertaking systematic research to find out things about business and management. Two phrases are important in this definition: 'systematic research' and 'to find out'. 'Systematic' suggests that research is based on logical relationships and not just beliefs (Ghauri *et al.*, 1995). As part of this your research will involve an explanation of the methods used to collect the data, argue why the results obtained are meaningful and explain any limitations that are associated with them. 'Finding out' suggests a multiplicity of possible purposes for your research. These may include describing, explaining, understanding, criticising and analysing (Ghauri *et al.*, 1995).

Easterby-Smith *et al.* (1991) argue that three things combine to make business and management a distinctive focus for research:

- the way in which managers (and researchers) draw on knowledge developed by other disciplines;
- the fact that managers tend to be powerful and busy people. As a consequence they are unlikely to allow research access unless they can see personal or commercial advantages;
- the requirement for the research to have some practical consequence. This means it needs either to contain the potential for taking some form of action or to take account of the practical consequences of the findings.

Thus not only does business and management research need to provide findings which advance knowledge, it also needs to provide a procedure for solving managerial problems and addressing business issues (Gill and Johnson, 1991). This is not to say that the satisfaction of your intellectual curiosity, for its own sake, is out of the question. Even that pursuit will normally have some practical implications.

Within these boundaries of advancing knowledge, solving managerial problems and addressing business issues, the purpose and the context of your research project can vary considerably. For some research projects your purpose may be to understand and explain the impact of something, such as a particular policy. You may undertake this research within an individual organisation and suggest appropriate action on the basis of your findings. For other research projects you may wish to explore the ways in which different organisations do things. In such projects your purpose may be to discover and better understand the underlying processes in a wider context, thereby providing greater understanding for practitioners. For yet other research projects you may wish to combine an in-depth investigation of an organisation within the context of a wider understanding of the processes that are operating.

Despite this variety, all business and management research projects can be placed on a continuum (Fig 1.1) according to their purpose and context. At one end of the continuum is research that is undertaken to understand the processes of business and management, and their outcomes. This is often termed *academic research*. At the other is research which is of direct and immediate relevance to managers, addresses issues which they see as important and is presented in ways which they understand and on which they can act. This is often termed *applied research*.

Wherever your research project lies on this academic-applied continuum, we believe that you should undertake your research with rigour. To do this you will need to pay careful attention to the entire research process.

Academic research ◄————————► Applied research	
Purpose:	*Purpose:*
● expand knowledge of processes of business and management	● improve understanding of particular business or management problem
● results in universal principles relating to the process and its relationship to outcomes	● results in solution to problem
	● new knowledge limited to problem
● findings of significance and value to society in general	● findings of practical relevance and value to manager(s) in organisation(s)
Context:	*Context:*
● undertaken by people based in universities	● undertaken by people based in a variety of settings including organisations and universities
● choice of topic and objectives determined by the researcher	● objectives negotiated with originator
● flexible timescales	● tight timescales

Fig 1.1 Academic and applied research
Sources: Authors' experience; Easterby-Smith et al., 1991; Hedrick et al., 1993; Johnson, 1996

1.3 THE RESEARCH PROCESS

Most research textbooks represent research as a multi-stage process which you must follow in order to undertake and complete your research project. The precise number of stages varies, but they usually include formulating and clarifying a topic, reviewing the literature, choosing a strategy, collecting data, analysing data and writing up. Articles you have read may also suggest that the research process is rational and straightforward. Unfortunately, this is very rarely true and the reality is considerably more messy. While you will need to pass through the stages outlined above, you will probably visit all of them more than once. Each time you revisit a stage you will need to reflect on the associated issues and refine your ideas. In addition, as highlighted by some text books, you will need to consider ethical and access issues during the process.

This textbook also presents the research process as a series of linked stages. At the start of this process it is vital that you spend time formulating and clarifying your research topic. This should be posed as one or a series of questions that your research must answer, and objectives that your research must address. However, we would also stress the continuing need to reflect on and revise your ideas and the way in which you are planning to progress your research. Often this will involve revisiting stages (including your research question(s) and objectives) and working through them again. There is also a need to plan ahead to ensure that the necessary preliminary work for later stages has been undertaken. This is emphasised by Fig 1.2, which also provides a schematic index to the remaining chapters of the book. The stages you will need to complete as part of your research project are emphasised in the centre of the chart. However be warned, the process is messier than a brief glance at Fig 1.2 suggests.

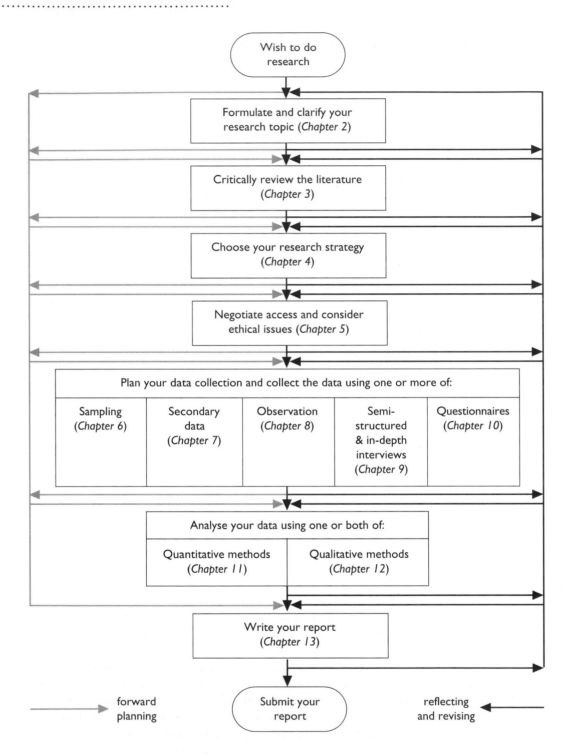

Fig 1.2 The research process

© Mark Saunders, Philip Lewis and Adrian Thornhill, 1997

1.4 THE STRUCTURE OF THIS BOOK

The purpose

As we stated earlier (Section 1.1) the overriding purpose of this book is to help you undertake research. This means that early on in your research project you will need to be clear about what you are doing, why you are doing it and the associated implications of what you are seeking to do. You will also need to ensure that you can show how your ideas relate to research that has already been undertaken in your topic area, and that you have a clear strategy for collecting and analysing your data. As part of this you will need to consider the validity and reliability of the data you intend to use, along with associated ethical and access issues. The appropriateness and suitability of the analysis techniques you choose to use will be of equal importance. Finally, you will need to write your research report as clearly and precisely as possible.

The structure of each chapter

Each of the subsequent chapters deals with part of the research process outlined in Fig 1.2. The ideas, techniques and methods are discussed using as little jargon as possible. Where appropriate you will find summaries of these using tables, checklists or diagrams. When new terms are introduced for the first time they are shown in italics and a definition or explanation follows shortly afterwards. The application of appropriate information technology is considered, in most instances as an integral part of the text. Discussion of information technology is not software specific but is concerned with the general principles. These will enable you to utilise whatever software you have available most effectively. Chapters have been cross-referenced as appropriate and an index provided to help you find your way around the book.

Included within the text of each chapter are a series of *worked examples*. These are based on actual research projects, often undertaken by our students and colleagues, in which points made in the text are illustrated. In many instances these worked examples illustrate possible pitfalls you may encounter while undertaking your research. These will help you understand the technique or idea and assess its suitability or appropriateness to your research. Where a pitfall has been illustrated it is to be hoped that it will help you to avoid the same mistake. There is also a summary of the key points of each chapter which you may look at before and after reading the chapter to ensure you have digested the main points.

To enable you to check that you have understood the chapter a series of *self-check questions* are included after the summary. These can all be answered without recourse to other (external) resources. Answers are provided to all the self-check questions at the end of the chapter. Each chapter also includes a research-based assignment which can be undertaken as part of your project. *Assignments* are designed to guide you through the entire research process (Fig 1.2). Completing the assignments for each chapter will enable you to generate all the material which you will need to include in your project report. Each assignment involves you in undertaking activities that are more complex than self-check questions, such as a library-based literature search or designing and piloting a questionnaire. They are presented in sufficient detail to enable you to focus on the techniques that are most appropriate to your research. However, as emphasised by Fig 1.2, you will almost certainly need to revisit and revise each assignment's answer as your research progresses.

Each chapter is accompanied by references, further reading and a case study. *Further reading* is included for two distinct reasons:

- to direct you to other work on the ideas contained within the chapter;
- to direct you to further examples of research where the ideas contained in the chapter have been used.

The precise reasons for the choice of further reading are also indicated.

Case studies are drawn from a variety of business and management research scenarios and have been based on the case study's authors' or their students' experiences when undertaking a research project. They have been written to highlight real issues that occur when undertaking business and management research. To help focus your thoughts or discussion on some of the pertinent issues, each case is followed by evaluative questions. A case study follows every chapter apart from Chapter 1.

An outline of the chapters

The book is organised in the following way.

Chapter 2 concerns the generation of ideas which will help you choose a suitable research topic and offers advice on what makes a good research topic. If you have already been given a research topic, perhaps by an organisation or tutor, you will need to refine it into one that is feasible and you should still read this chapter. After you have generated and refined your idea, the chapter discusses how to turn this idea into a clear research question(s) and related objectives. (Research questions and objectives are referred to throughout the book.) Finally, the chapter provides advice on how to write a research proposal.

The importance of the critical literature review to your research is outlined in Chapter 3. This chapter outlines what a critical review needs to include and the range of primary, secondary and tertiary literature sources available. It explains the purpose of reviewing the literature, discusses a range of search strategies, and contains advice on how to plan and undertake your search and write your review. The processes of identifying key words and searching, including using the Internet, are outlined. The chapter also offers advice on how to record items and evaluate their relevance.

Chapter 4 examines different ways of approaching research. It considers various strategies for conducting research and, crucially, the issue of the credibility of your research findings and conclusions.

Chapter 5 explores issues related to gaining access and research ethics. It offers advice on how to gain access to both organisations and individuals. Potential ethical issues are discussed in relation to each stage of the research process and different data collection methods.

A range of the probability and non-probability sampling techniques available for use in your research are explained in Chapter 6. The chapter considers why sampling is necessary and looks at issues of sample size and response rates. Advice on how to relate your choice of sampling techniques to your research topic is given and techniques for assessing the representativeness of those who respond are discussed.

Chapters 7, 8, 9 and 10 are concerned with different methods of obtaining data. The use of secondary data is discussed in Chapter 7 which introduces the various sources of data that are likely to be available and suggests ways in which they can be used. Advantages and disadvantages of secondary data are discussed, and a range of techniques for locating these data are suggested. The chapter also offers advice on how to evaluate the suitability of secondary data for your research.

In contrast, Chapter 8 is concerned with collecting primary data through observation. The chapter examines two types of observation: participant observation and structured observation. Practical advice on using each is offered and particular attention is given to ensuring that the data you obtain are both valid and reliable.

Chapter 9 is also concerned with collecting primary data, this time using semi-structured and in-depth interviews. The appropriateness of using these interviews in relation to your research strategy is discussed. Advice on how to undertake such interviews is offered, including the conduct of group interviews. Again, particular attention is given to ensuring that the data collected are both reliable and valid.

Chapter 10 is the final chapter concerned with collecting data. It introduces you to the use of both self-administered and interviewer-administered questionnaires and explores their respective advantages and disadvantages. Practical advice is offered on the process of designing, piloting and administering questionnaires to enhance their response rates. Particular attention is once again given to ensuring that the data collected are both reliable and valid.

Analysis of data is covered in Chapters 11 and 12. Chapter 11 outlines and illustrates the main issues that you need to consider when preparing quantitative data for analysis and when analysing this data by computer. Different types of data are defined and advice is given on how to create a data matrix and code data. Practical advice is also offered on the analysis of these data. The most appropriate diagrams to explore and illustrate data are discussed and suggestions made about which statistics to use to describe data, explore relationships and explore trends.

Chapter 12 outlines and discusses the main approaches available to you to analyse qualitative data. The nature of qualitative data is discussed and an overview of the analysis process provided. Strategies relating to the use of predicted theoretical explanations, the use of grounded theory and quantifying qualitative data are discussed. The chapter also considers the use of computer-based text retrievers and managers.

Chapter 13 helps you with the structure, content and style of your final project report. Above all, it encourages you to see writing as an intrinsic part of the research process which should not be left until everything else is completed.

1.5 HOW TO USE THIS BOOK

This book is written with a progressive logic, which means that terms and concepts are defined when they are first introduced. One implication of this is that it is sensible for you to start at the beginning and work your way through the text and worked examples, self-check questions, case studies and case-study questions. You can do this in a variety of ways depending on your reasons for using this book. However, this approach may not necessarily be suitable for your purposes and you may wish to dip into particular sections of the book. If this is true for you then you will need to use the book in a different way. Suggestions for three of the more common ways in which you might wish to use this book are given below.

As part of a research methods course or for self-study

If you are using this book as part of a research methods course or for self-study, it is probable that you will follow the chapter order quite closely. Groups of chapters within which we believe you can switch the order without affecting the logic of the flow too much are:

- those chapters associated with data collection (Chapters 7, 8, 9 and 10);
- those associated with data analysis (Chapters 11 and 12).

In addition, you might wish to read Chapter 13 on writing before starting to draft your critical review of the literature (Chapter 3).

As you work through the book we would recommend that you attempt all the self-check questions and those questions associated with the case studies. Your answers to the self-check questions can be assessed using the answers at the end of each chapter. However we hope you will actually have a go at the question before reading the answer! If you need more information on an idea or a technique, then first look at the references in the further reading section.

Appropriate assignments, when grouped together, will provide a useful *aide-mémoire* for assessed work. Such work might involve you in just planning a research project or, alternatively, in planning and undertaking a small research project of your own.

As a guide through the research process

If you are intending to use this book to guide you through the research process for a research project you are undertaking, such as your dissertation, we recommend you read the entire book quickly before starting your research. That way you will have a good overview of the entire process, including the range of techniques available, and will be better able to plan your work.

After having read the book once we suggest you work your way through it again following the chapter order. This time you should attempt the self-check questions and those questions associated with each case study to ensure that you have understood the material contained in each chapter before applying it to your own research project. Your responses to self-check questions can be assessed using the answers at the end of each chapter.

If you are still unsure as to whether a particular technique or idea is relevant, then look in the further reading for other examples of research where these have been used. If you need more information on an idea or a technique then, again, start with the references in the further reading section.

Material in some of the chapters is likely to prove less relevant to some research topics than others. However, you should beware of choosing inappropriate techniques simply because you are happy using them. Completing the assignments for Chapters 2 to 12 will enable you to generate all the material which you will need to include in your project report. It will also help you focus on the techniques and ideas that are most appropriate to your research. When you have also completed the assignment for Chapter 13 you will have written your research report.

As a reference source

It may be that you wish to use this book now or subsequently as a reference source. If this is the case, there is an extensive index which will point you to the appropriate page or pages. You should also find the contents pages a useful guide. In addition, we have tried to help you use the book in this way by including cross-references between sections in Chapters as appropriate. Do follow these up as necessary. If you need more information on an idea or a technique, then begin by consulting the references in the further reading section.

1.6 SUMMARY

- This book is designed to help you undertake a research project, whether you are an undergraduate or postgraduate student of business and management or a manager. It is designed as an introductory text and will guide you through the entire research process.
- Business and management research involves undertaking systematic research to find out things. The findings are designed to advance knowledge, provide procedures for solving managerial problems and address business issues.
- All business and management research projects can be placed on an academic-applied continuum according to their purpose and context.
- Wherever your research project lies on this continuum, you should undertake your research with rigour. To do this you will need to pay careful attention to the entire research process.
- In this book research is represented as a multi-stage process; however this process is rarely straightforward and will involve both reflecting on and revising stages already undertaken, and also forward planning.
- Each chapter contains advice with worked examples, self-check questions, an assignment and a case study with questions. Answers to all self-check questions are at the end of the appropriate chapter. Completing the assignments for Chapters 2 to 12 will enable you to generate all the material which you will need to include in your

project report. When you have also completed the assignment for Chapter 13 you will have written your research report.

■ The book can be used as part of a taught research methods course, for self-study, as a guide through the research process or for reference.

References

Easterby-Smith, M., Thorpe, R. and Lowe, A. (1991) *Management Research: An Introduction*, London, Sage.

Ghauri, P., Grønhaug, K. and Kristianslund, I. (1995) *Research Methods in Business Studies: A Practical Guide*, London, Prentice Hall.

Gill, J. and Johnson, P. (1991) *Research Methods for Managers*, London, Paul Chapman.

Hedrick, T.E., Bickmann, L. and Rog, D.J. (1993) *Applied Research Design*, Newbury Park, California, Sage.

Jankowicz, A.D. (1995) *Business Research Projects* (2nd edn), London, Chapman & Hall.

Johnson, G. (1996) 'The debate begins', *BAM News*, 6, 1–2.

Further Reading

Easterby-Smith, M., Thorpe, R. and Lowe, A. (1991) *Management Research: An Introduction*, London, Sage. Chapter 1 provides a very clear and readable introduction to management research and explains why it is distinctive from other forms of research.

CHAPTER 2

Formulating and clarifying the research topic

The principal objective of this chapter is to assist you in the generation of ideas which will help you choose a suitable research topic. Help is also given in identifying the attributes of a good research topic.

After you have generated and refined your idea, the chapter shows you how to turn this idea into a research topic which has clear research questions and objectives.

Finally, the chapter gives advice on how to write your research proposal.

2.1 INTRODUCTION

Before you start your research you need to have at least some idea of what you want to do. This is probably the most difficult, and yet the most important, part of your research project. Up to now most of your studies have been concerned with answering questions that other people have set. This chapter is therefore concerned with how to formulate and clarify your research topic and your research question(s) and objectives. If you are not clear about what you are going to research it is difficult to plan how you are going to research it. This reminds us of a favourite quote from *Alice's Adventures in Wonderland*. Alice asks the Cheshire Cat (Carroll, 1989: 63–4):

> 'Would you tell me, please, which way I ought to walk from here?'
> 'That depends a good deal on where you want to get to,' said the Cat.
> 'I don't much care where,' said Alice.
> 'Then it doesn't matter which way you walk,' said the Cat.

Formulating and clarifying the research topic is therefore the starting point of your research project (Ghauri *et al.*, 1995, Smith and Dainty, 1991). Once you are clear about this you will be able to choose the most appropriate research strategy and data collection and analysis techniques. The formulating and clarifying process is time consuming and will probably take you up blind alleys. However, without spending time on this stage you are far less likely to achieve a successful research project (Raimond, 1993).

In the initial stages of the formulating and clarifying process you will be generating and refining research ideas (Section 2.3). It may be that you have already been given a research idea, perhaps by an organisation or tutor. Even if this has happened, you will still need to refine the idea into one that is feasible. Once you have done this you will need to turn the idea into research questions and objectives (Section 2.4) and write the research proposal for your project (Section 2.5).

However, before starting the formulating and clarifying process, you need to understand what makes a good research topic. For this reason we begin this chapter (Section 2.2) with a discussion of the attributes required for a good research topic.

2.2 ATTRIBUTES OF A GOOD RESEARCH TOPIC

The attributes of a business and management research topic do not vary a great deal between universities (Raimond, 1993), although there will be differences in the emphasis placed on different attributes. If you are undertaking your research project as part of a course of study, the most important attribute will be that it meets the examining body's requirements and, in particular, that it is at the correct level. This means that you must choose your topic with care. For example, some universities require students to collect their own data as part of their research project, while others allow them to base their project on data that have already been collected. You, therefore, need to check the assessment criteria for your research project and ensure that your choice of topic will enable you to meet these criteria. If you are unsure, you should discuss your uncertainties with your project tutor.

In addition, your research topic must be something you are capable of undertaking and one that excites your imagination. Capability can be considered in a variety of ways. At the personal level, you need to feel comfortable that you have, or can develop, the skills that will be required to research the topic. We hope that you will develop your research skills as part of undertaking your research project. However, some skills, for example foreign languages, may be impossible to acquire in the time you have available. As well as having the necessary skills, you also need to have a genuine interest in the topic. Most research projects are undertaken over at least a six-month period. A topic in which you are only vaguely interested at the start is likely to become a topic in which you have no interest and for which you will fail to produce your best work.

Your ability to find the financial and time resources to undertake research on the topic will also have an impact on your capability. Some topics are unlikely to be possible to complete in the time allowed by your course of study. This may be because they require you to measure the impact of an intervention over a long period. Similarly, topics which are likely to require you to travel widely or need expensive equipment should be disregarded unless financial resources permit.

Capability also means you must be reasonably certain of gaining access to any data you might need to collect. Gill and Johnson (1991) argue that this is usually relatively straightforward to assess. They point out that many people start with ideas where access to data will prove difficult. Certain, more sensitive, subjects, such as financial performance or decision making by senior managers, provide potentially fascinating topics. However, they may present considerable access problems. You should, therefore, discuss this with your project tutor after reading Sections 5.2 and 5.3.

For most topics it is important that the issues within the research are capable of being linked to theory (Raimond, 1993; Yin, 1994). Initially, theory may just be based on the reading you have undertaken in your study to date. However, as part of your assessment criteria you are almost certain to be asked to set your topic in context (Section 3.2). As a consequence, you will need to have a broader knowledge of the literature and undertake further reading as part of defining your research question(s) and objectives (Section 2.4).

Most project tutors will argue that one of the attributes of a good topic is a clearly defined research question(s) and objectives (Section 2.4). These will, along with a good knowledge of the literature, enable you to assess the extent to which your research is likely to provide *fresh insights* into the topic. Many students believe this is going to be difficult. Fortunately, as pointed out by Phillips and Pugh (1994), there are many ways in which such insights can be defined as 'fresh' (Section 2.5).

If you have already been given a research idea (perhaps by an organisation), you will need to ensure that your questions and objectives relate clearly to the idea (Kervin, 1992). It is also important that your topic has a *symmetry of potential outcomes*, that is, your results will be of similar value whatever you find out (Gill and Johnson, 1991). Without this symmetry you may spend a considerable amount of time researching your topic only to find an answer which is of little importance.

● ●

WORKED EXAMPLE: *Ensuring symmetry of potential outcomes*

Karmen was a part-time student. Her initial research topic was concerned with finding out if there was any relationship between the levels of stress experienced by social workers and the number of years they had been employed as social workers. If she established that there was a link between these factors this would be an interesting finding; if, however, she discovered no relationship the finding would be less interesting and would have no real practical relevance to her organisation.

She therefore decided to amend her topic so that it became exploring and understanding the impact of a forthcoming stress management course on the relative levels of stress experienced by social workers before the course. The results of this research would be interesting and important whether or not the course had an impact.

● ●

It is almost inevitable that the extent to which these attributes apply to your research topic will depend on your topic and the reasons for which you are undertaking the research. However, most of these attributes will apply. For this reason, it is important that you check and continue to check any potential research topic against the summary checklist in Table 2.1.

☑ Does the topic fit the specifications and meet the standards set by the examining institution?

☑ Is the topic something with which you are really fascinated?

☑ Does your research topic contain issues that have a clear link to theory?

☑ Do you have, or can you develop within the research project timeframe, the necessary research skills to undertake the topic?

☑ Is the research topic achievable within the available time?

☑ Is the research topic achievable within the financial resources that are likely to be available?

☑ Are you reasonably certain of being able to gain access to data you are likely to require for this topic?

☑ Are you able to state your research question(s) and objectives clearly?

☑ Will your proposed research be able to provide fresh insights on this topic?

☑ Does your research topic relate clearly to the idea you have been given (perhaps by an organisation)?

☑ Are the findings for this research topic likely to be symmetrical, that is, of similar value what ever the outcome?

Table 2.1 Checklist of attributes of a good research topic

2.3 GENERATING AND REFINING RESEARCH IDEAS

Some business and management students are expected to generate and refine their own research ideas. Others, particularly those on professional and post-experience courses, may be provided with a research idea by an organisation or their university. In the initial stages of their research they are expected to refine this to a clear and feasible idea which meets the requirements of the examining organisation. If you have already been given a research idea we believe you will still find it useful to read the next subsection, which deals with generating research ideas. Many of the techniques which can be used for generating research ideas can also be used for the refining process.

Generating research ideas

If you have not been given an initial *research idea* there is a range of techniques that can be used to find and select a topic which you would like to research. They can be thought of as those which are predominantly *rational thinking* and those which involve more *creative thinking* (Table 2.2). The precise techniques which you choose to use and the order in which you use them is entirely up to you. However, like Raimond (1993), we believe you should use both rational and creative techniques, choosing those which you believe are going to be of most use to you, and which you will enjoy using. By using one or more creative techniques you are more likely to ensure that your heart, as well as your head, is in your research project. In our experience, it is usually better to use a variety of techniques.

In order to do this you will need to have some understanding of the techniques, and the ways in which they work. We therefore outline the more frequently used techniques in Table 2.2 and suggest possible ways in which they might be used to generate research ideas. These techniques will generate one of two outcomes:

■ one or more possible research project ideas that you might undertake;

■ absolute panic because nothing in which you are interested or which seems suitable has come to mind (Jankowicz, 1995).

In either instance, but especially the latter, we suggest you talk to your project tutor.

Rational thinking	Creative thinking
● Examining own strengths and interests ● Looking at past research projects ● Discussion ● Searching the literature	● Keeping a notebook of ideas ● Exploring personal preferences using past research projects ● Relevance trees ● Brainstorming

Table 2.2 More frequently used techniques for generating and refining research ideas

Examining own strengths and interests

It is important that you choose a topic in which you are likely to do well and, if possible, already have some academic knowledge. Jankowicz (1995) suggests that one way of doing this is to look at those assignments for which you have received good grades, since most of these assignments are also likely to be the topics in which you were interested (Table 2.1). They will provide you with an area in which to search and find a research idea. In addition you may, as part of your reading, be able to focus more precisely on the sort of ideas about which you wish to conduct your research.

Linked to your subject interest is the need to think about your future. If you plan to work in financial management, it would be sensible to choose a research project in the financial management field. One part of your course that will inevitably be discussed at any job interview is your research project. A project in the same field will provide you with a clear opportunity to display your depth of knowledge and your enthusiasm.

Looking at past research project titles

Many of our students have found looking at *past research project titles* to be a useful way of generating research ideas. For undergraduate and taught master's degrees these are often called *dissertations*. For research degrees they are termed *theses*. A common way of doing this is to scan a list of past project titles (such as those in Appendix 1) for anything that captures your imagination. Titles that look interesting or which grab your attention should be noted down, as should any thoughts you have about the title in relation to your own research idea. In this process the fact that the title is poorly worded or the project report received a low mark is immaterial. What matters is the fact that you have found a topic that interests you. Based on this you can think of new ideas in the same general area which will enable you to provide fresh insights.

Scanning actual research projects may also produce research ideas. However, you need to beware. The fact that a project is in your library is no guarantee of the quality of the arguments and observations it contains. In many universities all research projects are placed in the library whether they obtained a bare pass or a distinction.

Discussion

Colleagues, friends and university tutors are all good sources of possible research project ideas. Often project tutors will have ideas for possible student projects which they will be pleased to discuss with you. In addition, ideas can be obtained by talking to practitioners and professional groups (Gill and Johnson, 1991). It is important that as well as discussing possible ideas you also make a note of them. What seemed like a good idea in the coffee shop may not be remembered quite so clearly after the following lecture!

Searching the literature

As part of your discussions, relevant literature may also be suggested. Howard and Sharp (1983) discuss types of literature which are of particular use for generating research ideas. These include:

■ articles in academic and professional journals;

■ reports;

■ books.

Of particular value are academic *review articles*. These articles contain both a considered review of the state of knowledge in that topic area and pointers towards areas where further research needs to be undertaken. In addition, you can browse recent publications, in particular journals, for possible research ideas (Section 3.5). For many topic areas your project tutor will be able to suggest possible recent review articles, or articles which contain recommendations for further work. *Reports* may also be of use. The most recently published are usually up to date and, again, often contain recommendations which may form the basis of your research idea. *Books*, by contrast, are less up to date than other written sources. They do, however, often contain a good overview of research that has been undertaken which may suggest ideas to you.

Searching for publications is only possible when you have at least some idea of the area in which you wish to undertake your research. One way of obtaining this is to re-examine your lecture notes and course textbooks, and note those subjects that appear most interesting (discussed earlier in this section) and the names of relevant authors. This will give you a basis on which to undertake a *preliminary search* (using techniques outlined in sections 3.4 and 3.5). When you obtain the articles, reports and other items it is often helpful to look for unfounded assertions and statements about the absence of research (Raimond, 1993), as these are likely to contain ideas which will enable you to provide fresh insights.

Keeping a notebook of ideas

One of the more creative techniques is to keep a *notebook of ideas*. All this involves is simply noting down any interesting research ideas as you think of them and, of equal importance, what sparked off your thought. You can then pursue the idea using more rational thinking techniques later. Mark keeps a notebook by his bed so he can jot down any flashes of inspiration which occur to him in the middle of the night!

Exploring personal preferences using past research projects

Another way of generating possible project ideas is to explore your *personal preferences* using past project reports from your university. To do this Raimond (1993) suggests you:

1 Select six research projects which you like.

2 For each of these six projects note down your first thoughts in response to three questions (if responses for different projects are the same this does not matter):

   a What appeals to you about the project?

   b What is good about the project?

   c Why is the project good?

3 Select three research projects that you do not like.

4 For each of these three projects note down your first thoughts in response to three questions (if responses for different projects are the same, or cannot be clearly expressed, this does not matter, note them down anyway):

   a What do you dislike about the project?

   b What is poor about the project?

   c Why is the project poor?

You now have a list of what you consider to be excellent and what you consider to be poor in research projects. This will not be the same as a list generated by anyone else. It is also very unlikely to match the attributes of a good research project (Table 2.1). But by examining this list you will begin to understand those project characteristics that are important to you and with which you feel comfortable. Of equal importance, you will have identified those with which you are uncomfortable and should avoid. These can be used as the parameters against which you can evaluate possible research ideas.

Relevance trees

Relevance trees may also prove useful in generating research topics. In this instance, their use is similar to that of mind mapping (Buzan and Buzan, 1995), in which you start with a broad concept from which you generate further (usually more specific) topics. Each of these topics forms a separate branch from which you can generate further, more detailed, sub-branches. As you proceed down the sub-branches more ideas are generated and recorded. These can then be examined and a number selected and combined to provide a research idea (Howard and Sharp, 1983).[1]

[1] This technique is discussed in more detail in Section 3.4, which also includes a worked example in which a relevance tree is used to help generate key words for a literature search.

Brainstorming

Brainstorming, taught as a problem-solving technique on many business and management courses, can also be used to generate and refine research ideas. It is best undertaken with a group of people, although you can brainstorm on your own. To brainstorm, Moody (1983) suggests you do the following.

1 Define your problem, that is, the sorts of ideas you are interested in, as precisely as possible. In the early stages of formulating a topic this may be as vague as: 'I am interested in marketing, but don't know what to do for my research topic'.

2 Ask for suggestions relating to the problem.

3 Record all suggestions observing the following rules:

- no suggestion should be criticised or evaluated in any way before all ideas have been considered;
- all suggestions, however unusual, should be recorded and considered;
- as many suggestions as possible should be recorded.

4 Review all the suggestions and explore what is meant by each.

5 Analyse the list of suggestions and decide which appeal to you most as research ideas and why.

WORKED EXAMPLE: *Brainstorming*

George's main interest was football. When he finished university he wanted to work in marketing, preferably for a sports manufacturer. He had examined his own strengths and discovered that his best marks were in marketing. He wanted to do his research project on some aspect of marketing, preferably linked to football, but had no real research idea. He asked three friends, all taking business studies degrees, to help him brainstorm the problem.

George began by explaining the problem in some detail. At first the suggestions emerged slowly. He noted them down on the whiteboard. Soon the board was covered with suggestions. George counted these and discovered there were over 100.

Reviewing individual suggestions produced nothing which any of the group felt to be of sufficient merit for a research project. However, one of George's friends pointed out that combining the suggestions of Premier League football, television rights and sponsorship might provide an idea which satisfied the assessment requirements of the project.

They discussed the suggestion further and George noted the research idea as: 'something about how exclusive television rights to satellite broadcasters would affect sports sponsorship, concentrating on Premier League football.'

George arranged to see his project tutor to discuss how to refine the idea they had just generated.

Refining research ideas

The Delphi technique

An additional approach which our students have found particularly useful in refining their research ideas is the *Delphi technique*. This involves using a group of people who are either involved or interested in your initial idea to generate and choose a more specific research idea (Robson, 1993). To use this technique you need to do the following.

1 Brief the members of the group about the research idea (they can make notes if they wish).

2 At the end of the briefing encourage group members to seek clarification and more information as appropriate.

3 Ask each member of the group, including the originator of the research idea, to generate independently up to three specific research ideas based on the idea that has been described (they can also be asked to provide a justification for their specific ideas).

4 Collect the research ideas in an unedited and non-attributable form and distribute them to all members of the group.

5 A second cycle of the process (stages 2 to 4) takes place in which individuals comment on the research ideas and revise their own contributions in the light of what others have said.

6 Subsequent cycles of the process take place until a consensus is reached. These either follow a similar pattern (stages 2 to 4) or use discussion, voting or some other method.

This process works well, not least because people enjoy trying to help one another. In addition it is very useful for moulding groups into a cohesive whole.

WORKED EXAMPLE: *Using a Delphi group*

Jenny explained to the group that her research idea was concerned with understanding the decision-making processes associated with mortgage applications and loan advances. Her briefing to the three other group members, and the questions which they asked her, considered aspects such as:

■ the influences on a potential first-time buyer to approach a specific financial institution;

■ the influence of face-to-face contact between potential borrower and potential lender on decision making.

The group then moved on to generate a number of more specific research ideas, among which were the following:

■ the factors that influenced potential first-time house purchasers to deal with particular financial institutions;

■ the effect of interpersonal contact on mortgage decisions;

■ the qualities that potential applicants look for in mortgage advisers.

These were considered and commented on by all the group members. At the end of the second cycle Jenny had, with the other students' agreement, refined her research idea to:

■ the way in which a range of factors influenced potential first-time buyers' choice of lending institution.

She now needed to pursue these ideas by undertaking a preliminary search of the literature.

The preliminary study

Even if you have been given a research idea, it is still necessary to refine it in order to turn it into a research project. Some authors, for example Bennett (1991), refer to this process as a *preliminary study*; others, for example Kervin (1992), refer to it as *exploratory research* (Section 4.2). For some research ideas this will be no more than a review of some of the literature. This can be thought of as the first iteration of your critical review of the literature (Fig 3.1). For others it may include revisiting the techniques discussed earlier in this section, as well as informal discussions with people who have personal experience of, and knowledge in the area of, your research ideas. In some cases *shadowing* employees who are likely to be important in your research may also provide insights. If you are planning on undertaking your research within an organisation it is important to gain a good understanding of your host organisation (Kervin, 1992). Whatever techniques you choose, the underlying purpose is to gain a greater understanding so that your research ideas can be refined.

At this stage you need to be testing your research ideas against the checklist in Table 2.1 and, where necessary, adapting them. It may be that after a preliminary study, or discussing your ideas with colleagues, you decide that the research idea is no longer feasible in the form in which you first envisaged it. If this is the case, do not be too downhearted. It is far better to revise your research ideas at this stage than to have to do it later, when you have undertaken far more work.

Integrating ideas

The integration of ideas from these techniques is essential if your research is to have a clear direction and you are to avoid a mismatch between objectives and your final research report. Jankowicz (1995: 34) suggests an integrative process which our students have found most useful. This he terms 'working up and narrowing down'. It involves classifying each research idea into first its area, then its field and finally the precise aspect in which you are interested. These represent an increasingly more detailed description of the research idea. Thus your initial area, based on examining your course work, might be accountancy. After browsing some recent journals and discussion with colleagues, this becomes more focused on the field of financial accounting methods. With further reading, the use of the Delphi technique and discussion with your project tutor, you decide to focus on the aspect of activity-based costing.

You will know when the process of generating and refining ideas is complete as you will be able to say, 'I'd like to do some research on . . .' Obviously there will still be a big gap between this and the point when you are ready to start serious work on your research. Sections 2.4 and 2.5 will ensure that you are ready to bridge that gap.

2.4 TURNING RESEARCH IDEAS INTO RESEARCH PROJECTS

Writing research questions

Much is made in this book of the importance of defining clear *research questions* at the beginning of the research process. The importance of this cannot be over-emphasised. One of the key criteria of your research success will be whether you have a set of clear conclusions drawn from the data you have collected. The extent to which you can do that will be determined largely by the clarity with which you have posed your initial research questions.

WORKED EXAMPLE: *Defining the research question*

Alex was a personnel officer, in his first post, in an advanced electronics company specialising in research. When he first joined the company he was surprised by the seemingly arbitrary way in which many of the personnel policies were formulated and conducted. They seemed to bear little relation to the strategic direction the company was taking.

Alex had studied corporate strategy as part of his business studies degree. He was familiar with some of the literature which suggested that operational areas such as personnel would benefit from tying their policies to corporate strategy. It was an area in which he was very interested. He wanted to do some research on corporate strategy in his organisation and the links with personnel policies. At the same time he needed to satisfy the requirements of his Institute of Personnel and Development course.

After talking this over with his project tutor Alex decided on the following research question: 'Why do my organisation's personnel policies not reflect the corporate strategy?'

Defining research questions, rather like generating research ideas (Section 2.3), is not a straightforward matter. It is important that the question is sufficiently involved to generate the sort of research project that is consistent with the standards expected of you (Table 2.1). A question which prompts a descriptive answer – for example: 'What proportion of graduates from public schools enter the civil service?' – is far easier to answer than: 'Why are graduates from public schools more likely to enter the civil service?' More will be said about the importance of theory in defining the research question later in this section, but beware of research questions that are too easy.

It is perhaps more likely that you fall into the trap of asking research questions that are too difficult. The question cited above – 'Why are graduates from public schools more likely to enter the civil service?' – is an example of this. It would probably be very difficult to gain sufficient access to the inner portals of the civil service to obtain a good grasp of the subtle, 'unofficial' processes that operate in staff selection which may favour one type of candidate over another. Over-reaching yourself in the definition of research questions is a danger.

The pitfall that you must avoid at all costs is asking research questions that will not generate fresh insights (Table 2.1). This raises the question of the extent to which you have consulted the relevant literature. It is perfectly legitimate to replicate research because you have a genuine concern about its applicability to your research setting (for example, your organisation). But it certainly is not legitimate to display your ignorance of the literature (Robson, 1993).

It is often a useful starting point in the writing of research questions to begin with one *general focus research question* which flows from your research idea. This may lead to several more detailed questions or the definition of research objectives. Table 2.3 has some examples of general focus research questions.

Research idea		General focus research question	
1	The sponsorship of county cricket clubs by commercial organisations	1	What benefit do commercial organisations derive from their sponsorship of county cricket clubs?
2	The adoption by manufacturing companies of 'flexible workforces'	2	Why do manufacturing companies divide their workforces into 'core' and 'peripheral' workers?
3	The loss of mutuality status by building societies and the effect on the future of the industry	3	Will the loss of mutuality status by building societies lead to them offering less attractive terms to borrowers and savers than mutual societies?
4	The future of trade unions	4	What are the strategies that trade unions should adopt to ensure their viability into the next century?

Table 2.3 Example research ideas and their derived focus research questions

Writing your research questions will in most cases be your individual concern, but it is useful to get other people to help you. An obvious source of guidance is your project tutor. Consulting your project tutor will avoid the pitfalls of the questions that are too easy, too difficult or have been answered before. Discussing your area of interest with your project tutor will ensure that your research questions become much clearer.

Before discussion with your project tutor you may wish to conduct a brainstorming session with your peers or use the Delphi technique (Section 2.3). Your research questions may flow from your initial examination of the relevant literature. As outlined in Section 2.3, journal articles reporting primary research will often end with a conclusion which includes what the author sees as the implications for future research of the work in the article. This may be phrased in the form of research questions. But even if it is not, it may suggest pertinent research questions to you.

Writing research objectives

Your research may begin with a general focus research question which then generates more detailed research questions, or you may use your general focus research question as a base from which you write a set of *research objectives*. Objectives are more broadly acceptable to the research community as evidence of the researcher's clear sense of purpose and direction. It may be that either are satisfactory. Do check if your examining body has a preference.

We contend that research objectives are likely to lead to greater specificity than are research questions. Table 2.4 illustrates this point.

Research question	Research objective
1 Why have organisations introduced team-briefing?	1 To identify organisations' objectives for team-briefing schemes
2 How can the effectiveness of team-briefing schemes be measured?	2 To establish suitable effectiveness criteria for team-briefing schemes
3 Has team briefing been effective?	3 To describe the extent to which the effectiveness criteria for team-briefing have been met
4 How can the effectiveness of team-briefing be explained?	4 To determine those factors associated with the effectiveness criteria for team-briefing being met
	5 To estimate whether some of those factors are more influential than others
5 Can the explanation be generalised?	6 To develop an explanatory theory that associates certain factors with the effectiveness of team-briefing schemes

Table 2.4 Phrasing research questions as research objectives

Table 2.4 summarises the objectives of some research conducted by one of our students. Expressing the first research question as an objective prompted consideration of the objectives of the organisations. This was useful because it led to the finding that there often were no clear objectives. This in itself was an interesting theoretical discovery.

The second and third objectives operationalise the matching research questions by introducing the notion of explicit effectiveness criteria. In a similar way the fourth and fifth objectives are specific about factors which lead to effectiveness in question four.

The biggest difference between the questions and objectives is illustrated by the way in which the fifth question becomes the sixth objective. They are similar, but differ in the way that the objective makes clear that a theory will be developed which will make a causal link between two sets of variables: effectiveness factors and team briefing success.

This is not to say that the research questions could not have been written with a similar amount of specificity. They could. Indeed, you may find it easier to write specific research questions than objectives. But we doubt whether the same level of precision could be achieved through the writing of research questions alone. Research objectives require more rigorous thinking which derives from the use of more formal language.

The importance of theory

Section 4.1 outlines the role of theory in helping you to decide your approach to research design. However, your consideration of theory should begin earlier than this. It should inform your definition of research questions and objectives. *Theory* is defined by Gill and Johnson (1991: 166) as 'a formulation regarding the cause and effect relationships between two or more variables, which may or may not have been tested'.

There is probably no word which is more misused and misunderstood in education than the word 'theory'. It is thought that material included in textbooks is theory whereas what is happening in the 'real world' is practice. The citing of references in students' written work is often seen by them to be theory. Students who saw earlier drafts of this book remarked that they were pleased that the book was not too theoretical. What they meant was that the book concentrated on giving a great deal of practical advice. Yet the book is full of theory. Advising you to carry out research in a particular way (variable *A*) is based on the theory that this will yield effective results (variable *B*). This is the cause and effect relationship referred to in the definition of theory cited above.

The definition demonstrates that 'theory' has a specific meaning. It refers to situations where if *A* is introduced *B* will be the consequence. Therefore, the marketing manager may theorise that the introduction of loyalty cards by a supermarket will lead to customers being less likely to shop regularly at a competitor supermarket. That is a theory. Yet the marketing manager would probably not recognise it as such. He is still less likely to refer to it as a theory, particularly in the company of fellow managers. Many managers are very dismissive of any talk that smacks of theory. It is thought of as something that is all very well to learn about at business school but bears little relation to what goes on in every day organisational life. Yet the loyalty card example shows that it has everything to do with what goes on in everyday organisational life.

Section 4.1 notes that every purposive decision we take is based on theory i.e. that certain consequences will flow from the decision. It follows from this that every managers' meeting which features a number of decisions will be a meeting which is highly *theory dependent* (Gill and Johnson, 1991). All that will be missing is a realisation of this fact. So, if theory is something that is so rooted in our everyday lives, it certainly is something that we need not be apprehensive about. If it is implicit in all our decisions and actions, then recognising its importance means making it explicit. In research the importance of theory must be recognised, therefore it must be made explicit.

Phillips and Pugh (1994) distinguish between research and what they call *intelligence gathering*. The latter is the gathering of facts: for example, what is the relative proportion of undergraduates to postgraduates reading this book? What is the current spend per employee on training in the UK? What provision do small businesses make for bad debts? This is often called descriptive research (Section 4.2) and may form part of your research project.

Phillips and Pugh contrast such 'what' questions with 'why' questions. Examples of these 'why' questions are: why do UK organisations spend less per head on training than German organisations? Why are new car purchasers reluctant to take out extended warranties on their vehicles? Why do some travellers still prefer to use cross-Channel ferries as opposed to the Channel Tunnel? Such questions go 'beyond description and require analysis'. They look for 'explanations, relationships, comparisons, predictions, generalisations and theories'. (Phillips and Pugh, 1994: 47).

It is a short step from the 'why' research question to the testing of an existing theory in a new situation or the development of your own theory. This may be expressed as a hypothesis that is to be tested (Section 4.1) or the eventual answer to your research question may be the development or amendment of a theory.

WORKED EXAMPLE: *Writing a research question based on theory*

David was a senior manager studying part time. He was worried that the many changes that had taken place in his organisation, including large-scale redundancies at all levels, meant that the nature of the relationship between the organisation and its employees was changing.

His reading led him to become fascinated by the idea of the psychological contract between the organisation and the employee: what each will give the other (e.g. security, loyalty, ambition, career progression) in return for work and employment over and above the normal terms and conditions which are part of the legal employment contract.

David's research question was: 'How are the structural changes in my organisation affecting the way in which employees think about the psychological contract they have with the organisation?'

David was asked to clarify the theory underpinning his research. He did so by explaining that redundancies created in employees a feeling of insecurity, such that they saw the employment relationship simply as a short-term 'wage–work bargain'. This meant that they were unprepared to put in the extra commitment normally associated with building a career.

Although intelligence gathering will play a part in your research, it is unlikely to be enough. You should be seeking to explain phenomena, analyse relationships, compare what is going on in different research settings, predict outcomes and generalise. Then you will be working at the theoretical level. This is a necessary requirement for most assessed research projects.

2.5 WRITING YOUR RESEARCH PROPOSAL

At the start of all courses or modules we give our students a plan of the work they will be doing. It includes the learning objectives, the content, the assessment strategy and the recommended reading. This is our statement of our side of the learning contract. Our students have a right to expect this.

However, when we insist on a proposal for a dissertation which is often the equivalent of at least two other modules, there is frequently a marked reluctance to produce anything other than what is strictly necessary. This is unsatisfactory. It is unfair to your project tutor, because you are not making entirely clear what it is you intend to do in your research. You are also being unfair to yourself, because you are not giving yourself the best opportunity to have your ideas and plans scrutinised and subjected to rigorous questioning.

Writing a research proposal is a crucial part of the research process. If you are applying for research funding, or if your proposal is going before an academic research committee, then you will know that you will need to put a great deal of time into the preparation of your proposal. But even if the official need for a proposal is not so vital, it is still a process which will repay very careful attention.

The purposes of the research proposal

Organising your ideas

Section 13.1 notes that writing can be the best way of clarifying our thoughts. This is a valuable purpose of the proposal. Not only will it clarify your thoughts, but it will help you to organise your ideas into a coherent statement of your research intent. Your reader will be looking for this.

Convincing your audience

However coherent your ideas and exciting your research plan, they count for little if the proposal reveals that what you are planning to do is simply not possible. As part of our research methods course for taught postgraduate students we have a three-stage assignment, the first stage of which is to write a proposal. This is then discussed with a project tutor. What usually happens is that this discussion is about how the plans can be amended so that something more modest in scope is attempted. Often work that is not achievable in the given timescale is proposed. If your proposal has not convinced your audience that the research you have proposed is achievable, then you will have saved yourself a great deal of time and frustration.

Contracting with your 'client'

If you are asked to carry out a research project for a commercial client, it is unthinkable that you would go ahead without a clear proposal which you would submit for approval. Acceptance of your proposal by the client would be part of the contract that existed between you. So it is with your proposal to your project tutor or academic committee. Acceptance implies that your proposal is satisfactory. While this is obviously no guarantee of subsequent success, it is something of a comfort to you to know that at least you started your research journey with an appropriate destination and journey plan. It is for you to ensure that you are not derailed!

The content of the research proposal

Title

This may be your first attempt at the title. It may change as your work progresses. At this stage it should closely mirror the content of your proposal.

Background

This is an important part of the proposal. It should tell the reader why you feel the research you are planning is worth the effort. This may be expressed in the form of a problem which needs solving or something which you find exciting and has aroused your curiosity. The reader will be looking for evidence here that there is sufficient interest from you to sustain you over the long months (or years) ahead.

This is also the section where you will demonstrate your knowledge of the relevant literature. Moreover, it will clarify where your proposal fits into the debate in the literature. You will be expected to show a clear link between the previous work that has been done in your field of research interest and the content of your proposal. In short, the literature should be your point of departure. This is not the same as the critical literature review (Section 3.2) which you will present in your final project report. It will just indicate the key literature sources from which you intend to draw your ideas.

Research questions and objectives

The background section should lead smoothly into a statement of your research question(s) and objectives. These should leave the reader in no doubt as to precisely what it is your research seeks to achieve.

Method

This and the background sections will be the longest sections of the proposal. It will detail precisely how you intend to go about achieving your research objectives. It will also justify your choice of method in the light of those objectives. These two aims may be met by dividing your method section into two parts:

- research design;
- data collection.

In the part on research design you will explain where you intend to carry out the research. If your earlier coverage has pointed out that your research is a single-organisation issue, then this will be self-evident. However, if your research topic is more generic you will wish to explain, for example, which sector(s) of the economy you have chosen to research and why you chose these sectors. You will also need to explain the identity of your research population (for example, managers or trade union officials) and why you chose this population.

This section should also include an explanation of the general way in which you intend to carry out the research. Will it be based on a survey; interviews; examination of secondary data; or a combination of methods? Here again, it is essential to explain why you have chosen your approach (Chapter 4). Your explanation should be based on the most effective way of meeting your research objectives.

The research design section gives an overall view of the method chosen and the reason for that choice. The data collection section goes into much more detail about how specifically the data are to be collected and associated issues of access and ethics (Chapter 5). For example, if you are using a survey approach you should specify your population and sample size. You should also clarify how the questionnaires will be distributed and how they will be analysed. If you are using interviews you should explain how you will access the interviewees, how many interviews will be conducted, their intended duration, whether these will be tape recorded and how they will be analysed. In short, you should demonstrate to your reader that you have thought carefully about all the issues regarding your method and their relationship to your research objectives. However, it is normally not necessary in the proposal to include precise details of the method you will employ, for example the content of the observation schedule or questionnaire questions.

Timescale

This will help you and your reader to decide on the viability of your research proposal. It will be helpful if you divide your research plan into stages. This will give you a clear idea as to what is possible in the given timescale. Experience has shown that, however well the researcher's time is organised, the whole process seems to take longer than anticipated.

WORKED EXAMPLE: *A research time scale*

As part of the final year of their undergraduate business studies degree all our students have to undertake an 8000- to 10 000-word research project. In order to assist them with their time management we discuss the following outline timescale with them:

Target date	Month number	Task to be achieved
start October	1	● Start thinking about research ideas (latest start date)
end November	2	● Literature read
		● Research questions/objectives clearly defined with reference to literature
end December	3	● Literature review drafted
		● Methodology literature read for dissertations involving secondary/primary data
end January	4	● Secondary/primary data collected and analysed (analysis techniques linked to the literature)
		● Literature review extended further
mid-February	5	● Further writing up and analysis
end March	6	● Draft completed including formatting bibliography etc.
mid-May	8	● Draft revised as necessary
end May	8	● Submission

Resources

This is another facet of viability (Table 2.1). It will allow you and the reader to assess whether what you are proposing can be resourced. Resource considerations may be categorised as finance, data access and equipment.

Conducting research costs money. This may be for travel, subsistence, help with data analysis or postage for questionnaires. Think through the expenses involved and ensure that you can meet them.

Assessors of your proposal will need to be convinced that you have access to the data you need to conduct your research. This may be unproblematic if you are carrying out research in your own organisation. Many academic committees wish to see written approval from host organisations in which researchers are planning to conduct research. You will also need to convince your reader of the possibility of obtaining a reasonable response to any questionnaire that you send.

It is surprising how many research proposals have ambitious plans for large-scale surveys with no thought given to how the data will be analysed. It is important that you convince the reader of your proposal that you have access to the computer hardware and software required to analyse your data. Moreover, it is necessary for you to demonstrate that you have the necessary skill to perform the analysis or that you have access to help.

References

It is not necessary to try and impress your proposal reader with an enormous list of references (Robson, 1993). A few literature sources to which you have referred in the background section and that relate to the previous work which is directly informing your own proposal should be all that is necessary.

Criteria for evaluating research proposals

The extent to which the components of the proposal fit together

Your rationale for conducting the research should include a study of the previously published research, including relevant theories in the topic area. This study should inform your research question(s) and objectives. Your proposed methodology should flow directly from these research questions and objectives. The time that you have allocated should be a direct reflection of the methods you employ, as should the resources which you need.

- -

WORKED EXAMPLE: *Fitting together the components of the research proposal*

Karl was fascinated by the idea of men seeking what had traditionally been thought of as 'women's jobs'. He read all that he could on this topic, including accounts of research that had been carried out in different countries. This helped Karl define his research question as: 'Why may employers discriminate against men seeking what had traditionally been thought of as "women's jobs"?'

He reasoned that research design based on asking employers why they discriminated would be ineffective at answering his research question. Therefore, he decided to apply for some 'women's jobs' himself and from the resultant interviews see if he could discover at first hand what the reasons might be. He also advertised in local newspapers for men who had been in similar situations to contact him.

Karl reckoned that a six-month period would allow him to apply and be interviewed for approximately 20 jobs. This would give him sufficient data from which to draw conclusions. He thought that this would also give him enough time to interview any male respondents to his advertisements.

The main resource which Karl needed was acting ability. Since he was a member of the University Drama Society, he possessed this in abundance!

The viability of the proposal

This is the answer to the question: 'Will this research be carried out satisfactorily within the timescale?'

The absence of pre-conceived ideas

Your research should be an exciting journey into the unknown. Don't be like the student who came to Phil to talk over a research proposal and said, 'Of course, I know what the answer will be'. When asked to explain the purpose of doing the research if he already knew the answer, he became rather defensive, and eventually looked for another project tutor and, probably, another topic.

2.6 SUMMARY

- The process of formulating and clarifying your research topic is the most important part of your research project.
- Attributes of a research topic do not vary a great deal between universities. The most important is that your research topic will meet the requirements of the examining body.
- Generating and refining research ideas can make use of a variety of techniques. It is important that you use a variety of techniques, including those which involve rational thinking and those which involve creative thinking.
- The ideas generated can be integrated subsequently using a technique such as working up and narrowing down.
- Clear research questions and objectives, based on the relevant literature, will act as a focus for the research which follows.
- Research can be distinguished from intelligence gathering. Research is theory dependent and goes beyond just asking 'what' questions.
- Writing a research proposal helps you to organise your ideas and can be thought of as a contract between you and the reader of the proposal
- The content of the research proposal should tell the reader what you want to do, why you want to do it, what you are trying to achieve and how you plan to achieve it.

Self-check questions and assignment

Self-check question 2.1
Why is it important to spend time formulating and clarifying your research topic?

Self-check question 2.2
You have decided to search the literature to 'try and come up some research ideas in the area of Operations Management'. How will you go about this?

Self-check question 2.3
A colleague of yours wishes to generate a research idea in the area of accounting. He has examined his own strengths and interests on the basis of his assignments and read some review articles, but has failed to find an idea by which he is excited. He comes and asks you for advice.

Suggest two techniques which your colleague could use and justify your choice.

Self-check question 2.4
You are interested in doing some research on the interface between business organisations and schools. Write three research questions which may be appropriate.

Self-check question 2.5
What may be the theory underpinning the decision by organisations who sponsor schools?

Self-check question 2.6
How would you demonstrate the influence of relevant theory in your research proposal?

Assignment 2:
Choosing your research topic and writing your research proposal

- If you have not been given a research idea, consider the techniques available for generating and refining research ideas. Choose a selection of those with which you feel most comfortable, making sure to include both rational and creative thinking techniques. Use these to try to generate a research idea or ideas. Once you have some research ideas, or if you have been unable to find an idea, talk to your project tutor.

- Evaluate your research ideas against the checklist of attributes of a good research project (Table 2.1).

- Refine your research ideas using a selection of the techniques available for generating and refining research ideas. Re-evaluate your research ideas against the checklist of attributes of a good research project (Table 2.1). Remember that it is better to revise (and in some situations discard) ideas which do not appear to be feasible at this stage. Integrate your ideas using the process of working up and narrowing down to form one research idea.

- Use your research idea to write a general focus research question. Where possible this should be a 'why' or a 'how' rather than a 'what' question.

- Use the general focus research question to write more detailed research questions and your research objectives.

● Write your research proposal making sure it includes a clear title and sections on:
- the background to your research;
- your research questions and objectives;
- the method you intend to use;
- the timescale for your research;
- the resources you require;
- references to any literature on which you have drawn.

References

Bennett, R. (1991) 'What is Management Research', in Smith, N.C. and Dainty, P. (eds) (1991) *The Management Research Handbook*, London, Routledge, pp. 67–77.

Buzan, T. with Buzan, B. (1995) *The Mind Map Book* (revised edition), London, BBC Books.

Carroll, L. (1989) *Alice's Adventures in Wonderland*, London, Hutchinson.

Ghauri, P. Grønhaug, K. and Kristianslund, I. (1995) *Research Methods in Business Studies: A Practical Guide*, London, Prentice-Hall.

Gill, J. and Johnson, P. (1991) *Research Methods for Managers*, London, Paul Chapman.

Howard, K. and Sharp, J.A. (1983) *The Management of a Student Research Project*, Aldershot, Gower.

Jankowicz, A.D. (1995) *Business Research Projects* (2nd edn), London, Chapman & Hall.

Kervin, J.B. (1992) *Methods for Business Research*, New York, HarperCollins.

Moody, P.E. (1983) *Decision Making: Proven Methods for Better Decisions*, London, McGraw-Hill.

Phillips, E.M. and Pugh, D.S. (1994) *How to Get a PhD* (2nd edn), Buckingham, Open University Press.

Raimond, P. (1993) *Management Projects*, London, Chapman & Hall.

Robson, C. (1993) *Real World Research*, Oxford, Blackwell.

Smith, N.C .and Dainty, P. (1991) *The Management Research Handbook*, London, Routledge.

Yin, R.K. (1994) *Case Study Research: Design and Methods* (2nd edn), Beverly Hills, California, Sage.

Further reading

Gill, J. and Johnson, P. (1991) *Research Methods for Managers*, London, Paul Chapman. Chapter 3 is a particularly clear account of the role of theory in research methods and is worth reading to gain a better understanding of this often misunderstood area.

Pugh, D. (1988) 'The Aston Research Programme', in Bryman, A. (ed.) *Doing Research in Organisations*, London, Routledge, pp. 123–35. This contains an interesting account of how research ideas developed in a large-scale research project.

Raimond, P. (1993) *Management Projects*, London, Chapman & Hall. Chapter 4 contains a useful discussion of techniques for helping to identify project ideas. It is particularly good for those techniques which we have classified as creative rather than rational.

Robson, C. (1993) *Real World Research*, Oxford, Blackwell. Appendix A is devoted to the writing of research proposals and is a very useful source of further information.

Case 2:
The use of internal and word-of-mouth recruitment methods

A few years ago Mark and Phil thought it would be fun to work together on a piece of research. They also hoped it would benefit their continuing development as researchers. Mark's research background has its origins in the recruitment and subsequent mobility of labour. His research methods skills emphasise the quantitative approach, although he had undertaken a variety of qualitative research projects. Phil's strength is as a mainstream HRM academic with a bias towards understanding the processes of everyday HRM. His research methods skills are mainly qualitative. Unlike many students, their research area was one in which they were aware of the literature. However, despite this, they were in a similar situation to many students. They wanted to undertake a new piece of work which would excite them and be of some practical benefit to organisations.

In the early 1990s Mark had carried out a survey of recruitment methods used by local authority employers. This had built on and developed research he had undertaken as part of his doctoral thesis approximately 10 years earlier. While discussing the findings in the coffee shop, Phil agreed to take a more detailed look to see if there was anything of practical significance for managers. During discussion a few weeks later, an issue emerged which they felt was fascinating. Throughout the previous decade there appeared to have been a dominance of internal and word-of-mouth recruitment. Internal recruitment is where recruitment is restricted to an organisation's existing employees. Word of mouth is where recruitment relies on the organisation's existing employees to tell other people in their social networks about the vacancies.

Through their discussion Phil and Mark developed a clear research idea which was in both their areas of academic strength. This was concerned with explaining why, given the centrality of equal opportunities to local authorities' recruitment, internal and word-of-mouth recruitment was so dominant. They felt this idea was fascinating because, on the face of it, both forms of recruitment were alien to the principle of equal opportunities. Quantitative evidence from Mark's survey showed that the phenomena of internal and word-of-mouth recruitment were dominant. Mark's experience of working in local authorities supported this. They now needed to refine the idea, develop clear research questions and objectives, and write their research proposal.

They adopted what they felt was a rational process. They both drafted outline proposals simultaneously and criticised each other's work. This led to an outline proposal which integrated their ideas and encompassed research questions and objectives.

Next they reviewed the literature to establish what work had been done on this aspect of recruitment. The overall conclusion from the empirical research, undertaken in all sectors of the economy, was that word-of-mouth and internal recruitment methods were still important. However, none of this work concentrated on local authorities. Moreover, they thought that awareness of the importance of equal opportunities would have grown since the time when the research was conducted. Their research proposal still seemed valid and the literature confirmed its relevance. In addition, reading the literature had suggested possible new research questions. However, they still needed to discuss their proposal with other people.

The first discussion was with an equal opportunities officer at a London borough. He was not excited by their research idea and commented that he was not surprised by the survey findings. These, he said, were due to the need to redeploy people who would otherwise be made redundant. The second discussion was with a personnel specialist from a large county authority. Her response can be paraphrased as, 'Well, what do you expect . . . the pay for manual positions is relatively low so there are few applicants . . . we therefore have to rely on word of mouth.'

Mark and Phil were depressed to say the least. They thought they had a fascinating research question. Yet the first two people they had discussed their ideas with had shown them the answer was obvious. They had spent a great deal of time refining their research proposal and in searching the literature. Their immediate reaction was to abandon the research completely. However, a few days later they opted to revise their research ideas. They decided to discard the local authorities and equal opportunities perspectives and focus on the notification channels used by employers. Their revised research question was: 'Why do organisations use word-of-mouth recruitment?'

Case-study questions

1 **a** Do you think that Phil and Mark had good reasons for choosing the research topic initially?

   b Give reasons for your answer.

2 Draft a possible first research question for Mark and Phil's idea as described in the first three paragraphs of the case study.

3 What lessons can you learn from Phil and Mark's experience?

4 To what extent do you feel that Mark and Phil's final research question meets the criteria outlined in Table 2.1.

Answers to self-check questions

Self-check question 2.1
There are numerous reasons you could include in your answer. Some of the more important include:

- without being clear what you are going to do, it is difficult to plan your research;
- to enable you to choose the most appropriate research strategy and data collection and analysis techniques;
- to ensure that your topic meets the examining body's requirements;

- to ensure that your topic is one that you are capable of doing and excites your imagination;
- to ensure that you will have sufficient time and money resources to undertake your topic;
- to ensure that you will be able to gain access to the data you require;
- to ensure that the issues in your topic are capable of being linked to theory.

Self-check question 2.2

One starting point would be to ask your project tutor for suggestions of possible recent review articles or articles containing recommendations for further work which he or she has read. Another would be to browse recent editions of operations management journals, such as the *International Journal of Operations and Production Management*, for possible research ideas. These would include both statements of the absence of research and unfounded assertions. Recent reports held in your library may be of use here.

You could also scan one or two recently published operations management textbooks for overviews of research that has been undertaken.

Self-check question 2.3

From the description given it would appear that your colleague has only considered rational thinking techniques. It would therefore seem sensible to suggest two creative thinking techniques, as it is to be hoped that these would generate an idea which would appeal to his heart. One technique which you could suggest is brainstorming, perhaps emphasising the need to do this with other colleagues. Exploring past research projects in the accountancy area would be another possibility. You might also suggest that he keeps a notebook of ideas.

Self-check question 2.4

Your answer will probably differ from that below. However, the sort of things you could be considering include:

- How do business organisations benefit from their liaison with schools?
- Why do business organisations undertake school liaison activities?
- To what degree do business organisations receive value for money in their schools liaison activities?

Self-check question 2.5

Undoubtedly organisations would be looking for a 'pay off'. This may be left undefined – that it is bound to be a 'good thing' – or it may be linked to a specific theory that it will create an image of the organisation as one that is community minded. This is a particularly important concept if the product or service is one that has community values, for example water or electricity.

Self-check question 2.6

Try including a subsection in the background section which is headed: 'How the previous published research has informed my research questions and objectives'. Then show how, say, a gap in the previous research which is there because nobody has pursued a particular approach before has led to your filling that gap.

CHAPTER 3

Critically reviewing the literature

The objectives of this chapter are to outline the importance and purpose of the critical literature review, and to introduce you to a range of search strategies. It will help you plan and undertake your search and write your review.

The chapter outlines what a critical review needs to include and discusses the range of primary, secondary and tertiary literature sources available.

The processes of identifying key words and searching, including using the Internet, are outlined.

Advice is offered on how to record items and evaluate their relevance.

3.1 INTRODUCTION

Two main reasons exist for reviewing the literature (Howard and Sharp, 1983). The first, the preliminary search which helps you generate and refine your research ideas, has already been discussed in Section 2.3. The second, often referred to as the *critical review*, is part of your research project proper. Most research textbooks, as well as your project tutor, will argue that this critical review of the literature is necessary. Although you may feel that you already have a good knowledge of your research area, you will find reviewing the literature both useful and informative. Project assessment criteria usually require you to demonstrate awareness of the current state of knowledge in your subject, its limitations and how your research fits in this wider context (Gill and Johnson, 1991). In Jankowicz's (1995: 128–9) words:

> 'Knowledge doesn't exist in a vacuum, and your work only has value in relation to other people's. Your work and your findings will be significant only to the extent that they're the same as, or different from, other people's work and findings.'

You therefore need to establish what research has been published in your chosen area and to try to identify any other research that might currently be in progress. The items you read and write about will enhance your subject knowledge and help you to clarify your research question(s) further. This process is called *critically reviewing the literature*.

For most research projects your literature search will be an early activity. Despite this early start, it is usually necessary to continue searching throughout your project's life. The

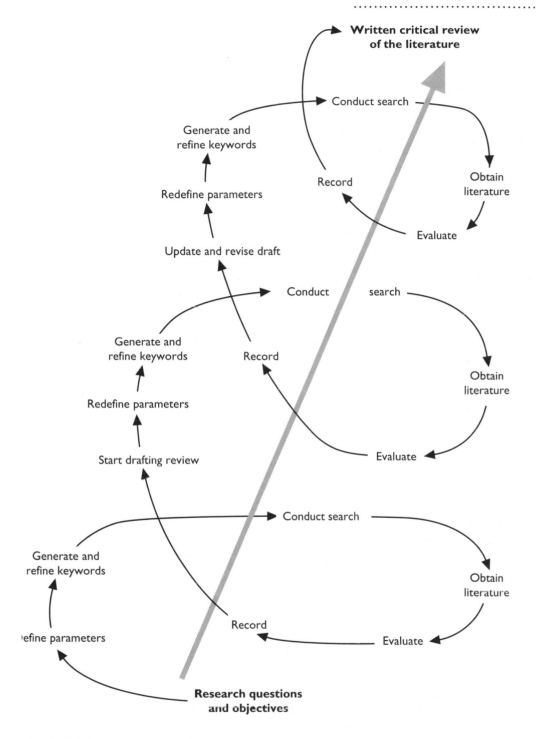

Fig 3.1 The literature review process

© Mark Saunders, Philip Lewis, Adrian Thornhill, Lynnette Bailey and Martin Jenkins, 1997

process can be likened to an upward spiral culminating in the final draft of a written critical literature review (Fig 3.1). In the initial stage of your literature review you will start to define the parameters to your research question(s) and objectives (Section 3.4). After generating key words and conducting your first search (Section 3.5) you will have a list of references to authors who have published on these subjects. Once these have been obtained, you can read and evaluate them (Section 3.6), record the ideas (Section 3.7) and start drafting your review. After the initial search you will be able to redefine your parameters more precisely and undertake further searches, keeping in mind your research question(s) and objectives. As your thoughts develop each subsequent search will be focused more precisely on material that is likely to be relevant. At the same time you will probably be refining your research question(s) and objectives in the light of your reading.

Unlike some academic disciplines, business and management research makes use of a wide range of literature. While your review is likely to include specific business disciplines such as finance, marketing, or human resource management, it is also likely to include other disciplines. Those most frequently consulted by our students include economics, psychology, sociology and geography. Given this, and the importance of the review to your research, it is vital for you to be aware of what a critical literature review is and the full range of literature available before you start the reviewing process. For these reasons we start this chapter by outlining what your critical review of the literature needs to include (Section 3.2) and the literature resources available (Section 3.3).

3.2 THE CRITICAL REVIEW

The purpose of the critical review

Your critical literature review will form the foundation on which your research is built. As you will have gathered from the introduction, its main purpose is to help you develop a good understanding and insight into relevant previous research and the trends that have emerged. You would not expect a scientific researcher inquiring into the causes of cot death to start the research without first reading about the findings of other cot death research. Likewise, you should not expect to start your research without first reading what other researchers in your area have already found out.

The precise purpose of your reading of the literature will depend on the approach you are intending to use in your research. For some research projects you will use the literature to help you identify theories and ideas which you will test using data. This is known as a *deductive approach* (Section 4.1) in which you develop a theoretical or conceptual framework which you subsequently test using data. For other research projects you will be planning to explore your data and develop theories from it which you will subsequently relate to the literature. This is known as an *inductive approach* (Section 4.1) and, although your research still has a clearly defined purpose with research question(s) and objectives, you do not start with any pre-determined theories or conceptual frameworks. We believe such an approach cannot be adopted without a competent knowledge of your subject area.

There is, however, no need to review all of the literature before collecting your data. You do not want your own ideas to be drowned out by the ideas in the literature. If your analysis is effective, new findings and theories will emerge which neither you nor anyone else had thought about (Strauss and Corbin, 1990). Despite this, when you write your critical review, you will need to show how your findings and the theories you have developed relate to the work that has gone before.

Your review also has a number of other purposes. Many of these have been highlighted by Borg and Gall (1989) in their book for students undertaking educational research and are, we believe, of equal relevance to business and management researchers.

- To help you further refine your research question(s) and objectives.
- To highlight research possibilities that have been overlooked implicitly in research to date.
- To discover explicit recommendations for further research. These can provide you with a superb justification for your own research question(s) and objectives.
- To help you avoid simply repeating work that has been done already.
- To sample current opinions in newspapers, professional and trade journals, thereby gaining insights into the aspects of your research question(s) and objectives that are considered newsworthy.
- To discover and provide an insight into research strategies (Section 4.2) and methodologies that may be appropriate to your own research question(s) and objectives.

The content of the critical review

As you begin to find, read and evaluate the literature, you will need to think how to combine the academic theories and ideas it contains to form the critical review which will appear in your project report. This will need to discuss critically the work that has already been undertaken in your area of research and reference that work (Appendix 2). It will draw out the key points and trends (recognising any omissions and bias) and present them in a logical way. In doing this you will provide readers of your project report with the necessary background knowledge to your research question(s) and objectives. It will also enable the readers to see your ideas against the background of previously published research in the area.

In writing your critical review you will therefore need to:

- show how your research relates to previously published research;
- assess the strengths and weaknesses of previous work including omissions or bias and take these into account in your arguments;
- justify your arguments by referencing previous research;
- through clear referencing enable those reading your project report to find the original work you cite.

In addition, by fully acknowledging the work of others you will avoid charges of *plagiarism* and the associated penalties.

The structure of the critical review

The literature review that you write for your project report should be a description and critical analysis of what other authors have written (Jankowicz, 1995). When drafting your review you need to focus on your research question(s) and objectives. One way of helping you focus is to think of your literature review as discussing how far the literature goes in answering your research question(s). The shortfall in the literature will be addressed, at least partially, in the remainder of your project report. Another way of helping you to focus is to ask yourself how your review relates to your objectives. If it does not, or only does partially, there is a need for a clearer focus on your objectives. The precise structure of the critical review is usually your choice, although you should check as it may be specified by your examining body. Three common structures are:

- a single chapter;
- a series of chapters;
- throughout the project report as you tackle various issues.

In all project reports you should return to the key issues from the literature in your conclusions (Section 13.3).

Within your critical review you will need to juxtapose different authors' ideas and form your own opinions and conclusions based on these. Although you will not be able to start writing until you have undertaken some reading, we recommend that you start drafting your review early (Fig 3.1). What you write can then be updated and revised as you read more.

A common mistake with critical literature reviews is that they become uncritical listings of previous research. Haywood and Wragg (1982: 2 cited by Bell, 1993: 35) describe this adeptly as:

> 'the furniture sale catalogue, in which everything merits a one paragraph entry no matter how skilfully it has been conducted: Bloggs (1975) found this, Smith (1976) found that, Jones (1977) found the other, Bloggs, Smith and Jones (1978) found happiness in heaven.'

Although there is no single structure that your critical review should take, our students have found it useful to think of the review as a funnel in which you do the following:

1 Start at a more general level before narrowing down to your specific research question(s) and objectives.
2 Provide a brief overview of key ideas.
3 Summarise in brief, compare and contrast the work of the key writers.
4 Narrow down to highlight the work most relevant to your research.
5 Provide a detailed account of the findings of this work.

6 Highlight those issues where your research will provide fresh insights.

7 Lead the reader into subsequent sections of your research report which explore these issues.

Whichever way you structure your review, you must demonstrate that you have read, understood and evaluated the items you have located. The key to writing a critical literature review is therefore to link together the different ideas you find in the literature to form a coherent and cohesive argument. Subsequent parts of your project report (Section 13.3) must follow on from this 'seamlessly as a continuation of the argument' (Jankowicz, 1995: 130).

WORKED EXAMPLE: *A critical review of the literature*

An article by Mark, published in the *International Journal of Manpower* (Saunders, 1993: 40–41), reviewed the vacancy notification and employee mobility literature. The following extract illustrates:

■ the overall structure of starting at a more general level before narrowing down;

■ the provision of a brief overview of (some of) the key ideas;

■ summarising, comparing and contrasting the work of key writers;

■ highlighting (some of) the most relevant work.

Employers recruit for two reasons, to replace employees (80%) and for expansion (20%) (Roper 1988). In both cases notification can be viewed as the point at which employer and job seeker labour searches interact (Dale 1987) and make contact (Watson 1989), where the employers' search for new employees links into those searching for employment within both the internal and the wider labour markets. For employees to be mobile within their company or between employers they need to be aware of vacancies. The key factor here is therefore the availability of information about job vacancies (for example Saunders 1985, Mortenson 1986). The methods adopted by an employer to search for potential new employees to fill a vacancy is based upon a series of factors. Crucial to the choice of notification method is the company policy regarding filling vacancies externally or internally (Salt 1990). Subsequent to this the employer will need to decide how and when to notify the vacancy, whether or not to short list an applicant and whether or not to offer the post (Herriot 1989).

The importance of this initial vacancy notification to the recruiter has been emphasised, particularly in the more prescriptive (HRM) literature. For example Mondy *et al.* (1987:42) state:

'Effective employee selection depends upon attracting the most qualified applicants. Time and money are wasted when the job search is conducted in the wrong place with the wrong methods.'

Wheeler (1988) identified associated advertising costs of over £370 million in the UK in 1987, the vast majority of this being spent in local and regional press. This excluded all associated costs such as the brochures, leaflets as well as other below the line costs such as staff time. Thus the HRM literature is concerned with how the employer reaches potential employees (Roper 1988). By contrast mobility and migration literature, such as Granovetter (1974), Saunders and Flowerdew (1987), have often focused on the impact on the person actively seeking a new post (the 'job seeker'), such as how choice of notification outlet directly influences applicant location. Theoretical job search and migration literature (principally North American) has been concerned with modelling this process using methods based upon stopping rule models (for example Seater 1979, Mortensen 1986). In focusing on job seekers rather than all potential employees they have excluded those notification methods aimed at people not searching for a job, such as the use of head hunters.

The importance to employers of factors likely to prevent potential applicants from applying and from taking up individual posts (that is factors preventing mobility between jobs) has also been cited in the HRM literature. However this has rarely been considered in any depth by UK textbooks on personnel management (Forster 1991a). To induce mobility employers may well offer incentives to the potential applicant(s) to overcome geographical inertia such as relocation assistance or golden handshakes for some very senior posts (Salt 1990). In the latter case the employee will usually need to move house, that is migrate. Migration specialists, in particular Geographers, have shown that wider institutional, legislative and labour market constraints are also likely to influence mobility and in particular the decision to migrate (Mondy et al. 1987). Other constraints such as those introduced by the Employment Protection Act are also likely to have an impact.

When an employer needs to go outside their organisation to find workers they must begin by identifying sources and methods of recruitment. HRM research and the more prescriptive literature both emphasise the impact and importance of choice of vacancy notification and methods used to encourage mobility for a company both in terms of the cost of recruitment, and equally in the cost of integrating and supporting new employees within the company (Forster and Munton 1990, Male and Clarke 1991). The crucial factor determining the subsequent stages of this process is the way in which potential applicants are made aware that a vacancy exists. To do this the most cost effective sources of recruitment and the appropriate incentives to encourage internal and external applications must be identified for each specific vacancy.

Subsequent to this the employer will need to select the most suitable candidate. HRM writers have argued that in the future employers will be likely to demand increasing mobility from employees within their company (Forster 1991a). Migration researchers have argued that, at a more aggregate level, the implications of this are considerable. They feel that there will be a similar increase in the number of job changes between companies requiring people to move house, that is migrate (Owen and Green 1992a). HRM research points to the need to provide a range of support mechanisms for new employees who, in addition to coping with a new job, will have moved to a new area would in many cases welcome support with the personal side of relocation (Forster 1991b).

Much of the HRM literature has therefore been concerned with the implications of the recruitment process for the employer; in particular how the employer can best manage it to ensure that quality people can be attracted to the organisation and the overall resourcing strategy met (Spellman 1992). Sisson (1989) argues that this takes two approaches; the most important of these in terms of articles published is largely prescriptive and concerned with techniques of personnel management. The latter is a critique and, whilst also from the manager's viewpoint, is concerned with the controls imposed and methods used to maximise employees' surplus value. By contrast the Migration literature has often taken the job seekers' viewpoint and considered the importance and impact of external factors. In addition the scale at which the process has been viewed has ranged from the individual to the international whilst the HRM literature has been principally concerned with the impact at the individual and company scales.

3.3 LITERATURE SOURCES AVAILABLE

An overview

The literature sources available to help you develop a good understanding of previous research can be divided into three categories: primary (published and unpublished), secondary and tertiary (Fig 3.2). In reality these categories often overlap; for example, primary literature sources including conference proceedings can appear in journals, and some books also contain indexes to primary and secondary literature (National Council for Education Technology, 1993).

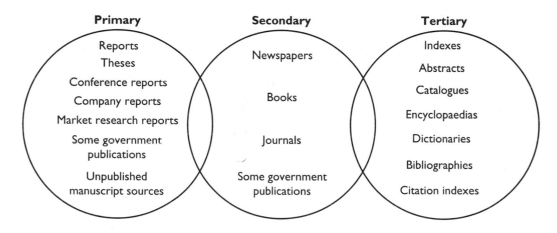

Fig 3.2 Literature sources available

Primary literature sources are the first occurrence of a piece of work. They include published sources such as reports and some central and local government publications such as white papers and planning documents. They also include unpublished manuscript sources such as letters, memos and committee minutes which may be analysed as data in their own right (Section 7.2).

Secondary literature sources such as books and journals are the subsequent publication of primary literature. These publications are aimed at a wider audience. They are easier to locate than primary literature as they are better covered by the tertiary literature.

Tertiary literature sources, also called *search tools*, are designed either to help locate primary and secondary literature or to provide an introduction to a topic. They therefore include indexes and abstracts as well as encyclopaedias and bibliographies.

Your use of these literature sources will depend on your research question(s) and objectives, the need for secondary data to answer them (Section 7.3) and the time available. For some research projects you may only use tertiary and secondary literature, for others you may need to locate primary literature as well. Most research projects will make the greatest use of secondary literature and so it is this we consider first, followed by the primary literature. Tertiary literature sources are not discussed until Section 3.5 as their major use is in conducting a literature search.

Secondary literature sources

The number of secondary literature sources available to you is expanding rapidly (Easterby-Smith *et al.*, 1991). Haythornthwaite (1990) gives a good general introduction to the wide range of sources available. Many new resources have appeared since 1990, especially in *electronic form* on CD-ROM and via the Internet. An increasing number of journals (such as the *Journal of Finance*) can be found on the Internet, while others (including the *Journal of Organisational Change Management*) are available on CD-ROM. The journal *Business Information Review* regularly includes reviews of recent developments. Your university's librarians will also be helpful here. They are likely to be aware of a wide range of secondary literature in business and management and will keep themselves up to date with new resources.

The main secondary literature sources that you are likely to use, along with those primary sources most frequently used by our students, are outlined in Table 3.1. The table is arranged by likely importance of the sources in placing your ideas in the context of earlier research. It therefore starts with the most important, refereed academic journals.

Journals

Journals are also known as *periodicals*, *serials* and *magazines* and are published on a regular basis. At present most are printed, but they are appearing increasingly in electronic form. Journals are a vital literature source for any research. The articles in them are easily accessible as they are well covered by tertiary literature and a good selection are kept for reference in most university libraries (Table 3.1). However, trade and some professional journals may only be partially covered by the tertiary literature (Table 3.2). You therefore need to browse these journals regularly to be sure of finding useful items (Section 3.5).

Articles in *refereed academic journals* (such as the *Journal of Management Studies*) are evaluated by academic peers before publication to assess their quality and suitability. These are usually the most useful for research projects as they will contain detailed reports of relevant earlier research. Not all academic journals are refereed. Most *other academic journals* will have an editor and possibly an editorial board with subject knowledge to select articles. The relevance and usefulness of such journals vary considerably and occasionally you may need to be wary of possible bias (Section 3.6).

Professional journals (such as *People Management*) are produced for their members by organisations such as the Institute of Personnel and Development, the Institute of Chartered Accountants and the American Marketing Association. They contain a mix of news-related items and more detailed articles. However, you need to exercise caution as articles can be biased towards the author's or the organisation's views. Articles are often of a more practical nature and more closely related to professional needs than those in academic journals. Some organisations will also produce newsletters or current awareness publications which you may find useful for up-to-date information. *Trade journals* fulfil a similar function to

Source	Frequency of publication	Format of publication	Coverage by abstracts and indexes (tertiary sources)	Likely availability
Refereed academic journal	Mainly monthly or quarterly	Mainly printed but increasingly available on microfiche, CD-ROM and the Internet	Well covered	Kept as reference in most university libraries; those not available locally can usually be obtained using inter-library loans
Other academic journal				
Professional journal	Mainly weekly or monthly		Not as good as academic and refereed journals, will probably need to browse actual copies of journal	Not as widely available in university libraries as academic and refereed journals; can be obtained using inter-library loans
Trade journal				
Newspapers	Mainly daily or weekly	All UK broadsheets now available on CD-ROM; also available on microfilm	Specialised indexes available; CD-ROM and Internet format easy to search using key words	Kept as reference in most university libraries
Books	Once, subsequent editions may be published	As for refereed academic journals	Well covered by abstracts and indexes	Widely available; those not available locally can be obtained using inter-library loans
Conference proceedings	Dependent on the conference, sometimes as part of a journal	As for refereed academic journals; may be published in book form	Depends on conference although often limited; specialist indexes sometimes available	Not widely held by university libraries; may be possible to obtain using inter-library loans
Reports	Once	As for refereed academic journals	Poor compared to most secondary sources, although some specialist indexes exist	
Theses	On the awarding of the research degree	Mainly printed but increasingly available on microfiche	Good for PhD and MPhil research degrees, otherwise poor	Usually obtained using inter-library loans; often only one copy

Table 3.1 Main primary and secondary literature sources
© Mark Saunders, Philip Lewis, Adrian Thornhill, Lynnette Bailey and Martin Jenkins, 1997

45

professional journals. They are published by trade organisations or aimed at particular industries or trades such as catering or mining. Often they focus on new products or services and news items. They rarely contain articles based on empirical research, although some provide summaries of research.

Newspapers

Newspapers are a good source of topical events, new developments within business and government, and recent statistical information such as share prices. They also produce special reports, such as the *Financial Times* industrial sector reports. Since the early 1990s the main broadsheet newspapers have been available on CD-ROM in most university libraries (and more recently on-line or via the Internet). As a consequence, finding items in these newspapers is quick and easy. Items in earlier issues are more difficult to access as they are usually stored on microfilm and need to be located using printed indexes. However, you need to be careful as newspapers may contain bias in their coverage, be it political, geographical or personal. Reporting can also be inaccurate and you may not pick up any subsequent amendments. In addition, the news presented is filtered depending on events at the time, with priority given to more headline-grabbing stories (Stewart and Kamins, 1993).

Books

Books or *monographs* are written for a specific audience. Some are aimed at the academic market, with a theoretical slant. Others, aimed at practising professionals, may be more applied in their content. The material in books is usually presented in a more ordered and accessible manner than that in journals, pulling together a wider range of topics. They are therefore particularly useful as introductory sources to help clarify your research question(s) and objectives or the research methods you intend to use. But beware, books may contain out of date material even by the time they are published.

Primary literature sources

Primary literature sources are more difficult to locate (Table 3.1). The most accessible, and those most likely to be of use in showing how your research relates to that of other people, are reports, conference proceedings and theses.

Reports

Reports include market research reports such as those produced by Mintel and Keynote, government reports and academic reports. Even if you are able to locate these, you may find it difficult to gain access to them as they are not as widely available as books (Section 7.4). Reports are not well indexed in the tertiary literature and you will need to rely on specific search tools such *British Reports, Translations and Theses* (Table 3.2).

Conference proceedings

Conference proceedings, sometimes referred to as *symposia*, are often published as unique titles within journals or as books. Most conferences will have a theme which is very specific but some have a wide-ranging overview. Proceedings are not well indexed by tertiary literature, so as with reports you may have to rely on specific search tools such as *Index to Conference Proceedings* (Table 3.2). If you do locate and are able to obtain the proceedings for a conference on the theme of your research, you will have a wealth of relevant information.

Theses

Theses are unique and so for a major research project can be a good source of detailed information; they will also be a good source of further references. Unfortunately they can be difficult to locate and, when found, difficult to access, as there may be only one copy at the awarding institution. Specific search tools are available such as *Index to Theses* and *British Reports, Translations and Theses* (Table 3.2). Only research degrees such as PhD and MPhil are well covered by these tertiary resources. Research undertaken as part of a taught master's degree is not covered as systematically.

3.4 PLANNING THE LITERATURE SEARCH

It is important that you plan this search carefully to ensure you locate relevant and up-to-date literature. This will enable you to establish what research has been previously published in your area and to relate your own research to it. All our students have found their literature search a time-consuming process which takes far longer than expected. Fortunately, time spent planning will be repaid in time saved when searching the literature. As you start to plan your search you need to beware of information overload! One of the easiest ways to achieve this is to start the main search for your critical review without a clearly defined research question(s), objectives and outline proposal (Sections 2.4 and 2.5). Before commencing your literature search we suggests you undertake further planning by:

- defining the parameters of your search;
- generating key words and search terms;
- discussing your ideas as widely as possible.

Defining parameters

For most research questions and objectives you will have a good idea of what subject matter is going to be relevant. You will, however, be less clear about the parameters within which you need to search. In particular, you need to be clear (Bell, 1993) about the following:

- language of publication (for example English);
- subject area (for example accountancy);
- business sector (for example manufacturing);
- geographical area (for example Europe);
- publication period (for example the last 10 years);
- literature type (for example journals and books).

One way of starting to firm up these parameters is by re-examining your lecture notes and course textbooks in the area of your research question. While doing this we suggest you make a note of subjects that appear most relevant to your research question and the names of relevant authors. These will be helpful when generating possible key words.

For example, if your research was on the marketing benefits of arts sponsorship to UK banking organisations, you might identify the subject area as marketing and sponsorship. Implicit in this is the need to think broadly. A common comment we hear from students who have attempted a literature search is 'there's nothing written on my research topic'. This is usually because they have identified one or more of their parameters too narrowly. We therefore recommend that if you encounter this problem you broaden one or more of your parameters to include material which your narrower search would not have located.

WORKED EXAMPLE: *Defining parameters for a research question*

Simon's research question was, 'How have green issues influenced the way in which man-ufacturers advertise cars?' To be certain of finding material, he defined each parameter in narrow and, in most instances, broader terms:

Parameter	Narrow	Broader
Language:	UK (e.g. Car)	UK and USA (e.g. Car and Automobile)
Subject area:	Green issues	Environmental issues
	Motor industry	Manufacturing
	Advertising	Marketing
Business sector:	Motor Industry	Manufacturing
Geographical area:	UK	Europe and North America
Publication period:	Last 5 years	Last 15 years
Literature type:	Academic journals and books	Journals and books

Generating key words

Undertaking reading of articles by key authors and recent review articles in your research area is also important at this stage. It will help you define your subject matter and suggest appropriate key words. Recent *review articles* are often helpful here. Their discussion of the current state of research for a particular topic will help you refine your key words. In addi-tion, they will probably contain references to other work which is pertinent to your

research question(s) and objectives. If you are unsure about review art
tutor should be able to point you in the right direction.

After re-reading your lecture notes, textbooks and undertaking t'
you will have a list of subjects that appear relevant to your research pr
to define precisely what is relevant to your research in terms of key v

The identification of *key words* or *search terms* is the most important p..
your search for relevant literature (Bell, 1993). Key words are the basic terms w..
describe your research question(s) and objectives and will be used to search the tertiary literature. Key words (which can include authors' surnames identified in the examination of
your lecture notes and course textbooks) can be identified using one or a number of different techniques in combination. Those found most useful by our students include:

- discussion with colleagues, your project tutor and librarians;
- initial reading;
- dictionaries, thesauruses, encyclopaedias and handbooks;
- brainstorming;
- relevance trees.

Discussion

We believe you should be taking every opportunity to discuss your research. In discussing
your work with others, either face to face, by electronic mail or letter, you will be sharing
your ideas, gaining feedback and obtaining new ideas and approaches.

Initial reading, dictionaries, encyclopaedias, handbooks and thesauruses

To produce the most relevant key words you may need to build on your brainstorming session with support materials such as *dictionaries, encyclopaedias, handbooks* and
thesauruses, both general and subject specific. These are also good starting points for new
topics with which you may be unfamiliar and for related subject areas. Initial reading, particularly of recent review articles, may be of help here. Project tutors, colleagues and
librarians can also be useful sources of ideas.

Brainstorming

Brainstorming has already been outlined as a technique for helping you develop your
research question (Section 2.3). However, it is also helpful for generating key words.
Either individually, or as part of a group, write down all the words and short phrases that
come to mind on your research topic. These are then evaluated and key words (and
phrases) selected.

RKED EXAMPLE: *Generating key words*

The research question of one of our overseas education management students asked: 'How do the actual management requirements of a school pupil record administration system differ from those suggested by the literature?' She brainstormed this question with her peer group. The resulting list included the following key words and phrases:

> schools, pupil records, administration, user requirements, computer,
> management information system, access, legislation, information, database,
> security, UK, Hong Kong, theories

These and others were evaluated by the group, all of whom were teachers in Hong Kong. As a result the following key words (and phrases) were selected:

> pupil records, management information system, computer, database,
> user requirement

Dictionaries and encyclopaedias were used subsequently to add to the choice of key words:

> student record, MIS, security

These were then used in combination to search the tertiary literature sources.

Relevance trees

Relevance trees provide a useful method of bringing some form of structure to your literature search and of guiding your search process (Howard and Sharp, 1983). They look similar to an organisation chart and are a hierarchical 'graph-like' arrangement of headings and subheadings. These headings and subheadings describe your research question(s) and objectives and may be key words (including authors' names) with which you can search. Relevance trees are often constructed after brainstorming. They enable you to decide either with help or on your own (Jankowicz, 1995):

■ which key words are directly relevant to your research question(s) and objectives;

■ which areas you will search first and which you will search later;

■ which areas are more important, as these tend to have more branches.

To construct a relevance tree you proceed as follows.

1 Start with your research question or objective at the top level.

2 Identify two or more subject areas which you think are important.

3 Further subdivide each main subject area into sub-areas which you think are of relevance.

4 Further divide the sub-areas into more precise sub-areas which you think are of relevance.

5 Identify those areas which you need to search immediately and those on which you particularly need to focus. Your project tutor will be of particular help here.

6 As your reading and reviewing progresses, add new areas to your relevance tree.

WORKED EXAMPLE: *Using a relevance tree*

Lily's research question asked, 'Is there a link between benchmarking and Total Quality Management?' After brainstorming her question, she decided to construct a relevance chart using the key words and phrases that had been generated:

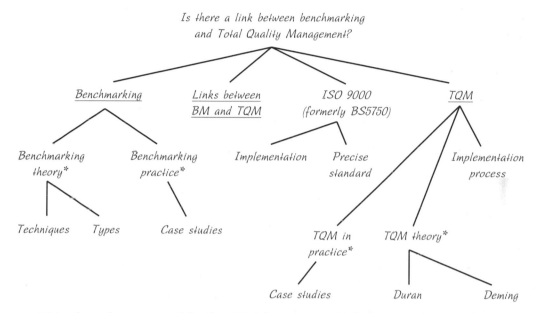

Using her relevance tree Lily identified those areas which she needed to search immediately (underlined) and those on which she particularly needed to focus (starred*).

3.5 CONDUCTING A LITERATURE SEARCH

Your literature search will probably be conducted using a variety of approaches:

- searching using tertiary literature sources;
- obtaining relevant literature (Section 3.6) referenced in articles you have already read;
- scanning and browsing secondary literature in your library;
- searching using the Internet.

Eventually you will be using a variety of these in tandem. However, we suggest that you start your search using tertiary literature sources and obtaining relevant literature that has been referenced in articles you have already read. Reading the articles you locate will enable you to refine your research question(s), objectives and the associated key words before searching using other approaches. It will also help you see more clearly how your research relates to previous research and will provide fresh insights.

Tertiary literature sources

A variety of tertiary literature is available to help you in your search. Most of these publications are called indexes and abstracts, and a selection will be held by your university library. An *index* will, as its name suggests, index articles from a range of journals and sometimes books, chapters from books, reports, theses, conferences and research. The information provided will be sufficient to locate the item; for example for journal articles:

- author or authors of the article;
- date of publication;
- title of the article;
- title of the journal;
- volume and part number of the journal issue;
- page numbers of the article.

Most index searches will be undertaken to find articles using key words, including the author's name. Occasionally you may wish to search by finding those authors who have referenced (cited) a key article after it has been published. A *citation index* enables you to do this, as it lists by author all other authors who have cited that author's publications subsequent to their publication.

An *abstract* provides the same information as an index but also includes a summary of the article, hence the term abstract. This abstract can be useful in helping you to assess the content and relevance of an article to your research before obtaining a copy. You should beware of using abstracts as a source of information for your research. They only contain a summary of the article and are likely to exclude much of relevance.

Indexes and abstracts are produced in printed and electronic (computerised) formats, the latter often being referred to as *databases*. This is the term we will use to refer to all electronic information sources. With the increasing amount of information available electronically, printed indexes and abstracts may be overlooked. Yet they are still a valuable resource, providing a varied and sometimes more specific range of information. Searching printed sources and databases is normally free, although some libraries may charge for printing from databases. One way round this is to take a computer disk on which to save the results of your search. This can subsequently be read into your wordprocessor.

Databases held at other institutions can be accessed via a telecommunications link or the Internet from many university libraries. Many of these will be paid for by subscription, but for pay-as-you-use databases the costs of the search may be passed on to the user. On-line databases provide a wealth of information, which may be updated daily or even several times during one day. This is an advantage over CD-ROMs which are usually updated quarterly.

It is advisable to obtain a librarian's help when using on-line databases because of the variety and lack of user-friendly software and the volume of information. It is also vital to have planned and prepared your search in advance so that time and money are not wasted.

To ensure maximum coverage in your search you need to use all appropriate abstracts and indexes. One mistake many people make is to restrict their searches to one or two business and management tertiary sources rather than using a variety. Some of those more frequently used are outlined in Table 3.2. New databases are being developed all the time, so it is worth asking a librarian for advice.

Name	Format	Coverage
ABI/Inform	CD-ROM, on-line	Indexes approximately 1000 international business and management journals. Also covers subjects such as engineering, law and medicine. Full text of selected articles from 500 journals may be available depending on subscription (CD-ROM updated monthly).
Anbar	CD-ROM, print	Abstracts of articles selected from more than 400 English-language publications on the basis of a significant contribution to knowledge (CD-ROM covers last six years).
British National Bibliography (BNB)	CD-ROM, print	Bibliographic information for books and serials (journals) deposited at the British Library by UK and Irish publishers since 1950.
British Reports, Translations and Theses	Print, microfiche	Detailed listings of research and practice reports produced by non-commercial publishers, local and national government, industry, research institutions and charities. Includes UK doctoral theses since 1970.
Business Periodicals Index	CD-ROM, print, on-line	Indexes English-language business periodicals (articles and book reviews). North American focus. Selection for indexing is by subscriber preference and has altered over time (since 1959).
Global Books in Print	CD-ROM	English language bibliographic information for books in print from most of the world!
Helecon	CD-ROM	Combined indexes from seven European databases on business and management. European focus (updated three times a year).
Index to Business Reports	Print	Indexes over 800 business reports published in business journals and newspapers each year (updated half-yearly).
Index to Conference Proceedings	Print, CD-ROM, on-line	Indexes all conference publications regardless of subject or language, held by British Library Document Supply Centre (updated monthly – print, quarterly – CD-ROM).
Index to Theses	CD-ROM, print	Indexes theses accepted for higher degrees by universities in Great Britain and Ireland and by the CNAA.
HMSO Monthly Catalogue	Print	Lists all publications published and distributed through HMSO (includes parliamentary, government department and European).
Research Index	Print, Internet	Indexes articles and news items of financial interest which appear in the UK national newspapers, professional and trade journals (updated frequently).
Sage Publications/SRM Database of Social Research Methodology	CD-ROM	Abstracts of methodological literature published in English, German, French and Dutch since 1970.
Social Science Citation Index	Print, on-line	Indexes 130 000 articles each year from over 1400 journals in behavioural and social sciences and selected articles from 3100 journals from physical and natural sciences.

Table 3.2 Tertiary literature sources and their coverage

Searching using tertiary literature

Once your key words have been identified, searching using tertiary literature is a relatively straightforward process. You need to do the following:

1 Ensure your key words match the controlled index language (unless you can use free-text searching).
2 Search appropriate printed and database sources.
3 Note the full reference of relevant items found.

Printed sources

Searching printed indexes and abstracts requires a different technique to electronic databases. The coverage of printed indexes tends to be smaller than that of databases. Unlike databases, it is normally only possible to search by author or one broad subject heading, although some cross-references may be included. Because they are paper based each issue or annual accumulation must be searched individually, which can be time consuming.

Databases

Most databases, in contrast, allow more precise searches using combinations of key words. These key words need to match the database's controlled index language of pre-selected terms and phrases or *descriptors*. If your key words do not match this vocabulary your search will be unsuccessful. Your first stage should therefore be to check your key words with the *index* or *browse* option. This is especially useful for checking how an author is indexed or whether hyphens should be used when entering terms. Some databases will also have a *thesaurus* which links words in the controlled index language to other terms. Some thesauruses will provide a definition of the term used as well as indicating other broader subject areas, more specific subject areas, or subjects related to the original term. Despite using these your searches may still be unsuccessful. The most frequent causes of failure are summarised in Table 3.3 as a checklist.

☑ Is the spelling incorrect? Behaviour is spelt with a 'u' in the UK but without in the USA.

☑ Is the language incorrect? Chemists in the UK but drug stores in the USA.

☑ Are you using incorrect terminology? In recent years some terms have been replaced by others, such as redundancy being replaced by downsizing.

☑ Are you using acronyms and abbreviations? For example UK for United Kingdom or ICI instead of Imperial Chemical Industries.

☑ Are you using jargon rather than accepted terminology? For example de-recruitment rather than redundancy.

☑ Are you using a word that is not in the controlled index language?

Table 3.3 Checklist for key words

Once individual key words have been checked, subsequent searches normally use a combination of key words linked using *Boolean logic*. This enables you to combine, limit or widen the variety of items found using *link terms* (Table 3.4). Boolean logic can also be used to construct searches using dates, journal titles and names of organisations or people. Initially it may be useful to limit your search to journal titles held by your library. It may also be valuable to narrow your search to specific years, especially if you are finding a wealth of items and need to concentrate on the most up-to-date. By contrast, searching by author allows you to broaden your search to find other work by known researchers in your area.

Some databases allow you to search on more than the controlled index language using *free-text searching*. This enables you to search the entire database rather than just the controlled vocabulary. Free-text searching is common for some electronic publications on CD-ROM and accessed via the Internet, in particular broadsheet newspapers and journals. These may not have a controlled index language. There are, however, problems with using a free-text search. The context of a key word may be inappropriate, leading to retrieval of irrelevant articles and information overload.

Link term	Purpose	Example	Outcome
AND	Narrows search	Recruitment and interviewing and skills	Only articles containing all three key words selected
OR	Widens search	Recruitment or selection	Articles with at least one key word selected
NOT	Excludes terms from search	Recruitment not selection	Selects articles containing the key word recruitment which do not contain the key word selection
* (truncation)	Uses word stems to pick up different words	Motivat*	Selects articles with: Motivate Motivation Motivating
? (wild card)	Picks up different spellings	behavio?r	Selects articles with: Behavior Behaviour

Table 3.4 Common link terms which use Boolean logic

WORKED EXAMPLE: *Searching printed and CD-ROM indexes and abstracts*

Matthew described his research project using the key words 'performance related pay' and 'organisational change'. As a technophobe he decided to use printed indexes rather than electronic databases. He chose *Anbar* and *Business Periodicals Index*. He checked his key words against each of these tertiary sources, and found they matched with *Anbar*. However, for *Business Periodicals Index* he needed to use 'Pay for Performance'. 'Organizational change' used the American spelling, but this did not matter with the printed index. Unfortunately he encountered problems when carrying out the search:

- there were large numbers of references under each index heading;
- many of the references were not relevant to his research;
- the search terms could not be combined to make his search more specific.

After discussing the problem, the librarian showed Matthew how to use the CD-ROM versions of these printed tertiary sources. Using the databases' indexes he checked his key words again. It was now crucial that he used the appropriate spelling, such as for organizational change. The link term AND enabled him to combine his key words and obtain a manageable list of references. Furthermore, he was able to print out the results of the search rather than noting them by hand.

Scanning and browsing

Any search will only find some of the relevant literature. You will therefore need to scan and browse the literature. New publications such as journals are unlikely to be indexed immediately in tertiary literature so you will need to *browse* these publications to gain an idea of their content. In contrast, *scanning* will involve you going through individual items such as a journal article to pick out points which relate to your own research. It is particularly important that you browse and scan trade and professional journals, as these are less likely to be covered by the tertiary literature.

To make browsing and scanning easier you should:

- identify when those journals that are the most relevant are published and regularly browse them;
- browse new book displays in libraries;
- scan new book reviews in journals and newspapers;
- scan publishers' new book catalogues where available;
- discuss your research with your project tutor and librarians who may be aware of other relevant literature.

Searching the Internet

The *Internet*, sometimes described as the *information superhighway*, is a worldwide network of computers which can provide access to a vast range of literature and other resources stored on computers around the world. Searching these will uncover further material with which you can compare and contrast your ideas. The places where these resources are stored are known as *sites*. Some of the resources may be of use either for your literature review or as secondary data (Chapter 7). As a student you are likely to have access to the Internet through your university's or another organisation's computer network. Alternatively, you can connect to the Internet as an individual subscriber using a microcomputer, modem and telephone.

Once you have decided to search the Internet there are a variety of approaches. These are summarised in Fig 3.3. Your first decision is whether to consult one of the many

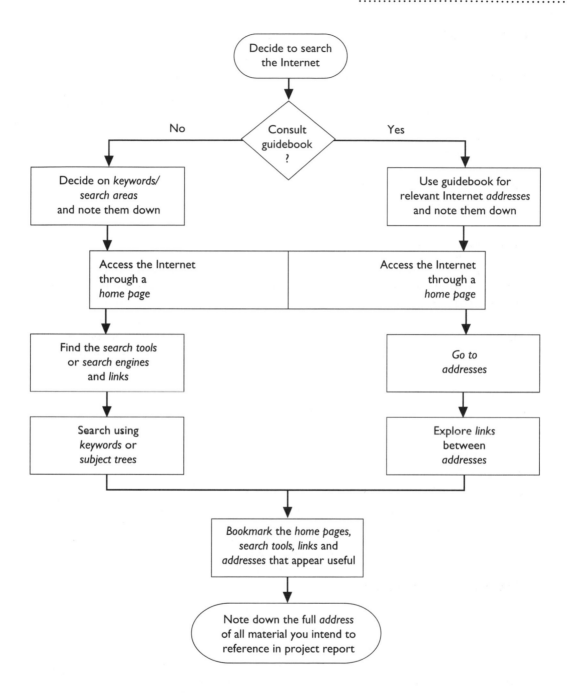

Fig 3.3 Searching the Internet

© Mark Saunders, Philip Lewis, Adrian Thornhill, Lynnette Bailey and Martin Jenkins, 1997

guidebooks. These are invaluable guides for an initial search and contain copious lists of evaluated resources and addresses of sites, for example Ellsworth and Ellsworth (1994) and Campbell and Campbell (1995). Searching and exploring are essential to find relevant material as it can literally appear and disappear overnight!

Home pages

Access to the Internet is through a home page. The *home page*, which can have multiple linked pages, is similar to a title or contents page. Although they often contain publicity for a company or institution, they are an excellent way of navigating around the Internet, as they bring a selection of Internet addresses and search tools together.

Addresses

Addresses of Internet sites (such as http://www.chelt.ac.uk) can be the quickest and most direct method of accessing these resources. Addresses can be obtained from many sources, the most frequently used of which are guide books, newspaper reviews, articles in journals, librarians and lecturers. A problem with going directly to one address is that your search is constrained by other people's ideas. Where there are connections (known as *links*) to other resources, you are limited by other people's ideas and the way they have linked pages.

Search tools

Search tools, often referred to as *search engines*, are probably the most important method of Internet searching for your literature review, as they will enable you to locate most current and up-to-date items. Although normally accessed through home pages, each search tool will have its own address. Most search tools search by key words or subject trees. A *subject tree* is similar to a contents page or index. Some are in the form of alphabetical subject lists, while others are in hierarchical groups of subjects which are then further subdivided with links to more narrowly focused subject groups.

Search tools are becoming more prolific and sophisticated all the time. Be careful, their use can be extremely time consuming. Your search will probably locate a mass of resources many of which will be irrelevant to you. It is also easy to become side-tracked to more interesting and glossy sites not relevant to your research needs!

Bookmarking

Once you have found a useful Internet site you need to note its address. This process, termed *bookmarking*, uses the software to note the Internet address and means you will be able to access it again directly. The vast amount of resources available and the fact that resources, home pages and sites can be added and deleted by their producers means it is vital to keep a record of the addresses (Section 3.7). These will be needed to reference your sources when you write your critical review (Section 3.2). When sufficient sites have been bookmarked it is possible to arrange them in whatever hierarchical way you wish.

3.6 OBTAINING AND EVALUATING THE LITERA

Obtaining the literature

Tertiary literature will provide you with details of what literature is avai
locate it. The next stage (Fig 3.1) is to obtain these items. To do this y
as follows:

1 Check your library catalogue to find out whether the appropriate publication is held by your library.

2 (for those publications that are held by your library) note their location:

   a locate the publication and scan it to discover if it is likely to be worth reading thoroughly,

   b browse other books and journals with similar class marks to see if they may also be of use.

3 (For those items that are not held by your library) order the item from another library on *inter-library loan*. As Bell (1993) points out, this is not a free service so make sure you really need it first. Our students have found that, in general, it is only worthwhile to inter-library loan articles from refereed journals and books.

Evaluating the literature

Two questions frequently asked by our students are, 'How do I know what I'm reading is relevant?' and 'How do I know when I've read enough?' Both of these are concerned with the process of evaluation. They involve defining the scope of your review and assessing the value of the items you have obtained in helping you answer your research question(s). Although there are no set ways of approaching these questions our students have found the following advice helpful.

You should, of course, read all the literature that is closely related to your research question(s) and objectives. The literature that is most likely to cause problems is that which is less closely related (Borg and Gall, 1989). For some research questions, particularly for new research areas, there is unlikely to be much closely related literature and so you will have to review more broadly. For research questions where research has been going on for some years, you may be able to focus on more closely related literature.

Assessing relevance

Assessing the relevance of the literature you have collected to your research depends on your research question(s) and objectives. You are looking for relevance, not critically assessing the ideas contained within the literature. Table 3.5 provides a checklist to help you in this process.

> ☑ How recent is the item?
>
> ☑ Is the item likely to have been superseded?
>
> ☑ Is the context sufficiently different to make it marginal to your research question(s) and objectives?
>
> ☑ Have you seen references to this item (or its author) in other items that were useful?
>
> ☑ Does the item support or contradict your arguments? For either, it will probably be worth reading!
>
> ☑ Does the item appear to be biased? Even if it is, it may still be relevant to your critical review.
>
> ☑ What are the methodological omissions within the work? Even if there are many, it still may be of relevance!
>
> ☑ Is the precision sufficient? Even if it is imprecise, it may be the only item you can find and so still be of relevance!

Table 3.5 Checklist for evaluating the relevance of literature
Sources: Authors' experience; Bell, 1993; Jankowicz, 1995; McNeill, 1990

Remember to make notes about the relevance of each item as you read it and the reasons you came to your conclusion. You may need to include your evaluation as part of your critical review.

Assessing sufficiency

Your assessment of whether you have read a sufficient amount is even more complex. It is impossible to read everything, as if you did you would never start to write your critical review, let alone your project report. Yet you need to be sure that your critical review discusses what research has already been undertaken and that you have positioned your research project in the wider context, citing the main writers in the field (Section 3.2). One clue that you have achieved this is when further searching provides mainly references to items you have already read. You also need to check what constitutes an acceptable amount of reading, in terms of both quality and quantity, with your project tutor.

3.7 RECORDING THE LITERATURE

The literature search, as you will now be aware, is a vital part of your research project, in which you will invest a great deal of time and effort. As you read each item you need to ask yourself how it contributes to your research question(s) and objectives and make *notes* with this focus (Bell, 1993). When doing this, many students photocopy articles and pages from books to ensure they have all the material. We believe that, even if you photocopy, you still need to make notes. The process of note making will help you think through the ideas in the literature in relation to your research.

In addition to making notes, Howard and Sharp (1983) identi
tion you need to record. These are:

- bibliographic details;
- brief summary of content;
- supplementary information.

Until the advent of inexpensive microcomputers it was usual
on to *index cards*. Database software provides a powerful and fl
for recording the literature, although it will probably mean noting it down and later transferring it to your database. Recording can seem very tedious, but it must be done. We have
seen many students frantically repeating searches for items that are crucial to their research
because they failed to record all the necessary details, either on index cards or in their database of references.

Bibliographic details

For some project reports you will be required to include a *bibliography*. Convention dictates this should include all the relevant items you consulted for your project including
those not referred to directly in the text. For others you will only be asked to include a list
of *references* for those items referred to directly in the text. The *bibliographic details* contained in both need to be sufficient to enable readers to find the original items. These are
summarised in Table 3.6.

Journal	Book	Chapter in an edited book
• Author(s)– surname, first name initials	• Author(s) – surname, first name initials	• Author(s) of chapter – surname, first name initials
• Year of publication (in brackets)	• Year of publication (in brackets)	• Year of publication (in brackets)
• Title of article	• Title and subtitle of book (underlined or in italics)	• Title of chapter
• Title of journal (underlined or in italics)	• Edition	• Author(s) of book – surname, first name initials
• Volume	• Place of publication	• Title and subtitle of book (underlined or in italics)
• Part/issue	• Publisher	• Edition
• Page numbers		• Place of publication
		• Publisher
		• Page numbers of chapter

Table 3.6 Bibliographic details required

If an item has been taken from an electronic source you need to record as much of the
information in Table 3.6 as is available along with details of format (e.g. CD-ROM). If you
located the item via the Internet you need to record the full address of the resource as well
(Appendix 2).

universities have a preferred *referencing style* that you must use in your project. This will normally be prescribed in your assessment criteria. Two of the most common styles are the *Harvard system* (which we have used in this book) and *footnotes*. Guidelines on using these are given in Appendix 2.

Brief summary

A brief summary of the content of each item on your index card or in your reference database will help you to locate the relevant items and facilitate reference to your notes and photocopies. This can be done by annotating each record with the key words used to locate the item and the abstract. It will also help you maintain consistency in your searches.

Supplementary information

As well as recording the details discussed earlier, other information may be worth recording. This can be anything you feel will be of value. In Table 3.7 we outline those that we have found most useful.

Information	Reason
ISBN	The identifier for any book and useful if the book has to be requested on inter-library loan
Class (Dewy Decimal) number	Useful to locate books in your university's library and as a pointer to finding other books on the same subject
Quotations	Always note useful quotations in full and with the page number of the quote; if possible also take a photocopy
Where it was found	Noting where you found the item is useful, especially if it is not in your university library and you could only take notes
The tertiary resource used	Useful to help identify resources for follow-up searches
Evaluative comments	Your personal notes on the value of the item to your research
When the item was consulted	Especially important for items found via the Internet as these may disappear without trace

Table 3.7 Supplementary information

3.8 SUMMARY

- A critical review of the literature is necessary to help you develop a thorough understanding and insight into previous research that relates to your research question(s) and objectives. Your review will set your research in context by critically discussing and referencing work that has already been undertaken, drawing out key points and presenting them in a logically argued way and highlighting those areas where you will provide fresh insights. It will lead the reader into subsequent sections of your project report.

- There is no one correct structure for a critical review, although it is helpful to think of it as a funnel in which you start at a more general level before narrowing down to your specific research question(s) and objectives.

- Literature sources can be divided into three categories: primary, secondary and tertiary. In reality, these categories often overlap. Your use of these resources will depend on your research question(s) and objectives. Some may use only tertiary and secondary literature. For others you may need to locate primary literature as well.

- When planning your literature search you need to:
  – have clearly defined research questions and objectives;
  – define the parameters of your search;
  – generate key words and search terms;
  – discuss your ideas as widely as possible.
  Techniques to help you in this include brainstorming and relevance trees.

- Your literature search will be undertaken using a variety of approaches in tandem. These will include:
  – searching using tertiary sources and the Internet;
  – following up references in articles you have already read;
  – scanning and browsing secondary literature in your library.

- Once obtained, the literature must be evaluated for their relevance to your research question(s) and objectives. Each item must be read and noted. Bibliographic details, a brief description of the content and appropriate supplementary information should also be recorded.

Self-check questions and assignment

Self-check question 3.1

The following extract and associated references are taken from the first draft of a critical literature review. The research project was concerned with the impact of direct insurers on the traditional motor insurer. List the problems with this extract in terms of its:

a content; **b** structure.

Jackson (1995) suggests that businesses must be developed from a customer rather than a product perspective. Lindesfarne (1995) demonstrates that direct selling gives the consumer increased control as it is up to them when and if they wish to respond to adverts or direct mail. MacKenzie (1995) comments that free gifts are useful for getting responses to adverts which is ultimately what all direct insurers need. Bowen (1995) suggests that this type of company can be split into three equally important parts: marketing, insurance and information technology. Motor insurance is particularly price sensitive because of its compulsory nature and its perception by many to have no real 'value' to themselves.

Bowen, I. (1994) 'Short Cut to Success', *Post Magazine*, 2 July, p. 26.
Jackson, D.R. (1995) 'Prudential's Prudent Parochialism', *Direct Marketing*, April, pp. 26–29.
Lindisfarne, I. (1995) 'Death of a Salesman', *Post Magazine*, 15 June, pp. 30–31
MacKenzie, G. (1995) 'Rise of the Freebie', *Post Magazine*, 2 February, p. 56

Self-check question 3.2
Outline the advice you would give a colleague on:

a how to plan her search;

b which literature to search first.

Self-check question 3.3
Brainstorm at least one of the following research questions, either on your own or with a colleague, and list the key words which you have generated.

a How effective is profit related pay as a motivator?

b How do the opportunities available to a first-time house buyer through interpersonal discussions influence the process of selecting a financial institution for the purposes of applying for a house purchase loan?

c To what extent do new methods of direct selling of financial services pose a threat to existing providers?

Self-check question 3.4
You are having considerable problems with finding relevant material for your research when searching databases. Suggest possible reasons why this might be so.

Self-check question 3.5
Rewrite the following passage as part of a critical literature review using the Harvard system of referencing:

Most of the writers[1] I've read on the European Union's future employment needs reckon that there's going to be an increase in the need for highly qualified employees. Yet the European Commission[2] have worked out that there's going to be fewer of these people about due to technological and economic changes and because there are fewer people are entering the labour market. Now that we're all in one 'single European market' these problems are likely to get even worse as some countries have a far higher demand for such people than they can supply internally[3].

[1] For example: Atkinson, J. (1989) 'Corporate Employment Policies for the Single European Market', *IMS Report No 179*, Sussex, Institute of Manpower Studies; Pearson, R. & Pike, G. (1989) 'The Graduate Labour Market in the 1990s', *IMS Report No. 167*, Sussex, Institute of Manpower Studies; Werner, H. (1990) 'Free movement of Labour in the Single European Market', Intereconomics, 25:2, 77–81.
[2] Commission of the European Communities (1991) *Employment in Europe*, COM, (89)339.
[3] Walwei, U. and Werner, H. (1993) 'Europeanising the Labour Market: Employee Mobility and Company Recruiting Methods', *Intereconomics*, Feb 3–10.

Assignment 3:
Critically reviewing the literature

- Consider your research question(s) and objectives. Use your lecture notes, course textbooks and relevant review articles to define both narrow and broader parameters of your literature search considering language, subject area, business sector, geographical area, publication period and literature type.

- Generate key words and search terms using one or a variety of techniques such as reading, brainstorming and relevance trees. Discuss your ideas widely, including with your project tutor and colleagues.

- Start your search using both printed and database tertiary sources to identify relevant secondary literature. Begin with those tertiary sources that abstract and index academic journal articles and books. At the same time, obtain relevant literature that has been referenced in articles you have already read.

- Expand your search via other sources such as the Internet and by browsing and scanning.

- Obtain copies of relevant items, read them and make notes. Remember also to record bibliographic details, a brief description of the content and supplementary information on an index card or in your references database.

- Start drafting your critical review as early as possible, keeping in mind its purpose.

- Continue to search the literature throughout your research project to ensure your review remains up to date.

References

Bell, J. (1993) *Doing Your Research Project* (2nd edn), Buckingham, Open University Press.

Borg, W.R. and Gall, M.D. (1989) *Educational Research: An Introduction* (5th edn), New York, Longman.

Campbell, D. and Campbell, M. (1995) *The Students' Guide to Doing Research on the Internet*, Reading, Massachusetts, Addison-Wesley.

Easterby-Smith, M., Thorpe, R. and Lowe, A. (1991) *Management Research: An Introduction*, London, Sage.

Ellsworth, J.H. and Ellsworth, M.V. (1994) *The Internet Business Book*, New York, John Wiley.

Gill, J. and Johnson, P. (1991) *Research Methods for Managers*, London, Paul Chapman.

Haythornthwaite, J. (ed.) (1990) *The Business Information Maze: An Essential Guide*, London, ASLIB.

Haywood, P. and Wragg, E.C. (1982) *Evaluating the Literature: Rediguide 2*, University of Nottingham School of Education, Nottingham.

Howard, K. and Sharp, J.A. (1983) *The Management of a Student Research Project*, Aldershot, Gower.

Jankowicz, A.D. (1995) *Business Research Projects* (2nd edn), London, Chapman & Hall.

McNeill, P. (1990) *Research Methods* (2nd edn), London, Routledge.

National Council for Education Technology (1993) *Information Skills in Action*, Coventry.

Saunders, M.N.K. (1993) 'Vacancy Notification and Employee Mobility', *International Journal of Manpower*, 14:6, 39–57.

Stewart, D.W. and Kamins, M.A. (1993) *Secondary Research: Information Sources and Methods* (2nd edn), Newbury Park, California, Sage.

Strauss, A. and Corbin, J. (1990) *Basics of Qualitative Research*, Newbury Park, California, Sage.

Further reading

Bell, J. (1993) *Doing Your Research Project* (2nd edn), Buckingham, Open University Press. Chapter 4 provides a good introduction to the process of reviewing the literature. The section on the critical review of the literature is especially helpful.

Campbell, D. and Campbell, M. (1995) *The Students' Guide to Doing Research on the Internet*, Reading, Massachusetts, Addison-Wesley. This contains a wealth of fascinating information on the Internet. However, by the time you read this book a substantial proportion will have probably changed, so look for a more recent edition!

Howard, K. and Sharp, J.A. (1983) *The Management of a Student Research Project*, Aldershot, Gower. Chapter 4 contains a useful in-depth discussion of the use of relevance trees in your literature search.

Jankowicz, A.D. (1995) *Business Research Projects* (2nd edn), London, Chapman & Hall. Chapter 8 provides a good discussion of reviewing and using the literature for business research projects.

Case 3:
The development of discount warehouse clubs

Jane was keen to start her research project early. She had decided on her dissertation topic – the development of discount warehouse clubs in the UK. She spent two days each week in the library over the vacation reading and noting all the articles she could find and wrote her literature review. In order to give her project tutor plenty of time to read the draft she sent it to him a week before the tutorial.

Jane arrived at her tutorial looking forward to her tutor's praise. 'Well Jane, you've obviously worked over the summer, but there's still a great deal of reading to be done . . .' Jane was crestfallen as her tutor explained the problems with her literature review. Every article was taken either from a trade magazine or newspaper and there was not a single mention of any academic underpinning. The review consisted almost entirely of quotations from the articles, a couple of paragraphs being devoted to each article. Although the ideas contained in the articles were summarised, they were not ordered in any logical manner and the purpose was unclear.

'Why didn't you use the CD-ROM abstract and indexes?' asked her tutor. 'I did . . . ,' Jane replied, 'but there's nothing written on the development of discount warehouse clubs in the UK.' After considerable discussion about how to search the literature and the purpose of the literature review in her project report, Jane went away feeling happier. She now knew that quotations should only be used sparingly in her review. The literature she had discovered in the trade magazines was still likely to be useful. Of most importance, she liked her tutor's suggestion of placing her research in the context of the spread of retailing innovation and, in particular, how innovations crossed from North America to the UK.

Over the next few months Jane diligently searched the tertiary literature and found many relevant items. Articles in the university library were noted. Those not available from the university library were obtained using inter-library loan. Appropriate sections from books on retailing innovation were photocopied. By February she had two lever-arch files full of information.

Jane began to redraft her literature review. This time she was determined to write a critical review. She made sure that her arguments flowed and that the review was focused on the transfer of retail innovations from North America to the UK. The work of different authors was clearly referenced and quotes were only included where they added significantly to her argument. She completed her draft, left it for a week, read it again and made further amendments. She was now ready to show it to her project tutor again.

This time Jane's project tutor seemed far more pleased. She suggested a few areas where points needed further explanation or justification, but that was all. Just as Jane was leaving she asked, 'You've got all the references together for your bibliography, haven't you?' Jane responded that she was going to do that next weekend and that she had noted them all down on the items as she was collecting them.

That weekend Jane sat down at her wordprocessor to type in her bibliography. She checked the format in the project assessment criteria and discovered that she should use the Harvard system. Working through her files she entered all the items she had read in alphabetical order, including those not directly referenced in the text. Unfortunately, she discovered three journal articles where the page numbers had been missed off by the photocopier when she had copied them. She decided to sort these out on Monday morning.

On Monday morning the library was packed and all the CD-ROM microcomputers were booked solid until 8 p.m. As Jane could not remember which database she had used she booked the most likely, *Anbar*, for 8 p.m. to 9 p.m., and went to the canteen. Over her coffee she tried to remember which key words she had used for her searches. At 8 p.m. she started to recreate her searches. Within 20 minutes she had found two of the three missing sets of page numbers. The third journal article did not appear to be indexed in *Anbar*. Then she remembered that she had also used *GeoAbstracts*. Jane located the CD-ROM and entered her search again. Within a few minutes she had found the missing page numbers.

In the following months Jane browsed the current periodicals section of the library. As relevant material was published she incorporated it into her literature review. Later that year she submitted her research project. It received a good upper second class mark.

> ### Case study questions
>
> 1 How might Jane have overcome the problems of only finding relevant articles in trade journals and newspapers?
>
> 2 Why did Jane type all the items she had in her files into her wordprocessor rather than just those she had referred to directly in the text?
>
> 3 What lessons can you learn from Jane's experience?

Answers to self-check questions

Self-check question 3.1

There are numerous problems with the content and structure of this extract. Some of the more obvious include:

- The content consists of predominantly trade magazines, in particular *Post Magazine*, and there are no references of academic substance. Some of the references to individual authors have discrepancies, for example was the article by Lindisfarne (or is it Lindesfarne?) published in 1994 or 1995?

- There is no real structure or argument in the extract. The extract is a list of what people have written with no attempt critically to evaluate or juxtapose the ideas.

Self-check question 3.2

A difficult one without knowing her research question! However, you could still advise her on the general principles. Your advice will probably include:

- Define the parameters of her research, considering language, subject area, business sector, geographical area, publication period and literature type.

    Generate key words and search terms using one or a variety of techniques such as reading, brainstorming or relevance trees.

    Discuss her ideas as widely as possible, including with her tutor, librarians and you.

- To start her search using tertiary sources to identify relevant secondary literature. She should commence with those tertiary sources that abstract and index academic journal articles and books.

    At the same time, she should obtain relevant literature that has been referenced in articles she has already read.

Self-check question 3.3

There are no incorrect answers with brainstorming! However, you might like to check the suitability of your key words by using them to search an appropriate database. We suggest you follow the approach outlined in Section 3.5 under 'Searching using the tertiary literature'.

Self-check question 3.4

There a variety of possible reasons including:

- one or more of the parameters of your search is defined too narrowly;

- the key words you have chosen do not appear in the controlled index language;
- your spelling of the key word is incorrect;
- the terminology you are using is incorrect;
- the acronyms you have chosen are not used by the database;
- you are using jargon rather than accepted terminology.

Self-check question 3.5

There are two parts to this answer: rewriting the text and using the Harvard system of referencing. Your text will inevitably differ from the answer given below due to your personal writing style. Don't worry about this too much, as it is discussed in far more detail in Section 13.5. The references should follow the same format.

The vast majority of writers on the European Union's (EU) future employment needs emphasise a growth in the requirements for highly qualified, specialist employees (Atkinson, 1989; Pearson and Pike, 1989; Werner, 1990). Such employees are forecast to become a scarce resource within the EU, due to technological change, the decline in young people entering the labour market and predictions that the economic climate will improve in the latter half of the 1990s (Commission of the European Communities, 1991). The completion of the Single European Market has magnified these problems. Demand for highly qualified labour in some states is forecast to be greater than supply, whereas in others the converse will be true (Walwei and Werner, 1993).

Atkinson, J. (1989) 'Corporate Employment Policies for the Single European Market', *IMS Report No 179*, Sussex, Institute of Manpower Studies.

Commission of the European Communities (1991) *Employment in Europe*, COM, (89)339.

Pearson, R. and Pike, G. (1989) 'The Graduate Labour Market in the 1990s', *IMS Report No. 167*, Sussex, Institute of Manpower Studies.

Walwei, U. and Werner, H. (1993) 'Europeanising the Labour Market: Employee Mobility and Company Recruiting Methods', *Intereconomics*, Feb, pp. 3–10.

Werner, H. (1990) 'Free Movement of Labour in the Single European Market', *Intereconomics*, 25:2, pp. 77–81.

CHAPTER 4

Deciding on the research approach and choosing a research strategy

The objectives of this chapter are to help you to examine different ways of approaching research. It will introduce you to different strategies that you may adopt in your research.

The chapter will then go on to help you to plan your research in such a way that your research findings and conclusions will appear credible to those who read them.

The chapter will end with a brief examination of the ethical considerations you should take into account in planning your research.

Our most important objective in this chapter is to encourage you to think creatively about the research strategy you may use to answer your research question(s) and objectives.

4.1 DIFFERING APPROACHES TO RESEARCH

Your research project will involve the use of theory. That theory may or may not be made explicit in the design of the research. Similarly, it may or may not be made explicit in your presentation of the findings and conclusions. However, your decision to read this book is based on a theory (albeit unstated) which you are subjecting to an *empirical test*. This theory is that reading a textbook on research methods will increase the likelihood that you will successfully complete your research project. The empirical test (which we hope will be prove the theory!) is simply the reading of the book and subsequent pursuit and submission of the project report.

You may want to make this research more rigorous. If this were so, you would involve a large sample of students; be clear about the conditions under which you would study the book; clarify what would constitute success in the completion of the project; and ensure that other variables which might 'contaminate' the results are controlled.

Positivism

This approach to research owes much to what we would think of as *scientific* research. It is what we will call the *positivist* approach. Robson (1993: 18–19) lists five sequential stages through which positivist research will go:

1 Deducing a *hypothesis* (a testable proposition about the relationship between two or more events or concepts) from the theory.

2 Expressing the hypothesis in operational terms (i.e. ones indicating exactly how the variables are to be measured) which propose a relationship between two specific variables.

3 Testing this operational hypothesis. This will involve an experiment or some other form of empirical inquiry.

4 Examining the specific outcome of the inquiry. It will either tend to confirm the theory or indicate the need for its modification.

5 If necessary, modifying the theory in the light of the findings. An attempt is then made to verify the revised theory by going back to the first step and repeating the whole cycle.

You can see that positivist research has a number of distinguishing features. It:

■ is *deductive* (theory tested by observation);

■ seeks to explain causal relationships between variables;

■ normally uses quantitative data;

■ employs controls to allow the testing of hypotheses;

■ uses a highly structured methodology to facilitate replication (Gill and Johnson, 1991).

Easterby-Smith *et al.* (1991: 23) list eight features of positivism:

1 *Independence.* The observer is independent of what is being observed.

2 *Value-freedom.* The choice of what to study, and how to study it, can be determined by objective criteria rather than by human beliefs and interests.

3 *Causality.* The aim of the social sciences should be to identify causal explanations and fundamental laws that explain regularities in human social behaviour.

4 *Hypothetico-deductive.* Science proceeds through a process of hypothesising fundamental laws and then deducing what kinds of observations will demonstrate the truth or falsity of these hypotheses.

5 *Operationalisation.* Concepts need to be operationalised in a way which enables facts to be measured quantitatively.

6 *Reductionism.* Problems as a whole are better understood if they are reduced to the simplest possible elements.

7 *Generalisation.* In order to be able to generalise about regularities in human social behaviour, it is necessary to select samples of sufficient size.

8 *Cross-sectional analysis.* Such regularities can most easily be identified by making comparisons of variations across samples.

An alternative approach to conducting research on the ways in which students complete their projects successfully would be to go ahead and collect some data. You could interview previously successful students, individually or in groups, without any clear theoretical position in mind. Your task then would be to make sense of the data you had collected by analysing those data. The result of this analysis would be the formulation of a theory, which may be, of course, that successful students tended to attribute their success to the study of research methods texts prior to undertaking their project. You may end up with the same theory, but you would have gone about the production of that theory in an *inductive* way: theory would follow data rather than vice versa as in the positivist approach.

Phenomenology

The *phenomenological* approach to research is so called because it is based on the way people experience social phenomena in the world in which they live. It can be contrasted with the positivist approach which treats the social world in the way it would be approached by the natural scientist, something with which the *phenomenologist* would feel uncomfortable.

Phenomenology is characterised by a focus on the meanings that research subjects attach to social phenomena; an attempt by the researcher to understand what is happening and why it is happening. Such research would be particularly concerned with the context in which such events were taking place. Therefore, the study of a small sample of subjects may be more appropriate than a large number as with the positivist approach. As can be seen in Chapter 9, researchers in this tradition are more likely to work with qualitative data and use a variety of methods to collect these data in order to establish different views of phenomena (Easterby-Smith *et al.*, 1991).

At this stage you may be asking yourself: 'So what? Why is the approach that I take to my research project important?' Easterby-Smith *et al.* (1991: 21) suggest three reasons. First, it enables you to take a more informed decision about your research design, which is 'more than simply the methods by which data are collected and analysed. It is the overall configuration of a piece of research: what kind of evidence is gathered and from where, and how such evidence is interpreted in order to provide good answers to the basic research question.'

Second, it will help you to think about those research approaches that will work for you and, crucially, those that will not. For example, if you are particularly interested in understanding why something is happening rather than being able to describe what is happening, it may be more appropriate to adopt the phenomenological approach than the positivist.

Third, a knowledge of the different research traditions enables you to adapt your research design to cater for constraints. These may be practical, involving, say, limited access to data. Or they may arise from a lack of prior knowledge of the subject. You simply may not be in a position to frame a hypothesis because you have insufficient understanding of the topic to do this.

Combining approaches to research

So far we have conveyed the impression that there are rigid divisions between the two approaches to research. This would be misleading. It is perfectly possible to combine approaches within the same piece of research.

WORKED EXAMPLE: *Positivist and phenomenological research*

One of our colleagues decided to conduct a research project on violence at work and its effects on the stress levels of staff. She considered the different ways she would approach the work were she to adopt:

■ the positivist approach;

■ the phenomenologist approach.

If she had decided to adopt a positivist approach to her work she would have done the following:

1 started with the hypothesis that violence at work exists;
2 decided to research a population in which she would have expected to find evidence of violence, for example a sizeable social security office;
3 administered a questionnaire to a large sample of staff in order to establish the extent of violence (either actually experienced or threatened) and the levels of stress experienced by them;
4 needed to have been particularly careful about how she defined violence;
5 standardised the stress responses of the staff, for example, days off sick or sessions with a counsellor.

On the other hand, if she had decided to adopt a phenomenologist approach she may have decided to interview some staff who had been subjected to violence at work. She may have been interested in their feelings about the events which they had experienced, how they coped with the problems which they experienced, and their views about the possible causes of the violence.

Either approach would have yielded valuable data about this problem. Neither approach should be thought of as better than the other. They are better at different things. It depends where her research emphasis lies.

At this point we should consider some of the possible advantages and disadvantages of the two approaches. These are summarised in Table 4.1.

	Positivism	**Phenomenology**
Advantages	• Economical collection of large amount of data • Clear theoretical focus for the research at the outset • Greater opportunity for researcher to retain control of research process • Easily comparable data	• Facilitates understanding of how and why • Enables researcher to be alive to changes which occur during the research process • Good at understanding social processes
Disadvantages	• Inflexible – direction often cannot be changed once data collection has started • Weak at understanding social processes • Often doesn't discover the meanings people attach to social phenomena	• Data collection can be time consuming • Data analysis is difficult • Researcher has to live with the uncertainty that clear patterns may not emerge • Generally perceived as less credible by 'non-researchers'

Table 4.1 Key advantages and disadvantages of the main approaches to research design

4.2 THE NEED FOR A CLEAR RESEARCH STRATEGY

Your *research strategy* will be a general plan of how you will go about answering the research question(s) you have set (the importance of clearly defining the research question cannot be over-emphasised). It will contain clear objectives, derived from your research question(s); specify the sources from which you intend to collect data; consider the constraints which you will inevitably have (e.g. access to data, time, location, money). Crucially, it should reflect the fact that you have thought carefully about why you are employing your particular strategy. It would be perfectly legitimate for your assessor to ask you why you chose to conduct your research in a particular organisation, why you chose the particular department, why you chose to talk to one group of staff rather than another, why you decided to adopt a phenomenological approach rather than a positivist one. You must have a valid reason for all your research strategy decisions. The justification should always be based on your research question(s) and objectives.

Not all the strategy decisions you take should always be so coldly rational. Hakim (1987) uses an architectural metaphor to illustrate the strategy choice process. She introduces the notion of the researcher's preferred style which, rather like the architect's, may reflect 'the architect's own preferences and ideas . . . and the stylistic preferences of those who pay for the work and have to live with the finished result' (Hakim, 1987: 1). This echoes the feelings of Buchanan *et al.* (1988: 59) who argue that 'needs, interests and preferences (of the researcher) . . . are typically overlooked but are central to the progress of fieldwork'. But a note of caution – it is important that your preferences don't lead to your changing the composition of the research question.

At this point we should make a clear distinction between strategy and *tactics*. The former is concerned with the overall approach you adopt, the latter is about the finer detail of data collection and analysis. Decisions about tactics will involve you being clear about the different data collection methods (e.g. questionnaires, interviews, focus groups, published data) which will be dealt with in detail in subsequent chapters. At this point we are concerned with general questions of strategy.

The different research strategies

Robson (1993) lists the three traditional research strategies as:

- experiment;
- survey;
- case study.

In addition to these three strategies we consider another two important ways of pursuing research: cross-sectional and longitudinal studies.

Again, these strategies should not be thought of as being mutually exclusive. This may seem to be an over-simplification of the way in which strategies may be categorised. Gill and Johnson (1991), for example, include quasi-experiment and action research. However, it is a useful way of representing the main research strategies.

Experiment

Experiment is a classical form of research which owes much to the natural sciences, although it features strongly in much social science research, particularly psychology. It will typically involve:

- the definition of a theoretical hypothesis;
- the selection of samples of individuals from known populations;
- allocation of samples to different experimental conditions;
- introduction of planned change on one or more of the variables;
- measurement on a small number of the variables;
- control of other variables.

* *

WORKED EXAMPLE: *Using the experimental strategy*

Deci (1972) studied the effect of external rewards and controls on the intrinsic motivation of individuals. He set up a laboratory study in which each subject participated in three one-hour sessions of puzzle solving. It had been established by an earlier experiment that the puzzles were intrinsically interesting. There were two participant groups: the experimental group and the control group. Both groups were asked to solve four puzzles during each of the three sessions. The only difference between the two groups was that the experimental group was paid one dollar per puzzle solved during the second session.

During each of the three sessions each group was left alone for an eight-minute 'free-choice period'. Deci reasoned that if the subjects continued puzzle solving in the 'free-choice period' (there were other activities to pursue, e.g. read magazines) then they must be intrinsically motivated to do so. In the event, the experimental group which had been given the external incentive spent less of their 'free' time puzzle solving. The result of this led Deci to theorise that the introduction of external incentives to intrinsically interesting tasks will lead to a decrease in intrinsic motivation – a theory with interesting implications for those introducing pay incentive schemes for employees who do jobs which they find intrinsically interesting!

Survey

The survey method is a popular and common strategy in business and management research. It is popular for some of the reasons mentioned earlier. It allows the collection of a large amount of data from a sizeable population in a highly economical way. Based most often on a questionnaire, these data are standardised, allowing easy comparison. In addition, the survey method is perceived as authoritative by people in general. This is because it is easily understood. Every day a news bulletin or a newspaper reports the results of a new survey which indicates, for example, that a certain percentage of the population thinks or behaves in a particular way.

Using a survey approach should give you more control over the research process. Much time will be spent in designing and piloting the questionnaire. Analysing the results, even with the aid of an appropriate computer package, will also be time consuming. But it will be your time – you will be independent. Many researchers complain that their progress is delayed by their dependence on others for information.

However, the data collected by the survey method may not be as wide ranging as those collected by qualitative research methods. There is a limit to the number of questions which any questionnaire can contain if the goodwill of the respondent is not to be presumed on too much. But perhaps the biggest drawback with the questionnaire method, as is emphasised in Section 10.2, is the capacity to do it badly!

The questionnaire, however, is not the only data collection device which belongs to the survey category. Structured observation, of the type most frequently associated with organisation and methods (O & M) research, and structured interviews, where standardised questions are put to all interviewees, also fall into this category. Observation methods are dealt with in detail in Chapter 8 and structured interviews in Section 10.5.

Case study

Robson (1993: 40) defines *case study* as the 'development of detailed, intensive knowledge about a single "case", or a small number of related "cases".' This strategy will be of particular interest to you if you wish to gain a rich understanding of the context of the research and the processes being enacted (Morris and Wood, 1991). The case-study approach also has considerable ability to generate answers to the question 'Why?' as well as 'What?' and 'How?' (Robson, 1993: 44) which tend to be questions addressed more by the survey method. The data collection methods employed may be various. They may include interviews, observation, documentary analysis and (as if to emphasise the dangers of constructing neat boxes in which to categorise the approaches, strategies and methods) questionnaires.

You may be suspicious of conducting case study research because of its 'unscientific' feel. We would argue that a case study can be a very worthwhile way of exploring existing theory. In addition, a simple, well-constructed case study can enable you to challenge an existing theory and also provide a source of new hypotheses (Emory and Cooper, 1991).

Cross-sectional and longitudinal studies

An important question to be asked in planning your research is, 'Do I want my research to be a "snapshot" taken at a particular time or do I want it to be more akin to a "diary" and be a representation of events over a given period?' (As always, of course, the answer should be, 'it depends on the research question'.) The 'snapshot' approach is what we call here *cross-sectional*, while the 'diary' perspective we call *longitudinal*.

We should emphasise that these time perspectives to research design are independent of whichever of the three main research strategies you are pursuing. So, for example, you may be studying the change in manufacturing processes in one company over a period of a year. This would be a longitudinal case study.

Cross-sectional studies

It is probable that your research may be cross-sectional, the study of a particular phenomenon (or phenomena) at a particular time. We say this because we recognise that most research projects undertaken for academic courses are necessarily time constrained. But the timescales on many courses do allow sufficient time for a longitudinal study, provided, of course, that you start it in plenty of time!

Cross-sectional studies often employ the survey strategy (Robson, 1993; Easterby-Smith *et al.*, 1991). They may be seeking to describe the incidence of a phenomenon (e.g. a survey of the IT skills possessed by managers in one organisation at a given point in time) or compare factors in different organisations (e.g. the relationship between expenditure on customer care training for sales assistants and sales revenue). But they may also use qualitative methods. Many case studies are based on interviews conducted over a short period.

Longitudinal studies

The main strength of longitudinal research is the capacity that it has to study change and development. Adams and Schvaneveldt (1991) point out that in observing people or events over time, the researcher is able to exercise a measure of control over variables being studied, provided that they are not affected by the research process itself. One of the best-known examples of this type of research comes from outside the world of business. It is the long-running television series *Seven Up*, which has charted the progress of a cohort of people every seven years of their life. Not only is this fascinating television, but it has provided the social scientist with a rich source of data on which to test and develop theories of human development.

Even with time constraints, it is possible to introduce a longitudinal element to your research. As Section 7.2 indicates, there is a massive amount of published data collected over time just waiting to be analysed! An example is the Workplace Industrial Relations Survey which was conducted in 1980, 1984 and 1990 (Millward *et al.*, 1992). From these surveys you would be able to gain valuable data which would give you a powerful insight into change in personnel management and industrial relations over a period of wide-ranging change. In longitudinal studies the basic question is: 'Has there been any change over a period of time?' (Dixon *et al.*, 1987).

Exploratory, descriptive and explanatory studies

Enquiries can be classified in terms of their purpose as well as by the research strategy used (Robson, 1993). The classification most often used is the threefold one of exploratory, descriptive and explanatory. In the same way as you may employ more than one strategy in your research project, so you may have more than one purpose. Indeed, as Robson (1993) points out, the purpose of your enquiry may change over time.

Exploratory studies

Exploratory studies are a valuable means of finding out 'what is happening; to seek new insights; to ask questions and to assess phenomena in a new light' (Robson, 1993: 42). They are particularly useful if you wish to clarify your understanding of a problem. Emory and Cooper (1991) argue that time is well spent on exploratory research as it may show that the research is not worth pursuing!

Emory and Cooper suggest three ways of conducting exploratory research:

- a search of the literature;
- talking to experts in the subject;
- conducting focus group interviews.

Exploratory research can be likened to the activities of the traveller or explorer (Adams and Schvaneveldt, 1991). Its great advantage is that it is flexible and adaptable to change. If you are conducting exploratory research you must be willing to change your direction as a result of new data which appear and new insights which occur to you. A quotation from the travel writer V.S. Naipaul (1989: 222) illustrates this point beautifully:

> 'I had been concerned, at the start of my own journey, to establish some lines of enquiry, to define a theme. The approach had its difficulties. At the back of my mind was always a worry that I would come to a place and all contacts would break down . . . If you travel on a theme, the theme has to develop with the travel. At the beginning your interests can be broad and scattered. But then they must be more focused; the different stages of a journey cannot simply be versions of one

another. And . . . this kind of travel depended on luck. It depended on the people you met, the little illuminations you had. As with the next day's issue of fast-moving daily newspaper, the shape of the character in hand was continually being changed by accidents along the way.'

Adams and Schvaneveldt (1991) reinforce this point by arguing that the flexibility inherent in exploratory research does not mean absence of direction to the enquiry. What is does mean is that the focus is initially broad and becomes progressively narrower as the research progresses.

Descriptive studies

The object of *descriptive research* is 'to portray an accurate profile of persons, events or situations' (Robson, 1993: 4). This may be an extension of, or a forerunner to, a piece of exploratory research. It is necessary to have a clear picture of the phenomena on which you wish to collect data prior to the collection of the data. One of the earliest and best-known examples of a descriptive survey is the Doomsday Book, which described the population of England in 1085.

Often project tutors are rather wary of work that is too descriptive. There is a danger of them saying, 'That's very interesting. . . but so what?' They will want you to go further and draw conclusions from your data. They will encourage you to develop the skills of evaluating data and synthesising ideas. These are higher-order skills than those of accurate description. Description in management and business research has a very clear place. But it should be thought of as a means to an end rather than an end in itself.

Explanatory studies

Studies which establish causal relationships between variables may be termed *explanatory studies*. The emphasis here is on studying a situation or a problem in order to explain the relationships between variables. You may find, for example, that a cursory analysis of quantitative data on manufacturing scrap rates shows a relationship between scrap rates and the age of the machine being operated. You could go ahead and subject the data to statistical tests such as correlation (discussed in Section 11.5) in order to get a clearer view of the relationship.

- -

WORKED EXAMPLE: *An explanatory study*

Phil studied individual performance related pay systems for managers. He was interested in explaining the relationship between success (a concept which needed to be given a working definition) of such systems and the factors that seemed to lead to such success. This research adopted a case-study approach in examining three organisations in some detail. The data collected were mainly qualitative, although some secondary quantitative data were used. What emerged was that the way in which implementing managers conducted the processes of assessing the performance of their managers, and translating these assessments into rewards, was more important than the design of such systems.

- -

4.3 MULTI-METHOD APPROACHES

These approaches and strategies obviously do not exist in isolation and therefore can be 'mixed and matched'. Not only can they, but it is often beneficial to do so. It is quite usual for a single study to combine quantitative and qualitative methods and to use primary and secondary data.

WORKED EXAMPLE: *Combining survey and case study methods*

We conducted an employee attitude survey in a small insurance company which used three different types of method. Two of these were qualitative and one quantitative. The research consisted of four stages:

1 In-depth interviews with senior managers in order to obtain a picture of the important issues we were likely to encounter in the research. This was essential contextual data.

2 Discussion groups with 6 to 10 employees representing different grades and occupations in the company. This was to establish the type of issues that were important to staff and would inform the content of the questionnaire.

3 A questionnaire which was administered to 100 of the 200 head office employees. We wanted to obtain the sort of data which would allow us to compare the attitudes of different employee groups: by age, gender, length of service, occupation and grade. This was particularly important to the company.

4 Semi-structured group interviews with further representative employee groups to clarify the content of some of the questionnaire results. This was essential to reach the meaning behind some of the data.

There are two major advantages to employing *multi-methods* in the same study. First, different methods can be used for different purposes in a study. You may wish to employ case-study methods, for example interviews, in order to get a feel for the key issues before embarking on a survey. This would give you confidence that you were addressing the most important issues.

The second advantage of using multi-methods is that it enables *triangulation* to take place. Triangulation refers to the use of different data collection methods within one study in order to ensure that the data are telling you what you think they are telling you. For example, semi-structured group interviews may be a valuable way of triangulating data collected by other means, such as a questionnaire.

Each method, tool or technique has its unique strengths and weaknesses (Smith, 1975). There is an inevitable relationship between the data collection method you employ and the results you obtain. In short, the results will be affected by the method used. The problem here is that it is impossible to ascertain the nature of that effect. Since all different methods will have different effects, it makes sense to use different methods to cancel out the 'method effect'. That will lead to greater confidence being placed in your conclusions.

The question that may occur to you at this stage is: 'How do I know which method to use in which situation?' There is no simple answer. We encourage you to use your imagination and think of research as a highly creative process. But above all, it is vital to have clear objectives for your study. It is a great temptation to think about the methods to be employed before the objectives are clarified.

WORKED EXAMPLE: *Using a multi-method approach*

Before discovering how the new supervisor learned to do her job, one of our students thought it was essential that he should have the clearest possible grasp of what the supervisor's job entailed.

This involved him in shadowing a new supervisor for a week, talking to night-shift supervisors to establish the differences in approach between day shift and night shift supervision, sending a questionnaire to supervisors in different locations in the company and interviewing the managers to whom those supervisors reported.

This gave our student a much better grasp of the content of the supervisor's job. It also did much to enhance his credibility in the eyes of the supervisors.

4.4 THE CREDIBILITY OF RESEARCH FINDINGS

Underpinning the above discussion on multi-method usage has been the issue of the credibility of research findings. This is neatly expressed by Raimond (1993: 55) when he subjects findings to the 'How do I know?' test: 'Will the evidence and my conclusions stand up to the closest scrutiny?'. How do you know that new supervisors learn their jobs by largely informal methods? How did we know that manual employees in our electronics factory had more negative feelings towards their employer than their clerical counterparts? The answer, of course, is that, in the literal sense of the question, you can't know. All you can do is to reduce the possibility of getting the answer wrong. This is where sound research design is important. This is aptly summarised by Rogers (1961, cited by Raimond, 1993: 55): 'scientific methodology needs to be seen for what it truly is, a way of preventing me from deceiving myself in regard to my creatively formed subjective hunches which have developed out of the relationship between me and my material'.

Reducing the possibility of getting the answer wrong means that attention has to be paid to two particular emphases on research design: reliability and validity.

Reliability

Reliability can be assessed by posing the following two questions (Easterby-Smith *et al.*, 1991: 41):

■ 'Will the measure yield the same results on different occasions? (positivist approach).

■ Will similar observations be made by different researchers on different occasions? (phenomenological approach).'

Threats to reliability

Robson (1993) asserts that there may be four threats to reliability. The first of these is *subject error*. If you are studying the degree of enthusiasm employees have for their work and their employer, it may be that you will find that a questionnaire completed at different times of the week may generate different results. Friday afternoons may show a different picture to Monday mornings! This should be easy to control. You should choose a 'neutral' time when employees may be expected to be neither on a 'high', looking forward to the weekend, or a 'low', with the working week in front of them.

Similarly, there may be *subject bias*. Interviewees may have been saying what they thought their bosses wanted them to say. This is a particular problem in organisations which are characterised by an authoritarian management style, or when there is a threat of employment insecurity. Researchers should be aware of this potential problem when designing research. For example, elaborate steps can be taken to ensure the anonymity of respondents to questionnaires, as Section 10.4 indicates. Care should also be taken when analysing the data to ensure that your data are telling you what you think they are telling you.

Third, there may have been *observer error*. In one piece of research we undertook, there were three of us conducting interviews with potential for at least three different approaches to eliciting answers. Introducing a high degree of structure to the interview schedule (Section 9.2) will lessen this threat to reliability.

Finally, there may have been *observer bias*. Here, of course, there may have been three different approaches to interpreting the replies!

There is more detail on how these threats to reliability may be reduced later in the book in the chapters dealing with specific data collection methods.

Validity

Validity is concerned with whether the findings are really about what they appear to be about. Is the relationship between two variables a *causal relationship*? For example, in a study of an electronics factory we found that employees' failure to look at new product displays was not caused by apathy but by lack of opportunity. This potential lack of validity in the conclusions was minimised by a research design which built in the opportunity for focus groups after the questionnaire results had been analysed.

Robson (1993) has also charted the threats to validity, which provides a useful way of thinking about this important topic.

Threats to validity

History

You may decide to study the opinions employees have about job security in a particular organisation. But if the research is conducted shortly after a major redundancy programme this may well have a dramatic, and quite misleading effect on the findings (unless, of course, the specific objective of the research was to find out about post-redundancy opinions).

Testing

Your research may include measuring how long it takes insurance clerks to deal with telephone enquiries from customers. If the clerks believe that the results of the research may disadvantage them in some way, then this is likely to affect the results.

Instrumentation

In the above example, the insurance clerks may have received an instruction that they were to take every opportunity to sell new policies between the time you tested the first batch and second batch of clerks. Consequently, the calls are likely to last longer.

Mortality

This refers to participants dropping out of studies. This was a major problem for one of our students who was studying the effects on the management styles of managers exposed to a year-long management development programme.

Maturation

In the management development example above, it could be that other events happening during the year have an effect on participants' management style.

Ambiguity about causal direction

One of our students was studying the effectiveness of performance appraisal in her organisation. One of her findings was that poor performance ratings of employees were associated with a negative attitude about appraisal among those same employees. What she was not clear about was whether the poor performance ratings were causing the negative attitude to appraisal, or whether the negative attitude to appraisal was causing the poor performance ratings.

Generalisability

This is sometimes referred to as external validity. A concern you may have in the design of your research is the extent to which your research results are generalisable, that is, your findings may be equally applicable to other research settings, such as other organisations. This is a particular worry if you are conducting case-study research in one or a small number of organisations. It may be particularly pertinent if the organisation is particularly 'different' in some way.

In such cases the purpose of your research will not be to produce a theory which is generalisable to all populations. Your task will be simply to try to explain what is going on in your particular research setting. It may be that you want to test the robustness of your conclusions by exposing them to other research settings in a follow-up study. In short, as long as you don't claim that your results, conclusions or theory can be generalised, then there is no problem.

Logic leaps and false assumptions

So far in this chapter we have shown that there are a host of decisions which need to be made in order for your research project to yield sufficient data of the sort which will result in valid conclusions being drawn. Those decisions necessitate careful thought from you. But more than just quantity of thought is involved. It is vital that your thought processes are of high quality. Your research design will be based on a flow of logic and a number of assumptions, all of which must stand up to the closest scrutiny.

These points have been illustrated skilfully by Raimond (1993). Raimond takes the research of Peters and Waterman on 'excellent' US companies and subjects it to just such scrutiny. The ideas of Peters and Waterman (1982) have been enormously influential in the last fifteen years. Their book is a management 'cookbook' which gives managers eight principles to which they must adhere if their organisations are to be successful. As such, it is fairly typical of a prescriptive type of writing in management books and journals which suggest that 'this is the way it should be done'.

Raimond's (1993) analysis of Peters and Waterman can be categorised into four 'logic steps':

Identification of the research population

This is similar to the point made about generalisability above. If the intention is to be able to generalise the conclusions across the whole population (in the Peters and Waterman case, all organisations), is the choice of population logical? If your research project is in the National Health Service, for example, it would be fanciful to assume that the findings were valid for software houses or advertising agencies.

Data collection

Is it logical to assume that the way you are collecting your data is going to yield valid data? If you interview top bosses you are likely to encounter the 'good news' syndrome. If you collect press cuttings from newspapers, how can you assume there has been no political bias put on them?

Data interpretation

It is here that there is probably the greatest danger of logic leaps and false assumptions. You will need to move from a position where you have a mountain of data, to one where you write a set of conclusions which are presented coherently. This is at the same time an intellectually challenging and a highly creative and exciting process.

You are likely to be using a theoretical framework against which you will analyse your data. If you are working deductively (from theory to data) this framework may have given rise to the hypothesis which you are testing in your research. One of our students studied the introduction of pay bonuses assessed by performance appraisal in the police service. Her hypothesis was based on Meyer *et al.*'s (1965) hypothesis that the non-pay benefits of appraisal (e.g. improvement of job performance) will be prejudiced by the introduction of pay considerations to the process, rendering the appraisal interview little more than a salary discussion.

On the other hand, you may be working inductively (from data to theory), in which case you may be using an established theoretical construct to help you make sense of your findings. For example, you may be studying the way in which different companies within the group in which you work formulate their business strategies. In order to structure your analysis you could use the categorisation of different types of organisational strategy suggested by Mintzberg and Waters (1989). This may lead you to conclude that the dominant strategy employed is a hybrid of those suggested by Mintzberg and Waters.

The important point to make here is that in both cases you are making assumptions about the appropriateness of the theory you are using. In both cases it is clear that the theory with which you are working will shape your conclusions. Therefore it is essential that you choose an appropriate theoretical framework. It is essential that you ask yourself, 'Why am I using this theory and not another which may be equally, or more, appropriate?'

We are making the assumption here that you will use a theory to analyse your data. For most undergraduate and postgraduate courses this is likely to be a requirement of your project tutor. Some professional courses may be more concerned with practical management reports. These emphasise the importance of the report's making viable recommendations which are the result of clear conclusions based on a set of findings. It is important that you clarify this point with the project tutor before commencing the research.

Development of conclusions

The question to ask yourself here is: 'Do my conclusions (or theory) stand up to the closest scrutiny?' If the declared theory in the police appraisal study is that the introduction of pay to the appraisal will lead to the process being useful for pay purposes only, does this apply to all police appraisals? Will it be true for younger, as well as older, police? For all different grades and locations? In other words, are you asking your readers to make logic leaps?

4.5 THE ETHICS OF RESEARCH DESIGN

Section 5.4 deals in more detail with the subject of research ethics. This has important implications for the negotiation of access to people and organisations and the collection of data. Here we will only address the ethical issues which you should consider when designing your research strategy.

Your choice of topic will be governed by ethical considerations. You may be particularly interested to study the consumer decision to buy flower bouquets. Although this may provide some interesting data collection challenges (who buys, for whom and why?) there are not the same ethical difficulties as will be involved in studying, say, the purchasing decision for funeral flowers. Your research design in the latter case may have to concentrate on data collection from the undertaker and, possibly, the purchaser at a time as distant from the death as delicacy permits. The ideal population, of course, may be the purchaser at a time as near as possible to the death. It is a matter of judgement as to whether the data collection strategy suggested by ethical considerations will yield data which are valid. The general ethical issue here is that the research design should not subject the research population to embarrassment or any other material disadvantage.

Your research design needs to consider the extent to which you should collect data from a research population which is unaware of the fact that they are the subject of research. There has been a recent dispute between solicitors and the Consumers' Association (CA). Telephone enquiries were conducted by the CA with a sample of solicitors for the purpose of assessing the accuracy of legal advice given and the cost of specified work. The calls were, allegedly, made without the CA's identity, or the purpose of the research, being disclosed (Gibb, 1995). It is for you to decide whether a similar strategy adopted in your project would be ethical, given that the publication of findings are likely to be rather less high profile than in the case of the CA.

It may be quite a different matter if you are collecting data from individuals, rather than from organisations as in the above example. This may be the case if you are conducting your research while working as an employee in an organisation. It may also be so if you are working on a student placement. In this case you would be researching as a *participant observer*. If the topic you were researching was one where it may be beneficial for your research if the fact that you were collecting data on individuals was not disclosed, then this poses a similar ethical dilemma. This will be discussed in more detail when we deal with observation as data collection method in Chapter 8.

4.6 SUMMARY

- The two main approaches to research are positivist and phenomenological. These should not be thought of as mutually exclusive. You can use both in combination on the same research project. The main influence on your choice of research approach should be your research question(s) and objectives.

- The main research strategies are experiment, survey and case study. Again, you should not think of these as discrete entities. They may be combined in the same research project.

- Research projects may be cross-sectional or longitudinal. In addition, they may be classed as exploratory, descriptive or explanatory.

- Multi-method approaches to research mean that different purposes may be served and that triangulation of results is facilitated.

- You should take care to ensure that your results are valid and reliable.

- You should always think carefully about the ethical issues implied by the choice of your research strategy.

Self-check questions and assignment

Self-check question 4.1
You have decided to undertake a project and have defined the main research question as: 'What are the opinions of consumers to a 10% reduction in weight, with the price remaining the same, of Snackers chocolate bars?' Write a hypothesis which you could test in your project.

Self-check question 4.2
You are about to embark on a year-long study of customer service training for sales assistants in two supermarket companies. The purpose of the research is to compare the way in which the training develops and its effectiveness. What measures would you need to take in the research design stage to ensure that the results were valid?

Self-check question 4.3
You are working in an organisation which has branches throughout the UK. The managing director is mindful of the fact that managers of the branches need to talk over common problems on a regular basis. That is why there have always been monthly meetings.

However, she is becoming increasingly concerned that these meetings are not cost effective. Too many managers see them as an unwelcome intrusion. They feel their time would be better spent pursuing their principal job objectives. Other managers see it as a 'day off': an opportunity to recharge the batteries.

She has asked you to carry out some research on the cost effectiveness of the monthly meetings. You have defined the research question you are seeking to answer as: 'What are the managers' opinions of the value of their monthly meetings?'

Your principal data collection method will be a questionnaire to all managers who attend the monthly meetings. But you are keen to triangulate your findings.

How could you do this?

Self-check question 4.4
You have started conducting interviews in a university with the university's hourly paid staff (e.g. porters, gardeners, caterers). The research objective is to establish the extent to which those employees feel a sense of 'belonging' to the university. You have

negotiated access to your interviewees through the heads of the respective departments. In each case you have been presented with a list of interviewees.

It soon becomes apparent to you that you are obtaining a rather rosier picture than you expected. The interviewees are all very positive about their jobs, their managers and the university. This make you suspicious. Are the hourly paid staff all as positive as this? Are you only being given the employees who can be relied on to tell the 'good news'? Have they been 'got at' by their manager?

There is a great risk that your results will not be valid.

What can you do?

Self-check question 4.5

You wish to study the way in which the job of the bank manager has changed over the past ten years. Your chosen research strategy is to have unstructured discussions with some bank managers who have been in banking for at least that ten-year period. You are asked by a small audience of peers and supervisors to explain why your chosen strategy is as valid as a questionnaire-based survey. What would be your answer?

Assignment 4:
Deciding on your research strategy

- Return to your research question(s) and objectives. Decide on whether you intend to pursue an approach which is deductive (your theory will be tested by observation) or inductive (the collection of your data will be followed by the development of theory). Explain clearly why you have decided on the approach chosen.

- Decide which of the strategies, experiment, survey or case study, is most appropriate for your research question(s) and objectives. Look at studies in the literature which are similar to your own. Which methods have been used? What explanations do the researchers give for their choice of strategy?

- Prepare notes on the constraints under which your research is being conducted. Do they, for example, preclude the pursuit of longitudinal research?

- How may you be able to combine different research methods in your study? Make notes on the advantages which such a multi-method approach would bring.

- List all the threats to reliability and validity contained in your research design.

References

Adams, G. and Schvaneveldt, J. (1991) *Understanding Research Methods* (2nd edn), New York, Longman.

Buchanan, D., Boddy, D. and McAlman, J. (1988) 'Getting In, Getting On, Getting Out and Getting Back', in Bryman, A. (ed.) *Doing research in organisations*, London, Routledge, pp. 53–67.

Deci, E.L. (1972) 'The Effects of Contingent and Non-Contingent Rewards and Controls on Intrinsic Motivation', *Organisational Behaviour and Human Performance*, 8, 217–19.

Dixon, B., Bouma, G. and Atkinson, G. (1987) *A Handbook of Social Science Research: A Comprehensive and Practical Guide for Students*, Oxford, Oxford University Press.

Easterby-Smith, M., Thorpe, R. and Lowe, A. (1991) *Management Research: An Introduction*, London, Sage.

Emory, C. and Cooper, D. (1991) *Business Research Methods* (4th edn), Homewood, Illinois, Richard D. Irwin.

Gibb, F. (1995) 'Consumer group accuses lawyers of shoddy service', *The Times*, 5 October.

Gill, J. and Johnson, P. (1991) *Research Methods for Managers*, London, Paul Chapman.

Hakim, C. (1987) *Research Design: Strategies and Choices in the Design of Social Research*, London, Allen and Unwin.

Jankowicz, A.D. (1995) *Business Research Projects* (2nd edn), London, Chapman & Hall.

Meyer, H., Kay, E. and French, J. (1965) 'Split Roles in Performance Appraisal', *Harvard Business Review*, 43: 1, 123–9.

Millward, N., Stevens, M., Smart, D. and Hawes, W.R. (1992) *Workplace Industrial Relations in Transition*, Aldershot, Dartmouth.

Mintzberg, H. and Waters, J. (1989) 'Of Strategies, Deliberate and Emergent', in Asch, D. and Bowman, C . (eds.) *Readings in Strategic Management*, Basingstoke, Macmillan Education, pp. 4–19.

Morris, T. and Wood, S. (1991) 'Testing the Survey Method: Continuity and Change in British Industrial Relations', *Work Employment and Society*, 5: 2, 259–82.

Naipaul, V.S. (1989) *A Turn in the South*, London, Penguin.

Peters, T. and Waterman, R. (1982) *In Search of Excellence*, New York, Harper & Row.

Raimond, P. (1993) *Management Projects*, London, Chapman & Hall.

Robson, C. (1993) *Real World Research*, Oxford, Blackwell.

Rogers, C.R. (1961) *On Becoming a Person*, London, Constable.

Smith, H. (1975) *Strategies of Social Research: The Methodological Imagination*, Englewood Cliffs, New Jersey, Prentice-Hall.

Further reading

Easterby-Smith, M., Thorpe, R. and Lowe, A. (1991) *Management Research: An Introduction*, London, Sage. Chapter 3 gives a comprehensive and highly readable introduction to different research approaches.

Gill, J. and Johnson, P. (1991) *Research Methods for Managers*, London, Paul Chapman. Chapters 3, 9 and 10 provide a detailed discussion of the choice of approach and strategy and the philosophical and theoretical assumptions underlying that choice.

Raimond, P. (1993) *Management Projects*, London, Chapman & Hall. Chapters 5 and 6 provide an excellent insight into the issue of validity and reliability.

Robson, C. (1993) *Real World Research*, Oxford, Blackwell. Chapters 3–7 give an excellent account of all the topics covered in this chapter. It is very readable, not least for the attractive and accessible way it is laid out. The examples are not drawn principally from management and business, but don't let that worry you.

Case 4:
The effectiveness of computer-based training at Falcon Insurance Company

(The techniques used in this case appear complicated when you first read about them. Do not worry, the case is included as an example of a research strategy not techniques. Further details on the techniques of observation, in-depth interviews and questionnaires can be found in Chapters 8, 9 and 10 respectively).

Ingrid works for Falcon Insurance, a large UK insurance company offering insurance in the life and motor markets. As part of its training portfolio Falcon Insurance was considering the introduction of computer-based training (CBT) for junior-level courses such as those in telephone manner. In order to make an informed decision about introducing CBT, Falcon needed to answer the question: was CBT, an effective training medium? After discussion with her project tutor Ingrid decided this would make a good research project. An extensive literature review enabled her to define the term 'effective' and generate four interrelated research questions:

- Was CBT effective for individual learning?
- Was CBT effective for group study?
- Was learning in groups more effective than self-study?
- Did a match of training media to learning style improve learning?

Ingrid wanted the research to provide both quantitative results which described the outcomes of CBT in relation to other forms of training, and qualitative results which explored trainees' opinions and behaviours and the meanings behind these outcomes.

In order to describe and explore the effect of CBT on learning, Ingrid decided to undertake a study which examined the impact of this type of training over an extended period. The independent variable was the training medium used, the dependent variable was the learning that took place. A review of the literature suggested that four distinct groups would be needed:

1 Self-study CBT: using the CBT software individually without a trainer to facilitate and provide input.

2 Group study CBT: using the same CBT medium but studying as a group of trainees without a trainer to facilitate and provide input.

3 Traditional training course: using the message and content of the CBT but applying it to a facilitated group in which no technology was used and the input was provided by a trainer.

4 Control group: where no training took place during the study period to provide a benchmark.

A representative sample of 120 Falcon Insurance employees was selected and 30 allocated to each group at random. Data were collected using a combination of questionnaires, observation and unstructured interviews (Table 1).

Group	Action taken:			
	immediately before training	during training	immediately after training	six months after training
1 Self-study CBT	Questionnaire and Learning Styles Questionnaire	Descriptive observation	Questionnaire and separate in-depth interview	Questionnaire
2 Group-study CBT	Questionnaire and Learning Styles Questionnaire	Descriptive observation	Questionnaire and separate in-depth interview	Questionnaire
3 Traditional training	Questionnaire and Learning Styles Questionnaire	Descriptive observation	Questionnaire and separate in-depth interview	Questionnaire
4 Control group	Questionnaire			Questionnaire

Table 1 The research strategy

Ingrid decided to use pre-tests and post-tests on each of the four distinct groups. These data would be collected using a questionnaire on three separate occasions: immediately before training, immediately after training and six months after training.

A confidential self-administered questionnaire, to measure quantitatively any changes in individuals' knowledge and understanding over the study period, was designed and pilot tested. Questions tested the respondents' knowledge and understanding that should have been developed by the training they would receive. The control group was also tested, despite receiving no training, to measure any change in knowledge and understanding due to other factors. In addition, questions were included to measure the trainees' reactions to various aspects of the training as well as attribute questions to assess the representativeness of the sample. The questionnaire was administered to all four groups for the pre-test and, with minor alterations, the post-test stages. In addition, all respondents who actually undertook some form of training were asked to complete a learning styles questionnaire.

An important part of Ingrid's research was to examine the social context of the groups studied and to provide additional data with which to compare and explore the results of the study. Descriptive observation was used to collect data on the behaviour of each of the three groups of trainees, paying particular attention to events and observed actions and behaviours. Observers were given a sheet on which they recorded this information in a structured manner using a pre-determined scheme. This scheme was developed to minimise the impact of subjectivity and inconsistency on the recorded response. Observations were recorded while observing each of the three trainee groups, the observer remaining only as such and not engaging with the group.

Ingrid used unstructured interviews to collect views about group learning from a stratified sample of trainees immediately after the training. In particular, she asked trainees to discuss their views on learning in a group and whether they preferred this to self-study. Trainees who had received group-study CBT were asked to discuss their views on the effectiveness of the medium in the group context and about the effect of group interaction in their particular session. Trainees were asked to consider whether or not they would put their learning into practice in their jobs. Finally, the trainees were asked to consider the match between their preferred learning style and the training they had received, and whether it had improved their learning.

Data collected from the questionnaire, observation and unstructured interviews were subsequently analysed.

Case-study questions

1 Which type(s) of research strategy are employed in this study?

2 What are the benefits of adding a longitudinal dimension to this research?

3 What are the benefits of using multiple methods of data collection?

4 a What threats to reliability are inherent in the research design?

  b How may these be overcome?

5 a What threats to validity are inherent in the research design?

  b How may these be overcome?

Answers to self-check questions

Self-check question 4.1
Probably the most realistic hypothesis here would be: 'Consumers of Snackers chocolate bars did not notice the difference between the current bar and its reduced weight successor'. Doubtless, that is what the Snackers' manufacturers would want confirmed!

Self-check question 4.2
This would be a longitudinal study. Therefore, the potential for some of the threats to validity explained in Section 4.4 is greater simply because they have longer to develop. You would need to make sure that most of these threats were controlled as much as possible. For example, you would need to:

- account for the existence of a significant event during the period of the research (wide-scale redundancies which may affect employee attitudes) in one of the companies but not the other;

- ensure that you use the same data collection devices in both companies;

- be aware of the 'mortality' problem. Some of the sales assistants will leave. You would be advised to replace them with assistants with similar characteristics, as far as possible.

Self-check question 4.3
The questionnaire will undoubtedly perform a valuable function in obtaining a

comprehensive amount of data which can be compared easily, say by district or age and gender. But you would add to the understanding of the problem if you observed managers' meetings. Who does most of the talking? What are the non-verbal behaviour patterns displayed by managers? Who turns up late? – or doesn't turn up at all!

You could also consider talking to managers in groups or individually. Your decision here would be whether to talk to them before or after the questionnaire, or both.

In addition, you could study the minutes of the meetings to discover who contributed the most. Who initiated the most discussions? What were the attendance patterns?

Self-check question 4.4

There is no easy answer to this question! You have to remember that being granted access to an organisation for the purpose of research is an act of goodwill on the part of managers and they do like to retain a certain amount of control. Selecting those whom researchers may interview is a classic way of managers retaining control. If this is the motive of the managers concerned, then they are unlikely to let you have free access to their employees.

What you could do is to ask to see all the employees in a particular department rather than a sample of employees. Alternatively, you could explain that your research was still uncovering new patterns of information and more interviews were necessary. This way you would penetrate deeper into the core of the employee group and may start seeing those who were rather less positive. All this assumes that you have the time to do this!

You could also be perfectly honest with the managers and confess your concern. If you did a sound job at the start of the research in convincing them that you are purely interested in academic research, and that all data will be anonymous, then you may have less of a problem.

Of course, there is always the possibility that the employees generally are positive and feel as if they really do 'belong'!

Self-check question 4.5

You would need to stress here that your principal interest would be in gaining a deep understanding of the changes in the manager's job and the reasons for the job having changed. You would discover what the managers thought of the changes and the ways in which they had responded to the changes. In other words, you would establish what you set out to establish and, no doubt, a good deal besides.

You will remember from Section 4.4 that validity is concerned with whether the findings are really about what they appear to be about. There is no reason that your discussions with managers should not be as valid as a questionnaire survey. But you should ensure that you talk to managers (and others) who are in a position to speak with authority on the subject. Your questioning should be skilful enough to elicit rich responses from your interviewees (see Chapter 9). You should be sensitive to the direction in which the discussion is moving. This will mean not being too directive, while still moving the interview in the direction you as the interviewer want.

Of course, you may alleviate any fears about validity by conducting a survey and interviews so that your findings can be triangulated!

CHAPTER 5

Negotiating access and research ethics

The objectives of this chapter are to explore issues related to gaining access and research ethics.

Advice is offered to help you gain access to organisations and to individual participants.

Potential ethical issues are considered at each stage of the research process to help you to anticipate and deal with these.

Ethical issues associated with particular data collection methods are also discussed so that you can consider these in relation to your proposed research methods.

5.1 INTRODUCTION

Access and ethics are critical aspects for the conduct of research. Many newcomers to research want to 'get on with it' once they have identified a topic area. Insufficient attention is likely to be paid to the very real problem of gaining access, and even less to the likelihood of ethical concerns arising in relation to the research project and their implications. These are aspects which require careful attention at the outset of any research project. Without this, what seem like good ideas for research may flounder and prove impractical or problematic once you attempt to carry them out.

The following section (5.2) of this chapter defines the types and levels of access and the issues associated with these. It discusses the key issues of feasibility and sufficiency in relation to gaining access and the effect of these on the nature and content of your research question and objectives. The following section (5.3) examines a number of proven strategies to help you to gain access to organisations and to intended participants within them. The next section (5.4) is devoted to a discussion of research ethics and the types of issues which are likely to occur at the various stages of your research project, and in relation to the use of particular research methods. Summary checklists are included on the issues of gaining access and anticipating and dealing with ethical concerns. These are designed to help you during the development of a research proposal and when you conduct your research project.

5.2 PROBLEMS ASSOCIATED WITH ACCESS

Your ability to collect data will depend on gaining access to its source, or to appropriate sources where there is a choice. The appropriateness of a source will of course depend on your research question(s), related objectives and strategy. The first level of access is *physical access* or entry (Gummesson, 1991). Gaining physical access can be difficult for a number of reasons. First, organisations or individuals may not be prepared to engage in additional, voluntary activities because of the time and resources required. Many organisations receive frequent requests for access and co-operation, and would find it impossible to agree to all or even some of these. Second, the request for access and co-operation may fail to interest the person who receives it. This may be for a number of reasons, related to:

- a lack of interest or perceived value in relation to the work of the organisation or the individual;
- the nature of the topic because of its potential sensitivity or because of concerns about the confidentiality of the information which would be required;
- perceptions about your credibility and doubts about your competence.

Third, the organisation may find itself in a difficult situation due to external events totally unrelated to any perceptions about the nature of the request or the person making it, so that there is no choice but to refuse access. Even where a particular organisational participant is prepared to offer access, this may be overruled at a higher level in the organisation. This may result in a 'false start' and an associated feeling of disappointment (Johnson, 1975). Where you are unable to gain this type of access you will therefore need to adopt a different case-study organisation, or even modify your research question(s) and objectives.

However, even where you are able to negotiate entry into an organisation, there are other levels of access which you will need to consider and plan for if your research strategy is to be realised successfully. Many writers see access as a *continuing* process and not an initial or single event (Gummesson, 1991; Marshall and Rossman, 1989; Robson, 1993). This may take two forms. First, access may be an iterative process, so that you gain entry to carry out part of your research and then seek further access in order to conduct another part. You may also seek to repeat your collection of data in different parts of the organisation, and therefore engage in the negotiation of access in each part (Marshall and Rossman, 1989). Second, those from whom you wish to collect data may be a different set of people to those who considered and agreed to your request for access. Physical access to an organisation will be formally granted through its management. However, it will also be necessary for you to gain informal acceptance from intended participants within the organisation in order to gain access to the data which they are able to provide (Robson, 1993).

Access may also refer to your ability to select a representative sample of organisational participants (or secondary data) in order to attempt to answer your research question(s) and objectives in an unbiased way and to produce reliable and valid data (Chapters 4 and 6). For example, we recall a well-known current affairs programme which broadcast a feature including short extracts of interviews conducted with employees of a case-study organisation. All of the interviewees' responses were very positive about the organisation. However, the reporter had prefixed the showing of these extracts by saying that it was the organisation which had selected all of the employees to be interviewed. The viewer was therefore left to wonder whether these very positive employees were typical of all those employed in the organisation, or whether they were providing an unreliable and untypical view of employee attitudes in this business.

We might refer to this broader meaning of access as *cognitive* access. Where you achieve this, you will have gained access to the data which you need your intended participants to share with you in order for you to understand their social reality and for you to be able to address your research question(s) and objectives. Simply obtaining physical access to an organisation will be inadequate unless you are also able to negotiate yourself into a position where you can reveal the reality of what is occurring in relation to your research question(s) and objectives. This fundamental point requires you to consider material included throughout this book; however, there are two specific issues which we will consider now. The first of these relates to whether you have sufficiently considered, and therefore fully realised, the extent and nature of the access which you will require in order to be able to answer your research question(s) and objectives. The second point relates to whether you are able to gain sufficient access in practice to answer your research question(s) and objectives. These two points may be linked in some instances. Your clarity of thought, which should result from sufficiently considering the nature of the access which you require, may be helpful in persuading organisations to grant entry, since they are more likely to be convinced about your credibility and competence.

Access is therefore likely to be a problematic area, in terms of gaining permission for physical access, maintaining that access and being able to create sufficient scope to address fully the research question(s) and objectives which guide your work. This suggests that the *feasibility* of your research will also be an important guiding principle, alongside the recognised hallmarks of good research outlined in a number of sources (Emory and Cooper, 1991; Marshall and Rossman, 1989; Sekaran, 1992). The issue of feasibility will determine the construction or refinement of your research question(s) and objectives and may sometimes lead to a clash with these hallmarks of good research. This has been recognised by Buchanan et al. (1988: 53–4):

> 'Fieldwork is permeated with the conflict between what is theoretically desirable on the one hand and what is practically possible on the other. It is desirable to ensure representativeness in the sample, uniformity of interview procedures, adequate data collection across the range of topics to be explored, and so on. But the members of organisations block access to information, constrain the time allowed for interviews, lose your questionnaires, go on holiday, and join other organisations in the middle of your unfinished study. In the conflict between the desirable and the possible, the possible always wins.'

The extent to which feasibility will affect the nature of your research, or at least the approach which you adopt, is made clear by Johnson (1975), who recognises that the reality of undertaking a research project may be to consider where you are likely to be able to gain access and develop a topic to fit the nature of this access.

A request to undertake research may involve you in seeking access to a range of participants based on an organisational sample. In order to select such a sample you will require access to organisational data, either directly or indirectly, through a request which outlines precisely how you require the sample to be selected (Chapter 6). Where you wish to undertake a longitudinal study, you will require access to the organisation and your research participants on more than one occasion. The difficulty of obtaining access in relation to these more *intrusive* methods and approaches has been recognised many times in the literature (for example Buchanan *et al.*, 1988; Johnson, 1975; Raimond, 1993).

5.3 STRATEGIES TO GAIN ACCESS

The preceding section has outlined problems associated with gaining access and the sufficiency of any access obtained. It has stressed the need to identify a feasible research question and objectives, from the perspective of gaining access. This section will outline and discuss a number of strategies which may help you to obtain physical and cognitive access to appropriate data. The discussion in this section will be applicable to you where you wish to gain *personal entry* to an organisation in order to use any of the methods listed in the preceding section. It will be less applicable where you send a self-administered, postal questionnaire to organisational participants, in situations where you do not need to gain physical access in order to identify participants. As Raimond (1993: 67) recognises, 'provided that people reply to the questionnaires, the problem of access to data is solved'. Even in this case, however, some of the points which follow will still apply to the way in which you construct the pre-survey contact and the written request to complete the questionnaire (see also Chapter 10).

The strategies to help you to gain access will be considered under the following headings:

- allowing yourself sufficient time;
- using existing contacts and developing new ones;
- providing a clear account of purpose and type of access required;
- overcoming organisational concerns to the granting of access;
- possible benefits to the organisation of granting you access;
- using suitable language;
- facilitating ease of reply when requesting access;
- developing your access on an incremental basis;
- establishing your credibility with intended participants.

Allowing yourself sufficient time

Physical access may take weeks or even months to arrange, and in many cases the time invested will not result in access being granted (Buchanan *et al.*, 1988). An approach to an organisation will either result in a reply or no response at all. A politely worded but clearly reasoned refusal at least informs you that access will not be granted. The non-reply situation means that if you wish to pursue the possibility of gaining access to a particular organisation, you will need to allow sufficient time before sending further correspondence or making a follow-up telephone call. Easterby-Smith *et al.* (1991) report the need to make up to four telephone calls in order to gain access. Great care must be taken in relation to this type of activity so that no grounds for offence are given. Seeking access to a large, complex organisation, where you do not have existing contacts, may also necessitate several telephone calls simply to make contact with the appropriate person, in order to ensure that your request for access will be considered by the right individual. In our experience this can take days or even a couple of weeks to achieve. You may also consider using e-mail, where you are able to, as a way of obtaining a reply.

If you can contact a participant directly, such as a manager, an exchange of correspondence may be sufficient to gain access. Here you should clearly set out what you require from this person and persuade him or her of the value of your work and your credibility. Even so, you will still need to allow time for your request to be received, considered and an interview meeting to be arranged at a convenient time for your research participant. This may take a number of weeks and you may have to wait longer to schedule the actual interview.

Where you are seeking access to a range of organisational participants to conduct a number of interviews, undertake a survey, engage in observation or use secondary data, your request may be passed 'up' the organisation for clearance and may be considered by a number of people. Where you are able to use a known contact in the organisation this may help, since you can probably feel assured that your request is being attended to, but the process is likely to take weeks rather than days. Where the organisation is prepared to consider granting access, it is likely that you will be asked to attend a meeting to discuss this. There may also be a delay after this stage while the case which you have made for access is evaluated in terms of its implications for the organisation, and it may be necessary to make a number of telephone calls to pursue your request politely.

In the situation where your intended participants are not the same people who grant you physical access, you will need to allow further time to gain their acceptance. This may involve you making *pre-survey contact* by telephone calls to these intended participants, or engaging in correspondence, or holding an explanatory meeting with them (discussed later). You may well need to allow a couple of weeks or more to establish contact with your intended participants and secure their co-operation, especially given any operational constraints which restrict their availability.

Once you have gained physical access to the organisation and to your participants, you will be concerned with gaining 'cognitive access'. Whichever method you are using to gather data will involve you in a time-consuming process, although some methods will require that more of your time be spent within the organisation to understand what is happening. The use of a questionnaire will mean less time spent in the organisation compared to the use of non-standardised interviews, whereas the use of observation techniques may result in even more time being spent to gather data (Bryman, 1988). Where you are involved in a situation of 'continuing access', as outlined in the section above, there will also be an issue related to the time which is required to negotiate, or re-negotiate, access at each stage, and you will need to consider how careful planning may help to minimise the possibility of any 'stop–go' approach to your research activity.

Using existing contacts and developing new ones

Other management and organisational researchers suggest that you are more likely to gain access where you are able to use *existing contacts* (Buchanan *et al.*, 1988; Easterby-Smith *et al.*, 1991; Johnson, 1975). Buchanan *et al.* (1988: 56) say that 'we have been most successful where we have a friend, relative or student working in the organisation'. We have also found this to be the case. In order to request access we have approached those whom we would consider to be professional colleagues, who may also be present or past students, course advisers, external examiners, or otherwise known to us through local, regional or national networks. Their knowledge of us means that they should be able to trust our stated intentions and the assurances given about the use of any data provided. It can also be useful to start a research project by utilising these existing contacts in order to establish a track record, which you can refer to in approaches which you make to other organisations where you do not have such contacts. This should help your credibility in the eyes of these new contacts.

The use of known contacts will depend to a large extent on your choice of research strategy and approach to selecting a sample, as suggested by your research question(s) and objectives. It will undoubtedly be easier to adopt this approach where you are using a case-study based research strategy and non-probability sampling (Section 6.3). This will certainly be the case where you undertake an in-depth study which focuses on a small, purposively selected sample. There will clearly be a high level of *convenience* in terms of gaining access through contacts who are familiar; however, these contacts may also be used as part of a quota sample, or in relation to purposive or snowball sampling (Section 6.3).

Jankowicz (1995) refers to the possibility of using your work placement organisation as a context for your research project, where this applies to your situation as a full-time undergraduate or postgraduate student. Where you have enjoyed a successful work placement, you will undoubtedly have made a number of contacts who may be able to be very helpful in terms of co-operating with you and granting access to data. You may have become interested in a particular topic because of the time which you spent in your placement organisation. If this applies to your situation, you can spend time reading theoretical work which may be relevant to this topic, then identify a research question and objectives, and plan a research project to pursue your interest within the context of your placement organisation. The combination of genuine interest in the topic and relatively easy access to organisational participants should help towards the production of a good-quality and useful piece of work.

Where you need to develop *new contacts*, consideration of the points discussed throughout this section will help you to cultivate these. In addition, you will need to be able to identify the most appropriate person to contact for help, either directly or indirectly. There may be a number of ways to do this, depending on your research topic. You may consider contacting the local branch of an appropriate professional association for the names and business addresses of key employees to contact in organisations where it would be suitable for you to conduct research. You could also contact this professional association at national level, if this is more appropriate to your research question(s) and objectives. It might also be appropriate to contact either an employers' association for a particular industry, or a trade union, at local or national level. Alternatively, it might be appropriate for you to contact one or more Chambers of Commerce, Training and Enterprise Councils or other employers' networks (Jankowicz, 1995).

You may also consider making a direct approach to an organisation in an attempt to identify the appropriate person to contact in relation to a particular research project. This has the advantage of potentially providing access to organisations which you would like to include in your research project; however, great care needs to be taken at each stage of this exercise.

WORKED EXAMPLE: *Identifying the appropriate person through whom to request access*

Adrian and another colleague identified a number of specific organisations which matched the criteria established for the types of business which they wished to include in a research project. Many of these were organisations where they did not have an appropriate contact, or indeed any contact at all. The different types of organisational structures in these organisations added to their difficulties in tracking down the most appropriate employee to contact in order to request access.

Available national directories were used to identify the corporate headquarters of each organisation. This part of the organisation was contacted by telephone. In each case the name of the researcher was given and also that of the institution through which they were conducting the research. A very brief explanation was provided in order to identify the name and location of that part of the organisation which dealt with the area of their research interest. This resulted in the researchers being provided with a telephone number or connected to that part of the organisation which the receptionist to whom they spoke thought was appropriate for the enquiry (see next paragraph). This initial telephone call was always ended by thanking the person for the help which had been provided.

At the next stage, the researchers again provided their name and that of the institution through which they were conducting the research. The purpose of the research was also briefly explained to the secretary who inevitably answered the telephone. The researchers asked for the name and business address of the person whom the secretary thought would be the most appropriate person to write to. In most cases the people to whom the researchers spoke at this stage were most helpful and provided some excellent leads.

Sometimes, particularly in relation to complex organisations, the researchers found that they were not talking to someone in the appropriate part of the organisation. They therefore asked the person to help by transferring the call. Sometimes this led to a series of calls to identify the right person. They always maintained politeness and thanked the person they spoke to for their help. They always gave their names and organisational location so as to reduce the risk of appearing to be threatening in any way. It was most important to create a positive attitude in what could be perceived as a tiresome enquiry.

The researchers chose to ask for the name and business address of hoped-for organisational 'leads', so that they could write a request to this person which could be considered when it was convenient, rather than attempt to talk to them at that point when it may well have not been a good time to make such a request. This process resulted in many successes and Adrian and his colleague have added a number of good contacts to their previous list. However, the key point to note is that great care needs to be exercised when using this approach.

Making this type of contact may result in identifying the person whom you wish to participate in your research. Alternatively, your reason for making contact with this person may be to ask them to grant you access to others in the organisation whom you wish to be your participants, or to secondary data. This second type of contact is sometimes referred to as a *broker* (Easterby-Smith *et al.*, 1991) or a *gatekeeper* (Gummesson, 1991; Marshall and Rossman, 1989). Easterby-Smith *et al.* (1991) suggest approaching an organisation's personnel manager because this person will have contacts across the organisation and can therefore be very helpful in terms of facilitating access. This type of contact may also be the functional manager or director of those staff to whom you would like access. Having identified an organisational broker or gatekeeper, you will have to persuade them about your credibility, overcome any issues they have about the sensitivity of your research project, and demonstrate the potential value of this for them.

Providing a clear account of purpose and type of access required

Providing a clear account of your requirements will allow your intended participants to be aware of what will be required from them (Robson, 1993). Asking for access and co-operation without being specific about your requirements will probably lead to a cautious attitude on their part, since the amount of time which could be required might prove to be disruptive. Even where the initial contact or request for access involves a telephone call, it is still probably advisable to send a letter which outlines your proposed research and requirements. Your *introductory letter* requesting access should outline in brief the purpose of your research, how the person being contacted might be able to help and what would be required. Healey (1991) suggests that the success of this letter will be helped by the use of short and clear sentences. Its tone should be polite and it should seek to generate interest on the part of intended respondents.

Establishing your credibility will be vital in order to gain access. The use of known contacts will mean that you can seek to trade on your existing level of credibility. However, when you are making contact with a potential participant for the first time, the nature of your approach will be highly significant in terms of beginning to establish credibility – or not doing so! Any telephone call or introductory letter will need to demonstrate your clarity of thought and purpose. A lack of preparation at this stage will be apparent and is likely to reduce the possibility of gaining access (see Section 9.4 for further consideration of these issues).

The presentation of the introductory letter will also serve to establish credibility. Healey (1991: 210) says: 'a well-designed and presented letter, typed on headed note paper, which is personally addressed with a hand-written signature, would seem to be a sensible way of trying to persuade . . . managers of businesses to co-operate.'

Overcoming organisational concerns to the granting of access

Organisational concerns may be placed into one of three categories. First, concerns about the amount of time or resources which will be involved in the request for access. Easterby-Smith *et al.* (1991) suggest that your request for access may be more likely to be accepted if the amount of time and resources required are kept to a minimum. As a complementary point to this, Healey (1991) reports earlier work which found that introductory letters containing multiple requests are also less likely to be successful. However, while access may be more likely to be achieved where your demands are kept to a minimum, there will still be a need to maintain honesty. For example, where you wish to conduct an interview you may be more likely to gain access if the time requested is kept within reason. However, falsely stating that it will last for only a short time and then deliberately exceeding this, is very likely to upset your participant and may prevent you gaining further access.

The second area of concern is related to *sensitivity* about the topic. We have found that organisations are less likely to co-operate where the topic of the research has a negative inference. Organisations do not normally wish to present themselves in a bad light. If this is likely to be the case, you will need to consider carefully the way in which your proposed research topic may be perceived by those whom you ask to grant access. In such cases you may be able to highlight a positive approach to the issue by, for example, emphasising that your work will be designed to identify individual and organisational learning in relation to the topic (a positive inference). You should avoid sending any request which appears to concentrate on aspects associated with non-achievement or failure if you are to gain access. Your request for access is therefore more likely to be favourably considered where you are able to outline a research topic which does not appear to be sensitive to the organisation (Easterby-Smith *et al.*, 1991).

The third area of concern is related to the *confidentiality* of the data which would have to be provided, and the *anonymity* of the organisation or individual participants. To overcome this concern, you will need to provide clear assurances about these aspects. One advantage of using an introductory letter is to give this guarantee in writing at the time of making the request for access, when this issue may be uppermost in the minds of those who will consider your approach. Once initial access has been granted you will need to repeat the assurance about anonymity to those who act as your participants. You will also need to consider how to maintain this when you write up your work in situations where particular participants could be indirectly identified (Bell, 1993) (Section 13.5).

Possible benefits to the organisation of granting you access

Apart from any general interest which is generated by the subject of your proposed research, you may find that it will have some level of *applicability* to the jobs of those whom you approach for access. Practitioners often wrestle with the same subject issues as researchers and may therefore welcome the opportunity to discuss their own analysis and course of action related to an issue, in a non-threatening, non-judgemental environment. A discussion may allow them to think through an issue and to reflect on the action which they have adopted to manage it. In our own interviews with practitioners we are pleased when told that the discussion has been of value to the interviewee.

For those who work in organisations where they are perhaps the only subject practitioner, this may be the first time they have had this type of opportunity. You therefore need to consider whether your proposed research topic may provide some advantage to those from whom you wish to gain access, although this does not mean that you should attempt to 'buy' your way in based on some promise about the potential value of your work. Where it is unlikely that your proposed research will suggest any advantage to those whose co-operation you seek, you will need to consider what alternative course of action to take. This may involve redesigning your research question(s) and objectives before seeking any access.

It may also help to offer a report of your findings to those who grant access. The intention would be to provide each of your participants with something of value and to fulfil any expectations about exchange between the provider and receiver of the research data, thereby prompting some of those whom you approach to grant access (Johnson, 1975). Buchanan *et al.* (1988) suggest that this type of report should be specially designed to be of use to those who participated, rather than, say, a copy of the document you need to submit for academic examination. They also suggest that feedback about this report may help you further with your research.

Using suitable language

Some researchers advise against referring to certain terms used in relation to research activity when making an approach to an organisation for access, because these may be perceived as threatening or not interesting to the potential participant (Buchanan *et al.*, 1988; Easterby-Smith *et al.*, 1991; Jankowicz, 1995). Buchanan *et al.* (1988: 57) suggest using 'learn from your experience' in place of research; 'conversation' instead of interview; and 'write an account' rather than publish. Easterby-Smith *et al.* (1991: 77) suggest that the term 'researcher' will have greater credibility than will 'student'.

Use of language will largely depend on the nature of the people you are contacting. Your language should be appropriate to the type of person being contacted, without any hint of being patronising, threatening or just boring. Given the vital role of initial telephone conversations or introductory letters, we would suggest allowing adequate time to consider and draft the wording of these, and using someone to check through your message. You are intending to engender interest in your research project and the initial point of contact needs to convey this.

WORKED EXAMPLE: *Introductory letter*

Department of Business and Finance

PO Box 220, The Park Campus

The Park, Cheltenham

Gloucestershire GL50 2QF

Telephone: 01242 543205

Fax: 01242 543208

Mr Geoffrey West
Personnel Policy Manager
Utility Co plc
South Avenue
Anytown

12th December 1995

Dear Mr West

THE POSITIVE MANAGEMENT OF REDUNDANCY

We are currently researching the above, in order to determine and share effective practices on this topical and sensitive issue. We are both attached to the Human Resource Management Research Centre within the College.

You have experience that would be of value to us and we would very much like to know your views on what it takes to get it right!

We are now arranging a further group of interviews with targeted practitioners who can give personal insights into specific redundancy programmes. We have already undertaken two groups of interviews involving senior personnel practitioners in 30 medium and large-scale organisations towards our target of 40.

An outline of the interview structure is attached, although it is not our intention to follow this slavishly. We will conduct interviews during January and February 1996 and envisage that these will take up to two hours.

We are aware of the need to treat our findings with the utmost confidentiality. No source, individual or organisational, will be identified or comment attributed without the express permission of the originator.

One of our intended outputs will be a report summarising our findings and we will be sending a copy of this to each of the participants in the study.

We hope you are able to help us and should be grateful if you would return the attached pro forma. We will contact you on receipt to confirm arrangements where you are able to participate. If you prefer to talk with us to agree a suitable time and venue please call us on the numbers above.

If you require any further information please do not hesitate to get in touch.

Yours sincerely

Adrian Thornhill   **Andrew Gibbons**

Dr Adrian Thornhill and Andrew Gibbons

Facilitating ease of reply when requesting access

We have found that the inclusion of a simple pro forma for use by recipients of our written requests for access generally ensures a reply. It may not be suitable in all cases and should be designed to fit the research method being used. But it is worth considering in cases where it is necessary for your recipient to draft their own letter to reply. Inclusion of a stamped or freepost, addressed envelope, or a fax number, or an e-mail address, may also facilitate a reply.

- -

WORKED EXAMPLE: *Pro forma to facilitate replies*

Variations of the following pro forma have been used successfully to facilitate replies from organisations whom we have requested to participate in research activity.

FOR THE ATTENTION OF K THORNHILL, THE BUSINESS SCHOOL

Dear Katie and Andrew

MANAGING CHANGE

❑ I am able to talk to you about managing change. I can be available to meet you at the following times, dates and locations . . .

Date/s   Time   Location/s

....
....
....
....

❑ Please contact me to arrange a suitable date, time and venue.

❑ I also recommend that you speak with . . .

....
....

❑ I am unable to talk to you about managing change.

❑ I do recommend that you speak with . . .

....
....

Yours sincerely,

Position:
Organisation:
Telephone:
Fax:
E-mail:

- -

Developing your access on an incremental basis

Reference has been made above to the strategy of achieving access by stages, as a means of overcoming organisational concerns about time-consuming, multiple requests. Johnson

(1975) provides an example of developing access on an incremental basis. He used a three-stage strategy to achieve his desired depth of access. The first stage involved a request to conduct interviews. This was the minimum requirement in order to commence his research. The next stage involved negotiating access to undertake observation. The final stage was, in effect, an extension to the second stage and involved gaining permission to tape record the interactions being observed.

There are potentially a number of advantages related to the use of this strategy. As suggested above, a request to an organisation for multiple access may be sufficient to cause managers to decline entry. Using an incremental strategy at least gains you access to a certain level of data. This strategy will also allow you the opportunity to develop a positive relationship with those who are prepared to grant initial access of a restricted nature. As you establish your credibility, you can develop the possibility of achieving a fuller level of access. A further advantage may follow from the opportunity which you have to design your request specifically for further access to the situation and opportunities which may become apparent from your initial level of access. On the other hand, this incremental process will be time consuming and you need to consider the amount of time which you will have for your research project before embarking on such a strategy.

Establishing your credibility with intended participants

In Section 5.2 we differentiated between physical and cognitive access. Just because you have been granted entry to an organisation, you will not be able to assume that those whom you wish to interview, survey or observe will be prepared to provide their co-operation. Indeed, assuming that this is going to happen raises an ethical issue which is considered in the next section. Robson (1993) says that gaining co-operation from these intended participants is a matter of developing relationships. This will mean repeating much of the process which you will have used to gain entry to the organisation. You will need to share with them the purpose of your research project, state how you believe that they will be able to help your study, and provide assurances about confidentiality and anonymity. This may involve writing to your intended participants or talking to them individually or in a group. Which of these means you use will depend on the intended research method, your opportunity to make contact with them, the numbers of participants involved and the nature of the setting. Where your intended method may be considered to be intrusive, you may need to exercise even greater care and take longer to gain acceptance. This might be the case, for example, where you wish to undertake observation. The extent to which you succeed in gaining cognitive access will depend on this effort.

WORKED EXAMPLE: *A request to participate in a discussion group*

Edcoll is holding a communications audit which we have been asked to undertake. In order to explore attitudes held by members of staff we will be holding a series of discussion groups. As a member of staff randomly selected by us to be invited to one of these discussion groups, your views will be important in order for us to be able to build up a clear picture of staff attitudes about internal communication. The attitudes revealed at these discussion groups will then be used by us to inform the design of a questionnaire to be sent to all members of staff.

Each discussion group should last no longer than one hour. Comments made during the discussion group will not be attributed to any individual or to the group and will only be used by us to inform the design of the questionnaire. On completion of the audit, key results will be communicated to all members of staff.

The discussion group which you have been invited to take part in will be held on:

(time, day, date, room, location)

If you will not be able to attend please can you contact one of us by (date), so that an appropriate alternative person can be invited in your place. Our telephone number is:

We very much hope that you can attend and look forward to seeing you.

(Signed by the members of the research team)

Summary checklist to help to gain access

- ☑ Allow yourself plenty of time.
- ☑ Consider using existing contacts, at least at the start of your research project, in order to gain access and gather data.
- ☑ Consider using your work placement organisation, where appropriate, as a case-study setting for your research project.
- ☑ Where you need to seek information about organisations which may be able to grant access, approach appropriate local and/or national employer or employee, professional or trade bodies to see if they can suggest contacts.
- ☑ Consider making a direct approach to an organisation to identify the most appropriate person to contact for access.
- ☑ Invest sufficient time to identify this person and be prepared to make a number of telephone calls to achieve this.
- ☑ Maintain politeness at all times.
- ☑ Even where your initial request for access involves a telephone conversation, it is advisable to follow this with an introductory letter to confirm your requirements.
- ☑ Always provide a clear account of your requirements when requesting access (at least your initial requirements).
- ☑ Outlining the purpose of your research project and demonstrating clarity of thought should help to establish your credibility and assist the goal of gaining access.

☑ The construction, tone and presentation of an introductory letter will also assist the establishment of your credibility and the goal of gaining access.

☑ Any request for access will need to consider and address organisational concerns relating to the amount of time or resources which would be involved on the part of the organisation, sensitivity about the topic, and confidentiality and anonymity.

☑ Consider possible benefits for the organisation should it grant access to you and the offer of a report summarising your findings to enhance your chance of achieving access.

☑ Exercise care and attention in your use of language, so that it is appropriate to the person who receives it without any hint of being patronising, threatening or boring.

☑ Include a simple pro forma for recipients of your request for access to use as a means to reply, and also send a stamped or freepost, addressed envelope, or e-mail address, plus a fax number where possible.

☑ Be prepared to attend a meeting to present and discuss your request for access.

☑ Be prepared to work through organisational gatekeepers in order to gain access to intended types of participants.

☑ Consider developing your access on an incremental basis where it is likely that a multiple request for access would lead to a refusal to gain any entry.

☑ Allow further time to contact intended participants and to develop a relationship with them in order to gain their acceptance, once physical access has been granted.

☑ Remember that some methods will require fairly lengthy periods of your time being spent within an organisation in order to gain 'cognitive access' to data.

5.4 RESEARCH ETHICS

Defining research ethics

Ethical concerns will emerge as you plan your research, seek access to organisations and to individuals, collect, analyse and report your data. In the context of research, *ethics* refers to the appropriateness of your behaviour in relation to the rights of those who become the subject of your work, or are affected by it. Wells (1994: 284) defines 'ethics in terms of a code of behaviour appropriate to academics and the conduct of research'. The appropriateness or acceptability of our behaviour as researchers will be affected by broader social norms of behaviour (Wells, 1994; Zikmund, 1994). A *social norm* indicates the type of behaviour which a person ought to adopt in a particular situation (Robson, 1993; Zikmund, 1994). However, as Wells (1994) recognises, the norms of behaviour which prevail will in reality allow for a range of ethical positions. You will therefore need to consider ethical issues throughout the period of your research and remain sensitive to the impact of your work on those whom you approach to help, those who provide access and co-operation and those affected by your results.

The conduct of your research may be guided by a code of ethics, and where you are a member of an educational institution or a professional association you should seek out the existence of such guidelines (Appendix 3). A *code of ethics* will provide you with a statement of principles and procedures for the conduct of your research. This will be helpful and, where followed, should ensure that you do not transgress behavioural norms established by your institution or association. However, there may well be other ethical issues which you need to consider during the conduct of your research.

The nature of business and management research means that you will be dependent on other people for access, as we have seen above. This will inevitably lead to a range of ethical issues. As Wells (1994: 290) puts it: 'In general, the closer the research is to actual individuals in real-world settings, the more likely are ethical questions to be raised.' Related to this, the nature of *power relationships* in business and management research will raise ethical issues which also need to be considered. Managers will be in a very powerful position in relation to researchers who request organisational access. We will consider these ethical issues related to business and management research in the discussion which follows.

Nature and scope of ethical issues in business and management

This discussion of ethical issues is divided into three subsections. First, ethical issues which arise during the design stage and when seeking initial access. Second, ethical issues during the data collection stage, when we will examine particular issues related to different methods. Third, ethical issues related to the analysis and reporting stages.

Ethical issues during the design and initial access stages

A number of management researchers state that ethical problems should be anticipated and dealt with during the design stage of any research project, perhaps by altering your research strategy or choice of methods, or by recognising the need to conduct your research in line with ethical principles. Evidence of consideration of these issues at this stage, through a discussion in your research proposal, should be one of the criteria against which your research proposal is judged (Emory and Cooper, 1991; Marshall and Rossman, 1989).

Ethical problems may also arise when seeking initial access. You should not attempt to apply any pressure on intended participants to grant access (Robson, 1993; Sekaran, 1992). This is unlikely to be the case where you are approaching a member of an organisation's management to request access. However, where you are undertaking a research project within your employing organisation, in relation to a part-time qualification, there may be a temptation to apply pressure on others (colleagues or subordinates) to cooperate. Individuals have a *right to privacy* which means that you will have to accept any refusal to take part (Emory and Cooper, 1991; Robson, 1993). Privacy may also be affected by the nature and timing of any approach which you make to intended participants – say by telephoning at 'unsociable' times, or, where possible, by 'confronting' intended participants.

Access to secondary data may also raise ethical problems in relation to privacy. Where you happen to obtain access to personal data about individuals who have not consented to let you have this (through personnel or client records) you will be obliged to treat this in the strictest confidence and not to abuse it in any way.

Research can involve an attempt to *deceive* intended participants in some way. This may be related to deceit over the real purpose of your research (Sekaran, 1992); or in relation to some undeclared sponsorship (Zikmund, 1994); or be related to an association with another organisation which will use any data gained for commercial advantage. This will cause embarrassment to those who promote your request for access within their employing organisation, as well as to yourself. In this respect, the widely used concept of *informed consent* refers to intended participants and gatekeepers (discussed earlier) being told 'the aims and nature of the research, who is undertaking it, who is funding it, its likely duration, why it is being undertaken, the possible consequences of the research, and how the results are to be disseminated' (Appendix 3). Participants can then provide their consent before entering into the process of providing data, either verbally or through an exchange of correspondence or by signing a form (Emory and Cooper, 1991; Robson, 1993). The consenting participant should also be made aware that they may refuse to answer a particular question or questions and withdraw at any time from the process if they wish (Appendix 3; Robson, 1993).

In the preceding section we discussed possible strategies to help you to gain access. One of these was related to possible benefits to an organisation of granting you access. You should be realistic about this. Where you are anxious to gain access you may be tempted to offer more than is feasible. Alternatively, you may offer to supply information arising from your work without intending to do this. Such behaviour would clearly be unethical and to compound this the effect of such action (or inaction) may result in a refusal to grant access to others who come after you.

Ethical issues during the data collection stage

The data collection stage is associated with a range of ethical issues. Some of these are general issues which will apply to whichever method is being used to collect data. Other issues are more specifically related to a particular method of collecting data. We will consider the issues related to all methods first and then examine issues related to particular methods of data collection.

Irrespective of method, there are a number of ethical principles to which you need to adhere. In the previous subsection we referred to the importance of not intruding on an intended participant's privacy. This was in relation to the participant's right not to take part. Once participants have agreed to take part in your research, they still maintain their right to privacy. This means that they have the right to withdraw as participants and that they may decline to take part in a particular aspect of your research. You should not ask them to participate in anything which will intrude on their privacy, where this goes beyond the scope of the access agreed. We also referred to rights in relation to deceit. Once access has been granted you should remain within the aims of your research project which you shared with your intended participant(s) (Zikmund, 1994). To do otherwise, without raising this with your participant(s) and re-negotiating access, would be, in effect, another type of deceit. This would be likely to cause upset and could result in the premature termination of your data collection. There are perhaps some situations where deception may be accepted in relation to 'covert' research and we will discuss this later in this subsection.

Another general ethical principle is related to the maintenance of your *objectivity*. During the data collection stage this means making sure that you collect your data accurately and fully – that you avoid exercising subjective selectivity in what you record. The importance of this action also relates to the validity and reliability of your work, which is discussed in Chapters 4, 6 and 7–10. Without objectively collected data your ability to analyse and report your work accurately will also be impaired. We return to this as an ethical issue in the next subsection. Obviously any invention of data is also a totally unacceptable and unethical course of action.

WORKED EXAMPLE: *The ethical dilemma of dubious data*

A famous debate about whether research data was invented concerns some of the work of one of the best-known British psychologists, Cyril Burt. His research concerned the relationship between IQ and genetic factors. He believed that 'individual differences in IQ are caused in part by genetic factors' (Morgan, 1995).

Claims about such a relationship are politically contentious and in the mid-1970s, after Burt's death, doubts were raised about the statistical reliability of some of Burt's data and about whether two of his research assistants had really existed. Because of the significance of the implications of Burt's work, a debate has continued to exist over two decades among those in his academic discipline about the data which he produced to justify his conclusions (*see* Mackintosh, 1995).

Confidentiality and *anonymity* have also been shown to be important in terms of gaining access to organisations and individuals (Section 5.3). Once promises about confidentiality and anonymity have been given it is of great importance to make sure that these are maintained. Easterby-Smith *et al.* (1991) raise the important point that, in a qualitatively based approach to primary data collection, points of significance will emerge as the research progresses and this will probably lead you to wish to explore these with other participants. However, they recognise that where you do this within an organisation it may lead to participants indirectly identifying which person was responsible for making the point which you wish to explore with them. This may result in harmful repercussions for the person whose openness allowed you to identify this point. Great care therefore needs to be exercised in maintaining each participant's right of anonymity. You will need to consider where the use of any data gained may have harmful consequences for the disclosing participant. Where you wish to get others to discuss such a potentially sensitive point, you may attempt to steer the discussion to see if they will raise it without in any way making clear that one of the other participants has already referred to it.

The ability to explore data or seek explanations through qualitatively based methods means that there will be greater scope for ethical issues to arise in relation to this approach to research (Easterby-Smith *et al.*, 1991). The general ethical issues which we considered above (*see also* Zikmund, 1994) may arise in relation to the use of quantitative research. However, in qualitatively based research, the resulting personal contact, scope to use non-standardised questions or observe on a 'face-to-face' basis, and capacity to develop your knowledge on an incremental basis mean that you will be able to exercise a greater level of control (Chapter 9). This contrasts with the use of a quantitative approach based on structured interviews or self-administered questionnaires (Chapter 10).

The relatively greater level of control associated with qualitatively based research methods should be exercised with care so that your behaviour remains within appropriate and acceptable parameters. In face-to-face *interviews* you should avoid over-zealous questioning and pressing your participant for a response, which may make the situation stressful for your participant (Sekaran, 1992). You should also make clear to your interview participant that they have the right to decline to respond to any question (Emory and Cooper, 1991). The nature of questions to be asked also requires consideration. Sekaran (1992) states that you should avoid asking questions which are in any way demeaning to your participant (Sections 9.4, 9.5 and 9.7 provide a fuller consideration of related issues). In face-to-face interviews it will clearly be necessary to arrange a time which is convenient for your participant; however, where you seek to conduct an interview by telephone (Sections 10.2 and 10.5) you should not attempt to do this at an unreasonable time of the day. In the interview situation, whether face-to-face or on the telephone, it would also be unethical to attempt to prolong the discussion when it is apparent that your participant needs to attend to the next part of their day's schedule (Zikmund, 1994).

The use of *observation* techniques raises its own ethical concerns (Section 8.3). The boundaries of what it is permissible to observe need to be clearly drawn. Without this type of agreement the principal participants may find that their actions are being constrained (Bryman, 1988). You should also avoid attempting to observe behaviour related to your participant's private life, such as personal telephone calls and so forth. Without this, the relationship between observer and the observed will break down, with the latter finding the process to be an intrusion on their right to privacy. There is, however, a second problem related to the use of this method. This is the issue of ' "reactivity" – the reaction on the part of those being investigated to the investigator and his or her research instruments' (Bryman, 1988: 112). This issue applies to a number of strategies and methods (Bryman, 1988), but is clearly a particular problem in observation.

A solution to this problem might be to undertake a *covert* study, so that those being observed are not aware of this fact. In a situation of likely reactivity to the presence of an observer, you might use this approach in a deceitful yet benign way, since to declare your purpose at the outset of your work might lead to non-participation or problems related to validity and reliability if those being observed altered their behaviour (Bryman, 1988; Gummesson, 1991; Wells, 1994). The rationale for this choice of approach would thus be related to a question of whether 'the ends justify the means' provided that other ethical aspects are considered (Wells 1994: 284). However, the ethical concern with deceiving those being observed may prevail over any pragmatic view (Bryman, 1988; Emory and Cooper, 1991). Indeed, the problem of reactivity may be a diminishing one where those being observed adapt to your presence as declared observer (Bryman, 1988). This adaptation is known as *habituation* (Section 8.6).

Where access is denied after being requested, you may have no other choice but to carry out covert observation – where this is practical (Gummesson, 1991). Irrespective of the reason for a deception occurring, Emory and Cooper (1991) suggest that after the observation has taken place you should inform those affected about what has occurred and why.

One group who may consider using a covert approach are those whom we refer to as 'practitioner-researchers' (Section 8.3). *Practitioner-researchers* may be part-time students undertaking a professional qualification. There are recognised advantages and disadvantages associated with this role. (Section 8.3). One of the possible disadvantages is related to your relationship with those from whom you will need to gain co-operation in order to obtain cognitive access to their data. This may be connected with the fact that your status is relatively junior to these colleagues, or that you are more senior to them. Any status difference may act to inhibit your intended data collection. One solution would therefore be to adopt a covert approach in order to seek to gain data. Thus you may decide to interview subordinate colleagues, organise focus group decisions through your managerial status, or observe interactions during meetings without declaring your research interest. The key question to consider is whether this approach will be more likely to yield trustworthy data than declaring your real purpose and acting overtly. The answer will depend on a number of factors:

- the existing nature of your relationships with those whom you wish to be your participants;
- the prevailing managerial style within the organisation or that part of it where these people work;
- the time and opportunity which you have to attempt to develop the trust and confidence of these intended participants in order to gain their co-operation.

Absolute assurances about the use of the data collected may also be critical to gain trust, and the time you invest in achieving this may be very worthwhile.

In comparison with the issues discussed in the preceding paragraphs, Dale *et al.* (1988: 57) believe that the 'ethical problems of survey research may be rather less difficult than those of qualitative research'. This is due to the nature of structured survey questions which are clearly not designed to explore responses; and the avoidance of the in-depth interview situation, where the ability to use probing questions leads to more revealing information (Dale *et al.*, 1988). Zikmund (1994) believes that the ethical issues linked with survey research are those associated with more general issues discussed above: privacy, deception, openness, confidentiality, and objectivity. Dale *et al.* (1988) point to particular ethical issues which arise in relation to the analysis of secondary data derived from survey research, and it is to the issues associated with the analysis and reporting stages of research that we now turn.

Ethical issues related to the analysis and reporting stages

The maintenance of your objectivity will be vital during the analysis stage to make sure that you do not misrepresent the data collected. This will include not being selective about which data to report or, where appropriate, avoiding misrepresentation of its statistical accuracy (Zikmund, 1994). A great deal of trust is placed in each researcher's integrity and it would clearly be a significant ethical issue were this to be open to question. The duty to represent your data honestly extends to the analysis and reporting stage of your research. Lack of objectivity at this stage will clearly distort your conclusions and any course of action which appears to stem from your work.

The ethical issues of confidentiality and anonymity also come to the fore during the reporting stage of your research. Wells (1994) recognises that it may be difficult to maintain the assurances which have been given. However, it is vital to attempt to ensure that these are maintained. Allowing a participating organisation to be identified by those who can 'piece together' the characteristics which you reveal may result in embarrassment and also in access being refused to those who seek it after you. Great care therefore needs to be exercised to avoid this situation. You also have the option of requesting permission from the organisation to use its name. To gain this permission you will undoubtedly need to let people in the organisation read your work to understand the context within which they will be named.

This level of care also needs to be exercised in making sure that the anonymity of individuals is maintained. Embarrassment and even harm could result from reporting data which is clearly attributable to a particular individual (Emory and Cooper, 1991; Robson, 1993). Care therefore needs to be taken to protect those who participated in your research.

- -

WORKED EXAMPLES: *Inadvertently revealing participants' identities*

The following examples demonstrate how the identities of research participants can be inadvertently revealed because of a lack of thought on the part of researchers presenting their findings:

■ reporting a comment made by a female accounts manager when in fact there is only one such person;

■ referring to a comment made by a member of the sales team, when in fact the data being reported could only have come from one person;

■ reporting data and comments related to a small section of staff, where it was possible to attribute the particular opinions being reported to specific individuals; or where there was a tendency on the part of other participants to seek to attribute these opinions because of the small numbers to whom these comments related.

- -

A further ethical concern stems from the use made by others of the conclusions which you reach, and any course of action which is explicitly referred to or implicitly suggested, based on your research data. How ethical will it be to use the data collected from a group of participants effectively to disadvantage them because of the decisions which are then made in the light of your research? On the other hand, there is a view which says that, while the anonymity of your participants should not be revealed, they cannot be exempt from the way in which research conclusions are then used to make decisions (Dale *et al.*, 1988). This is clearly a very tricky ethical issue!

Where you are aware that your findings may be used to make a decision which could adversely affect the collective interests of your participants, it may be ethical to refer to this possibility, even though it reduces the level of access which you achieve. An alternative position is to construct your research question(s) and objectives to avoid this possibility, or to ensure that decisions taken as a result of your research should only have positive consequences for the collective interests of those who participate.

You may find that this alternative is not open to you, perhaps because you are a part-time student in employment and your employing organisation directs your choice of research topic. If so, it will be more honest to concede to your participants that you are in effect acting as an internal consultant rather than as a (dispassionate) researcher.

This discussion about the impact of research on the collective interests of those who participate brings us back to the reference made above to the particular ethical issues which arise in relation to the analysis of secondary data derived from survey research. Dale *et al.* (1988) point out that, where survey results are subsequently used as secondary data, the original assurances provided to those who participated in the research may be set aside, with the result that the collective interests of participants may be disadvantaged through this use of data. The use of data for secondary purposes therefore also leads to ethical concerns of potentially significant proportions and you will need to consider these in the way in which you make use of this type of data.

Summary checklist to anticipate and deal with ethical issues

- ☑ Attempt to recognise potential ethical issues which will affect your proposed research.
- ☑ Utilise your university's code on research ethics to guide the design and conduct of your research (if one is not available use Appendix 3).
- ☑ Anticipate ethical issues at the design stage of your research and discuss how you will seek to control these in your research proposal.
- ☑ Seek consent through the use of openness and honesty, rather than by deception.
- ☑ Do not exaggerate the likely benefits of your research for participating organisations or individuals.
- ☑ Respect others' rights to privacy at all stages of your research project.
- ☑ Maintain objectivity and quality in relation to the processes you use to collect data.
- ☑ Recognise that the nature of a qualitatively based approach to research will mean that there is greater scope for ethical issues to arise, and seek to avoid the particular problems related to interviews and observation.
- ☑ Avoid referring to data gained from a particular participant when talking to others, where this would allow the individual to be identified with potentially harmful consequences to that person.
- ☑ Covert research should only be used where reactivity is considered to be a significant issue or where access is denied (and a covert presence is practical). However, other ethical aspects of your research should still be respected when using this approach.
- ☑ Maintain your objectivity during the stages of analysing and reporting your research.
- ☑ Maintain the assurances which you gave to participating organisations with regard to confidentiality of the data obtained and their organisational anonymity.
- ☑ Protect individual participants by taking great care to ensure their anonymity in relation to anything to which you refer in your research project report, dissertation or thesis.
- ☑ Consider how the collective interests of your research participants may be adversely affected by the nature of the data which you are proposing to collect, and alter the nature of your research question(s) and objectives where this possibility is likely to be the case. Alternatively, declare this possibility to those whom you wish to participate in your proposed research.

5.5 SUMMARY

- Access and ethics are critical aspects for the conduct of research.

- Different types and levels of access have been identified which help us to understand the problem of gaining entry: physical access to an organisation; access to intended participants; continuing access in order to carry out further parts of your research or to be able to repeat the collection of data in another part of the organisation; cognitive access in order to get sufficiently close to find out valid and reliable data.

- Feasibility has been recognised to be an important determinant of what you choose to research and how you undertake the research.

- Strategies to help you gain access to organisations and to intended participants within them have been described and discussed.

- Research ethics refer to the appropriateness of your behaviour in relation to the rights of those who become the subject of your work or are affected by the work.

- Potential ethical issues should be recognised and considered from the outset of your research and be one of the criteria against which your research proposal is judged.

- Ethical concerns are likely to occur at all stages of your research project: when seeking access, during data collection, as you analyse data, and when you report it.

- Qualitative research is likely to lead to a greater range of ethical concerns in comparison to quantitative research, although all research methods have specific ethical issues associated with them.

- Ethical concerns are also associated with the 'power relationship' between the researcher and those who grant access, and the researcher's role (as external researcher, practitioner-researcher or internal consultant).

Self-check questions and assignment

Self-check question 5.1
How can you differentiate between types of access, and why is it important to do this?

Self-check question 5.2
What do you understand by the use of the terms 'feasibility' and 'sufficiency' when applied to the question of access?

Self-check question 5.3
Which strategies to help gain access are likely to apply to the following scenarios:

a an 'external' researcher seeking direct access to managers who will be the research participants;

b an 'external' researcher seeking access through an organisational gatekeeper/broker to his or her intended participants;

c a practitioner-researcher planning to undertake a research project within his or her employing organisation?

Self-check question 5.4
What are the principal ethical issues you will need to consider irrespective of the particular research methods which you use?

Self-check question 5.5
What problems may you encounter in attempting to protect the interests of participating organisations and individuals despite the assurances which you provide?

Assignment 5:
Negotiating access and addressing ethical issues

- Consider the following aspects:
    - Which types of data will you require in order to be able to answer your proposed research question(s) and objectives sufficiently?
    - Which research methods will you attempt to use to yield this data?
    - What type(s) of access will you require in order to be able to collect data?
    - What problems are you likely to encounter in gaining access?
    - Which strategies to gain access will be useful to help you to overcome these problems?
- Depending on the type of access envisaged and your research status (i.e. as external researcher or practitioner-researcher), produce appropriate requests for organisational access, together with a return pro forma, and/or requests to intended participants for their co-operation.
- Describe the ethical issues which are likely to affect your proposed research project. Discuss how you may seek to overcome or control these. This should be undertaken in relation to the various stages of your research project.
- Note down your answers.

References

Bell, J. (1993) *Doing Your Research Project* (2nd edn), Buckingham, Open University Press.

Bryman, A. (1988) *Quantity and Quality in Social Research*, London, Unwin Hyman.

Buchanan, D., Boddy, D. and McCalman, J. (1988) 'Getting In, Getting On, Getting Out and Getting Back', in Bryman, A. (ed.) *Doing Research in Organisations*, London, Routledge, pp. 53–67.

Dale, A., Arber, S. and Procter, M. (1988) *Doing Secondary Research*, London, Unwin Hyman.

Easterby-Smith, M., Thorpe, R. and Lowe, A. (1991) *Management Research: An Introduction*, London, Sage.

Emory, C. and Cooper, D. (1991) *Business Research Methods* (4th edn), Homewood, Illinois, Richard D. Irwin.

Gummesson, E. (1991) *Qualitative Methods in Management Research*, Newbury Park, California, Sage.

Healey, M.J. (1991) 'Obtaining Information from Businesses', in Healey, M.J. (ed.) *Economic Activity and Land Use*, Harlow, Longman, pp. 193–251.

Jankowicz, A.D. (1995) *Business Research Projects for Students* (2nd edn), London, Chapman & Hall.

Johnson, J.M. (1975) *Doing Field Research*, New York, Free Press.

Mackintosh, N. (ed.) (1995) *Cyril Burt: Fraud or Framed?*, Oxford, Oxford University Press.

Marshall, C. and Rossman, G.B. (1989) *Designing Qualitative Research*, Newbury Park, California, Sage.

Morgan, M. (1995) 'The case of the dubious data', *The Guardian,* 4 August, Second section, pp. 10–11.

Raimond, P. (1993) *Management Projects*, London, Chapman & Hall.

Robson, C. (1993) *Real World Research*, Oxford, Blackwell.

Sekaran, U. (1992) *Research Methods for Business: A Skill-Building Approach* (2nd edn), New York, John Wiley.

Wells, P. (1994) 'Ethics in Business and Management Research', in Wass, V.J. and Wells, P.E. (eds.) *Principles and Practice in Business and Management Research*, Aldershot, Dartmouth, pp. 277–97.

Zikmund, W.G. (1994) *Business Research Methods*, Fort Worth, Dryden Press.

Further Reading

Buchanan, D., Boddy, D. and McCalman, J. (1988) 'Getting In, Getting On, Getting Out and Getting Back', in Bryman, A. (ed.) *Doing Research in Organisations*, London, Routledge, pp. 53–67. This provides a highly readable and very useful account of the negotiation of access. Other chapters in Bryman's book also consider issues related to access and research ethics.

Gummesson, E. (1991) *Qualitative Methods in Management Research*, Newbury Park, California, Sage. Chapter 2 provides a very useful examination of access and researcher roles and some highly valuable means of differentiating types of access.

Miles, M.B. and Huberman, A.M. (1994) *Qualitative Data Analysis*, Thousand Oaks, Sage. Chapter 11 provides a very useful examination of a range of ethical issues principally from the perspective of their implications for data analysis.

Wells, P. (1994) 'Ethics in Business and Management Research', in Wass, V.J. and Wells, P.E. (eds.) *Principles and Practice in Business and Management Research*, Aldershot, Dartmouth, pp. 277–98. This provides a very useful exploration of ethics in a range of subject areas, as well as a discussion of a number of key issues related to business research.

Zikmund, W.G. (1994) *Business Research Methods*, Fort Worth, Dryden Press. Chapter 4 very usefully examines ethical issues associated with business research from the perspective of the rights and obligations of participants, researchers and clients.

Case 5:
The effects of a merger in a major UK building society

Jackie, a final year student, was in the early stages of her research project. She was a full-time student on a business studies degree course which required a placement to be undertaken in the penultimate year. Jackie's placement organisation was the regional office of a national building society. The organisation had been very supportive of placement students from the course, and had taken at least one student for the past three years. Jackie gained a variety of experience by moving round different departments during her time there. When she left, the regional manager, Mrs Sterling, indicated that she would be prepared to help, if she could, with data for Jackie's research project.

Jackie had indicated to her project tutor that she had become interested in the future of building societies in general, and particularly the implications of the merging of organisations. During her placement, Jackie's host organisation had announced the intention to merge with another organisation. Jackie and her project tutor discussed the possibility of investigating the operational implications of such mergers. Jackie indicated that Mrs Sterling would be willing to be interviewed to give an industry perspective. She agreed that she would draft possible questions to use in an interview for discussion with her project tutor.

A short time later Jackie was at a nightclub with some of the people that she had worked with while on her placement. One of these, Simon, was concerned with personnel issues and had just attended a briefing course at the organisation's head office. The issue of the merger was the main topic of conversation throughout the evening. During the evening, when Jackie and Simon were slightly apart from the rest of the group, he mentioned that when the organisations merge they were going to close five branches in that region. He commented that the issue of redundancies among staff was something he was not looking forward to dealing with. A while later he asked Jackie not to mention any of their conversation to the others as it was not common knowledge.

Later when Jackie compiled her objectives she reflected on these conversations with her work colleagues. Some of the problems and issues associated with the merger were obvious to her from her research, but she thought it would add something original to her research project if she could get specific information on branch closures and redundancies. She decided that this was something she must include, and drafted some objectives based on her discussions with her work placement colleagues.

Jackie heard that Mrs Sterling was going on holiday for a couple of weeks, and so telephoned Mrs Sterling's secretary on Tuesday to arrange to see her on Friday. The secretary was very helpful and told Jackie she could probably see Mrs Sterling for half an hour between meetings. Before leaving university, Jackie jotted down the questions for her interview and left them for her project tutor.

When the time of the appointment arrived, Mrs Sterling was late but pleased to see Jackie. Jackie explained she had come with some questions for her research project. Mrs Sterling asked if it would be possible to see her at another time as she had to attend another meeting shortly. Jackie said it would only take a few minutes, and asked her first question. However, when Jackie asked a question about the implications of closing five branches in the region, and the numbers of staff involved in redundancies, Mrs Sterling checked her watch and said she would have to leave.

Jackie asked if she could make an appointment after Mrs Sterling returned from holiday. Mrs Sterling indicated that she would ask her secretary to contact Jackie, although she was very busy at the moment.

When Jackie returned to university she wrote up the answers that she received from Mrs Sterling. As she didn't get all the information she had wanted from the interview, she included some of the information that she had obtained from Simon and the others to fill in the gaps, as she was sure that was what Mrs Sterling would have told her anyway. Jackie forwarded this to her project tutor, and indicated she might be seeing Mrs Sterling again. Jackie later received a message that her project tutor wanted to see her.

Case-study questions

1 a What are the issues of access that Jackie does not address?

   b Give reasons for your answer.

2 What procedures related to access should Jackie have followed?

3 a Where has Jackie failed to consider the ethical implications of her actions?

   b What are the implications for her research?

4 a What might be the consequences of Jackie's actions for all the parties involved:

- now;

- if Jackie had made her work generally available?

   b How could this have been avoided?

Answers to self-check questions

Self-check question 5.1

The types of access to which we have referred in this chapter are: physical entry or initial access to an organisational setting; continuing access which recognises that researchers often need to develop their access on an incremental basis; and cognitive access where you will be concerned to gain the co-operation of individual participants once you have achieved access to the organisation in which they work. We also referred to personal access, which allows you to consider whether you actually need to meet with participants in order to carry out an aspect of your research as opposed to corresponding with them or sending them a self-administered, postal questionnaire. Access is strategically related to the success of your research project and needs to be carefully planned. In relation to many research designs it will need to be thought of as a multi-faceted aspect and not a single event.

Self-check question 5.2

Gaining access can be problematic for researchers, for a number of reasons. The concept of feasibility recognises this and suggests that in order to be able to conduct your research it will be necessary to design it with access clearly in mind. You may care to look again at the references to the work of Buchanan et al. (1988) and Johnson (1975) in Section 5.2 which demonstrate the relationship between research design and feasibility.

	Scenario a	Scenario b	Scenario c
Allowing yourself sufficient time to gain access	Universally true in all cases. The practitioner-researcher will be going through a very similar process to those who wish to gain access from the outside in terms of contacting intended participants, meeting with them to explain the research, providing assurances etc. The only exception will be related to a covert approach, although sufficient time for planning etc. will of course still be required.		
Using any existing contacts	Where possible.		Yes
Developing new ones	Probably necessary.		This may still apply within large, complex organisations, depending on the nature of the research.
Providing a clear account of the purpose of your research and what type of access you require, with the intention of establishing your credibility	Definitely necessary.		Still necessary although easier to achieve (verbally or internal memo) with familiar colleagues. Less easy with unfamiliar colleagues, which suggests just as much care as for external researchers.
Overcoming organisational concerns in relation to the granting of access	Definitely necessary.	Absolutely necessary. This may be *the* major problem to overcome since you are asking for access to a range of employees.	Should not be a problem unless you propose to undertake research on a highly sensitive topic to the organisation! We know of students whose proposal has been used *within* their organisation.
Outlining possible benefits of granting access to you and any tangible outcome from doing so	Probably useful.		Work-based research projects contain material of value to the organisation, although they may largely be theoretically based.
Using suitable language	Definitely necessary.		Still necessary at the level of participants in the organisation.
Facilitating ease of reply when requesting access	Definitely useful.		Might be useful to consider in relation to certain internal participants.
Developing your access on an incremental basis	Should not be necessary, although you may wish to undertake subsequent work.	Definitely worth considering.	Might be a useful strategy depending on the nature of the research and the work setting.
Establishing your credibility in the eyes of your intended participants	Access is not being sought at 'lower' levels within the organisation.	Definitely necessary.	May still be necessary with unfamiliar participants in the organisation.

Table 5.1: Considering access

Sufficiency refers to another issue related to access. In Section 5.2 we stated that there are two aspects to the issue of sufficiency. The first of these relates to whether you have sufficiently considered and, therefore, fully realised the extent and nature of the access which you will require in order to be able to answer your research question(s) and objectives. The second aspect relates to whether you are able to gain sufficient access in practice in order to be able to answer your research question(s) and objectives.

Self-check question 5.3

We may consider the three particular scenarios outlined in the question through Table 5.1. **Self-check question 5.4**

The principal ethical issues you will need to consider irrespective of which research methods you use are:

- to respect intended and actual participants' rights to privacy;
- to avoid deceiving participants about why you are undertaking the research, its purpose and how the data collected will be used;
- maintaining your objectivity during the data collection, analysis and reporting stages;
- respecting assurances provided to organisations about the confidentiality of (certain types) of data;
- respecting assurances given to organisations and individuals about their anonymity;
- to consider the collective interests of participants in the way you use the data which they provide.

Self-check question 5.5

A number of ethical problems might emerge. These are considered in turn. You may wish to explore a point made by one of your participants, but to do so might lead to harmful consequences for this person were the point to be attributed to them.

It may be possible for some people who read your work to identify a participating organisation, although you do not actually name it. This may cause embarrassment to the organisation.

Individual participants may also be identified by the nature of the comments which you report, again leading to harmful consequences for them.

Your report may also lead to action being taken within an organisation which adversely affects those who were kind enough to act as participants in your research.

Finally, others may seek to re-use any survey data which you collect and this might be to the disadvantage of those who provided the data by responding to your questionnaire.

CHAPTER 6

Selecting samples

The objectives of this chapter are to introduce you to a range of probability and non-probability sampling techniques, help you decide how they can play a part in your research project and provide advice on their use.

The chapter considers why sampling is necessary and looks at the issues of sample size and response rates. The relationship between your research question(s) and objectives and the techniques you use is also considered.

Practical advice is offered about assessing the representativeness of respondents and the possible need to combine techniques within a research project illustrated.

6.1 INTRODUCTION

Whatever your research question(s) and objectives you will need to collect data to answer them. If you collect and analyse data from every possible case or group member this is termed a *census*. However, for many research questions and objectives it will be impossible for you either to collect or to analyse all the data available to you due to restrictions of time, money and often access. *Sampling* techniques provide a range of methods that enable you to reduce the amount of data you need to collect by considering only data from a subgroup rather than all possible cases. Some research questions will require sample data to make generalisations about all the cases from which your sample has been selected. For example, if you asked a sample of consumers what they thought of a new chocolate bar and 75 per cent said that they thought it was too expensive, you might infer that 75 per cent of all consumers felt that way. Other research questions may not involve such generalisations. However, even if you are undertaking case-study research within a large organisation using in-depth interviews, you will still need to select your case-study (sample) organisation and a group (sample) of employees and managers to interview. Techniques for selecting samples will therefore still be important.

The full set of cases from which the sample is taken is called the *population*. In sampling the term population is not used in its normal sense, as the full set of cases need not necessarily be people. For research to discover relative levels of service from staff in burger bars throughout the country, the population from which you would select your sample would be all burger bars in the country. Alternatively, you might need to establish the 'life' of long-life batteries produced over the past month by a particular manufacturer. Here the population would be all the long-life batteries produced over the past month by that manufacturer.

The need to sample

For some research questions it is possible to survey an entire population as it is of a manageable size. However, you should not assume that a census survey will necessarily provide more useful results than a well-planned sample survey. Sampling provides a valid alternative to a census when:

- it would be impractical for you to survey the entire population;
- your budget constraints prevent a survey of the entire population;
- your time constraints prevent a survey of the entire population;
- you have collected all the data but need the results quickly.

For all research questions where it would be impractical for you to survey the whole population, you need to select a sample. This will be important whether you plan to use a predominantly qualitative or a quantitative research strategy. You might only be able to obtain permission to collect data from two or three organisations. Alternatively, testing an entire population of products to destruction so as to establish the crash protection provided by cars would be impractical for any manufacturer.

With other research questions it might be theoretically possible for you to be able to survey the whole population, but the overall cost will prevent it. It is obviously cheaper for you to collect, enter (if you are analysing the data using a computer) and check data from 250 employees than from 2500, even though the cost per unit of your study (in this case employee) is likely to be higher than with a census. Your costs will be made up of new costs such as sample selection, and the fact that overhead costs such as survey design and setting up computer software for data entry are spread over a smaller number of cases.

Sampling also saves time, an important consideration when you have tight deadlines. The organisation of data collection is more manageable as fewer people are involved. As you have less data to enter the results will be available more quickly. Occasionally, to save time, surveys collect data from the entire population but only analyse a sample of the data collected. For reasons of economy this procedure was adopted for hard to code questions, such as occupation and industry, in the United Kingdom 1991 Census. Data were collected from the total population for all questions but, for the hard to code questions, only 10 per cent of these data were coded using a detailed coding scheme (Section 11.2). These 10 per cent were entered into the computer and subsequently analysed (Dale, 1993).

Many researchers, for example Moser and Kalton (1986) and Henry (1990), argue that using sampling enables a higher overall accuracy than does a census. The smaller number of cases for which you need to collect data means that more time can be spent designing and piloting the means of collecting these data. Collecting data from fewer cases also means that you can collect more detailed information. In addition, if you are employing people to collect the data (perhaps as interviewers) you can use higher-quality staff. You also can spend more time chasing up data from the more difficult cases. Once your data have been collected, proportionally more time can be devoted to checking and testing the data for accuracy prior to analysis.

An overview of sampling techniques

The sampling techniques available to you can be divided into two types:

- probability or representative sampling;
- non-probability or judgemental sampling.

In *probability samples* the chance, or probability, of each case being selected from the population is known and is usually equal for all cases. This means that it is possible to answer research questions and achieve objectives which require you to estimate statistically the characteristics of the population from the sample. As a consequence, probability sampling is often associated with survey and, to a lesser extent, experiment research (Section 4.2). For *non-probability samples* the probability of each case being selected from the total population is not known, and it is impossible to answer research questions or objectives that require you to make statistical inferences about the characteristics of the population. You may still be able to generalise from non-probability samples about the population, but not on statistical grounds. For this reason non-probability sampling (other than quota sampling) is more frequently used for case-study research (Section 4.2). However, with both types of sample you can answer other forms of research questions, such as 'What attributes attract people to jobs?' or 'How are financial institutions adapting the services they provide to meet recent legislation?'.

Subsequent sections of this chapter outline a variety of probability (Section 6.2) and non-probability (Section 6.3) sampling techniques, discuss their advantages and disadvantages and give examples of when you might use them. Although each technique is discussed separately, for many research projects you will need to use a variety of sampling techniques at different stages. This is illustrated by the case study.

6.2 PROBABILITY SAMPLING

Probability sampling is most commonly associated with survey-based research where you need to make inferences from your sample about a population to answer your research question(s) or meet your objectives. The process of probability of sampling can be divided into four stages:

1 Identify a suitable sampling frame based on your research question(s) or objectives.
2 Decide on a suitable sample size.
3 Select the most appropriate sampling technique and select the sample.
4 Check that the sample is representative of the population.

Each of these stages will be considered in turn. However, for populations of less than 50 cases, Henry (1990) advises against probability sampling. He argues that you should collect data on the entire population, as the influence of a single extreme case on subsequent statistical analyses is more pronounced than for larger samples.

Identifying a suitable sampling frame

The *sampling frame* for any probability sample is a complete list of all the cases in the population from which your sample will be drawn. If your research question or objective is concerned with members of a local video club, your sampling frame will be the complete membership list for that video club. If your research question or objective is concerned with registered nursing homes in a local area, your sampling frame will be a complete list of all registered nursing homes in that area. For both, you then select your sample from this list. The completeness of your sampling frame is very important. An incomplete or inaccurate list means that some cases will have been excluded and so it will be impossible for every case in the population to have a chance of selection. As a consequence, your sample may not be representative of the total population.

Where no suitable list exists you will have to compile your own sampling frame. It is important to ensure that the sampling frame is unbiased, current and accurate. You might decide to use a telephone directory as the sampling frame from which to select a sample of typical UK householders. However, the telephone directory only covers subscribers in one geographical area who own a telephone. Your survey will therefore be biased towards householders who are telephone subscribers. Because the telephone directory is only published annually the sampling frame will be out of date (*non-current*). As some householders choose to be ex-directory, it will be inaccurate as it does not include all those who own telephones. This means that you will be selecting a sample of telephone subscribers at the date the directory was compiled who chose not to be ex-directory!

In recent years a number of organisations have been established which specialise in selling lists of names and addresses for surveys. These lists include a wide range of people such as company directors, chief executives, marketing managers, production managers and personnel managers, for public, private and non-profit-making organisations. They are usually in a format suitable for being read by wordprocessing and database computer software and can easily be merged into standard letters such as those included with questionnaires (Section 10.4). Because you pay for such lists by the case (individual address) the organisations which provide them usually select your sample. It is therefore important to establish precisely how they will select your sample as well as how the list was compiled and when it was last revised. From this you will be able to assess the currency and accuracy of your sample and whether or not any bias is likely to exist.

Deciding on a suitable sample size

Generalisations about populations from data collected using any sample are based on probability. The larger your sample size, the lower the likely error in generalising to the population. Probability sampling is therefore a compromise between the accuracy of your findings and the amount of time and money you invest in collecting, checking and analysing the data. Your choice of sample size within this compromise is governed by:

- the confidence you need to have in your data, that is, the level of certainty that the characteristics of the data collected will represent the characteristics of the total population;

- the margin of error that you can tolerate, that is, the accuracy you require for any estimates made from your sample;

- the types of analyses you are going to undertake, in particular the number of categories into which you wish to subdivide your data, as many statistical techniques have a minimum threshold of data cases for each cell (for example chi square, Section 11.5);

and to a lesser extent:

- the size of the total population from which your sample is being drawn.

Given these competing influences, it is not surprising that the final sample size is almost always a matter of judgement rather than calculation (Hoinville *et al.*, 1978). For many research questions and objectives your need to undertake particular statistical analyses (Section 11.5) will determine the threshold sample size for individual categories. These will impact on the overall sample size. In such instances the Economist's (1993) advice of a minimum number of 30 for statistical analyses provides a useful rule of thumb for the smallest number in each category within your overall sample. Where the population in the category is less than 30, and you wish to undertake your analysis at this level of detail, you should normally collect data from all cases in that category.

Researchers normally work to a 95 per cent level of certainty. This means that if your sample was selected 100 times at least 95 of these samples would be certain to represent the characteristics of the population. The margin of error describes the precision of your estimates of the population. Table 6.1 provides a rough guide to the different *minimum sample sizes* required from different sizes of population at the 95 per cent level of certainty. It assumes that data are collected from all cases in the sample (full details of the calculation for minimum sample size and adjusted minimum sample size are given in Appendix 4). For most business and management research, researchers are content to estimate the population's characteristics to within plus or minus 3 to 5 per cent of its true values. This means that if 45 per cent of your sample are in a certain category then your estimate for the total population within the same category will be 45 per cent plus or minus the margin of error; somewhere between 42 and 48 per cent for a 3 per cent margin of error.

As you can see from Table 6.1, the smaller the sample and, to a far lesser extent, the smaller the proportion of the total population sampled, the greater the margin of error. Within this the relative impact of sample size on the margin of error decreases for larger sample sizes. DeVaus (1991) argues that it is for this reason that many market research companies limit their sample sizes to approximately 2000. Unfortunately for many sample surveys a 100 per cent response rate is unlikely and so your sample will need to be larger to ensure sufficient responses for the margin of error you require.

Population	Margin of error			
	5%	3%	2%	1%
50	44	48	49	50
100	79	91	96	99
150	108	132	141	148
200	132	168	185	196
250	151	203	226	244
300	168	234	267	291
400	196	291	434	384
500	217	340	414	475
750	254	440	571	696
1 000	278	516	706	906
2 000	322	696	1091	1655
5 000	357	879	1622	3288
10 000	370	964	1936	4899
100 000	383	1056	2345	8762
1 000 000	384	1066	2395	9513
10 000 000	384	1067	2400	9595

Table 6.1 Sample sizes for different sizes of population at a 95% level of certainty (assuming data are collected from all cases in the sample)

The importance of a high response rate

The most important aspect of a probability sample is that it represents the population. A perfect *representative sample* is one that exactly represents the population from which it is taken. If 60 per cent of your sample were small service-sector companies then, provided that the sample was representative, you would expect 60 per cent of the population to be small service-sector companies. You therefore need to obtain as high a response rate as possible to ensure your sample is representative.

In reality you are likely to have non-responses. Non-respondents are different from the rest of the population because they have refused to be involved in your research for whatever reason. As a consequence, your respondents will not be representative of the total population and the data you collect may be biased. In addition, any non-responses will necessitate extra respondents being found to reach the required sample size, thereby increasing the cost of your survey.

You should therefore analyse the refusals to respond to both individual questions and entire surveys to check for bias (Section 11.2). Non-response is due to three interrelated problems:

- refusal to respond;
- ineligibility to respond;
- non-contact.

The most common reason for non-response is that your respondent refuses to answer a question or be involved in your research but does not give a reason. Such non-response can be minimised by paying careful attention to the methods used to collect your data (Chapters 8, 9 and 10). Alternatively, some of your selected respondents may not meet your research requirements and so will be *ineligible* to respond. Non-contact creates a further problem; the fact that some respondents are *unreachable* means they will not be represented in the data you collect.

As part of your research report you will need to include your *response rate*. A common way of doing this excludes ineligible respondents and those who, despite repeated attempts (Sections 9.3 and 10.5), were unreachable (deVaus, 1991):

$$\text{response rate} = \frac{\text{total number of responses}}{\text{total number in sample} - (\text{ineligible} + \text{unreachable})}$$

Even after ineligible and unreachable respondents have been excluded it is probable that you will still have some non-responses. You therefore need to be able to assess how representative your data are, and to allow for the impact of non-response in your calculations of sample size. These issues are explored in subsequent sections.

Estimating response rates and actual sample size required

With all probability samples it is important that your sample size is large enough to provide you with the necessary confidence in your data. The margin of error must therefore be within acceptable limits and you must ensure that you will be able to undertake your analysis at the level of detail required. You therefore need to estimate the likely *response rate*, that is, the proportion of cases from your sample who will respond or from which data will be collected and increase the sample size accordingly. Once you have an estimate of the likely response rate, and the minimum or the adjusted minimum sample size, the *actual sample size* you require can be calculated using the following formula:

$$n^a = \frac{n \times 100}{re\%}$$

where: n^a is the actual sample size required

n is the minimum (or adjusted minimum) sample size (see table 6.1 or appendix 4)

$re\%$ is the estimated response rate expressed as a percentage

• •

WORKED EXAMPLE: *Calculation of actual sample size*

For a survey of consultants you calculate that an adjusted minimum sample size of 439 is required. Given an estimated response rate of 30% the actual sample size can be calculated:

$$n^a = \frac{439 \times 100}{30}$$

$$= \frac{43900}{30}$$

$$= 1463$$

Your actual sample therefore needs to be 1463 consultants. In practice this would be rounded to either 1400 or 1500 consultants, depending on time and money available. The likelihood of 70 per cent non-response means that you should include a check that the sample is representative when you design the data collection method.

If you are collecting your sample data from a secondary source (Section 7.2) within an organisation which has already granted you access, your response rate should be virtually 100 per cent. In research Mark recently undertook he established that all the data he required were available from employees' personnel files. Once access had been granted to these files by the organisation, he was ensured of virtually a 100 per cent response rate. His actual sample size was therefore the same as his minimum sample size.

In contrast, estimating the likely response rate from a sample to which you will be sending a questionnaire or interviewing is more difficult. One way of obtaining this estimate is to consider the response rates achieved for similar surveys that have already been undertaken and base your estimate on these. Alternatively, you can err on the side of caution. For postal surveys a response rate of approximately 30 per cent is reasonable (Owen and Jones, 1990). For interviews you should expect a response rate of approximately 50 per cent (Kervin, 1992).

However beware, response rates can vary considerably when collecting primary data. Research by Dillman (1978) recorded response rates of between 50 per cent and 92 per cent for questionnaire surveys and of between 73 and 99 per cent for telephone interviews. More recent work by Healey (1991) also records a wide variation in response rates. He suggests lower average response rates of about 50 per cent for postal surveys and 75 per cent for face-to-face interviews. The former rate concurs with a recent questionnaire survey we undertook for a multinational organisation which had an overall response rate of 52%. In our survey, response rates for individual sites varied from 41 to 100 per cent, again emphasising variability. Our examination of response rates to recent business surveys reveals rates as low as 15 to 20 per cent for postal surveys, some authors citing respondents' questionnaire fatigue as a contributory factor! Fortunately a number of different techniques, depending on your data collection method, can be used to enhance your response rate. These are discussed with the data collection method in the appropriate sections (9.3 and 10.5).

Selecting the most appropriate sampling technique and the sample

Once you have chosen a suitable sampling frame and established the actual sample size required, you need to select the most appropriate sampling technique to obtain a representative sample. Five main techniques can be used to select a probability sample:

- simple random;
- systematic;
- stratified random;
- cluster;
- multi-stage.

Sample technique	Sampling frame required	Size of sample needed	Geographical area to which suited	Relative cost	Ease of explaining to support workers	Advantages compared with simple random
Simple random	Accurate and easily accessible	Better with over a few hundred	Concentrated if face-to-face contact required, otherwise does not matter	High if large sample size or sampling frame not computerised	Relatively difficult to explain	–
Systematic	Accurate, easily accessible and not containing periodic patterns; actual list not always needed	Suitable for all sizes	Concentrated if face-to-face contact required, otherwise does not matter	Low	Relatively easy to explain	Normally no difference
Stratified random	Accurate, easily accessible, divisible into relevant strata (see comments for simple random and systematic as appropriate)	See comments for simple random and systematic as appropriate	Concentrated if face-to-face contact required, otherwise does not matter	Low, providing lists of relevant strata available	Relatively difficult to explain (once strata decided see comments for simple random and systematic as appropriate)	Better comparison across strata; differential response rates may necessitate re-weighting
Cluster	Accurate, easily accessible, relates to relevant clusters not individual population members	As large as practical	Dispersed if face-to-face contact required and geographically based clusters used	Low, providing lists of relevant clusters available	Relatively difficult to explain until clusters selected	Quick but reduced precision
Multi-stage	Initial stages: geographical. Final stage: only needed for geographical areas selected, see comments for simple random and systematic as appropriate	Initial stages: as large as practicable. Final stage: see comments for simple random and systematic as appropriate	Dispersed if face-to-face contact required, otherwise no need to use this technique!	Low, as sampling frame for actual survey population only required for final stage	Initial stages: relatively difficult to explain. Final stage: see comments for simple random and systematic as appropriate	Difficult to adjust for differential response rates. Substantial errors possible!

Table 6.2 Impact of various factors on choice of probability sampling techniques

© *Mark Saunders, Philip Lewis and Adrian Thornhill, 1997*

Your choice of technique depends on your research question(s) and your objectives, the structure of the sampling frame, the size of the sample you need, the geographical area of your survey and, if you are using support workers, the ease of explaining the technique. The impact of each of these is summarised in Table 6.2.

Simple random sampling

Simple random sampling involves you selecting the sample at random from the sampling frame using either random number tables (Appendix 5) or a computer. To do this you:

1 Number each of the cases in your sampling frame with a unique number. The first case is numbered 0, the second 1 and so on.

2 Select cases using random numbers (Table 6.3, Appendix 5) until your actual sample size is reached.

78 41	11 62	72 18	66 69	58 71	31 90	51 36	78 09	41 00
70 50	58 19	68 26	75 69	04 00	25 29	16 72	35 73	55 85
32 78	14 47	01 **55**	10 91	83 21	13 32	59 53	03 38	79 32
71 60	20 53	86 78	50 57	42 30	73 48	68 09	16 35	21 87
35 30	15 57	99 96	33 25	56 43	65 67	51 45	37 99	54 89
09 08	05 41	66 54	01 49	97 34	38 85	85 23	34 62	60 58
02 59	34 51	98 71	31 54	28 85	23 84	49 07	33 71	17 88
20 13	44 15	22 95						

Table 6.3 Extract from random number tables

It is usual to select your first random number at random (closing your eyes and pointing with your finger is a good way!) as this ensures that the set of random numbers obtained for different samples is unlikely to be the same. If you do not, you will obtain sets of numbers which are random but identical.

Starting with this number you read off the random numbers (and select the cases) in a regular and systematic manner until your sample size is reached. If the same number is read off a second time it must be disregarded as you need different cases. This means you are not putting each case's number back into the sampling frame after it has been selected and is termed *sampling without replacement*. Alternatively, a number might be selected which is outside the range of those in your sampling frame. If this happens you simply ignore it and continue reading off numbers until your sample size is reached.

You can use a computer program such as a spreadsheet to generate and print out random numbers. However, you must ensure that the numbers generated are within your range and that if a number is repeated it is ignored and replaced. If details of the population are stored on the computer it is possible to generate a sample of randomly selected cases. For telephone interviews many market research companies now use computer-aided telephone interviewing (CATI) software to select telephone numbers at random from an existing database and dial each respondent in turn.

Random numbers allow you to select your sample without bias. The sample selected can therefore be said to be representative of the whole population. However, the selection which simple random sampling provides is more evenly dispersed throughout the population for samples of more than a few hundred cases. The first few hundred cases selected using simple random sampling normally consist of bunches of cases whose numbers are close together, followed by a gap and then further bunching. For over a few hundred cases this pattern occurs far less frequently. Because of the technique's random nature it is therefore possible that the chance occurrence of such patterns will result in certain parts of a population being over- or under-represented.

WORKED EXAMPLE: *Simple random sampling*

You have a population of 5011 supermarket customers, all of whom use the supermarket's charge card for their weekly purchases. You wish to find out why they use the charge card. There is insufficient time to interview all of them and so you decide to interview a sample. Your calculations reveal that to obtain acceptable levels of confidence and accuracy you need an actual sample size of approximately 360 customers. You decide to select them using simple random sampling.

First you give each of the cases (customers) in the sampling frame a unique number. In order for each number to be made up in exactly the same way, you use 5011 four-digit numbers starting with 0000 through to 5010. So customer 677 is given the number 0676.

The first random number you select is 55 (shown in bold and italics in Table 6.3). Starting with this number you read off the random numbers in a regular and systematic manner (in this example continuing along the line):

5510 9183 2113 3259 5303 3879 3271 6020

until 360 different cases have been selected. These form your random sample. Numbers selected which are outside the range of those in your sampling frame (such as 5510, 9183, 5303 and 6020) are simply ignored.

Simple random sampling is best used when you have an accurate and easily accessible sampling frame which lists the entire population, preferably stored on a computer. While you can often obtain these for employees within organisations or members of clubs or societies, adequate lists are often not available for types of organisations. If your population covers a large geographical area, random selection means that selected cases are likely to be dispersed throughout the area. As a consequence, this form of sampling is not suitable if you are undertaking a survey which covers a large geographical area and requires face-to-face contact due to the associated high travel costs. Simple random sampling would still be suitable for a geographically dispersed area if you used an alternative technique of collecting data such as postal questionnaires or telephone interviewing (Chapter 10).

Systematic sampling

Systematic sampling involves you selecting the sample at regular intervals from the sampling frame. To do this you:

1 Number each of the cases in your sampling frame with a unique number. The first case is numbered 0, the second 1 and so on.

2 Select the first case using a random number.

3 Calculate the sampling fraction.

4 Select subsequent cases systematically using the sampling fraction to determine the frequency of selection.

To calculate the *sampling fraction*, that is, the proportion of the total population that you need to select, you use the formula:

$$\text{Sampling fraction} = \frac{\text{actual sample size}}{\text{total population}}$$

If your sampling fraction is $\frac{1}{3}$ you need to select one in every three cases, that is every third case from the sampling frame. Unfortunately, your calculation will usually result in a more complicated fraction. In these instances it is normally acceptable to round your population down to the nearest ten (or hundred) and increase your minimum sample size until a simpler sampling fraction can be calculated.

On its own, selecting one in every three would not be random, as every third case would be bound to be selected, whereas those in-between would have no chance of selection. To overcome this a random number is used to decide where to start on the sampling frame. If your sampling fraction is $\frac{1}{3}$ the starting point must be one of the first three cases. You therefore select a random number (in this example a one-digit random number between 0 and 2) as described earlier and use this as the starting point.

Once you have selected your first case at random you then select, in this example, every third case until you have gone right through your sampling frame. As with simple random sampling, you can use a computer to generate the first random and subsequent numbers that are in the sample.

In some instances it is not necessary to construct a list for your sampling frame. Research that Mark undertook for a local authority required data to be collected about every tenth client of a social services department. Although these data were not held on computer, they were available from each client's manual file. The files were stored in alphabetical order and, once the first file (client) was selected at random, it was easy to extract every tenth file (client) thereafter. This process had the additional advantage that it was easy to explain to social services' employees, although Mark still had to explain to inquisitive employees that he needed a representative sample and so their 'interesting' clients might not be selected!

WORKED EXAMPLE: *Systematic sampling*

You have a population of approximately 1500 patients and wish to find out their attitudes to a new voucher scheme. There is insufficient time and money to collect data from all of them using a questionnaire and so you decide to send the questionnaire to a sample. Your calculation of sample size reveals that, to obtain acceptable levels of confidence and accuracy, you need an actual sample size of approximately 300 patients to whom you will send the questionnaire. You decide to select them using systematic sampling.

First you need to work out the sampling fraction:

$$\frac{300}{1500}$$

$$= \frac{1}{5}$$

Your sampling fraction is therefore $\frac{1}{5}$. This means that you need to select every fifth patient from the sampling frame.

You use a random number to decide where to start on the sampling frame. As your sampling fraction is $\frac{1}{5}$ the starting point must be one of the first five patients. You therefore select a one-digit random number between 0 and 4.

Once you have selected your first patient at random you select every fifth patient until you have gone right through your sampling frame. If the random number you selected was two, then you would select the following patient numbers:

2 7 12 17 22 27 32 37 and so on until 300 patients had been selected

Despite the advantages, you must be careful when using existing lists as sampling frames. You need to ensure that the lists do not contain periodic patterns.

A high street bank needs you to undertake a sample survey of individual customers with joint bank accounts. A sampling fraction of $\frac{1}{4}$ means that you will need to select every fourth customer on the list. The names on the customer lists, which you intend to use as the sampling frame are arranged alphabetically by account with males followed by females (Table 6.4). If you start with a male customer all those in your sample will be male. Conversely, if you start with a female customer all those in your sample will be female. As a consequence your sample will be biased (Table 6.4). This sampling frame is therefore not suitable without re-ordering or stratifying (discussed later).

Number	Customer	Sample	Number	Customer	Sample
000	Mr L Baker	*M*	006	Mr E Saunders	
001	Mrs B Baker		007	Mrs M Saunders	*F*
002	Mr S Davis		008	Mr J Smith	*M*
003	Mrs P Davis	*F*	009	Mrs K Smith	
004	Mr J Lewis	*M*	010	Mr J Thornhill	
005	Mrs P Lewis		011	Mrs A Thornhill	*F*

M all male sample selected if start with 000, *F* all female sample selected if start with 003

Table 6.4 The impact of periodic patterns on systematic sampling

Unlike simple random sampling, systematic sampling works equally well with a small or large number of cases. However, if your population covers a large geographical area the random selection means that the sample cases are likely to be dispersed throughout the area. As a consequence, systematic sampling is only suitable for geographically dispersed cases if you do not require face-to-face contact when collecting your data.

Stratified random sampling

Stratified random sampling is a modification of random sampling in which you divide the population into two or more relevant and significant strata based on one or a number of attributes. In effect, your sampling frame is divided into a number of subsets. A random sample (simple or systematic) is then drawn from each of the strata. As a consequence, stratified sampling shares many of the advantages and disadvantages of simple random and systematic sampling.

Dividing the population into a series of relevant strata means that the sample is more likely to be representative, as you can ensure that each of the strata is represented proportionally within your sample. However, it is only possible to do this if you are aware of, and can easily distinguish, significant strata in your sampling frame. In addition, the extra stage in the sampling procedure means that it is likely to take longer, be more expensive, and be more difficult to explain than simple random or systematic sampling.

In some instances, as pointed out by deVaus (1991), your sampling frame will already be divided into strata. A sampling frame of employee names which is in alphabetical order will automatically ensure that, if systematic sampling is used (discussed earlier), employees will be sampled in the correct proportion to the letter with which their name begins. Similarly membership lists which are ordered by date of joining will automatically result in stratification by length of membership if systematic sampling is used. Therefore if you are using simple random sampling or your sampling frame contains periodic patterns, you will need to stratify it. To do this you:

1 Choose the stratification variable or variables.

2 Divide the sampling frame into the discrete strata.

3 Number each of the cases within each strata with a unique number, as discussed earlier.

4 Select your sample using either simple random or systematic sampling, as discussed earlier.

The stratification variable (or variables) chosen should represent the discrete characteristic (or characteristics) for which you want to ensure correct representation within the sample.

WORKED EXAMPLE: *Stratified random sampling*

In the survey of joint bank account holders discussed earlier, an important strata would be each account customer's gender and so the sampling frame is divided into two discrete strata: females and males. Within each strata the individual cases are numbered:

| | Female strata | | | Male strata | |
Number	Customer	Selected	Number	Customer	Selected
000	Mrs B Baker		000	Mr L Baker	
001	Mrs P Davis	✓	001	Mr S Davis	
002	Mrs P Lewis		002	Mr J Lewis	
003	Mrs M Saunders		003	Mr E Saunders	✓
004	Mrs K Smith		004	Mr J Smith	
005	Mrs A Thornhill	✓	005	Mr J Thornhill	
006	Mrs D Woollons		006	Mr J Woollons	
007	Mrs F Wordden		007	Mr F Wordden	✓

You decide to select a systematic sample. A sampling fraction of ¼ means that you will need to select every fourth customer on the list. As indicated by the ticks (✓) random numbers select the first cases from the female (1) and male (3) strata. Subsequently every fourth customer in each strata is selected.

Samples can be stratified using more than one characteristic. You may wish stratify a sample of an organisation's employees by both department and salary grade. To do this you would:

1 Divide the sampling frame into the discrete departments.

2 Within each department divide the sampling frame into discrete salary grades.

3 Number each of the cases within each salary grade within each department with a unique number as discussed earlier.

4 Select your sample using either simple random or systematic sampling as discussed earlier.

In some instances the relative sizes of different strata mean that in order to have sufficient data for analysis you need to select larger samples from the strata with smaller populations. Here the different sample sizes must be taken into account when aggregating data from each of the strata to obtain an overall picture. The more sophisticated statistical analysis software packages enable you to do this by differentially weighting the responses for each strata (Section 11.2).

Cluster sampling

Cluster sampling is, on the surface, similar to stratified sampling as you need to divide the population into discrete groups prior to sampling (Henry, 1990). The groups are termed *clusters* in this form of sampling and can be based on any naturally occurring grouping. For example you could group your data by type of manufacturing firm or geographical area.

For cluster sampling your sampling frame is the complete list of clusters rather than a complete list of individual cases within the population. You then select a few clusters, normally using simple random sampling. Data are then collected from every case within the selected clusters. The technique has three main stages:

1 Choose the cluster grouping for your sampling frame.

2 Number each of the clusters with a unique number. The first cluster is numbered 0, the second 1 and so on.

3 Select your sample clusters using simple random sampling, as discussed earlier.

WORKED EXAMPLE: *Cluster sampling*

You need to select a sample of firms to undertake a survey about the use of photocopiers. As you have limited resources with which to pay for travel and other associated data collection costs, you decide to interview firms in four geographical areas selected from a cluster grouping of local authority areas. A list of all local authority areas forms the sampling frame. Each of the local authority areas (clusters) is given a unique number, the first being 0, the second 1 and so on. The four sample clusters are selected from a sampling frame of local authority districts using simple random sampling.

Your sample is all firms within the selected clusters. For this research the appropriate telephone directories would probably provide a suitable list of all firms in each cluster.

Selecting clusters randomly makes cluster sampling a probability sampling technique. However, the technique normally results in a sample which represents the total population less accurately than stratified sampling. Restricting the sample to a few relatively compact geographical sub-areas (clusters) maximises the number of interviews you can undertake within the resources available. However, it may also reduce the representativeness of your sample. For this reason you need to maximise the number of sub-areas to allow for variations in the population within the available resources. Your choice is between a large sample from a few discrete subgroups and a smaller sample distributed over the whole group. It is a trade-off between the amount of precision lost by using a few subgroups and the amount gained from a larger sample size.

Multi-stage sampling

Multi-stage sampling, sometimes called *multi-stage cluster sampling*, is a development of cluster sampling. It is normally used to overcome problems associated with a geographically dispersed population when face-to-face contact is needed, or where it is expensive and time consuming to construct a sampling frame for a large geographical area. However, as with cluster sampling you can use it for any discrete group, including those which are not geographically based. The technique can be divided into four phases:

Phase 1:

a Choose your sampling frame of relevant discrete groups.

b Number each of the groups with a unique number. The first group is numbered 0, the second 1 and so on.

c Select a small sample using simple random sampling, as discussed earlier.

139

Phase 2: for selected groups:

a Choose your sampling frame of relevant discrete subgroups.

b Number each of the subgroups with a unique number, as described in phase 1.

b Select a small sample using simple random sampling, as discussed earlier.

Phase 3: repeat phase 2 if necessary.

Phase 4: for final selection of subgroups:

a Choose your sampling frame of relevant discrete subgroups.

b Number each of the subgroups with a unique number as described in phase 1.

c Select a sample using simple random or systematic sampling, as discussed earlier.

WORKED EXAMPLE: *Multi-stage sampling*

A market research organisation needs you to interview a sample of 400 households in England and Wales. The electoral register provides a possible sampling frame. Selecting 400 households using either systematic or simple random sampling would probably result in these 400 households being dispersed throughout England and Wales. The time and cost of travelling to and interviewing your sample would be enormous. By using multi-stage sampling these problems can be overcome.

In the first stage the geographical area (England and Wales) is split into discrete subareas (counties). These form the sampling frame. After numbering, a small number of counties are selected using simple random sampling. Since each case (household) is located in a county each has an equal chance of being selected for the final sample.

As the counties selected are still too large, the selected counties are subdivided into smaller geographically discrete areas (electoral wards) which form the next sampling frame (stage 2). Another simple random sample is selected. A larger number of wards are selected to allow for likely important variations in households between wards.

A sampling frame is generated for each ward using a combination of the electoral register and the Post Office's postcode address file. The cases (households) which will be interviewed are then selected using either simple random or systematic techniques.

Because multi-stage sampling relies on a series of different sampling frames, you need to ensure that they are all appropriate and available. In order to minimise the impact of selecting smaller and smaller subgroups on the representativeness of your sample, you can apply stratified sampling techniques (discussed earlier). This technique can be further refined to take account of the relative size of the subgroups. It is discussed in greater detail by Hoinville *et al.* (1978). As you have selected your sub-areas using different sampling frames, you only need a sampling frame which lists all the members of the population for those subgroups you finally select. This provides considerable savings in time and money.

Checking that the sample is representative

Often it is possible to compare data you collect from your sample with data from another source for the population. For example, you can compare data on the age and socio-economic characteristics of respondents in a marketing survey with these characteristics for the population in the UK as recorded by the 1991 Census. If there is no statistically significant difference, then the sample is representative with respect to these characteristics.

When working within an organisation comparisons can also be made. In a recent survey we undertook of all types of employees in a multinational organisation we asked closed questions about salary grade, gender, length of service and place of work. Possible responses to each question were designed to provide sufficient detail to compare the characteristics of our sample with the characteristics of the entire population of employees as recorded by the organisation's computerised personnel system. At the same time we kept the categories sufficiently broad to preserve, and so as to be seen to preserve, the confidentiality of individual respondents. The two questions on length of service and salary grade from a recent questionnaire we developed illustrate this:

58 How long have you worked for *Organisation's name*?

    up to 3 years ❑   over 3 years to 10 years ❑   over 10 years ❑

59 Which one of the following best describes your job?

Technical/clerical (grades 1–3)	❑	Senior Management (grades 12–14)	❑
Supervisor (grades 4–5)	❑	Directorate (grades 15–17)	❑
Professional (grades 6–8)	❑	Other (please say)	❑
Management (grades 9–11)	❑	....	

We found that there was no statistically significant difference between the proportions of respondents in each of the length of service groups and the data obtained from the computerised personnel database. This meant that our sample was representative of all employees with respect to length of service. However, those responding were (statistically) significantly more likely to be in professional and managerial grades than in technical, clerical or supervisory grades. We therefore added a note of caution about the representativeness of our findings.

6.3 NON-PROBABILITY SAMPLING

The techniques for selecting samples discussed earlier have all been based on the assumption that your sample will be statistically chosen at random. As a consequence, it is possible to specify the probability that any case will be included in the sample. However, within some business research, such as market surveys and case-study research, this is often not possible and so your sample must be selected some other way. Non-probability sampling provides a range of alternative techniques based on your subjective judgement. In the exploratory stages of some research projects, such as a pilot survey, a non-probability sample may be the most practical, although it will not allow the extent of the problem to be determined. Subsequent to this, probability sampling techniques may be used. For other business and management research projects your research question(s), objectives and choice of research strategy (Sections 4.1 to 4.3) may dictate non-probability sampling. To answer your research question(s) and meet your objectives you may need to undertake an in-depth study which focuses on a small, perhaps single, sample selected purposively. This would provide you with an information-rich case study in which to explore your research question. Alternatively, limited resources or the inability to specify a sampling frame may dictate the use of one or a number of non-probability sampling techniques.

Selecting the most appropriate sampling technique and the sample

A range of non-probability sampling techniques are available which should not be discounted as they can provide sensible alternatives to select cases to answer your research question(s) and address your objectives. At one end of this range is quota sampling which, like probability samples, tries to represent the total population. Quota sampling has similar requirements for sample size as probabilistic sampling techniques.

At the other end are techniques based on the need to obtain a sample as quickly as possible where you have little control over the content and there is no attempt to obtain a representative sample. These include convenience and self-selection sampling techniques. Purposive sampling and snowball sampling techniques lie between these extremes (Table 6.5). For these techniques the issue of sample size is ambiguous. Unlike quota and probability samples, there are no rules. Rather it depends on your research question(s) and objectives; in particular, what you need to find out, what will be useful, what will have credibility and what can be done within your available resources (Patton, 1990). This is particularly so where you are intending to collect qualitative data. The validity and understanding that you will gain from your data will be more to do with your data collection and analysis skills than the size of your sample (Patton, 1990). As such, it is the logic behind your sample selection that is important.

Quota sampling

Quota sampling is entirely non-random and is normally used for interview surveys. It is based on the idea that your sample will represent the population, as the variability in your sample for various quota variables is the same as that in the population. Quota sampling is therefore a type of stratified sample in which selection of cases within strata is entirely non-random (Barnett, 1991). To select a quota sample you:

1 Divide the population into specific groups.
2 Calculate a quota for each group based on relevant and available data.
3 Give each interviewer an *assignment* which states the number of cases in each quota from which they must collect data.
4 Combine the data collected by interviewers to provide the full sample.

Sample type	Likelihood of sample being representative	Types of research in which useful	Relative costs	C sa
Quota	Reasonable to high, although dependent on selection of quota variables	Where costs constrained/ data needed very quickly so an alternative to probability sampling needed	Moderately high to reasonable	Rel:
Purposive	Low, although dependent on researcher's choices: **Extreme case** **Heterogeneous** **Homogenous** **Critical case** **Typical case**	Where working with very small samples focus: unusual or special focus: key themes focus: in-depth focus: importance of case focus: illustrative	Reasonable	Reasonable
Snowball	Low, but cases will have characteristics desired	Where difficulties exist in identifying cases	Reasonable	Quite low
Self-selection	Low, but cases self-selected	Where exploratory research needed	Low	Low
Convenience	Very low	Where very little variation in population	Low	Low

Table 6.4 Impact of various factors on choice of non-probability sample techniques
Source: Developed from Kervin, 1992 and Patton, 1990

Quota sampling has a number of advantages over the probabilistic techniques. In particular, it is less costly and can be set up very quickly. If, as with television audience research surveys, your data collection needs to be undertaken very quickly, then quota sampling may be the only possibility. In addition, it does not require a sampling frame and may therefore be the only technique you can use if that is not available.

Quota sampling is normally used for large populations. For small populations it is usually possible to obtain a sampling frame. Decisions on sample size are governed by the need to have sufficient responses in each quota to enable subsequent statistical analyses to be undertaken. This normally necessitates a sample size of between 2000 and 5000.

Calculations of quotas are based on relevant and available data, and are usually relative to the proportions in which they occur in the population. Without sensible and relevant quotas, data collected may be biased. For many market research projects quota are derived from census data. Your choice of quota is dependent on two main factors:

- usefulness as a means of stratifying the data;
- ability to overcome likely variations between groups in their availability for interview.

Where pensioners are likely to have different opinions to those of working couples, for example, a quota which does not ensure that these differences are captured may result in the data being biased, as it would probably be easier to collect the data from pensioners. Quotas used in market research surveys usually include measures of age, gender and socioeconomic status or social class. These may be supplemented by additional quotas dictated by the research question(s) and objectives.

Once you have given each interviewer their particular assignment, they decide whom to interview until they have completed their quota. You then combine the data from this assignment with that collected by other interviewers to provide the full sample. Because the interviewers can choose within quota boundaries whom they interview, your quota sample may be subject to bias. Interviewers tend to choose respondents who are easily accessible and who appear willing to answer the survey. Clear controls may therefore be needed. In addition, it has been known for interviewers to fill in quotas incorrectly. This is not to say that your quota sample will not produce good results; they can and often do! However, you cannot measure the level of certainty or margins of error as the sample is not probability based.

WORKED EXAMPLE: *Devising a quota sample*

A market research survey requires you to interview a sample of people representing people aged 20–64 who are in employment. No sampling frame is available. You wish to disaggregate your findings into groups dependent on respondents' age and type of employment. Previous research suggests that gender will also have an impact on responses and so you need to make sure that those interviewed in each group also reflect the proportions of males and females in the population. Fortunately, the Census contains a breakdown of the number of people in employment by gender, age and socioeconomic status. You decide to use these data to obtain your quota.

As you wish to analyse the data for individual age and socioeconomic status groups, it is important that each of these categories has sufficient respondents (at least 30) to enable meaningful statistical analyses. You calculate that a 5% quota for each of the groups will provide sufficient numbers for all groups, provided that your analyses are not also disaggregated by gender. This gives you the following quotas:

Gender	Age group	Socioeconomic status	Population	Quota
Male	20–29	Professional	1121	56
		Managers/employers	798	40
		Intermediate and junior non-manual	910	43
		Skilled manual	1611	79
		Semi-skilled manual	1260	63
		Unskilled manual	503	25
	30–44	Professional	2143	107
		Managers/employers	2327	116
		Intermediate and junior non-manual	799	40
		Skilled manual	2141	107
		Semi-skilled manual	1924	96
		Unskilled manual	498	25
	45–64	Professional	1661	83
		Managers/employers	2397	120
		Intermediate and junior non-manual	999	49
		Skilled manual	2001	100
		Semi-skilled manual	1761	88
		Unskilled manual	576	29

Gender	Age group	Socioeconomic status	Population	Quota
Female	20–29	Professional	881	44
		Managers/employers	678	34
		Intermediate and junior non-manual	2158	108
		Skilled manual	175	9
		Semi-skilled manual	963	48
		Unskilled manual	357	18
	30–44	Professional	1638	82
		Managers/employers	976	49
		Intermediate and junior non-manual	2842	142
		Skilled manual	221	11
		Semi-skilled manual	1180	59
		Unskilled manual	879	41
	45–64	Professional	882	44
		Managers/employers	784	39
		Intermediate and junior non-manual	2197	110
		Skilled manual	157	8
		Semi-skilled manual	942	47
		Unskilled manual	816	41
Total sample			44156	2200

These are then divided into assignments of 50 people for each interviewer.

Purposive sampling

Purposive or *judgemental sampling* enables you to use your judgement to select cases which will best enable you to answer your research question(s) and meet your objectives. This form of sample is often used when working with very small samples, such as in case-study research, and when you wish to select cases that are particularly informative (Neuman, 1991). Purposive sampling may also be used by researchers following the grounded theory approach. For such research, findings from data collected from your initial sample inform the way you extend your sample into subsequent cases (Section 12.6). Such samples cannot, however, be considered to be statistically representative of the total population. The logic on which you base your strategy for selecting cases for a purposive sample should be dependent on your research question(s) and objectives. The more common strategies are discussed below.

- *Extreme case* sampling focuses on unusual or special cases on the basis that the data collected about these unusual or extreme outcomes will enable you to learn the most and answer your research question(s) and meet your objectives most effectively. This is often based on the premise that findings from extreme cases will be relevant in understanding or explaining more typical cases (Patton, 1990). Peters and Waterman's research (1982) on excellent companies was based on a purposive sample of extreme (excellent) companies.

- *Heterogeneous* or *maximum variation* sampling enables you to collect data to describe and explain the key themes that can be observed. Although this might appear to be a contradiction, as a small sample may contain cases which are completely different, Patton (1990) argues that this is in fact a strength. Any patterns that do emerge are likely to be of particular interest and value and represent the key themes. In addition, the data collected should enable you to document uniqueness. To ensure maximum variation within a sample, Patton (1990) suggests that you identify your diverse characteristics (sample selection criteria) prior to selecting your sample.

■ In direct contrast to heterogeneous, *homogenous* sampling focuses on one particular subgroup in which all the sample members are similar. This enables you to study the group in great depth.

■ *Critical case* sampling selects critical cases, on the basis that they can make a point dramatically or because they are important. The focus of data collection is to understand what is happening in each critical case so that logical generalisations can be made. Patton (1990) outlines a number of clues that suggest critical cases. These can be summarised by the questions:

   – If it happens there, will it happen everywhere?

   – If they are having problems, can you be sure that everyone will have problems?

   – If they cannot understand the process, is it likely that no one will be able to understand the process?

■ In contrast, *typical case* sampling is usually employed as part of a research project to provide an illustrative profile using a representative case. Such a sample enables you to provide an illustration of what is 'typical' to those who will be reading your research report and may be unfamiliar with the subject matter. It is not intended to be definitive.

WORKED EXAMPLE: *Purposive sampling*

Phil was undertaking case-study research in three organisations in the financial sector. He needed to interview managers to discover their organisations' objectives for a particular pay system and the extent to which the system seemed to be successful. He decided to talk to three homogenous samples of managers:

■ senior general managers and personnel directors (the policy designers), to establish pay objectives and the extent to which they felt these had been achieved;

■ line managers (the policy operators), to establish their views on the pay system's objectives and the level of success being achieved;

■ middle and junior managers reporting directly to these line managers (the policy recipients) to test their perceptions of the pay system's objectives and the extent to which they considered it successful.

Where appropriate Phil also interviewed trade union officials.

Snowball sampling

Snowball sampling is commonly used when it is difficult to identify members of the desired population, for example people who are working while claiming unemployment benefit. You therefore need to:

1 Make contact with one or two cases in the population.

2 Ask these cases to identify further cases.

3 Ask these new cases to identify further new cases (and so on).

The main problem is making initial contact. Once you have done this, these cases identify further members of the population who then identify further members and so the sample snowballs. For such samples the problems of representativeness are huge, as respondents are most likely to identify other potential respondents who are similar to themselves. The next problem is to find these new cases. However, for populations which are difficult to identify, snowball sampling may provide the only possibility.

Self-selection sampling

Self-selection sampling occurs when you allow a case, usually an individual, to identify their desire to take part in the research. You therefore:

1 Publicise your need for cases, either by advertising through appropriate media or asking them to take part.

2 Collect data from those who respond.

Cases that self-select often do so because of their feelings or opinions about the research question(s) or stated objectives. In some instances, as in research undertaken by Adrian and colleagues on the positive management of redundancy, this is exactly what the researcher wants. In this research a letter in the personnel trade press generated a list of self-selected organisations who were interested in the research topic, considered it important and were willing to devote time to being interviewed.

Convenience sampling

Convenience sampling involves selecting those cases which are easiest to obtain for your sample. The sample selection process is continued until your required sample size has been reached. Although this technique of sampling is widely used, it is prone to bias and influences which are beyond your control, as the cases only appear in the sample because of the ease of obtaining them. Often the sample is intended to represent the total population, for example managers taking an MBA course as a surrogate for all managers! In such instances the choice of sample is likely to have biased the sample meaning that subsequent generalisations are likely to be at best flawed. These problems are less important where there is little variation in the population and such samples often serve as pilots to studies using more structured samples.

6.4 SUMMARY

- Your choice of sampling techniques is dependent on the feasibility and sensibility of collecting data to answer your research question(s) and address your objectives from the entire population. For populations of 50 or under there is often no need to sample if you are considering probability sampling.

- Choice of sampling technique or techniques is dependent on your research question(s) and objectives:
  - research question(s) and objectives which need you to estimate statistically the characteristics of the population from a sample require probability samples;
  - research question(s) and objectives that do not require such generalisations can make use of non-probability sampling techniques.

- Factors such as the confidence that is needed in the findings, accuracy required and likely categories for analyses will affect the size of the sample that needs to be collected:
  - statistical analysis usually requires a minimum sample size of 30;
  - research question(s) and objectives which do not require statistical estimation may need far smaller samples.

- Sample size and the technique used are also influenced by the availability of resources, in particular financial support and time available to select the sample and collect, enter into a computer and analyse the data.

- Probability sampling techniques all necessitate some form of sampling frame, so they are often more time consuming than non-probability techniques.

- Where it is not possible to construct a sampling frame you will need to use non-probability sampling techniques.

- Non-probability sampling techniques also provide you with the opportunity to select your sample purposively and to reach difficult-to-identify members of the population.

- For many research projects you will need to use a combination of different sampling techniques.

- All your choices will be dependent on your ability to gain access to organisations. The considerations summarised earlier must therefore be tempered with an understanding of what is practically possible.

Self-check questions and assignment

Self-check question 6.1

Identify a suitable sampling frame for each of the following research questions:

a How do company directors of manufacturing firms of over 500 employees think a specified piece of legislation will affect their companies?

b Which factors are important in accountants' decisions regarding working in mainland Europe?

c How do employees at Cheltenham Gardens Ltd think the proposed introduction of compulsory Saturday working will affect their working lives?

Self-check question 6.2

You have been asked to select a sample of manufacturing firms using the sampling frame below. This also lists the value of their annual output in tens of thousands of pounds over the past year. To help you in selecting your sample the firms have been numbered from 0 to 99.

	Output		Output		Output		Output		Output
0	1163	20	1072	40	1257	60	1300	80	1034
1	10	21	7	41	29	61	39	81	55
2	57	22	92	42	84	62	73	82	66
3	149	23	105	43	97	63	161	83	165
4	205	24	157	44	265	64	275	84	301
5	163	25	214	45	187	65	170	85	161
6	1359	26	1440	46	1872	66	1598	86	1341
7	330	27	390	47	454	67	378	87	431
8	2097	28	1935	48	1822	68	1634	88	1756
9	1059	29	998	49	1091	69	1101	89	907
10	1037	30	1298	50	1251	70	1070	90	1158
11	59	31	10	51	9	71	37	91	27
12	68	32	70	52	93	72	88	92	66
13	166	33	159	53	103	73	102	93	147
14	302	34	276	54	264	74	157	94	203
15	161	35	215	55	189	75	168	95	163
16	1298	36	1450	56	1862	76	1602	96	1339
17	329	37	387	57	449	77	381	97	429
18	2103	38	1934	58	1799	78	1598	98	1760
19	1061	39	1000	59	1089	79	1099	99	898

a Select two simple random samples, each of twenty firms, and mark those firms selected for each sample on the sampling frame.

b Describe and compare the pattern on the sampling frame of each of the samples selected.

c Calculate the average (mean) annual output in tens of thousands of pounds over the past year for each of the samples selected.

d Given that the true average annual output is £6 608 900, is there any bias in either of the samples selected?

Self-check question 6.3

You have been asked to select a 10 per cent sample of firms from the sampling frame used for Question 6.2.

a Select a 10 per cent systematic sample and mark those firms selected for the sample on the sampling frame.

b Calculate the average (mean) annual output in tens of thousands of pounds over the past year for your sample.

c Given that the true average annual output is £6 608 900, why does systematic sampling provide such a poor estimate of the annual output in this case?

Self-check question 6.4

You need to undertake a face-to-face interview survey of managing directors of small to medium-sized organisations. From the data you collect you need to be able to generalise about the attitude of such managing directors to recent changes in government policy towards these firms. Your generalisations need to be accurate to within plus or minus 5 per cent. Unfortunately you have limited resources to pay for interviewers, travelling and other associated costs.

a How many managing directors will you need to interview?

b You have been given the choice between cluster or multi-stage sampling. Which technique would you choose for this research? You should give reasons for your choice.

Self-check question 6.5

You have been asked to undertake a survey of residents' opinions regarding the siting of a new supermarket in an inner-city suburb (estimated catchment population 111 376 at the last census). The age and gender distribution of the catchment population at the last census is listed below:

Gender	Age group							
	0–4	5–15	16–19	20–29	30–44	45–59/64*	60/65#–74	75+
Males	3498	7106	4884	7656	9812	12892	4972	2684
Females	3461	6923	6952	9460	8152	9152	9284	4488

*59 females, 64 males, #60 females, 65 males

a Devise a quota for a quota sample using these data.

b What other data would you like to include to overcome likely variations between groups in their availability for interview and replicate the total population more precisely? Give reasons for your answer.

c What problems might you encounter in using interviewers?

Self-check question 6.6

For each of the following research questions it has not been possible for you to obtain a sampling frame. Suggest the most suitable non-probability sampling technique to obtain the necessary data, giving reasons for your choice.

a What support do people sleeping rough believe they require from social services?

b Which television advertisements do people remember watching last weekend?

c How do employers' opinions vary regarding the impact of European Union legislation on employee recruitment?

d How are manufacturing companies planning to respond to the introduction of road tolls?

e Would users of the squash club be prepared to pay a 10 per cent increase in subscriptions to help fund two extra courts (answer needed by tomorrow morning!)?

Assignment 6:
Using sampling as part of your research

- Consider your research question(s) and objectives. You need to decide whether you will be able to collect data on the entire population or will need to collect data from a sample.

- If you decide that you need to sample you must establish whether your research question(s) and objectives require probability sampling. If they do, make sure that a suitable sampling frame is available or can be devised and calculate the actual sample size required, taking into account likely response rates. If your research question(s) and objectives do not require probability sampling or you are unable to obtain a suitable sampling frame, you will need to use non-probability sampling.

- Select the most appropriate sampling technique or techniques after considering the advantages and disadvantages of all suitable techniques and undertaking further reading as necessary.

- Select your sample or samples following the technique or techniques as outlined in this chapter.

- Remember to note down the reasons for your choices when you make them, as you will need to justify your choices when you write about your research methodology.

References

Barnett, V. (1991) *Sample Survey Principles and Method*, London, Edward Arnold.

Dale, A. (1993) 'Fieldwork and Data Processing', in Dale, A. and Marsh, C. (eds) *The 1991 Census User's Guide*, London, HMSO, pp. 84–110.

deVaus, D.A. (1991) *Surveys in Social Research* (3rd edn), London, UCL Press and Allen & Unwin.

Dillman, D.A. (1978) *Mail and Telephone Surveys: The Total Design Method*, New York, Wiley.

The Economist (1993) *The Economist Numbers Guide*, London, Hamish Hamilton.

Healey, M.J. (1991) 'Obtaining information from Businesses', in Healey, M.J. (ed.) *Economic Activity and Land Use: The Changing Information Base for Local and Regional Studies*, Harlow, Longman, pp. 193–250.

Henry, G.T. (1990) *Practical sampling*, Newbury Park, California, Sage.

Hoinville, G., Jowell, R. and Associates (1978) *Survey Research Practice*, London, Heinemann.

Kervin, J.B. (1992) *Methods for Business Research,* New York, HarperCollins.

Moser, C.A. and Kalton, G. (1986) *Survey Methods in Social Investigation* (2nd edn), Aldershot, Gower.

Neuman, W.L. (1991) *Social Research Methods*, London, Allyn and Bacon.

Owen, F. and Jones, R. (1990) *Statistics* (3rd edn), London, Pitman Publishing.

Patton, M.Q. (1990) *Qualitative Evaluation and Research Methods* (2nd edn), Newbury Park, California, Sage.

Peters, T. and Waterman, R. (1982) *In Search of Excellence*, New York, Harper & Row.

Robson, C. (1993) *Real World Research*, Oxford, Blackwell.

Further Reading

Barnett, V. (1991) *Sample Survey Principles and Method*, London, Edward Arnold. Chapters 2, 5 and 6 provide an explanation of the statistics behind probability sampling and quota sampling as well as the techniques.

deVaus, D.A. (1991) *Surveys in social research* (3rd edn), London, UCL Press and Allen & Unwin. Chapter 5 provides a useful overview of both probability and non-probability sampling techniques.

Henry, G.T. (1990) *Practical Sampling*, Newbury Park, California, Sage. This provides a useful discussion of probability sampling techniques and interesting examples. Discussion of non-probability sampling techniques is relatively limited.

Hoinville, G., Jowell, R. and Associates (1978) *Survey Research Practice*, London, Heinemann. Chapter 4 provides a useful discussion of the practical aspects of probability sampling techniques, although it is very limited on non-probability sampling techniques.

Moser, C.A. and Kalton, G. (1986) *Survey Methods in Social Investigation* (2nd edn), Aldershot, Gower. This is one of the definitive texts on survey methods. Chapters 4 to 8 inclusive are particularly useful for their discussion on the impact of sample size, probability sampling and quota sampling, and discussion of the problem of non-response.

Patton, M.Q. (1990) *Qualitative Evaluation and Research Methods* (2nd edn), Newbury Park, California, Sage. Chapter 9 contains a useful discussion of non-probability sampling techniques with examples.

Wass, V.J. (1994) 'Minimizing and Managing Bias in a Mail Survey: A Study of Redundant Miners', in Wass, V.J. and Wells, P.E. *Principles and Practice in Business and Management Research*, Aldershot, Dartmouth, pp. 91–121. This includes a useful account of the realities of sample selection for a postal questionnaire survey.

Case 6:
Change management at Hattersley Electrics.

Hattersley Electrics is a division of the Hattersley Group Plc, a UK-based manufacturing conglomerate whose main markets were, until recently, the high-tech aerospace and defence industries. In recent years the division has been hit by both the recession in the airline industry and the contraction in defence spending by European governments. In order to overcome this Hattersley Electrics has embarked on a process of repositioning itself within the electronics marketplace in the niche of advanced civilian communications equipment. As part of this it has changed its manufacturing foci and chosen to downsize and restructure its workforce.

Initially the workforce were not resistant to change due to the extensive efforts made by management to keep them involved and informed at all stages. This involved restructuring the division (Fig 1) into cells and reducing the workforce from 380 to 250. After this restructuring the works council informed the division's management team that the workforce were concerned about the longer-term effects of these changes, in particular the possible loss of employment, future job security, a lack of division identity, a lack of direction from senior management and a lack of employee involvement in recent decisions.

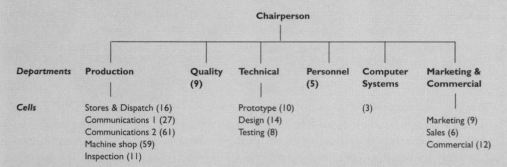

Figures in brackets refer to number of employees including managers

Fig 1 Organisational structure of Hattersley Group Plc Electrics Division

A consultancy group was hired by the management team and set three objectives to be achieved (at a 95 per cent level of certainty) within a fixed budget and a timescale of 10 weeks from start to finish. These were to establish the following:

1 The views of the division's managers and employees about the effectiveness of change at Hattersley Electrics.

2 General perceptions of the division's managers and staff about general aspects of the experience of the changes at Hattersley Electrics.

3 Whether there were any differences in general perceptions between departments and between managers and employees.

The agreed methodology involved three stages of data collection. Interviews were undertaken with the division's chairperson and six managers and a sample of employees. One employee was selected at random from each cell. These interviews were to enable the consultants to understand the background to the changes, and to establish the full variety of opinions regarding its effectiveness. In addition, they covered a range of other issues associated with general aspects of the experience of the changes.

A questionnaire was distributed, reflecting the issues generated by interviews in the first stage, to 50 per cent of company managers and employees. This sample was selected from a sampling frame generated from the personnel department's staff database and was stratified by department and cell. Within each cell employees were listed in order of seniority. All employees other than those in the production department received a questionnaire; 28 per cent of those employees in the production department received a questionnaire. The numbers sampled in each cell are given in Fig 2. Overall there was a 97.6 per cent response rate to the questionnaire, two non-responses coming from the computer systems department and one from the production department.

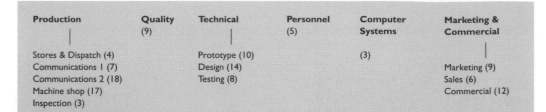

Production	Quality (9)	Technical	Personnel (5)	Computer Systems	Marketing & Commercial
Stores & Dispatch (4)		Prototype (10)		(3)	
Communications 1 (7)		Design (14)			Marketing (9)
Communications 2 (18)		Testing (8)			Sales (6)
Machine shop (17)					Commercial (12)
Inspection (3)					

Fig 2 Number of managers and employees in each cell who received a questionnaire

After the analysis of the questionnaire, three follow-up group interviews were undertaken, each group consisting of five or six people. One group consisted of production employees, another of managers from all departments, and a third of employees from all departments other than production. In the interviews issues that had arisen during the analysis of the questionnaire were probed and clarified.

Case-study questions

1 **a** Name the sampling techniques used at each of the three stages.

 b List possible reasons for the choice of each of these techniques.

2 Given the quoted response rate of 97.6 per cent, what is the accuracy (margin of error) of the questionnaire results for the division likely to have been?

3 **a** What issues will need to be taken into account when generalising from the questionnaire results to:

 ● all employees in each department of the Electrics division?

 ● all employees in the Electrics division?

 b Give reasons for your answers.

4 **a** Would it be possible to use the results from the three sample surveys outlined in this case to generalise about the management of change in the Hattersley PLC group?

 b Give reasons for your answer.

Answers to self-check questions

Self-check question 6.1

a A complete list of all directors of large manufacturing firms could be purchased from an organisation which specialised in selling such lists to use as the sampling frame. Alternatively, a list which only contained those selected for the sample could be purchased to reduce costs. These data are usually in a format suitable for being read by wordprocessing and database computer software and so they could easily be merged into standard letters such as those included with questionnaires.

b A complete list of accountants, or one which only contained those selected for the sample, could be purchased from an organisation which specialised in selling such lists. Care would need to be taken regarding the precise composition of the list to ensure that it included those in private practice as well as those working for organisations. Alternatively, if the research was only interested in qualified accountants, then the professional accountancy bodies' yearbooks, which list all their members and their addresses, could be used as the sampling frame.

c The personnel records or payroll of Cheltenham Gardens Ltd could be used. Either would provide an up-to-date list of all employees with their addresses.

Self-check question 6.2

a Your answer will depend on the random numbers you selected. However, the process you follow to select the samples is likely to be similar to that outlined. Starting at randomly selected points two sets of 20 two-digit random numbers are read from the random number tables (Appendix 3). If a number is selected twice it is disregarded. Two possible sets are:

Sample 1: 38 41 14 59 53 03 52 86 21 88 55 87 85 90 74 18 89 40 84 71

Sample 2: 28 00 06 70 81 76 36 65 30 27 92 73 20 87 58 15 69 22 77 31

These are then marked on the sampling frame (sample 1 is enclosed by a box, sample 2 is shaded), as shown below:

0	1163	20	1072	40	1257	60	1300	80	1034
1	10	21	7	41	29	61	39	81	55
2	57	22	92	42	84	62	73	82	66
3	149	23	105	43	97	63	161	83	165
4	205	24	157	44	265	64	275	84	301
5	163	25	214	45	187	65	170	85	161
6	1359	26	1440	46	1872	66	1598	86	1341
7	330	27	390	47	454	67	378	87	431
8	2097	28	1935	48	1822	68	1634	88	1756
9	1059	29	998	49	1091	69	1101	89	907
10	1037	30	1298	50	1251	70	1070	90	1158
11	59	31	10	51	9	71	37	91	27
12	68	32	70	52	93	72	88	92	66
13	166	33	159	53	103	73	102	93	147
14	302	34	276	54	264	74	157	94	203
15	161	35	215	55	189	75	168	95	163
16	1298	36	1450	56	1862	76	1602	96	1339
17	329	37	387	57	449	77	381	97	429
18	2103	38	1934	58	1799	78	1598	98	1760
19	1061	39	1000	59	1089	79	1099	99	898

b Your samples will probably produce patterns which cluster around certain numbers in the sampling frame, although the amount of clustering may differ, as illustrated by samples 1 and 2 above.

c The average (mean) annual output in tens of thousands of pounds will depend entirely on your sample. For the two samples selected the averages are:
Sample 1 (boxed): £6 752 000   Sample 2 (shaded): £7 853 500

d There is no bias in either of the samples as both have been selected at random. However, the average annual output calculated from sample 1 represents the total population more closely than that calculated from sample 2, although this has occurred entirely at random.

Self-check question 6.3

a Your answer will depend on the random number you select as the starting point for your systematic sample. However, the process you followed to select your sample is likely to be similar to that outlined. As a 10 per cent sample has been requested the sampling fraction is $1/10$. Your starting point is selected using a random number between 0 and 9, in this case 2. Once the firm numbered 2 has been selected every 10th firm is selected:

2 12 22 32 42 52 62 72 82 92

These are marked with a box on the sampling frame and will result in a regular pattern whatever the starting point:

0	1163	20	1072	40	1257	60	1300	80	1034
1	10	21	7	41	29	61	39	81	55
2	57	22	92	42	84	62	73	82	66
3	149	23	105	43	97	63	161	83	165
4	205	24	157	44	265	64	275	84	301
5	163	25	214	45	187	65	170	85	161
6	1359	26	1440	46	1872	66	1598	86	1341
7	330	27	390	47	454	67	378	87	431
8	2097	28	1935	48	1822	68	1634	88	1756
9	1059	29	998	49	1091	69	1101	89	907
10	1037	30	1298	50	1251	70	1070	90	1158
11	59	31	10	51	9	71	37	91	27
12	68	32	70	52	93	72	88	92	66
13	166	33	159	53	103	73	102	93	147
14	302	34	276	54	264	74	157	94	203
15	161	35	215	55	189	75	168	95	163
16	1298	36	1450	56	1862	76	1602	96	1339
17	329	37	387	57	449	77	381	97	429
18	2103	38	1934	58	1799	78	1598	98	1760
19	1061	39	1000	59	1089	79	1099	99	898

b The average (mean) annual output of firms for your sample will depend on where you started your systematic sample. For the sample selected above it is £757 000.

c Systematic sampling has provided a poor estimate of the annual output because there is an underlying pattern in the data which has resulted in firms with similar levels of output being selected.

Self-check question 6.4

a If you assume that there are at least 100 000 managing directors of small to medium-sized organisations from which to select your sample, you will need to interview approximately 380 to make generalisations which are accurate to within plus or minus 5 per cent (Table 6.1).

b Either cluster or multi-stage sampling could be suitable, what is important is the reasoning behind your choice. This choice between cluster and multi-stage sampling is dependent on the amount of limited resources and time you have available. Using multi-stage sampling will take longer than cluster sampling as more sampling stages will need to be undertaken. However, the results are more likely to be representative of the total population due to the possibility of stratifying the samples from the sub-areas.

Self-check question 6.5

a Before deciding on your quota you will need to consider the possible inclusion of residents aged under 16 in your quota. Often in such research projects residents aged under 5 (and those aged 5 to 15) are excluded. You would need a quota of between 2 000 and 5 000 residents to obtain a reasonable accuracy. These should be divided proportionally between the groupings as illustrated in the possible quota below:

Gender	Age group					
	16–19	**20–29**	**30–44**	**45–59/64**	**60/65–74**	**75+**
Male	108	169	217	285	110	59
Female	154	209	180	203	205	99

b Data on social class, employment status, socioeconomic status or car ownership could also be used as further quotas. These data are available from the census and are likely to affect shopping habits.

c Interviewers might choose respondents who were easily accessible or appeared willing to answer the questions. In addition, they might fill in their quota incorrectly or make up the data.

Self-check question 6.6

a Either snowball sampling, as it would be difficult to identify members of the desired population or, possibly, convenience sampling due to initial difficulties in finding members of the desired population.

b Quota sampling to ensure that the variability in the population as a whole was represented.

c Purposive sampling to ensure that the full variety of responses were obtained from a range of respondents from the population.

d Self-selection sampling, as it requires people who are interested in the topic.

e Convenience sampling due to the very short timescales available and the need to have at least some idea of members' opinions.

CHAPTER 7

Using secondary data

The objectives of this chapter are to introduce you to the variety of secondary data that are likely to be available and to suggest ways in which these can be used to help you answer your research question(s) and meet your objectives.

The chapter outlines the advantages and disadvantages of using secondary data and suggests a range of techniques, including published guides, for locating these data.

Practical advice is offered on how to evaluate the suitability of secondary data for answering your research question(s) and achieving your objectives. This pays special attention to the issues of coverage, validity, reliability and measurement bias.

7.1 INTRODUCTION

When considering how to answer their research question(s) or meet their objectives, few researchers consider the possibility of re-analysing data that have already been collected for some other purpose (Hakim, 1982). Such data are known as *secondary data*. Most researchers automatically think in terms of collecting new *(primary) data* specifically for that purpose. Yet, despite this, secondary data can provide a useful source from which to answer, or begin to answer, your research question(s).

Secondary data include both raw data and published summaries. Most organisations collect and store a variety of data to support their operations; for example payroll details, copies of letters, minutes of meetings and accounts of sales of goods or services. Quality daily newspapers contain a wealth of data, including reports about takeover bids and companies' share prices. Government departments undertake surveys and publish official statistics covering social, demographic and economic topics. Consumer research organisations collect data which are used subsequently by different clients. Trade organisations survey their members on topics such as sales which are subsequently aggregated and published.

Some of these data, in particular documents such as company minutes, are only available from the organisations which produce them and so access will need to be negotiated

(Section 5.3). Others, including government surveys such as the population census, are widely available in published form and on CD-ROM in university libraries. An increasing variety have been deposited in and are available from data archives (Dale et al., 1988). In addition, a rapidly increasing number of on-line computer databases can be accessed via the Internet (Section 3.5).

For certain types of research project, such as those requiring national or international comparisons, secondary data will probably provide the main source to answer your research question(s) and address your objectives. However, if you are undertaking your research project as part of a course of study, we recommend that you check the examination regulations before deciding to rely entirely on secondary data. You may be required to collect primary data for your research project. Most research questions are answered using some combination of secondary and primary data. Where limited appropriate secondary data are available, you will have to rely mainly on data you collect yourself.

In this chapter we examine the different types of secondary data that are likely to be available to help you to answer your research question(s) and meet your objectives, how you might use them (Section 7.2) and a range of methods, including published guides, for locating these data (Section 7.3). We then consider the advantages and disadvantages of using secondary data (Section 7.4) and discuss ways of evaluating their validity and reliability (Section 7.5). We do not attempt to provide a comprehensive list of secondary data sources, as this would be an impossible task within the space available.

7.2 TYPES OF SECONDARY DATA AND USES IN RESEARCH

Secondary data include both quantitative and qualitative data and can be used in both descriptive and explanatory research. The data you use may be *raw data*, where there has been little if any processing, or *compiled data*, which has received some form of selection or summarising (Kervin, 1992). Within business and management research such data are mostly used in case-study and survey-type research. However, there is no reason not to include secondary data in experimental research.

Different researchers (for example Bryman, 1989; Dale *et al.*, 1988; Hakim, 1982; Robson, 1993) have generated a variety of classifications for secondary data. These classifications do not, however, capture the full variety of data. We have therefore built on their ideas to create three main subgroups of secondary data: documentary data, survey-based data and those compiled from multiple sources (Fig 7.1).

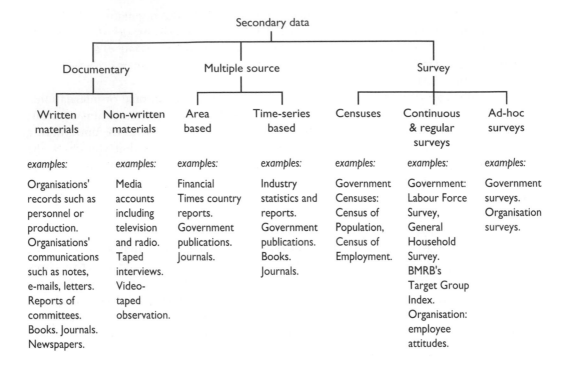

Fig 7.1 Types of secondary data
© Mark Saunders, Philip Lewis and Adrian Thornhill, 1997

Documentary secondary data

Documentary secondary data are often used in research projects which also use primary data collection methods. However, you can use them on their own or with other sources of secondary data, in particular for historical research. Research based almost exclusively on documentary secondary data is termed *archival research* and, although this term has historical connotations, it can refer to recent as well as historical documents (Bryman, 1989). Documentary secondary data include *written documents* such as notices, correspondence, minutes of meetings, reports to shareholders, diaries, transcripts of speeches and administrative and public records. Written documents can also include books, journal and magazine articles and newspapers. These can be important raw data sources in their own right, as well as a storage medium for compiled data. You could use written documents to provide qualitative data such as managers' espoused reasons for decisions. They could also be used to generate statistical measures, such as data on absenteeism and profitability derived from company records (Bryman, 1989). Documentary secondary data also include *non-written documents* (Fig 7.1) such as tape and video recordings, pictures, drawings, films and television programmes (Robson, 1993). These data can be analysed both quantitatively and qualitatively. In addition, they can be used to help triangulate findings based on other data such as written documents and primary data collected through observation, interviews or questionnaires (Chapters 8, 9 and 10).

For your research project the documentary sources you have available will depend on whether you have been granted access to an organisation's records as well as your success in locating library, data archive and commercial sources (Section 7.4). Access to an organisation's data will be dependent on gatekeepers within that organisation (Section 5.3). In our experience those research projects that make use of documentary secondary data often do so as part of a within-company research project or a case study of a particular organisation.

WORKED EXAMPLE: *Using documentary secondary data*

You are interested in the impact of private-sector values on the organisational culture of UK local authorities. As part of this research you wish to discover whether there has been a shift from recruiting people with only public-sector experience to recruiting those with at least some private-sector experience. To provide quantitative data about changes you have gained access to individual employees' personnel records (documentary secondary data) over a 15-year period in the local authority where you undertook your work placement. These contain the date that each vacancy was filled, how it was notified, and the age, gender, qualifications and previous occupation of the successful applicant.

Your next stage will be to abstract data for each externally notified vacancy and match these with data from vacancy advertisement invoice instructions (also documentary secondary data). The latter will enable you to obtain a complete list of all notification outlets used for each vacancy. Once your data have been combined you will be able to analyse these data quantitatively.

Survey-based secondary data

Survey-based secondary data refers usually to data collected by questionnaires (Chapter 10) which have already been analysed for their original purpose. Such data can refer to organisations, people or households (Hakim, 1982). They are made available as compiled data tables or as a computer-readable matrix of raw data (Section 11.2) for secondary analysis.

Survey-based secondary data will have been collected through one of three distinct types of survey: censuses, continuous/regular surveys or ad hoc surveys (Fig 7.1). *Censuses* are usually carried out by governments and are unique because, unlike surveys, participation is obligatory (Hakim, 1982). As a consequence they provide very good coverage of the population surveyed. They include population censuses, which have been carried out every ten years in the UK since 1801 with the exception of 1941 (Marsh, 1993), and others such as the UK Census of Employment. The latter was carried out annually between 1971 and 1978. Since then the frequency of the Census of Employment has depended on the overall employment situation, although it is normally administered every two or three years (Mort, 1992). The data from censuses conducted by many governments are intended to meet the needs of government departments as well as local government. As a consequence they are usually clearly defined, well documented and of a high quality. Such data are easily accessible in compiled form and widely used by other organisations and individual researchers.

Continuous and regular surveys are those surveys, excluding censuses, that are repeated over time (Hakim, 1982). They include surveys where data are collected throughout the year, such as the UK General Household Survey (Foster *et al.*, 1995), and those repeated at regular intervals. The latter includes the Labour Force Survey which is undertaken annually by member states throughout the European Union with a core set of questions. This means that some comparative data are available for member states; although access to these data is limited by European and individual countries' legislation (Dale *et al.*, 1988). Regular surveys are also carried out by non-governmental bodies, including general-purpose market research surveys such as British Market Research Bureau International's (BMRB) Target Group Index. Because of the Target Group Index's commercial nature the data are very expensive. However, BMRB has provided copies of reports (usually over three years old) to between 20 and 30 UK university libraries. Many large organisations undertake regular surveys, a common example being the employee attitude survey. However, because of the sensitive nature of this information it is often difficult to gain access to such survey data, especially in its raw form.

Census and continuous and regular survey data provide a useful resource with which to compare or set in context your own research findings. Aggregate data are often available on CD-ROMs or in published form in libraries (Section 7.3), in particular for government surveys. If you are undertaking research in one UK organisation, you could use these data to place your case-study organisation within the context of its industry group or division using the Census of Employment. Aggregated results of the Census of Employment can be found in *Labour Market Trends* (formerly the *Employment Gazette*). Alternatively, you might explore issues already highlighted by data from an organisation survey through in-depth interviews.

Survey secondary data may be available in sufficient detail to provide the main data set from which to answer your research question(s) and meet your objectives. Alternatively, they may be the only way in which you can obtain the required data. If your research question is concerned with national variations in consumer spending, it is unlikely that you will be able to collect sufficient data. You will therefore need to rely on secondary data such as the Family Expenditure Survey (King, 1995). For some research questions and objectives suitable data will be available in published form. For others you may need more disaggregated data. This may be available on CD-ROM, via the Internet (Section 3.4) or from archives (Section 7.3). We have found that for most business and management research involving secondary data you are unlikely to find all the data you require from one survey. Rather, your research project is likely to involve detective work in which you build your own multiple source data set using different data items from a variety of surveys and other secondary data sources. As with all detective work, finding data that helps answer a research question or meet an objective is immensely satisfying.

Ad hoc surveys are usually one-off surveys and are far more specific in their subject matter. They include data from questionnaires which have been undertaken by independent researchers as well as surveys undertaken by organisations and governments. Because of their ad hoc nature you will probably find it more difficult to discover relevant surveys. However, it may be that an organisation in which you are undertaking research has conducted its own questionnaire on an issue related to your research. Some organisations will provide you with a report containing aggregated data, others may be willing to let you re-analyse the raw data from this ad hoc survey. Alternatively, you may be able to gain access to and use raw data from an ad hoc survey which has been deposited in an archive.

WORKED EXAMPLE: *Integrating secondary and primary data*

One of our colleagues, Sue, is undertaking research on the impact of European Union legislation on employee mobility between member states. In particular she is interested in how legislation relating to the mutual recognition of qualifications has affected those working in the accountancy profession. This legislation should mean that an accountant who has qualified in any European Union state can, after an aptitude test and a period of adaptation, apply to have her or his qualification recognised by another member state.

As part of her research, Sue has undertaken a series of in-depth interviews with UK accountants at different stages of their careers. These have explored their attitudes to working elsewhere in the European Union. Within the interviews Sue has concentrated on the importance of mutual recognition of qualifications relative to other factors such as the accountants' need to move their families and their foreign language ability.

Sue's survey data have been set in context by analysing a variety of published secondary data. Published tables from the International Passenger Survey (for example, Office of Population Censuses and Surveys, 1994) have been re-analysed to ascertain the level of professional migration out of and into the UK. These aggregate data have also been used to ascertain the proportion of professional migrants whose family move with them when they migrate. Secondary data have been used to explore the frequency of applications for mutual recognition of qualifications in the UK. Unpublished tables, obtained from the Department of Trade and Industry, have provided details regarding how many accountants and other professionals have applied to have their qualifications recognised by UK professions.

Multiple-source secondary data

Multiple-source secondary data can be based entirely on documentary or on survey data or can be an amalgam of the two. The key factor is that different data sets have been combined to form another data set before you access the data. One of the more common types of multiple source data you are likely to come across in document form are various compilations of company information such as *The Times 1000 1996* (Barrow, 1995). This contains comparable quantitative and qualitative data on the top 1000 UK and European companies and top 100 companies for other regions of the world. Other multiple-source secondary data include the various share-price listings for different stock markets in the financial pages of quality newspapers. These are available in most university libraries, including back copies on microfilm or CD-ROM. However, you need to beware of relying on CD-ROM copies for tabular data or diagrams, as many only contain the text of articles.

The way in which a multiple-source data set has been compiled will dictate the sorts of research question(s) or objectives with which you can use it. One method of compilation is to extract and combine selected comparable variables from a number of surveys or from the same survey which has been repeated a number of times to provide a *time series* of data. For short research projects this is one of the few ways in which you will be able to obtain data over a long period to undertake a *longitudinal* study. Other ways of obtaining time-series data are to use a series of company documents such as appointment letters, or public and administrative records, to create your own longitudinal secondary data set. Examples include the UK Employment Department's stoppages at work data held by the ESRC Data Archive, and those derived by researchers from nineteenth-century population census returns which, in the UK, are accessible to the public after 100 years (Hakim, 1982).

Data can also be compiled for the same population over time using a series of 'snap shots' to form *cohort studies*. Such studies are relatively rare due to the difficulty of maintaining contact with members of the cohort from year to year. An example is the television series *Seven Up* (already mentioned in Section 4.2) which has followed a cohort since they were school children at seven-year intervals for over 40 years.

Secondary data from different sources can also be combined if they have the same geographical basis to form *area-based* data sets (Hakim, 1982). Such data sets usually draw together quantifiable information and statistics and are commonly produced by governments for their country. Area-based multiple source data sets are usually available in published form for the countries and component standard economic planning regions. Those more widely used by our students include the UK's *Annual Abstract of Statistics* (Dennis, 1995), *Regional Trends* (Church, 1995) and the journal *Labour Market Trends*. Area-based multiple-source data sets are also available from data archives such as the ESRC Data Archive. These include data such as the Labour Force Survey (ESRC Data Archive, 1995a).

7.3 LOCATING SECONDARY DATA

Unless you are approaching your research project with the intention of analysing one specific secondary data set which you already know well, your first step will be to ascertain whether the data you need are available. This will be guided by your research question(s), objectives and the literature you have reviewed. For many research projects you are likely to be unsure as to whether the data you require are available as secondary data. Fortunately there are a number of pointers to the sorts of data that are likely to be available.

The breadth of data discussed in the previous sections only serves to emphasise the variety of possible locations in which such data may be found. Finding relevant secondary data requires detective work which has two interlinked stages:

1 Establishing that the sort of data you require are likely to be available as secondary data.

2 Locating the precise data you require.

The availability of secondary data

There are a number of clues to whether the secondary data you require are likely to be available. As part of your literature review you will have already read books and journal articles on your chosen topic. Where these have made use of secondary data, they will provide you with an idea of the sort of data that is available. In addition, these books and articles should contain full references to the sources of the data. Where these refer to published secondary data such as multiple-source or survey reports, it is usually relatively easy to track down the original source.

References for unpublished and documentary secondary data are often less specific, referring to 'unpublished survey results' or an 'in-house company survey'. Although these may be insufficient to locate or access the actual secondary data, they still provide useful clues about the sort of data that might be found within organisations and which might prove useful.

Textbooks which discuss organisational record systems such as Evans' (1991) *Computers and Personnel Systems* can provide you with valuable clues about the sort of documentary secondary data that are likely to exist within organisations.

Tertiary literature such as indexes and catalogues can also help you locate secondary data (Sections 3.2 to 3.4). Data archive catalogues, in particular the ESRC Data Archive at the University of Essex, may prove a useful source of the sorts of secondary data available.[1] This Archive holds over 5000 computer-readable social science and humanities data sets for further analysis by the research community (ESRC Data Archive, 1995b). These data have been acquired from academic, commercial and government sources and relate mainly to post-war Britain. The complete catalogue of these can be accessed via the Internet (Section 3.5) using the ESRC's home page.[2] However, it should be remembered that the supply of data and documentation for all of the Archive's data sets is charged at cost and there may be additional administrative and royalty charges.

Informal discussions are also often a useful source. Acknowledged experts, colleagues, librarians or your project adviser may well have knowledge of the sorts of data that might be available (Stewart and Kamins, 1993). In addition there are a range of published guides to secondary data sources. Five of the general and business guides which we, and our

[1] There are numerous other data archives in Europe and the USA. The ESRC has access to data held in many European archives through its membership of the Council for European Social Science Data Archive. The central repository for data archives in the USA is the Inter-university Consortium for Political and Social Research (ICPSR) at the University of Michigan. Copies of the ICPSR catalogue are obtainable from the ESRC Data Archive (ESRC Data Archive, 1995b).

[2] The Internet address for the ESRC home page is http://sosig.esrc.bris.ac.uk/esrc/esrc.html

students, have found most useful are outlined in Table 7.1. However, there are also subject-specific guides which provide more detail on sources for particular subject areas such as marketing and finance.

Guide	Coverage
Central Statistical Office (1995) *Guide to Official Statistics*, London, HMSO.	Official statistics produced by UK government.
Croner (no date) *A–Z of Business Information sources*, Kingston, Croner Publications.	Loose-leaf, regularly updated. Alphabetical list of subjects showing relevant sources including trade associations and institutional sources; UK focus.
Smith, G. (annual) (ed.) *Business Information Yearbook*, Headland, Headland Press.	Annual survey. Covers company and market information, on-line business information, and a who's who in business information.
Mort, D. (1992) *UK Statistics – A Guide for Business Users*, Aldershot, Ashgate.	Official statistics collected by UK government; unofficial statistics such as those collected by major survey organisations; who produce these data.
Mort, D. (1992) *European Market Information: A Handbook for Managers*, London, Pitman Publishing.	General unofficial and official statistical publications on a country-by-country basis; who produce these data.
ASLIB (1982) *ASLIB Directory of Information Sources in the United Kingdom – Volume 1: Science, Technology and Commerce*, London, ASLIB.	Lists specialist libraries with specific subject collections in the UK.

Table 7.1 Published guides to possible secondary data sources

Finding secondary data

Once you have ascertained that secondary data are likely to exist you need to find their precise location. For secondary data published by governments this will be relatively straightforward. Precise references are often given in published guides (Table 7.1) and, where other researchers have made use of them, a full reference should exist. Locating published secondary data which are likely to be held by libraries or secondary data held in archives is relatively straightforward. Specialist libraries with specific subject collections such as market research reports can usually be located using the *ASLIB Directory* (Table 7.1). If you are unsure where to start, confess your ignorance and ask a librarian. This will usually result in a great deal of helpful advice, as well as saving you time. Once the appropriate abstracting tool or catalogue has been located and its use demonstrated, it can be searched for using similar techniques to those employed in your literature search (Section 3.5).

Data which are held by organisations are more difficult to locate. For within-organisation data we have found that the information or data manager within the appropriate department is most likely to know the precise secondary data that are held. This is the person who will also help or hinder your eventual access to the data and can be thought of as the *gatekeeper* to the information (Section 5.3).

Data on the Internet can be located using *search tools* where you search for all possible locations that match key words associated with your research question(s) or objectives

(Section 3.5). However, although the amount of data on the Internet is increasing rapidly, much of it is, in our experience, of dubious quality. Searching for relevant data is often very time consuming. The vast majority of data are, at the time of writing, North American rather than European in focus. UK government departments in particular have included far less data than have those in the United States.

Once you have located a possible secondary data set you need to be certain that it will meet your needs. For documentary data or data in a published form, the easiest way is to obtain and evaluate a sample copy. For survey data which is available in computer-readable form, this is likely to involve some cost. One alternative is to obtain and evaluate detailed variable definitions for the data set (which include how they are coded (Section 11.2)) and the documentation which describe how the data were collected. This evaluation process is discussed in Section 7.5.

WORKED EXAMPLE: *Establishing that the secondary data you require are available*

Dunkerley (1988) undertook a three-year historical research project on the naval dockyard in the Devonport area of the City of Plymouth. The proposed research strategy used interviews with dockyard workers as well as secondary data sources, including:

- enumerators' books for population censuses from 1851;
- records relating to dockyard employment, labour relations and skills;
- Admiralty and Treasury papers;
- Poor law records;
- a sample of local newspapers.

Initially it had been assumed that these secondary data would be readily available. Unfortunately, much of the secondary data that it had been assumed were available locally had been destroyed during enemy action in the Second World War. In addition, data that still existed had been obscurely catalogued in the Public Records Office at Kew, London. This made these data difficult to find.

Although copies of enumerators' books for the population censuses were available locally, the use of census material 'proved more difficult than had been imagined' (Dunkerley, 1988: 86). Data collected differed between successive censuses. In addition, the 100-year confidentiality rule meant that the enumerators' books were not available for more recent censuses.

As a consequence of these and other problems, a rethink of the aims and methods of the research was undertaken before proceeding further.

7.4 ADVANTAGES AND DISADVANTAGES OF SECONDARY DATA

Advantages

May have fewer resource requirements

For many research questions and objectives the main advantage of using secondary data is the enormous saving in resources, in particular your time and money (Ghauri *et al.*, 1995). In general, it is much less expensive to use secondary data than to collect the data yourself. As a consequence, you may be able to analyse far larger data sets such as those collected by government surveys. You will also have more time to think about theoretical aims and substantive issues, as your data will already be collected; and you can subsequently spend more time, and effort, analysing and interpreting the data.

Unobtrusive

If you need your data quickly, secondary data may be the only viable alternative. In addition, they are likely to provide higher quality data than could be obtained by collecting your own (Stewart and Kamins, 1993). Using secondary data within organisations may also have the advantage that, because it has already been collected, it provides an unobtrusive measure (Robson, 1993).

Longitudinal studies may be feasible

For many research projects time constraints mean that secondary data provide the only possibility of undertaking longitudinal studies. This can be done either by creating your own or by using an existing multiple-source data set (Section 7.2). Comparative research may also be possible if comparable data are available. You may find this to be of particular use for research questions and objectives which require regional or international comparisons. However, you need to ensure that the data you are comparing were collected and recorded using methods that are comparable. Comparisons relying on unpublished data, such as those from a census, are likely to be expensive as tabulations will have to be specially prepared. In addition, your research is dependent on access being granted by the owners of the data, principally governments (Dale *et al.*, 1988).

Can provide comparative and contextual data

Often it can be useful to compare data you have collected with secondary data. This means that you can place your own findings within a more general context or, alternatively, triangulate your findings (Section 4.3). If you have undertaken a sample survey, perhaps of potential customers, secondary data such as the census can be used to assess the generalisability of the findings; in other words, how representative these data are of the total population (Section 6.2).

Can result in unforeseen discoveries

Re-analysing secondary data can also lead to unforeseen or unexpected new discoveries. Dale *et al.* (1988) cite establishing the link between smoking and lung cancer as an example of such a serendipitous discovery. In this example the link was established through secondary analysis of medical records which had not been collected with the intention of exploring any such relationship.

Disadvantages

May have been collected for a purpose which does not match your need

Data which you collect yourself will be collected with a specific purpose in mind: to answer your research question(s) and meet your objectives. Unfortunately, secondary data will have been collected for a specific purpose which may not match the needs of your research question(s) or objectives (Stewart and Kamins, 1993). As a consequence, the data you are considering may be inappropriate to your research question (Table 7.1). If this is the case then you need to find an alternative source or collect the data yourself! More probably, you will only be able partially to answer your research question or address your objectives. A common reason for this is that the data were collected a few years earlier and so are not current. Where this is the case, such as in a research project which is examining an issue within an organisation, you are likely to have to combine secondary and primary data.

Access may be difficult or costly

Where data have been collected for commercial reasons, gaining access may be difficult or costly. Market research reports, such as those produced by Mintel or Keynote, may cost hundreds of pounds. If the report you require is not available in your library they can rarely be borrowed on inter-library loan and you will need to identify (Section 7.3) and visit the library that holds that collection.

Aggregations and definitions may be unsuitable

The fact that secondary data were collected for a particular purpose may result in other, including ethical (Section 5.4), problems. Much of the secondary data you use are likely to be in published reports. As part of the compilation process, data will have been aggregated in some way. These aggregations, while meeting the requirements of the original research, may not be quite so suitable for your research. The definitions of data variables may not be the most appropriate for your research question(s) or objectives. In addition, where you are intending to combine data sets, definitions may differ markedly or have been revised over time.

· ·

WORKED EXAMPLE: *Changing definitions*

A report in *Labour Market Trends* (Fenwick and Denman, 1995) details 31 changes which could have affected the comparability of the UK's monthly count of unemployment claimants between 1979 and 1994. Of these, Employment Department statisticians calculate that nine had a significant numerical impact on comparisons over time:

Date	Change	Effect on count (+ increase, – decrease)
October 1979	Weekly attendance for registration replaced by fortnightly attendance.	+20 000
November 1981	Older men who received long-term rate of supplementary benefit no longer required to sign as available for work.	–37 000
October 1982	Basis of count altered from registering unemployed to claiming benefits.	–190 000
April 1983*	Men aged 60+ no longer required to sign on to receive national insurance credits.	–108 000
June 1983*	Men aged 60+ who received long-term rate of supplementary benefit no longer required to sign on.	–54 000
July 1985	Corrective action due to discrepancies in figures for Northern Ireland.	–5 000
March 1986	Compilation and publication of figures delayed to correct for previous over-recording.	–50 000
September 1988	16- and 17-year-old people no longer entitled to unemployment benefit.	–40 000
July 1989	Men covered by Redundant Mineworkers Scheme no longer required to sign on.	–15 500
February 1994	Northern Ireland benefits system fully integrated with rest of UK.	–1500

Source: Labour Market Trends 1995, *Office for National Statistics. Crown Copyright 1995. Reproduced by permission of the Controller of HMSO and the Office for National Statistics.*

*Fenwick and Denman (1995) argue that these should be treated as one change as both are the effect of the 1983 budget.

Initial purpose may affect how data are presented

When using data which are presented as part of a report, you also need to be aware of the purpose of that report and the impact that this will have on the way the data are presented. This is especially so for internal organisational documents and external documents such as published company reports and newspaper reports. Reichman (1962, cited by Stewart and Kamins, 1993) emphasises this point referring to newspapers, although the sentiments apply to many documents. He argues that newspapers select what they consider to be the most significant points and emphasise these at the expense of supporting data. This, Reichman states, is not a criticism, as the purpose of the reporting is to bring these points to the attention of readers rather than provide a full and detailed account. For these reasons you must carefully evaluate any secondary data you intend to use. Possible ways of doing this are discussed in the next section (7.5).

7.5 EVALUATING SECONDARY DATA SOURCES

Secondary data must be viewed with the same caution as any primary data you collect. You need to be sure that:

- it will enable you to answer your research question(s) and meet your objectives;
- the benefits associated with its use will be greater than the costs;
- you will be allowed access to the data (Section 5.3).

Secondary sources which appear relevant at first may on closer examination not be appropriate to your research question(s) or objectives. It is therefore important to evaluate the suitability of secondary data sources for your research.

Stewart and Kamins (1993) argue that, if you are using secondary data, you are at an advantage compared to researchers using primary data. Because the data already exist you can evaluate them prior to use. The time you spend evaluating any potential secondary data source is time well spent, as rejecting unsuitable data earlier can save much wasted time later! Such investigations are even more important when you have a number of possible secondary data sources you could use. Most authors suggest a range of validity and reliability criteria (Section 4.4) against which you can evaluate potential secondary data. These, we believe, can be incorporated into a three-stage process:

1 Assess the overall suitability of the secondary data source to your research question(s) and objectives, paying particular attention to:

- measurement validity,
- coverage, including unmeasured variables.

(If you consider the data are definitely unsuitable at this stage, do not proceed with subsequent stages.)

2 Evaluate the precise suitability of the data for analyses you need to answer your research question(s) and meet your objectives, paying particular attention to:

- validity and reliability,
- measurement bias.

(If you consider the data are definitely unsuitable at this stage do not proceed with stage 3.)

3 Make a judgement as to whether to use the data based on an assessment of the costs and benefits of using these secondary data in comparison to alternative sources.

Alongside this process you also need to consider the accessibility of the secondary data. For some secondary data sources, in particular those available in your library, this will not be a problem. It may, however, necessitate long hours working in the library if the sources are 'for reference only'. For other data sources, such as those within organisations, you need to obtain permission before gaining access. This will be necessary even if you are working for the organisation. These issues are discussed in Section 5.3, so we can now consider the evaluation process in more detail.

Overall suitability

Measurement validity

One of the most important criteria for the suitability of any data set is *measurement validity*. Secondary data that fails to provide you with the information you need to answer your research question(s) or meet your objectives will result in invalid answers (Kervin, 1992). Often when you are using secondary survey data you will find that the measures used do not quite match those which you need (Jacob, 1994). For example, a manufacturing organisation may record monthly sales whereas you are interested in monthly orders. This may cause you a problem when you undertake your analyses believing you have found a relationship with sales, whereas in fact your relationship is with the number of orders. Alternatively, you may be using minutes of company meetings as a proxy for what actually happened in those meetings. Minutes of meetings can provide a summary of what happened at the meeting from the chair's viewpoint!

Unfortunately, there are no clear solutions to problems of measurement invalidity. All you can do is try to evaluate the extent of the data's validity and make your own decision. A common way of doing this is to examine how other researchers have coped with this problem for a similar secondary data set in a similar context. If they found that the measures, while not exact, were suitable, then you can be more certain that they will be suitable for your research question(s) and objectives. If they had problems then you may be able to incorporate their suggestions as to how to overcome them. Your literature search (Sections 3.4 and 3.5) will probably have identified other such studies already.

Coverage and unmeasured variables

The other important suitability criterion is *coverage*. You need to be sure that the secondary data cover the population about which you need data, for the time period you need and contains data variables which will enable you to answer your research question(s) and meet your objectives. For all secondary data sets coverage will be concerned with two issues:

- ensuring unwanted data are or can be excluded;
- ensuring that sufficient data remain for analyses to be undertaken once unwanted data have been excluded (Hakim, 1982).

When analysing secondary survey data you will need to exclude those data which are not relevant to your research question(s) or objectives. Service companies, for example, need to be excluded if you are only concerned with manufacturing companies. However, in doing this it may be that insufficient data remain to undertake the quantitative analyses you require (Sections 11.4 and 11.5). For documentary sources you will need to ensure that the data contained relates to the population identified in your research. For example, check that the minutes are of board meetings and that they cover the required time period. Where you are intending to undertake a longitudinal study, you also need to ensure that the data are available for the entire period in which you are interested.

Some secondary data sets, in particular for survey data, may not include variables you have identified as necessary for your analysis. These are termed *unmeasured variables*.

Their absence may not be particularly important if you are undertaking descriptive research. However, it could drastically affect the outcome of explanatory research as a potentially important variable has been excluded.

Precise suitability

Reliability and validity

The *reliability* and *validity* (Section 4.4) you ascribe to secondary data are a function of the method by which the data were collected and the source. You can make a quick assessment by looking at the source of the data. Survey data from large, well-known organisations, such as that found in Mintel and Keynote market research reports, are likely to be reliable. The continued existence of such organisations is dependent on the credibility of their data. As a consequence, their procedures for collecting and compiling the data are likely to be well thought through and accurate. Survey data from government organisations are also likely to be reliable for similar reasons. However, you will probably find the validity of documentary data such as organisations' records more difficult to assess. While organisations may argue that their records are reliable, there are often inconsistencies and inaccuracies. You therefore need to examine the method by which the data were collected and try to ascertain the precision needed by the original (primary) user.

For all secondary data a detailed assessment of the validity and reliability will involve you in an assessment of the method or methods used to collect the data (Dale *et al.*, 1988). These are usually discussed in the methodology section of the report. Your assessment will involve looking at who were responsible for collecting or recording the information and examining the context in which the data were collected. From this you should gain some feeling regarding the likelihood of potential errors or biases. In addition, you need to look at the process by which the data were selected and collected or recorded. Where sampling has been used to select cases (usually for surveys), the sampling procedure adopted and the associated sampling error and response rates (Section 6.2) will also give clues to validity. Secondary data collected through a survey with a high response rate are also likely to be more reliable than those with a low response rate. However, commercial providers of high-quality, reliable data sets may be unwilling to disclose details about how data were collected. This is particularly the case where these organisations see the methodology as important to their competitive advantage.

For some documentary sources, such as transcripts of interviews or meetings, it is unlikely that there will be a formal methodology describing how the data were collected. The reliability of these data will therefore be difficult to assess, although you may be able to discover the context in which the data were collected. The fact that you did not collect and were not present when these data were collected will also affect your analyses. Dale *et al.* (1988) argue that analyses of in-depth interview data require an understanding derived from participating in social interactions that cannot be fully recorded on tape or by transcript.

Validity and reliability of collection methods for survey data will be easier to assess where you have a clear explanation of the methodology used to collect the data. This needs to include a clear explanation of any sampling techniques used and response rates (discussed earlier), as well as a copy of the survey instrument which will usually be a questionnaire. By examining the questions by which data were collected you will gain a further indication of the validity.

Where data have been compiled, such as in a report, you need to pay careful attention to how these data were analysed and how the results are reported. Where percentages (or proportions) are used without actually giving the totals on which these figures are based, you need to examine the data very carefully. For example, a 50 per cent increase in the number of clients from two to three for a small company may be of less relevance than the 20 per cent increase in the number of clients from 1000 to 1200 for a larger company in the same market! Similarly, where quotations appear to be used selectively without other supporting evidence you should beware as the data may be unreliable.

WORKED EXAMPLE: *Graphical distortion of data*

One of our undergraduate students examined the use of diagrams and tables in company reports as part of her dissertation. Based on a sample of 47 companies' reports she found that 68 per cent of companies used at least one form of graph and all companies used tables.

Of considerable interest was the finding that 47 per cent of diagrams used to present key financial information had distorted the data. This was done either by overstating or understating the size of the bar or graphic that represented each value in some way. One of the more frequently used techniques, not starting the value axis at zero, is illustrated below:

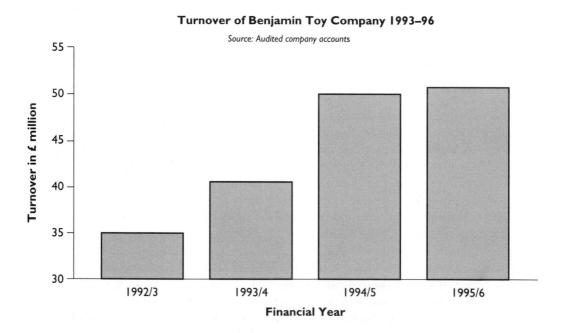

Turnover of Benjamin Toy Company 1993–96

Source: Audited company accounts

Measurement bias

Measurement bias can occur for two reasons (Kervin, 1992):

- deliberate or intentional distortion of data;
- changes in the way data are collected.

Deliberate distortion occurs when data are recorded inaccurately on purpose and is most common for secondary data sources such as organisational records. Managers may deliberately fail to record minor accidents so as to improve safety reports for their departments. Data which have been collected to further a particular cause or the interests of a particular group are more likely to be suspect, as the purpose of the study may be to reach a pre-determined conclusion (Jacob, 1994). Reports of consumer satisfaction surveys may deliberately play down negative comments so as to make the service appear better to their target audience of senior managers and shareholders.

Other distortion may be deliberate but not intended for any advantage. Employees keeping time diaries may only record the approximate time spent on their main duties rather than accounting precisely for every minute. People responding to a structured interview (questionnaire) may adjust their responses to please the interviewer (Section 10.2).

Unfortunately, measurement bias resulting from deliberate distortion is difficult to detect. While you should adopt a neutral stance about the possibility of bias, you still need to look for pressures on the original source which might have biased the data. For written documents, such as minutes, reports and memos, the intended target audience may suggest possible bias as indicated earlier in this section. Therefore, where possible you will need to triangulate the findings with other data sources. Where data from two or more independent sources suggest similar conclusions you can have more confidence that the data on which they are based are not distorted. Conversely, where data suggest different conclusions you need to be more wary of the results.

Changes in the way in which data were collected can also introduce changes in measurement bias. Provided that the method of collecting data remains constant in terms of the people collecting it and the procedures used, the measurement biases should remain constant. Once the method is altered, perhaps through a new procedure of taking minutes or a new data collection form, then the bias also changes. This is very important for longitudinal data sets such as the UK's Retail Price Index where you are interested in trends rather than actual numbers. Your detection of biases is dependent on discovering that the way data are recorded has changed. Within-company sources are less likely to have documented these changes than government-sponsored sources.

- -

WORKED EXAMPLE: *Assessing the suitability of published data*

As part of your research project you wish to establish how the cost of living has altered over the last 15 years for low to medium income households. Other research which you have read as part of your literature review has utilised the UK Central Statistical Office's (CSO) Retail Prices Index. Searching through the 1994 edition of *Economic Trends* (CSO, 1994) you come across Table 2.1 – Prices. You decide to assess the suitability of this data, an extract from which follows:

Year	General Index of Retail Prices[2]	
	All items	**Total food**
1980	70.7	76.1
1981	79.1	82.5
1982	85.9	89.0
1983	89.8	91.8
1984	94.3	97.0
1985	100.0	100.0
1986	103.4	103.3
1987	107.7	106.4
1988	113.0	110.1
1989	121.8	116.4
1990	133.3	125.7
1991	141.1	132.2
1992	146.4	135.0

Extract from Table 2.1 – Prices

Source: Economic Trends 1994, *Office for National Statistics. Crown Copyright 1994. Reproduced by permission of the Controller of HMSO and the Office for National Statistics.*

[2] The index numbers given here are for comparative purposes only and should not be regarded as accurate to the last digit shown. The official Retail Prices Index is shown in Table 2.2.

Initial examination of the data's overall suitability reveals two problems:

■ The data refers to the General Index of Retail Prices rather than the Retail Prices Index. This means that it may not be the precise data referred to in the literature. The note (2) confirms that the data do not meet your requirements, and directs you to Table 2.2.

■ The data are not sufficiently up to date, 1992 being the most recent year.

For these reasons you decide not to use the data in this table but consult the equivalent of Table 2.2 in a more recent edition.

Examination of the appendices in the more recent edition provides you with detail about how the Retail Prices Index is calculated. The data source is credible, having been compiled by the UK government's Central Statistical Office. However, the appendix states that changes in prices are measured with the exception of certain higher-income households. You conclude that the index is therefore suitable for low to medium income households.

In addition, the methodology for calculating the index is clearly described and suggests that it will be precisely suitable. The one problem you have is that the appendix states that the data measure changes in prices and are not a cost-of-living index. However, because other researchers have shown that the Retail Price Index provides a reasonable surrogate for cost of living, you decide to use the data from the more recent edition.

Overall suitability:

☑ Does the data set contain the information you require to answer your research question(s) and meet your objectives?

☑ Do the measures used match those you require?

☑ Is the data set a proxy for the data you really need?

☑ Does the data set cover the population which is the subject of your research?

☑ Can data about the population which is the subject of your research be separated from unwanted data?

☑ Are the data sufficiently up to date?

☑ Are data available for all the variables you require to answer your research question(s) and meet your objectives?

Precise suitability:

☑ How reliable is the data set you are thinking of using?

☑ How credible is the data source?

☑ Is the methodology clearly described?

    ☑ If sampling was used what was the procedure and what were the associated sampling errors and response rates?

    ☑ Who were responsible for collecting or recording the data?

    ☑ (For surveys) is a copy of the questionnaire or interview checklist included?

    ☑ (For compiled data) are you clear how the data were analysed and compiled?

☑ Are the data likely to contain measurement bias?

    ☑ What was the original purpose for which the data were collected?

    ☑ Who were the target audience and what was their relationship to the data collector or compiler?

    ☑ Have there been any documented changes in the way the data are measured or recorded, including definition changes?

    ☑ How consistent are the data obtained from this source when compared with data from other sources?

☑ Are you happy that the data have been recorded accurately?

Costs and benefits:

☑ What are the financial and time costs of obtaining these data?

☑ Have the data already been entered into a computer?

☑ Do the overall benefits of using this secondary data source outweigh the associated costs?

Table 7.2 Checklist to evaluate secondary data sources
Sources: Authors' experience; Dale et al., 1988; Jacob, 1994; Kervin, 1992; Stewart and Kamins, 1993

Costs and benefits

Kervin (1992) argues that the final criterion for assessing secondary data is a comparison of the costs of acquiring them with the benefits they will bring. Costs include both time and the financial resources you will need to devote to obtaining the data. Some data will be available in your local library and so will be free, although you will have to pay for any photocopying you need. Other data will require lengthy negotiations before access is granted (Section 5.3). Even then the granting of access may not be certain (Stewart and Kamins, 1993). Data from market research companies or special tabulations from government surveys will have to be ordered and will normally be charged for; as a consequence these will be relatively costly.

Benefits from data can be assessed in terms of the extent to which they will enable you to answer your research question(s) and meet your objectives. You will be able to form a judgement on the benefits from your assessment of the data set's overall and precise suitability (discussed earlier in this section). This assessment is summarised as a checklist of questions in Table 7.2. An important additional benefit is the form in which you receive the data. If the data are already in computer-readable form this will save you considerable time, as you will not need to re-enter the data before analysis (Sections 11.2 and 12.8). However, when assessing the costs and benefits you must remember that data which are not completely reliable and contain some bias are better than no data at all, if they enable you to start to answer your research question(s) and achieve your objectives.

7.6 SUMMARY

- Data that have already been collected for some other purpose, perhaps processed and subsequently stored, are termed secondary data. There are three main types of secondary data: documentary, survey and those from multiple sources.

- Most research projects require some combination of secondary and primary data to answer your research question(s) and meet your objectives. You can use secondary data in a variety of ways. These include:
  - to provide your main data set;
  - to provide longitudinal (time-series) data;
  - to provide area-based data;
  - to compare with, or set in context, your own research findings.

- Any secondary data you use will have been collected for a specific purpose. This purpose may not match that of your research. In addition, the secondary data are likely to be less current than any data you collect yourself.

- Finding the secondary data you require is a matter of detective work. This will involve you in:
  - establishing if the sort of data you require are likely to be available;
  - locating the precise data.

- Once located you must assess secondary data sources to ensure their overall suitability for your research question(s) and objectives. In particular, you need to pay attention to the measurement validity and coverage of the data.

- You must also evaluate the precise suitability of the secondary data. Your evaluation should include both reliability and any likely measurement bias. You can then make a judgement on the basis of the costs and benefits of using the data in comparison to alternative sources.

- When assessing costs and benefits you need to be mindful that secondary data which are not completely reliable and contain some bias are better than no data at all if they enable you partially to answer your research question(s) and meet your objectives.

Self-check questions and assignment

Self-check question 7.1
Give three examples of different situations where you might use secondary data as part of your research.

Self-check question 7.2
You are undertaking a research project as part of your course. Your initial research question is: 'How has the UK's import and export trade with other countries altered since its entry into the European Union?'

List the arguments that you would use to convince someone of the suitability of using secondary data to answer this research question.

Self-check question 7.3
Suggest possible secondary data that would help you answer the following research questions. How would you locate these secondary data?

a To what extent do organisations' employee relocation policies meet the needs of employees?

b How have consumer spending patterns in the UK altered in the last 10 years?

c How have governments' attitudes to the public sector altered since 1979?

Self-check question 7.4
As part of case-study research based in a manufacturing company with over 500 customers, you have been given access to an internal market research report. This was undertaken by the company's marketing department. The report presents the results of a recent customer survey as percentages. The section in the report which describes how the data were collected and analysed is reproduced below:

'Data were collected from a sample of current customers selected from our customer database. The data were collected using a telephone questionnaire administered by marketing department staff. 25 customers responded resulting in a 12.5% response rate. These data were analysed using the SNAP

```
computer software. Additional qualitative data based on in-
depth interviews with customers were also included.'
```

a Do you consider these data are likely to be reliable?

b Give reasons for your answer.

Assignment 7:
Assessing the suitability of secondary data for your research

● Consider your research question(s) and objectives. Decide whether you need to use secondary data or a combination of primary and secondary data to answer your question. (If you decide that you need only to use secondary data and you are undertaking this research as part of a course of study, check your course's examination regulations to ensure that this is permissible.)

● If you decide that you need to use secondary data, make sure that you are clear why and how you intend to use these data.

● Locate the secondary data you require and make sure that permission for them to be used for your research is likely to be granted. Evaluate the suitability of the data for answering your research question and make your judgement based on assessment of their suitability, other benefits and the associated costs.

● Note down the reasons for your choices, including the possibilities and limitations of the data. You will need to justify your choices when you write your research methodology.

References

Barrow, M. (1995) *The Times 1000 1996*, London, Times Books.

Bryman, A. (1989) *Research Methods and Organisation Studies*, London, Unwin Hyman.

Central Statistical Office (1994) *Economic Trends Annual Supplement 1994 edition*, London, HMSO.

Church, J. (1995) (ed.) *Regional Trends 30*, London, HMSO.

Dale, A., Arber, S. and Proctor, M. (1988) *Doing Secondary Analysis*, London, Unwin Hyman.

Dennis, G. (1995) (ed.) *Annual Abstract of Statistics 1995*, London, HMSO.

Dunkerley, D. (1988) 'Historical Methods and Organizational Analysis', in Bryman, A. (ed.) *Doing Research in Organisations*, London, Routledge, pp. 82–95.

ESRC Data Archive (1995a) *ESRC Data Archive Abbreviated Catalogue*, Colchester, ESRC Data Archive.

ESRC Data Archive (1995b) *The ESRC Data Archive: Sharing and Preserving Research Data*, Colchester, ESRC Data Archive.

Evans, A. (1991) *Computers and Personnel Systems: A Practical Guide,* London, Institute of Personnel Management.

Fenwick, D. and Denman, J. (1995) 'The Monthly Claimant Unemployment Count: Change and Consistency' *Labour Market Trends*, November, 397–400.

Foster, K., Jackson B., Thomas, M., Hunter, P. and Bennett, N. (1995) *General Household Survey 1993*, London, HMSO.

Ghauri, P., Grønhaugh, K. and Kristianslund, I. (1995) *Research Methods in Business Studies: A Practical Guide*, London, Prentice Hall.

Hakim, C. (1982) *Secondary Analysis in Social Research*, London, Allen & Unwin.

Jacob, H. (1994) 'Using Published Data: Errors and Remedies', in Lewis-Beck, M.S. *Research Practice*, London, Sage and Toppan Publishing, pp. 339–89.

Kervin, J.B. (1992) *Methods for Business Research*, New York, HarperCollins.

King, J. (1995) (ed.) *Family Spending – a report on the 1994–95 Family Expenditure Survey*, London, HMSO.

Marsh, C. (1993) 'An Overview', in Dale, A. and Marsh, C. (eds.) *The 1991 Census User's Guide*, London, HMSO, pp. 1–15.

Mort, D. (1992) *UK Statistics – a guide for Business Users*, Aldershot, Ashgate.

Office of Population Censuses and Surveys (1994) *International Migration 1992*, London, HMSO.

Reichman, C.S. (1962) *Use and Abuse of Statistics*, New York, Oxford University Press.

Robson, C. (1993) *Real World Research*, Oxford, Blackwell.

Stewart, D.W. and Kamins, M.A. (1993) *Secondary Research: Information Sources and Methods* (2nd edn), Newbury Park, California, Sage.

Thomas, P. and Smith, K. (1995) 'Results of the 1993 Census of Employment', *Employment Gazette*, October, 369–77.

Further reading

Bryman, A. (1989) *Research Methods and Organisation Studies*, London, Unwin Hyman. Chapter 9 contains a good discussion with a series of examples of how archival research and secondary analysis of survey data have been used in management and business research.

Dale, A., Arber, S. and Proctor, M. (1988) *Doing Secondary Analysis*, London, Unwin Hyman. This includes useful discussions on the benefits and costs of using secondary data (Chapter 3) and how to choose and order a secondary data set using the ESRC Data Archive as an example (Chapter 5).

Dunkerley, D. (1988) 'Historical Methods and Organizational Analysis', in Bryman, A. (ed.) *Doing Research in Organisations*, London, Routledge, pp. 82–95. This provides an open and honest account of the realities of doing historical research on an organisation using secondary data.

Hakim, C. (1982) *Secondary Analysis in Social Research*, London, Allen & Unwin. Although published in 1982, this still contains a wealth of useful information on UK-based census and survey data sets.

Stewart, D.W. and Kamins, M.A. (1993) *Secondary Research: Information Sources and Methods* (2nd edn), Newbury Park, California, Sage. This provides a good discussion on the evaluation of secondary data (Chapter 2). It also provides a wealth of information on US government and non-government data sets and their acquisition.

Case 7:
The involvement of auditors in preliminary profit announcements

Each year UK companies publish and issue an annual report and audited accounts which are sent to numerous shareholders and other users. The process may take as long as three months from the end of the company's accounting period. This delay could create problems: investors would be without up-to-date information and the probability of insider trading is therefore increased the longer the delay between the data being prepared and the accounts being published.

For these two reasons the London Stock Exchange requires listed companies to issue preliminary profit announcements or 'Prelims'. Prelims are brief (usually only about four pages long) announcements, made by companies to the financial markets, giving estimates of the financial performance of the company during the year, and should, in principle at least, represent a summary of the information to be included in the subsequent full annual report and accounts.

Tony and Jim had a good knowledge of the literature. Previous research had shown that the release of prelims had a significant impact on the share price of a company and that stock market analysts ranked prelims as their most important source of information. Yet despite this, prelims were relatively lightly regulated by the stock market.

They hypothesised that the content of prelims was more likely to differ from that in the annual accounts the greater the period between the time that they were released and the publication of the annual accounts. A large sample survey of current company practice was therefore planned.

Companies have to issue their prelims through the Stock Exchange Regulatory News Service (RNS) which controls the dissemination of price-sensitive information to the financial markets. Many large financial institutions have on-line real-time access to the RNS. Using a contact in one of these companies, Tony and Jim were able to negotiate (for a nominal fee) access to an RNS terminal for a few days. This enabled them to collect the relevant data on their sample of prelims. Luckily the RNS system allows users to print out the various data, so they were also able to obtain hard copies which they could take away and analyse later. Data were collected on the release dates of 178 Prelims and copies of 166 of these were obtained. Unfortunately, it was only possible to obtain the corresponding subsequent annual report and audited accounts for 148 of these companies. Data were then compared between the 148 prelims and their related full annual reports (which were issued subsequently) and differences in financial data noted, as well as the time lag between the prelims being released and the accounts being published

In collecting the data, Tony and Jim were interested in the fact that some companies specifically mentioned that their prelims had been issued after the audit of the full accounts had been completed and others did not. In practice, most companies made no mention of the audit. A substantial minority said the audit had not been completed and 32 per cent said that it had been finished and that the auditors had signed their audit report.

Tony and Jim were aware of several reports which discussed the issues involved with prelims and made recommendations for improving their regulation. These reports actually asserted that when the majority of prelims were released, the audit of the accounts was incomplete. These reports also suggested that some companies were disclosing that they were releasing their prelims after the final audit had been completed. Tony and Jim knew that these assumptions could be tested. If it was found that these reports were based on incorrect assumptions, this could significantly undermine the validity of many of the recommendations they were making.

They decided to re-examine the data to see if they could find more specific evidence about the extent to which prelims were audited. Even though the prelims contained very little mention of the audit, the associated (and subsequent) full annual report and accounts included the date on which the audit had been signed off. This represented the end of the audit work. Since they already had the date of the release of the prelims, they simply had to go back and compare this date with the date the audit report was signed.

They found that the majority (56 per cent) of prelims had been issued after the audit report had been signed. This appeared to be fairly strong evidence that the assumption that the audit of the accounts was incomplete when the majority of prelims were released was not correct.

Case-study questions

1 a Identify data sources used by Tony and Jim in this research.

   b Which of these are secondary data and which are primary data?

   c Give reasons for your answers.

2 a What other methods (if any) do you think Tony and Jim could have used to obtain the data they needed to test their hypothesis?

   b Give reasons for your answer.

3 What were the problems faced by Tony and Jim in using these secondary data?

4 What lessons can you learn from Tony's and Jim's experience?

Answers to self-check questions

Self-check question 7.1

Although it would be impossible to list all possible situations, the key features which should appear in your examples are listed below:

- to compare findings from your primary data;
- to place findings from your primary data in a wider context;
- to triangulate findings from other data sources;

- to provide the main data set where you wish to undertake research over a long time period, undertake historical research or undertake comparative research on a national or international scale with limited resources.

Self-check question 7.2

The arguments you have listed should focus on the following issues:

- The study suggested by the research question requires historical data so that changes which have already happened can be explored. These data will, by definition, already have been collected.

- The timescale of the research (if part of a course) will be relatively short term. One solution for longitudinal studies in a short timeframe is to use secondary data.

- The research question suggests an international comparative study. Given your likely limited resources, secondary data will provide the only feasible data sources.

Self-check question 7.3

a The secondary data required for this research question relate to organisations' employee relocation policies. The research question assumes that these sorts of data are likely to be available from organisations. Textbooks, research papers and informal discussions would enable you to confirm that these data were likely to be available. Informal discussions with individuals responsible for the personnel function in organisations would also confirm the existence and availability for research of such data.

b The secondary data required for this research question relate to consumer spending patterns in the UK. As these appear to be the sort of data in which the government would be interested, they may well be available in published form. Examination of various published guides (both governmental and non-governmental sources) would reveal that these data were collected by the annual Family Expenditure Survey and Summary, results of which are published (for example King, 1995). These reports could then be borrowed either from your library or by using inter-library loan. In addition, the ESRC Data Archive Catalogue could be searched. This would reveal that data from the survey had been deposited with the archive.

c The secondary data required for this research question are less clear. What you require is some source from which you can infer past and present government attitudes. Transcripts of ministers' speeches (such as in *Hansard*) and newspaper reports might prove useful. However, to establish suitable secondary sources for this research question you would need to pay careful attention to those used by other researchers. These would be outlined in research papers and textbooks. Informal discussions could also prove useful.

Self-check question 7.4

a The data are unlikely to be reliable.

b Your judgement should be based on a combination of the following reasons:

- Initial examination of the report reveals that it is an internally conducted survey. As this has been undertaken by the marketing department of a large manufacturing company, you might assume that those undertaking the research had considerable expertise. As a consequence you might conclude that the report contains credible data. However, you need to take account of the following:

- The methodology is not clearly described, in particular:
  - the sampling procedure and associated sampling errors are not given;
  - it does not appear to contain a copy of the questionnaire, which means that it is impossible to check for bias in the way questions were worded;
  - the methodology for the qualitative in-depth interviews is not described.
- In addition, the information provided in the methodology suggests that the data may be unreliable:
  - the reported response rate of 12.5 per cent is very low for a telephone survey (Section 6.2);
  - responses from 25 people mean that all tables and statistical analyses in the report are based on a maximum of 25 people. This is may be too few for reliable results (Sections 6.2 and 11.5).

CHAPTER 8

Collecting primary data through observation

The objectives of this chapter are to introduce you to observation as a data collection method. This will help you decide whether observation can play a part in your research design.

The chapter examines two types of observation: participant observation and structured observation. The differing origins and applications of both are considered, together with some practical advice on data collection and analysis for both types.

Particular attention is given to the threats to validity and reliability faced by the two types of observation.

8.1 INTRODUCTION TO OBSERVATION

If your research question(s) and objectives are concerned with what people do, an obvious way in which to discover this is to watch them do it. This is essentially what observation involves: the systematic observation, recording, description, analysis and interpretation of people's behaviour.

The two types of observation examined in this chapter are very different. *Participant observation* is qualitative and derives from the work of social anthropology early in the twentieth century. Its emphasis is on discovering the meanings which people attach to their actions. By contrast, *structured observation* is quantitative and is more concerned with the frequency of those actions.

A common theme in this book is our effort to discourage you from thinking of the various research methods as the sole means which you should employ in your study. This is also true of observation methods. It may meet the demands of your research question(s) and objectives to use both participant and structured observation in your study, either as the main methods of data collection or to supplement other methods.

8.2 PARTICIPANT OBSERVATION: AN INTRODUCTION

What is participant observation?

If you have studied sociology or anthropology in the past you are certain to be familiar with *participant observation*. This is where 'the researcher attempts to participate fully in the lives and activities of subjects and thus becomes a member of their group, organisation or community. This enables the researcher to share their experiences by not merely observing what is happening but also feeling it' (Gill and Johnson, 1991: 109). It has been used extensively in these disciplines to attempt to get the root of 'what is going on' in a wide range of social settings.

Participant observation has its roots in social anthropology, but it was the Chicago school of social research that encouraged its students to study by observation the constantly changing social phenomena of Chicago in the 1920s and 1930s.

Participant observation has been used much less in management and business research. However, this does not mean to say that it has limited value for management and business researchers. Indeed, it can be a very valuable tool, usually as the principal research method, but possibly in combination with other methods.

Delbridge and Kirkpatrick (1994: 37) note that participant observation implies a research strategy of '*immersion* [by the researcher] in the research setting, with the objective of sharing in people's lives while attempting to learn their symbolic world'. It is worth dwelling on this explanation. Whichever role you adopt as the participant observer (the choices open to you will be discussed later), there will be a high level of immersion. This is quite different to data collection by means of questionnaire, where you probably will know little of the context in which the respondents' comments are set or the delicate nuances of meaning with which the respondents garnish their responses. In participant observation the purpose is to discover those delicate nuances of meaning. As Delbridge and Kirkpatrick (1994: 39) state: 'in the social sciences we cannot hope to adequately explain the behaviour of social actors unless we at least try to understand their meanings'.

This last comment gives a clue to the point Delbridge and Kirkpatrick make about 'attempting to learn the [respondent's] symbolic world'. Some understanding of this point is vital if you are to convince yourself and others of the value of using participant observation.

The symbolic frame of reference is located with the school of sociology known as *symbolic interactionism*. In symbolic interactionism the individual derives a sense of identity from interaction and communication with others. Through this process of interaction and communication individuals respond to others and adjust their understandings and behaviour as they 'negotiate' a shared sense of order and reality with others. Central to this process is the notion that people continually change in the light of the social circumstances in which they find themselves. The transition from full-time student to career employee is one example of this. (How often have you heard people say, 'they're so different since they've worked at that new place'?) The individual's sense of identity is constantly being constructed and reconstructed as he or she moves through differing social contexts and encounters different situations and different people.

This is a necessarily brief explanation of symbolic interactionism. But we hope you can see why Delbridge and Kirkpatrick (1994: 37) think participant observation is about 'attempting to learn the [respondent's] symbolic world'. It is a quest for understanding the identity of the individual but, more importantly, it is about trying to get to the bottom of the processes by which individuals constantly construct and reconstruct their identity.

WORKED EXAMPLE: *Discovering the meanings respondents convey in their responses*

The head office of a large company operating in a town with a world-famous horse-racing festival was plagued annually by some of the more junior staff going sick at the time of the festival. Over the years there had been attempts to cure the problem by 'making examples' of particular employees. But nothing had succeeded. It seemed that the absentees always had a valid reason for their absence. Yet managers were convinced that many absentees attended the horse-racing festival.

Sarah was intrigued to discover why this phenomenon was occurring. Discovering the answer to this research question would heighten considerably Sarah's knowledge and understanding of employee absenteeism.

Answering the research question entailed Sarah working in the sections which were staffed mainly by junior employees. Sarah needed to 'become one of them' (as far as it was possible to do this). She needed to immerse herself in the social context of the junior employees' work.

A period of immersion as the participant observer enabled Sarah to unravel the complicated social processes by which junior staff 'negotiated' with one another to cover the work of absentees. Sarah also learned that staff consider taking time off work as a 'legitimate perk'. Often in their past, schools, colleges and employers had 'turned a blind eye' to this practice.

N.B. It may have occurred to you that this example may be thought of as ethically rather dubious research. The ethical implications of participant observation are discussed in Section 8.3.

Situations in which participant observation has been used

One of the most famous examples of participant observation is that of Whyte (1955) who lived among a poor Italian-American community in order to understand 'street corner society'. A celebrated business example is the work of Roy (1952). Roy worked in a machine shop for ten months as an employee. He wanted to understand how and why his 'fellow workers' operated the piece-work bonus system. Rather more colourfully, Rosen (1991) worked as a participant observer in a Philadelphia advertising agency. Rosen was working within the theoretical domain of dramaturgy. He wanted to understand how organisations used social drama to create and sustain power relationships and social structures.

These may strike you as rather elaborate examples which suggest little relevance to you as you contemplate your own research project. Yet this would be a disappointing conclusion. You may already be a member of an organisation which promises a fertile territory for research. This may be your employing organisation or a social body of which you are a member. One of Phil's students undertook research in his church community. He was a member of the church council and conducted observational research on the way in which decisions were reached in council meetings. A more specific focus was adopted by another of our students. She was a member of a school governing body. Her specific hypothesis was that the head teacher possessed the decision-making power. Her study confirmed this hypothesis. All the significant decisions were in effect taken prior to governors' meetings as a consequence of the head teacher canvassing the support of those committee members whom he defined as 'influential'.

So, adopting the participant observer role as an existing member of an organisation does present opportunities to you. But it also has its dangers. We will deal with these later.

8.3 PARTICIPANT OBSERVATION: RESEARCHER ROLES

We have explained what participant observation is, but we have not explained clearly what participant observers do. A number of questions may have occurred to you. For example, should the participant observer keep their purpose concealed? Does the participant observer need to be an employee or an organisational member, albeit temporarily? Can the participant observer just observe? The answers here are not straightforward. The role you play as participant observer will be determined by a number of factors. But before examining those factors, we need to look at the different roles in which the participant observer may be cast.

Gill and Johnson (1991) develop a fourfold categorisation of the role the participant observer can adopt. The roles are:

- complete participant;
- complete observer;
- observer as participant;
- participant as observer.

The first two of these roles – complete participant and complete observer – involve you, as the researcher, in concealing your identity. This has the significant advantage of you not conditioning the behaviour of the research subjects you are studying. The second two – observer as participant and participant as observer – entail you revealing your purpose to those with whom you are mixing in the research setting. Ethically, the latter two roles are less problematic.

Complete participant

The *complete participant* role sees you as the researcher attempting to become a member of the group in which you are performing research. You do not reveal your true purpose to the group members. You may be able to justify this role on pure research grounds in the light of your research question(s) and objectives. For example, you may be interested to know the extent of lunchtime drinking in a particular work setting. You would probably be keen to discover which particular employees drink at lunchtimes, what they drink and how much they drink, and how they explain their drinking. Were you to explain your research objectives to the group you wished to study it's rather unlikely that they would co-operate, since lunchtime drinking would usually be discouraged by employers. In addition, they may see your research activity as prying.

This example raises questions of ethics. You are in a position where you are 'spying' on people who have probably become your friends as well as colleagues. They may have learned to trust you with information which they would not share were they to know your true purpose. On these grounds alone you may agree with us that this is a role which the researcher should not adopt.

There are also objections on pure research grounds. You may work so hard at gaining the trust of your 'colleagues' and value that trust when it is gained that you lose sight of your research purpose. The objective, detached perspective that all researchers need will be lost.

Complete observer

Here too you would not reveal the purpose of your activity to those you were observing. But, unlike the complete participant role, you do not take part in the activities of the group. For example, the *complete observer* role may be used in studying consumer behaviour in supermarkets. Your research question may concern your wish to observe consumers at the checkout. Which checkouts do they choose? How much interaction is there with fellow shoppers and the cashier? How do they appear to be influenced by the attitude of the cashier? What level of impatience is displayed when delays are experienced? This behaviour may be observed by the researcher being located near the checkout in an unobtrusive way. The patterns of behaviour displayed may be the precursor to research by structured observation (Section 8.5). This would be the exploratory stage of this research.

Observer as participant

You may adopt the role of *observer as participant* in an outward-bound course to assist team building if you were attending to observe without taking part in the activities in the same way as the 'real' candidates. In other words, you would be a 'spectator'. However, your identity as a researcher would be clear to all concerned. They would know your purpose, as would the trainers running the course. This would present the advantage of you being able to focus on your researcher role. For example, you would be able to jot down insights as they occurred to you. You would be able to concentrate on your discussions with the participants. What you would lose, of course, would be the emotional involvement: really knowing what it feels like to be on the receiving end of the experience.

Participant as observer

In the role of *participant as observer* you reveal your purpose as a researcher. Both you and the subjects are aware of the fact that it is a fieldwork relationship (Ackroyd and Hughes, 1992). You are particularly interested to gain the trust of the group. This was the role adopted by the sociologist Punch (1993) in his study of police work in Amsterdam. Because of the trust developed by Punch with police officers whom he was researching, he was able to gain admission to activities which otherwise would have been 'out of bounds' to him. Because his identity as researcher was clear he could ask questions of his subjects to enhance his understanding. Robson (1993: 197) argues that this leads to another advantage of this role. This is that key informants are likely to adopt a perspective of *analytic reflection* on the processes in which they are involved.

WORKED EXAMPLE: *Adopting the participant as observer role*

Your research project is concerned with you wishing to understand what the experience of a one-day assessment centre is like for the graduates who attend these as prospective employees.

You decide that there is no better way of doing this than 'getting in on the action' and being a guinea pig. You negotiate access with the company managers who are running the assessment centre. You also explain your research to the graduates who are there 'for real'. You become involved in all the activities and speak to as many of your fellow graduates as possible in order to discover their feelings about the experience. At the end of the day you are utterly exhausted!

Practitioner-researcher

This may be the participant observer role you are most likely to adopt. If you are a part-time student, or if you are undertaking research as part of your job, you will be surrounded by exciting opportunities to pursue business and management research. You are unlikely to encounter one of the most difficult hurdles which the participant observer has to overcome: that of negotiating research access. Indeed, like many people in such a position, you may be asked to research a particular problem by your employer which lends itself to this methodological approach.

Another advantage is your knowledge of the organisation and all this implies about understanding the complexity of what goes on in that organisation. It isn't necessary to spend a good deal of valuable time in 'learning the context' in the same way as the outsider does. But that advantage carries with it a significant disadvantage. You must be very conscious of the assumptions and pre-conceptions that you carry around with you. This is an inevitable consequence of knowing the organisation well. It can prevent you from exploring issues which would enrich the research.

Familiarity has other problems. When we were doing case-study work in a manufacturing company, we found it very useful to ask 'basic' questions revealing our ignorance about the industry and the organisation. These 'basic' questions are ones which as the practitioner-researcher you would be less likely to ask because you would feel that you should know the answers.

There is also the problem of status. As a junior employee you may feel that working with more senior colleagues inhibits your interactions as practitioner-researcher. The same may be true if you are more senior than your colleagues.

A more practical problem is that of time. Combining two roles at work is obviously very demanding, particularly as the participant observer role may involve you in much data recording 'after hours'. This activity is hidden from those who determine your workload. They may not appreciate the demands which your researcher role is making on you. For this reason, Robson (1993) makes much of practitioner-researchers negotiating a proportion of their 'work time' to devote to their research.

There are no easy answers to these problems. All you can do is to be aware of the threats to the quality of your data by being too close to your research setting. But it is a problem which besets much participant observer research. As will now be obvious to you, all methods have their strengths and weaknesses.

Factors which will determine the choice of participant observer role

The purpose of your research

You should always be guided by the appropriateness of the method for the research question(s) and objectives. A research question about developing an understanding of a phenomenon about which the research subjects would be naturally defensive is one that lends itself to the complete participant role. Discovering what it is like to be a participant on a particular training course is more appropriate to the participant as observer role.

The time you have to devote to your research

Some of the roles covered above may be very time consuming. If you are to develop a rich and deep understanding of an organisational phenomenon it will need much careful study. A period of attachment to the organisation will often be necessary. But many full-time courses have placement opportunities which may be used for this purpose. In addition, most full-time students now have part-time jobs which provide wonderful opportunities to understand the 'meanings' which their fellow employees, for whom the work is their main occupation, attach to a variety of organisational processes. What is needed is a creative perspective on what constitutes research and research opportunities. The possibilities are endless.

The degree to which you feel suited to participant observation

Delbridge and Kirkpatrick (1994) note that not everybody is suited to this type of research. Much of it relies on the building of relationships with others. A certain amount of personal flexibility is also needed. As the participant observer you have to be 'all things to all people'. Your own personality must be suppressed to a great extent. This is not something with which you may feel comfortable.

Organisational access

This may present a problem for some researchers. It is obviously a key issue. More is said about gaining access to organisations for research in Section 5.3.

Ethical considerations

The degree to which you reveal your identity as the researcher will be dictated by ethical considerations. The topic of ethics in research is dealt with in detail in Section 5.4.

8.4 PARTICIPANT OBSERVATION: DATA COLLECTION AND ANALYSIS

Delbridge and Kirkpatrick (1994) categorise the types of data generated by participant observation as primary, secondary and experiential.

Primary observations are those where you would note what happened or what was said at the time. Keeping a diary is a good way of doing this.

Secondary observations are statements by observers of what happened or was said. This necessarily involves those observers' interpretations.

Experiential data are those data on your feelings and perceptions as you experience the process you are researching. Keeping a diary of these perceptions proves a valuable source of data when the time comes to write up your research. This may also include notes on how you feel your values have intervened, or changed, over the research process.

Finally, you will also collect data on factors material to the research setting, for example roles played by key participants and how these may have changed; organisational structures; communication patterns.

Data collection

What will be clear from the types of data you will collect as the participant observer is that formal set-piece interviewing is unlikely to take place. Such 'interviewing' that does take place is likely to be informal discussion. It will be part of the overall approach of asking questions which should be adopted in this research method. These questions are of two types (Robson, 1993): first, to informants to clarify the situations you have observed; and second, to yourself to clarify the situation and the accounts given of the situation.

WORKED EXAMPLE: *A diary account*

For a period of ten months between 1944 and 1945, Donald Roy worked on the factory floor as a production operative in order to study how workers restricted production. He kept a diary, an extract of which is reproduced below as an example of a narrative account (Roy, 1952: 432). The 'technical' content of the piece is irrelevant. What is important is to get a feel for a narrative account.

'On April 7 I was able to enjoy four hours of "free time".

I turned out 43 pieces in the four hours from 3 to 7, averaging nearly 11 an hour or \$2.085 per hour). At 7 o'clock there were only 23 pieces left in the lot, and I knew there would be no point in building up a kitty for Monday if Joe punched off the job before I got to work. I could not go ahead with the next order . . . because the new ruling made presentation of a work order to the stock-chaser necessary before material could be brought up. So I was stymied and could do nothing for the rest of the day. I had 43 pieces plus 11 from yesterday's kitty to turn in for a total of 54.'

Of course, the data you collect depend on your research question(s) and objectives which have given a particular focus to your observation. Robson (1993) suggests that your data may well be classed as *descriptive observation* and *narrative account*. In descriptive observation you may concentrate on observing the physical setting; the key participants and their activities; particular events and their sequence; and the attendant processes and emotions involved. This description may be the basis for your writing of a narrative account, in much the same way as an investigative journalist may write one. But Robson (1993) makes the point forcefully that the researcher must go much further than the journalist. Your job as the researcher is to go on to develop a framework or theory which will help you understand, and explain to others, what is going on in the research setting you are studying.

How you record your data will depend to a great extent on the role you play as the participant observer. The more 'open' you are the more possible it will be for you to make notes at the time the event is being observed or reported. In any event, there is one golden rule: recording must take place on the same day as the fieldwork in order that you do not forget valuable data. The importance placed on this by one complete participant observer, working in a bakery, is evident from the following quotation:

'Right from the start I found it impossible to keep everything I wanted in my head until the end of the day . . . and had to take rough notes as I was going along. But I was 'stuck on the line', and had nowhere to retire to privately to note things down. Eventually, the wheeze of using innocently provided lavatory cubicles occurred to me. Looking back, all my notes for that third summer were on Bronco toilet paper! Apart from the awkward tendency for pencilled notes to be self-erasing from hard toilet paper . . . my frequent requests for 'time out' after interesting happenings or conversations in the bakehouse and the amount of time that I was spending in the lavatory began to get noticed'

Ditton (1977), cited in Bryman (1989: 145)

Data analysis

We deal with data analysis in more depth in Chapters 11 and 12. But you should bear in mind that in participant observation research your data collection and analysis activity may be part of the same process. That is, you will be carrying out analysis and collection of data simultaneously. Let us say you were acting as the complete participant observer in attempting to establish 'what is going on' in terms of sex discrimination at the workplace in which you were researching. You would observe informal banter, hear conversations of a discriminatory nature, talk to those who approved and disapproved of the activity. All this would be part of your everyday work. You may mix socially with colleagues in situations where discriminatory attitudes and behaviour may be evident. All these events would yield data which you would record, as far as possible, on the spot, or at least write up soon afterwards. You would turn these rough notes into something rather more systematic along the lines of the procedures suggested in Section 12.4. What would be emerging is what the investigative journalist may call 'promising lines of enquiry' which you may wish to follow up in your continued observation. But remember, the journalist is interested in the story, you are interested in generating a theory to help you understand 'what is going on'. This will lead you to adopt the researcher's equivalent of 'promising lines of enquiry'. A common approach to this is what's called *analytic induction*.

- -

WORKED EXAMPLE: *Using analytic induction*

As a result of data already collected, you form an initial hypothesis that pilfering at the workplace at which you were researching was restricted to a group of employees who mixed socially outside work and they defined this as an extension of their social activities. You search for further evidence to support this hypothesis.

You find that the pilfering group included colleagues who do not mix socially, although these 'new' pilferers do define this as an extension of their own individual social activities.

You redefine your hypothesis to state that pilferers at your workplace define their workplace pilfering as an extension of their social activities, i.e. they make no distinction in this respect between work and non-work situations.

Further data collection supports this refined hypothesis.

N.B. This worked example is a simplified version of analytic induction. It only involves *one* redefinition of the hypothesis, whereas several may be involved. Moreover, an alternative to the redefining of the hypothesis is redefining the phenomenon to be explained so that the particular instance which casts doubt on the hypothesis is excluded (Denzin, 1970).

- -

Threats to reliability and validity

Gill and Johnson (1991) argue that participant observation is very high on *ecological validity* because it involves studying social phenomena in their natural contexts. Nonetheless, participant observation is subject to the same threats to validity as noted in

Section 4.4 (e.g. history and maturation), although the fact that your study is likely to be over an extended period will overcome most of these.

The greatest threat to the reliability of your research conclusions produced as a result of a participant observation study is that of *observer bias*. As Delbridge and Kirkpatrick (1994: 43) note: 'because we are part of the social world we are studying we cannot detach ourselves from it, or for that matter avoid relying on our common sense knowledge and life experiences when we try to interpret it'.

The propensity that we all have for our own perceptions to colour our interpretation of what we believe to be 'true' is well known. What we advocate here is that we cannot avoid observer bias. All we can do is to be aware of the threat to reliability it poses and seek to control it.

The first way in which this may be done is to revert to the process of asking yourself questions about your conclusions: 'Did she really mean that?' 'What other interpretations could I have put on this?' The second way is that adopted by our student who was researching decision-making power in a school governing body. Her approach was to use *informant verification*. After each of her informal discussions with fellow PTA members she wrote these up, including her own conclusions as the meanings of the discussions in the light of her research hypothesis. She then presented the written accounts to her informants for them to verify the content. Not only is this a form of *triangulation*, but it can be a source of new interpretations which have not occurred to the researcher. This method of triangulation is also one that can be used with more formal interview results.

Advantages and disadvantages of participant observation

Before leaving the subject of participant observation, we summarise some of the advantages and disadvantages of this method.

Advantages of participant observation

- It is good at explaining 'what is going on' in particular social situations.
- It heightens the researcher's awareness of significant social processes.
- It is particularly useful for researchers working within their own organisations.
- Some participant observation affords the researcher the opportunity to experience 'for real' the emotions of those who are being researched.
- Virtually all data collected are useful.

Disadvantages of participant observation

- It can be very time consuming.
- It can pose difficult ethical dilemmas for the researcher.
- There can be high levels of role conflict for the researcher (e.g. 'colleague' versus researcher).

- The closeness of the researcher to the situation being observed can lead to significant observer bias.

- The participant observer role is a very demanding one to which not all researchers will be suited.

- Access to organisations may be difficult.

- Data recording is often very difficult for the researcher.

8.5 STRUCTURED OBSERVATION: AN INTRODUCTION

So far this chapter might have given you the impression that research using observational techniques is unsystematic and unstructured. This need not be the case. A sound research design based on clear research questions and objectives using participant observation should be highly systematic. But it would be true to say that the degree of pre-determined structure in participant observation may not be that high. After all, one of the strengths of this method is its responsiveness.

In contrast, structured observation is systematic and has a high level of pre-determined structure. If you use this method in your data collection strategy you will be adopting a more detached stance. Your concern would be in quantifying behaviour. As such, structured observation may form only a part of your data collection approach, because its function is to tell you how often things happen rather than why they happen. Once again, we see that all research methods have their place in an overall research strategy. What is important is choosing the method which meets the research question(s) and objectives.

Situations in which structured observation may be used

The most powerful image which occurs to many people when they think of structured observation is that of the 'time and motion' study expert. This inscrutable figure stalked the factory floor, complete with clipboard and pencil, making notes on what tasks machine operators were performing and how long these tasks took. This may seem to you a long way from the definition of research that we have assumed in this book. Isn't it simply fact finding? Yes it is. But establishing straightforward facts may play an important role in answering your research question(s) and objectives. This is straightforward descriptive research, as Section 4.2 notes.

- -

WORKED EXAMPLE: *Using self-completion diaries*

As part of a review of staffing levels in residential homes for elderly people, Mark needed to establish:

- how much time care assistants actually spent on various caring activities;

- how the pattern of caring activities varied throughout a 24-hour day;
- how much time care assistants felt that they needed to undertake their caring activities adequately.

Ideally this would have involved structured observation of each care assistant throughout their working day. Unfortunately there were insufficient resources and so, in consultation with care assistants and their managers, a self-completion diary form was devised. In the extract below 'act.' refers to actual time spent on each activity, 'adeq.' refers to the amount of time that care assistants felt they needed to undertake their caring activities adequately.

Care Assistant's name:

Residential home:

Date: Time started work: a.m. / p.m.

hour ⇨	1		2		3		4		
minutes taken ⇨	act.	adeq.	act.	adeq.	act.	adeq.	act.	adeq.	
activity ⇩									
washing / bathing									
dressing / undressing									
eating / drinking									
continence / toiletting									
personal hygiene									
mobility / lifting									
medication									
counselling									
social interaction									

After pilot testing of the diary form, care assistants received training on its completion. This focused on the importance of being honest, precise definitions of activities and how to fill in the form. A definition of each activity was also provided. Data were subsequently collected from ten residential homes over a two-week period.

One of the best-known examples of managerial research which used structured observation as part of its data collection approach was the study of the work of senior managers by Mintzberg (1973). This led to Mintzberg's casting doubt on the long-held theory that managerial work was a rational process of planning, controlling and directing. He studied what five chief executives actually did during one working week. He did this by direct observation and the recording of events on three pre-determined coding schedules. This followed a period of 'unstructured' observation in which the categories of activity which formed the basis of the coding schedules he used were developed. So Mintzberg 'grounded' (*see* Section 12.6 for an explanation of grounded theory) his structured observation on data collected in the period of participant observation.

Of course, studying what jobholders of the type not normally 'observed' actually do in their everyday lives lends itself to approaches other than observation. Self-completion of diaries is one approach that is often used. But involvement of the researcher in the process lends a degree of impartiality and thoroughness. This has benefits for reliability and validity that may not be evident when the jobholder is the 'observer'.

Advantages and disadvantages of structured observation

As with other research methods, structured observation has its advantages and disadvantages.

Advantages of structured observation

- It can be used by anyone after suitable training in the use of the measuring instrument. Therefore, you could delegate this extremely time-consuming task. In addition, structured observation may be carried out simultaneously in different locations. This would present the opportunity of comparison between locations.

- It should yield highly *reliable* results by virtue of its replicability. We will deal with threats to reliability in Section 8.7, but suffice to say here that the easier the observation instrument to use and understand, the more reliable the results will be.

- Structured observation is capable of more than simply observing the frequency of events. It is also possible to record the relationship between events. For example, is the visit to the retail chemist's counter to present a prescription preceded by an examination of merchandise unrelated to the prescription transaction?

- The method allows the collection of data at the time they occur in their natural setting. Therefore there is no need to depend on 'second-hand' accounts of phenomena from respondents who put their own interpretation on events.

- Structured observation secures information which most participants would ignore because to them it was too mundane or irrelevant.

Disadvantages of structured observation

■ The observer must be in the research setting when the phenomena under study are taking place.

■ Research results are limited to overt action or surface indicators from which the observer must make inferences.

■ Data are slow and expensive to collect.

8.6 STRUCTURED OBSERVATION: DATA COLLECTION AND ANALYSIS

Using coding schedules to collect data

One of the key decisions you will need to make before undertaking structured observation is whether you use an 'off-the-shelf' coding schedule or design your own. You will hardly be surprised to hear us say that this should depend on your research question(s) and objectives. What follows are two sets of guidelines for assessing the suitability of existing, tailor-made coding schedules.

Choosing an 'off-the-shelf' coding schedule

There are a number of questions you should ask yourself when choosing an 'off-the-shelf' coding schedule. These are detailed in Table 8.1.

☑ For what purpose was the coding schedule developed? Is it consistent with your research question(s) and objectives? (It should be.)

☑ Is there overlap between the behaviours to be observed? (There should not be.)

☑ Are all behaviours in which you are interested covered by the schedule? (They should be.)

☑ Are the behaviours sufficiently clearly specified so that all observers will place behaviours in the same category? (They should be.)

☑ Is any observer interpretation necessary? (It should not be.)

☑ Are codes to be used indicated on the recording form to avoid the necessity for memorisation by the observer? (They should be)

☑ Will the behaviours to be observed be relevant to the inferences you make? (They should be.)

☑ Have all sources of observer bias been eliminated? (They should have been.)

Table 8.1 Checklist of questions to ask when choosing an 'off the shelf' coding schedule
Source: developed from Walker, 1985

One of the most frequent uses of established coding schedules in management and business is for recording interpersonal interactions in social situations such as meetings or negotiations. This lends itself to structured observation particularly well. Fig 8.1 is an example of just such an off-the-shelf coding schedule which may be used for this purpose.

Nature of group:						
Nature of activity:						
Date: Name of observer:						
Initial arrangement of group:						
C D B E A F						
Name of group members (or reference letters)						
	A	B	C	D	E	F
Taking initiative – e.g. attempted leadership, seeking suggestions, offering directions						
Brainstorming – e.g. offering ideas or suggestions however valid						
Offering positive ideas – e.g. making helpful suggestions, attempting to problem-solve						
Drawing in others – e.g. encouraging contributions, seeking ideas and opinions						
Being responsive to others – e.g. giving encouragement and support, building on ideas						
Harmonising – e.g. acting as peacemaker, calming things down, compromising						
Challenging – e.g. seeking justification, showing disagreement in a *constructive* way						
Being obstructive – e.g. criticising, putting others down, blocking contributions						
Clarifying/summarising – e.g. linking ideas, checking progress, clarifying objectives/proposals						
Performing group roles – e.g. spokesperson, recorder, time-keeper, humorist						
Other comments						

Fig 8.1 Recording sheet for observing behaviour in groups
Source: Mullins, 1996: 228. © L.J. Mullins 1996.

Designing your own coding schedule

We would encourage you to use an off-the-shelf coding schedule if you can find one that is suitable. Not only will it save you a lot of time, but it will be tried and tested. Therefore, it should make your results and conclusions more reliable and valid.

However, you may decide that no off-the-shelf coding schedule is suitable for your purposes. In this case you will need to develop your own schedule. Table 8.2 contains useful guidelines for this activity. The observation categories in your schedule should be devised to be consistent with your research question(s) and objectives. To ensure ease of use and reliability, the categories should reflect the attributes shown in Table 8.2.

Attribute	Comment
Focused	Don't observe and record all that is going on. Only concern yourself with what is strictly relevant.
Unambiguous	Therefore requiring the absolute minimum of observer interpretation.
Non-context dependent	The observer's job is more difficult if the coding of behaviours is dependent on the context in which the behaviour occurs. It may be essential for your research question(s) and objectives to record contextual data, but this should be kept to a minimum.
Explicitly defined	Provide examples for the observer (even if this is you) of behaviours which fall into each category and those that don't.
Exhaustive	Ensure that it is always possible to make a coding for those behaviours you wish to observe.
Mutually exclusive	Ensure that there is no overlap between behaviour categories.
Easy to record	The observer must be able quickly to tick the correct box without having to memorise appropriate categories.

Table 8.2: Guidelines for developing your own coding schedule
Source: developed from Robson, 1993

An alternative to the use of an off-the-shelf coding schedule or the development of your own may be a combination of the two. If this is the option that seems most appropriate in the light of your research question(s) and objectives, we recommend that you still use the checklist in Table 8.1 and the guidelines in Table 8.2 to ensure that your schedule is as valid and reliable as possible.

Data analysis

The complexity of your analysis will depend on your research question(s) and objectives. It may be that you are using Fig 8.1 to establish the amount of interactions by category in order to relate the result to the output of the meeting. This may enable you to conclude that 'positive' behaviours (e.g. brainstorming) may be more strongly associated with meetings which make clear decisions than are 'negative' behaviours (e.g. being obstructive). Simple manual analysis may be sufficient for this purpose.

Alternatively, you may be using Fig 8.1 to see what patterns emerge. It may be that the amount of interactions vary by the nature of the group or its activity, or that seating position is associated with the amount of contributions. Patterns reflecting relationships between amounts of interaction categories may become evident (for example when 'drawing in others' was high 'clarifying/summarising' was also high). This level of analysis is obviously more complex and will need a computer to calculate the cross-classifications. Section 11.2 contains guidance on preparing data for quantitative analysis by computer.

Threats to validity and reliability

The main threats here are ones of reliability. This section deals with three of these: subject error, time error and observer effects.

Subject error

Subject error may cause your data to be unreliable. You may be concerned with observing the output of sales administrators as measured by the amount of orders they process in a day. Subject error may be evident if you chose administrators in a section which was short staffed due to illness. This may mean that they were having to spend more time answering telephones, and less time processing orders, as there were fewer people available to handle telephone calls. The message here is clear: choose subjects who in as many respects as possible are 'normal' examples of the population under study.

Time error

Closely related to the issue of subject error is that of *time error*. It is essential that the time at which you conduct the observation does not provide data which are untypical of the total time period in which you are interested. So the output of the insurance administrators may be less in the immediate hour before lunch as their energy levels are lower. If you were interested in the amount of customers using a retail shop, you would need to conduct observations at different times of the day and week to provide a valid picture of total customer flow.

Observer effect

One of the most powerful threats to the validity and reliability of data collected through observation is that of *observer effect*. This is quite simply that the process of the observer's observation of behaviour changes the nature of that behaviour, due to the fact that the subject is conscious of being observed. The simplest way to overcome this effect is for the observation to take place in secret. But this is often not possible, even if it were ethically sound to do so.

Robson (1993) notes two strategies for overcoming observer effect. The first, *minimal interaction*, means that the observer tries as much as possible to 'melt into the background' – having as little interaction as possible with the subjects of the observation. This may involve sitting in an unobtrusive position in the room and avoiding eye contact with those being observed. The second strategy is *habituation*, where the subjects being observed become familiar with the process of observation so that they take it for granted. Those of you who use a tape recorder to record discussions may notice that initially the respondent is very wary of the machine. But after a short period this apprehension wears off and the machine is not noticed.

Adopting a strategy of habituation to reduce observer effect may mean that several observation sessions are necessary in the same research setting with the same subjects. As the observer effect diminishes, so the interaction will settle down into a predictable pattern.

8.7 SUMMARY

- Participant observation is a method in which researchers participate in the lives and activities of those whom they are studying. It is used to attempt to get to the root of 'what is going on' in a wide range of social settings.

- You may use the participant observation method in a student placement or you may already be a member of an organisation which will enable you to adopt the role of the practitioner-researcher.

- Participant observation means that you adopt a number of potential roles, differentiated by the degree to which your identity is concealed from the subjects of the research and the degree to which you participate in the events you are studying.

- Participant observation must avoid the trap of mere story telling. The purpose is to develop theory.

- A prevalent form of data analysis used in participant observation is analytic induction, which may lead to an initial hypothesis being re-developed more than once.

- Structured observation is concerned with the frequency of events. It is characterised by a high level of pre-determined structure and quantitative analysis.

- A choice may be made between off-the-shelf coding schedules and a schedule which you design for your own purpose. Alternatively you may decide to use a 'hybrid'.

- The main threats to reliability and validity inherent in structured observation are subject error, time error and observer effects.

Self-check questions and assignment

Self-check question 8.1
You have been asked to give a presentation to a group of managers at the accountancy firm in which you are hoping to negotiate access for research. You wish to pursue the research question: 'What are the informal rules which govern the way in which trainee accountants work and how do they learn these rules?'

You realise that talk of 'attempting to learn the trainee accountants' symbolic world' would do little to help your cause with this group of non-research-minded business people. But you wish to point out some of the benefits to the organisation which your research may yield. Outline what you believe these would be.

Self-check question 8.2

You are a building society branch manager. You feel your staff are too reluctant to generate sales 'leads' from ordinary investors and borrowers which may be passed on to the society's consultants in order that they can attempt to sell life insurance policies, pensions and unit trusts. You would like to understand the reasons for their reluctance. As the participant observer, how would you go about this?

Self-check question 8.3

You are conducting your research project on the extent to which staff become involved in the decision-making processes conducted by a newly privatised regional electricity supplier. Staff 'involvement' is a new idea in the company and senior managers want to ascertain how it is working.

A main part of the involvement strategy is to have regular team meetings where staff can have their say. You have been given access to these meetings. You decide that you will observe the meetings to gain some feel for how they are working.

How would you record your observations?

Self-check question 8.4

Look again at Fig 8.1 and Table 8.1. Ask the questions contained in Table 8.1 of the coding schedule in Fig 8.1. How well does it match?

Assignment 8: Deciding on the appropriateness of observation

● Return to your research question(s) and objectives. Decide on how appropriate it would be to use observation as part of your research strategy. If you decide that this is appropriate, explain the relationship between your research question(s) and objectives and observation. If you decide that using observation is not appropriate, justify your decision.

● Look again at the previous paragraph and ensure that you have responded for both participant observation and structured observation *separately*.

● If you decide that participant observation is appropriate, what practical problems do you foresee? Are you likely to be faced with any moral dilemmas? How may you overcome both sets of problems?

● If you decide that participant observation is appropriate, what threats to validity and reliability are you likely to encounter? How may you overcome these?

● If you decide that structured observation is appropriate, what practical problems do you foresee? How may you overcome these?

● If you decide that structured observation is appropriate, what threats to validity and reliability are you likely to encounter? How may you overcome these?

● If you decide that structured observation is appropriate, design your own research instrument.

References

Ackroyd, S. and Hughes, J. (1992) *Data Collection in Context* (2nd edn), London, Longman.

Bryman, A. (1989) *Research Methods and Organisation Studies*, London, Unwin Hyman.

Delbridge, R. and Kirkpatrick, I. (1994) 'Theory and Practice of Participant Observation', in Wass, V. and Wells, P. (eds) *Principles and Practice in Business and Management Research*, Aldershot, Dartmouth, pp. 35–62.

Denzin, N. (1970) *The Research Act: A Theoretical Introduction to Sociological Methods*, Chicago, Aldine.

Ditton, J. (1977) *Part-Time Crime: An Ethnography of Fiddling and Pilferage*, London, Macmillan.

Gill, J. and Johnson, P. (1991) *Research Methods for Managers*, London, Paul Chapman.

Mintzberg, H. (1973) *The Nature of Managerial Work*, New York, Harper and Row.

Mullins, L. (1996) *Management and Organisational Behaviour* (4th edn), London, Pitman Publishing.

Punch, M. (1993) Observation and the Police: The Research Experience', in Hammersley, M. *Social Research Philosophy, Politics and Practice*, London, Sage, pp. 181–99.

Robson, C. (1993) *Real World Research*, Oxford, Blackwell.

Rosen, M. (1991) 'Breakfast at Spiro's: Dramaturgy and Dominance', in Frost, P., Moore, L., Louis, M., Lundberg, C. and Martin, J. (eds) *Reframing Organisational Culture*, Newbury Park, California, Sage, pp. 77–89.

Roy, D. (1952) 'Quota restriction and goldbricking in a machine shop', *American Journal of Sociology*, 57, 427–42.

Walker, R. (1985) *Doing Research: A Handbook for Teachers*, London, Methuen.

Whyte, W. (1955) *Street Corner Society* (2nd edn), Chicago, University of Chicago Press.

Further Reading

Ackroyd, S. and Hughes, J. (1992) *Data Collection in Context* (2nd edn), London, Longman. Chapter 6 contains a helpful analysis of the origins of, and problems with, participant observation. It also has a full analysis of symbolic interactionism.

Hammersley, M. and Atkinson, P. (1983) *Ethnography Principles in Practice*, London, Routledge. Chapters 4 and 8 on field relations and data analysis in participant observation are well worth reading.

Mintzberg, H. (1973) *The Nature of Managerial Work*, New York, Harper and Row. Appendix C has a full account of the methodology which Mintzberg employed. You will be struck by how such a seemingly simple methodology can lead to such important conclusions.

Punch, M. (1993) 'Observation and the Police: The Research Experience', in Hammersley, M. (ed.) *Social Research Philosophy, Politics and Practice*, London, Sage, pp. 181–99. An absorbing account of fieldwork experience with the Amsterdam police which makes riveting reading. Particularly good at the process of negotiating relationships with fellow participants.

Robson, C. (1993) *Real World Research*, Oxford, Blackwell. Chapter 8 is a most thorough and practical guide to observational methods. There is an interesting section at the end of the chapter on inter-observer reliability which you should look at if you intend to use a number of observers.

Taylor, S. and Bogdan, R. (1984) *Introduction to Qualitative Research Methods: The Search for Meanings*, New York, John Wiley. Chapters 2 and 3 are very practical accounts of how to approach and conduct participant observation.

Case 8:
Manufacturing strategy change in a textile company

Huw was a part-time student who combined his studies with his work as a freelance consultant and writer. After graduating from business school a number of contracts arose that enabled him to become self-employed. He had developed a passionate interest in manufacturing at university and was keen to research the then developing field of manufacturing strategy, in particular the aspects of change associated with this. This he believed would also strengthen his position as a consultant.

Within six months Huw had the chance to join a team of consultants hired to develop a manufacturing strategy. The company involved manufactured textiles for export in the North of England and employed approximately 400 people. It had a traditional management style and was heavily unionised. When a new managing director was appointed he quickly became concerned about the production function's ability to respond to the changing requirements of the marketplace. Different consultants were invited to tender for a contract to help the company to develop and implement a new manufacturing strategy. A chief factor in the appointment of the successful consulting team was the emphasis placed on facilitating the existing management team to develop their own manufacturing strategy. The consultant team was involved for 24 months, initially for three days a week, reducing gradually to one day a week after 12 months. The team comprised a senior academic consultant with extensive industrial experience, a freelance consultant with interests in organisational change and Huw.

The consulting contract represented an ideal opportunity for Huw to engage in participant observation research, although this was not part of his original plan. The other consultants in the team also had research interests and they were all comfortable with each other pursuing individual research interests. This was cleared with the managing director on the condition that the company was disguised in research outputs. The team spent several weeks gaining a thorough understanding of the organisation, meeting with managers at all levels, listening to them and probing key issues. Consequently managers were trained and helped to develop and implement their own strategy. Simultaneously the team became involved in meetings over several months helping to resolve short-term issues facing the company. This gained the team significant credibility and helped with access to data; they were readily provided with a wide range of reports, memos and strategic documents.

Huw recorded observations in his notebook throughout the meetings. On the right-hand page he would record observations regarding his participant role and on the left his reflections as an observer. The observer reflections were noted during meetings afterwards in the hotel and at home. This was an onerous task. The consulting team spent much time preparing for meetings and reviewing how they went; because all the team had research interests, this was a great stimulus for reflection.

Analytic induction was continuing and iterative but took the following underlying logic:

- A list of 'activities' in which the team were involved in their consulting role was developed, e.g. understanding the organisation, education, various change activities, and team preparation and review time. The duration of these activities was also mapped out using diary records of when meetings took place.

- The role the consultants played in each activity was described from notes, memos, reports and a handful of interviews with the other team members where gaps were evident.

- 'Observations' were noted for each activity. This was often an intuitive approach, noting points based on gut feel and interest.

- A set of 'reflections' then emerged which drew out unifying themes across the set of observations.

- 'Conceptualisation' then took place, where links were made between the different reflections, and between the reflections and literature.

As a result of the research Huw gained a much deeper understanding of the change process that took place. This helped him forge a link between models of manufacturing strategy in the literature and models of change theory.

Case-study questions

1 Describe the type of participant observation role adopted.
2 What were the advantages/disadvantages of Huw's approach?
3 What are the merits of Huw's approach to recording data?
4 What were the strengths of Huw's approach to analytic induction?

Answers to self-check questions

Self-check question 8.1

The research question is very broad. It allows you plenty of scope to discover a host of interesting things about the world of the trainee accountant. Without doubt, one of the things you will emerge with is a clear understanding about what they like about their work and what they don't like. This has practical implications for the sort of people that the firm ought to recruit, how they should be trained and rewarded. You may learn about some of the short-cuts practised by all occupations which may not be in the interest of the client. By the same token, you will probably discover aspects of good practice which managers can disseminate to other accountants. The list of practical implications is endless.

All this assumes, of course, that you will supply the managers with some post-research feedback. This does raise issues of confidentiality which you must have thought through beforehand.

Self-check question 8.2

This is a difficult one. The question of status may be a factor. But this would depend on your relationship with the staff. If you are, say, of similar age and have an open, friendly, 'one of the team' relationship with them, then it may not be too difficult. The element of threat which would attend a less open relationship would not be present.

You could set aside a time each day to work on the counter in order to really get to know what life is like for them. Even if you have done their job, you may have forgotten what is like! It may have changed since your day. Direct conversations about lead generation would probably not feature in your research times. But you would need to have a period of reflection after each 'research session' to think about the implications for your research question of what you have just experienced.

Self-check question 8.3

You may start your meeting attendance with an unstructured approach where you simply get the 'feel' of what is happening. Analysis of the data you have collected will allow you to develop an observational instrument which can be used in further meetings you attend. This instrument would be based on a coding schedule which allowed you to record, among other things, the number of contributions by each person at the meeting and the content of that contribution.

You would need to make sure that all those attending the meetings understand fully the purpose of your research. You would also be well advised to ensure that your findings are communicated to them.

Self-check question 8.4

Clearly there are some question marks about the coding schedule in fig 8.1. There does appear to be some overlap in the behavioural categories covered in the schedule. For example, it could be difficult to distinguish between what is 'offering directions' (taking initiative) and 'offering ideas' (brainstorming). It may be even more difficult to draw a distinction between 'offering suggestions' (brainstorming) and 'making helpful suggestions' (offering positive ideas). Similarly, there does not appear to be much difference between the behaviours in 'drawing in others' and 'being responsive to others'. You may argue that the first is defined by *invitation*, the second by *response*. But making the distinction when the interactions are coming thick and fast in the research setting will be much less easy.

The point about all this potential confusion is that different observers may make different estimations. This obviously has potentially harmful implications for the reliability of the coding schedule.

A much smaller point is how the observer indicates on the schedule the occurrence of a particular interaction.

CHAPTER 9

Collecting primary data using semi-structured and in-depth interviews

The objectives of this chapter are to explore the uses and limitations of semi-structured and in-depth interviews and how to undertake them.

Ways of classifying research interviews are described which are synthesised in order to help you to understand the purpose of each type.

The appropriateness of using semi-structured and in-depth interviews in relation to the purposes of research and the choice of your research strategy is discussed.

Situations favouring the use of semi-structured and in-depth interviews are discussed.

The chapter examines problem areas of data quality, researcher's competence and logistical and resource issues. Practical advice is offered on how to overcome these.

Issues and advantages associated with group interviews are also discussed.

9.1 INTRODUCTION

An interview is a purposeful discussion between two or more people (Kahn and Cannell, 1957). The use of interviews can help you to gather valid and reliable data which are relevant to your research question(s) and objectives. Where you have not yet formulated such a research question and objectives, an interview(s) may help you to achieve this. In reality, the research interview is a general term for several types of interview. This fact is significant since the nature of any interview should be consistent with your research question(s) and objectives, the purpose of your research and the research strategy which you have adopted. We define types of interview in the next section of this chapter (9.2) and show how these are related to particular research purposes. In order to provide a typology of research interviews we briefly outline all types in the next section, although the chapter will be concerned with those which we refer to as semi-structured and in-depth interviews.

Section 9.3 considers situations favouring the use of semi-structured and in-depth interviews. The following three sections examine issues associated with the use of these types of interview. Section 9.4 identifies data-quality issues associated with their use and discusses how to overcome them. Section 9.5 considers the areas of competence which you will need to develop. Section 9.6 discusses logistical and resource issues and how to manage these. Throughout the discussion of issues related to the use of semi-structured and in-depth interviews the focus is centred on what you will need to consider in order to be able to conduct these interviews. To draw this consideration together, a checklist is presented in Section 9.7 which offers you advice about how to conduct these types of research interview. Finally, Section 9.8 considers the particular advantages and issues associated with the use of group interviews.

9.2 TYPES OF INTERVIEW AND THEIR LINK TO THE PURPOSES OF RESEARCH AND RESEARCH STRATEGY

Types of interview

Interviews may be highly formalised and structured, using standardised questions for each respondent (Chapter 10), or they may be informal and unstructured conversations. In between there are intermediate positions. One typology which is commonly used is thus related to the level of formality and structure, whereby interviews may be categorised as either:

■ structured interviews (Chapter 10);

■ semi-structured interviews; or

■ unstructured interviews.

Another typology (Healey, 1991; Healey and Rawlinson, 1993; Healey and Rawlinson, 1994) differentiates between:

■ standardised interviews; and

■ non-standardised interviews.

Robson (1993), based on the work of Powney and Watts (1987), refers to a different typology:

■ respondent interviews;

■ informant interviews.

There is overlap between these different typologies, although consideration of each typology adds to our overall understanding of the nature of research interviews.

Structured interviews use questionnaires based on a predetermined and *standardised* or identical set of questions (Chapter 10). You read out each question and then record the response on a standardised schedule, usually with pre-coded answers (Sections 10.4 and 11.2). While there is social interaction between you and the respondent, such as explanations which you will need to provide, you should read out the questions in the same tone of voice so that you do not indicate any bias.

By comparison, semi-structured and unstructured interviews are *non-standardised*. In *semi-structured interviews* the researcher will have a list of themes and questions to be covered, although these may vary from interview to interview. This means that you may omit some questions in particular interviews given the specific organisational context which is encountered in relation to the research topic. The order of questions may also be varied depending on the flow of the conversation. On the other hand, additional questions may be required to explore your research question and objectives given the nature of events within particular organisations. The nature of the questions and the ensuing discussion means that data will be recorded by note taking, or perhaps by tape recording the conversation (Section 9.5).

Unstructured interviews are informal. You would use these to explore in depth a general area in which you are interested. We therefore refer to these as *in-depth interviews* in this chapter and elsewhere in the book. There is no pre-determined list of questions to work through in this situation, although you need to have a clear idea about the aspects you want to explore. The interviewee is given the opportunity to talk freely about events, behaviour and beliefs in relation to the topic area, so that this type of interaction is sometimes called *non-directive*. It has been labelled as an *informant interview* since it is the interviewee's perceptions which guide the conduct of the interview. In comparison, a *respondent interview* is one where the interviewer directs the interview and the interviewee responds to the questions of the researcher (Easterby-Smith *et al.*, 1991; Ghauri *et al.*, 1995; Healey and Rawlinson, 1994; Robson, 1993).

Links to the purpose of research and research strategy

Each type of interview outlined above has a different purpose. Structured or standardised interviews can be used in survey research to gather data which will then be the subject of quantitative analysis (Sections 11.3 to 11.5). Semi-structured and in-depth, or non-standardised, interviews are used in qualitative research in order to conduct exploratory discussions to reveal and understand not only the 'what' and the 'how', but also to place more emphasis on exploring the 'why'.

In Chapter 4 we outlined various ways in which your research can be classified. One classification is related to exploratory, descriptive and explanatory studies (Sections 4.2). By examining the respective categories within this classification, we can see how the various types of interview may be used to gather information for, and assist the progress of, each kind of study:

■ In an exploratory study, in-depth interviews can be very helpful to 'find out what is happening [and] to seek new insights' (Robson, 1993: 42). Semi-structured interviews may also be used in relation to an exploratory study.

■ In descriptive studies structured interviews can be used as a means to identify general patterns.

- In an explanatory study, semi-structured interviews may be used in order to understand the relationships between variables, such as those revealed from a descriptive study (Section 4.2). Structured interviews may also be used in relation to an explanatory study, in a statistical sense (Section 11.5).

This is summarised in Table 9.1.

	Exploratory	Descriptive	Explanatory
Structured		✓✓	✓
Semi-structured	✓		✓✓
In-depth	✓✓		

✓✓ = more frequent, ✓ = less frequent

Table 9.1 Uses of different types of interview in each of the main research categories

Your research may incorporate more than one type of interview. In a quantitative approach to research, for example, you may decide to use in-depth or non-standardised interviews initially to identify variables. The data you gather from such exploratory interviews will be used in the design of your questionnaire or structured interview (Section 4.2). Semi-structured interviews may be used to explore and explain themes which have emerged from the use of your questionnaire (Wass and Wells, 1994). In addition to this staged approach, Healey and Rawlinson (1994: 130) state that a combination of styles may be used within one interview: 'one section of an interview may ask a common set of factual questions . . . while in another section a semi-structured qualitative approach may be used to explore [responses]'. Wass and Wells (1994) make the point that interviews, presumably semi-structured or in-depth ones, may also be used as a means to validate findings from the use of questionnaires. We can therefore see that the various types of interview have a number of potentially valuable uses in terms of undertaking your research project. The key point for you to consider is the need for consistency between the research question and objectives, the strategy to be employed and the methods of data collection used – their fitness for purpose.

WORKED EXAMPLE: *Using interviews in a research project*

During a research project to survey employee attitudes in a public sector organisation, the use of interviews was considered for each stage of this undertaking. The first stage of data collection consisted of a series of in-depth interviews, which were undertaken with a representative cross-section of employees, to reveal variables to be tested empirically at the second stage of the research project. A number of decisions were made about these in-depth interviews during the initial planning phase:

- to obtain personnel data relating to job categories and grades, gender, age and length of service in order to select a representative sample;
- to combine similar employee categories and to use group interviews in order to overcome time constraints and the researchers' capacity to handle the data to be collected. As a result six group interviews were arranged, consisting of about ten participants in each group, in order to cover all employee categories;
- not to mix managerial and non-managerial participants within a group because this could have meant that non-managerial employees would be reluctant to take part.

At the next stage of the research project a decision had to be taken about whether to use a questionnaire or structured and standardised interviews. Because the number of employees in the organisational sample to be surveyed exceeded 30, it was decided that it would be more efficient to use a questionnaire rather than interviews (Wass and Wells, 1994).

After the analysis of the questionnaire data, a further stage used a series of semi-structured interviews in order to explore and explain the findings obtained through the survey. These were also conducted as group interviews. Care was again needed in relation to the representativeness, size and composition of each group as well as the setting for the discussion to occur.

9.3 SITUATIONS FAVOURING INTERVIEWS

There are many situations in which the use of interviews as a method of data collection may be advantageous, taking into account the points made in the previous section. These situations may be grouped into four categories:

- the nature of the approach to research;
- the significance of establishing personal contact;
- the nature of the data collection questions;
- length of time required and completeness of the process.

These are examined in turn.

The nature of the approach to research

We have discussed the way in which research can be classified according to its purpose. Where you are undertaking an exploratory study, or a study which includes an exploratory element, it is likely that you will include interviews in your approach (Emory and Cooper, 1991). Similarly, an explanatory study is also likely to include interviews in order to infer causal relationships between variables (Sections 4.2 and 10.4). Essentially, where it is necessary for you to understand the reasons for the decisions which your research participants have taken, or to understand the reasons for their attitudes and opinions, it will be necessary for you to conduct an in-depth interview.

Semi-structured and in-depth interviews also provide you with the opportunity to probe answers, where you want your interviewees to explain, or build on, their responses. This is important if you are adopting a phenomenological approach, where you will be concerned to understand the meanings which respondents ascribe to various phenomena (Section 4.1). Interviewees may use words or ideas in a particular way and the opportunity to probe these meanings will add significance and depth to the data obtained. It may also lead the discussion into areas which you had not previously considered but which are significant for your understanding, and in order for you to address the research question(s) and objectives which you have set, or indeed to help you to formulate such a question. It also affords interviewees an opportunity to hear themselves 'thinking aloud' about things they may not have previously considered. The result should be that you are able to collect a rich set of data.

The significance of establishing personal contact

We have found that managers are more likely to agree to be interviewed, rather than complete a questionnaire, especially where the interview topic is seen to be interesting and relevant to their own current work. An interview provides them with an opportunity to reflect on events without needing to write them down. Other researchers report similar conclusions, where participants prefer to be interviewed rather than fill in a questionnaire (Healey, 1991, citing North et al., 1983), and where interviewees value the opportunity for feedback from the interviewer and the personal assurance which can be given about the way in which information will be used (Zikmund, 1994).

Potential research participants who receive a questionnaire through the post may be reluctant to complete it for a number of reasons. They may feel that it is not appropriate to provide sensitive and confidential information to someone they have never met. They may also not completely trust the way in which the information provided is to be used. They may be reluctant to spend time providing written explanatory answers, where these are requested, especially if the meaning of any question is not entirely clear. The use of personal interviews, where appropriate, may therefore achieve a higher response rate than using questionnaires. Healey (1991: 206) also makes the point that 'the interviewer . . . has more control over who answers the questions', in comparison to a questionnaire which may be passed from one person to another.

The nature of the questions

An interview will undoubtedly be the most advantageous approach to attempt to obtain data in the following circumstances (Easterby-Smith et al., 1991; Healey, 1991; Jankowicz, 1995):

- where there are a large number of questions to be answered;
- where the questions are either complex or open-ended;
- where the order and logic of questioning may need to be varied.

A semi-structured or in-depth interview will be most appropriate for the latter two types of situation.

● ●

WORKED EXAMPLE: *The need to vary the order and logic of questioning*

Adrian undertook a series of interviews, along with another colleague, into the management of redundancy in 40 organisations. It soon became evident that it would not be meaningful to ask exactly the same questions in each organisation. For example, some organisations only made employees redundant through a compulsory approach, whereas some other organisations relied on obtaining volunteers for redundancy. Another significant variable was associated with whether the organisation recognised trade unions in respect of any category of employees, or if it was non-unionised.

The impact of these and other variables meant that it was meaningless to ask exactly the same questions at each interview, even though many questions remained applicable in all cases and the underlying intention was to ensure consistency between interviews. It was not until each interview had started that they were able to learn which of these different variables operated within the particular organisation. The conclusion is that a semi-structured or in-depth interview can allow for the flexibility which may well be required.

● ●

Length of time required and completeness of the process

Apart from the difficulty of trying to design a viable questionnaire schedule to cope with questions which are complex, or open-ended or large in number, the time needed to obtain the required data may mean that an interview is in any case the best or only alternative. In our experience, where expectations have been clearly established about the length of time required, and participants understand and agree with the objectives of the research interview, they have generally been willing to agree to be interviewed. Some negotiation is, in any case, possible and the interview can be arranged at a time when the interviewee will be under least pressure. We have found that our respondents tend to be generous with their time, and sometimes where interviews have been arranged to start at mid-morning they arrange for lunch which can allow the discussion and exploration of issues to continue. However, for those of you who fancy a free lunch, we do not want to falsely raise your expectations and the start time for an interview shouldn't be set with this in mind!

Your aim will be to obtain answers to all of the questions which you ask, and Zikmund (1994) believes that, where you skilfully conduct the event, an interview is more likely to achieve this than the use of a self-administered or telephone questionnaire. Where your respondent does not provide an answer to a particular question or questions in an interview, you should be able to form some indication of why a response could not be provided. This may even lead you to modify the question or compose another where this would be appropriate. Section 5.4 provides a consideration of the ethical issues associated with seeking to obtain answers.

While there are a number of situations favouring the use of interviews, there are also a number of issues associated with them. The next three sections will describe issues associated with semi-structured and in-depth interviews, and discuss how you can manage them, under the following headings:

■ data-quality issues;

■ the researcher's interviewing competence;

■ logistical and resource issues.

9.4 DATA-QUALITY ISSUES AND HOW TO OVERCOME THEM

Data-quality issues

A number of data-quality issues can be identified in relation to the use of semi-structured and in-depth interviews, related to:

■ reliability;

■ forms of bias;

■ validity and generalisability.

These are discussed in turn.

The lack of standardisation in these interviews may lead to concerns about *reliability* (Robson, 1993). In relation to these interviews, reliability is concerned with whether alternative interviewers would reveal similar information (Easterby-Smith *et al.*, 1991; Healey and Rawlinson, 1994). The concern about reliability in these types of interview is also related to issues of bias. There are various types of bias to consider. The first of these is related to *interviewer bias*. This is where the comments, tone or non-verbal behaviour of the interviewer creates bias in the way that interviewees respond to the questions being asked. This may be where you may attempt to impose your own beliefs and frame of reference through the questions which you ask. It is also possible that you will demonstrate bias in the way you interpret responses (Easterby-Smith *et al.*, 1991). Where you are unable to develop the trust of the interviewee, or perhaps where your credibility is seen to be lacking, the value of the information given may also be limited, raising doubts about its validity and reliability.

Related to this is *interviewee* or *response bias*. This type of bias may be caused by perceptions about the interviewer, as referred to above, or in relation to perceived interviewer bias. However, the cause of this type of bias is not necessarily linked to any perception related to the interviewer. Taking part in an interview is an intrusive process. This is especially true in the case of in-depth or semi-structured interviews, where your aim will be to explore events or to seek explanations. The interviewee may, in principle, be willing to participate but may nevertheless be sensitive to the in-depth exploration of certain themes. Interviewees may therefore choose not to reveal and discuss an aspect of the topic which you wish to explore, because this would lead to probing questions which would intrude on sensitive information which they do not wish, or are not empowered, to discuss with you. The outcome of this may be that interviewees provide a partial 'picture' of the situation which casts themselves in a 'socially desirable' role, or the organisation which they work for in a positive or even negative fashion.

Bias may also result from the nature of the individuals or organisational participants who agree to be interviewed. The time-consuming requirements of the interview process may result in a reduction in willingness to take part on behalf of some of those whom you would like to talk to. This may bias your sample from whom data are collected (Robson, 1993). This is an issue which you will need to consider carefully and attempt to overcome through the approach taken to sampling (Section 6.3).

There is also likely to be an issue about the generalisability of the findings from qualitatively based interview studies, although the validity of such studies is not raised as an issue. If we consider *validity* first, this refers to the extent to which 'the researcher [has] gained full access to the knowledge and meanings of informants' (Easterby Smith *et al.*, 1991: 41). The high level of validity which is possible in relation to carefully conducted qualitative interviews is made clear by the following quotation:

> 'the main reason for the potential superiority of qualitative approaches for obtaining information is that the flexible and responsive interaction which is possible between interviewer and respondent(s) allows meanings to be probed, topics to be covered from a variety of angles and questions made clear to respondents.'
>
> Sykes, 1991: 8, cited in Healey and Rawlinson, 1994: 132.

However, qualitative research using semi-structured or in-depth interviews will not be able to be used to make *generalisations* about the entire population (whatever this may relate to in the context of the research topic) where this is based on a small and unrepresentative number of cases. This will be the situation in a case-study approach (Yin, 1994).

Overcoming data-quality issues

Reliability

One response to the issue of reliability is that the findings from using non-standardised research methods are not necessarily intended to be repeatable since they reflect reality at the time they were collected, in a situation which may be subject to change (Marshall and Rossman, 1989). The assumption behind this type of research is that the circumstances to be explored are complex and dynamic. The value of using this non-standardised approach is derived from the flexibility which you may use to explore the complexity of the topic. Therefore an attempt to ensure that qualitative, non-standardised research could be replicated by other researchers would not be realistic or feasible without undermining the strength of this type of research. Marshall and Rossman (1989) suggest that researchers using a qualitative, non-standardised approach need to make this clear – perhaps to transform an aspect perceived to be a weakness by some into a strength, based on realistic assumptions about the ability to replicate research findings.

However, they suggest that where you use this approach you should make and retain notes relating to the design of the research, the reasons underpinning the choice of strategy and methods, and the data obtained. Justification of the choice of your research strategy and methods should initially be discussed in your research proposal. These records can be referred to by other researchers in order to understand the processes which you used, and to enable them to re-use the data which you collected. The use of a qualitative approach should not lead to a lack of rigour in relation to the research process – if anything, greater rigour is required to overcome the views of those who may be wedded to the value of quantitative research to the exclusion of any other approach.

Interviewer and interviewee bias

Overcoming these forms of bias is integral to the way in which the interview is conducted. In order to attempt to avoid the sources of bias discussed earlier, you need to consider the following points:

- your own preparation and readiness for the interview;
- the level of information supplied to the interviewee;
- the appropriateness of your appearance at the interview;
- the nature of the opening comments to be made when the interview commences;
- your approach to questioning;
- the impact of your behaviour during the course of the interview;
- your ability to demonstrate attentive listening skills;
- your scope to test understanding;
- your approach to recording information.

The relationship between these aspects and the management of interviewer and interviewee bias will be explored in the discussion which follows. The aim in relation to each of these aspects will be to demonstrate your credibility and to obtain the confidence of the interviewee.

Preparation and readiness for the interview

You need to be knowledgeable about the organisational or situational context. A search in your university library (Sections 3.4 and 3.5) may reveal journal articles written by senior employees of the organisation, which is participating in your research. There may also be other material about the organisation, and this is particularly likely to be found in the 'trade' press and the quality newspapers. It may also be appropriate to look at company reports and other publications, or financial data relating to the organisation. The ability to draw on this type of knowledge in the interview should help to demonstrate your credibility and thereby encourage the interviewee to offer a more detailed account of the topic under discussion. A further benefit of this is made clear by Healey and Rawlinson (1994: 136): 'A well informed interviewer has a basis for assessing the accuracy of some of the information offered.'

Your level of knowledge about your research question(s) and objectives should also help to establish your credibility in the view of the research participant. This knowledge may be gleaned through the review of the literature associated with the research. As you undertake a number of interviews you will also be able to draw on the initial analysis which you make of data previously collected.

Level of information supplied to the interviewee

Credibility may also be promoted through the supply of relevant information to participants before the interview. Providing participants with a list of the interview themes before the event, where this is appropriate, should help this aim, and also promote validity and reliability through enabling the interviewee to consider the information being requested and allowing them the opportunity to assemble supporting organisational documentation from their files. We can testify to this approach and to the value in allowing participants to prepare themselves for the discussion in which they are to engage. Access to organisational documentation also allows for triangulation of the interview data provided (Sections 7.2 and 7.4). Our experience is that participants are generally willing to supply a photocopy of such material, although of course it is sometimes necessary to conceal confidential or personal details.

- -

WORKED EXAMPLE: *Interview themes*

You have been asked to undertake semi-structured interviews with a number of employees to ascertain their views about the nature and efficiency of internal communication within an organisation. This subject is felt to be significant in relation to both customer service and employee commitment perspectives. You have been requested to provide a list of themes which you wish to explore with interviewees. After some deliberation and reading you come up with the following list of themes which you wish to explore during the course of these interviews.

- What interviewees understand by the term internal communication.
- Nature and sources of internal communications received.
- Perceptions about the channels used for internal communication and their impact on its intended purpose.
- Value of internal communication in providing information about performance (of the organisation and more locally) and strategic direction.
- Use and impact of internal communication on the work of the interviewee's department.
- Affect of internal communication on the work of the interviewee.
- Scope for upward communication.
- Impact of upward communication on organisational procedures and practices.
- Perceptions about improving the processes, content and efficiency of internal communication in relation to the twin foci of the research.

These can be used as your guide through the substantive part of the interview.

- -

Interview themes may be derived from the literature which you read; the theories which you consider; your experience of a particular topic; common sense; discussion with co-workers, fellow students, tutors and research participants; or some combination of these approaches. You will need to have some notion of the themes which you wish to discuss with your participants, even if you intend to commence with exploratory, in-depth interviews and adopt a grounded theory approach to your research project (Section 12.6). Without some focus your work will clearly lack a sense of direction and purpose. It will be necessary for you to formulate a focus if your work is to make progress. You should therefore commence with a set of themes which reflect the variables being studied, which you can explore to see if you can identify and test relationships between them.

Appropriateness of the researcher's appearance at the interview

Your appearance may affect the interviewee's perception of you. Where this has an adverse affect on your credibility in the view of the interviewee, or results in a failure to gain their confidence, the resulting bias may affect the reliability of the information provided. Robson (1993) advises researchers to adopt a similar style of dress to those to be interviewed. Essentially, you will need to wear clothing which will be generally acceptable for the setting within which the interview is to occur.

Nature of the opening comments to be made when the interview commences

Where the interviewee has not met you before, the first few minutes of conversation may have a significant impact on the outcome of the interview – again related to the issue of your credibility and the level of the interviewee's confidence. The interview is likely to occur in a setting which is unfamiliar to you, but it will nevertheless be your responsibility to shape the start of the discussion. You will need to establish your credibility and gain the interviewee's confidence. The interviewee may have some uncertainties about sharing information and the manner in which this data may be used. Alternatively, they may still need clarification about the exact nature of the data which you wish to obtain. There may also be a degree of curiosity on the part of the interviewee and probably a genuine level of interest in the research, related to the reason that the request to participate was accepted. This curiosity and interest will offer an opening for both parties to start a conversation, probably before the intended discussion commences. You may find it appropriate to follow up by demonstrating interest in the interviewee and asking about their role within the host organisation (Ghauri *et al.*, 1995). However, you need to make sure that these opening moves to demonstrate credibility and friendliness, and to relax and develop a positive relationship, are not over-stated, so that too much time is used and the interviewee starts to become bored or restive.

The commencement of the intended discussion needs to be shaped by you. This will be your opportunity to allay, wherever possible, the interviewee's uncertainties in providing information. The following example provides a structure which might be appropriate to commence an interview and to fulfil this purpose.

WORKED EXAMPLE: *Opening a semi-structured interview*

As part of a research project, a series of semi-structured interviews was undertaken with participants from a range of organisations. In order to cover a number of aspects felt to be important at the start of each interview, the following points were followed on each occasion:

- The participant was thanked for considering the request for access and agreeing to the meeting.

- The objectives for the discussion were briefly outlined.

- Confidentiality and anonymity were stressed by stating that nothing said by the participant would be attributed to them or their employing organisation without first seeking and obtaining permission.

- The participant was told about the nature of the outputs to which the research was intended to lead. This provided further assurance about the way in which the information derived from the research was to be used. It was at this point that the offer of any written documentation to the interviewee could be made verbally, where this was appropriate, and when this was intended to occur.

- Before the substantive discussion got under way, the final point was to indicate the way in which the interviewer would like the meeting to be conducted and the themes to be covered.

All of these points were dealt with in a couple of minutes.

Healey and Rawlinson (1994) say that an assurance from you that confidential information is not being sought should make interviewees more relaxed and open in the information that they are willing to discuss. Combined with assurances about anonymity, this should increase the level of confidence in your trustworthiness and reduce the possibility of interviewee or response bias. You may also demonstrate your commitment to confidentiality by not naming other organisations who have participated in your research, or by talking about the data you obtained from them.

Approach to questioning

When conducted appropriately, your approach to questioning should reduce the scope for bias during the interview and increase the reliability of the information obtained. Your questions need to be clearly phrased, so that the interviewee can understand them, and you should ask them in a neutral tone of voice. Easterby-Smith *et al.* (1991) point out that the use of open questions (Section 9.5) should help to avoid bias. These can then be followed up by the use of appropriately worded probing questions (Section 9.5) which will help you to explore the topic and produce a fuller account. Conversely, questions which seek to lead the interviewee or which indicate bias on your part should be avoided. Perceived interviewer bias may well lead to interviewee or response bias. Long questions or those which are in fact made up of two or more questions should be avoided if you are to obtain a response to each aspect which you are interested to explore (Robson, 1993).

Questions should also avoid too many theoretical concepts or jargon, since your understanding of such terms may vary from that of your interviewees. Where theoretical concepts or specific terminology need to be used, you will have to ensure that the interviewee understands your intended meaning (Easterby Smith *et al.*, 1991; Ghauri *et al.*, 1995). For example, when Adrian and another colleague conducted interviews about the 'survivors' of redundancies, one participant initially thought that this referred to those made redundant but who had managed to overcome and 'survive' the experience – which is a very understandable interpretation. In fact, the meaning was related to employees who remained in the organisation! The term 'survivor syndrome' has now become accepted jargon by those interested in this area, but most people would not specifically relate it to those who stay in employment. You will therefore need to exercise great care in the way that you use similar jargon which you take for granted but which others do not.

Healey and Rawlinson (1994: 138) suggest that 'it is usually best to leave sensitive questions until near the end of an interview because this allows a greater time for the respondent to build up trust and confidence in the researchers'. They report cases where the first part of an interview is used by participants to assess the level of trust which can be placed in the researcher. A colleague of ours recalled an occasion when this type of treatment was particularly noticeable: for the first hour of a two-hour interview it appeared to him that the participants were convinced that he was really there to offer them a consultancy service. When they accepted that he wasn't about to try to sell them something, the mood of the meeting changed and they became much more relaxed and open! Once this position has been reached and you wish to seek responses to potentially sensitive questions, Ghauri *et al.* (1995) point out that the wording of these deserves very particular attention in order to avoid any negative inferences related to, for example, responsibility for failure or error. Care taken over the exploration of sensitive questions should help towards the compilation of a fuller and more reliable account.

Nature and impact of the interviewer's behaviour during the course of the interview

Appropriate behaviour by the researcher should also reduce the scope for bias during the interview. Comments or non-verbal behaviour, such as gestures, which indicate any bias in your thinking should be avoided. A neutral (but not a disinterested) response should be projected to the interviewee's answers in order not to provide any lead which may result in bias. Robson (1993) says that you should enjoy the opportunity, or at least appear to do so. A suggestion of boredom on your part is hardly likely to encourage your interviewee!

Your posture and tone of voice may also encourage or inhibit the flow of the discussion. You should sit slightly inclined towards the interviewee and adopt an open posture, avoiding folded arms. This should provide a signal of attentiveness to your interviewee (Torrington, 1991). Tone of voice can also provide signals to the interviewee. You need to project interest and enthusiasm through your voice, avoiding any impression of anxiety, disbelief, astonishment or other negative signals.

Demonstration of attentive listening skills

The purpose of a semi-structured or in-depth interview will be to understand the participant's explanations and meanings. This type of interaction will not be typical of many of the conversations which you normally engage in, where those involved often compete to speak rather than concentrate on listening. You therefore need to recognise that different skills will be emphasised in this kind of interaction. Torrington (1991: 43) says that listening involves people being 'on the look-out for signals and willing to spend the time needed to listen and build understanding, deliberately holding back our own thoughts, which would divert or compete with the other's'.

It will be necessary for you to explore and probe explanations and meanings, but you must also provide the interviewee with reasonable time to develop their responses, and you must avoid projecting your own views (Easterby-Smith *et al.*, 1991; Ghauri *et al.*, 1995; Robson, 1993). Careful listening should allow you to identify comments which are significant to the research topic and to explore these with the interviewee (Torrington, 1991).

Scope to test understanding

You may test your understanding by summarising an explanation provided by the interviewee. This will allow the interviewee to 'evaluate the adequacy of the interpretation and correct where necessary' (Healey and Rawlinson, 1994: 138). This can be a powerful tool for avoiding a biased or incomplete interpretation. It may also act as a means to further explore and probe the interviewee's responses.

In addition to this opportunity to test understanding at the interview, you may also ask the interviewee to read through the factual account which you need to produce of the interview. Where the interviewee is prepared to undertake this, it will provide a further opportunity for you to test your understanding and for the interviewee to add any further points of relevance which may occur to them.

Approach to recording data

A full record of the interview should be compiled as soon as possible after it has occurred (Healey, 1991; Healey and Rawlinson, 1994; Robson, 1993). Where you do not do this, the exact nature of explanations provided may be lost as well as general points of value. There is also the possibility that you may mix up data from different interviews, where you carry out a number of these within a short period and you do not complete a record of each one at the time it takes place (Ghauri *et al.*, 1995). Either situation will clearly lead to an issue about the trustworthiness of the data. You therefore need to allocate time to write up a full set of notes soon after the event. Recording information is considered further in Section 9.5.

As a final note to this particular discussion, we need to recognise that it is often difficult to attempt to control bias in all cases. Other factors may become significant. For example, there may be misinterpretation of responses because of cultural differences between the interviewee and the interviewer (Marshall and Rossman, 1989). This issue is not exclusively related to interviews and can be associated with a number of data collection methods. For example, we encountered it in relation to the interpretation of the data produced from a cross-national survey. An in-depth interview at least offers the opportunity to explore meanings, including those which may be culturally specific, but you will need to be aware of cultural differences and their implications (*see*, for example, Hofstede, 1991).

Generalisability

In the previous subsection which described data-quality issues relating to semi-structured and in-depth interviews, we stated that there is likely to be a concern surrounding the generalisability of findings from qualitative research, based on the use of a small and unrepresentative number of cases. However, two arguments have been advanced which seek to clarify and modify the approach often adopted to the generalisability or transferability of qualitative research. The first of these relates to the situation where a single case study is used because of the in-depth nature of the research. Bryman (1988: 90) states that 'within a case study a wide range of different people and activities are invariably examined so that the contrast with survey samples is not as acute as it appears at first glance'. The single case may in fact encompass a number of settings, where for example it involves a study in a large organisation with sites across the country, or even around the world. By comparison, Bryman (1988) points out that many survey samples may be restricted to one particular locality. A well-completed and rigorous case study is thus more likely to be useful in other contexts than one which lacks such rigour.

The second argument with the approach which questions the generalisability of qualitative research or a case study is related to the significance of this type of research to theoretical propositions (Bryman, 1988; Yin, 1994). Where you are able to relate your research project to existing theory, you will be in a position to demonstrate that your findings will have a broader significance than the case or cases which form the basis of your work (Marshall and Rossman, 1989). It will clearly be up to you to establish this relationship to existing theory in order to be able to demonstrate the broader significance of your particular case-study findings.

This relationship will allow your study to test the applicability of existing theory to the setting(s) you are examining and, where this is found wanting, to suggest why. It will also allow theoretical propositions to be advanced which can then be tested in another context. However, as Bryman (1988) points out, this also has implications for the relationship between theory and research, since the application of theory will be necessary before the researcher embarks on the collection of data (Section 12.4).

9.5 THE RESEARCHER'S INTERVIEWING COMPETENCE

There are several areas where you need to develop and demonstrate competence in relation to the conduct of semi-structured and in-depth research interviews. These areas are:

- opening the interview;
- using appropriate language;
- questioning;
- listening;
- testing and summarising understanding;
- behavioural cues;
- recording data.

Most of these areas of competence have been discussed in relation to overcoming inter-viewer and interviewee bias in Section 9.4. A list of competences is also contained in Table 9.3. However, there is scope to discuss further approaches to questioning and record-ing information in order to be able to develop your competence.

Questioning

Even in an in-depth interview, as well as in a semi-structured one, you will need to consider your approach to questioning. Allowing the interviewee to talk freely throughout an in-depth interview is unlikely to lead to a clearly focused discussion on issues relevant to the research topic (Easterby-Smith *et al.*, 1991; Robson, 1993), unless the purpose is simply to discover important concerns relating to the topic at a given time. It will therefore be nec-essary to devise relevant interview themes (Section 9.4), even though you can adopt a flexible approach about the way these are dealt with during the interview. This approach demands a significant level of competence on your part. Formulating appropriate questions to explore areas in which you are interested will be critical to achieving success in this type of interviewing. We will now discuss the types of questions which you will use during semi-structured and in-depth interviews.

Open questions

The use of *open questions* will allow participants to define and describe a situation or event. An open question is designed to encourage the interviewee to provide an extensive and developmental answer and may be used to reveal attitudes or obtain facts (Grummitt 1980). They encourage interviewees to reply as they wish. An open question is likely to start with, or include, one of the following words: what, how, or why. Examples of open questions include:

- 'What methods have been used to make employees redundant?'
- 'How has corporate strategy changed over the past five years?'
- 'Why did the organisation introduce its marketing strategy?'

Probing questions

Probing questions can be used to explore responses which are of significance to the research topic. They may be worded like open questions but request a particular *focus* or direction. Examples of this type of question include:

- 'Why did you choose to make compulsory redundancies?'
- 'What external factors caused the corporate strategy to change?'
- 'How would you evaluate the success of the new marketing strategy?'

These questions may be prefaced with, for example, 'That's interesting . . .'; 'Tell me more about . . .'

Probing questions may also be used to seek an *explanation* where you do not understand the interviewee's meaning or where the response does not reveal the reasoning involved. Examples of this type of question include:

- 'What do you mean by "bumping" as a means to help to secure volunteers for redundancy?'
- 'What is the relationship between the new statutory requirements which you referred to and the organisation's decision to set up its corporate affairs department?'

Use of *reflection* may also help you to probe a theme. This is where you will 'reflect' a statement made by the interviewee by paraphrasing their words. An example of this might be:

- 'Why don't you think that the employees understand the organisation's mission statement?'

The intention will be to encourage exploration of the point made without offering a view or judgement on your part.

Where an open question does not reveal a relevant response, you may also probe the area of interest by using a *supplementary* question which finds a way of rephrasing the original question (Torrington, 1991).

Specific and closed questions

These types of questions may be used to obtain specific information or to confirm a fact or opinion and are more generally used in questionnaires (Section 10.4). Examples of these types of question include:

- 'How many people responded to the customer survey?'

This question is designed to obtain a specific piece of data.

- 'Did I hear you say that the new warehouse opened on 25 March?'

This is a closed question seeking a yes or no answer.

In phrasing questions, remember that you should avoid using leading or proposing types of questions in order to control any bias which may result from their use (Section 9.4).

Recording information

The need to create a full record of the interview soon after its occurrence was identified in Section 9.4 as one of the means of controlling bias and producing reliable data for analysis. This particular discussion looks briefly at the need to develop the skill of making notes during the interview and evaluates the use of tape recorders. Most people have their own means of making notes, which may range from an attempt to create a verbatim account to a diagrammatic style which records key words and phrases, or perhaps some combination of these styles. The task of note making in this situation will be a demanding one. As you seek to test your understanding of what your interviewee has told you, this will allow some time to complete your notes concurrently in relation to the particular aspect being discussed. Most interviewees recognise the demands of the task and act accordingly. However, the interview will not be the occasion to perfect your style and you may be advised to practise in a simulated situation; for example by watching an interview on television and attempting to produce a set of notes.

One option is to tape record the interview. However, the disadvantages of doing so may outweigh the advantages. These are considered in Table 9.2.

Advantages	Disadvantages
• Allows interviewer to concentrate on questioning and listening	• May adversely affect the relationship between interviewee and interviewer (possibility of 'focusing' on the recorder)
• Allows questions formulated at an interview to be accurately recorded for use in later interviews where appropriate	• May inhibit some interviewee responses and reduce reliability
• Can re-listen to the interview	• Possibility of a technical problem
• Accurate and unbiased record provided	• Disruption to discussion when changing tapes
• Allows direct quotes to be used	• Time required to transcribe the tape
• Permanent record for others to use	

Table 9.2 Advantages and disadvantages of tape recording the interview
Sources: authors' experience; Easterby-Smith et al., 1991; Ghauri et al., 1995; Healey and Rawlinson, 1994

Permission should always be sought to tape record an interview. Healey and Rawlinson (1994) report an earlier study which advises that you should explain why you would prefer to use a recorder rather than simply requesting permission. Where it is likely to have a detrimental effect it is better not to use a recorder. However, some interviewees may adapt quickly to the use of the recorder.

Where a recorder is used it will still be necessary for you to continue to listen attentively. You are advised to make notes even when using a tape recorder in order to maintain your concentration and focus (Ghauri *et al.*, 1995). It is more ethical to allow your interviewee to maintain control over the tape recorder, so that if you ask a question which they are prepared to respond to, but only if their words are not tape recorded, they have the option to switch it off (see the discussion of ethical issues in Section 5.4). It will therefore be necessary to make notes in this situation.

9.6 LOGISTICAL AND RESOURCE ISSUES AND HOW TO MANAGE THESE

Logistical and resource issues

Interviewing is a time-consuming process. Where the purpose of the interview is to explore themes or explain findings, the process may call for a fairly lengthy discussion. In such cases, the time required to obtain data is unlikely to be less than one hour and could easily exceed this, perhaps taking two hours or longer. This may have an adverse impact on the number and representativeness of those who are willing to be interview participants, as we discussed above. Where managers or other potential participants receive frequent requests to participate in research projects, they will clearly need to consider how much of their time they may be willing to devote to such activities. This issue may arise in relation to either the completion of a questionnaire or participation in an interview. However, there will be more flexibility about when and where to fill in a questionnaire. It is therefore incumbent on you to establish credibility with, and engender the interest of, potential interviewees.

Your choice of an approach which involves data collection through interviewing will have particular resource issues. Conducting interviews may become a costly process where it is necessary to travel to the location of participants, although this can be kept to a minimum by cluster sampling (Section 6.2). Interviews are almost certainly likely to be more expensive than using self-administered or telephone questionnaires to collect data. The choice of method should nevertheless be determined by the nature of the research question(s) and objectives and not by cost considerations. This highlights the need to examine the feasibility of the proposed question(s) and research strategy in relation to resource constraints, including time available and expense, before proceeding to the collection of data. Where your research question(s) and objectives require you to undertake semi-structured or in-depth interviews, you need to consider the logistics of scheduling interviews. Thought needs to be given to the number of interviews to be arranged within a given period, the time required to compose notes and/or transcribe tape recordings of each one, and to undertake an initial analysis of the data collected (Section 12.3).

Managing logistical and resource issues

In the preceding subsection the issue of time required to collect data through interviewing was raised. You need to consider very carefully the amount of time which will be required to conduct an interview. In our experience the time required to undertake research interviews is usually under-estimated. The likely time required should be clearly referred to in any initial contact, and it may be better to suggest that interviews are envisaged to last up to, say, one, one-and-a-half or two hours, so that a willing participant sets aside sufficient time, and they then may be in a position to recoup time not required for a shorter interview should this be the case. Some negotiation is in any case possible with an interested participant who feels unable to agree to a request for, say, two hours but who is prepared to agree to a briefer meeting. The interview can also be arranged at a time when the interviewee will be under least pressure. Another possible strategy is to arrange two or more shorter interviews in order to explore a topic thoroughly. This might have the added advantage of allowing participants to reflect on the themes raised and questions being asked, and, therefore, to provide a fuller account and more accurate set of data. It may be beneficial to arrange an initial meeting with a potential participant to discuss this request, where you will be able to establish your credibility. A series of exploratory interviews may then be agreed.

Consideration also needs to be given to the number of interviews which may be undertaken in a given period. It is easy to over-estimate what is practically possible. One of our colleagues arranged two interviews in London during the course of a day, which involved travelling some miles across the city during the lunch hour. Given the total travelling time to and from London, the time to find the appropriate buildings, the transfer time during a busy period, the time to conduct the interviews, as well as the need to maintain concentration, probe responses, make initial notes and then to write these up without too much time elapsing, a decision was subsequently taken not to conduct more than one interview per day where significant travel was involved, even though this necessitated more journeys and greater expense. These are all factors which need to be considered in the scheduling of in-depth interviews. Where you are involved in a study at one establishment, it may be more practical to undertake a number of interviews in one day, although there is still a need to maintain concentration, make notes and write up information, and conduct your initial analysis. Phil found that undertaking three interviews per day in this type of study was enough.

The nature of semi-structured or in-depth interviews also has implications for the management of the time available during the meeting. The use of open-ended questions and reliance on informant responses means that, while you must remain responsive to the objectives of the interview and the time constraint, interviewees need the opportunity to provide developmental answers. You should avoid making frequent interruptions but will need to cover the themes and questions indicated and probe responses in the time available (Ghauri *et al.*, 1995). The intensive nature of the discussion and the need to optimise your understanding of what has been revealed mean that time must be found to write up notes as soon as possible after an interview. Where a tape recorder has been used time will be required to produce a transcription, and Robson (1993) states that a one-hour recording may take up to ten hours to transcribe.

9.7 A CHECKLIST FOR USING SEMI-STRUCTURED AND IN-DEPTH INTERVIEWS

Following the discussion about types of research interview (Section 9.2), this chapter has considered situations favouring their use (Section 9.3) and issues relating to data quality (Section 9.4), the level of competence required by the researcher (Section 9.5) and resources (Section 9.6). Throughout this discussion the focus has been on what you will need to consider in order to be able to conduct semi-structured or in-depth interviews. The checklist in Table 9.3 is an attempt to present the key points from the discussion above in order to help you think about when to and how to conduct these types of research interview. You may use the checklist as a means to test your understanding of the points included in the table, to indicate where you need to return to a section of the text above to reinforce this.

Deciding whether to use these types of interview:

☑ Does the purpose of your research suggest using semi-structured and/or in-depth interviews?

☑ Will it help to seek personal contact in terms of gaining access to participants and their data?

☑ Are your data collection questions large in number, complex or open-ended, or will there be a need to vary the order and logic of questioning?

☑ Will it help to be able to probe interviewees' responses to build on or seek explanation of their answers?

☑ Will the data collection process with each individual involve a relatively lengthy period of time?

Aspects to consider before conducting a semi-structured or in-depth interview:

☑ How will you seek to minimise issues related to the reliability of your work and its usefulness for other researchers?

☑ How will you seek to minimise forms of interviewer bias (related to your role and conduct), interviewee bias (the level of access which you gain to the data of those whom you interview) and sampling bias?

☑ What is the aim of your research interview? How can you prepare yourself to gain access to the data which you hope your participants will be able to share with you? What is the focus of your in-depth interview, or what are the themes which you wish to explore or seek explanations for during a semi-structured interview?

☑ What type of information, if any, will it be useful to send to your interviewee prior to the interview?

☑ What did you agree to supply to your interviewee when you arranged the interview? Has this been supplied?

☑ How will your appearance during the interview affect the willingness of the interviewee to share data?

☑ How will your level of preparation and knowledge (in relation to the research context and your research question) affect the willingness of the interviewee to share data?

☑ How would you like to record the data which is revealed to you during the interview? Where this involves using a tape recorder, have you raised this as a request and provided a reason for it helping you to use this technique?

Opening the interview:

☑ How will you prepare yourself to be able to commence the interview with confidence and purpose?

☑ What will you tell your interviewee about youself and the purpose of your research?

☑ What concerns, or need for clarification, may your interviewee have?

☑ How will you seek to overcome these concerns or provide this clarification?

☑ In particular, how do you intend to use the data to which you are given access?

☑ How do you intend to record the data which is shared with you? What rights will your interviewee have in relation to the use of a tape recorder where they have agreed in principle to let you use one?

Table 9.3 Checklist for the use of semi-structured and in-depth interviews

☑ How long will you have to conduct the interview?

☑ How do you wish to conduct (or structure) the interview?

Conducting the interview:

☑ How will you use appropriate language and tone of voice, and avoid jargon when asking questions or discussing themes?

☑ How will you ask appropriately worded open questions to obtain relevant data?

☑ How will you ask appropriately worded probing questions to build on, clarify or explain your interviewee's responses?

☑ How will you avoid asking leading questions which may introduce forms of bias?

☑ How will you order questions, where the early introduction of sensitive issues may introduce interviewee bias?

☑ How will you avoid over-zealously asking questions and pressing your interviewee for a response where it should be clear that they do not wish to provide one?

☑ How will you listen attentively and demonstrate this to your interviewee?

☑ How will you test and summarise your understanding of the data which is shared with you in order to ensure its accuracy?

☑ How will you allow your interviewee to maintain control over the use of a tape recorder, where used, if they wish to exercise this?

☑ How will you carry out a number of tasks at the same time, including listening, note taking and the identification of areas which need to be probed further?

☑ How will you identify actions and comments made by your interviewee which indicate an aspect of the discussion which should be explored in order to reveal the reason for the response?

☑ How will you avoid projecting your own views or feelings through your actions or comments?

☑ How will you maintain a check on the interview themes which you intend to cover and steer the discussion where appropriate to raise and explore these aspects?

☑ How will you draw the interview to a close within the agreed time limit and thank the interviewee for their time and the data they have shared with you?

Recording the information:

☑ How will you remember the interviewee's responses for long enough to make an accurate record?

☑ Has your schedule of work been formulated to permit you to find sufficient time to write up your notes and analyse them before undertaking further data collection?

☑ How will you organise your material so that you retain a copy of your original notes, an extended version of your notes after writing them up or a transcript of relevant material, and a set of additional notes or memos relating to the interview and your learning from that particular experience?

Table 9.3 Checklist for the use of semi-structured and in-depth interviews (*continued*)

9.8 A FINAL WORD ABOUT GROUP INTERVIEWS

We can also differentiate interviews according to whether there are one or more participants. While the discussion in this chapter relates to both one-to-one and group interviews, the latter category poses particular problems as well as providing advantages in certain circumstances. In a *group interview* you will act as facilitator and manager of the discussion. The interview is likely be relatively unstructured and to be fairly free flowing (Zikmund, 1994), although of course where you use this method you will have particular themes which you wish to explore. The onus will be placed firmly on you to explain its purpose, encourage participants to relax and to initiate the discussion (Easterby-Smith *et al.*, 1991), although the opportunity for you to develop the level of rapport which is possible in one-to-one interviews will not be present. Once established the discussion will need to be managed, in order to encourage involvement by all members of the group and to maintain its intended focus. A high level of skill will therefore be required from you to be able to conduct this type of discussion successfully.

Despite these difficulties there are distinct advantages. Because of the presence of several participants, this type of situation allows for a variety of points of view to emerge and for the group to respond to and discuss these views. A dynamic group can generate or respond to a number of ideas and evaluate them, thus helping you to explain or explore concepts. They can also generate numbers of key themes which become the subject of a survey. For example, in an attitude survey the initial use of focus group interviews, as these are often referred to, can lead to a 'bottom-up' generation of concerns and issues which helps to establish the survey and also to involve those who will be asked to provide the data which will be vital for its success. Focus group interviews are also used in market research to test reactions to products and in a range of other contexts. Their use may allow you to adopt an interview-based strategy which can more easily be related to a representative sample, particularly where the research project is being conducted within a specific organisation or in relation to a clearly defined population. This may help to establish the credibility of this research where an attempt is made to overcome issues of bias associated with interviews in general and this type in particular.

If you are thinking about using group interviews, consideration of the following specific issues may help.

- Where your research project (or part of it) occurs within an organisation, the request to participate in a group interview may be received by individuals as an instruction rather than something about which they may exercise choice. This may be the case where an organisation is acting as a host for your research and the request is sent out on official notepaper or in the name of a manager, or where you work in the organisation. In our experience participants often welcome the chance to 'have their say'. But where any request may be perceived as indicating lack of choice, to gain their confidence you will need to exercise care over the wording to be used and in your introduction to the group when the interview occurs in order to provide a clear assurance about confidentiality.

- The effect of gathering people together may be to inhibit possible contributions. This may be related to lack of trust, perceptions about status differences or because of the dominance of certain individuals. The nature and selection of each group will affect the first two elements. We would advise using a *horizontal slice* through an organisation to select a sample of people who have a similar status and similar work experiences. (Using a *vertical slice* would introduce perceptions about status differences and variations in work experience.) In this way group interviews can be conducted at a number of levels within an organisation. A reference may be made about the nature of the group to provide reassurance, and you may consider asking people to introduce themselves by their first name without referring to their exact job.

- Where one or two people dominate the discussion you should carefully seek to reduce their contributions and bring others in. Torrington (1991) suggests that this may be attempted in a general way:

  - 'What do you think, Barry?'

  - 'What do other people think about this?'

  or more specifically:

  - 'How does Sally's point relate to the one which you raised, Sheila?'

  A question posed to other group members should also have the effect of inhibiting the contribution of a dominant member:

  - 'What do you think about John's suggestion?'

- You will need to ensure that participants understand each other's contributions and that you develop an accurate understanding of the points being made. Asking a participant to clarify the meaning of a particular contribution, where it has not been understood, and testing understanding through summarising should help to ensure this.

- You will need to consider the location and setting for a group interview. It is advisable to conduct the interview in a neutral setting rather than, say, in a manager's office, where participants may not feel relaxed. There should be no likelihood of interruption or being overheard. You should consider the layout of the seating in the room where the interview is to be held. Arrange the seating in a circular fashion so that everyone will be facing inward and so that they will be an equal distance from the central point of this circle.

- The demands of conducting this type of interview and the potential wealth of ideas which may flow from it mean that it may be difficult to manage the process and note key points at the same time. We have managed to overcome this by using two interviewers, where one person facilitates the discussion and the other person makes notes. Where you cannot use this approach you need to write up notes almost immediately so as not to lose data. We would not advise one person to undertake interviews like this 'back to back' because of the danger of losing or confusing data.

9.9 SUMMARY

- In-depth interviews are difficult to conduct properly.
- Interviews can be differentiated according to the level of structure and standardisation adopted. Different types of interview are useful for different research purposes.
- You can use in-depth and semi-structured interviews to explore topics and explain other findings.
- Your research design may incorporate more than one type of interview.
- In-depth and semi-structured interviews can be used in quantitative as well as qualitative research.
- There are situations favouring in-depth interviews which will lead you to use this method. Apart from the nature of your research strategy, these are related to the significance of establishing personal contact; the nature of your data collection questions; and the length of time required from those who provide data.
- Data-quality issues, your level of competence and logistical and resource matters will all need to be considered when you use in-depth and semi-structured interviews.
- Apart from one-to-one interviews, you may consider using group interviews. There may be particular advantages associated with group interviews, but these are considerably more difficult to manage than one-to-one interviews.

Self-check questions and assignment

Self-check question 9.1
What type of interview would you use in each of the following situations:

a a market research project?

b a research project seeking to understand whether trade union attitudes have changed?

c following the analysis of a questionnaire?

Self-check question 9.2
What are the advantages of using semi-structured and in-depth interviews?

Self-check question 9.3
During a presentation of your proposal to undertake a research project which will be qualitatively based using semi-structured or in-depth interviews, you feel that you have dealt well with the relationship between the purpose of the research and the proposed methodology when one of the panel leans forward and asks you to discuss the trustworthiness and usefulness of your work for other researchers. This is clearly a challenge to see if you can defend such a qualitative approach. How do you respond?

Self-check question 9.4
Having quizzed you about the trustworthiness and usefulness of your work for other researchers, the panel member decides that one more testing question is in order. He

explains that qualitatively based work isn't an easy option. 'It isn't an easier alternative for those who want to avoid quantitative work,' he says. 'How can we be sure that you're competent to be involved in interview work, especially where the external credibility of this organisation may be affected by the impression which you create in the field?' How will you respond to this concern?

Self-check question 9.5
What are the key issues to consider when planning to use semi-structured or in-depth interviews?

Self-check question 9.6
What are the key areas of competence which you need to develop in order to conduct an interview successfully?

Assignment 9:
Using semi-structured or in-depth interviews in your research

- Review your research question(s) and objectives. How appropriate would it be to use semi-structured or in-depth interviews to collect data? Where it is appropriate, explain the relationship between your research question(s) and objectives and the use of semi-structured or in-depth interviews. Where this type of interviewing is not appropriate, justify your decision.

- If you decide that semi-structured or in-depth interviews are appropriate, what practical problems do you foresee? How may you attempt to overcome these practical problems?

- What threats to the trustworthiness of the data collected are you likely to encounter? How may you overcome these?

- Draft a list of interview themes to be explored, and thoroughly compare these with your research question(s) and objectives.

- Ask your project tutor to comment on your judgement about the use of semi-structured or in-depth interviews, the issues and threats which you have identified, your suggestions to overcome these, and the fit between your interview themes and the research question(s) and objectives.

References

Bryman, A. (1988) *Quantity and Quality in Social Research*, London, Unwin Hyman.

Easterby-Smith, M., Thorpe, R. and Lowe, A. (1991) *Management Research: An Introduction*, London, Sage.

Emory, C. and Cooper, D. (1991) *Business Research Methods* (4th edn), Homewood, Illinois, Richard D. Irwin.

Ghauri, P.N., Grønhaug, K. and Kristianslund, I. (1995) *Research Methods in Business Studies: A Practical Guide*, London, Prentice-Hall.

Grummitt, J. (1980) *Interviewing Skills*, London, The Industrial Society.

Healey, M.J. (1991) 'Obtaining Information from Businesses', in Healey, M.J. (ed.) *Economic Activity and Land Use*, Harlow, Longman, pp. 193–251.

Healey, M.J. and Rawlinson, M.B. (1993) 'Interviewing Business Owners and Managers: A Review of Methods and Techniques', *Geoforum*, 24: 3, 339–55.

Healey, M.J. and Rawlinson, M.B. (1994) 'Interviewing Techniques in Business and Management Research', in Wass, V.J. and Wells, P.E. *Principles and Practice in Business and Management Research*, Aldershot, Dartmouth, pp. 123–46.

Hofstede, G. (1991) *Cultures and Organisations*, London, McGraw-Hill.

Jankowicz, A.D. (1995) *Business Research Projects for Students* (2nd edn), London, Chapman & Hall.

Kahn, R. and Cannell, C. (1957) *The Dynamics of Interviewing*, New York and Chichester, John Wiley.

Marshall, C. and Rossman, G.B. (1989) *Designing Qualitative Research*, Newbury Park, California, Sage.

North, D.J., Leigh, R. and Gough, J. (1983) 'Monitoring Industrial Change at the Local Level: Some Comments on Methods and Data Sources', in Healey, M.J. (ed.) *Urban and Regional Industrial Research: The Changing UK Data Base*, Norwich, Geo Books, pp. 111–29.

Powney, J. and Watts, M. (1987) *Interviewing in Educational Research*, London, Routledge and Kegan Paul.

Robson, C. (1993) *Real World Research*, Oxford, Blackwell.

Sykes, W. (1991) 'Taking stock: issues from the literature in validity and reliability in qualitative research', *Journal of Market Research Society*, 33, 3–12.

Torrington, D. (1991) *Management Face to Face*, London, Prentice Hall.

Wass, V. and Wells, P. (1994) 'Research Methods in Action: An Introduction', in Wass, V.J. and Wells, P.E. *Principles and Practice in Business and Management Research*, Aldershot, Dartmouth, pp. 1–34.

Yin, R.K. (1994) *Case Study Research: Design and Methods* (2nd edn), Beverly Hills, California, Sage.

Zikmund, W.G. (1994) *Business Research Methods*, Fort Worth, Dryden Press.

Further Reading

Easterby-Smith, M., Thorpe, R. and Lowe, A. (1991) *Management Research: An Introduction*, London, Sage. Chapter 5 provides a very useful and highly readable overview of qualitative methods. This includes in-depth interviews and other methods to supplement them.

Krueger, R.C. (1994) *Focus Groups: A Practical Guide for Applied Research* (2nd edn), London, Sage. A very useful work for those considering the use of this method.

Marshall, C. and Rossman, G.B. (1989) *Designing Qualitative Research*, Newbury Park, California, Sage. This provides many excellent insights into the design of qualitative research and the methods associated with it.

Healey, M.J. and Rawlinson, M.B. (1994) 'Interviewing Techniques in Business and Management research', in Wass, V.J. and Wells, P.E. *Principles and Practice in Business and Management Research*, Aldershot, Dartmouth, pp. 123–46. This is an excellent contribution and a 'must' for those of you intending to use qualitative research and interviews.

Case 9:
The practices and styles of public relations practitioners

Public relations (PR) practitioners are a significant and growing group in the UK. Some of them operate internationally with great sophistication to improve their companies' profiles and stock exchange status. Some peddle sex stories to the tabloid press. Another group in politics, known as 'spin doctors', are hired to make political moves more acceptable. However, in the UK there has been very little substantive research into PR practices and styles. This is partly because of the lack of a UK journal dedicated to research in public relations and partly because PR has traditionally been subsumed within the discipline of marketing.

Valerie designed a case study which sought to examine the practices and styles of public relations practitioners. However, it was recognised that this group included a wide range of people from publicity technicians to corporate communications professionals. The first stage of the research project was designed to examine the practices and styles of public relations practitioners through the eyes of those they interact with most frequently – namely journalists. The second stage was designed to gauge public relations practitioners' own assessments of the way they operate.

A theoretical basis for this study was established by using the model devised by Grunig and Hunt (1984). This identified a number of public relations styles based on research conducted in the USA:

- Press agency – little research, main aim to get firm/product mentions in the media, truth not vital. Emphasis on one-way communication.

- Public information – some research, main aim to get media exposure, truth matters. Emphasis on one-way communication.

- Two-way asymmetric – founded on research, aim to seek behaviour change, can be manipulative.

- Two-way symmetric – held to be the most ethical, sophisticated and far-reaching in that there is dialogue, negotiation and compromise to try and achieve understanding.

This research project, therefore, was exceedingly ambitious in seeking to recognise and verify the existence of such styles and relationships in the context of public relations practices in the UK. It also faced potential barriers of cultural misunderstanding, based as it was in an unfamiliar area of analysis. Degree-level courses in public relations, which have progressed from the practical to the academic, have only been running at UK universities for the past few years. Graduates with a knowledge of Grunig and Hunt's and others' key theories are only beginning to percolate into a few PR consultancies and in-house departments. The majority of public relations people have only a general degree or a CAMS certificate, or are promoted from secretaries and assistants. Grunig and Hunt's model is, however, seminal to judging PR as either a craft, using technician-level thinking, or as something one could rightly call a profession. Because the terminology of the study was not familiar to many people it was decided that semi-structured interviews would be the best mode of approach in order to overcome these barriers by providing interpretation and clarification as necessary. However, the selection of interview subjects posed equal problems:

- there were time constraints to this research project;
- PR practitioners interact with all the media, using slightly different techniques with each;
- PR consultancies in certain locations such as London practise internationally and at a higher level of sophistication than others;
- Tunstall's (1972) important work on journalistic practice in the UK indicated that there were also great differences in the standards and approach of journalists working for different specialist areas.

The decision was taken to concentrate the first part of the research on newspaper journalists and to follow this up with journalists from radio and television. The journalists would be drawn half from national publications in London and half from the regional press; and four different specialisms would be covered, namely general news, women's interest pages, business pages and political journalism. A major factor in this decision was Valerie's background in newspapers as well as in public relations, since it was important that in seeking out subjects the interviewer could be seen to have a background which was relevant and credible.

The choice of specialisms was made for the following reasons. The news section receives the widest variety of PR news releases and personal contacts. The women's pages receive the most concentrated approaches from public relations practitioners in the consumer goods areas. The business pages receive the most sophisticated forms of PR aimed at enhancing the credibility, image and stock market standing of major firms. The political journalists receive the most intensive PR pressures of a governmental, party political and general lobby type.

The ideal targets to select, however, are rarely the simplest. The journalists who would best be able to illustrate the type and level of PR approaches they received would of necessity be working long, anti-social hours; would have very busy and often unpredictable diaries; could frequently be protected by filter-style secretaries; and might possibly self-select because of polarised views about public relations practice.

It therefore took approximately eight months to make appointments with 25 journalists who constituted the right spectrum and balance – 25 who agreed to be interviewed out of some 120 contacted overall. However, a random element entered the selection, in that if a first phone call to a certain newspaper asking for a named person was unsuccessful, the caller would always ask if a second name from that specialism was there, or, failing that, if any of the journalists from an alternative specialism would be prepared to take the call. If a journalist agreed to help with the study, a confirmatory letter would be sent and the appointment double checked.

The use of a tape recorder during each interview did not prove an obstacle, since all of the subjects were well used to this interview format themselves and appeared quickly able to ignore a very discreet form of this technology. They were also promised anonymity.

In a pilot test interview it had been found that a broad approach to the topic – 'What do you consider to be the style of relationship between journalists and public relations officers?' – worked best, followed by questions on what they perceived the role of public relations practitioners to be. Many answers were reflected back to test understanding and to clarify what the journalists felt to be the most important factors of certain interactive processes between them and public relations practitioners. But the most successful ingredient of all was the critical incident technique: in recounting what they felt to be the best and the worst examples of treatment by public relations practitioners they had experienced, the journalists usually became much more expansive and revealing. These questions were posed at a later stage in the meeting when some rapport had been established, and often acted as a corrective to one or two somewhat guarded initial statements.

Both the interviewer and interviewees appreciated the dangers of generalising from the particular. Yet it was easier than Valerie had anticipated to delineate differences between reported approaches of public relations practitioners as press agents, and those who had a more sophisticated and more long-term approach to the building of positive media coverage and relationships. In the majority of cases it was the journalists who volunteered the information about when and how far they had ever felt in the position of being manipulated by public relations practitioners. But those few who had to be asked if they had ever had this experience were not resentful of the inference and appeared to accept the existence of manipulative practice as a recognised by-product of public relations.

References

Grunig, J. and Hunt, T. (1984) *Managing Public Relations*, New York, Reinhart and Winston.

Tunstall, J. (1972) 'News Organisation Goals and Specialist News Gathering Journalists', in McQuail, D. *Sociology of Mass Communications*, London, Penguin, pp. 259–80.

Case-study questions

1 What are the strengths of the design of this research project? Give reasons for your answer.

2 What are the weaknesses of the design of this research project? Give reasons for your answer. How would you seek to overcome them?

3 What reasons would you advance for using semi-structured or in-depth interviews in relation to this research project?

4 What data-quality issues are evident in relation to the conduct of this research project?

5 How were these data-quality issues managed during the period of the research project referred to above?

6 What logistical and resource issues are associated with the research project and what are the implications of these for its conduct?

Answers to self-check questions

Self-check question 9.1

The type of interview which is likely to be used in each of these situations is as follows:

a A standardised and structured interview where the aim is to develop response patterns from the views of people. The interview schedule might be designed to combine styles, so that comments made by interviewees in relation to specific questions could also be recorded.

b The situation outlined suggests an exploratory approach to research and therefore an in-depth interview would be most appropriate.

c The situation outlined here suggests that an explanatory approach is required in relation to the data collected and in this case a semi-structured interview is likely to be appropriate.

Self-check question 9.2

Reasons which suggest the use of interviews include:

- the exploratory or explanatory nature of your research;
- situations where it will be significant to establish personal contact, in relation to interviewee sensitivity about the nature of the information to be provided and the use to be made of this;
- situations where the researcher needs to exercise control over the nature of those who supply data;
- situations where there are a large number of questions to be answered;
- situations where questions are complex or open-ended;
- situations where the order and logic of questioning may need to be varied.

Self-check question 9.3

Certainly politely! Your response needs to show that you are aware of the issues relating to reliability, bias and generalisability which might arise. It would be useful to discuss how these might be overcome through the following: the design of the research; the keeping of records or a diary in relation to the processes and key incidents of the research project as well as the recording of data collected; attempts to control bias through the process of collecting data; and the relationship of the research to theory.

Self-check question 9.4

Perhaps it will be wise to say that you understand his position. You realise that any approach to research calls for particular types of competence. Your previous answer touching on interviewee bias has highlighted the need to establish credibility and gain the interviewee's confidence. While competence will need to be developed over a period of time, allowing for any classroom simulations and dry runs with colleagues, probably the best approach will be your level of preparation before embarking on interview work. This relates first to the nature of the approach made to those who you would like to participate in the research project and the information supplied to them; second to your intellectual preparation related to the topic to be explored and the particular context of the organisations participating in the research;

third to your ability to conduct an interview. You also recognise that piloting the interview themes will be a crucial element towards building your competence.

Self-check question 9.5
Key issues to consider are the following:

- Planning to minimise the occurrence of forms of bias where these are within your control, related to interviewer bias, interviewee bias and sampling bias.

- Considering your aim in requesting the research interview and how you can seek to prepare yourself in order to gain access to the data which you hope your participants will be able to share with you.

- Devising interview themes which you wish to explore or seek explanations for during the interview.

- Sending a list of your interview themes to your interviewee before the interview, where this is considered appropriate.

- Requesting permission, and providing a reason, where you would like to use a tape recorder during the interview.

- Making sure that your level of preparation and knowledge (in relation to the research context and your research question(s) and objectives) is satisfactory in order to establish your credibility when you meet your interviewee.

- Considering how your intended appearance during the interview will affect the willingness of the interviewee to share data.

Self-check question 9.6
There are several areas where you need to develop and demonstrate competence in relation to the conduct of semi-structured and in-depth research interviews. These areas are:

- opening the interview;
- using appropriate language;
- questioning;
- listening;
- testing and summarising understanding;
- behavioural cues;
- recording data.

CHAPTER 10

Collecting primary data using questionnaires

The objectives of this chapter are to introduce you to questionnaires as a data collection method, help you decide whether they can play a part in your research project and provide advice on their design.

The chapter examines both self-administered and interviewer-administered questionnaires and explores their advantages and disadvantages. Their relationships to your research question(s) and objectives are considered.

Practical advice is offered on the process of designing, piloting and administering questionnaires to enhance response rates and the validity and reliability of the data collected.

10.1 INTRODUCTION

The greatest use of questionnaires is made by the survey strategy (Section 4.2). However, both experiment and case-study research strategies can make use of these techniques. There are various definitions of the term questionnaire (Oppenheim, 1992). Some authors (for example Kervin, 1992) reserve it exclusively for surveys where the person answering the question actually records their own answers. Others (for example Bell, 1993) use it as a more general term to include interviews which are administered either face to face or by telephone.

In this book we use *questionnaire* as a general term to include all techniques of data collection in which each person is asked to respond to the same set of questions in a predetermined order (deVaus, 1991). It therefore includes both structured interviews and telephone questionnaires as well as those in which the questions are answered without an interviewer being present. The range of techniques which fall under this broad heading are outlined in the next section (10.2), along with their relative advantages and disadvantages.

The use of questionnaires is discussed in many research methods texts. These range from those which devote a few pages to those which specify precisely how you should construct and use them, such as Dillman's (1978) *Total Design Method*. Perhaps not surprisingly, questionnaires are one of the most widely used survey data collection techniques. Because each person (*respondent*) is asked to respond to the same set of questions, it provides an efficient way of collecting responses from a large sample prior to quantitative analysis (Chapter 11). However, before you decide to use a questionnaire we would like to sound a note of caution. Many authors (for example Bell, 1993; Oppenheim, 1992) argue it is far harder to produce a good questionnaire than you might think. You need to ensure that it will collect the precise data you require to answer your research question(s) and achieve your objectives. This is of paramount importance, as you are unlikely to be able to go back to people and collect additional data using another questionnaire. These issues are discussed in Section 10.3.

The design of your questionnaire will affect the response rate and the reliability and validity of the data you collect. Response rates, validity and reliability can be maximised by:

- careful design of individual questions;
- clear layout of the questionnaire form;
- lucid explanation of the purpose of the questionnaire;
- pilot testing.

Together these form the content of Section 10.4 in which we discuss designing your survey. Administering the actual questionnaire is considered in Section 10.5.

10.2 AN OVERVIEW OF QUESTIONNAIRE TECHNIQUES

When to use questionnaires

We have found that many people use a questionnaire to collect data without considering other methods such as examination of secondary sources (Chapter 7), observation (Chapter 8), semi-structured or in-depth interviews (Chapter 9). Our advice is to evaluate all possible data collection methods and choose those most appropriate to your research question(s) and objectives. Questionnaires are not particularly good for exploratory or other research which requires large numbers of open-ended questions (Sections 9.2 and 9.3). They work best with standardised questions which you can be confident will be interpreted the same way by all respondents (Robson, 1993).

Questionnaires can therefore be used for descriptive or explanatory research. *Descriptive research*, such as that undertaken using attitude and opinion questionnaires and questionnaires on organisational practices, will enable you to identify and describe the variability in different phenomena. In contrast, *explanatory* or *analytical research* will enable you to examine and explain relationships between variables, in particular cause and effect relationships. These two purposes have different research design requirements (Gill and Johnson, 1991) which we will discuss later (Section 10.3).

Although questionnaires may be used as the only data collection method, it is often better to link them with other methods in a *multi-method* approach (Section 4.3). For example, a questionnaire to discover customers' attitudes can be complemented by in-depth interviews to explore and understand these attitudes (Section 9.3). In addition, questionnaires, if worded correctly, usually require less skill and sensitivity to administer than do semi-structured or in-depth interviews (Jankowicz, 1995).

Types of questionnaire

The design of a questionnaire differs according to how it is administered, in particular the amount of contact you have with the respondents (Fig 10.1). *Self-administered questionnaires* are usually completed by the respondents. Such questionnaires are either posted to respondents who return them by post after completion (*postal* or *mail questionnaires*), or delivered by hand to each respondent and collected later (*delivery and collection questionnaires*). Responses to *interviewer-administered questionnaires* are recorded by the interviewer on the basis of each respondent's answers. A growing number of surveys, particularly in the area of market research, contact respondents and administer questionnaires using the telephone. These are known as *telephone questionnaires*. The final category, *structured interviews* (sometimes known as *interview schedules*), refers to those questionnaires where interviewers physically meet respondents and ask the questions face to face. These differ from semi-structured and in-depth interviews (Section 9.2) as there is a defined schedule of questions from which interviewers should not deviate.

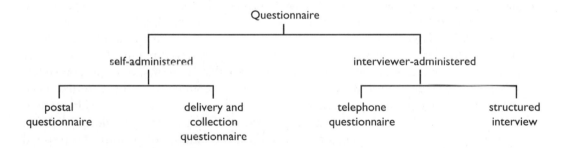

Fig 10.1 Types of questionnaire

The choice of questionnaire

Your choice of questionnaire will be influenced by a variety of factors related to your research question(s) and objectives (Table 10.1), in particular the:

- characteristics of the respondents from which you wish to collect data;
- importance of reaching a particular person as respondent;
- importance of respondents' answers not being contaminated or distorted;
- size of sample you require for your analysis, taking into account the likely response rate;
- types of questions you need to ask to collect your data;
- number of questions you need to ask to collect your data.

These factors will not apply equally to your choice of questionnaire, and for some research questions or objectives may not apply at all. The type of questionnaire you choose will dictate how sure you can be that the respondent is the person whom you wish to answer the questions and thus determine the reliability of responses (Table 10.1). Even if you address a postal questionnaire to a company manager by name, you have no way of ensuring that person will be the respondent. It could be completed by an assistant or someone else! With delivery and collection questionnaires you can sometimes check who has answered the questions at collection. By contrast, interviewer-administered questionnaires enable you to ensure that the respondent is the person you want. This improves the reliability of your data. In addition, you can record who were non-respondents, thereby avoiding unknown bias caused by refusals.

Any *contamination* of respondents' answers will reduce your data's reliability (Table 10.1). Respondents to self-administered questionnaires are relatively unlikely to answer to please you or because they believe certain responses are more *socially desirable* (Dillman, 1978). They may, however, discuss their answers with others, thereby contaminating their response. Respondents to telephone questionnaires and structured interviews are more likely to answer to please due to contact with you, although the impact of this can be minimised by good interviewing technique (Section 9.5). Responses can also be contaminated or distorted when recorded. In extreme instances interviewers may invent responses. For this reason random checks of interviewers are often made by survey organisations (Moser and Kalton, 1986).

The type of questionnaire you choose will affect the number of people who respond (Section 6.2). Interviewer-administered questionnaires will usually have a higher response rate than self-administered questionnaires (Table 10.1). The size of your sample and the way in which it is selected will have implications for the confidence you can have in your data and the extent to which you can generalise (Section 6.2).

Longer questionnaires are best presented as a structured interview. In addition they can include more complicated questions than can telephone questionnaires or self-administered questionnaires (Oppenheim, 1992). The presence of an interviewer means that it is also easier to route different subgroups of respondents to answer different questions using a filter question (Section 10.4). The suitability of different types of question also differs between techniques.

Attribute	Type of questionnaire			
	Postal	Delivery and collection	Telephone	Structured interview
Population's characteristics for which suitable	Literate individuals who can be contacted by post; selected by name, household or organisation etc.		Individuals who can be telephoned; selected by name, household or organisation etc.	Any; selected by name, household, organisation or in the street etc.
Confidence that the right person has responded	Low	Low, but can be checked at collection	High	High
Likelihood of contamination or distortion of respondent's answer	May be contaminated by consultation with others		Occasionally distorted or invented by interviewer	Occasionally contaminated by consultation with others or distorted/invented by interviewer
Size of sample	Large, can be geographically dispersed	Dependent on number of field workers	Dependent on number of interviewers	
Likely response rate*	Variable, 30% reasonable	Moderately high, 30–50% reasonable	High, 50–70% reasonable	High, 50–70% reasonable
Feasible length of questionnaire	6–8 A4 pages		Up to half an hour	Variable depending on location
Suitable types of question	Closed questions but not too complex, only simple sequencing, must be of interest to respondent		Open and closed questions, but only simple questions, complicated sequencing acceptable	Open and closed questions, including complicated questions, complicated sequencing acceptable
Time taken to complete data collection	4–8 weeks from posting (depending on number of follow-ups)	Dependent on sample size, number of field workers etc.	Dependent on sample size, number of interviewers etc., but slower than self-administered for sample size	
Main financial resource implications	Outward and return postage, photocopying, clerical support, data entry	Field workers, travel, photocopying, clerical support, data entry	Interviewers, telephone calls, clerical support; photocopying and data entry if not using CATI$, computers if using CATI	Interviewers, travel, clerical support; photocopying and data entry if not using CAPI£; computers if using CAPI
Role of the interviewer/field worker	None	Delivery and collection of questionnaires, enhancing respondent participation	Enhancing respondent participation, guiding the respondent through the questionnaire, answering respondents' questions	
Ease of automating data input# (only suitable with large numbers of respondents)	Closed questions can be designed so that responses can be entered using optical mark readers after questionnaire has been returned		Response to all questions can be entered at time of collection using CATI$	Response to all questions can be entered at time of collection using CAPI£

Table 10.1 Main attributes of questionnaires

*Discussed in Chapter 6   #Discussed in Section 11.2   £Computer aided personal interviewing $Computer aided telephone interviewing
Source: developed from Dillman, 1978; Oppenheim, 1992; deVaus, 1991

Your choice of questionnaire will also be affected by the resources you have available (Table 10.1), in particular the:

- time available to complete the data collection;
- financial implications of data collection and entry;
- availability of interviewers and field workers to assist;
- ease of automating data entry.

Time needed for data collection increases markedly for delivery and collection questionnaires and structured interviews where the samples are geographically dispersed (Table 10.1). One way in which you can overcome this constraint is to select your sample using cluster sampling (Section 6.2). Unless *computer aided personal interviewing (CAPI)* or *computer aided telephone interviewing (CATI)* are used, you will need to consider the costs of reproducing the questionnaire, clerical support and entering the data for computer analysis. For postal and telephone questionnaires cost estimates for postage and telephone calls will need to be included. If you are working for an organisation postage costs may be reduced by using *freepost* for questionnaire return. This means that you pay postage and a small handling charge only for those questionnaires which are returned by post.

Virtually all data collected by questionnaires are analysed by computer. Once your data have been coded and entered into the computer you will be able to explore and analyse it far more quickly and thoroughly than by hand (Section 11.2). As a rough rule, you should analyse questionnaire data by computer if it has been collected from 30 or more respondents. For larger surveys you may wish to automate the input of data. For self-administered questionnaires this can be done for closed questions where respondents select and mark their answer from a prescribed list.

WORKED EXAMPLE: *Closed question designed for an optical mark reader*

The following question is typical of those used for large-scale market research. Similar questions can be found in many postal questionnaires. Respondents are given clear instructions on how to mark their responses on the questionnaire:

Please use a pencil to mark your answer as a solid box like this: [▬▬]
If you make a mistake use an eraser to rub out your answer.

I Please mark all the types of music which you regularly listen to:	Pop/Rock	[ ]
	Reggae	[ ]
	New Age	[ ]
	Jazz	[ ]
	Classical	[ ]
	Easy listening	[ ]
	Other	[ ]
	(please describe:)	

....

The mark is read using an *optical mark reader* which recognises and converts marks into data at rates sometimes exceeding 200 pages a minute. Data for interviewer administered questionnaires can be entered directly into the computer at the time of interview using CATI or CAPI software. With both types of software you read the questions to the respondent from the screen and record their answers directly into the computer. Because of the costs of computers, software and pre-survey programming, CATI and CAPI are only financially viable for very large surveys or where repeated use of the computers and software will be made.

In reality, you are almost certain to have to make compromises in your choice of questionnaire. These will be unique to your research. This is emphasised by Dillman (1978). He argues that the question of which type of questionnaire is most suitable cannot be answered in isolation from your research question(s) and objectives and the population you are surveying.

10.3 DECIDING WHAT DATA NEED TO BE COLLECTED

Research design requirements

Unlike in-depth and semi-structured interviews (Chapter 9), the questions you ask in questionnaires need to be defined precisely before data collection. Whereas you can prompt and explore issues further with in-depth and semi-structured interviews, this will not be possible for questionnaires. In addition, the questionnaire offers only one chance to collect the data, as it is often difficult to identify respondents or return to collect additional information. This means that the time you spend planning precisely what data you need to collect, how you intend to analyse them (Chapter 11) and designing your questionnaire to meet these requirements is crucial if you are to answer your research question(s) and meet your objectives.

For most management and business research the data you collect using questionnaires will be used for either descriptive or explanatory purposes. For questions where the main purpose is to describe the population's characteristics either at a fixed time or at a series of times to enable comparisons, you will normally need to administer your questionnaire to a sample. The sample needs to be as representative and accurate as possible, as it will be used to generalise about the total population (Sections 6.1 to 6.3). Where possible your findings will also need to be related to earlier research. It is important that you select the appropriate characteristics to answer your research question(s) and address your objectives. You therefore need to have:

- reviewed the literature carefully;
- discussed your ideas with colleagues, your project tutor and other interested parties.

For research involving organisations we have found it essential to understand the organisations in which we are undertaking the research. Without this it is easy to make mistakes, such as using the wrong terminology, and to collect useless data. For many research projects this can be achieved through reading company publications, observation (Chapter 8) and in-depth and semi-structured interviews (Chapter 9).

Explanatory research requires data to test a theory or theories. This means that, in addition to those issues raised for descriptive research, you need to define the theories you wish to test as relationships between variables before designing your questionnaire. You therefore need to have reviewed the literature carefully, discussed your ideas widely and conceptualised your own research clearly (Ghauri *et al.*, 1995). In particular you need to be clear about which:

- relationships you think are likely to exist between variables;
- variables are *dependent*, that is, change in response to changes in other variables;
- variables are *independent*, that is, cause changes in dependent variables;
- variables are *extraneous*, that is, might also cause changes in dependent variables, thereby providing an alternative explanation to your independent variables.

WORKED EXAMPLE: *Defining theories in terms of relationships between variables*

As part of her research Han wished to test the theory that the incidence of repetitive strain injury (RSI) was linked to the number of rest periods that keyboard operators took each working day.

The relationship that was thought to exist between the variables was that the incidence of RSI was higher when fewer or no rest periods were taken each day. The dependent variable was the incidence of RSI and the independent variable was the number of rest periods taken each day. Han thought that extraneous variables such as the use of proper seating and wrist rests might also influence the incidence of RSI. Data were therefore collected on these variables as well.

As these relationships are likely to be tested through statistical analysis (Section 11.5) of the data collected by your questionnaire, you need to be clear about the way they will be measured at the design stage. Where possible you should ensure measures are compatible with those used in other relevant research so that comparisons can be made (Section 11.2).

Types of variable

The sorts of data that can be collected through questionnaires have been grouped by Dillman (1978) into four distinct types of variable:

- attitudes;
- beliefs;
- behaviour;
- attributes.

These distinctions are important as they will influence the way your questions are worded. *Attitude* variables record how respondents feel about something. They differ from *belief* variables where you record what respondents think or believe is true or false. As a consequence, questions about belief should imply neither good or bad, only an assessment of what the respondent thinks. Although these two sorts of data can appear similar, it is important to specify precisely which you need to ensure that your questions collect the data you need.

In contrast, data on behaviours and attributes are more straightforward to collect (Robson, 1993). When recording what respondents do, you are recording their *behaviour*. This differs from respondents' beliefs because you are recording a concrete experience. Behavioural variables contain data on what people (or their organisations) did in the past, do now, or will do in the future. By contrast, *attribute* variables contain data about the respondents' characteristics. They are best thought of as something a respondent possesses, rather than something a respondent does (Dillman, 1978) and are used to explore how attitudes, beliefs and behaviour differ between respondents as well as to check that the data collected are representative of the total population (Section 6.2). Attributes include characteristics such as age, gender, marital status, education, occupation and income.

WORKED EXAMPLE: *Attitude, belief, behaviour and attribute questions*

You have been asked to undertake an anonymous survey of financial advisers' ethical values. In particular, your sponsors are interested in the advice given to clients. After some deliberation you come up with three questions which address the issue of putting the client's interests before their own:

2 How do you feel about the following statement? 'Financial advisers should place their client's interest before their own.'

	strongly agree ❑
(please tick the appropriate box)	mildly agree ❑
	neither agree or disagree ❑
	mildly disagree ❑
	strongly disagree ❑

3 In general, do financial advisers place their client's interests before their own?

	always yes ❑
(please tick the appropriate box)	usually yes ❑
	sometimes yes ❑
	seldom yes ❑
	never yes ❑

4 How often do you place your client's interests before your own?

	80–100% of my time ❑
(please tick the appropriate box)	60–79% of my time ❑
	40–59% of my time ❑
	20–39% of my time ❑
	0–19% of my time ❑

Your choice of question or questions to include in your questionnaire will depend on whether your need to collect data on financial advisers' attitudes, beliefs or behaviours. Question 2 is designed to collect data on respondents' attitudes to financial advisers placing their client's interest before their own. It therefore asks respondents how they feel. In contrast, question 3 asks respondents whether financial advisers in general place their client's interests before their own. It is therefore concerned with their individual beliefs. Question 4 focuses on how often the respondent actually places their client's interests before their own. Unlike the previous questions, it is concerned with their actual behaviour rather than their beliefs or their attitudes.

To answer your research question(s) and meet your objectives you also need to collect data to explore how ethical values differed between subgroupings of financial advisers. One theory you have is that ethical values are related to age. To test this you need to collect data on the attribute age. After further deliberation you come up with question 5:

5 How old are you?

	less than 30 years	❏
(please tick the appropriate box)	30 to less than 40 years	❏
	40 to less than 50 years	❏
	50 to less than 60 years	❏
	60 years or over	❏

Ensuring that essential data are collected

A problem experienced by many students and organisations we work with is how to ensure that the data collected will enable the research question(s) to be answered and the objectives achieved. Although no method is infallible, one way is to create a data requirements table (Table 10.2). This summarises the outcome of a process:

1 Decide whether the main outcome of your research is descriptive or explanatory.

2 Subdivide each research question or objective into more specific investigative questions about which you need to gather data.

3 Repeat the second stage if you feel the investigative questions are not sufficiently precise.

4 Identify the variables about which you will need to collect data to answer each investigative question.

5 Establish how to measure the data for each variable.

Research question/objective:			
Type of research:			
Investigative questions:	**Variable(s) required:**	**Detail in which data measured:**	**Check included in questionnaire** ✓

Table 10.2 Data requirements table

Investigative questions are the questions that you need to answer in order satisfactorily to answer each research question and meet each objective (Emory and Cooper, 1991). They need to be generated with regard to your research question(s) and objectives. For some investigative questions you will need to subdivide your first attempt into more detailed investigative questions. For each you need to be clear whether you are interested in respondents' attitudes, beliefs, behaviour or attributes (discussed earlier), as what appears to be a need to collect one sort of variable frequently turns out to be a need for another (Dillman, 1978). We have found the literature review, discussions with interested parties and pilot studies to be of help here.

You then need to identify the variables about which you need to collect data to answer each investigative question, and decide the detail at which these are measured. Once again, the review of the literature and associated research can suggest possibilities. However, if you are unsure about the detail needed you should measure at the more precise level. Although this is more time consuming, it will give you flexibility in your analyses. In these you will be able to use computer software to group or combine data (Section 11.2).

Once your table is complete it must be checked to make sure that all data necessary to answer your investigative questions are included. When checking you need to be disciplined and also ensure that only data that are essential to answering your research question(s) and meeting your objectives are included. We added the final column to remind us to check that our questionnaire actually includes a question which collects the data!

WORKED EXAMPLE: *Data requirements table*

One of our postgraduate students was asked to discover staff attitudes to the possible introduction of a no-smoking policy at her workplace. Discussion with senior management and colleagues and reading relevant literature helped her to firm up her objective and investigative questions. A selection of these are included in the extract from her table of data requirements:

Research question/objective: *To establish employees' attitudes to the possible introduction of a no smoking policy at their workplace*

Type of research: *Predominantly descriptive, although wish to examine differences between employees*

Investigative questions:	Variable(s) required:	Detail in which data measured:	Check included in questionnaire ✓
Do employees feel that they should be able to smoke in their office if they want to as a right? (attitude)	*attitude of employee to smoking in their office as a right*	*feel . . . should be allowed, should not be allowed, no strong feelings*	
Do employees feel that a smoking room should be provided by the employer for smokers if smoking in offices is banned? (attitude)	*attitude of employee to the provision of a smoking room for smokers*	*feel . . . very strongly that it should, quite strongly that it should, no strong opinions, quite strongly that it should not, very strongly that it should not*	

Would employees accept a smoking ban at work if it were agreed by the majority of people? (behaviour)	likely behaviour of employee regarding the acceptance of a ban	would . . . accept with no preconditions, accept if a smoking room was provided, not accept without additional conditions (specify conditions), would not accept whatever the conditions	
Do employee attitudes differ depending on — age? (attribute) — whether or not a smoker? (behaviour)	(attitude of employee outlined above) age of employee smoker	(included above) to nearest 5 year band (youngest 16, non smoker, smokes but not in office, smokes in office	
How representative are the responses? (attributes)	age of employee gender of employee job	(included above) male, female senior management, management supervisory, other	

10.4 DESIGNING THE QUESTIONNAIRE

The validity and reliability of the data you collect and the response rate you achieve depend, to a large extent, on the design of your questions, the structure of your questionnaire and the rigour of your pilot testing (all discussed in this section). This means that each part of the design stage is likely to involve substantial rewriting in order to get the questionnaire right. We therefore recommend that you use a wordprocessor.

Designing individual questions

The design of each question should be determined by the data you need to collect (Section 10.3). When designing individual questions researchers do one of three things (Bourque and Clark, 1994):

- adopt questions used in other questionnaires;
- adapt questions used in other questionnaires;
- develop their own questions.

Adopting or adapting questions may be necessary if you wish to replicate, or compare your findings with, another study. This can allow reliability to be assessed. It is also more efficient than developing your own questions, provided that you can still collect the data you need to answer your research question(s) and meet your objectives. However, before you adopt questions beware! There are a vast number of poor questions in circulation, so always assess each question carefully. In addition, you need to check whether or not they are under copyright. If they are, you need to obtain the author's permission to use them. Even where there is no formal copyright, you should note where you obtained the questions and give credit to their author.

Initially you only need to consider the type and wording of individual questions rather than the order in which they will appear on the form. Clear wording of questions using terms which are likely to be familiar to and understood by respondents can improve the validity of the questionnaire. Most types of questionnaire include a combination of open and closed questions. *Open questions* allow respondents to give answers in their own way (Fink, 1995a). *Closed questions* provide a number of alternative answers from which the respondent is instructed to choose (deVaus, 1991). The latter are usually quicker and easier to answer as they require minimal writing. Responses are also easier to compare as they have been predetermined. Youngman (1986, cited in Bell, 1993) identifies six types of closed questions which we discuss later:

- list – where the respondent is offered a list of items, any of which may be selected;
- category – where only one response can be selected from a given set of categories;
- ranking – where the respondent is asked to place something in order;
- scale – in which a scaling device is used to record responses;
- quantity – to which the response is a number giving the amount;
- grid – where responses to two or more questions can be recorded using the same matrix.

Before data analysis you will need to group and code responses to each question. Detailed coding guidance is given in Section 11.2. You are strongly advised to read the whole of Chapter 11 before designing your questions.

Open questions

Open questions are widely used in in-depth and semi-structured interviews (Section 9.5). In questionnaires they are useful if you are unsure of the response, such as in exploratory research, when you require a detailed answer or when you want to find out what is uppermost in the respondent's mind. An example of an open question (from a self-administered questionnaire) is:

6 Please list up to **three** things you like about your job:

1..

2..

3..

With open questions the precise wording of the question and the amount of space partially determine the length and fullness of response. However, if you leave too much space the question becomes off-putting. Question 6 collects data about what each respondent believes they like about their job. Thus if salary had been the reason uppermost in their mind this would probably have been recorded first. Unfortunately, for large-scale questionnaire surveys responses to open questions are extremely time consuming to code (Section 11.2). You should therefore keep their use to a minimum.

List questions

List questions offer the respondent a list of responses, any of which they can choose. Such questions are useful when you need to be sure that the respondent has considered all possible responses. However, the list of responses must be defined clearly and be meaningful to the respondent. For structured interviews it is often helpful to present the respondent with a *prompt card* listing all responses. The response categories you can use vary widely and include 'yes/no', 'agree/disagree', and 'applies/does not apply' along with 'don't know' or 'not sure'. If you intend to use what you hope is a compete list you may wish to add a catch-all category of 'other'. This has been included in question 7 to illustrate this point although, in reality, the question does not contain a complete list of services.

7 Please tick ☑ the box in the provided column for services you provided as a Home Care Assistant for this client in the past month.
If you have not provided a particular service or are not sure place a tick ☑ in the appropriate box.

Service	Provided	Not provided	Not sure
cleaning rooms	☑	☐	☐
shopping	☑	☐	☐
bed making	☐	☑	☐
laundry	☐	☑	☐
other (please describe):..			

Question 7 collects data on the behaviour of the home care assistant, in this instance the services they provided for a particular client. In this question, taken from a self-completion questionnaire, the 'don't know' category has been replaced by 'not sure' as this is less threatening. In some list questions, negative response boxes are omitted and negative responses are inferred from each unmarked response. If you choose to do this beware, non-response could also indicate uncertainty or that an item does not apply!

Category questions

In contrast, *category questions* are designed so that each respondent's answer can fit only one category. Such questions are particularly useful if you need to collect data about behaviour or attributes. The number of categories that you can include without affecting the accuracy of responses is dependent on the type of questionnaire. Self-administered questionnaires and telephone questionnaires should usually have no more than five response categories (Fink, 1995a). Structured interviews can have more categories provided that a *prompt card* is used or, as in question 8, the interviewer categorises the responses.

8   How often do you visit this shopping centre?

Interviewer: listen to the respondent's answer and tick ✓ as appropriate.

☐	first visit	2 or more times a week	☑
☐	once a week	less than once a week to fortnightly	☐
☐	less than fortnightly to once a month	less often	☐

You should arrange responses in a logical order so that it is easy to locate the response category which corresponds to each respondent's answer. Your categories should be *mutually exclusive* (not overlapping) and cover all possible responses. The layout of your questionnaire should make it clear which boxes refer to which response category by placing them close to the appropriate text.

WORKED EXAMPLE: *Use of a prompt card as part of a structured interview*

As part of a market research questionnaire interviewers asked the following question:

Which of the following daily newspapers have you read during the past month?
Show respondent card three with the names of the newspapers. Read out names of the newspapers one at a time. Record their response with a ✓ in the appropriate box.

	read	not read	don't know
The Daily Telegraph	❏	❏	❏
The Times	❏	❏	❏
The Daily Express	❏	❏	❏
The Sun	❏	❏	❏
The Daily Mirror	❏	❏	❏
The Guardian	❏	❏	❏
The Daily Mail	❏	❏	❏
The Financial Times	❏	❏	❏
The Star	❏	❏	❏

Card three was given to the respondent before reading out the newspaper names and collected back after the question had been completed:

3

The Daily Telegraph

THE TIMES

The Daily Express

The Sun

The Daily
Mirror

the Guardian

The Daily Mail

THE FINANCIAL TIMES

**The
Star**

Ranking questions

A *ranking question* asks the respondent to place things in rank order. This means that you can discover their relative importance to the respondent. In question 9, taken from a postal questionnaire, the respondents are asked their beliefs about the relative importance of a series of features when choosing a new car. The catch-all feature of 'other' is included to allow respondents to add one other feature.

9 Please number each of the factors listed below in order of importance to you in your choice of a new car. Number the most important 1, the next 2 and so on. If a factor has no importance at all please leave blank.

factor	importance
acceleration	⬜
boot size	⬜
depreciation	⬜
safety features	⬜
fuel economy	⬜
price	⬜
driving enjoyment	⬜
other	⬜

(⬑ please describe)

With such questions you need to ensure that the instructions are clear and will be understood by the respondent. In general respondents find ranking more than seven or eight items takes too much effort, so you should keep your list to this length or shorter (Kervin, 1992). Respondents can rank accurately only when they can see or remember all items. This can be overcome with face-to-face questionnaires by using prompt cards on which you list all of the features to be ranked. However, telephone questionnaires should only ask respondents to rank a maximum of three or four items as the respondent will need to rely on their memory (Kervin, 1992).

Scale questions

Scale or *rating* questions are often used to collect attitude and belief data. The most common approach is the *Likert-style* rating scale, in which you ask the respondent how strongly they agree or disagree with a statement or series of statements on a four- or five-point scale. If you intend to use a series of statements you should keep the same order of response categories to avoid confusing respondents (Kervin, 1992).

10 For the following statement please tick ☑ the box which matches your view most closely.

	agree	tend to agree	tend to disagree	disagree
I feel that employees' views have influenced the decisions taken by management	❑	❑	❑	❑

Question 10 has been taken from a delivery and collection questionnaire to employees in an organisation and is designed to collect attitude data. In this question a four-point scale has been used to force respondents to express their feelings. By contrast, question 11, also from a delivery and collection questionnaire, allows respondents to 'sit on the fence' by ticking the 'about average' category. It also includes a clearly separated 'don't know' category for those employees who are unsure. This question is designed to collect data on what employees believed happened.

11 For the following statement please tick ☑ the box which matches your view most closely.

	very often	fairly often	about average	not too often	not at all often	don't know
I believe that employees' views have influenced the decisions taken by management	❑	❑	❑	❑	❑	❑

You can expand this form of question further to record finer shades of attitudes and beliefs. However, respondents to telephone questionnaires find it difficult to distinguish between values on scales of more than five points plus 'don't know'.

In question 12 the respondent's attitude is captured on a 10-point *numeric scale*. In such questions it is important that the numbers reflect the feeling of the respondent, thus 1 reflects poor value for money and 10 good value for money. These end categories (and sometimes the middle) are labelled. An additional category of 'not sure' or 'don't know' can be added and should be slightly separated from the scale.

12 For the following statement please circle ◯ the number which matches your view most closely.

This concert was good value for money	strongly disgree	1	2	3	4	5	6	7	8	9	10	strongly agree

Another variation is the *semantic differential* scale. These are often used in consumer research to determine underlying attitudes. The respondent is asked to rate a single object or idea on a series of bi-polar scales. Each *bi-polar scale* is described by a pair of opposite adjectives (question 13) designed to capture respondents' attitudes towards service. For these scales you should vary the position of positive and negative adjectives from left to right to reduce the tendency to read only the attribute on the left (Kervin, 1992).

13 On each of the lines below place a *X* to show how you feel about the service you received at our restaurant.

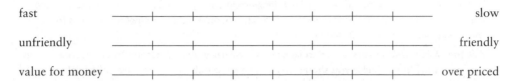

fast ——|——|——|——|——|——|——|—— slow

unfriendly ——|——|——|——|——|——|——|—— friendly

value for money ——|——|——|——|——|——|——|—— over priced

You can combine individual scaling questions to build a scale to measure a concept such as customer loyalty. A detailed explanation of three of the most common scaling techniques (Likert, Guttman and Thurstone) can be found in Oppenheim (1992).

Quantity questions

The response to a *quantity question* is a number which gives the amount of a characteristic. For this reason they tend to be used to collect behaviour or attribute data. A common quantity question which collects attribute data is:

14 What is your year of birth? | 1 | 9 | | |

(for example for 1974 write:) | 1 | 9 | 7 | 4 |

Because the data collected by this question could be entered into the computer without coding, it can also be termed a *self-coded* question.

Grid

A *grid* or *matrix* enables you to record the responses to two or more similar questions at the same time. The 1991 British Census form was designed using a matrix format. Questions were listed down the left-hand side of the page and each household member was listed across the top. The response to each question for each household member was then recorded in the cell where the row and column met. Although using a grid saves space, research cited by Collins and White (1995) suggests that respondents have difficulties comprehending these designs and that it is a barrier to response.

Question wording

The wording of each question will need careful consideration to ensure that the responses are valid, that is, they measure what you think they do. Your questions will need to be checked within the context for which they were written rather than in abstract. Given this, the checklist in Table 10.3 should help you avoid the most obvious problems associated with wording which threaten the validity of responses.

☑ Does your question collect data at the right level of detail to answer your investigative question as specified in your data requirements table?

☑ Will respondents have the necessary knowledge to answer your question? A question on the implications of a piece of European Union legislation would yield meaningless answers from those who were unaware of that legislation.

☑ Are the words used in your question familiar and will they be understood by all respondents in the same way? In particular, you should avoid using jargon, abbreviations and colloquialisms.

☑ Are there any words which sound similar and might be confused with those used in your question? This is a particular problem with interviewer-administered questionnaires.

☑ Are there any words in your question which might cause offence? These might result in biased responses or a lower response rate.

☑ Can your question be shortened? Long questions are often difficult to understand, especially in interviewer-administered questionnaires as the respondent needs to remember the whole question. As a consequence they often result in no response at all.

☑ Are you asking more than one question at the same time? The question 'How often do you visit your mother and father?' contains two separate questions, one about each parent, so responses would probably be impossible to interpret.

☑ Does your question include a negative or double negative? Questions which include the word 'not' are sometimes difficult to understand. The question 'Would you rather not use a non-medicated shampoo?' is far easier to understand as 'Would you rather use a medicated shampoo?'.

☑ Is your question unambiguous? This can arise from poor sentence structure, using words with several different meanings or having an unclear investigative question. If you ask 'When did you leave school?' some respondents might state the year, others might give their age, while those still in education might give the time of day! Ambiguity can also occur in category questions. If you ask employers how many employees they have on their payroll and categorise their answers into three groups (up to 100, 100 to 250, 250 plus), they will not be clear which group to choose if they have 100 or 250 employees.

☑ Does your question imply that a certain answer is correct? If it does the question is biased and will need to be reworded, such as with the question 'Many people believe that too little money is spent on our Health Service. Do you believe this to be the case?'. For this question respondents are more likely to answer 'yes' to agree with and please the interviewer.

☑ Does your question prevent certain answers from being given? If it does, the question is biased and will need to be reworded. The question 'Is this the first time you have pretended to be sick?' infers that the respondent has pretended to be sick whether they answer yes or no!

☑ Is your question likely to embarrass the respondent? If it is, then you either need to reword it or place it towards the end of the survey when you will hopefully have gained the respondent's confidence. Questions on income can either be asked as precise amounts (more embarrassing), using a quantity question, or income bands (less embarrassing), using a category question.

☑ Have you incorporated advice appropriate for your type of questionnaire (such as the maximum number of categories) outlined in the earlier discussion of question types?

☑ Are the instructions on how to record each answer clear?

Table 10.3 Checklist for question wording

Question coding

If you are planning to analyse your data by computer it will need to be coded before entry. For quantity questions, actual numbers can be used as codes. For other questions you will need to design a coding scheme. Whenever possible you should establish the coding scheme before collecting data and incorporate it into your questionnaire. This should take account of relevant existing coding schemes to enable comparisons with other data sets (Section 11.2).

For most closed questions you should be able to add codes to response categories. These can be printed on the questionnaire, thereby *pre-coding* the question and removing the need to code after data collection. Two ways of doing this are illustrated by questions 15 and 16 which collect data on the respondents' beliefs.

	Excellent	Good	Reasonable	Poor	Awful
15 Is the service you receive?					
(please circle ◯ the number)	1	2	3	4	5
	Excellent	Good	Reasonable	Poor	Awful
16 Is the service you receive?					
(please tick ☑ the box)	❏ 5	❏ 1	❏ 3	❏ 2	❏ 4

The codes allocated to response categories will affect your analyses. In question 15 an ordered scale of numbers has been allocated to adjacent responses. This will make it far easier to aggregate responses using a computer (Section 11.2) to 'satisfactory' (1, 2 or 3) and 'unsatisfactory' (4 or 5) compared with the codes in question 16. We therefore recommend that you do not allocate codes as in question 16.

For open questions you will need to reserve space on your data collection form to code responses after data collection. Question 17 has been designed to collect attribute data in a sample survey of 5000 people. Theoretically there could be hundreds of possible responses and so sufficient spaces are left in the 'for Office use only' box.

17 In what country were you born? ....

> for Office use only
> ☐ ☐ ☐

Open questions which generate lists of responses are likely to require more complex coding using either the multiple response or multiple-dichotomy method. These are discussed in Section 11.2 and we recommend you read this before designing your questions.

Designing the survey form

The order and flow of questions

When constructing your questionnaire it is a good idea to spend time considering the order and flow of your questions. These should be logical to the respondent (and interviewer) rather than following the order in your data requirements table (Table 10.2). To assist the flow of the survey it may be necessary to include *filter questions*. These identify those respondents for whom the following question or questions are not applicable, so they can skip those questions. They can be programmed into CAPI and CATI software so that skipped questions are never displayed on the screen and as a consequence never asked (Saris, 1994). In the following example the answer to question 18 determines whether or not questions 19 to 23 will be answered. (Questions 18 and 19 both collect data on attributes.)

18 Are you currently registered as unemployed?   Yes   ☐ 1

No   ☐ 2

If "no" go to question 24

19 How long have you been registered

as unemployed? |__|__| years |__|__| months

(for example for no years and six months write:) |__| 0 | years |__| 6 | months

Where you need to introduce new topics, phrases such as 'the following questions refer to . . .' or 'I am now going to ask you about . . .' are useful. As when wording your questions, you should remember the particular population for whom your questionnaire is designed. For interviewer-administered questionnaires you will have to include instructions for the interviewer. The checklist in Table 10.4 should help you avoid the most obvious problems associated with question order and flow. For some questionnaires the advice contained may be contradictory. Where this is the case you need to decide what is most important for your particular population.

☑ Are questions at the beginning of your questionnaire more straightforward and ones the respondent will enjoy answering? Questions about attributes and behaviours are usually more straightforward to answer than those collecting data on attitudes or beliefs.

☑ Are questions at the beginning of your questionnaire obviously relevant to the stated purpose of your questionnaire? For example, questions requesting contextual information may appear irrelevant.

☑ Are more complex questions and topics towards the middle of your questionnaire? By this stage most respondents should be completing the survey with confidence but not yet be bored or tired.

☑ Are personal and sensitive questions towards the end of your questionnaire, and their purpose clearly explained? On being asked these a respondent may refuse to answer; however, if they are at the end of an interviewer-administered questionnaire you will still have the rest of the data!

☑ Are filter questions and routeing instructions easy to follow so that there is a clear route through the questionnaire?

☑ (For interviewer-administered questionnaires) are instructions to the interviewer easy to follow?

☑ Are questions grouped into obvious sections which will make sense to the respondent?

☑ Have you re-examined the wording of each question and ensured it is consistent with the position in the questionnaire as well as the data you require?

Table 10.4 Checklist for question order

WORKED EXAMPLE: *Introducing a series of scale questions in a telephone questionnaire*

As part of a telephone questionnaire you need to collect data on respondents' attitudes to motorway service stations. To do this you ask respondents to rate a series of statements on a Likert-type scale. Because the survey will be conducted by telephone the scale has been restricted to four categories: strongly agree, agree, disagree, strongly disagree.

In order to make the questionnaire easy for the interviewer to follow, instructions are in italics and the words that need to be read to the respondent in bold. An extract is given below:

Now I'm going to read you several statements. Please tell me whether you strongly agree, agree, disagree or strongly disagree with each.

Interviewer: read out statements 20 to 29 one at a time and after each ask. . .

Do you strongly agree, agree, disagree or strongly disagree? *Record respondent's response with a tick ✓*

	strongly agree	agree	disagree	strongly disagree
20 I wish there were a greater number of service stations on motorways	❏ 4	❏ 3	❏ 2	❏ 1

The layout of the questionnaire

Layout is important for both self-administered and interviewer-administered questionnaires. Interviewer-administered questionnaires should be designed to make reading questions and filling in responses easy. The layout of self-administered questionnaires should, in addition, be attractive to encourage the respondent to fill it in and return it while not appearing too long.

The length of your questionnaire will affect your response rate. DeVaus (1991) argues that optimal length will depend on your population, your research question(s) and your objectives. The more specialised the population and the more relevant the topic, the longer your questionnaire can be. Although the general rule is to keep questionnaires as short as possible, we have found that for within-organisation self-administered questionnaires an optimal length is six to eight A4 pages. Telephone questionnaires can last up to half an hour, whereas structured interviews vary from only a few minutes in the street to far longer in a more comfortable environment (Section 9.6).

One way in which you can reduce length without reducing legibility is to record answers to questions with the same set of possible responses as a table. Usually you place questions in the rows and responses in the columns. Instructions on how to answer the question and column headings are given above the grid and on each subsequent page, as illustrated by questions 22 and 23. These were designed to collect data on respondents' behaviour using a delivery and collection questionnaire.

For each of the following statements please tick the box which most closely matches your experience . . .

	monthly	every 3 months	every 6 months	less often	never
22 I receive a company site newsletter . . .	☐	☐	☐	☐	☐
23 I receive other company publications . . .	☐	☐	☐	☐	☐

Table 10.5 summarises the most important layout issues as a checklist.

☑ (For self-administered questionnaires) do questions appear squashed on the page? This will discourage the respondent from reading it and reduce the response rate. Unfortunately a thick questionnaire is equally off-putting!

☑ (For self-administered questionnaires) is the questionnaire going to be printed on good-quality paper? This will imply that the survey is important.

☑ (For self-administered questionnaires) is the questionnaire going to be printed on warm pastel coloured paper? Warm pastel shades such as yellow and pink generate more responses than cool colours such as green or blue. White is a good neutral colour, but bright or fluorescent colours should be avoided.

☑ (Fo structured interviews) will the questions and instructions be printed on one side of the paper only? You will find it difficult to read the questions on back pages if you are using a questionnaire attached to a clipboard!

☑ Is your questionnaire easy to read? Questionnaires should be typed in 12 point or 10 point using a plain font. Excessively long and excessively short lines reduce legibility. Similarly, respondents find CAPITALS and *italics* more difficult to read.

☑ Is your questionnaire laid out in a format that respondents are accustomed to reading? Research has shown that many people skim read questionnaires (Collins and White, 1995). Instructions that can be read one line at a time from left to right moving down the page are therefore more likely to be followed correctly.

Table 10.5 Checklist for questionnaire layout

Explaining the purpose of the questionnaire

The covering letter

Most self-administered questionnaires are accompanied by a *covering letter* which explains the purpose of the survey. This is the first part of the questionnaire that a respondent should look at. Unfortunately, some of your sample will ignore it while others use it to decide whether or not to answer the accompanying questionnaire.

Research by Dillman (1978) and others has shown that the messages contained in a self-administered questionnaire's covering letter will affect the response rate. The results of this research are summarised in Table 10.6.

Type of paper:	good-quality, official letterhead, including telephone number
Maximum length of letter:	one side (12 point font size if possible)
Salutation:	use recipient's title and name (if possible)
First set of messages:	what research is about, why it is useful
Second set of messages:	why recipient is important, how long it will take to complete
Third set of messages:	promises of confidentiality or anonymity
Fourth set of messages:	how results will be used; token reward or charity donation for participation (if any)
Final set of messages:	whom to contact if there are any queries
Closing remarks:	thank recipient for their help
Signature:	yours, by hand, in blue
Name and title:	yours, including forename and surname

Table 10.6 Structure of a covering letter
Source: developed from Dillman, 1978

For some research projects you may also send a letter before administering your questionnaire. This will be used by the respondent to decide whether or not to grant you access. As a consequence, it is often the only opportunity you have to convince the respondent to participate in your research. Ways of ensuring this are discussed in Section 5.4.

Introducing the questionnaire

At the start of your questionnaire you need to explain clearly and concisely why you want the respondent to complete the survey. Dillman (1978) argues that, to achieve as high a response rate as possible, this should be done on the first page of the questionnaire in addition to the covering letter. He suggests that as well as a summary of the main messages in the covering letter (Table 10.6), you include the following:

- a clear, unbiased title which conveys the topic of the questionnaire and makes it sound interesting;
- a subtitle which conveys the research nature of the topic (optional);
- a neutral graphic illustration or logo to add interest and set the questionnaire apart (self-administered questionnaires).

In addition, it is helpful to include the return name and address at the end of the questionnaire.
Interviewer-administered questionnaires will require this information to be phrased as a short introduction which the interviewer can read to each respondent. A template for this (developed from deVaus, 1991: 123) is given in the next paragraph:

'Good morning/afternoon/evening. My name is (your name) from (your organisation). We are doing a research project to find out (brief description of purpose of the research). Your telephone number was drawn at random. The questions I need to ask will take about (number) minutes. If you have any queries I will be happy to answer them. (pause). Please can I ask you the questions now?'

WORKED EXAMPLE: *Introducing a self administered questionnaire*

Dave and Mark were researching which job attributes attracted people to junior non-manual vacancies in a local labour market. As part of this research 10 local employers agreed to include a questionnaire with each job application form they sent to prospective applicants.

The employers requested that the introduction to the questionnaire emphasised that responses were confidential and would not be passed on to the employing organisation.

JOB SEEKER QUESTIONNAIRE
What influences you in your search for a job

This survey is part of a research project to understand better what influences people such as you in your search for a job. Please answer the questions freely. You cannot be identified from the information you provide. The project is not attached to the employing organisation and your responses will not be given to that organisation.

ALL THE INFORMATION YOU PROVIDE WILL BE TREATED IN THE STRICTEST CONFIDENCE

The questionnaire should take you about five minutes to complete. Please answer the questions in the space provided. Try and complete the questions at a time when you are unlikely to be disturbed. Also do not spend too long on any one question. Your first thoughts are usually your best!

Even if you feel the items covered may not apply directly to you in your search for a job, please do not ignore them. Your answers are essential in building an accurate picture of what people find important when looking for a job.

WHEN YOU HAVE COMPLETED THE QUESTIONNAIRE PLEASE RETURN IT TO US IN THE ENCLOSED FREEPOST ENVELOPE

We hope you find completing the questionnaire enjoyable, and thank you for taking the time to help us. If you have any queries or would like further information about this project please call us on 01242 532987.

Thank you for your help

David Dawson and Mark Saunders
Human Resource Management Research Centre
Cheltenham & Gloucester College of Higher Education

Pilot testing

Before using your questionnaire to collect data it should be pilot tested. The purpose of the *pilot test* is to refine the questionnaire so that respondents will have no difficulties in answering the questions and there will be no problems in recording the data. In addition, it will enable you to obtain some assessment of the questions' validity and the reliability of the data collected. Preliminary analysis using the pilot test data can be undertaken to ensure that the data collected will enable your investigative questions to be answered. You should test your questionnaire with a group as similar as possible to the final population in your sample. For any research project there is a temptation to skip the pilot test. We would endorse Bell's (1993: 84) advice: 'however pressed for time you are, do your best to give the questionnaire a trial run' as, without a trial run, you have no way of knowing that your questionnaire will succeed.

The number of people on whom you pilot your questionnaire, and the number of pilot tests you conduct, are dependent on your research question(s), your objectives, the size of your research project, the time and money resources you have available, and how well you have initially designed your questionnaire. Very large questionnaire surveys such as the British Census will have numerous field trials, starting with individual questions and working to larger and more rigorous pilots of later drafts.

For smaller-scale questionnaires you are unlikely to have sufficient financial or time resources for such testing. However, it is still important that you test your questionnaire. The number of people you choose should be sufficient to include any significant variations in your population which you feel are likely to affect responses. For most questionnaires this means that the minimum number for a pilot is 10 (Fink, 1995b). Occasionally you may be extremely pushed for time. In such instances it is better to pilot test the questionnaire using friends or family than not at all!

As part of your pilot you should check each completed pilot questionnaire to ensure that respondents have had no problems understanding or answering questions and have followed all instructions correctly (Fink, 1995b). Their responses will provide you with an idea of the validity of the questions. For self-administered questionnaires additional information about problems can be obtained by giving respondents a further short questionnaire. Bell (1993) suggests you should use this to find out:

- how long the questionnaire took to complete;
- the clarity of instructions;
- which, if any, questions were unclear or ambiguous;
- which, if any, questions the respondent felt uneasy about answering;
- whether in their opinion there were any significant topic omissions;
- whether the layout was clear and attractive;
- any other comments.

Interviewer-administered questionnaires need to be tested with the respondents for all these points other than layout. One way of doing this is to form an assessment as each questionnaire progresses. Another is to interview any interviewers you are employing. However, you can also check by asking the respondent additional questions at the end of their interview. In addition, you will need to pilot test the questionnaire with interviewers to discover whether:

- there are any questions for which visual aids should have been provided;
- they have difficulty in finding their way through the questionnaire;
- they are recording answers correctly.

Once you have completed pilot testing you should write to your respondents thanking them for their help.

Questionnaire reliability is concerned with the stability of responses to your questionnaire over time (Easterby-Smith *et al.*, 1991). Even where respondents can be identified this is often difficult. External factors and thus responses are likely to change over time. However, some sense of reliability can be obtained by comparing responses to similar questions. Where questions are included for this purpose, usually in longer questionnaires, they are called *check questions*.

10.5 ADMINISTERING THE QUESTIONNAIRE

Once your questionnaire is designed, pilot tested and amended and your sample selected, it can be used to collect data. This final stage is called *administering* the questionnaire. As part of this you will need to gain access to your sample (Sections 5.2 and 5.3). The process of administering a questionnaire differs for each of the four types, as we will now see.

Postal questionnaires

For postal questionnaires it is important to have a clear timetable which identifies the tasks that need to be done and the resources that will be required. A good response depends on the recipient being motivated to answer the questionnaire and post it back. Although the covering letter (Section 10.4) and good design will help ensure a high level of response, the actual administration process is also important. Our advice (developed from deVaus, 1991) can be split into six stages:

1 Ensure that questionnaires and letters are printed and envelopes addressed.

2 Contact recipients by post, telephone or e-mail and advise them to expect a questionnaire – a *pre-survey contact* (see Section 5.3). This stage is often omitted for cost reasons.

3 Post the survey with a covering letter and a return envelope (and fax cover sheet). You should make sure that this will arrive when recipients are likely to be receptive. For most organisations Fridays and days surrounding major public holidays have been shown to be a poor time.

4 Post (or e-mail) the *first follow-up* one week after posting out the survey to all recipients. For postal questionnaires this should take the form of a postcard designed to thank early respondents and remind rather than persuade non-respondents.

5 Post the *second follow-up* to people who have not responded after three weeks. This should contain another copy of the questionnaire, a new return envelope and a new covering letter. The covering letter should be reworded to emphasise further the importance of completing the questionnaire. For anonymous questionnaires a second follow-up will not be possible, as you should not be able to tell who has responded!

6 A *third follow-up* can also be used if time allows or your response rate is low. For this it may be possible to use recorded delivery (post), telephone calls, or even calling in person to emphasise the importance of responding.

DeVaus (1991) also advises placing a unique *identification number* on each questionnaire which is recorded on your list of recipients. This makes it easy to check who has responded. However, identification numbers should not be used if you have assured respondents that their replies will be anonymous!

Delivery and collection questionnaires

The administration of delivery and collection questionnaires is very similar to that of postal questionnaires. However, you or field staff will deliver and call to collect the questionnaire. It is therefore important that your covering letter states when the questionnaire is likely to be collected. As with postal questionnaires, follow-ups can be used, calling at a variety of times of day and on different days to try to catch the respondent.

A variation of this process which we have used widely in organisations allows for delivery and collection of questionnaires the same day and eliminates the need for a follow-up. The stages are:

1 Ensure that all questionnaires and covering letters are printed and a collection box is ready.

2 Contact respondents by internal post or telephone advising them to attend a meeting or one of a series of meetings to be held (preferably) in the organisation's time (Section 5.3).

3 At the meeting or meetings hand out the questionnaire with a covering letter to each respondent.

4 Introduce the questionnaire and stress its anonymous or confidential nature.

5 Ensure respondents place their completed questionnaires in a collection box before they leave the meeting.

Although this adds to costs, as employees are completing the questionnaire in work time, response rates as high as 98 per cent are achievable!

Telephone questionnaires

The quality of data collected using telephone questionnaires will be affected by the researcher's competence in conducting interviews. This is discussed in Section 9.5. Once your sample has been selected you need to:

1 Ensure that all questionnaires are printed or, for CATI, that the software has been programmed and tested.

2 Where possible and resources allow, contact respondents by post, e-mail or telephone advising them to expect a telephone call (Section 5.3).

3 Telephone each respondent, recording the date and time of call and whether or not the questionnaire was completed. You should note any specific times that have been arranged for call-backs. For calls which were not successful you should note the reason, such as no reply or telephone disconnected.

4 For unsuccessful calls where there was no reply, try three more times, each at a different time and on a different day, and note the same information.

5 Make call-back calls at the time arranged.

Structured interviews

Conducting structured interviews uses many of the skills required for in-depth and semi-structured interviews (Section 9.5). Issues such as interviewer appearance and preparedness are important and will affect the response rate (Section 9.4). However, once your sample has been selected you need to:

1 Ensure that all questionnaires are printed or, for CAPI, that the software has been programmed and tested.

2 (For probability samples – Section 6.3) contact respondents by post, e-mail or telephone advising them to expect an interviewer to call within the next week (Section 5.3). This stage is often omitted for cost reasons.

3 (For large-scale surveys) divide the sample into groups which are of a manageable size (50–100) for one interviewer.

4 Contact each respondent or potential respondent in person, recording the date and time of contact and whether or not the interview was completed. You should note down any specific times that have been arranged for return visits. For contacts which were not successful you should note down the reason.

5 (For probability samples) try unsuccessful contacts at least twice more, each at a different time and on a different day, and note down the same information.

6 Visit respondents at the times arranged for return visits.

10.6 SUMMARY

- Questionnaires collect data by asking people to respond to exactly the same set of questions. They are often used as part of a survey strategy to collect descriptive and explanatory data about attitudes, beliefs, behaviours and attributes. Data collected are normally coded and analysed by computer.

- Your choice of questionnaire will be influenced by your research question(s) and objectives and the resources that you have available. The four main types are postal, delivery and collection, telephone and structured interview.

- Before designing a questionnaire you must know precisely what data you need to collect to answer your research question(s) and meet your objectives. One way of helping to ensure that you collect this data is to use a data requirements table.

- The validity and reliability of the data you collect and the response rate you achieve depend, to a large extent, on the design of your questions, the structure of your questionnaire and the rigour of your pilot testing.

- When designing your questionnaire you should consider the wording of individual questions before you think about the order in which they appear. Questions can be divided into open and closed. The six types of closed questions are list, category, ranking, scale, quantity and grid.

- Wherever possible, closed questions should be pre-coded on your questionnaire to facilitate analysis.

- The order and flow of questions in the questionnaire should be logical to the respondent. This can be helped by filter questions and linking phrases.

- The questionnaire should be laid out so it is easy to read and the responses are easy to fill in.

- Questionnaires must be carefully introduced to the respondent to ensure a high response rate. For self-administered questionnaires this should take the form of a covering letter, for interviewer-administered questionnaires this will be done by the interviewer.

- All questionnaires should be pilot tested before collecting data to assess the validity and reliability of the questions.

- Administration of questionnaires will differ depending on the type of questionnaire.

Self-check questions and assignment

Self-check question 10.1
In what circumstances would you choose to use a delivery and collection questionnaire rather than a postal questionnaire? Give reasons for your answer.

Self-check question 10.2

The following questions have been taken from a questionnaire about flexibility of labour.

i Do you agree or disagree with the use of nil hours contracts by employers?

(please tick appropriate box)

strongly agree	☐ 4
agree	☐ 3
disagree	☐ 2
strongly disagree	☐ 1

ii Have you ever been employed on a nil hours contract?

(please tick appropriate box)

yes	☐ 1
no	☐ 2
not sure	☐ 3

iii What is your marital status?

(please tick the appropriate box)

single	☐ 1
married or living in long term relationship	☐ 2
widowed	☐ 3
divorced	☐ 4
other	☐ 5

.... (⇐ please describe)

iv Please describe what you think would be the main impact on employees of a nil hours contract?

for Office use only
☐ ☐ ☐

For each question identify:

a the sort of data that is being collected;

b the type of question.

You should give reasons for your answers.

Self-check question 10.3

You are undertaking research on the use of children's book clubs by householders. As part of this you have already undertaken in-depth interviews with households who belong and do not belong to children's book clubs. This, along with a literature review, has suggested a number of investigative questions from which you start to construct a table of data requirements.

a For each investigative question listed, decide whether you will need to collect data on attitudes, beliefs, behaviours or attributes.

b Complete the table of data requirements for each of the investigative questions already listed. (You can embellish the scenario to help in your choice of variables required and how the data will be measured as you feel necessary).

Research question/objective: *To establish householders' opinions about children's book clubs?*			
Type of research: *Predominantly descriptive, although wish to explain differences between householders*			
Investigative questions:	**Variable(s) required:**	**Detail in which data measured:**	**Check included in questionnaire ✓**
a. do householders think that children's book clubs are a good or a bad idea?			
b. what things do householders like most about children's book clubs?			
c. would householders be interested in an all ages book club?			
d. how much do households spend on children's books a year?			
e. do households' responses differ depending on: i. number of children? ii. if already members of a children's book club?			

Self-check question 10.4

Design pre-coded or self-coded questions to collect data for each of the investigative questions in self-check question 10.3. *Note:* you will need to answer self-check question 10.3 first (or use the answer at the end of this chapter).

Self-check question 10.5

You work for a major consumer research bureau which has been commissioned by 11 major UK companies to design and administer a telephone questionnaire. The purpose of this questionnaire is to describe and explain relationships between adult consumers' lifestyles, opinions and purchasing intentions. Write the introduction to this telephone questionnaire to be read by an interviewer to each respondent. You can embellish the scenario and include any other relevant information you wish.

Self-check question 10.6

You have been asked by a well-known national charity, 'Work for All', to carry out research into the effects of long-term unemployment throughout the UK. The charity intends to use the findings of this research as part of a major campaign to highlight public awareness about the effects of long-term unemployment. The charity has drawn up a list of names and addresses of people who are or were long-term unemployed with whom they have had contact over the past six months. Write a covering letter to accompany the postal questionnaire. You can embellish the scenario and include any other relevant information you wish.

Self-check question 10.7

You have been asked to give a presentation to a group of managers at an oil exploration company to gain access to undertake your research. As part of the presentation you outline your methodology, which includes piloting the questionnaire. In the ensuing question and answer session one of the managers asks you to justify the need for a pilot study, arguing that 'given the time constraints the pilot can be left out'. List the arguments that you would use to convince him that pilot testing is essential to your methodology.

Assignment 10:
Using a questionnaire in your research

- Return to your research question(s) and objectives. Decide on how appropriate it would be to use questionnaires as part of your research strategy. If you do decide this is appropriate, note down the reasons for thinking it will be sensible to collect at least some of your data in this way. If you decide that using a questionnaire is not appropriate, justify your decision.

- If you decide that using a questionnaire is appropriate, re-read Chapter 6 on sampling and in conjunction with this chapter decide which of the four types of questionnaire will be most appropriate. Note down your choice of questionnaire and the reasons for this choice.

- Construct a data requirements table and work out precisely what data you need to answer your investigative questions. Remember you will need to relate your investigative questions and data requirements back to the literature you have reviewed and any preliminary research you have already undertaken.

- Design the separate questions to collect the data specified in your data requirements table. Wherever possible try to use closed questions and adhere to the suggestions in the question wording checklist. If you are intending to analyse your questionnaire by computer, read Section 11.2 and pre-code questions on the questionnaire whenever possible.

- Order your questions to make reading the questions and filling in the responses as logical as possible to the respondent. Wherever possible try to adhere to the checklist for layout. Remember, interviewer-administered questionnaires will need instructions for the interviewer.

- Write the introduction to your questionnaire and, where appropriate, a covering letter.

- Pilot test your questionnaire with as similar a group as possible to the final group in your sample. Pay special attention to issues of validity and reliability.

- Administer your questionnaire and remember to send out a follow-up survey to non-respondents whenever possible.

References

Bell, J. (1993) *Doing your Research Project* (2nd edn), Buckingham, Open University Press.

Bourque, L.B. and Clark, V.A. (1994) 'Processing Data: The Survey Example', in Lewis-Beck, M.S. *Research Practice*, London, Sage, pp. 1–88.

Collins, D. and White, A. (1995) 'Making the next Census form more respondent-friendly', *Social Survey Methodology Bulletin*, 37, July, 8–14.

deVaus, D.A. (1991) *Surveys in Social Research* (3rd edn), London, UCL Press and Allen & Unwin.

Dillman, D.A. (1978) *Mail and Telephone Surveys: The Total Design Method*, New York, Wiley.

Easterby-Smith, M., Thorpe, R. and Lowe, A. (1991) *Management Research: An Introduction*, London, Sage.

Emory, C.W. and Cooper, D.R. (1991) *Business Research Methods* (4th edn), Boston, Irwin.

Fink, A. (1995a) *How to Ask Survey Questions*, Thousand Oaks, California, Sage.

Fink, A. (1995b) *The Survey Handbook*, Thousand Oaks, California, Sage.

Ghauri, P., Grønhaugh, K. and Kristianslund, I. (1995) *Research Methods in Business Studies: A Practical Guide*, London, Prentice-Hall.

Gill, J. and Johnson, P. (1991) *Research Methods for Managers*, London, Paul Chapman.

Jankowicz, A.D. (1995) *Business Research Projects* (2nd edn), London, Chapman & Hall.

Kervin, J.B. (1992) *Methods for Business Research*, New York, HarperCollins.

Moser, C.A. and Kalton, G. (1986) *Survey Methods in Social Investigation* (2nd edn), Aldershot, Gower.

Oppenheim, A.N. (1992) *Questionnaire Design, Interviewing and Attitude Measurement* (new edition), London, Pinter.

Robson, C. (1993) *Real World Research*, Oxford, Blackwell.

Saris, W.E. (1994) 'Computer-Assisted Interviewing', in Lewis-Beck, M.S. *Research Practice*, London, Sage, pp. 163–250.

Youngman, M.B. (1986) *Analysing Questionnaires*, Nottingham, University of Nottingham School of Education.

Further reading

Collins, D. and White, A. (1995) 'Making the next Census form more respondent-friendly', *Social Survey Methodology Bulletin*, 37, July, 8–14. This provides a useful discussion of how to make the order, flow and layout of self-administered questionnaires more respondent friendly, thereby improving response rates and accuracy.

Craig, P.B. (1991) 'Designing and Using Mail Questionnaires', in Smith, N.C. and Dainty, P. (eds) *The Management Research Handbook*, London, Routledge, pp. 181–9. This provides a useful discussion of the realities of applying Dillman's Total Design Method to management research.

deVaus, D.A. (1991) *Surveys in Social Research* (3rd edn), London, UCL Press and Allen & Unwin. Chapters 6 and 7 provide a detailed guide to constructing and administering questionnaires respectively.

Dillman, D.A. (1978) *Mail and Telephone Surveys: The Total Design Method*, New York, Wiley. This contains a detailed analysis of how to design postal questionnaires and telephone interviews to maximise response rates using the Total Design Method. It is also worthwhile reading Craig (1991) to obtain a realistic view of this approach.

Fink, A. (1995) *The Survey Handbook*, Thousand Oaks, California, Sage. This contains a series of useful checklists and a stage-by-stage guide to the survey process.

Oppenheim, A.N. (1992) *Questionnaire Design, Interviewing and Attitude Measurement* (new edition), London, Pinter. Chapters 10, 11 and 12 are particularly useful if you wish to explore attitude scaling in greater depth.

Wass, V.J. (1994) 'Minimizing and Managing Bias in a Mail Survey: A Study of Redundant

Miners', in Wass, V.J. and Wells, P.E. *Principles and Practice in Business and Management Research*, Aldershot, Dartmouth, pp. 91–121. This contains an excellent discussion and provides a good case study of the issues of controlling for bias when using a postal questionnaire.

Case 10:
The provision of leisure activities for younger people in rural areas

A report from the chairperson of the 'vandalism working party' was the last item on the agenda of the Littlebury town council meeting. Following extensive consultation with representatives of the local population, the group concluded that boredom among the town's young people was a major problem and undoubtedly a contributory factor to the unprecedented rise in vandalism.

A number of preliminary suggestions had been made of projects which might be of interest to young people within the town and help to combat the problem. But the working party had agreed that if they were really going to attract the support of the young people, they needed to have concrete information about what they wanted to see in the town. They believed that there was a need for a survey.

The chairperson reported that, following contact with the business school of the local university, a leisure management undergraduate had expressed interest in carrying out a survey as part of her research project. She was interested in looking at the provision of leisure activities for young people in small rural towns, and had met with him to discuss her preliminary ideas. They had agreed that a survey of the young people in Littlebury could be carried out and that its objectives would be:

● to find out what the town's young people did in their spare time;

● to establish what leisure activities they would like to have available in the town;

● to establish their potential interest in some of the ideas proposed by the working party;

● to compare leisure activities and preferences of different age groups.

The chairperson was able to report that funding such a survey would not be a problem as a group of local business people had agreed to support the costs of reproducing the questionnaires and sending them out. He concluded his report by seeking the council's agreement to proceed with the survey. There was unanimous support and the meeting closed on a very positive note.

The student decided to collect her data using a postal questionnaire. She designed the survey and pilot tested it on five members of the local youth club who all thought it was fine. (A copy of the questionnaire is included at the end of this case.) The 400 questionnaires were sent out to young people aged 11 to 18 living in the town and 187 usable responses were returned. She attributed the relatively high response rate to the high profile given to the survey in the town's local paper.

The results indicated that there was very little support for the existing clubs and societies in the town, with the exception of the youth club and the leisure centre. Membership of the youth club was predominantly from inhabitants of the town's two council estates. However, it was not clear which activities held at the leisure centre were patronised by young people. Football and tennis were the most popular sporting activities in all age groups. Shopping and listening to pop music proved to be the most popular out-of-school pastimes for all ages, while the younger groups preferred to watch videos.

Of the ideas proposed by the working party, the coffee shop and swimming pool proved most popular overall, but especially among younger girls who accounted for 58% of total responses. The younger boys said that the video games centre would be visited most frequently. Working respondents had a different pattern of response, suggesting that their interests were very different from those of their counterparts at school. Unfortunately, these people made up less than 10% of respondents and it was felt that more information was needed here. The answers to question 8 were hardly revolutionary and suggested that the best thing the town could do for all age groups was to attract some of the retail multiples to its high street and open a night club!

Overall, the working party was disappointed by the results. Although there was a much clearer picture of what the town's young people did with their spare time, the group did not feel any closer to finding out what would capture their interest and reduce the boredom.

Littlebury Leisure Survey

Please answer all of the following questions by ticking the appropriate boxes

1 **How often do you use the following in Littlebury:**

	more than once a week	once a week	once a month	less than once a month	never
The leisure centre	☐	☐	☐	☐	☐
The youth centre	☐	☐	☐	☐	☐
The library	☐	☐	☐	☐	☐
Church	☐	☐	☐	☐	☐

2 **Do you belong to any of the following:**

Girl Guides	yes ☐	no ☐
The army cadets	yes ☐	no ☐
The air training corps	yes ☐	no ☐
The theatre club	yes ☐	no ☐
Boy souts	yes ☐	no ☐
Youth club	yes ☐	no ☐

3 Which of the following sports do you play regularly outside school:

Aerobics	☐	Martial arts	☐
Badminton	☐	Riding	☐
Basketball	☐	Rugby	☐
Boxing	☐	Sailing	☐
Cycling	☐	Self Defense	☐
Cricket	☐	Swimming	☐
Football	☐	Table tennis	☐
Gymnastics	☐	Tennis	☐

Any other: please state which...

4 Do you belong to any other clubs or societies in Littlebury?

Please state which...

....

5 Which of the following do you do regularly?

Watch videos	☐	Listen to pop music	☐	Go to discos	☐
Play music	☐	Go shopping	☐	Voluntary work	☐

6 Please list up to 3 other things which you do regularly in your spare time

....

....

....

7 If the following were available in Littlebury, how often would you use them?

	more than once a week	once a week	once a month	less than once a month	never
Indoor swimming pool	☐	☐	☐	☐	☐
Drama club	☐	☐	☐	☐	☐
Coffee shop	☐	☐	☐	☐	☐
Video game centre	☐	☐	☐	☐	☐
Sailing club	☐	☐	☐	☐	☐
Karting club	☐	☐	☐	☐	☐
Any other: please state which					
....	☐	☐	☐	☐	☐

8 Please complete the following sentence:

'The one thing I would really like to be able to do in Littlebury in my spare time is

....,'

9 Please tell us about yourself:

How old are you?.............................   Are you male ☐ or female ☐?

If you're still at school, which school do you attend?..

If you've left school are you: employed full time   ☐

employed part time   ☐

not employed   ☐

10 Please tell us your postcode   GL__ _ _ _

Thank you very much for helping us. Please return this form as soon as possible in the envelope provided. If it reaches us by April 1st you will be included in the draw for the first prize of £25.00! Good luck.

Case-study questions

1 Why were the working party 'disappointed with the results'?

2 Amend the questions so that the data collected meets the working party's objectives more closely.

3 What other changes would you make to the questionnaire?

4 In what ways could the method used to pilot the questionnaire be improved?

5 Do you think that a postal questionnaire was the best way of collecting these data? (Give reasons for your answer).

Answers to self-check questions

Self-check question 10.1

When you:

- wanted to check that the person whom you wished to answer the questions had actually answered the questions;

- have sufficient resources to devote to delivery and collection and the geographical area over which the questionnaire is administered is small;

- can use field workers to enhance response rates. Delivery and collection questionnaires have a moderately high response rate of between 30 and 50% compared to 30% offered on average by a postal questionnaire;

- are administering a questionnaire to an organisation's employees and require a very high response rate. By administering the questionnaire to groups of employees in work time and collecting it on completion, response rates of up to 98% can be achieved.

Self-check question 10.2

a i Attitude data; the question is asking how the respondent *feels* about the use of nil hours contracts by employees.

ii Behaviour data: the question is asking about the *concrete experience* of being employed on a nil hours contract.

iii Attribute data: the question is asking about the respondent's characteristics, in Dillman's (1978: 83) phrase, '*something they possess*'.

iv Belief data: the question is asking the respondent what they *think* or believe would be the impact on employees. It does not imply either good or bad.

b i Scale question using a Likert-type scale in which respondents are asked how strongly they agree or disagree with the statement.

ii Category question in which the respondent's answer can fit only one answer.

iii Category question as before.

iv Open question in which respondents can give their own answer in their own way.

Self-check question 10.3

Although your answer is unlikely to be precisely the same, the completed table of data requirements below should enable you to check you are on the right lines.

> **Research question/objective:** *To establish householders' opinions about children's book clubs?*
>
> **Type of research:** *Predominantly descriptive, although wish to explain differences between householders*

Investigative questions:	Variable(s) required:	Detail in which data measured:	Check included in questionnaire ✓	
do householders think that children's book clubs are a good or a bad idea? (attitude – this is because you are really asking how householders feel)	attitude to children's book clubs	very good idea, good idea, neither a good or a bad idea, bad idea, very bad idea		
what things do householders like most about children's book clubs? (belief)	what householders like about children's book clubs	get them to rank following things (generated from earlier in-depth interviews): monthly magazine, lower prices, credit, choice, special offers, shopping at home		
would householders be interested in an all ages book club? (behaviour)	interest in a book club which was for both adults and children	interested, not interested, may be interested		
how much do households spend on children's books a year? (behaviour)	amount spent on children's books by adults and children per year by household	(answers to the nearest £) £0 to £10, £11 to £20, £21 to £30, £31 to £50, £51 to £100, £101 and over		
do households' responses differ depending on: ● *number of children?* (attribute)	number of children aged under 16	actual number		
● *if already members of a children's book club?* (behaviour)	children's book club member	yes, no		

Self-check question 10.4

a Please complete the following statement by ticking the phrase that matches your feelings most closely . . .

I feel children's book clubs are . . .

. . . a very good idea	☐ 5
. . . a good idea	☐ 4
. . . neither a good or a bad idea	☐ 3
. . . a bad idea	☐ 2
. . . a very bad idea	☐ 1

b Please number each of the features of children's book clubs listed below in order of how much you like them. Number the most important 1, the next 2 and so on. The feature you like the least should be given the highest number.

feature	how much liked
monthly magazine	☐
lower prices	☐
credit	☐
choice	☐
special offers	☐
shopping at home	☐

c Would you be interested in a book club which was for both adults and children?

(please tick the appropriate box)

yes	☐ 1
no	☐ 2
not sure	☐ 3

d How much money is spent in total on children's books by all the adults and children living in your household each year?

(please tick the appropriate box)

£0 to £10	☐ 1
£11 to £20	☐ 2
£21 to £30	☐ 3
£31 to £50	☐ 4
£51 to £100	☐ 5
over £100	☐ 6

e i How many children aged under 16 are there living in your household? ⬚⬚ children

(for example for 3 write:) |⬚ *3*| children

ii Is any person living in your household a member of a children's book club?   Yes ☐ 1

(please tick the appropriate box)   No ☐ 2

Self-check question 10.5

Although the precise wording of your answer is likely to differ it would probably be something like this:

Good morning/afternoon/evening. My name is _____ from Saunders and Dawson Consumer Research. We are doing an important national survey covering lifestyles, opinions and likely future purchases of adult consumers. Your telephone number has been selected at random. The questions I need to ask you will take about 15* minutes. If you have any queries I will be happy to answer them (*pause*). Please can I ask you the first question now?

*The total time should not be more than 30 minutes.

Self-check question 10.6

Although the precise wording of your answer is likely to differ, it would probably be something like this:

Work for All

Registered Charity No: 123456789

M&D Ltd

M&D Market Research Ltd
St Richard's House
Malvern
Worcestershire WR14 12Z
☎ *01684 56789101*
Fax 01684 56789102

Respondent's name
Respondent's address

Today's date

Dear *title name*

Work for All is conducting research into the effects of long-term unemployment. This is an issue of great importance within the UK and yet little is currently known about the consequences.

You are one of a small number of people who are being asked to give your opinion on this issue. You were selected at random from Work for All's list of contacts. In order that the results will truly represent people who have experienced long-term unemployment, it is important that your questionnaire is completed and returned.

285

All the information you give us will be totally confidential. You will notice that your name and address do not appear on the questionnaire and that there is no identification number.

The results of this research will be passed to Work for All who will be mounting a major campaign to highlight public awareness about the effects of long-term unemployment in the new year.

If you have any questions you wish to ask or there is anything you wish to discuss, please do not hesitate to telephone me, or my assistant Dave Dawson, on 01684 56789101 during the day. You can call me at home on 01242 123456789 evenings and weekends.

Thank you for your help.

Yours sincerely

Mark NK Saunders

Dr Mark NK Saunders
Project Manager

Self-check question 10.7

Despite the time constraints, pilot testing is essential to your methodology for the following reasons:

- to find out how long the questionnaire takes to complete;
- to check that respondents understand and can follow the instructions on the questionnaire (including filter questions);
- to ensure that all respondents understand the wording of individual questions in the same way and that there are no unclear or ambiguous questions;
- to ensure that you have the same understanding of the wording of individual questions as have the respondents;
- to check that respondents have no problems in answering questions; for example:
  - all possible answers are covered in list questions,
  - if there are any questions that respondents feel uneasy about answering;
- to discover if there are any major topic omissions;
- to provide an idea of the validity of the questions that are being asked;
- to provide an idea of the reliability of the questions by checking responses from individual respondents to similar questions;
- to check that the layout appears clear and attractive;
- to provide limited test data so you can check that the proposed analyses will work.

CHAPTER 11

Analysing quantitative data

The objectives of this chapter are to outline and illustrate the main issues that you need to consider when preparing quantitative data for analysis and when analysing these data by computer.

The chapter defines four types of data (descriptive, ranked, continuous and discrete) and discusses how to create a data matrix and code data.

Practical advice is offered on the most appropriate diagrams to explore and illustrate different aspects of variables for the four types of data.

Advice is also offered on which statistics to use to describe individual variables and to explore relationships and trends for variables for the four types of data.

11.1 INTRODUCTION

Virtually all research will involve some numerical data, or contain data that could usefully be quantified to help you answer your research question(s) and meet your objectives. *Quantitative data* refers to all such data and can be a product of all three main types of research strategy (Section 4.2). It can range from simple counts such as the frequency of occurrences to more complex data such as test scores or prices. To be useful these data need to be analysed and interpreted. Quantitative analysis techniques assist this process. These range from creating simple tables or diagrams which show the frequency of occurrence, through establishing statistical relationships between variables to complex statistical modelling.

Until the advent of powerful personal computers data were analysed either by hand or using mainframe computers. The former of these was extremely time consuming and prone to error, the latter expensive. Fortunately the by-hand or calculator 'number crunching' and 'charting' elements of quantitative analysis have been incorporated into relatively inexpensive personal computer-based analytical software. These range from spreadsheets such as Excel, Lotus 123 and SuperCalc to more advanced data management and statistical analysis software packages such as Minitab, SAS, SPSS for Windows and Statview. As a consequence, it is no longer necessary for you to be able to draw presentation-quality diagrams or calculate statistics by hand as these can be done by computer. However, if your analyses are to be straightforward and of any value you need to:

■ have prepared your data with quantitative analyses in mind;

■ be aware of and know when to use different charting and statistical techniques.

Robson (1993: 310) summarises this, arguing that quantitative data analysis is:

'a field where it is not at all difficult to carry out an analysis which is simply wrong, or inappropriate for your purposes. And the negative side of readily available analytical software is that it becomes that much easier to generate elegantly presented rubbish.'

He also emphasises the need to seek advice regarding statistical analyses, a sentiment which we support strongly.

This chapter builds on the ideas outlined in earlier chapters about data collection. It assumes that you will use a personal computer (with at least a spreadsheet) to analyse all but the most simple quantitative data. It does not focus on one particular piece of analytical software, as there are numerous books already published which concentrate on specific software packages (for example Babbie and Halley, 1995; Morris, 1993; Robson, 1993). Likewise, it does not attempt to provide an in-depth discussion of the wide range of graphical and statistical techniques available or to cover more complex statistical modelling, as these are already covered elsewhere (for example Fox and Long, 1990; Hays, 1994). Rather, it discusses issues that need to be considered at the planning and analysis stages of your research project and outlines analytical techniques our students have found to be of most use. In particular the chapter is concerned with the process of:

■ preparing your data for analysis by computer (Section 11.2);

■ choosing the most appropriate tables and diagrams to explore and present your data (Section 11.3);

■ choosing the most appropriate statistics to describe your data (Section 11.4);

■ choosing the most appropriate statistics to examine relationships and trends in your data (Section 11.5).

11.2 PREPARING DATA FOR ANALYSIS

If you intend to undertake quantitative analysis we recommend you consider:

■ the type of data (level of numerical measurement);

■ the format in which your data will be input to the analytical software;

■ the impact of data coding on subsequent analyses (for different data types);

■ the need to weight cases;

■ the methods you intend to use to check data for errors.

Ideally all of these should be considered before obtaining your data. This is equally important for both primary and secondary data analysis, although you obviously have far greater control over the type, format and coding of primary data. We will now consider each of these.

Data types

Many business statistics textbooks classify quantitative data into *data types* using a hierarchy of measurement, often in ascending order of numerical precision (Morris, 1993; Saunders and Cooper, 1993). These different *levels of numerical measurement* dictate the range of techniques available to you for the presentation, summary and analysis of your data. They are discussed in more detail in subsequent sections of this chapter.

Quantitative data can be divided into two distinct groups: categorical and quantifiable (Fig 11.1). *Categorical data* refer to data whose values cannot be measured numerically but can either be classified into sets (categories) according to the characteristics in which you are interested, or placed in rank order. They can be further subdivided into descriptive and ranked. A car manufacturer might categorise the cars it produces as hatchback, saloon and estate. These are known as *descriptive* (or *nominal*) *data*, as it is impossible to measure the category numerically or rank it. For virtually all analyses the categories should be unambiguous and not overlapping. This will prevent questions arising as to which category an individual case belongs to. Although these data are purely descriptive, you can count them to establish which category has the most and whether cases are spread evenly between categories (Morris, 1993). *Ranked* (or *ordinal*) *data* are more precise. In such instances you know the definite position of each case within your data set, although the actual numerical measures (such as scores) on which the position is based are not recorded.

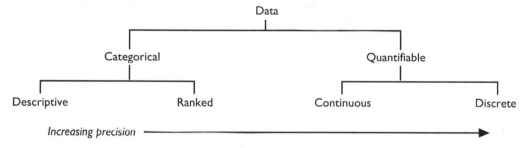

Fig 11.1 Types of data and levels of numerical measurement

Quantifiable data are those whose values you actually measure numerically as quantities. This means that quantifiable data are more precise than categorical as you can assign each data value a position on a numerical scale.[1] Within this group there is, again, a subdivision: continuous and discrete (Fig 11.1). *Continuous data* are those whose values can theoretically take any value (sometimes within a restricted range) provided that you can measure them accurately enough (Morris, 1993). Data such as furnace temperature,

---

[1] Some text books (for example Fink, 1995) use an alternative hierarchy of measurement: nominal, ordinal, interval and ratio. Nominal equates to descriptive and ordinal to ranked data. If you have interval data you can, in addition to ranking, state the difference between any two data values precisely. For ratio data you can also calculate the relative difference between any two data values, that is, the ratio.

delivery distance and length of service are therefore continuous data. *Discrete data* can, by contrast, be measured precisely. Each case takes one of a finite number of values from a scale which measures changes in discrete units. These data are often whole numbers (integers) such as compact disc players manufactured or customers served. However, in some instances (for example UK shoe size), discrete data will include non-integer values.

Definitions of discrete and continuous data are, in reality, dependent on how your data values are measured. The number of customers served by a large organisation is strictly discrete data, as you are unlikely to get a part customer! However, for a large organisation with many customers you might treat this as continuous data; the discrete measuring units are minute compared with the total number being measured.

The more precise the level of measurement, the greater the range of analytical techniques available to you. Data which have been collected and coded using precise numerical measurements can be regrouped to a less precise level where they can also be analysed. For example, a student's score in a test could be recorded as the actual mark (discrete data) or as the position in their class (ranked data). By contrast, less precise data cannot be made more precise. Therefore, if you are not sure about the level of precision you require it is usually better to collect data at the highest level possible, and regroup it if necessary.

● ●

WORKED EXAMPLE: *Levels of numerical measurement*

As part of a marketing survey, individual customers were asked to rank up to five features of a new product in order of importance to them. Data collected were therefore categorical and ranked. Initial analyses made use of the ranked data. Unfortunately, a substantial minority of customers had ticked, rather than ranked, those features of importance to them.

All responses which had originally been ranked were therefore recoded to 'of some importance'. This reduced the precision of measurement from ranked to descriptive, but enabled all responses to be used in subsequent analyses.

● ●

Data layout

Some primary data collection methods, such as computer-aided personal interviewing (CAPI) and computer-aided telephone interviewing (CATI), automatically enter and save data to a computer file at the time of collection. Secondary data (Section 7.3) accessed from CD-ROMs or via the Internet may also be saved to a file, removing the need for re-entering. For such data it is often possible to specify a data layout compatible with your analytical software. For other data collection methods you will have to prepare and enter your data for computer analysis. You therefore need to be clear about the precise data layout requirements of your analytical software.

Virtually all analytical software will accept your data if it is entered in table format. This table is called a *data matrix* (Table 11.1). Once data have been entered into your analytical software it is usually possible to save them in a format that can be read by other software. Within a data matrix each column usually represents a single *variable* for which you have obtained data. Each matrix row contains the variables for an individual *case*, that

	ID	age	gender	service	employed
case 1	1	27	1	2	1
case 2	2	19	2	1	2
case 3	3	24	2	3	1

Table 11.1 A simple data matrix

is, an individual unit for which data have been obtained. If your data have been collected using a survey each row will contain the data from one survey form. Alternatively, for longitudinal data such as a company's share price over time, each row (case) will be a different time period. Secondary data that have already been stored in computer-readable form will almost always be held as a large data matrix. For such data sets you usually select the subset of variables and cases you require and save these on a disk as a separate matrix. If you are entering your own data they are typed directly into your chosen analytical software one case (row) at a time. We recommend that you save your data regularly as you are entering it, to minimise the chances of deleting it all by accident! In addition, you should keep a back-up or security copy on a separate disk.

In Table 11.1 the first variable (ID) is the *survey form identifier*. This means you can link data for each case in your matrix to the survey form when error checking (discussed later). The second variable (age) contains quantifiable data: the age of each respondent (case) at the time of the survey. Subsequent variables contain the remaining data: the third (gender) records this descriptive data using code 1 for male and 2 for female; the fourth (service) records each case's length of service to the nearest year with their most recent employer. The final variable (employed) records whether each case is (code 1) or is not (code 2) currently in employment. Codes can therefore have different meanings for different variables. Larger data sets with more data variables and cases are recorded using larger data matrices. Although data matrices store data using one column for each variable, this may not be the same as one column for each question for data collected using surveys.

If you intend to enter data into a spreadsheet the first variable is in column A, the second in column B and so on. Each cell in the first row (1) should contain a short variable name to enable you to identify each variable. Subsequent rows (2 onwards) will each contain the data for one case. Statistical analysis software follows the same logic, although the variable names are usually displayed 'above' the first row, as in Table 11.1.

WORKED EXAMPLE: *Data input*

As part of a marketing interview survey, you need to discover which of four products (tomato ketchup, brown sauce, soy sauce, vinegar) have been purchased within the last month by consumers. You therefore need to collect four data items from each respondent:

- tomato ketchup purchased within the last month?   Yes/No
- brown sauce purchased within the last month?   Yes/No
- soy sauce purchased within the last month?   Yes/No
- vinegar purchased within the last month?   Yes/No

Each of these data items is a separate variable. However, the data are collected using one question:

	item	purchased	not purchased	not sure
I Which of the following	tomato ketchup	❏ 1	❏ 2	❏ 3
items have you purchased	brown sauce	❏ 1	❏ 2	❏ 3
within the last month	soy sauce	❏ 1	❏ 2	❏ 3
	vinegar	❏ 1	❏ 2	❏ 3

The data collected from each respondent will form four separate variables in the data matrix using numerical codes (1 = purchased, 2 = not purchased, 3 = not sure). This is known as multiple dichotomy coding:

	tomato	brown	soy	vinegar
respondent	1	1	1	2

Question 2 (below) could theoretically have millions of possible responses for each of the 'things'. The number that each respondent mentions may also vary. Our experience suggests that virtually all respondents will select five or less. Space therefore has to be left to code up to five responses after data have been collected.

2 List the things you like about

your current job

....

....

....

....

....

for Office use only

❑❑❑❑

❑❑❑❑

❑❑❑❑

❑❑❑❑

❑❑❑❑

The *multiple dichotomy* method uses a separate variable for each different answer. For question 2 a separate variable could be used for each 'thing' listed, for example salary, location, colleagues, hours, holidays, car and so on. You would subsequently code each variable as 'listed' or 'not listed' for each case. This makes it easy to calculate the number of responses for each 'thing' (deVaus, 1991). The alternative, the *multiple response method*, uses the same number of variables as the maximum number of different responses from any one case. For question 2 these might be named 'like1', 'like2', 'like3', 'like4' and 'like5'. Each of these variables would use the same codes and could include any of the responses as a category. Statistical analysis software often contains special multiple-response procedures to analyse such data.

Coding

All data types should, with few exceptions, be recorded using numerical codes. This enables you to enter the data quickly and with fewer errors. It also makes subsequent analyses, in particular those which require recoding of data to create new variables, more straightforward. Unfortunately, analyses of limited meaning are also easier, such as calculating a mean (average) gender from codes 1 and 2! A common exception to using a numerical code for categorical data is where a postcode is used as the code for a geographical reference. If you are using a spreadsheet you will need to keep a list of codes for each variable. Statistical analysis software can store these so that each code is automatically labelled.

Coding quantifiable data

Actual numbers are often used as codes for quantifiable data, even though this level of precision may not be required. Once you have entered your data as a matrix you can use analytical software to group or combine data to form additional variables with less detailed categories. This process is referred to as *recoding*. A UK employee's salary could be coded to the nearest pound and entered into the matrix as 23543 (discrete data). Later, recoding could be used to place it in a group of similar salaries, £20 000 to £24 999 (categorical data).

Coding categorical data

Codes are often applied to categorical data with little thought, although you can design a coding scheme which will make subsequent analyses far simpler. For many secondary data sources (such as government surveys), a suitable coding scheme will have already been devised when the data were first collected. However, for some secondary and all primary data you will need to decide on a coding scheme. Before this you need to establish the highest level of precision required by your analyses.

Existing coding schemes can be used for many variables. These include industrial classification (Central Statistical Office, 1992), occupation (Office of Population Censuses and Surveys, 1990a, b), social class (Office of Population Censuses and Surveys, 1991), marital status and ethnic group (Office of Population Censuses and Surveys and General

Registrar's Office for Scotland, 1992) as well as social attitude variables (Jowell *et al.*, 1994). Wherever possible we recommend you use these as they:

■ save time;

■ are normally well tested;

■ enable comparisons of your results with other (often larger) surveys.

These codes should be included on your data collection form as *pre-set codes* provided that there are a limited number of categories (Section 10.4) which will be understood by the person filling in the form. Even if you decide not to use an existing coding scheme, perhaps because of a lack of detail, you should ensure that your codes are still compatible. This means that you will be able to compare your data with those already collected.

Coding at data collection occurs when there are a limited range of well established categories into which the data can be placed. These are included on your data collection form and the correct category is selected by the person filling in the form.

Coding after data collection is necessary when you are unclear of the likely responses or there are a large number of possible responses in the coding scheme. To ensure that the coding scheme captures the variety in responses (and will work!) it is better to wait until data from the first 50 to 100 cases are available and then develop the coding scheme. This is called the *code book*. As when designing your data collection method(s) (Chapters 7, 8, 9 and 10) it is essential to be clear about the intended analyses, in particular the:

■ level of precision required;

■ coding schemes used by surveys with which comparisons are to be made.

To create your code book for each variable you:

1 Examine the data and establish broad groupings.

2 Subdivide the broad groupings into increasingly specific subgroups dependent on your intended analyses.

3 Allocate codes to all categories at the most precise level of detail required.

4 Note the actual responses which are allocated to each category and produce a code book.

5 Ensure that those categories which may need to be aggregated together are given adjacent codes to facilitate recoding.

Coding missing data

Each variable for each case in your data set should have a code, even if no data have been collected. The choice of code is up to you, although some statistical analysis software have a code which is used by default. A *missing data* code is used to indicate why data are missing. DeVaus (1991) identifies four main reasons for missing data:

■ the data were not required, perhaps due to a skip generated by a filter question in a survey;

■ the question was not answered as the respondent had no opinion (a *non-response*);

- the data were not available for some other reason;
- leaving part of a question in a survey blank infers an answer; in such cases the data are not classified as missing.

Statistical analysis software often reserves a special code for missing data. Cases with missing data can then be excluded from subsequent analyses when necessary. For some analyses it may be necessary to distinguish between reasons for missing data using different codes.

WORKED EXAMPLE: *Creating a code book and coding multiple responses*

As part of research on vacancy notification procedures, Mark collected data from personnel files about how vacancies were notified by the employer. These data specified the precise notification outlets used and can be thought of as the answer to the question: 'Which outlets did you use to notify this vacancy?' The data included over 100 different outlets for over 1500 vacancies, although the maximum number of outlets used for any one vacancy was eight.

Once data had been collected Mark devised a hierarchical coding scheme based on the type and geographical circulation of each notification outlet. Codes were allocated to each outlet as shown in the extract below.

Extract from coding scheme used to classify notification outlets

Code	Outlet	Subgrouping	Grouping
1	Internal vacancy sheet		Internal
6	Job Centre		
7	Careers office		Employment agencies
8	Professional Executive Register		
9	Private sector employment agency		
11	Oxford Mail		
12	Swindon Evening Advertiser	Daily	
13	Wantage Evening Advertiser		
20	Herald Series		Local newspapers
21	Wiltshire Gazette	Weekly	
22	Oxford Times		
26	Oxford Journal	Free	
27	Oxford Star		
40	Daily Mail		
41	Daily Telegraph	Daily	

42	The Times
43	The Guardian
50	Sunday Times
60	Public Finance and Accounting
61	Opportunities
62	Local Government Chronicle
63	Municipal Journal
70	Quantity Surveyors Weekly
72	Architects Journal
75	Surveyor
81	The Planner
82	Planning
90	Solicitors Journal
91	Law Society Gazette

Sunday — National newspapers

Public service journals and magazines

Planning

Legal — Professional journals and magazines

Notification codes for each vacancy were entered into eight (the maximum number of notification outlets used) variables in the data matrix using the multiple-response method for coding. This meant that any notification outlet could appear in any of the eight variables. When less than eight outlets were used the code 0 was entered in the remaining outlet variables. The first vacancy in the extract below was notified through outlets 1, 90, 91 and 61; the next through outlets 90, 91, 63, 41, 1, 7 and 8; and so on. No significance was attached to the order of variables to which outlets were coded:

outlet 1	outlet 2	outlet 3	outlet 4	outlet 5	outlet 6	outlet 7	outlet 8
1	90	91	61	0	0	0	0
90	91	63	41	1	7	8	0
6	23	22	1	11	0	0	0

The hierarchical coding scheme meant that notification outlets could subsequently be recoded into groupings such as those indicated above, as well as local, regional or national, to facilitate a range of different analyses. These were undertaken using statistical analysis software.

Weighting cases

Most data you use will be a sample. For some forms of probability sampling such as strat-ified random sampling (Section 6.2) you may have used a different sampling fraction for each strata. Alternatively, you may have obtained a different response rate for each of the strata. To obtain an accurate overall picture you will need to take account of these differ-ences in response rates between strata. A common method of achieving this is to use cases from those strata which have lower proportions of responses to represent more than one case in your analysis. Most statistical analysis software allows you to do this by *weighting cases*. To *weight* the cases you:

1 Calculate the percentage of the population responding for each strata.

2 Establish which strata had the highest percentage of the population responding.

3 Calculate the weight for each strata using the formula:

$$\text{weight} = \frac{\text{highest proportion of population responding for any strata}}{\text{proportion of population responding in strata for which calculating weight}}$$

(*Note:* if your calculations are correct this will always result in the weight for the strata with the highest proportion of the population responding being 1.)

4 Apply the appropriate weight to each case.

Beware, many authors (for example Hays, 1994) question the validity of using statistics to make inferences from your sample if you have weighted cases.

• •

WORKED EXAMPLE: *Weighting cases*

To select your sample for a survey, you have used stratified random sampling. The per-centage of each strata's population that responded is given below:

Upper strata: 90%
Lower strata: 65%

To account for the differences in the response rates between strata you decide to weight the cases prior to analysis.

The weight for the Upper strata is: $\dfrac{90}{90} = 1$

This means that each case in the Upper strata will count as 1 case in your analysis.

The weight for the Lower strata is: $\dfrac{90}{65} = 1.38$

This means that each case in the Lower strata will count for 1.38 cases in your analysis.
     You enter these as a separate variable in your data set and use the statistical analysis software to apply the weights.

• •

Checking for errors

No matter how carefully you code and subsequently enter data, there will always be some errors. The main methods to check data for errors are:

- Look for illegitimate codes. In any coding scheme only certain numbers are allocated. Other numbers are therefore errors. Common errors are the inclusion of letters O and o instead of zero, letters l or I instead of one, and number 7 instead of one.

- Look for illogical relationships. For example, if a person is coded to the professional socioeconomic group and their social class is unskilled manual, an error has occurred.

- Check that rules in filter questions are followed. Certain responses to filter questions (Section 10.4) mean that other variables should be coded as missing values. If this has not happened there has been an error.

For each possible error you need to discover whether it occurred at coding or data entry and then correct it. By giving each case a unique identifier (normally a number) it is possible to link the matrix to the original data. You must remember to write the identifier on the data collection form and enter it along with the other data into the matrix.

Data checking is very time consuming and so is often not undertaken. Beware, not doing this is very dangerous and can result in incorrect results from which false conclusions are drawn!

11.3 EXPLORING AND PRESENTING DATA

Once your data have been entered and checked for errors, you are ready to start your analysis. We have found Tukey's (1977) *exploratory data analysis* approach useful in these initial stages. This approach emphasises the use of diagrams to explore and understand your data. As you would expect, we believe it is important to keep your research question(s) and objectives in mind when exploring your data. However, the exploratory data analysis approach also formalises the common practice of looking for other relationships in data which your research was not initially designed to test. This should not be discounted as it may suggest other fruitful avenues for analysis. In addition, computers make this relatively easy and quick.

Even at this stage it is important that you structure and label clearly each diagram and table to avoid possible misinterpretation. Table 11.2 summarises the points to remember when designing a diagram or table as a checklist.

We have found it best to begin exploratory analysis by looking at individual variables and their components. The key aspects you may need to consider will be guided by your research question(s) and objectives and are likely to include (Sparrow, 1989):

- specific values;
- limits of components (highest and lowest);
- trends over time;

For both diagrams and tables:
☑ Does it have a brief but clear and descriptive title?
☑ Are the units of measurement used clearly stated?
☑ Are the sources of data used clearly stated?
☑ Are there notes to explain abbreviations and unusual terminology?
☑ Does it state the size of the sample on which the values in the table are based?

For diagrams:
☑ Does it have clear axis labels?
☑ Are bars and their components in the same logical sequence?
☑ Is more dense shading used for smaller areas?
☑ Is a key or legend included (where necessary)?

For tables:
☑ Does it have clear column and row headings?
☑ Are columns and rows in a logical sequence?

Table 11.2 Checklist for diagrams and tables

- proportions;
- distributions.

Once you have explored these you can then begin to compare and look for relationships between variables considering in addition (Sparrow, 1989):

- conjunctions (the point where values for two or more variables intersect);
- totals (accumulations);
- interdependence and relationships.

These are summarised in Table 11.3. Most analytical software contains procedures to create tables and diagrams. Your choice will depend on those aspects of the data you wish to emphasise and the level of measurement at which the data were recorded. This section is concerned only with tables and two-dimensional diagrams available on most spreadsheets (Table 11.3). Three-dimensional diagrams are not discussed as these can hinder interpretation. Those tables and diagrams most pertinent to your research question(s) and objectives will eventually appear in your research report to support your arguments. You should therefore save a disk copy of all tables and diagrams you create.

Exploring and presenting individual variables

To show specific values

The simplest way of summarising data for individual variables so that specific values can be read is to use a *table (frequency distribution)*. For descriptive data the table summarises the number of cases (frequency) in each category. For variables where there are likely to be a large number of categories (or values for quantifiable data), you will need to group the data into categories that reflect your research question(s) and objectives.

To:	Categorical		Quantifiable	
	Descriptive	Ranked	Continuous	Discrete
show one variable so that any **specific** value can be read easily	table/frequency distribution (data often grouped)			
show the frequency of occurrences of categories or values for one variable so that highest and lowest (**limits**) are clear	bar chart (data may need grouping)		histogram or frequency polygon (data must be grouped)	bar chart or pictogram (data may need grouping)
show the **trend** for a variable		line graph or bar chart	line graph or histogram	line graph or bar chart
show the **proportion** of occurrences of categories or values for one variable	pie chart (data may need grouping)		histogram or pie chart (data must be grouped)	pie chart (data may need grouping)
show the **distribution** of values for one variable			frequency polygon or histogram (data must be grouped)	frequency polygon or bar chart (data may need grouping)
show the **interdependence** between two or more variables so that any **specific** value can be read easily	contingency table/cross-tabulation (data often grouped)			
compare the frequency of occurrences of categories or values for two or more variables so that totals highest and lowest (**limits**) are clear	multiple bar chart (continuous data must be grouped, other data may need grouping)			
compare the **trends** for two or more variables so that **conjunctions** are clear		multiple line graph or multiple bar chart		
compare the **proportions** of occurrences of categories or values for two or more variables	comparative pie charts or percentage component bar chart (continuous data must be grouped, other data may need grouping)			
compare the frequency of occurrences of categories or values for two or more variables so that totals (**accumulations**) are clear	stacked bar chart (continuous data must be grouped, other data may need grouping)			
compare the **proportions** and totals (**accumulations**) of occurrences of categories or values for two or more variables	comparative proportional pie charts (continuous data must be grouped, other data may need grouping)			
show the **relationship** between cases for two variables		scatter graph/scatter plot		

Table 11.3 Data presentation by data type – a summary
© Mark Saunders, Philip Lewis and Adrian Thornhill, 1997

To show limits

Tables attach no visual significance to highest or lowest values unless emphasised by different fonts. Diagrams can provide visual clues, although both categorical and quantifiable data may need grouping (Sparrow, 1989). For categorical and discrete data, bar charts and pictograms are both suitable. However, bar charts provide a more accurate representation and are used for most research reports. In a *bar chart*, sometimes called a *column chart*, the height of the bars represent the frequency of occurrence (Fig 11.2). Bars are separated by clear gaps, usually half the width of the bars or less.

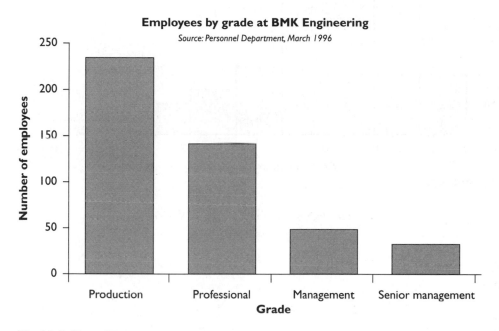

Fig 11.2 Bar chart

Most researchers use a histogram for continuous data. Before this can be drawn, data will need to be grouped into class intervals. In a *histogram* the area of each bar represents the frequency of occurrence and the continuous nature of the data is emphasised by the absence of gaps between the bars. For equal-width class intervals the height of your bar still represents the frequency of occurrences (Fig 11.3) and so limits are easy to distinguish. For histograms with unequal class interval widths this is not the case.

Analytical software treats histograms for data of equal-width class intervals as a variation of a bar chart. Unfortunately, few spreadsheets will cope automatically with the calculations required to draw histograms for unequal class intervals. As a consequence you may have to use a bar chart due to the limitations of your analytical software.

Frequency polygons are used less often to illustrate limits. Most analytical software treats them as a version of a line graph (Fig 11.4) in which the lines are extended to meet the horizontal axis, provided that the class widths are equal.

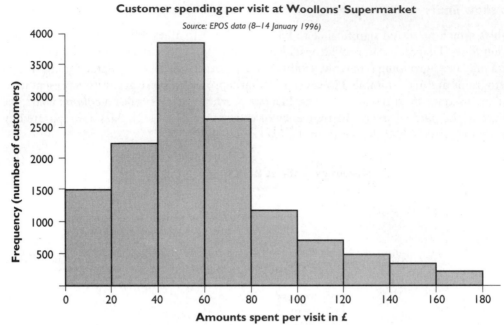

Customer spending per visit at Woollons' Supermarket

Source: EPOS data (8–14 January 1996)

Fig 11.3 Histogram

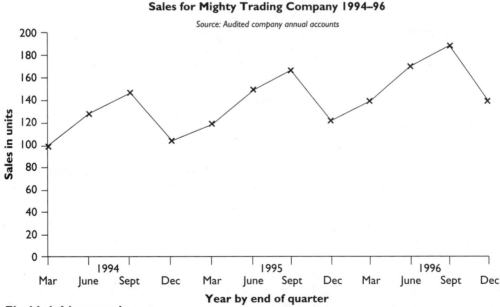

Sales for Mighty Trading Company 1994–96

Source: Audited company annual accounts

Fig 11.4 Line graph

To show the trend

Trends can only be presented for variables containing quantifiable (and occasionally ranked) longitudinal data. The most suitable diagram for exploring the trend is a *line graph*

(Sparrow, 1989) in which your data values for each time period are joined with a line to represent the trend (Fig 11.4). You can also use bar charts (Fig 11.2) to show trends between discrete time periods and histograms (Fig 11.3) for continuous time periods. The trend can also be calculated using time series analysis (Section 11.5).

MNS Ltd: Breakdown of sales by region 199–

Source: Sales returns

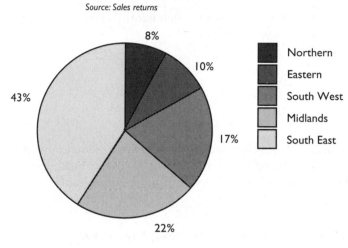

Total sales = £12.8 million

Fig 11.5 Pie chart

To show proportions

Research has shown that the most suitable diagram to emphasise the proportion or share of occurrences is the pie chart (Sparrow, 1989). A *pie chart* is divided into proportional segments according to the share each has of the total value (Fig 11.5). For continuous and some discrete and categorical data, you will need to group data before drawing the pie chart, as it is difficult to interpret pie charts with more than 10 segments (Saunders and Cooper, 1993).

To show the distribution of values

Before using many statistical tests it is necessary to establish the distribution of values for variables containing quantifiable data (Sections 11.4, 11.5). This can be seen by plotting either a frequency polygon or a histogram (Fig 11.3) for continuous data or a frequency polygon or bar chart for discrete data (Fig 11.2). If your diagram shows a bunching to the left and a long tail to the right, as in Fig 11.3, the data are *positively skewed*. If the converse is true the data are *negatively skewed*. If your data are equally distributed either side of the highest frequency, then they are *symmetrically distributed*. A special form of the symmetric distribution, in which the data can be plotted as a bell-shaped curve, is known as the *normal distribution*.

● ●

WORKED EXAMPLE: *Exploring and presenting data for individual variables*

As part of audience research, people attending a play at a provincial theatre were asked to complete a short questionnaire. This collected responses to 25 questions including:

3 How many plays (including this one) have you seen at this theatre in the past year? ____ ____

	strongly disagree	disagree	agree	strongly agree
11 This play is good value for money	☐ 1	☐ 2	☐ 3	☐ 4

24 How old are you?

Under 18	☐ 1	35 to 64	☐ 3
18 to 34	☐ 2	Over 65	☐ 4

Exploratory analyses were undertaken using analytical software and diagrams generated. For question 3, which collected discrete data, the aspects that were most important were the distribution of values and the highest and lowest (limits) numbers of plays seen. A bar chart was therefore drawn:

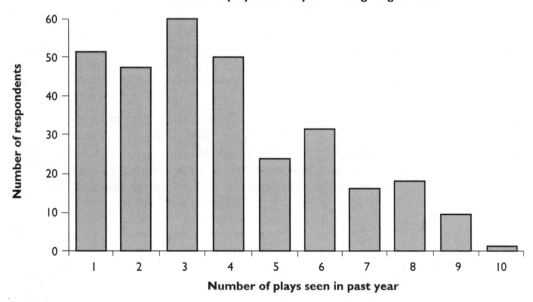

Number of plays seen in year ending August 1993

Note: based on 305 responses; no respondents attended more than 10 plays

Source: Audience questionnaire survey, August 1993

This emphasised that the most frequent number of plays seen by respondents was three and the least frequent 10. It also showed that the distribution was positively skewed towards lower numbers of plays seen.

For question 11 (categorical data) the most important aspect was the proportions of people agreeing and disagreeing with the statement. A pie chart was therefore drawn using similar shadings for the two agree categories and for the two disagree categories:

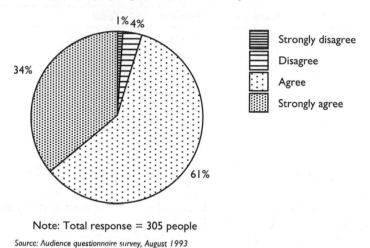

Proportion of respondents agreeing and disagreeing with the statement 'This play is good value for money'

Note: Total response = 305 people

Source: Audience questionnaire survey, August 1993

This emphasised that the vast majority (95%) agreed that the play was good value for money. Percentages were included on the chart to emphasise the specific proportions.

Question 24 collected data on each respondent's age. This question had grouped continuous data into four unequal-width age groups. For this analysis the most important aspect was the specific number of respondents in each age category and so a table was constructed:

Age of respondents

Age group	Number
less than 18	13
18 to 34	63
35 to 64	160
65 plus	64
Total	300

Note: 5 people did not respond
Source: Audience questionnaire survey, August 1993

Comparing variables

To show specific values and interdependence

As with individual variables, the best method of finding specific data values is a table. This is known as a *contingency table* or *cross-tabulation* (Table 11.4) and also enables you to examine interdependence between the variables. For variables where there are likely to be a large number of categories (or values for quantifiable data), you may need to group the data to prevent the table from becoming too large.

Number of insurance claims by gender 199–

Number of claims	Male	Female	Total
0	10 032	13 478	23 510
1	2 156	1 430	3 586
2	120	25	145
3	13	4	17
Total	12 321	14 937	27 258

*No clients had more than 3 claims
Source: KJD Insurance Services

Table 11.4 Contingency table

Most statistical analysis software allows you to add totals and row and column percentages when designing your table. Statistical analyses such as chi square can also be undertaken at the same time (Section 11.5).

To compare highest and lowest

Comparisons of variables which emphasise the highest and lowest rather than precise values are best explored using a *multiple bar chart* (Sparrow, 1989). As with a bar chart, continuous data, or data where there are many values or categories, need to be grouped. Within any multiple bar chart you are likely to find it easiest to compare between adjacent bars. Thus, Fig 11.6 has been drawn to emphasise comparisons between years rather than companies.

To compare proportions

Comparison of proportions between variables uses either a *percentage component bar chart* or two or more pie charts. Either type of diagram can be used for all data types, provided that continuous data, and data where there are more than 10 values or categories, are grouped. Percentage component bar charts are more straightforward to draw than comparative pie charts using most spreadsheets. Within your percentage component bar chart comparisons will be easiest between adjacent bars. The chart in Fig 11.7 has been drawn to compare proportions of each type of response between products. Consumers' responses for each product therefore form a single bar.

To compare trends and conjunctions

The most suitable diagram to compare trends for two or more quantifiable (or occasionally ranked) variables is a *multiple line graph* where one line represents each variable

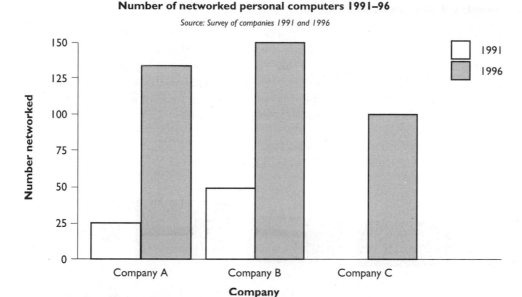

Fig 11.6 Multiple bar chart

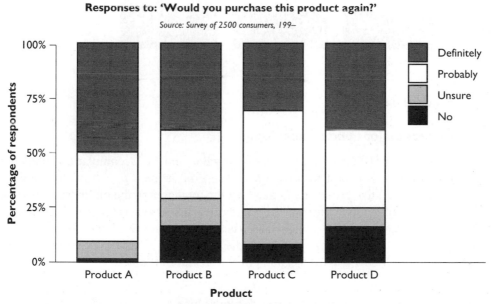

Fig 11.7 Percentage component bar chart

(Sparrow, 1989). You can also use multiple bar charts (Fig 11.6) in which bars for the same time period are placed adjacent to each other.

If you need to look for conjunctions in the trends, that is, where values for two or more variables intersect, this is where the lines on a multiple line graph cross.

To compare accumulations (totals)

Comparison of accumulations (totals) between variables uses a variation of the bar chart. A *stacked bar chart* can be used for all data types, provided that continuous data and data where there are more than 10 possible values or categories are grouped. As with percentage component bar charts, the design of the stacked bar chart is dictated by the totals you want to compare. For this reason in Fig 11.8 sales for each quarter have been stacked to give annual totals which can be compared between companies.

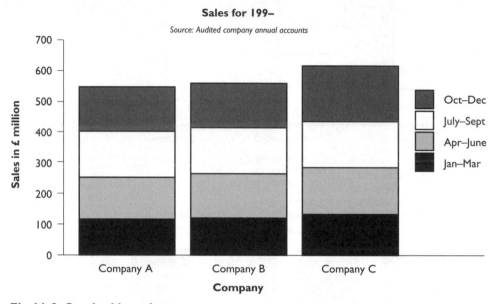

Fig 11.8 Stacked bar chart

To compare proportions and accumulations

To compare both proportions of each category or value and the accumulation totals for two or more variables, it is best to use *comparative proportional pie charts* for all data types. For each comparative proportional pie chart the total area of the pie chart represents the total for that variable. By contrast, the angle of each segment represents the relative proportion of a category within the variable (Fig 11.4). Because of the complexity of drawing comparative proportional pie charts they are rarely used for exploratory data analysis, although they can be used to good effect in research reports.

To show the relationship between cases for variables

You can explore possible relationships between ranked and quantifiable data variables by plotting one variable against another. This is called a *scatter graph* or *scatter plot* and each cross (point) represents the values for one case (Fig 11.9). Convention dictates that you plot the *dependent variable*, that is, the variable that changes in response to changes in the other (*independent*) variable, on the vertical axis. The strength of the relationship is indicated by the closeness of the points to an imaginary line. If as the values for one variable increase so

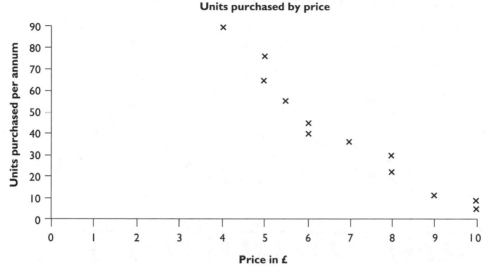

Fig 11.9 Scatter graph

do those for the other, you have a positive relationship. If as the values for one variable decrease, those for the other variable increase, you have a negative relationship. Thus in Fig 11.9 there is a negative relationship between the two variables. The strength of this relationship can be assessed statistically using techniques such as correlation or regression (Section 11.5).

WORKED EXAMPLE: *Comparing variables*

An independent ice-cream manufacturer has kept records of monthly sales of ice cream for 1994 and 1995. In addition, the company has obtained longitudinal data on average (mean) daily hours of sunshine for each month for the same period from their local weather station. As part of your research project you need to explore data on sales of the three best-selling flavours (vanilla, strawberry and chocolate), paying particular attention to:

■ comparative trends in sales;

■ the relationship between sales and amount of sunshine.

To compare trends in sales between the three flavours you plot a multiple line graph (see page 310).

This indicates that sales for all flavours of ice cream are following a seasonal pattern but with an overall upwards trend. It also shows that sales of vanilla ice cream are highest and that those of chocolate have overtaken strawberry. The multiple line graph highlights the conjunction when sales of chocolate first exceeded strawberry, September 1995.

To show relationships between sales and amount of sunshine, you plot scatter graphs for sales of each ice-cream flavour against average (mean) daily hours of sunshine for each month. You plot sales on the vertical axis as you presume these are dependent on the amount of sunshine, as for example on page 310.

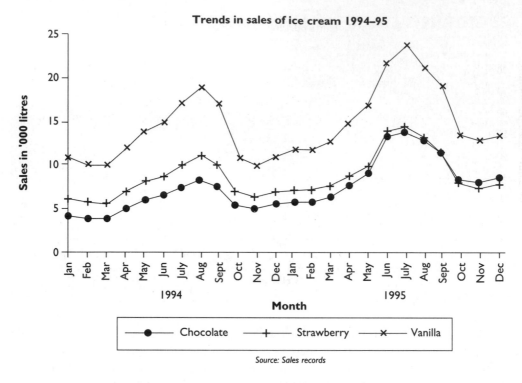

Trends in sales of ice cream 1994–95

Source: Sales records

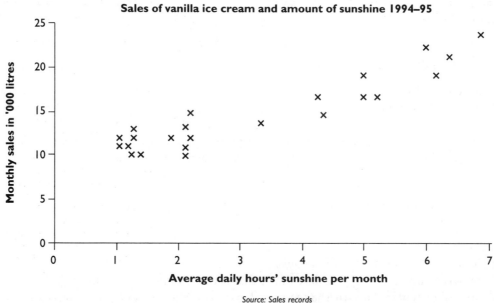

Sales of vanilla ice cream and amount of sunshine 1994–95

Source: Sales records

The scatter graph shows that there is a positive relationship between the amount of sunshine and sales of vanilla flavour ice cream. Subsequent scatter plots reveal similar relationships for strawberry and chocolate flavours.

11.4 DESCRIBING DATA USING STATISTICS

The exploratory data analysis approach (Section 11.3) emphasised the use of diagrams to understand your data. *Descriptive statistics* enable you to describe (and compare) variables numerically. Your choice of statistics, although limited by the type of data (Table 11.5) should be guided by your research question(s) and objectives. Statistics to describe a variable focus on two aspects:

- the central tendency;
- the dispersion.

These are summarised in Table 11.5. Those most pertinent to your research question(s) and objectives will eventually be quoted in your research report as support for your arguments.

To calculate a measure of:		Categorical		Quantifiable	
		Descriptive	Ranked	Continuous	Discrete
central tendency which ...	... represents the value which occurs most frequently	mode			
	... represents the middle value			median	
	... includes all data values (average)			mean	
dispersion which ...	... states the difference between the highest and lowest values			range (data need not be normally distributed but must be placed in rank order)	
	... states the difference within the middle 50% of values			inter-quartile range (data need not be normally distributed but but must be placed in rank order)	
	... states the difference within another fraction of the values			deciles or percentiles (data need not be normally distributed but must be placed in rank order)	
	... describes the extent by which data values differ from the mean			variance or more usually the standard deviation (data should be normally distributed)	
	... compares the extent by which data values differ from the mean between variables			coefficient of variation (data should be normally distributed)	

Table 11.5 Descriptive statistics by data type – a summary
© Mark Saunders, Philip Lewis and Adrian Thornhill, 1997

Describing the central tendency

When describing data for both samples and populations quantitatively, it is usual to provide some general impression of values that could be seen as common, middling or average. These are termed measures of *central tendency* and are discussed in virtually all statistics textbooks. The three ways of measuring the central tendency most used in business research are the:

■ most frequent value (mode);

■ middle value or mid-point after the data have been ranked (median);

■ value often known as the average which includes all data values in its calculation (mean).

However beware: if you have used numerical codes most analytical software can calculate all three measures whether or not they are appropriate!

To represent the value which occurs most frequently

The *mode* is the value that occurs most frequently. For descriptive data, the mode is the only measure of central tendency that can be sensibly interpreted. You might read in a report that the most common (*modal*) colour of motor cars sold last year was red or that the two most common makes were Ford and Vauxhall (it is possible to have more than one mode). The mode can be calculated for variables where there are likely to be a large number of categories (or values for quantifiable data), although it may be less useful. One solution is to group the data into suitable categories and quote the most frequently occurring or *modal group*.

To represent the middle value

If you have quantitative data it is also possible to calculate the middle or *median* value by ranking all the values in ascending order and finding the mid-point (or *50th percentile*) in the distribution. For variables which have an even number of data values the median will occur halfway between the two middle data values. The median has the advantage that it is not affected by extreme values in the distribution.

To include all data values

The most frequently used measure of central tendency is the *mean* or *average* which includes all data values in its calculation. However, it is usually only possible to calculate a meaningful mean using quantifiable data.

The value of your mean is unduly influenced by extreme data values in skewed distributions (Section 11.3). In such distributions the mean tends to be drawn towards the long tail of extreme data values and may be less representative of the central tendency. For this and other reasons Hays (1994) suggests that the median may be a more useful descriptive statistic. However, because the mean is the building block for many of the statistical tests used to explore relationships (Section 11.5), it is usual to include it as at least one of the measures of central tendency for quantifiable data in your report. This is, of course, provided that it makes sense!

● ●

WORKED EXAMPLE: *Measuring the central tendency*

As part of your research project, you have obtained secondary data from the *Annual Abstract of Statistics* (Dennis *et al.*, 1995 Table 15.2 on the 1993 distribution of annual income in the UK):

Income in £s	Number of incomes in '000s		Income in £	Number of incomes in '000s
3501 – 4000	716		10001 – 12000	2800
4001 – 4500	699		12001 – 15000	3420
4501 – 5000	829		15001 – 20000	3810
5001 – 5500	851		20001 – 30000	3140
5501 – 6000	814		30001 – 50000	1230
6001 – 7000	1710		50001 – 100000	335
7001 – 8000	1800		100001+	95
8001 – 10000	3130			

Total number of incomes = 25 400 000; total income before tax = £373 700 000 000

Source: *Annual Abstract of Statistics, Office for National Statistics. 1995 Crown Copyright 1995. Reproduced by permission of the Controller of HMSO and the Office for National Statistics*

Your exploratory analysis has revealed a positively skewed distribution (long tail to the right):

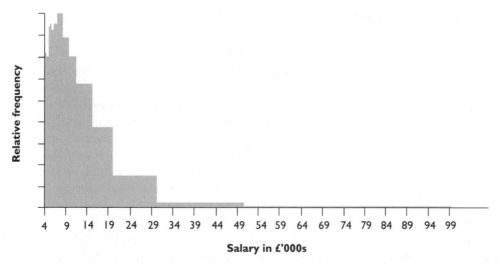

From the table the largest single group of people is those earning £15 001–£20 000 per year. This is the modal income group (most commonly occurring). However, the usefulness of this statistic is limited due to the variety of class widths for income. By definition, half the people will have below the median income (approximately £11 500) and half will

313

have above it. However, there are 95 000 people earning over £100 000 per year. As a consequence, mean income (£14 712) is pulled towards higher incomes. This is represented by the skewed shape of the distribution.

You need to decide which of the these measures of central tendency to include in your research report. As the mode makes little sense, you quote the median and mean when interpreting the data:

1993 incomes within the UK were positively skewed. Although mean income was £14 712, half the population had an annual income less than £11 500 (median). Grouping of the published data means it is not possible to calculate a meaningful mode.

Describing the dispersion

As well as describing the central tendency for a variable, it is important to describe how the data values are dispersed around the central tendency. As you can see from Table 11.5, this is only possible for quantifiable data. Two of the most frequently used ways of describing the dispersion are the:

- difference within the middle 50 per cent of values (inter-quartile range);
- extent to which values differ from the mean (standard deviation).

Although these *measures of dispersion* are only suitable for quantifiable data, most statistical analysis software will also calculate them for categorical data if you have used numerical codes!

To state the difference between values

In order to get a quick impression of the distribution of data values for a variable, you could simply calculate the difference between the lowest and the highest values, that is, the *range*. However, this statistic is rarely used in research reports as it only represents the extreme values.

A more frequently used statistic is the *inter-quartile range*. As we discussed earlier, the median divides the range into two. The range can be further divided into four equal sections called *quartiles*. The lower quartile is the value below which a quarter of your data values will fall, the upper quartile is the value above which a quarter of your data values will fall. As you would expect, the remaining half of your data values will fall between the lower and upper quartiles. The difference between the upper and lower quartiles is the inter-quartile range (Saunders and Cooper, 1993). As a consequence, it is only concerned with the middle 50 per cent of data values and ignores extreme values.

You can also calculate the range for other fractions of a variable's distribution. One alternative is to divide your distribution using *percentiles*. These split your distribution into 100 equal parts. Obviously, the lower quartile is the 25th percentile and the upper quartile the 75th percentile. However, you could calculate a range between the 10th and 90th percentiles so as to include 80 per cent of your data values. Another alternative is to divide the range into 10 equal parts, called *deciles*.

To describe and compare the extent to which values differ from the mean

Conceptually and statistically in research it is important to look at the extent to which the data values for a variable are *spread* around their mean, as this is what you need to know to assess its usefulness as a typical value for the distribution (Saunders and Cooper, 1993). If your data values are all close to the mean, then the mean is more typical than if they vary widely. To describe the extent of spread of quantifiable data you use the *standard deviation*. If your data are a sample (Section 6.1) this is calculated using a slightly different formula than if your data are a population, although if your sample is larger than about 30 cases there is little difference in the two statistics (Morris, 1993).

You may need to compare the relative spread of data between distributions of different magnitudes (for example, one may be measured in hundreds of tonnes, the other in billions of tonnes). To make a meaningful comparison you will need to take account of these different magnitudes. A common way of doing this is to:

1 Divide the standard deviation by the mean.

2 Then multiply your answer by 100.

This results in a statistic called the *coefficient of variation* (Saunders and Cooper, 1993). The values of this statistic can then be compared. The distribution with the largest coefficient of variation has the largest relative spread of data.

● ●

WORKED EXAMPLE: *Describing variables and comparing their dispersion*

A bank collects data on the total value of transactions at each of its main and sub-branches. The mean value of total transactions at the main branches are five times as high as those at the sub-branches. This makes it difficult to compare the relative spread in total value of transactions between the two types of branches. Calculating the coefficients of variation reveals that there is relatively more variation in the total value of transactions at the main branches than at the sub-branches:

Branch type	Mean total transaction value	Standard deviation	Coefficient of variation
Main	£6 000 000	£1 417 000	23.62
Sub	£1 200 000	£217 000	18.08

This is because the coefficient of variation for the main branches is larger (23.62) than the coefficient for the sub-branches (18.08).

● ●

11.5 EXAMINING RELATIONSHIPS AND TRENDS USING STATISTICS

One of the questions you are most likely to ask in your analysis is, 'How does a variable relate to another variable?' In statistical analysis you normally answer this question by testing the likelihood of the relationship occurring by chance, that is, its significance. The way in which this significance is tested can be thought of as answering one from a series of questions, depending on the data type:

■ Are these variables significantly associated?

■ Are these groups significantly different?

■ What is the strength of the relationship between these variables and is it significant?

■ If I know the values of the independent variables, how well (significantly) can I predict the values of the dependent variable?

These are summarised in table 11.6 along with statistics to help examine trends.

To:	Categorical		Quantifiable	
	Descriptive	**Ranked**	**Continuous**	**Discrete**
test whether two variables are significantly associated	chi square (data may need grouping)		chi square if variables grouped into discrete classes	
test whether two groups (categories) are significantly different			independent *t*-test or paired *t*-test (often used to test for changes over time)	
test whether three or more groups (categories) are significantly different			analysis of variance (ANOVA)	
assess the strength of relationship between two variables		Spearman's Rank Correlation Coefficient	Pearson's Product Moment Correlation Coefficient (PMCC)	
assess the strength of a relationship between one dependent and one or more independent variables			regression coefficient	
predict the value of a dependent variable from one or more independent variables			regression equation	
compare relative changes over time			index numbers	
determine the trend over time of a series of data			time series: moving averages, regression equation	

Table 11.6 Statistics to examine relationships and trends by data type – a summary
© Mark Saunders, Philip Lewis and Adrian Thornhill, 1997

Testing for significant relationships

Testing the probability of a relationship between variables having occurred by chance is known as *significance testing*. As part of your research project you might have collected sample data to examine the relationship between two variables. Once you have entered data into the analytical software, chosen the statistic and run the program, an answer will appear as if by magic! With most statistical analysis software this will consist of a test statistic, the degrees of freedom and based on these the probability of your test result occurring by chance. If the probability of your test statistic having occurred by chance is very low (usually 0.05 or lower[2]), then you have a significant relationship. If the probability of obtaining the test statistic by chance is higher than 0.05, then you conclude that the relationship is not significant. There may still be a relationship between the variables under such circumstances, but you cannot make the conclusion with any certainty.

The significance of the relationship indicated by the test statistic on sample data is determined in part by your sample size (Section 6.2). As a consequence it is very difficult to obtain a significant test statistic with a small sample. Fortunately, the impact of sample size declines rapidly for samples over about 30 cases.

To test whether two variables are significantly associated

Often descriptive or quantifiable data will be summarised as a two way contingency table (such as Table 11.4). The *chi square test* enables you to find out if the values for the two variables are independent or associated. It is based on a comparison of the observed values in the table with what might be expected if the two distributions were entirely independent. Therefore you are testing whether the data in your table differ significantly from those which you would expect if the two variables were independent of each other.

The test relies on:

- the categories used in the contingency table being mutually exclusive so each observation falls into only one category or class interval;
- no more than 20 per cent of the cells in the table having expected values of less than five. For contingency tables of two rows and two columns it is preferable to have no expected values of less than 10 (Hays, 1994).

If the latter assumption is not met, the accepted solution is to combine rows and columns.

The chi square test calculates the probability that two variables are independent. Most statistical analysis software does this automatically. However, if you are using a spreadsheet you will need to look up the probability in a critical values of chi square table using your calculated chi square value and the degrees of freedom[3]. This table is included in most statistics textbooks. A probability of 0.05 means that there is only a 5 per cent chance that the variables are independent of each other. Therefore a probability of 0.05 or smaller means you can be at least 95 per cent certain that your two variables are significantly associated.

WORKED EXAMPLE: *Testing whether two variables are significantly associated*

As part of your research you wish to discover if there is a significant association between grade of the respondent and gender. Earlier analysis has indicated that there are 760

---

[2] A probability of 0.05 means that the probability of your test result occurring by chance is 5 in 100, that is, 1 in 20.

[3] Degrees of freedom are calculated by (number of rows in the table − 1) × (number of columns in the table − 1)

respondents in your sample with no missing data for either variable. However, it has also highlighted the small numbers of respondents in the lowest grade and very small numbers in the three highest grade categories:

gender	grade 1	grade 2	grade 3	grade 4	grade 5	grade 6	grade 7
male	13	52	100	45	15	3	1
female	27	233	209	49	12	0	1

Bearing in mind the assumptions of the chi square test, you decide to combine categories to give three new grades: lower (grades one and two), middle (grade three) and higher (grades four, five, six and seven). The statistical analysis software creates a new data table and provides the following output:

	lower grade	middle grade	higher grade	row totals
male	65	100	64	229 (30.1%)
female	260	209	62	531 (69.9%)
column totals	325 (42.8%)	309 (40.7%)	126 (16.6%)	760 (100%)

Chi square = 42.13, degrees of freedom = 2, probability <.001.

As can be seen, there is an overall chi square value of 42.13 with 2 degrees of freedom. This means that the probability of the values in your table occurring by chance is less than 0.001. You therefore conclude that the variables gender and grade are significantly associated.

To explore this association further, you examine the cell values in relation to the row and column totals. You find that 27.9 per cent of males are in higher grades. This is high compared to the column totals which indicate that only 16.6 per cent of the total sample were in higher grades. The row totals indicate that males in the sample represent 30.1 per cent of the total. Yet column frequencies show that males represented just over half (50.8 per cent) of the higher grades. Thus males are over-represented (and females under-represented) in higher grades.

To test whether two groups are significantly different

If a quantifiable variable can be divided into two distinct groups using a descriptive variable, you can assess whether or not the groups are significantly different using an *independent groups t-test*. This compares the difference in the means of the two groups using a measure of the spread of the scores. If the two variables are significantly different this will be represented by a larger *t* statistic with a probability of less than 0.05.

Alternatively you might have quantifiable data for two variables which measure the same feature but under different conditions. Your research could focus on the effects of an intervention such as employee counselling. As a consequence, you would have pairs of data that measure work performance before and after counselling for each case. To assess whether or not your two groups (each half of the pair) are significantly different, you would use a *paired t-test*. Although the calculation of this is slightly different, your interpretation would be the same as that for the independent groups *t*-test.

Although the *t*-test assumes the data are normally distributed (Section 11.3) this can be ignored without too many problems even with sample sizes of less than 30 (Hays, 1994). The assumption that the data for the two groups have the same variance (standard deviation squared) can also be ignored, provided that the two samples are of similar size (Hays, 1994).

WORKED EXAMPLE: *Testing whether two groups are significantly different*

As part of your research project you need to compare the performance of two international companies' European subsidiaries to see if there is a significant difference in average (mean) share yield between the two companies. You decide to use the following secondary data from the financial pages of a national newspaper:

Company A subsidiaries	Yield	Company B subsidiaries	Yield
France	6.2	Belgium	5.4
Germany	6.2	Denmark	5.7
Italy	5.9	Eire	7.2
Portugal	4.8	Luxembourg	4.8
Spain	4.5	Netherlands	6.0
United Kingdom	5.8	Norway	6.0
		Sweden	5.7
		Switzerland	5.1

Source: The National Newspaper, 8 July 199X

After defining the two groups (Company A and Company B) using the descriptive variable, you use a *t*-test to find out if there is a significant difference between average yields for the two international companies.

Your statistical analysis software provides you with the means and standard deviations for the two groups as well as the *t* value, degrees of freedom and probability:

	Company A	Company B
Mean	5.57	5.74
Standard deviation	0.73	0.73

t value = 0.43, degrees of freedom = 12, probability = 0.672

As the standard deviations for both sectors are the same, the assumption that the two variables have the same variance is satisfied. The *t* value is only 0.43 with 12 degrees of freedom. A probability of 0.672 (much greater than 0.05) indicates that there is no significant difference between the two groups. You conclude in your research report that there is no significant difference in average (mean) yields between Company A and Company B.

To test whether three or more groups are significantly different

If a quantifiable variable is divided into three or more distinct groups using a descriptive variable, you can assess whether these groups are significantly different using *one-way analysis of variance* or *one-way ANOVA* (Table 11.6). As you can gather from its name, ANOVA analyses the variations within and between groups of data by comparing means. These differences are represented by the *F ratio* or *F statistic*. If the means are significantly different between groups this will be represented by a large *F* ratio with a probability of less than 0.05.

Hays (1994) lists the following assumptions which need to be met before using one-way ANOVA:

- Each data value is independent and does not relate to any of the other data values. This means that you should not use one-way ANOVA where data values are related in some way, such as the same person being tested repeatedly.

- The data for each group are normally distributed (Section 11.3). This assumption is not particularly important provided that the number of cases in each group is large (30 or more).

- The data for each group have the same variance (standard deviation squared). However, provided that the number of cases in the largest group is not more than 1.5 times that of the smallest group, this appears to have very little effect on the test results.

WORKED EXAMPLE: *Testing whether three groups are significantly different*

Andy and a colleague were interested to discover if there were significant differences in job satisfaction across three groups of employees (managers, administrators, shopfloor workers) within a manufacturing organisation. They decided to measure job satisfaction using a tried and tested scale based on five questions which resulted in a job satisfaction score (quantifiable data) for each employee.

After ensuring that the assumptions of one-way ANOVA were satisfied, they analysed their data using statistical analysis software. The output included the following:

```
ANALYSIS OF VARIANCE

Source            D.F.      Sum of        Mean       F Ratio    F Prob.
                            Squares       Squares

Between Groups      2      455.7512      227.8756     24.3952    <.0001

Within Groups     614     5735.3834       9.3410

Total             616     6191.1345
```

This output shows that the *F* ratio value of 24.3952 with 2 and 614 degrees of freedom (DF) has a probability of occurrence by chance of less than 0.0001 if there is no significant difference between the three groups. Andy and his colleague therefore concluded that there was a significant difference in job satisfaction between managers, administrators, and shopfloor workers.

Assessing the strength of relationship

As part of your exploratory data analysis you will already have plotted the relationship between cases for two ranked or quantifiable variables using a scatter graph (Fig 11.9). Such relationships might include those between weekly sales of a new product and those of a similar established product, or age of employees and their length of service with the company. These examples emphasise the fact that your data can contain two sorts of relationship:

- those where a change in one variable is accompanied by a change in another variable but it is not clear which variable caused the other to change – a *correlation*.
- those where a change in one or more (independent) variables causes a change in another (dependent) variable – a *cause and effect* relationship (Saunders and Cooper, 1993).

To assess the strength of relationship between pairs of variables

A *correlation coefficient* enables you to quantify the strength of the relationship between two ranked or quantifiable variables. This coefficient (represented by the letter *r*) can take on any value between –1 and +1 (Fig 11.10). A value of +1 represents a perfect *positive correlation*. This means that the two variables are precisely related and that as values of one variable increase, values of the other variable will increase. By contrast, a value of –1 represents a perfect *negative correlation*. Again, this means the two variables are precisely related, however as the values of one variable increase the other's decrease. Correlation coefficients between +1 and –1 represent weaker positive and negative correlations, a value of 0 meaning the variables are perfectly independent. Within business research it is extremely unusual to obtain perfect correlations.

Fig 11.10 Values of the correlation coefficient

For data collected from a sample you will need to know the probability of your correlation coefficient having occurred by chance. Most statistical analysis software calculates this probability automatically. As outlined earlier, if this probability is very low (usually less than 0.05) then you have a significant relationship. If the probability is greater than 0.05 then your relationship is not significant.

If both your variables contain quantifiable data you should use *Pearson's product moment correlation coefficient (PMCC)* to assess the strength of relationship (Table 11.6). However, if one of your variables contains rank data you will need to rank the other variable and use *Spearman's rank correlation coefficient*. Although this uses a different formula to calculate the correlation coefficient, it is interpreted in the same way.

● ●

WORKED EXAMPLE: *Assessing the strength of relationship between pairs of variables*

As part of their market research a company has collected data on the number of newspaper advertisements, number of enquiries and number of sales for a product. These data have been entered into their statistical analysis software. They wish to discover whether there are any relationships between the following pairs of these variables:

■ number of newspaper advertisements   and   number of enquires
■ number of newspaper advertisements   and   number of sales
■ number of enquiries   and   number of sales

As the data are quantifiable, they program the statistical analysis software to calculate Pearson's product moment correlation coefficients for all pairs of variables. The output is provided in the form of a correlation matrix:

```
Correlation Coefficients

                advert        enquiry        sales

advert          1.0000        0.3441*        0.2030

enquiry         0.3441*       1.0000         0.7002**

sales           0.2030        0.7002**       1.0000

* significance <.05, **significance <.01
```

The matrix is symmetrical because correlation only implies a relationship rather than a cause and effect relationship. The value in each cell of the matrix is the correlation coefficient. Thus the correlation between the variable 'advert' and the variable 'enquiry' is 0.3441. This coefficient shows that there is a fairly weak but positive relationship between the number of newspaper advertisements and the number of enquiries. The * indicates that the probability of this correlation coefficient occurring by chance is less than 0.05 (5 per cent). This correlation is therefore significant.

Using the data in this matrix, the company concludes that there is a highly significant strong positive relationship between the number of enquiries and the number of sales ($r =$

0.7002) and a significant but weaker relationship between the number of newspaper advertisements and the number of enquiries ($r = 0.3441$). However, there is no significant relationship between the number of newspaper advertisements and the number of sales.

To assess the strength of a cause and effect relationship between variables

In contrast to the correlation coefficient, the *regression coefficient* (sometimes known as the *coefficient of determination*) enables you to assess the strength of relationship between a quantifiable dependent variable and one or more quantifiable independent variables. For a dependent variable and one (or perhaps two) independent variables, you will have probably already plotted this relationship on a scatter graph. If you have more than two independent variables this is unlikely, as it is very difficult to represent four or more scatter graph axes visually!

The regression coefficient (represented by the letter R^2) can take on any value between 0 and +1. It measures the proportion of the variation in a dependent variable (amount of sales) that can be explained statistically by the independent variable (marketing expenditure) or variables (marketing expenditure, number of sales staff etc.). This means that if all the variation in amount of sales can be explained by the marketing expenditure and the number of sales staff, the regression coefficient will be 1. If 50 per cent of the variation can be explained the regression coefficient will be 0.5, and if none of the variation can be explained the coefficient will be 0. Within our research we have rarely obtained a regression coefficient above 0.8.

The process of calculating a regression coefficient using one independent variable is normally termed regression. Calculating the regression coefficient using two or more independent variables is termed multiple *regression*. The calculations and interpretation required by *multiple* regression are relatively complicated and we advise you to use statistical analysis software and consult a detailed statistics textbook or computer manual such as Norusis (1992). Most statistical analysis software will calculate the significance of the regression coefficient for sample data automatically. A very low significance value (usually 0.05) means that your coefficient is unlikely to have occurred by chance. A value greater than 0.05 means you can conclude that your regression coefficient is not significant.

WORKED EXAMPLE: *Assessing a cause and effect relationship*

As part of your research you wish to assess the relationship between all the employees' annual salaries and the number of years they have been employed by the organisation. You believe that annual salary will be dependent on the number of years for which they have been employed (the independent variable).

You enter the data into your analytical software and calculate a regression coefficient (R^2) of 0.37.

As you are using data from the population rather than a sample, the probability of the coefficient occurring by chance is 0. You therefore conclude that 37 per cent of the variation in employees' salaries can be explained by the number of years they have been employed by the organisation.

To predict the value of a variable from one or more other variables

Regression analysis can also be used to predict the values of a dependent variable given the values of one or more independent variables by calculating a *regression equation*. You may wish to predict the amount of sales for a specified marketing expenditure and number of sales staff. You would represent this as a regression equation:

amount of sales $= a + (b_1 \times$ marketing expenditure$) + (b_2 \times$ number of sales staff$)$

Using regression analysis you would calculate the values of a, and b_1 and b_2 from data you had already collected on amount of sales, marketing expenditure and number of sales staff. A specified marketing expenditure and number of sales staff could then be substituted into the regression equation to predict the amount of sales that would be generated.

The regression coefficient (discussed earlier) can be used as a measure of how good a predictor your regression equation is likely to be. If your equation is a perfect predictor then the regression coefficient will be 1. If the equation can only predict 50 per cent of the variation then the regression coefficient will be 0.5, and if the equation predicts none of the variation the coefficient will be 0.

WORKED EXAMPLE: *Forecasting journey time*

A minicab firm needs to establish the relationship between the time a journey takes (dependent variable) and the distance travelled in towns and the country (independent variables) in order to be able to provide their customers with an estimate of journey time. To do this they have collected data for a sample of 250 journeys on the miles travelled in towns, the miles travelled in the country and the time taken in minutes. The data are entered into statistical analysis software and a multiple regression performed. The output includes the following statistics:

```
R Square = 0.60459   F = 24.14   Signif F = 0.0012
Variables in the Equation
Variable           B
town               2.7651
country            1.3453
constant (a)       4.7452
```

The 'variables in the equation' are substituted into the regression equation (after rounding the values of a and b):

journey time $= 4.7 + (2.8 \times$ town miles$) + (1.3 \times$ country miles$)$

The time for any journey, such as one of **2** town miles and **3** country miles can now be estimated:

$$4.7 + (2.8 \times 2) + (1.3 \times 3)$$
$$= 12.9 \text{ minutes}$$

However, care should be taken with these estimates as, while the values in the equation are unlikely to have occurred by chance (Signif F = 0.0012), they only explain just over 60 per cent (R^2 of 0.60459) of the variation in the journey time.

Examining trends

When examining longitudinal data the first thing we recommend you do is to draw a line graph to obtain a visual representation of the trend (Fig 11.4). After this statistical analyses can be undertaken. Two of the more common uses of such analyses are to:

■ compare trends for variables measured in different units or of different magnitudes;

■ determine the long-term trend and forecast future values for a variable.

These are summarised in Table 11.6.

To compare trends

To answer some research question(s) and meet some objectives you may need to compare trends between two or more variables measured in different units or at different magnitudes. To compare changes in prices of fuel oil and coal over time is difficult as the prices are recorded for different units (litres and tonnes). One way of overcoming this is to use *index numbers* and compare the relative changes in prices rather than actual figures. Index numbers are also widely used in business publications and by organisations. The Financial Times share indices and the Index of Retail Prices are well-known examples.

Although such indices can involve quite complex calculations, they all compare change over time against a base period. The *base period* is normally given the value of 100 (or 1000 in the case of many share indices) and change calculated relative to this. Thus a value greater than 100 would represent an increase relative to the base period and a value less than 100 a decrease.

To calculate simple index numbers for each case of a longitudinal variable you use the following formula:

$$\text{Index number for case} = \frac{\text{data value for case}}{\text{data value for base period}} \times 100$$

Thus if a company's sales were 125 000 units in 1995 (base period) and 150 000 units in 1996, the index number for 1995 would be 100 and for 1996 it would be 120.

To determine the trend and forecasting

The trend can be estimated by drawing a freehand line through the data on a line graph. However, these data are often subject to variations such as seasonal variations (Fig 11.4) and so this method is not very accurate. A straightforward way of overcoming this is to calculate a moving average for the *time series* of data values. Calculating a *moving average* involves replacing each value in the time series with the mean of that value and those values directly preceding and following it (Saunders and Cooper, 1993). This smoothes out the variation in the data so that you can see the trend more clearly. The calculation of a moving average is relatively straightforward using either a spreadsheet or statistical analysis software.

Once the trend has been established it is possible to forecast future values by continuing the trend forward for time periods for which data have not been collected. This involves calculating the *long-term trend*, that is, the amount by which values are changing each time period after variations have been smoothed out. Once again, this is relatively straightforward to calculate using analytical software (Saunders and Cooper, 1993). Forecasting can also be undertaken using other statistical methods including regression (Section 11.5).

11.6 SUMMARY

- Data for quantitative analysis can be collected and subsequently coded at different levels of numerical measurement. The data type (precision of measurement) will constrain the data presentation, summary and analysis techniques you can use.

- Data are entered for computer analysis as a data matrix in which each column usually represents a variable and each row a case. Your first variable should be a unique identifier to facilitate error checking.

- All data should, with few exceptions, be recorded using numerical codes to facilitate analyses.

- Where possible you should use existing coding schemes to enable comparisons.

- For primary data you should include pre-set codes on the data collection form to minimise coding after collection. For variables where responses are not known you will need to develop a code book after data have been collected for the first 50 to 100 cases.

- You should enter codes for all data values, including missing data.

- The data matrix must be checked for errors.

- Your initial analysis should explore data using both tables and diagrams. Your choice of table or diagram will be influenced by your research question(s) and objectives, the aspects of the data you wish to emphasise and the level of measurement at which the data were recorded. This may involve using:
  - tables to show specific values;
  - bar charts, multiple bar charts and histograms to show limits (highest and lowest values);

– line graphs to show trends;

– pie charts and percentage component bar charts to show proportions;

– scatter graphs to show relationships between variables.

■ Subsequent analyses will involve describing your data and exploring relationships using statistics. As before, your choice of statistics will be influenced by your research question(s) and objectives and the level of measurement at which the data were recorded. Your analysis may involve using statistics such as:

– the mean, median and mode to describe the central tendency;

– the inter-quartile range and the standard deviation to describe the dispersion;

– chi square to test whether two variables are significantly associated;

– *t*-tests and ANOVA to test whether groups are significantly different;

– correlation and regression to assess the strength of relationships between variables;

– regression analysis to predict values.

■ Longitudinal data may necessitate selecting different statistical techniques such as:

– index numbers to compare trends between two or more variables measured in different units or at different magnitudes;

– moving averages and regression analysis to determine the trend and forecast.

Self-check questions and assignment

Self-check question 11.1

The following secondary data have been obtained from the Park Trading Company's audited annual accounts:

Year	Income (£)	Expenditure (£)
1988	11 000 000	9 500 000
1989	15 200 000	12 900 000
1990	17 050 000	14 000 000
1991	17 900 000	14 900 000
1992	19 000 000	16 100 000
1993	18 700 000	17 200 000
1994	17 100 000	18 100 000
1995	17 700 000	19 500 000
1996	19 900 000	20 000 000

a Which are the variables and which are the cases?

b Sketch a possible data matrix for these data for entering into a spreadsheet.

Self-check question 11.2

a How many variables will be generated from the following question?

Please tell me up to five things you like about the
Home Care Service.

....

....

....

....

....

for **Office use**

b How would you go about devising a coding scheme for these variables from a survey of 500
Home Care Service clients?

Self-check question 11.3

a Illustrate the data from the Park Trading Company's audited annual accounts (self-check
question 11.1) to show trends in income and expenditure.

b What does your diagram emphasise?

c What diagram would you use to emphasise the years with the lowest and highest
income?

Self-check question 11.4

As part of research into the impact of television advertising on donations by credit card to a
major disaster appeal, data have been collected on the number of viewers reached and the
number of donations each day for the past two weeks.

a Which diagram or diagrams would you use to explore these data?

b Give reasons for your choice.

Self-check question 11.5

a What measures of central tendency and dispersion would you choose to describe the Park
Trading Company's income (self-check question 11.1) over the period 1988–96?

b Give reasons for your choice.

Self-check question 11.6

A colleague has collected data from a sample of 103 students. He presents you with the
following output from the statistical analysis software:

Information technology facilities at this University are....

	good	reasonable	poor	row totals
undergraduate	63	18	5	86 (83.5%)
postgraduate	6	4	7	17 (16.5%)
column totals	69 (67.0%)	22 (21.4%)	12 (11.6%)	103

Chi square = 18.33, degrees of freedom = 2, probability <0.01.

Explain what this tells you about undergraduate and postgraduate students' opinion of the information technology facilities.

Self-check question 11.7

Briefly describe when you would use regression analysis and correlation analysis using examples to illustrate your answer.

Self-check question 11.8

a Use an appropriate technique to compare the following data on share prices for two financial service companies over the past six months, using the period six months ago as the base period.

	EJ Investment Holdings	AE Financial Services
price 6 months ago	10 pence	587 pence
price 4 months ago	12 pence	613 pence
price 2 months ago	13 pence	658 pence
current price	14 pence	690 pence

b Which company's share prices have increased most in the last six months? Quote relevant statistics to justify your answer.

Assignment 11
Analysing your quantitative data

- Examine the technique(s) you are proposing to use to collect data to answer your research question. You need to decide whether you are collecting any data that could usefully be analysed quantitatively.

- If you decide that your data should be analysed quantitatively, you must ensure that the data collection methods you intend to use have been designed to make analysis by computer as straightforward as possible. In particular, you need to pay attention to the coding scheme for each variable and the layout of your data matrix.

- Once your data have been entered into a computer you will need to explore and present them. Bearing your research question(s) in mind, you should select the most appropriate diagrams and tables after considering the suitability of all possible techniques. Remember to label your diagrams clearly and keep a copy, as they may form part of your research report.

- Once you are familiar with your data, describe and explore relationships using those statistical techniques which best help you to answer your research question(s) and are suitable for the data type. Remember to keep an annotated copy of your analyses, as you will need to quote statistics to justify statements you make in the findings section of your research report.

References

Babbie, E. and Halley, F. (1995) *Adventures in Social Research: Data Analysis using SPSS for Windows*, London, Pine Forge Press.

Central Statistical Office (1992) *Standard Industrial Classification of Economic Activities*, London, HMSO.

Dennis, G., Pearson, N. and Ukueku, C. (eds.) (1995) *Annual Abstract of Statistics*, London, HMSO.

deVaus, D.A. (1991) *Surveys in Social Research* (3rd edn), London, UCL Press and Allen & Unwin.

Fink, A. (1995) *How to Analyze Survey Data*, Thousand Oaks, California, Sage.

Fox, J. and Long, J.S. (eds.) (1990) *Modern Methods of Data Analysis*, Newbury Park, California, Sage.

Hays, W.L. (1994) *Statistics* (4th edn), London, Holt-Saunders.

Jowell, R., Curtice, J., Brook, L. and Ahrendt, D. (1994) *British Social Attitudes – the 11th Report*, Aldershot, Dartmouth.

Morris, C. (1993) *Quantitative Approaches in Business Studies* (3rd edn), London, Pitman Publishing.

Norusis, M.J. (1992) *SPSS for Windows Base System User's Guide*, Chicago, SPSS Inc.

Office of Population Censuses and Surveys (1990a) *Standard Occupational Classification, Volume 1*, London, HMSO.

Office of Population Censuses and Surveys (1990b) *Standard Occupational Classification, Volume 2*, London, HMSO.

Office of Population Censuses and Surveys (1991) *Standard Occupational Classification, Volume 3*, London, HMSO.

Office of Population Censuses and Surveys and General Registrar's Office for Scotland (1992) *1991 Census Definitions Great Britain*, London, HMSO.

Robson, C. (1993) *Real World Research*, Oxford, Blackwell.

Saunders, M.N.K. and Cooper, S.A. (1993) *Understanding Business Statistics*, London, DP Publications.

Sparrow, J. (1989) 'Graphic displays in information systems: some data properties influencing the effectiveness of alternate forms', *Behaviour and Information Technology*, 8: 1, 43–56.

Tukey, J.W. (1977) *Exploratory Data Analysis*, Reading, Massachusetts, Addison-Wesley.

Further reading

deVaus, D.A. (1991) *Surveys in Social Research* (3rd edn), London, UCL Press and Allen & Unwin. Chapter 14 contains an excellent discussion on techniques for coding data.

Hays, W.L. (1994) *Statistics* (4th edn), London, Holt-Saunders. This provides detailed discussions of statistics, emphasising both the theoretical and applied aspects. This book is aimed at the first-year postgraduate student who will probably have already taken an undergraduate statistics module.

Morris, C. (1993) *Quantitative Approaches in Business Studies* (3rd edn), London, Pitman Publishing. This provides an introduction to the use of mathematical and statistical techniques and diagrams in business. Guidance is given on using the Lotus 123 spreadsheet and Minitab statistical analysis software.

Norusis, M.J. (1992) *SPSS for Windows Base System User's Guide*, Chicago, SPSS Inc. An excellent introduction to the SPSS statistical analysis software as well as explaining the statistical techniques clearly.

Robson, C. (1993) *Real World Research*, Oxford, Blackwell. Chapter 11 provides an introduction to quantitative data analysis and guidance on using the Statview statistical analysis software.

Saunders, M.N.K. and Cooper, S.A. (1993) *Understanding Business Statistics*, London, DP Publications. A basic introduction to the use of mathematical and statistical techniques and diagrams in business. Guidance is provided on using spreadsheets to undertake the calculations.

Case 11:
The marketing of Arts festivals

Jemma was interested in utilising secondary data from her placement organisation as part of her undergraduate research project on the marketing of Arts festivals. In particular she was interested in:

- the extent to which audiences associated events with their sponsors;
- the socioeconomic status of those attending;
- the importance of different media for finding out about events.

Her placement organisation had undertaken a questionnaire survey with attendees at the local Arts festival and agreed that Jemma could use the data for her research project. The data had already been entered into a spreadsheet. A copy of a completed questionnaire is included below.

The
Anyshire
Echo

**ANYTOWN
FESTIVAL OF ARTS**

AUDIENCE QUESTIONNAIRE

Please help us to continue to improve the Arts Festival by completing the questionnaire below.

When you have completed it, please hand it to the Box Office or the Friends Information Desk or send it back to us **by 10th September** and you can enter a **free prize draw** for one of four £30 record tokens.

It takes just five minutes to answer the questions, and your opinions will help us plan next year's festival.

Please return your completed questionnaire to the address below (N.B. no stamp is needed)

FREEPOST 12345
Town Hall
Town Square
Anytown
AN50 2BD

To enter the free prize draw please write your name and address below:

Mrs Lily Anners

Name: ....

15, Anytown Road

Address: ....

Anytown

....

AN34 7MS

Postcode: ....

(N.B. this information will not be passed on to any other organisation.)

PART 1: Please answer these questions by putting a <u>circle</u> around the appropriate number

1 Which Festival event have you attended

Ruskin's Poetry Reading and Arias by Candlelight

2 Where do you live?

In Anytown	①	30 to less than 50 miles away	2
under 10 miles away	3	50 to less than 100 miles away	4
10 to less than 20 miles away	5	over 100 miles away	6
20 to less than 30 miles away	7		

3 What age are you?

Under 18	1	35 to 44	3	over 60	5
19 to 30	2	45 to 60	④		

4 Are you . . .

Female ? ①   Male? 2

5 Are you currently....

Unemployed?	1	In full time paid professional employment?	5
Retired?	②	In full time non professional employment?	6
A housewife?	3	In part-time paid employment?	⑦
A student?	4	Other? (please say)....................................	8

6 Which of the following organisations do you associate with this festival?

The Anytown Bank	1	Murial's Bookstores	6
Anytown Borough Council	2	Good Deal Records	⑦
The Anyshire Echo	③	Midshire Bank	8
Steven's Computers Ltd	4	Other (please say)............................	9
VHT Record Stores	5		

7 Did you take advantage of any of the following discounts when booking?

Early booking	1	Poetry pass	4	
Friends discount	2	Anyshire Echo pass	5	
Group discount	3	Student discount	6	*None of these*

PART 2: Please read the statements below; decide whether you agree, strongly agree, disagree or strongly disagree; then *circle* the number below your choice:

8 I found it easy to book/buy tickets for the Festival	strongly disagree	disagree	agree	strongly agree
	1	2	3	④

9 The event(s) I came to was/were good value for money	1	②	3	④
		one		*other*

PART 3: Please comment on the following:

10 Is there anything you would like to change to improve the Festival (i.e. the times, the programme, etc.)? *The battle for the best seats nearest the speakers. The middle classes are seen at their most devious here – sneaking in and laying coats on seats etc!!*

11 What did you think of the event you came to? *Good*

12 How did you find out about the Festival? *Programmes available in Book shop*

Case-study questions

1 On looking at the questionnaire Jemma noticed some problems with the way in which some questions had been coded.

 a What were these problems?

 b How might these have been overcome at the survey design stage?

2 a Which of the questions were likely to be most useful to Jemma for her research project?

 b How could Jemma have minimised the impact on her analysis of any coding problems with these questions?

3 Which diagrams, tables and statistics would you recommend Jemma to use to analyse those questions which were useful to her research project? (You should state precisely what your recommended diagrams, tables and statistics will enable Jemma to find out.)

Answers to self-check questions

Self-check question 11.1

a The variables are 'income', 'expenditure' and 'year'. There is no real need for a separate case identifier as the variable 'year' can also fulfil this function. Each case (year) is represented by one row of data.

b When the data are entered into a spreadsheet the first column will be the case identifier, for these data the year. Income and expenditure should not be entered with the £ sign as this can be formatted subsequently using the spreadsheet.

year (ID)	income	expenditure
1988	11000000	9500000
1989	15200000	12900000
1990	17100000	14000000
1991	17900000	14900000
1992	19000000	16100000
1993	18700000	17200000
1994	17100000	18100000
1995	17700000	19500000
1996	19900000	20000000

Self-check question 11.2

a There is no one correct answer to this question as the number of variables will depend on the method used to code this descriptive data. If you choose the multiple-response method five variables will be generated. If the multiple-dichotomy method is used the number of variables will depend on the number of different responses.

b Your first priority is to decide on the level of detail of your intended analyses. Your coding scheme should, if possible, be based on an existing coding scheme. If this is of insufficient detail then it should be designed to be compatible to enable comparisons. To design the coding scheme you need to take the responses from the first 50 to 100 cases and establish broad groupings. These can be subdivided into increasingly specific subgroups until the detail is sufficient for the intended analysis. Codes can then be allocated to these subgroups. If you ensure that similar responses receive adjacent codes this will make any subsequent grouping easier. The actual responses that correspond to each code should be noted in a code book. Codes should be allocated to data on the data collection form in the 'for Office use' box. These codes need to include missing data, such as when four or less 'things' have been mentioned.

Self-check question 11.3

a

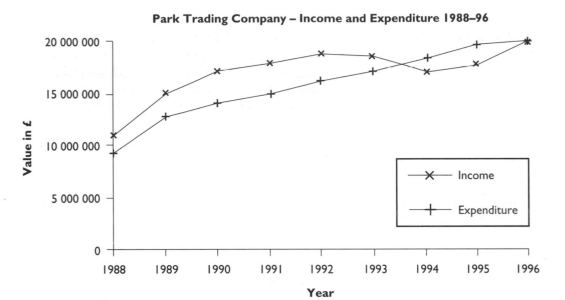

Park Trading Company – Income and Expenditure 1988–96

Source: Audited annual accounts

b Your diagram (hopefully) emphasises the upward trends of expenditure and to a lesser extent income. It also highlights the conjunction where income falls below expenditure in 1994.

c To emphasise the years with the lowest and highest income, you would probably use a histogram because the data are continuous. A frequency polygon would also be suitable.

Self-check question 11.4

a You would probably use a scatter graph in which number of donations would be the dependent variable and number of viewers reached by the advertisement the independent variable.

b This would enable you to see if there was any relationship between number of viewers reached and number of donations.

Self-check question 11.5

a The first thing you need to do is establish the data type. As it is quantifiable, you could theoretically use all three measures of central tendency and both the standard deviation and inter-quartile range. However, you would probably calculate the mean and perhaps the median as measures of central tendency, and the standard deviation and perhaps the inter-quartile range as measures of dispersion.

b The mean would be chosen because it includes all data values. The median might be chosen to represent the middle income over the 1988–96 period. The mode would be of little use for these data as each year has different income values.

If you had chosen the mean you would probably choose the standard deviation as this describes the dispersion of data values around the mean. The inter-quartile range is normally chosen where there are extreme data values which need to be ignored. This is not the case for these data.

Self-check question 11.6

The probability of a chi square value of 18.33 with 2 degrees of freedom occurring by chance for these data is less than 0.01. This means that there is a significant association between type of student and their opinion of the information technology facilities.

To explore this association further, you examine the cell values in relation to the row and column totals. Of the postgraduates, 41.1 per cent thought the information technology facilities were poor. This is high compared to the column totals, which indicate that only 11.6 per cent of total students thought the information technology facilities were poor. The column frequencies indicate that undergraduates represent 91.3 per cent of those students who thought information technology facilities were good. Yet only 83.5 per cent of the total students thought information technology facilities were good. Thus postgraduate students have a poorer opinion of information technology facilities than do undergraduate students.

Self-check question 11.7

Your answer needs to emphasise that correlation analysis is used to establish whether a change in one variable is accompanied by a change in another. In contrast, regression analysis is used to establish whether a change in a dependent variable is caused by changes in one or more independent variables; in other words, a cause and effect relationship.

Although it is impossible to list all the examples you might use to illustrate your answer, you should make sure that your examples for regression illustrate a dependent and one or more independent variables.

Self-check question 11.8

a These quantitative data are of different magnitudes. Therefore the most appropriate technique to compare these data is index numbers. The index numbers for the two companies are:

	EJ Investment Holdings	AE Financial Services
price 6 months ago	100	100.0
price 4 months ago	120	104.4
price 2 months ago	130	112.1
current price	140	117.5

b The price of AE Financial Services' shares has increased by 103 pence compared to an increase of four pence for EJ Investment Holdings' share price. However, the proportional increase in prices has been greatest for EJ Investment Holdings. Using six months ago as the base period (with a base index number of 100), the index for EJ Investment Holdings' share price is now 140 while the index for AE Financial Services' share price is 117.5.

CHAPTER 12

Analysing qualitative data

The objectives of this chapter are to outline and discuss the main approaches available to you to analyse qualitative data.

The nature of qualitative data is discussed and an overview of the process of qualitative analysis is provided.

Analytical strategies and procedures related to the use of predicted theoretical explanations and to the use of grounded theory are described and discussed.

Quantifying qualitative data as a means of analysis is briefly considered.

The chapter also considers the use of computer-based text retrievers and text managers.

12.1 INTRODUCTION

This chapter is designed to help you analyse the qualitative data which you collect. However, it commences by considering the nature of qualitative data so that you can recognise the issues associated with attempting to analyse systematically and rigorously this type of data (Section 12.2). Section 12.3 provides an overview of the process of qualitative analysis. In reading this overview you will recognise the interrelated and interactive nature of qualitative data collection and analysis. The stages of the process of qualitative analysis outlined in this overview demonstrate that you will need to undertake your data collection and analysis in a systematic and well planned manner, in order to be able to analyse your data rigorously and draw verifiable conclusions from them.

It is possible to approach qualitative data collection and analysis from either a deductive or an inductive perspective (Section 12.4). We therefore consider analytical strategies and procedures which commence with theoretical propositions, which can be tested against the data collected (Section 12.5). We also discuss the use of a 'grounded theory' approach and the main implications associated with this particular qualitative research strategy (Section 12.6). The final approach which we consider to help you to analyse some of your qualitative data is the use of quantification (Section 12.7). The advent of powerful personal computers has made a significant impact on the way in which qualitative data can be processed and analysed, and the use of software to facilitate this is therefore also discussed (Section 12.8).

12.2 UNDERSTANDING QUALITATIVE DATA

A key distinction is drawn between qualitative and quantitative research (for example Bryman, 1988; Easterby-Smith *et al.*, 1991). However, attempts to define the distinctiveness of qualitative research, and therefore the way in which it can be distinguished from quantitative research, can be problematic (Silverman, 1993). Nevertheless, when we look at the data produced by qualitative research we are able to draw some significant distinctions compared to those which result from quantitative work. These are helpful in terms of understanding what is necessary in order to be able to analyse this data meaningfully. Table 12.1 highlights three distinct differences between quantitative and qualitative data.

Quantitative data	Qualitative data
● Based on meanings derived from numbers	● Based on meanings expressed through words
● Collection results in numerical and standardised data	● Collection results in non-standardised data requiring classification into categories
● Analysis conducted through the use of diagrams and statistics	● Analysis conducted through the use of conceptualisation

Table 12.1 Distinctions between quantitative and qualitative data
Source: developed from Dey, 1993; Healey and Rawlinson, 1994; authors' experience

While 'number depends on meaning' (Dey, 1993: 28) it is not always the case that meaning is dependent on number. Dey (1993: 28) points out that: 'The more ambiguous and elastic our concepts, the less possible it is to quantify our data in a meaningful way'. Qualitative data are associated with such concepts and are characterised by their richness and fullness based on your opportunity to explore a subject in as real a manner as is possible (Robson, 1993). A contrast can thus be drawn between the 'thin' abstraction or description which results from quantitative data collection and the 'thick' or 'thorough' abstraction or description associated with qualitative data (Dey, 1993; Robson, 1993).

The nature of qualitative data therefore has implications for both its collection and analysis. To be able to capture the richness and fullness associated with qualitative data, it cannot be collected in a standardised way, like that of quantitative data. During analysis, however, the non-standardised and complex nature of the data which you have collected will need to be classified into categories before it can be meaningfully analysed (discussed later), otherwise the most that can result will be an impressionistic view of what it means. While it may be possible to make some use of diagrams and statistics at this stage, such as the frequency of occurrence of certain categories of data (Sections 11.3 and 11.4), the way in which you are likely to analyse the qualitative data which you collect is through the creation of a conceptual framework. This may be formulated before or during your data collection (discussed later).

The analysis of qualitative data involves a demanding process and should not be seen as an 'easy option'. Yin (1994) refers to colleagues who leave the data which they collect unanalysed for periods of time because of their uncertainty about the analytical process required.

Where you have been through the various stages of formulating and clarifying your research topic (Chapter 2), reviewing appropriate literature (Chapter 3), deciding on a research strategy (Chapter 4), considering access and ethical issues and negotiating the former (Chapter 5) and collecting your data (Chapters 6 to 10), you clearly do not wish to be halted by an inability to analyse this type of data. Equally, you will not wish to be 'marked down' because the analysis of the data collected is perceived to be a weak aspect of your work and one which casts doubt on the thoroughness and validity of the conclusions which you draw from the data.

Indeed, two further aspects spring from this cautionary note. First, you should take the advice of Marshall and Rossman (1989), who include data analysis as one of the issues which you should consider at the time you are formulating a proposal to undertake qualitative research. Second, the act of analysing qualitative data is very likely to occur at the same time as you collect these data as well as afterwards, and this is a matter which we discuss in detail below. This leads us to the next section, which provides an overview of qualitative analysis as a process.

12.3 AN OVERVIEW OF QUALITATIVE ANALYSIS

The features of qualitative data outlined above indicate the problematic nature of qualitative analysis. To add to this, or because of it, there is no standardised approach to the analysis of qualitative data. There are many qualitative research traditions or approaches, with the result that there are also different strategies to deal with the data collected (Dey, 1993; Miles and Huberman, 1994; Tesch, 1990; Robson, 1993). Phenomenologists, for example, resist categorising or coding their data, preferring to work from the transcripts of interviews (Miles and Huberman, 1994). Using the transcripts or notes of qualitative interviews or observations by thoroughly reading and re-reading them is one approach to analysing this type of data. However, this approach may cause you problems in relation to the elements of the numbered list which follows in the next paragraph.

The approach adopted in this chapter involves disaggregating the mass of qualitative data which you collect, as you collect it, into meaningful and related parts or *categories*. This will allow you systematically to rearrange and rigorously analyse these data. Adopting this approach essentially means transforming the nature of the data which you collect in order to allow you to:

1 Comprehend and manage it.

2 Merge related data drawn from different transcripts and notes.

3 Identify key themes or patterns from it for further exploration.

4 Develop and/or test hypotheses based on these apparent patterns or relationships.

5 Draw and verify conclusions (Dey, 1993; Miles and Huberman, 1994).

The process discussed below involves the following activities:

- categorisation;
- 'unitising' data;
- recognising relationships and developing the categories you are using to facilitate this;
- developing and testing hypotheses to reach conclusions.

Categorisation

The first activity involves classifying your data into meaningful *categories*, which may be derived from this data (*see* Sections 12.5 and 12.6 for a discussion of this aspect) and which should in any case 'fit' what you have revealed. These categories are in effect labels which you will use to rearrange your data. They provide you with an emergent structure which is relevant to your research project to analyse your data further.

The identification of these categories will be guided by the purpose of your research, as expressed through your research question(s) and objectives. Another analyst, for example, with a different purpose, may be able to derive different categories from the same data depending on their research objectives (Dey, 1993). Strauss and Corbin (1990) suggest that there are three main sources from which to derive names for these categories:

- you devise them;
- they come from terms used in existing theory and the literature;
- or they are based on terms used by your participants ('*in vivo*' codes).

However, the categories which you devise need to be part of a coherent set so that they provide you with a well-structured, analytical framework to pursue your analysis. Dey (1993: 96–7) states 'that categories must have two aspects, an internal aspect – they must be meaningful in relation to the data – and an external aspect – they must be meaningful in relation to the other categories'.

'Unitising' data

The next activity of the analytical process will be to attach relevant 'bits' or 'chunks' of your data, which we will refer to as *units* of data, to the appropriate category or categories which you have devised. A unit of data may be a number of words, a sentence, a number of sentences, a complete paragraph or some other chunk of textual data which fits the category.

You may use a computer to help you to process your data (Section 12.8) or you may use a manual approach. Where you use the second approach, you can label a unit of data with the appropriate category (or categories) in the margin of the transcript or set of notes. These may then be cut up and stuck onto a data card, or otherwise transferred, and filed so that you end up with piles of related units of data. An alternative is to index categories by recording where they occur in your transcripts or notes on cards headed with particular category labels (Easterby-Smith *et al.*, 1991). Undertaking this stage of the analytical process means that you are engaging in a selective process guided by the purpose of your research, which has the effect of reducing and rearranging your data into a more manageable and comprehensible form.

WORKED EXAMPLE: *Extract of an interview with analytical categories*

The categories listed below were initially used to label the following interview extract.

Some initial categories

RED:	Redundancy
RED/STR:	Redundancy strategy
RED/STR/ISS:	Redundancy strategy issues
RED/STR/VOL:	Voluntary redundancy strategy
RED/STR/COM:	Compulsory redundancy strategy
RED/CON:	Redundancy consultation
RED/MGT:	Redundancy management
RED/MGT/ROLE:	Redundancy management roles
SUR:	Survivors
SUR/REAC:	Survivors' reactions
SUR/REAC/PSY:	Psychological reactions
SUR/REAC/BEH:	Behavioural reactions

SUR/STR/LINK: This category was created to denote a link or relationship between other two categories: survivors' reactions and the choice of redundancy strategy.

Extract

RED/CONS	"The first stage is to find out what particular employees want for themselves and how they want this to happen.
RED/CONS	Staff are seen by their line manager and/or a member of personnel. An employee might want to talk to someone from personnel
RED/MGT/ROLE	rather than talk with their line manager – well, you know, for obvious reasons, at least as they see it – and this would be acceptable to the organisation.
RED/STR/VOL	This meeting provides them with the opportunity to opt for voluntary redundancy.
RED/STR/ISS	We do not categorise employees into anything like core or non-core although we will tell a group of employees something like 'there are 4 of you in this particular function and we only need
RED/CONS	2 of you, so you think about what should happen'.
RED/CONS	Sometimes when we attempt to give employees a choice about who might leave, they actually ask us to make the choice. This
RED/STR/COM	is one such situation where a compulsory selection will occur.
SUR/STR/LINK	We prefer to avoid this compulsory selection because of the
SUR/REAC/PSY	impact on those who survive – negative feelings, guilt and so on."

One way of achieving this reduction and rearrangement of your data, depending on the suitability of the data, is to use one or more of the analytical techniques described by Miles and Huberman (1994). These include a range of different matrices, charts, graphs and networks to use as a means to arrange and display your data. Use of these may allow you to recognise emergent patterns in your data which will provide you with an indication about how to further your data collection. We advise you to consult Miles and Huberman (1994) to see how any of these techniques may assist you in the conduct of your analytical process.

Recognising relationships and developing categories

Generating categories and reorganising your data according to them, or designing a suitable matrix and placing the data gathered within its cells, means that you are engaging in the process of analysing of your data (Dey, 1993; Miles and Huberman, 1994; Yin, 1994). This analysis will continue as you search for key themes and patterns or relationships in your rearranged data. This may lead you to alter your categories and to continue to rearrange your data as you search for meaning in your data set. You may decide to 'subdivide or integrate categories as ways of refining or focusing [your] analysis' (Dey, 1993: 95).

There may be practical reasons for seeking to divide or join your initial categories. Some categories, for example, may attract large numbers of units of data and prove to be too broad for further analysis without being subdivided. You may also gain new insights within existing categories which suggest new ones. A related piece of advice is to keep an up-to-date definition of each of the categories you are using, so that you can maintain consistency when assigning these to units of data as you continue to undertake interviews or observations (Miles and Huberman, 1994).

WORKED EXAMPLE: *Assigning data to and developing categories*

'After each interview, I transcribed the interview verbatim and filed its material according to the categorisation then in use. The material was typically in the form of paragraphs [that] were cross-classified to several categories. As I filed each statement, I compared it with previous statements in that category and kept running notes on the content of the category. The categories changed over time; some disappeared and were merged under more general titles. Some emerged out of previous categories that became too heterogeneous. Some categories became parts of matched pairs or triads in which any given comment would typically be filed in each constituent category. For example, comments [that] described instances of lax work or bad workmanship also typically mentioned abusive management. Similarly, statements that described devising one's own procedures also typically included statements of satisfaction with the autonomy that provided. This helped to reveal connections between categories.'

Source: Hodson, 1991, cited in Erlandson et al., 1993 at p. 119. Reprinted by permission of Sage Publications.

Developing and testing hypotheses

As you seek to reveal patterns within your data and to recognise relationships between categories, you will be able to develop hypotheses in order to test these. A *hypothesis* is defined by Silverman (1993: 1) as 'a testable proposition'. The appearance of an *apparent* relationship or connection between categories will need to be tested if you are to be able to conclude that there is an *actual* relationship.

WORKED EXAMPLES: *Research hypotheses*

During the process of qualitative data analysis a researcher evaluating the effectiveness of employee communication within a particular organisation formulated the following hypothesis:

- the credibility of employee communication depends on managerial action in the organisation.

A research student exploring mortgage borrowers' decision making drew up this hypothesis:

- potential mortgage borrowers' choice of lending institution is strongly affected by the level of customer service which they receive during the initial inquiry stage.

Another researcher investigating cause-related marketing formulated the following hypothesis:

- companies engaging in cause-related marketing are principally motivated by altruism.

A relationship is evident in each of these hypotheses. Each hypothesis was used to test the relationship within it through the data which had been collected or which was to be collected.

It is important to test the hypotheses which inductively emerge from the data by seeking alternative explanations and negative examples which do not conform to the pattern or relationship being tested (Marshall and Rossman, 1989). Alternative explanations frequently exist and only by testing the propositions which you identify will you be able to move towards formulating valid conclusions and an explanatory theory, even a simple one (Dey, 1993; Miles and Huberman, 1994). Dey (1993: 48) points out that 'the association of one variable with another is not sufficient ground for inferring a causal or any other connection between them'. The existence of an intervening variable may offer a more valid explanation of an association which is apparent in your data.

WORKED EXAMPLE: *The impact of an intervening variable*

A research project was established to look at legal issues arising from redundancies in organisations in a number of industries. A relationship appeared to emerge between organisations in a particular industry and the frequency of Industrial Tribunal applications. This could have led the researchers to conclude that managerial competence in relation to this process was lower in this industry when compared to the other industries in the study.

In reality, the firms included in the study from this particular industry had a much higher incidence of using a compulsory approach to declaring redundancies than those organisations in the other industries in the study. These organisations tended to use a voluntary approach to secure redundancies. The use of this compulsory strategy turned out to be highly associated with applications to Industrial Tribunals, especially when compared with a voluntary approach. The variable of redundancy strategy proved to be a much more valid way of explaining the apparent association which initially emerged, rather than any explanation linked to managerial competence or any other variable.

By rigorously testing your propositions and hypotheses against your data, looking for alternative explanations and seeking to explain why negative cases occur, you will be able to move towards the development of valid and well-grounded conclusions. Thus the validity of your conclusions will be verified by their ability to withstand alternative explanations and the nature of negative cases.

The interactive nature of the process

The course of events outlined above demonstrates that data collection, data analysis and the development and verification of relationships and conclusions are very much an interrelated and interactive set of processes. Analysis occurs during the collection of data as well as after it. This analysis helps to shape the direction of data collection, especially where you are following a grounded theory approach (Section 12.6). As hypotheses or propositions emerge from your data, or if you commence your data collection with a theoretical framework or propositions already worked out (Section 12.5), you will seek to test these as you compare them against the cases in your study (Erlandson *et al.*, 1993; Glaser and Strauss, 1967). The key point here is the relative flexibility which this type of process permits you.

The interactive nature of data collection and analysis allows you to recognise important themes, patterns and relationships as you collect data; in other words, to allow these to emerge from the process of data collection and analysis. As a result you will be able to re-categorise your existing data to see if these themes, patterns and relationships are present in the cases where you have already collected data, as well as adjust your future data collection approach to see if they exist in cases where you intend to conduct your research (Strauss and Corbin, 1990). In comparison, the collection of data before its analysis during a quantitative research study may prevent this course of action.

The concurrent process of data collection and analysis also has implications for the way in which you will need to manage your time, and organise your data and related documentation. It will be necessary to arrange interviews or observations with enough time between them to allow yourself sufficient time to write up or type in a transcript, or set of notes, and to analyse this before proceeding to your next data collection session (Easterby-Smith *et al.*, 1991; Erlandson *et al.*, 1993). Where you conduct a small number of interviews in one day, you will need time during the evening to undertake some initial analysis on these before carrying out further interviews. You may also be able to find a little time between interviews to carry out a cursory level of analysis. However, there is a clear limit to the value of continuing to undertake interviews or observations without properly analysing these in the manner described above.

Analytical aids

In addition to writing or typing up the recording or notes made of a research session and assigning units of data to appropriate categories, it will also help your analysis if you make a record of additional information. This will help you to recall the context and content of the interview or observation. You may also consider other techniques aimed at helping you to analyse your qualitative data, such as those outlined by Riley (1990). Various researchers have advanced methods to help you to record information which will usefully supplement your written-up notes or transcripts and your categorised data (for example Glaser, 1978; Miles and Huberman, 1994; Riley, 1990; Robson, 1993; Strauss and Corbin, 1990). We consider the following suggestions:

- summaries, including those for interviews, observations and documents, and also interim ones;
- self-memos;
- a researcher's diary.

Summaries

After you have written up your notes, or produced a transcript, of an interview or observation session, you can produce a *summary* of the key points which emerge from undertaking this activity. At this point you will be conversant with the principal themes which have emerged from the interview or observation and how you would like to explore these further in forthcoming data collection sessions. You may be able to identify apparent relationships between themes which you wish to note down so that you can return to these to seek to establish their validity. It will also be useful to make some comments about the person(s) you interviewed or observed, the setting in which this occurred, and whether anything occurred during the interview or observation which might have affected the nature of the data which you collected. For example, Adrian recalls an interview where the first part was conducted with two participants before they were joined by their manager. It was noticeable that after this person had joined the interview process the first two deferred and said very little. The interview was considered to be highly valuable and all the questions asked were fully answered. However, it was worth recording this incident in a post-transcript summary in case any divergence appeared between the nature of the data in the two parts of the interview. Once you have produced a summary of the key points which emerge from the interview or observation and its context, you should attach a copy to the set of your written-up notes or transcript for further reference (Miles and Huberman, 1994; Riley, 1990; Robson, 1993).

Qualitative research may also involve the use of organisational documentation. This may be an important source of data in its own right (for example using minutes of meetings, internal reports, planning documents and schedules), or you may use such documentation as a means of triangulating other data which you collect (Section 7.2). Where you use any sort of documentation you can also produce a summary which describes the purpose of the document, how it relates to your work and why it is significant, as well as providing a list of the key points which it contains. This type of summary may be useful when you undertake further analysis if you want to refer to sources of data (i.e. the document) as well as the way in which your data have been categorised into their component parts.

An *interim summary* is an attempt by you to take stock of your progress to date through the production of a written paper which looks at the following aspects:

- what you have found out so far;
- what level of confidence you have in your findings and conclusions to date;
- what you need to do in order to improve the quality of your data and/or seek to substantiate your apparent conclusions, or to seek alternative explanations;
- how you will seek to achieve the needs identified by the above interim analysis.

This can become a working document to which you make continued reference as your research project continues to progress (Miles and Huberman, 1994; Riley, 1990; Robson, 1993).

Self-memos

Self-memos allow you to make a record of the ideas which occur to you about any aspect of your research, as you think of them. Where you omit to record any idea as it occurs to you it may well be lost. There are a number of occasions when you will want to write yourself a memo: when you are writing up interview or observation notes, or producing a transcript of these; when you are categorising these data; as you continue to categorise and analyse these data; and when you engage in the process of writing. Ideas may also occur as you engage in an interview or observation session. In this case you may very briefly record the idea as a margin note and write it as a memo to yourself after the event. Similarly, ideas may occur as you work through a documentary source.

It may be useful to carry a reporter's notebook in order to be able to record your ideas, whenever and wherever they occur. When you are undertaking the production of notes, a transcript or any aspect of qualitative analysis, such a notebook can be ready to hand to record your ideas.

These memos may vary in length from a few words to one or more pages. They can be written as simple notes – they do not need to be formally set out. Miles and Huberman (1994) suggest, however, that it will be useful to date them and provide cross-references to appropriate places in your written-up notes or transcripts, where appropriate. Alternatively, an idea which is not grounded in any data (which may nevertheless prove to be useful) should be recorded as such. Memos should be filed together, not with notes or transcripts, and may themselves be categorised where this will help you undertake later stages of your qualitative analysis. Memos may also be updated as your research progresses, so that your bank of ideas continues to have currency and relevance (Glaser, 1978; Robson, 1993).

Researcher's diary

An alternative approach to recording your ideas about your research is to maintain a *researcher's diary*. You may of course maintain such a diary alongside the creation of self-memos. Its purpose will be similar to the creation of self-memos: to record your ideas and your reflections on these, and to act as an *aide-mémoire* on your intentions about the direction of your research. However, its chronological format may help you to identify the development of certain ideas (such as data categories or hypotheses), the way in which your research methodology developed, as well as providing an approach which suits the way in which you like to think (Riley, 1990).

12.4 STRATEGIES FOR QUALITATIVE ANALYSIS

In providing an overview of qualitative analysis, it has become apparent that there are different approaches to the commencement of this process. These relate to whether you start from a deductive or an inductive perspective. Where you commence your research project from a *deductive* position, you will seek to use existing theory to shape the approach which you adopt to the qualitative research process and to aspects of data analysis. On the other hand, where you commence your research project from an *inductive* position, you will seek to build up a theory which is adequately grounded in a number of relevant cases. The design of qualitative research requires you to recognise this choice and to devise an appropriate strategy to guide your research project.

Yin (1994) has identified analytical strategies related to these two approaches which you may use to analyse qualitative research:

- using a theoretical or descriptive framework to analyse qualitative data;
- exploring qualitative data without a pre-determined theoretical or descriptive framework.

Using a theoretical or descriptive framework

Yin (1994) suggests that, where you have made use of existing theory to formulate your research question(s) and objectives, you should also use the theoretical propositions which helped you do this as a means to devise a framework to help you to organise and direct your data analysis. This approach demonstrates a preference for commencing with and utilising theory in qualitative research, rather than allowing it to develop from the work.

There is a debate about this approach as applied to qualitative analysis (Bryman, 1988). Bryman (1988: 81) sums up the argument against it as: 'The prior specification of a theory tends to be disfavoured because of the possibility of introducing a premature closure on the issues to be investigated, as well as the possibility of the theoretical constructs departing excessively from the views of participants in a social setting.' If this occurs when you use a theoretical framework to design and analyse your research, you will clearly need to adapt your approach (Section 12.5). For example, Phil commenced a research project by adopting a deductive approach but found that the theoretical framework he adopted did not yield a sufficiently convincing answer to his research questions and objectives. He therefore decided to reanalyse his data inductively. This revealed themes which had not figured prominently in the deductive analysis. A combination of the two approaches generated a more convincing answer to the research questions and objectives. However, commencing from a theoretical perspective may help you to get started, link your research into the existing body of knowledge in your subject area, and provide you with an initial analytical framework.

To devise a theoretical or descriptive framework you need to identify the main variables, components, themes and issues in your research project and the predicted or presumed relationships between them (Miles and Huberman, 1994; Robson, 1993; Yin, 1994). A descriptive framework will rely more on your previous experience and what you expect to occur, although it is of course possible to develop an explanatory framework based on a mixture of theory and your own expectations. You will use this framework as the means to start and direct the analysis of your data. We advise you to use Miles and Huberman (1994) to consider further how to develop a theoretical or descriptive framework where you believe that this approach will be suitable as a means to approach your research and its analysis.

Exploring without a pre-determined theoretical or descriptive framework

The alternative analytical strategy to the previous approach is to start to collect the data and then explore them to see which themes or issues to follow up and concentrate on (Glaser and Strauss, 1967; Robson, 1993; Schatzman and Strauss, 1973; Strauss and Corbin, 1990; Yin, 1994). Yin (1994) believes that this may be a difficult strategy to follow and may not lead to success for someone who is an inexperienced researcher. Robson (1993) agrees that this is likely to be the case where you simply go ahead and collect data without examining it to assess which themes are emerging from the data being gathered. However, using this strategy successfully is likely to involve a lengthy period of time and be resource intensive.

Where you commence your data collection with this strategy – related initially to an exploratory purpose – you will need to analyse the data as you collect them (Section 12.3) and develop a conceptual framework to guide your subsequent work. This strategy is referred to as a *grounded* approach because of the nature of the theory or explanation which emerges as a result of the research process. Strauss and Corbin (1990) emphasise the following aspects of this approach:

■ that grounded theory is an inductive approach;

■ theory emerges from the process of data collection and analysis;

■ therefore you do not commence such a study with a defined theoretical framework;

■ instead, you identify relationships between your data and develop questions and hypotheses to test these.

You will, however, need to commence this strategy with a clear research purpose.

Yin (1994) differentiates between the explanatory and exploratory purposes of research in relation to this type of strategy because his approach to explanation building, which commences with a theoretical proposition (Section 12.5), may appear to be similar to this inductive, 'grounded' theory approach (Section 12.6). Yin states that his hypothesis-testing approach is related to *explanatory* case studies, while the hypothesis-generating approach developed by Glaser and Strauss (1967) is relevant for *exploratory* studies. If we accept this distinction, it may help us to understand that the suitability of using an emergent, grounded approach is relevant for a particular research purpose, at least in the initial stages of such a research project. However, we feel that the use of this strategy is not suitable where you lack research experience.

The relationship between strategy and process

While the process for analysing qualitative data, which we outlined in Section 12.3, may be applicable to both of the analytical strategies described in this section, its use will vary according to whether you commence from a deductive or an inductive perspective. In the next two sections we therefore go on to describe and discuss specific analytical procedures in relation to these strategies and how these affect the process outlined in Section 12.3.

12.5 ANALYTICAL PROCEDURES BASED ON PREDICTED THEORETICAL OR CONCEPTUAL EXPLANATIONS

This section will first outline the specific analytical procedures described by Yin (1994) which are particularly applicable to qualitative analysis. It will then examine how the process for analysing qualitative data (Section 12.3) is affected by the deductive perspective which underpins these specific analytical procedures.

Theoretically based procedures

Yin's (1994) preference for devising theoretical propositions before data collection as a means to analyse data leads to a number of specific analytical procedures to achieve this. These are briefly described and discussed in turn, although you are strongly advised to consult his work (see further reading) to gain a fuller appreciation of these techniques than we are able to provide here.

Pattern matching

The first analytical procedure is termed *pattern matching* and essentially involves predicting a pattern of outcomes based on theoretical propositions to explain what you expect to find.

Using this approach you will first need to establish a conceptual or analytical framework, utilising existing theory, and then test the adequacy of the framework as a means to explain your findings. If the pattern of your data matches that which has been predicted through the conceptual framework you will have found an explanation, where possible threats to the validity of your conclusions can be discounted. Examples are provided in relation to two variations of this procedure which we now describe.

These variations depend on the nature of the variables being considered. The first of these is associated with a set of *dependent* variables where you suggest the likely outcomes arising from another, *independent* variable. For example, based on theoretical propositions drawn from appropriate literature, you specify a number of related outcomes (dependent variables) which you expect to find as a result of the implementation of a particular change management programme (independent variable) in an organisation where you intend to undertake research. Having specified these expected outcomes, you then engage in the process of data collection and analysis. Where your predicted outcomes are found, then it is likely that your theoretically based explanation is appropriate to explain your findings. If, however, you reveal one or more outcomes which have not been predicted by your explanation, then you will need to seek an alternative one (Yin, 1994).

The second explanatory variation is associated with variables which are independent of each other. In this case you would identify a number of *alternative* explanations to explain the pattern of outcomes which you expect to find. As a consequence, only one of these predicted explanations may be valid. In other words, if one explanation is found to explain your findings then the others may be discarded. Where you find a match between one of these predicted explanations and the pattern of your outcomes, you will have evidence to suggest that this is indeed an explanation for your findings. Further evidence that this is a correct explanation will flow from finding the same pattern of outcomes related to other similar cases (Yin, 1994).

WORKED EXAMPLE: *Alternative predicted explanations*

The objective of your research project is to explain why productivity has increased in a case-study organisation even though a number of factors have been held constant (technology, numbers of staff employed, pay rates and bonuses, and the order book) during the period of the increase in productivity. You suggest two alternative explanations based on different theoretical propositions to explain this increase in productivity in the organisation. Your explanations are related to the following propositions.

First, that the increase is due to better management which has been able to generate greater employee commitment, where this proposition is based on theory related to strategic and human resource management.

Second, that the increase is due to fears about change and uncertainty in the future, where this proposition is, in addition, based on theory related to organisational behaviour and change management.

These propositions offer you two possible and exclusive reasons why the described phenomenon has occurred, so that where evidence can be found to support one of these, the other which doesn't match your outcomes can be discounted.

Explanation building

Another approach to pattern matching, which Yin (1994) refers to as a special type, involves an attempt to build an explanation while collecting data and analysing them, rather than testing a predicted explanation as set out above. Yin (1994) recognises that this procedure, which he labels *explanation building*, appears to be similar to the grounded theory approach, which we discuss later (Section 12.6). However he differentiates between the two, since the explanation building approach is still designed to test a theoretical explanation, albeit in an iterative manner, rather than to generate 'grounded' theory (Section 12.6). This explanation-building procedure is designed to go through the following stages (Yin, 1994; Robson, 1993):

1 Devising a theoretical proposition which you will then seek to test.

2 Undertaking data collection through an initial case study in order to be able to compare the findings from this in relation to this theoretical proposition.

3 Where necessary amending this theoretical proposition in light of the findings from the initial case study.

4 Undertaking a further round of data collection in order to compare the findings from this in relation to the revised theoretical proposition.

5 Where necessary amending this theoretical proposition in light of the findings from this second case study.

6 Undertaking further iterations of this process until a satisfactory explanation is derived.

Impact of a deductive approach on the process

In relation to pattern matching and explanation building, you will still be able to follow the general process outlined earlier for analysing qualitative data (Section 12.3), with some modification. First, you will be in a position to commence your data collection with a well-defined research question and objectives, and a clear framework and propositions, derived from the theory which you will have used. Second, with regard to sampling (Section 6.3), you will be in a position to identify the number and type of organisations to which you wish to gain access in order to undertake data collection. However, this strategy should not be used as a means to adopt a less than rigorous approach to selecting sufficient cases through which to test the propositions which have been advanced and for you to seek to answer your research question(s) and objectives. Third, the use of this literature and the theory within it will shape the data collection questions which you wish to ask those who participate in your research project (Section 3.2). It is also to be expected that categories for analysis will emerge from the nature of these interview questions. Therefore, you will be able to commence data collection with an initial set of categories derived from your theoretical propositions/hypotheses and conceptual framework linked to your research question and objectives (Marshall and Rossman, 1989; Miles and Huberman, 1994).

Of course, these categories may be subject to change depending on their appropriateness for the data which your participants provide (Dey, 1993). However, where your predicted theoretical explanations appear to fit the data being revealed, your predetermined categories may prove to be useful, subject to some revision and development (Miles and Huberman, 1994).

Your use of this analytical strategy will, of course, also provide you with key themes and patterns to search for in your data. Therefore, as you carry out your research and conduct analysis through attaching units of data to categories, and examine these for emergent patterns, your analysis will be guided by the theoretical propositions and explanations with which you commenced. Your hypotheses will still need to be tested rigourously – associated with the thoroughness with which you carry out this analytical process and by seeking alternative explanations and negative examples which do not conform to the pattern or association being tested for.

However, the use of predicted explanations should mean that the pathway to an answer to your research question(s) and objectives should be a more defined one. This will, of course, depend on two factors: first, your level of thoroughness in using existing theory to define clearly the theoretical propositions and conceptual framework which will guide your research project; second, the appropriateness of these theoretical propositions and the conceptual framework for the data which you reveal.

In summary, this section has briefly analysed two of the analytical procedures suggested by Yin (1994) for case-study analysis which are particularly relevant to the analysis of qualitative data. The use of these procedures is underpinned by the need to specify theoretical propositions before the commencement of data collection and analysis. Even in explanation building a theoretical proposition is initially advanced, although this may be revised through the iterative stages of the process. It has also been shown that the general process outlined earlier for analysing qualitative data will be useful to you in carrying out these deductive analytical procedures. However, the stages of this process related to devising categories and identifying patterns should be more apparent, at least initially, because this approach is based on existing theory.

12.6 ANALYTICAL PROCEDURES TO GENERATE 'GROUNDED THEORY'

There may be a number of good reasons for adopting a grounded theory approach to your research project and the analysis of the data which are produced. First, as we discussed in Section 12.4, you may commence on an exploratory project seeking to generate a direction for further work. Second, the scope of your research may be constrained by adopting restrictive theoretical propositions which do not reflect your participants' views and experience (Bryman, 1988). In this case the use of a theoretically based approach to qualitative analysis would prove to be inadequate. The use of a grounded theory approach in such a case should allow a good 'fit' to develop between the social reality of the research participants and the theory which emerges – it will be 'grounded' in that reality. This relationship should also mean that the theory can be understood by those who participated in the research process. Third, the theory may be used to suggest subsequent, appropriate action to be taken because it is specially derived from the events and circumstances of the setting in which the research was conducted. Finally, the theory's generalisability may also be tested in other contexts (Glaser and Strauss, 1967; Strauss and Corbin, 1990).

However, you should not draw the conclusion that you may use a grounded approach as a means of avoiding a proper level of preparation before commencing your research project. Grounded theorists do not jump into a subject area without a competent level of knowledge about that area. Their research will commence with a clearly defined purpose, even though this may be altered by the nature of the data which they collect. For example, Hodson (1991, cited in Erlandson *et al.*, 1993) reported that his initial purpose was focused on organisational sabotage, although the research process led him to develop and seek to verify a hypothesis related to more subtle forms of not co-operating with the employer. The avoidance of a pre-determined theoretical basis to this type of approach is related to the desire to search for and recognise meanings in the data. It is not to avoid the burden of producing this before the process of data collection! You should seek to compare your grounded explanations to existing theory once these have emerged. The use of a grounded theory approach will also involve you in a lengthy period of data collection and concurrent analysis in order to analyse a theme adequately or derive a well-grounded theory. Strauss and Corbin (1990) suggest that this process is likely to take months to complete.

The procedures related to a grounded approach are therefore designed to develop an explanation or a theory. They are not designed to test existing theory (Strauss and Corbin, 1990). In comparison to the strategy of testing existing theory (Section 12.5), the advocates of grounded theory lay down fairly precise procedures to be adopted in relation to each of the stages of the qualitative analysis process which was outlined in general terms in Section 12.3. Without paying particular attention to the nature of the procedures outlined for grounded theory, you may not produce a research report which is sufficiently rigorous to substantiate the analysis or theory which you are seeking to advance. In the grounded theory approach of Strauss and Corbin (1990), the disaggregation of data into units is called *open coding*; the process of recognising relationships between categories is referred to as *axial coding*; and the integration of categories to produce a theory is labelled *selective coding*. We will briefly outline each of these in turn, drawing on the work of Strauss and Corbin (1990).

Open coding

Open coding is essentially the first stage of the qualitative analysis process outlined in Section 12.3. The data which you collect will be disaggregated into conceptual units and provided with a label. The same label or name will be given to similar units of data. However, because this process commences without a basis in existing theory, the result may be the creation of a multitude of conceptual labels related to the lower level of focus and structure with which you commenced your research. These code labels will therefore need to be compared and placed into broader, related groupings or categories. Strauss and Corbin (1990) suggest that there are three main sources for deriving names for these categories: you devise them; they come from terms used in existing theory and the literature;

or they are based on terms used by your participants ('*in vivo*' codes). However, they counsel against names being derived from existing theory and literature in a grounded approach. This is because their use in the written account of your research may lead readers to interpret these according to their previous understanding of such theoretical concepts, rather than the particular meaning which you have now placed on such terms.

Because the emphasis in a grounded theory approach is to derive meaning from the subjects being studied, your approach to open coding or data categorisation will be affected by this. In Section 12.3 we stated that a unit of data may relate to a few words, a sentence or number of sentences, or a paragraph. The need to understand meanings and to generate categories to encompass these in a grounded theory approach will therefore probably lead you to conduct your early analysis by looking at smaller rather than larger units of data. The categorisation which you derive from your data will indicate significant themes and issues and help you to consider where data collection should be focused in the future (Strauss and Corbin, 1990).

Axial coding

This stage refers to the process of looking for relationships between the categories of data which have emerged from open coding. As relationships between categories are recognised, they are rearranged into a hierarchical form, with the emergence of subcategories. The essence of this approach is to explore and explain a phenomenon (the subject of your research project, or one of them) by identifying what is happening and why; the environmental factors which affect this (such as economic, technological, political, legal, social and cultural ones); how it is being managed within the context being examined; and what the outcomes are of the action which has been taken. Clearly, there will be a relationship between these aspects, or categories, and the purpose of your analysis will be to explain this.

Once these relationships have been recognised you will then seek to verify them against the actual data which you have collected. Strauss and Corbin (1990) recommend that you undertake this by formulating questions or statements, which can then be phrased as hypotheses, to test these apparent relationships. As you undertake this process you will be looking for evidence which support these questions and also for negative cases which will demonstrate variations to these relationships.

Selective coding

Strauss and Corbin (1990) suggest that after a lengthy period of data collection, which may take several months, you will have developed a number of principal categories and related subcategories. The stage which follows is called selective coding. This is intended to identify one of these principal categories, which becomes known as the core category, in order to relate the other categories to this with the intention of developing a grounded theory. In the previous stage the emphasis was on recognising the relationships between categories and their subcategories. In this stage the emphasis is on recognising the relationships between the principal categories which have emerged from this grounded approach in order to develop an explanatory theory. We strongly advise you to consult Strauss and Corbin (1990) where you are considering the use of this approach in order to familiarise yourself with the procedural steps.

Implications of using a grounded theory approach

A number of implications have emerged from this brief outline of the main procedures involved in the use of a grounded theory approach. These may be summarised by saying that the use of a grounded theory approach will involve you in a process which will be time consuming, intensive and reflective. Before you commit yourself to this particular approach, you will need to consider the amount of time which you will have to conduct your research project, the level of competence which you will need to use an inductive approach, your access to data, and the logistical implications of immersing yourself in such an intensive approach to research. There may also be a concern that little of significance will emerge at the end of the research process, and this will be an important aspect for you to consider when determining the focus of your research if you use this approach.

12.7 A NOTE ON QUANTIFYING YOUR QUALITATIVE DATA

There may be occasions when you decide to quantify some of your qualitative data. This is likely to be the case when you wish to count the frequency of certain events, or of particular reasons which have been given, or in relation to specific references to a phenomenon. These frequencies can then be shown using a table or diagram (Section 11.3). This form of representation will provide you with the capacity to display a large amount of data which you will be able to discuss through the use of text.

This approach to describing and presenting your data will provide you with a very useful supplement to the principal means of analysing your qualitative data discussed above. It may also enable you to undertake other quantitative analyses, such as those discussed in Sections 11.4 to 11.6. However, it is indeed a supplementary means of achieving this, and there is clearly only limited purpose in collecting qualitative data if you intend to ignore the nature and value of these data by reducing most of them to a simplified form.

WORKED EXAMPLE: *Recording frequencies of mention*

One of our colleagues, Mike, undertook a series of semi-structured interviews with a sample of 12 managers in an organisation to evaluate the extent to which this organisation had adopted its espoused model of managing human resources. During the analysis of these interviews he recorded which of these human resource initiatives were referred to by the managers whom he interviewed. The nature of these data meant that they could be tabulated to show these frequencies clearly. An extract of the table which Mike created is shown below.

HR Initiatives	HRM Practices identified by Senior/Line Managers (n=12)													
	1	2	3	4	5	6	7	8	9	10	11	12	Total	%
Developing flexible staff base														
Restructuring			✓										1	8
New style (professional) contracts	✓										✓		2	17
Develop a skills mix														
Effective staff development														
Creation of Professional Development Unit	✓			✓									2	17
Appointment of Professional Development Tutor														
Funding staff development at 2% of payroll	✓			✓									2	17
Performance appraisal for all	✓		✓										2	17
Goal-oriented rewarded and appraisal														
Performance-linked pay scheme			✓	✓							✓		3	25
Generating staff commitment														
Ensuring equal opportunity			✓		✓								2	17
High quality support staff structure														
Introduce quality improvement programme														
Customer care for personnel department														
Harmonisation of staff terms and conditions														
Identification of HR needs from strategic plan														
Targeted appointments														
Development of robust HR MIS System			✓										1	8
Staff development review scheme	✓	✓	✓	✓	✓	✓	✓			✓	✓		9	75
Devolving staff development budgets									✓		✓		2	17
Investors In People		✓						✓					2	17
Induction programme			✓										1	8
Line management training			✓										1	8
In-house training programmes			✓										1	8
Nurturing staff from within			✓										1	8
Devolvement to line managers										✓	✓		2	17
Personnel/Policy Handbook			✓	✓									2	17
Formal structures to support HR function			✓										1	8
Transfer of payroll to personnel														
Harassment policy				✓									1	8
Grading review and promotion policy									✓		✓		2	17
Direct communication										✓			1	8
Communication audit			✓										1	8
Common Interest Groups			✓										1	8

Source: Millmore, 1995

This form of display provides a clear illustration of the level and pattern of references to particular initiatives, and is therefore a valuable and concise form of representation. It does not, however, describe the complete data and it might be misleading to attempt to draw conclusions from the table by itself.

12.8 USING A COMPUTER FOR QUALITATIVE ANALYSIS

Qualitative analysis computer software helps you in your role as a qualitative analyst by acting as an aid to:

- project management;
- coding and retrieval;
- data management;
- hypothesis building and theorising.

What this software does, and does very well, is file, retrieve (find), cut and paste, and display your data in useful and helpful ways. The fact that it does all of this very quickly means that you will have more time to think about linkages and their meaning. Qualitative analysis software is a tool, rather like a washing machine. It performs tedious and time-consuming operations, thus releasing you and your brain for creative thinking and the generation of ideas.

Project management

Your data, whether in the form of text or other non-textual 'documents' (such as video tapes, audio tapes, photographs etc.) need to be organised in such a way that access to them is both quick and accurate. In doing this, a good qualitative analysis program will display an index of documents, with facilities to select and retrieve individual documents. Computer-readable text-based documents can be displayed in full, so that units of text can be selected for operations such as editing, indexing (coding or categorising) or note making (memos), simply by highlighting and without affecting the primary document.

One of the most powerful tools in a qualitative analysis software is the ability swiftly to search any number of documents for specified units of data or codes. Such a process would, if undertaken manually, require the reading through of each document, a burdensome process if there are many documents in the research project.

Furthermore, the ability to use the software to cluster units of text containing the words you select, and to display the cluster in a window together with reference to the *source* or *primary documents*, replaces the tedious and expensive process of multiple photocopying, slicing copies into dozens of little paper slips and annotating each one before sticking them on to data cards and filing them in piles, or sticking them in appropriate places on a vast 'clipboard'. This process can be undertaken without any damage to your primary data, which are still held in the original primary documents.

Coding and retrieval

If all your data are wordprocessed, or in some other computer-readable form, it will be possible for your primary documents to be accessed directly by the software. The software can search the text itself and allocate codes to specified units of text. The more powerful software such as ATLAS/*ti* and NUD.IST can display the documents on screen in your chosen format.

The identification of text units is usually by line number, although more powerful software offers you the facility of choosing the most appropriate size of text unit for your type of data (for example sentence, paragraph, utterance) (Section 12.3) simply by highlighting the appropriate section of text in the document window.

Data are coded by selecting a unit of text, and directing it either to a new or an existing code 'address'. A text unit may be directed to any number of code addresses. For example, the text unit 'and I wouldn't dream of asking advice from that supervisor, he's only just joined this place after finishing college' could be encoded under 'attitudes to managers', 'trust', 'employee relations', 'older respondents' etc. In order that categories (or codes) in a hierarchical system can be readily traced by their location in the hierarchy, they may also be allocated a code number.

Some software offers a facility for coding non-computer-readable data such as video tapes, audio tapes, maps, photographs or archive texts.

Data management

As your research project progresses, you will quickly gather more and more data. These need to be managed in such a way that they can readily be accessed and reviewed. You will have primary data, index codes and memos. The qualitative analysis software will retrieve and display all or any of these individually, in specified groups or clusters, and will indicate cross-references or links between them. Some more powerful software, such as ATLAS/*ti*, incorporates a *linked window system* whereby the selection of a unit of text from the primary document results in the automatic display of its code, any memos associated with it, and the text of cross-references from other primary documents. *System closure* is often also available, whereby your notes and memos are themselves open to the same search-and-retrieve procedures as the primary documents.

Hypothesis building and testing

The foundation of *hypothesis building* lies in discovering links between elements of your data. The development of a theory is then the process of making sense of these links. Only you can do the latter, but the qualitative analysis software can help you to discover the links and, with graphic facilities, can display them for you. Two basic ways of organising and linking your data are available.

The first of these involves a *hierarchical organisation*. This is where your data may be classified in a few broad themes, then each theme classified into a number of subcategories, and each of these into subsubcategories, and so on. It is similar to the coding used for quantitative data analysis (Section 11.2). For example (Fig 12.1), you may classify your data under the broad themes of 'Values', 'Concepts' and 'Strategies'. On reviewing all the data under 'Strategies', you may wish to divide them into 'Mature' and 'Immature', or 'Long term" and 'Short term". Your 'Values' theme may fall naturally into, say, 'Internal' and 'External', and then you may identify several subcategories such as 'Duty', 'Trust' and 'Liking'.

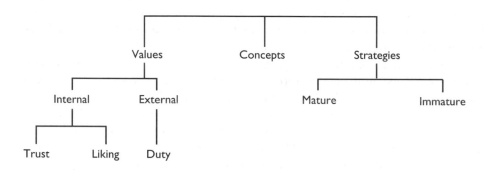

Fig 12.1 Hierarchical organisation and linking of data

An alternative approach is to code each section of data as you work through it, and later on discover ways of gathering together similar categories that can be grouped together under common headings, which can in turn be grouped together in broad themes, and so on. For example, in the case above you might identify the concepts of 'Duty', 'Trust' and 'Liking' from your reading of the data, and then decide to group all these under a common heading of 'Values'. Later you may wish to have distinct subheadings under 'Values' which you call 'Internal' and 'External', allocating to them your original categories accordingly. The NUD.IST, ATLAS/*ti* and INSPIRATION software, for instance, all offer this style of organisation.

The second way of organising and linking your data involves a *network organisation*. This is where your categories may be more flexibly linked to one another, without the rigidity implicit in the hierarchical structure discussed above. In particular, the ability to represent your data graphically can be a very powerful aid to theory building, and INSPIRATION offers an extremely varied network facility, with publishable quality printing. ATLAS/*ti* has, in addition, a library of code and linkage icons, so that you can see at a glance the nature of the relationships between categories. Networks can be rearranged in whatever way suits your developing research project. INSPIRATION and ATLAS/*ti* offer both networks and hierarchies, with tools for automatically moving between them.

Choosing appropriate software

Weitzman and Miles (1995) review over 20 programmes, from straightforward text retrievers and managers through to conceptual network builders, and we advise you to consult this review. Your choice of software will be dictated by the following factors:

- cost and access;
- type of data;
- your own preferred style of analysis.

We advise you to experiment with several software packages before you commit your entire research project. A search of the Internet will uncover opportunities to obtain public domain demonstration disks for quite a few of these software programs, including NUD.IST, ATLAS/*ti* and INSPIRATION. Check with the information technology specialists at your university to discover what software is already available and try it out. Some universities offer introductory courses.

12.9 SUMMARY

- Qualitative data is based on meanings expressed through words. It results in the collection of non-standardised data which requires classification, and is analysed through the use of conceptualisation.

- The process of qualitative analysis involves the development of data categories, allocating units of your original data to appropriate categories, recognising relationships within and between categories of data, and developing and testing hypotheses to produce well-grounded conclusions.

- The process of data analysis and data collection is necessarily an interactive one.

- There are a number of aids which you may use to help you through the process of qualitative analysis, including interview, observation, document and interim summaries, self memos and maintaining a researcher's diary.

- Different qualitative analytical strategies can be identified, related to using either predicted theoretical explanations or a grounded theory approach. The use of these strategies has implications for the procedures involved in the analysis of qualitative data.

- Quantifying some categories of qualitative data may help you to analyse them.

- The use of computer software can help you to perform four basic and useful functions during qualitative analysis, related to: project management; coding and retrieval; data management; and hypothesis building and theorising.

Self-check questions and assignment

Self-check question 12.1
Why do we describe qualitative analysis as an 'interactive process'?

Self-check question 12.2
What types of data will you need to retain and file while you are undertaking qualitative research?

Self-check question 12.3
How would you differentiate between a deductive and an inductive analytical strategy?

Self-check question 12.4
What are the main implications of using a deductive analytical strategy for the way in which you conduct the process of qualitative analysis?

Self-check question 12.5
What are the main implications of using an inductive analytical strategy for the way in which you conduct the process of qualitative analysis?

Assignment 12
Analysing qualitative data

- Undertake an initial semi-structured or in-depth interview related to your research project, transcribe this interview and make a few copies of your transcript.

- Where your research project is based on a deductive strategy, develop a provisional set of categories from your research question(s) and objectives, conceptual framework, research themes and initial propositions. Produce a description of each of these categories. Evaluate these categories to see if they appear to form a coherent set in relation to the aim of your research.

- Using one of the transcript copies, attempt to allocate units of data to appropriate categories by writing their code labels alongside the text in the left-hand margin. Again, evaluate this provisional set of categories and modify any which appear to be inappropriate.

- Where your research project is based on an inductive strategy, work through one of the transcript copies and seek to identify categories related to your research purpose. Write appropriate code labels for these categories alongside the text in the left-hand margin. List these categories and their labels, and produce a description for each of the categories which you have devised.

- Once you have allocated units of data to the set of categories in use, cut these out and transfer them to an appropriately labelled index card (reference to the interview, location of the text in the transcript, the date and so forth). Read through the units of data within each category.

- Commence your analysis of this categorised data by asking questions of it, such as those which follow. What are the points of interest which emerge within each category? How will you seek to follow these up during your next data collection session? How does the material which has been revealed through this interview relate to any theoretical explanation or initial propositions with which you commenced your data collection? Are any connections evident between the categories?

- Produce a summary of the interview and attach it to a copy of the transcript. Memo any ideas which you have and file these.
- Repeat the procedure for the remaining qualitative data and revise your ideas as necessary.

References

Bryman, A. (1988) *Quantity and Quality in Social Research*, London, Unwin Hyman.

Dey, I. (1993) *Qualitative Data Analysis*, London, Routledge.

Easterby-Smith, M., Thorpe, R. and Lowe, A. (1991) *Management Research: An Introduction*, London, Sage.

Erlandson, D.A., Harris, E.L., Skipper, B.L. and Allen, S.D. (1993) *Doing Naturalistic Inquiry*, Newbury Park, California, Sage.

Glaser, B. (1978) *Theoretical Sensitivity: Advances in the Methodology of Grounded Theory*, Mill Valley, California, Sociology Press.

Glaser, B. and Strauss, A. (1967) *The Discovery of Grounded Theory*, Chicago, Aldine.

Healey, M.J. and Rawlinson, M.B. (1994) 'Interviewing Techniques in Business and Management Research', in Wass, V.J. and Wells, P.E. (ed.) *Principles and Practice in Business and Management Research*, Aldershot, Dartmouth, Chapter 5.

Hodson, R. (1991) 'The Active Worker: Compliance and Autonomy at the Workplace', *Journal of Contemporary Ethnography*, 20: 1, 47–8.

Marshall, C. and Rossman, G.B. (1989) *Designing Qualitative Research*, Newbury Park, California, Sage.

Miles, M.B. and Huberman, A.M. (1994) *Qualitative Data Analysis* (2nd edn), Thousand Oaks, California, Sage.

Millmore, M. (1995) *HRM in C&GCHE?: Assessing the current state of play*, Unpublished MA Dissertation, Cheltenham, Cheltenham & Gloucester College of Higher Education.

Riley, J. (1990) *Getting the Most from your Data: A Handbook of Practical Ideas on How to Analyse Qualitative Data*, Bristol, Technical and Educational Services Ltd.

Robson, C. (1993) *Real World Research*, Oxford, Blackwell.

Schatzman, L. and Strauss, A. (1973) *Field Research: Strategies for a Natural Sociology*, Englewood Cliffs, New Jersey, Prentice-Hall.

Silverman, D. (1993) *Interpreting Qualitative Data*, London, Sage.

Strauss, A. and Corbin, J. (1990) *Basics of Qualitative Research*, Newbury Park, California, Sage.

Tesch, R. (1990) *Qualitative Research: Analysis Types and Software Tools*, New York, Falmer.

Weitzman, E.A. and Miles, M.B. (1995) *Computer Programs for Qualitative Data Analysis*, Thousand Oaks, California, Sage.

Yin, R.K. (1994) *Case Study Research: Design and Methods* (2nd edn), Thousand Oaks, California, Sage.

Further Reading

Dey, I. (1993) *Qualitative Data Analysis*, London, Routledge. This provides a very thorough discussion of the stages of qualitative analysis without being bound to any of the approaches referred to in the sources below.

Miles, M.B. and Huberman A.M. (1994) *Qualitative Data Analysis* (2nd edn), Thousand Oaks, California, Sage. An excellent source of reference to the elements involved in qualitative research, as well as offering a number of particular techniques which may help you to analyse your data.

Strauss, A. and Corbin, J. (1990) *Basics of Qualitative Research*, Newbury Park, California, Sage. A very thorough introduction to the grounded theory approach.

Weitzman, E.A. and Miles, M.B. (1995) *Computer Programs for Qualitative Data Analysis*, Thousand Oaks, California, Sage. A review of over twenty programmes.

Yin, R.K. (1994) *Case Study Research: Design and Methods* (2nd edn), Thousand Oaks, California, Sage. Chapter 5 very usefully examines analytical strategies and procedures based on a deductive approach.

Case 12:
Communicating bad news at Abco

Fiona undertook an interview in an organisation undergoing a period of change. Communicating change was one of the major issues which had to be confronted in the organisation. One of Fiona's research questions was: 'How can the communication of bad news be managed to reduce its potentially adverse impact?'. The following extract is part of an in-depth interview which relates to this research question.

Does Abco have a close knit community here in Southtown?

Yes, there is, but there's much more of a community in Northtown, and even more in Eastown, than there is in Southtown. There's a couple of reasons for this: people in Northtown tend to socialise outside of work, after work, and they do in Eastown as well. People live very locally at both sites. People who work in Southtown live all over the place, they can live sixty miles away. There are even people who live in Netherford, which is sixty-five, seventy miles away and they commute every day. So it's not quite so easy for people to intermingle, but yes, they do associate very well. And the industry itself is a very close knit one. They know people from other companies and there are lots of people who are in dual income relationships, or whatever you call it, whose partners work also in industry or the same company, we've got one whose partner works for Cyco and the other one works in Abco. So there is quite a lot of that going on and people are fairly close and identify very closely.

Do you find that there's a problem with rumours and informal communication?

We did at the beginning, because in a place like Northtown, word just shot around, and people were sometimes – I wouldn't say deliberately – starting rumours, but I think when you are frightened and concerned about your job or whatever, you do start reading into things which people say, and sometimes you're reading things that aren't meant to be there or just aren't there. So there's quite a lot of supposition made.

But these are bright people and it does not take them long to work things out. In most companies, if you've got issues going around the place there are usually a limited number of solutions. And if people think about these issues they will come up with the solutions and they will probably come up will the preferred solution in the same way as management will. So what happens is people say, well yeah I knew that was going to happen. Well yeah there is a good likelihood that they will.

That's one of the dangers of being very open about the processes and the solutions, and the options and the issues. You have to just face up to the fact that the grapevine may sometimes work against you. I think that what we've done in our communications has been so good that we've been able to be very sensitive to what the needs and fears will be.

If you're closing somewhere down, like Northtown, with 2000 people and it's the second largest employer in the area, the effect on the infrastructure is huge. It's not just the effect on the individuals who work there – that's bad enough – but there's all sorts of other things that happen, like the retailers who lose business and so on. People in the area also get quite angry about it, because they see the prices of their houses goes down.

Was any training given on the delivery of bad news?

Yes, but it was not that sophisticated. It was really just getting people used to the idea that when they get to do this, that they have to think about how they talk to the individual and what they're going to say. It's not the sort of thing when you hand someone a letter in a pub and say you've got to read that and mine's a pint. You know you have to be a bit more sensitive than that.

It was also stressed that it had to be done on an individual basis, and people had to be aware of the support mechanisms that were available. In the United States, for example, managers had to be taught about the security angle, because it's not uncommon for disaffected employees who have been fired to come back and shoot the person that did it to them!

Really?

Yeah, it happened at a couple of places in the United States. In one company someone came in and shot four people.

What we learn is put in a manual. This stuff includes the states people go through, like denial and despair; how to prepare, for example don't do it on a Friday; lots of dos and don'ts, whatever; why people are different; the processes people go through. There's also lots of handouts and it gives you all sorts of advice on the logistics of breaking bad news.

But handling some cases is more difficult than most. There have been quite a few people who have been identified as high flyers but we haven't been able to find a job for them and they are so angry about it because they didn't expect the news. So what to do when you meet this situation? Well don't mess about; get to the point straight away; don't come in and go, 'how's the family'; be clear about it.

Try and avoid using words like fire and terminate but don't get into arguments about it. That's one thing you have to make sure the person realises – that the decision has been made, nothing can be done.

You also need to know how people might react, common questions they might ask and how to answer them etc.

Do you think the training was useful in practice?

I think managers realised that it is important and it has been obligatory for them. But I think some of the logistics are quite difficult. Last week, last Thursday in fact, we got everyone in Product Development together in the United States, and what they had done was to tell everyone the previous Monday whether they had a job or not and that created an awful lot of hype and excitement and trepidation among people. Because they had so many people, they had to walk people from one part of the building to the other, I mean it's a big building, so people could see them being walked across and could see how they reacted afterwards so it was a bit public and that's when it's a bit dangerous to do it all at once.

What could be done to improve the training about breaking bad news?

Make it longer, more chance to practise what we tell them as theory. We could test their ability to do it – test them in a realistic situation before we ask them to do it for real. Maybe we could do more about breaking this news to those who have to do this to those they've been working with for years. They're likely to be friends. It's difficult, hard to do this in this situation. We need to recognise the difficulties – evaluate what we do – this should improve this training.

Case-study questions

Given the focus of the research question above, conduct the following process to commence the analysis of this qualitative data.

1 Devise categories to label this data and 'unitise' or code this data using these categories.

2 Which passages of text would you avoid categorising, if any, and why?

3 Do any relationships or patterns begin to emerge in the data, and if so what are these?

4 What are the important themes which you feel stand out in your categorisation which you would seek to explore in subsequent interviews?

Answers to self-check questions

Self-check question 12.1

There are a number of reasons for describing qualitative analysis as an 'interactive process'. Analysis needs to occur during the collection of data as well as after it. This helps to shape the direction of data collection, especially where you are following a grounded theory approach. The interactive nature of data collection and analysis allows you to recognise important themes, patterns and relationships as you collect data. As a result you will be able to re-categorise your existing data to see if these themes, patterns and relationships are present in the cases where you have already collected data. In addition, you will be able to adjust your future data collection approach to see if they exist in cases where you intend to conduct your research.

Self-check question 12.2

You will generate three broad types of data which you will need to retain and file as the result of undertaking qualitative research.

The first of these may be referred to as raw data files. These are your original notes and tapes made during the conduct of interviews or observations, or from consulting documentation. In addition, you will also retain transcripts and written-up notes of interviews and observations, although these may also be contained in a computer file.

The second of these are analytical files containing your categorised data. These may of course also be contained in a computer file.

The third of these may be referred to as a supporting file, or indeed it may be different files, containing working papers, self-memos, interim reports and so forth. Again, these may also be contained in a computer file. You are well advised to keep all of this until the end of your research project.

Eventually you will create a fourth file – containing your finished work!

Self-check question 12.3

A *deductive* analytical strategy is one where you will seek to use existing theory to shape the approach which you adopt to the qualitative research process and to aspects of data analysis. An *inductive* analytical strategy is one where you will seek to build up a theory which is adequately grounded in a number of relevant cases. The design of qualitative research requires you to recognise this choice and to devise an appropriate strategy to guide your research project.

Self-check question 12.4

There are a number of implications of using a deductive analytical strategy for the way in which you conduct the process of qualitative analysis:

- You will be in a position to commence your data collection with a well-defined research question and objectives, and a clear framework and propositions, derived from the theory which you will have used.

- With regard to sampling, you will be in a position to identify the number and type of organisations to which you wish to gain access in order to undertake data collection to answer your research question(s) and objectives.

- The use of literature and the theory within it will shape the data collection questions which you wish to ask those who participate in your research project.

- You will be able to commence data collection with an initial set of categories derived from your theoretical propositions/hypotheses and conceptual framework linked to your research question(s) and objectives.

- This strategy will provide you with key themes and patterns to search for in your data, and your analysis will be guided by the theoretical propositions and explanations with which you commenced.

Self-check question 12.5

The main implications of using an inductive analytical strategy for the process of qualitative analysis are likely to be related to:

- managing and categorising a large number of code labels which are likely to emerge from the data which you collect;

- working with smaller rather than larger units of data;

- recognising significant themes and issues during early analysis to help you to consider where data collection should be focused in the future;

- recognising the relationships between categories and rearranging these into a hierarchical form, with the emergence of subcategories;

- seeking to verify apparent relationships against the actual data which you have collected; understanding how negative cases broaden (or threaten) your emerging explanation;

- recognising the relationships between the principal categories which have emerged from this grounded approach in order to develop an explanatory theory;

- being rigorous in your use of the procedures which are advocated by grounded theorists in order to be able to produce a research report containing findings which are sufficiently 'grounded' to substantiate the analysis or theory which you are seeking to advance.

CHAPTER 13

Writing your project report

The main objective of this chapter is to encourage you to view the writing of the final project report as an exciting prospect which enables you to do two things: first, to present an authoritative account of your research and second, to reflect on all you have learned while conducting the research.

The chapter gives advice on how to begin the writing of your report and on the adoption of appropriate format, structure and style.

The need for continual revision is stressed and there are guidelines on ensuring that your report meets the necessary assessment criteria.

13.1 INTRODUCTION

Some of you may view the process of writing your project report as an exciting prospect. However, it is more likely that you will approach this stage of your research with a mixture of resignation and trepidation. This is a great pity. We believe that writing about your work is the most effective way of clarifying your thoughts. This suggests that writing should not be seen as the last stage of your research. It should be thought of as something which is continuous throughout the research process.

Writing is a powerful way of learning (Griffiths, 1993). Most teachers will tell you that the best way to learn is to teach. This is because of the necessity to understand thoroughly something yourself before you can begin to explain it to others. This is the position you are in as the writer of your project report. You have to explain a highly complex set of ideas and facts to an audience which you must assume has little or no knowledge of your subject. There is another problem here which has a parallel with teaching. Often, the more familiar you are with a subject, the more difficult it is to explain it to others with no knowledge of that subject. You will be so familiar with your subject that, like the teacher, you will find it difficult to put yourself in the place of the reader. The result of this is that you may fail to explain something that you assume the reader will know. Even worse, you may leave out important material which should be included.

But why do most of us view writing with such concern? Veroff (1992) argues that much of this is rooted in the experience we have of writing. Many of us are afraid of exposing our efforts to an audience which we feel will be more likely to criticise than encourage.

369

In our education much of our writing has been little more than rehashing the ideas of others. This has taught us to think of writing as a boring, repetitive process. Some of us are impatient. We are unwilling to devote the time and energy (and inevitable frustration) which is needed for writing.

We agree with Phillips and Pugh (1994) who note that writing is the only time when we really think. This suggests that writing your project report is something which should not be left until every other part of your research has been completed – but more of that in the next section.

13.2 GETTING STARTED

If writing is synonymous with thinking, it follows that writing is something you should do throughout the whole research process. Section 2.4 emphasises the need for clear ideas in writing about research questions and objectives. If you have done this already you will know the difficulty of committing your vague ideas to paper and amending them continually until they express your ideas with brevity, clarity and accuracy. However, there is no reason why your research proposal and plan should be the last writing you do before you finally write up your research in the project report. We encourage you to write as a continual process throughout the research.

Many researchers find it helpful to write the critical review of the literature (Section 3.2) early on in their research. This has clear benefits. It starts you writing on a part of the research process which necessarily comes early on in that process. And it focuses your thinking on the way in which the literature will inform the research strategy you adopt. You will be pleased you wrote this part of the report when the time pressure is on as the submission deadline for your report approaches. Don't worry that early writing of the literature review means that later relevant publications are ignored in your review. They can always be incorporated at a later date. This is one of the advantages of using a word-processor: a topic which we will cover later in this section.

Having discouraged you from thinking of writing as a process you leave until the end of your research, this section goes on to consider a number of practical hints to help you to get started.

Create time for your writing

Writing is not an activity that can be allocated an odd half-hour whenever it is convenient. It requires sustained concentration. The amount of time needed to make real progress in your writing is dependent on the way in which you prefer to work. Most people find that it takes a day to write about 2000 words, but we all work in different ways. Once some people have started, they prefer to continue until they drop from exhaustion! Others like to set a strict timetable where three or four hours a day are devoted to writing. Whichever category you fall into, make sure that you have time for writing allocated in your diary. We have found that it is helpful to have blocks of time where writing can take place on successive days. This ensures a degree of continuity of ideas, which isn't easy to maintain if you keep having to 'think your way back' into your research.

Write when your mind is fresh

We have emphasised so far in this chapter that writing should be a highly creative process. It is important, therefore, that you write at the time of day when your mind is at its freshest. All of us have jobs to do during the day which require little or no creativity. Arrange your day so that the uncreative jobs are done at the time when you are at your least mentally alert.

Find a regular writing place

Most of us have one place where we do our writing. It is so important that we often cannot write in unfamiliar surroundings. If this is the case with you, it is essential that you combine this psychological comfort with a few practical features of your writing place which will enhance your productivity. One of the most important of these is to ensure that you are not interrupted. A simple 'do not disturb' sign on the door usually works wonders. You may, like Phil, find a telephone answering machine a useful investment. Remove all distractions, such as television, magazines and computer games, from the room. It may be that you need background noise, even your personal stereo, to help you concentrate. One person's distractions are another person's necessities. What is important is to know what distracts you and to remove those distractions.

Set goals and achieve them

This is the height of self-discipline. Most writers set themselves targets for the period of writing. Usually this is a set number of words. It is better to be realistic about these goals. If you are too ambitious the quality of your work may suffer as you rush to meet the goal. You may be as self-disciplined as Mark who sets himself sub-goals during the day and rewards the achievement of these goals with coffee breaks. What is important is that you see this as entering into a contract with yourself. If you break this contract by not meeting your goal you are the one who should feel guilty. You may like to enter into a similar arrangement with a close friend, on the understanding that each of you will insist on the other meeting their goal.

Use a wordprocessor

The wordprocessor has revolutionised writing. There are still some who prefer to write in longhand before wordprocessing the final report. However, for those of us who 'think on screen', the main advantage of the wordprocessor is that enables us to keep amending copy without having to fill the wastepaper basket with numerous unsatisfactory attempts. In addition, the wordprocessor enables you to keep updating your project report as you develop new ideas or become dissatisfied with old ones. There is, however, a potential problem here. The ease with which you can keep inserting and deleting text means that relevant *flagging material* will need to be changed. At its simplest this may be the contents page or the announcement at the beginning of a chapter that the chapter will cover certain ground. But this is just as likely to be an obscure reference buried in the text to a table which you have deleted, thus making the reference redundant. So it is important to make these amendments at the same time as you amend text in the main body of your project report.

WORKED EXAMPLE: *Using the wordprocessor to save time*

Phil made interview notes in longhand during the interviews which he conducted with managers about the pay system in their organisations. He was particularly careful to note verbatim especially relevant comments from the managers.

Phil ensured that he wordprocessed these notes, either on the return train journey at the end of the day or at home in the evening.

When writing the project report Phil found the wordprocessed notes invaluable. He wanted to use some of the verbatim quotes to illustrate key arguments that he was developing from the data. He was able to insert many of these into the report, thus saving time and ensuring accuracy of transcription.

One other advantage of the wordprocessor may have occurred to you. Most packages have a word-count facility. You can use this to check your progress towards the word goal you have set yourself for the writing session.

The necessity to keep *back-up* or *security copies* of your work on separate disks should go without saying. However, do learn from the experience of one of our students who lost all his research material as a consequence of not keeping adequate back-up copies. This led to him having to abandon completely his research project.

Generate a plan

Few of us can sit down and write without a great deal of thought and planning. We all have our own systems for doing this. However, most people find it essential to construct a plan before they start writing. Veroff (1992) describes the *clustering method*. This may be familiar to you. The method's stages are:

1 write the main topic in the middle of a sheet of paper;

2 jot down the other ideas which occur to you at other points on the page;

3 as the page begins to fill up, relationships between the ideas suggest themselves and lines between the ideas may be drawn;

4 this allows you to group the ideas into discrete but related 'chunks' which enables you to devise an outline structure for a section, or chapter.

This chapter started out as just such a pencilled plan written on four pieces of A4 held together with sticky tape. It is essential to bring your ideas into some form of order at the outset. This will give you encouragement to start writing.

Finish the writing session on a high point

Many writers prefer to finish their writing session while they are in the middle of a section to which they will look forward to returning. This eases the way in next time. The worst thing you can do is to leave a complex part half-way through. It will be difficult to pick up the threads.

Get friends to read your work

Writing is creative and exciting, but checking your work is not. The importance of getting someone else to read through your material cannot be over emphasised. Your project tutor should not be the first person who reads your report, even in its draft form.

Ask your friend to be constructively critical. They must be prepared to tell you about things they don't understand in the text; to point out omissions, spelling, punctuation and grammatical errors. Overall, they must tell you whether the piece of writing makes sense and achieves its purpose.

This is not an easy process for you or your critical friend. Most of us are sensitive to criticism, particularly when the consequence of it is the necessity to do a lot more work. Many of us are also hesitant about giving criticism. However, if your project report does not communicate to the reader in the way it should you will get it back for revision work in the long run. It is much better to try to ensure that this does not happen.

13.3 STRUCTURING YOUR REPORT

Suggested structure

Most writers agree with Robson (1993) on the general structure to adopt for a project report which is the end product of your research. This is:

- Abstract
- Introduction
- Literature review
- Method
- Results

- Conclusions
- References
- Appendices.

Phillips and Pugh (1994) note that each of these general sections can be subdivided into one or more relevant chapters, depending on the topic and the way in which you want to present your particular *storyline*. This is a vital point. Your structure should have a logical flow. Readers should know the journey on which they are being taken and they should know at all times the point in the journey which has been reached. Above all, the structure you adopt should enable your readers, having read the report, to identify the storyline clearly.

We will now explain how to distinguish between these broad sections by outlining their purpose and content.

The abstract

The *abstract* is probably the most important part of your report because it may be the only part that some will read. It is a short summary of the complete content of the project report. This enables those who are not sure whether they wish to read the complete report, to make an informed decision. For those who intend to read the whole report, the abstract prepares them for what is to come. It should contain four short paragraphs with the answers to the following questions:

1 What were my research questions and why were these important?

2 How did I go about answering the research question(s)?

3 What did I find out in response to my research question(s)?

4 What conclusions do I draw regarding my research question(s)?

Smith (1991) lists five principles for the writing of a good abstract. He argues the following:

- It should be short. Try to keep it to a maximum of two sides of A4.

- It must be self-contained. Since it may be the only part of your report that some people see, it follows that it must summarise the complete content of your report.

- It must satisfy your reader's needs. Your reader must be told about the problem, or central issue, which the research addressed and the method adopted to pursue the issue. It must also contain a brief statement of the main results and conclusions.

- It must convey the same emphasis as the report, with the consequence that the reader should gain an accurate impression of the report's contents from the abstract.

- It should be objective, precise and easy to read. The project report contents page should give you the outline structure for the abstract. Summarising each section should give you an accurate résumé of the content of the report. Do ensure that you stick to what you have written in the report. The abstract is not the place for elaborating any of your main themes. Be objective. You will need to write several drafts before you eliminate every word that is not absolutely necessary. The purpose is to convey the content of your report in as clear and brief a way as possible.

Writing a good abstract is difficult. The obvious thing to do is to write it after you have finished the report. We suggest that you draft it at the start of your writing so that you have your storyline abundantly clear in your mind. You can then amend the draft when you have finished the report so that it conforms to the five principles above.

The introductory chapter

The *introduction* should give the reader a clear idea of the central issue of concern in your research and why you thought that this was worth studying. It should incorporate a full statement of your research question(s) and research objectives. It is also important to include in this chapter a 'route map' to guide the reader through the rest of the report. This will give brief details of the content of each chapter and present an overview of how your storyline unfolds.

This will usually be a fairly brief chapter, but it is very important.

The literature review

Section 3.2 deals in detail with the writing of a literature review. All that it is necessary to comment on here is the position of this chapter in the project report. We suggest that this is placed before the methodology chapter.

The main purpose of your literature review is to show the reader how your study supplements the work that has already been done on your topic. The literature review, therefore, may inform directly any specific hypotheses that your research was designed to test. These hypotheses will also suggest a particular research approach, strategy and data collection methods. If, on the other hand, you are working inductively (i.e. from data to theory) your literature review may also have implications for the way in which you conduct your research.

The title of your literature review chapter should reflect the content of the chapter. It may draw on one of the main themes in the review (for example: 'A review of published research on insider dealings'). We recommend that you do not call it simply 'literature review'. It may be that your literature is reviewed in more than one chapter. This might be the case, for example, if you were using more than one body of literature in your research.

- -

WORKED EXAMPLE: *Using the literature review to inform the research questions*

Paul was fascinated by the way in which organisations pursued policies of rewarding their employees on the basis of individual merit, because the literature showed that these policies often seemed not to produce the results which the organisations wanted.

Many items of the literature which Paul covered in his review were American psychological studies which paid no attention to the organisational context in which merit pay policies were pursued. Paul used his literature review to argue that there was a gap in the literature which his research could fill.

Paul wanted to explore his theory that the success of merit pay schemes was dependent on an organisational context which was consistent with the aims of the scheme.

- -

The method chapter

This should be a detailed chapter giving the reader sufficient information to make an estimate of the reliability and validity of your methods. Table 13.1 provides a useful checklist of the points you should include in the method chapter.

Setting:

☑ What was the research setting?

☑ Why did you choose that particular setting?

Participants:

☑ How many?

☑ How were they selected?

☑ What were their characteristics?

☑ How were refusals/non-returns handled?

Materials:

☑ What tests/scales/interview or observation schedules/questionnaires were used?

☑ How were purpose-made instruments developed?

☑ How were the resulting data analysed?

Procedures:

☑ What were the characteristics of the interviewers and observers and how were they trained?

☑ How valid and reliable do you think the procedures were?

☑ What instructions were given to participants?

☑ How many interviews/observations/questionnaires were there; how long did they last; where did they take place?

☑ When was the research carried out?

Table 13.1 Checklist of points for inclusion in the method chapter
Source: developed from Robson, 1993

The results chapter(s)

It may well be that your report will contain more than one results chapter. For example, if your hypothesis is that the effectiveness of a management process is dependent on organisational context, you may wish to have a chapter on organisational context and another on the operation of the process. The question you should ask yourself is: 'Is more than one results chapter necessary to communicate my findings clearly?'

The results chapter is probably the most straightforward chapter to write. It is your opportunity to report the facts which your research discovered. These may be in the form of either quantitative or qualitative data analysis or a combination of both. This is where you will include such tables and graphs that will illustrate your findings (do not put these in the appendices). The chapter may also contain verbatim quotes from interviewees or sections of narrative account which illustrate periods of unstructured observation.

There are two important points to bear in mind when writing your results. The first is to stress that the purpose is to present facts. It is normally not appropriate in this chapter to begin to offer opinions on the facts. This is for the following chapter. Many of us become confused about the difference between findings and conclusions. One way of overcoming the confusion is to draw up a table with two columns. The first should be headed 'what I found out' and the second 'what judgements I have formed as a result of what I found out'. The first list is entirely factual (for example, 66 per cent of respondents indicated they preferred to receive paper memos rather than e-mail messages) and therefore the content of your findings chapter. The second list will be your judgements based on what you found out (for example, it appears that traditional forms of communication are still preferred to electronic) and therefore the content of your conclusions section.

The second point links to the first. Drawing up a table will lead you to a consideration of the way in which you present your findings. The purpose of your project report is to communicate the answer to your research question(s) to your audience in as clear a manner as possible. Therefore you should structure your findings in a clear, logical and easily understood manner. There are many ways of doing this. One of the simplest is to return to the research objectives and let these dictate the order in which you present your findings. Alternatively, you may prefer to report your findings thematically. You could present the themes in descending order of importance. Whichever method you choose should be obvious to the reader. As with the literature review, the chapter(s) devoted to research should be titled in an interesting way which reflects the content of the findings.

The conclusions chapter(s)

Logically, for each finding there should be at least one conclusion. This suggests that the *conclusions* chapter(s) (often called discussion) should be at least as long as the findings chapter(s). This is certainly the case. Findings presented without reflective thought run the risk of your reader asking 'So what?'.

The conclusions chapter (which, again, should have a more interesting title than 'conclusions') is where you have the opportunity to shine. It is your conclusions which will demonstrate whether you have answered the research question(s) and show the degree of insight you have exhibited in reaching your conclusions.

You may find that the clearest way to present your conclusions is to follow a similar structure to the one used in your findings section. If that structure reflects the research objectives, then it should make certain that your conclusions will address the research question(s). Drawing up a matrix similar to that in Fig 13.1 may help you in structuring your findings and conclusions.

An alternative approach to the matrix is to draw a *mindmap* which places the findings randomly on a blank page and links conclusions to these findings by way of lines and arrows (Buzan with Buzan, 1995). For some of you this may be a more creative approach which enables you to associate groups of findings with conclusions and vice versa.

Answering the research question(s) and research objectives and, if appropriate, supporting or otherwise the research hypotheses are the main purposes of the conclusions chapter. This is where you will consider the findings presented in the previous chapter. You

Research questions	Results (what factual information did I discover in relation to the specific research questions?)	Conclusions (what judgements can I make about the results in relation to the specific research questions?)
What are the operational differences between different shifts in the production plant?	Cases of indiscipline in the last six months have been twice as frequent on the night shift as on the day shift	The night shift indiscipline problems may be due to the reluctance of operators to work on this shift

Fig 13.1 A matrix plan for the results and conclusions chapters

should also return to your literature review and ask yourself, 'What do my conclusions add to the understanding of the topic displayed in the literature?'.

It may be that there are practical implications arising from your findings. In a management report this would normally form the content of a chapter specifically devoted to recommendations. We suggest you check with your project tutor to find out whether this is expected. In the reports which students are required to prepare on some professional courses this is an important requirement. For academic degree programmes it is often unnecessary.

Even if you do not specify any practical implications of your research, you may comment in the conclusions chapter on what your research implies for any future research. This is a logical extension of a section in the conclusions chapter which should be devoted to the limitations of your research. These limitations may be the size of sample, the snap-shot nature of the research or the restriction to one geographical area of an organisation. Virtually all research has its limitations. This section should not be seen as a confession of your weaknesses, but as a mature reflection on the degree to which your findings and conclusions can be said to be the 'truth'.

References

A range of conventions is used to reference the material of other writers' material which you have cited in your text. Appendix 2 illustrates the two most popular, the Harvard and footnotes systems. However, we suggest that you consult your project tutor about the system which is appropriate for your report.

It is a good idea to start your references section at the beginning of the writing process and add to it as you go along. It will be a tedious and time-consuming task if left until you have completed the main body of the text. If you do leave this until the end, the time spent on compiling the reference section is time which would be better spent on checking and amending your report.

Appendices

In general, *appendices* should be kept to the minimum. If they are so important that your reader's understanding of the points you are making in the text makes their inclusion in the report necessary, then they should be in the main body of the text. If, on the other hand, the material is 'interesting to know', rather than 'essential to know', then it should be in the appendices. Many people feel tempted to include appendices to 'pad out' a project report. Resist this temptation. Your readers will not be reading your report for leisure purposes. They will be pressed for time and will probably not look at your appendices. Your report will stand or fall on the quality of the main text. However, your appendices should include a blank copy of your questionnaire, interview or observation schedule.

The management report

You may have wondered why we made no reference to recommendations in the report structure. In a typical *management report* this may be the most important section. The hard-pressed executive reading your report may turn to your recommendations first to see what action needs to be taken to tackle the issue.

Whether you include a recommendation section depends on the objectives of your research. If you are doing exploratory research you may well write recommendations, among which will be suggestions for the pursuit of further research. However, if your research is designed to explain or describe, recommendations are less likely. For example, a research question 'Why do small engineering companies in the UK reinvest less of their profits in their businesses than their German counterparts?' may imply clear points for action. However, strictly speaking, recommendations are outside the scope of the research question, which is to discover 'Why?' not 'What can be done about it?'. The message is clear. If you want your research to change the situation you are researching, then include the need to develop recommendations in your research objectives.

Length of the project report

You will probably have guidelines on the number of words your project report should contain. Do stick to these. However interesting your report, your tutors will have others to read so they will not thank you for exceeding the limit. Indeed, if you can meet your research objectives fully in a clear and absorbing report which is significantly shorter than the word limit, so much the better. Reports which exceed the word limit are usually excessively verbose. It is more difficult to be succinct. Don't fall into the trap of writing a long report because you didn't have the time to write a shorter one.

13.4 ORGANISING THE PROJECT REPORT'S CONTENT

Choosing a title

This is the part of the project report on which most of us spend the least time. Yet it is the only knowledge that many people have of the project. Day (1989) thinks a good *title* is one that reflects the content of the project report in the fewest possible words. Try choosing a title then ask a colleague who knows your subject what they think the title describes. If their description matches your content, then stick with your title.

Tell a clear story

Be prepared for your project tutor to ask you, 'What's your main *storyline*?'. Your storyline (your central argument or thesis) should be clear, simple and straightforward. It should be so clear that you can stop the next person you see walking towards you and tell that person what your project report's storyline is and they will say, 'Yes, I understand that'. This is where writing the abstract helps. It forces you to think clearly about the storyline because you have to summarise it in so few words.

A simple format for developing the storyline is shown in Fig 13.2.

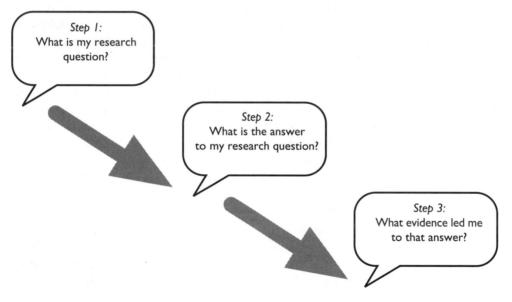

Fig 13.2 A format for developing the storyline
Source: developed from Raimond, 1993

WORKED EXAMPLE: *Developing a storyline*

Step one:
I wanted to know whether, as the literature suggested, an organisation's structure is determined by its strategies.

Step two:
The answer is that organisation structures are in part determined by strategies and in part by *ad hoc* factors which owe little to strategy considerations.

Step three:
I based this answer on interviews with senior managers in three large UK organisations and examination of the minutes of meetings at which structural issues were discussed. The particular focus was on the removal of management positions from the organisational hierarchy.

Helping the reader find all the information

Dividing your work

One of us once received the first draft of a 20 000-word project report which had virtually no divisions except the chapters. It was like looking at a road map of Britain which did not illustrate any road numbers or towns. It was just as difficult to find your way around that report as it would be to journey from Southampton to Harrogate using the townless road map. The content of the project report seemed fine. However, it was hard to be sure about this because it was so difficult to spot any gaps in the ground it covered. What was needed were some signposts and some town names. Don't think about how you can put in all your information. Instead, concentrate on helping readers get all the information out.

The message is simple. Divide your work in such a way that it is easy for readers to find their way round it and for them always to be clear where they are, where they have come from and where they are going.

To do this you may find it helpful to return to the matrix idea in Fig 13.1. You will see that each column of the matrix represents the broad content of a chapter. The cells indicate the way in which the chapters may be divided. Each division may have a subdivision.

We hope that you have noticed that we have employed a similar system in this book. Each chapter section is identified by large, bold upper case letters. The subheadings are bold lower case and further divisions of the subsection content are denoted by bold, lower case italics and normal, lower case italics. Smith (1991) explains various ways of organising and signposting text. It is not important which way you do this as long as your approach is consistent, it helps the reader around the report and matches those specified by your examining institution.

Previewing and summarising chapters

A further way in which you can signpost your work is to 'top and tail' each chapter. This is to include a few words at the beginning of the chapter (Smith, 1991) which provides a description of how the chapter is to contribute to answering the research question, the methods used in this part of the study and the points that are covered. At the end of each chapter it is useful if readers have a brief summary of the content of the chapter and a very brief indication of how this content links to the following chapter. This may seem like repetition. But it helps readers on their journey through your report and ensures that you, the writer, are on the correct road.

Tables and diagrams

Your readers will find your project report more accessible and easier to read if you present some of your data and ideas in *tables* and *diagrams*. It is not only numerical data which can be presented in tabular form. You can also present ideas which can be easily compared. Table 13.1 is an example of this.

Don't be tempted to put your numerical tables in the appendices. They will probably be some of your most important data. Include them and comment on them within the text. Your commentary should note the significance of the data in the tables. It should not simply describe the table's contents.

Section 11.3 (and in particular Table 11.2) has detail on the presentation of tables and diagrams.

A final note of caution. To avoid confusing your readers, do make sure that you have introduced the table or graphic before it appears in the text.

One report or two?

Many researchers on management topics face the dilemma of having to write for two audiences: the academic audience, who possibly will mark and grade the report for a degree or a diploma, and the organisation's managers, who will be interested in the practical benefit which the report promises. This raises the thorny question: 'For whom should the report be written?'.

Many people have resolved this dilemma by writing two reports, one for each audience. The academic report will usually be much longer and contain contextual description which the organisational audience does not require. Similarly, those managers reading the report will probably be less interested than the academic audience in the literature review and the development of theory. If the research question did not imply the necessity for recommendations for future action, these may need to be written for the organisational version.

Fortunately, the advent of wordprocessors makes this job easy. Some careful cutting and pasting will be necessary. However, what should always be kept in mind is the audience that each specific report is addressing. Take care not to fall between two stools. Make sure the style and content of each report are applicable to its audience.

13.5 DEVELOPING AN APPROPRIATE WRITING STYLE

Much of your concern in writing your project report will be about *what* you write. In this section of the chapter we ask you to think about the *way* you write. Your writing style is just as important as the content, structure and layout of your report. It is true that 'good writing can't cure bad thought' (Phillips and Pugh, 1994: 66). However, bad writing can spoil the effect of good thought.

Clarity and simplicity

The . . . lack of ready intelligibility [in scholarly writing], I believe, usually has little or nothing to do with the complexity of the subject matter, and nothing at all to do with profundity of thought. It has to do almost entirely with certain confusions of the academic writer about his own status . . . To overcome the academic prose you first of all have to overcome the academic pose.'

Wright Mills, 1970: 239–40

Phil tells a story which reinforces the point made by Wright Mills in the above quotation. He was asked by a student to comment on her thesis in progress which was about the impact of a particular job advertising strategy. He thought it was written in an over-elaborate and academic way. After many suggestions for amendments, Phil came across a sentence which explained that the strategy his student was studying 'was characterised by factors congruent with the results of a lifestyle analysis of the target market'. Phil thought this was too wordy and academic. He suggested making it simpler. His student examined the sentence at length and declared she could see no way of improving it. Phil thought that it could say, 'it was a strategy which matched the lifestyles of those at which it was aimed'. His student protested. She agreed that it was shorter and clearer but protested that it was less 'academic'. We think that clarity and simplicity are more important than wishing to appear academic. Your project report is a piece of communication.

Phillips and Pugh (1994) advise that you should aim to provide readers with a report that they can't put down until 2.00 a.m. or later for fear of spoiling the flow. (If you are reading this chapter at 2.30 a.m. we have succeeded!)

Write simple sentences

A common source of lack of clarity is the confusing sentence. This is often because it is too long. A simple rule to adopt is: one idea – one sentence. Mark reads his work out loud. If the sentences are too long he runs out of breath! This is another useful guide to sentence length.

● ●

WORKED EXAMPLE: *Writing clearer sentences*

'While it is true to say that researchers have illusions of academic grandeur when they sit down to write their project report, and who can blame them because they have had to demonstrate skill and resilience to get to this point in their studies, they nonetheless must consider that writing a project report is an exercise in communication and nobody likes reading a lot of ideas which are expressed in such a confusing and pretentious way that nobody can understand them, let alone the poor tutor who has to plough through it all to try and make some sense of it.'

There appear to be at least six separate ideas in this sentence. It contains 101 words (when marking, we sometimes come across sentences with over 150!). In addition, it contains a common way of introducing multiple ideas in to a sentence: the embedded clause. In the sentence above the embedded clause is 'and who can blame them because they have had to demonstrate skill and resilience to get to this point in their studies'. The give-away is the first word in the sentence, 'While'. This invites an embedded clause. The point here is that potentially rich ideas become buried in the literary undergrowth. Dig them up and replant them. Let them breathe in a sentence of their own.

The sentence needs to be clearer and simpler. However, it should not lose any of its meaning. Halving the amount of words and dividing up the sentence into smaller clearer sentences results in the following:

> 'Researchers have illusions of academic grandeur when they write their project report. This is understandable. They have demonstrated skill and resilience to reach this point in their studies. However, writing a project report is an exercise in communication. Nobody likes confusing and pretentious writing which is difficult to understand. Pity the tutor who has to make sense of it.'

Avoid jargon

Jargon should not be confused with technical terminology. Some technical terms are unavoidable. To assist your reader, it is best to put a glossary of such terms in the appendices. However, do not assume that your reader will have such a full knowledge as you of the subject and, in particular, the context. Here, and in all cases, try to put yourself in the position of the reader. Phil makes this point to MBA students who use their organisations as vehicles to write assignments. He asks them to 'mark' past (anonymous) assignments. They are usually horrified at the assumptions that their fellow students make about the tutor's prior knowledge.

What can be avoided is the sort of jargon which the *Oxford English Dictionary* defines as 'gibberish' and 'debased language'. You will know the sort of phrases: 'ongoing situation'; 'going down the route of'; 'at the end of the day'; 'the bottom line'; 'at this moment in time'. It is not just that they are ugly, but they are not clear and simple. For example, 'now' is much clearer and simpler than 'at this moment in time'.

Check your spelling and grammar

Spelling and *grammar* are still a problem for many of us, in spite of the wordprocessor's spelling and grammar checkers. The spell checker won't correct your 'moral' when you wished to say 'morale' or sort out when you should write 'practise' rather than 'practice'. This is where the friend who is reading your draft can help, provided that friend is a competent speller. However, tutors tend to be more patient with errors of this kind than those which reflect carelessness. The point remains that spelling and grammar errors detract from the quality of your presentation and the authority of your ideas.

The ten commandments of good writing

Day (1989) provides a useful checklist for those of us who make the sort of *grammatical errors* which threaten the credibility of our writing. He demonstrates cleverly the error in each of the points listed in Table 13.2.

Often we write:	The correct way is:
1 Each pronoun should agree with **their** antecedent.	Each pronoun should agree with **its** antecedent.
2 Just between you and **I**, case is important.	Just between you and **me**, case is important.
3 A preposition is a poor word to end a sentence **with**.	A preposition is a poor word **with which** to end a sentence.
4 Verbs **has** to agree with their subject.	Verbs **have** to agree with their subject.
5 Don't use **no** double negatives.	Don't use double negatives.
6 Remember **to never split** an infinitive.	Remember **never to split** an infinitive.
7 When dangling, don't use participles.	Don't use dangling participles.
8 Join clauses good, like a conjunction should.	Conjunctions should join clauses.
9 Don't write a run on sentence it is difficult when you got to punctuate it so it makes sense when the reader reads what you wrote.	Don't write a run on sentence. It is difficult to punctuate it so that it makes sense to the reader.
10 About sentence fragments.	What about sentence fragments? (!)
11 The data **is** included in this section.	The data **are** included in this section

Table 13.2 Common grammatical errors
Source: developed from Day, 1989

It is not our intention here to conduct an English grammar lesson. Some of the common errors in Table 13.2 are self-explanatory.

You may argue that the *split infinitive* is not often thought of as an error these days. However, 'to boldly go' ahead with your project report ignoring this rule risks irritating your reader – something you can ill afford to do. You want the reader to concentrate on your ideas.

Day's *dangling participle* warning is amusingly illustrated by the draft questionnaire shown to us by a student. This asked for 'the amount of people you employ in your organisation, broken down by sex'. We wrote on our copy: 'We haven't got people in that category: they've not got the energy when they work here!' (Remember that when writing your questionnaire!)

Some of the more obvious grammatical errors you can spot by reading your text aloud to yourself. You need not know the grammatical rules, the words often just sound wrong.

Person, tense and gender

Traditionally, academic writing has been dry and unexciting. This is partly because the convention has been to write impersonally, in the past *tense* and in the *passive voice* (e.g. interviews were conducted following the administration of questionnaires).

The writer was expected to be distanced from the text. This convention is no longer as strong. It is a matter of preferred style rather than rules. The research approach which dominates your methods may dictate your choice of *personal pronoun*. Section 4.1 lists 'the observer is independent of what is being observed' as one feature of positivism. It follows from this that an impersonal style is more appropriate. By contrast, Section 8.2 notes that the participant observer 'participates in the daily life of people under study'. The researcher is an intrinsic part of the research process. Use of the first person seems more logical here. However, style is important. Use of the term 'the author' sounds too impersonal and stilted. Excessive use of 'I' and 'we' may raise questions in your readers' minds about your ability to stand outside your data and be objective.

Day (1989) identifies rules for the correct use of tense. He suggests that the present tense should be used when referring to previously published work (e.g. Day identifies). When referring to your present results (e.g. I found that . . .) you should use the past tense. Although he notes exceptions to this rule, it serves as a useful guide.

Day (1989) and Becker (1986) both stridently attack the passive voice (e.g. it was found that) and champion the use of the *active voice* (e.g. I found that). Certainly it is clearer, shorter and unambiguous. It is a good idea to check with your project tutor here which is most likely to be acceptable.

Finally, a note about the use of language which assumes the *gender* of a classification of people. The most obvious example of this is the constant reference to managers as 'he'. Not only is this inaccurate in many organisations, but it gives offence to many people of both sexes. Those offended will probably include your readers! It is simple enough to avoid (e.g. 'I propose to interview each executive unless he refuses' becomes 'I propose to interview each executive unless I receive a refusal') but often less easy to spot. The further reading section in the first draft of this chapter referred to Becker as a 'master craftsman'. These notes on language and gender prompted us to change it to 'an expert in the field'.

Preserving anonymity

You may have given the participants (and the organisations) from whom you collected data an undertaking that you would not disclose their identity in anything you write. In this case you will need to conceal their identity in your project report. The usual way of doing this is to invent pseudonyms for organisations and not to name individual participants. This should not detract from the impact of your report.

Similarly, your sponsoring organisation(s) may have requested sight of your report before it is submitted. Should there be misgivings about the content of the report you should be able to alleviate these by the use of pseudonyms. For example, Mark and Adrian referred to a service sector company from which they had obtained data as 'Servco'. This is usually a better option than significant text changes.

13.6 THE NEED FOR CONTINUAL REVISION

Adrian recently asked a group of undergraduate students how many of them did more than one draft of their assignment papers. He did not expect that many would reply that they did more than once. What he did not predict was that many of them had not even thought that this was necessary.

Submitting the first attempt is partly due to the heavy assessment loads on many courses which means that students are constantly having to 'keep up with the clock'. On part-time courses, students have so many demands in their paid employment that writing an assignment just once is all that is possible. Becker (1986) argues that this is the way most of us learned to write at school. The paper is usually only seen by the teacher. The arrangement is a private one.

However, project reports are different. They will be seen by an audience much wider than one tutor. They will usually be lodged in the library to be read by succeeding students. You will be judged on the quality of your work. For that reason we urge you most strongly to polish your work with successive drafts until you are happy that you can do no better.

The final version of this chapter (which, incidentally, was read by five people and is the last of nine or ten drafts) contains guidelines that you can use to evaluate your first draft. These are summarised in Table 13.3 as a checklist.

☑ Is there a clear structure?

☑ Is there a clear storyline?

☑ Does your abstract reflect accurately the whole content of the report?

☑ Does your introduction state clearly the research question(s) and/or objectives?

☑ Does your literature review inform the later content of the report?

☑ Are your methods clearly explained?

☑ Have you made a clear distinction between findings and conclusions in the two relevant chapters?

☑ Have you checked all your references and presented these in the required manner?

☑ Is there any text material which should be in the appendices and vice versa?

☑ Does your title accurately reflect your content?

☑ Have you divided your text throughout with suitable headings?

☑ Does each chapter have a preview and a summary?

☑ Are you happy that your writing is clear, simple and direct?

☑ Have you eliminated all jargon?

☑ Have you checked spelling and grammar?

☑ Have you checked for assumptions about gender?

☑ Is your report in a format which will be acceptable to the assessing body?

Table 13.3 Checklist for the first draft of the project report

Having been through this checklist you may decide to make minor alterations to your text. On the other hand, you may want to rewrite sections or move sections within chapters to other chapters. Keep asking yourself: 'How easy can I make the reader's task?'.

After each successive draft do leave time for your thoughts to mature. It is amazing how something you wrote a few days before will now make no sense to you. However, you will also be impressed with the clarity and insight of some passages.

Having completed a second draft you may now feel confident enough to give it to your colleague or friend to read. Ask your reader to use the checklist above to which you can add specific points which you feel are important (e.g. are my arguments well reasoned?).

13.7 MEETING THE ASSESSMENT CRITERIA

Your readers will be assessing your work against the assessment criteria which apply to your research programme. Therefore it is essential that you familiarise yourself with these criteria. Easterby-Smith *et al.* (1991) cite Bloom's (1956) well-known taxonomy of educational objectives to illustrate the level which project reports should attain. At the lower levels project reports should show *knowledge* and *understanding* of the topic covered. At the intermediate levels they should contain evidence of *application* and *analysis*. Application is thought of as the ability to apply certain principles and rules in particular situations. Your methodology section should be the principal vehicle for demonstrating application. Analysis may be illustrated by your ability to break down your data and clarify the nature of the component parts and the relationship between them. Whatever your assessment criteria, it is certain that you will be expected to demonstrate your ability at these lower and intermediate levels.

The higher levels are *synthesis* and *evaluation*. Rowntree (1977: 103) defines synthesis as 'the ability to arrange and assemble various elements so as to make a new statement or plan or conclusion – a unique communication'. The emphasis put on conclusions and, in particular, on the development of a storyline in your project report suggests that we feel that you should be showing evidence of synthesis. Evaluation refers to 'the ability to judge materials or methods in terms of internal accuracy and consistency or by comparison with external criteria' (Rowntree 1977: 103). You have the chance to show this ability not only in the literature review but in the awareness of the limitations of your own research, which we have suggested in Section 13.3 that you should include in your conclusions.

In summary, we think that each of the levels of educational objectives should be demonstrated in your project report.

13.8 SUMMARY

- Writing is a powerful way of clarifying your thinking.
- Writing is a creative process which requires the right conditions if it is to produce successful results.
- Your project report should have a clear structure which enables you develop a clear storyline.
- Your report should be laid out in such a way that your reader finds all the information readily accessible.
- You should try to develop a clear, simple writing style which will make reading the report an easy and enjoyable experience.
- Spelling and grammatical errors should be avoided.
- Don't think of your first draft as your last. Be prepared to rewrite your report several times until you think it is the best you can do.

Self-check questions and assignment

Self-check question 13.1
Your project tutor has returned your draft project report with the suggestion that you make a clearer distinction between your results and your findings. How will you go about this?

Self-check question 13.2
Why is it considered good practice to acknowledge the limitations of your research in the project report?

Self-check question 13.3
Look again at the quote from Wright Mills cited early in Section 13.5 (p 383). Rewrite this so that his idea is communicated to the reader in the clearest way possible.

Self-check question 13.4
There are other problems that must be avoided when repositioning sections of your report in the re-drafting processes. What are they?

Assignment 13
Writing your research report

- Design a clear structure for your report which fits broadly the structure suggested in Section 13.3. Ensure that the structure you design accommodates a clear storyline.

- Write the report's abstract. Remember that you will need to rewrite this when you have finished your first draft.

- Compile the main body of the report. How will you ensure that the literature review relates to the following chapters? What method will you adopt to make the distinction between result and conclusions?

- If you are using a wordprocessor remember to make regular back-up copies of your work on separate disks.

- Give your report the 'reader-friendly' test to ensure that the style is easy to read and free from avoidable errors.

References

Becker, H. (1986) *Writing for Social Scientists*, Chicago, University of Chicago Press.

Bloom, B. (1956) (ed.) *Taxonomy of Educational Objectives: Cognitive Domain*, New York, McKay.

Buzan, T. with Buzan, B. (1995) *The Mindmap Book* (revised edition), London, BBC Books.

Day, R. (1989) *How to Write and Publish a Scientific Paper* (3rd edn), Cambridge, Cambridge University Press.

Easterby-Smith, M., Thorpe, R. and Lowe, A. (1991) *Management Research: An Introduction*, London, Sage.

Griffiths, M. (1993) 'Productive writing', *The New Academic*, Autumn, 29–30.

Phillips, E. and Pugh, D. (1994) *How to get a PhD* (2nd edn), Buckingham, Open University Press.

Raimond, P. (1993) *Management Projects*, London, Chapman & Hall.

Robson, C. (1993) *Real World Research*, Oxford, Blackwell.

Rowntree, D. (1977) *Assessing Students: how shall we know them?*, London, Harper and Row.

Smith, C.B. (1991) *A Guide to Business Research*, Chicago, Nelson-Hall.

Veroff, J. (1992) 'Writing', in Rudestam, K. and Newton, R. (eds) *Surviving your Dissertation,* Newbury Park, California, Sage, pp. 145–67.

Wright Mills, C. (1970) *The Sociological Imagination*, London, Pelican.

Further reading

Becker, H. (1986) *Writing for Social Scientists*, Chicago, University of Chicago Press. A highly readable book, full of anecdotes, from an expert in the field. It is rich in ideas about how writing may be improved. Most of these have been developed by Becker from his own writing and teaching. Such is the emphasis that Becker puts on rewriting that the title would more accurately be 'Rewriting for Social Scientists'.

Day, R. (1989) *How to Write and Publish a Scientific Paper* (3rd edn), Cambridge, Cambridge University Press. This takes the reader through the whole process with a host of useful advice. It is funny and irreverent but none the less valuable for that!

Smith, C.B. (1991) *A Guide to Business Research*, Chicago, Nelson-Hall. Chapters 7 to 10 provide an excellent introduction to writing for business and management researchers.

Case 13:
The impact of office automation on social relations between staff

Lata had worked hard on her research. She was pleased with the project report she had submitted and was quietly confident that it would receive a good grade. But this was not to be. She was horrified when she received a note from Louise, her course tutor, telling her that her report had been referred back for substantial reworking. Lata went to see Louise immediately. She told the story of how her research had developed from the time she had first discussed it with Eddie, her project tutor, to the time her report was submitted. This is that story.

'My research question was: 'What have been the effects of office automation on the social relations between staff?'. I was conducting a case study in Midshire, a large local authority. My data collection methods were questionnaire and semi-structured interviews.

I was enthusiastic about my research. In the early days I had frequent meetings with Eddie. I wanted to start collecting data immediately. However, Eddie counselled caution. He was concerned that I should think more thoroughly about my research objectives and the questions I was going to ask in my questionnaire. To be honest, I became impatient with Eddie's approach, which I thought was too fussy.

I went ahead and collected the data. I had piloted the questionnaire with friends whom I met when working in Midshire's education department. I was pleased with the response rate of over 60%. I then went ahead and conducted my interviews. I interviewed those people I was friendly with and who would be more likely to give up their time. I suppose that by the time I had finished my data collection I had not seen Eddie for several months.

I had taken Eddie's advice not to leave all my writing until the last minute. I was determined to write up my research as I went along. Early on in my research I had written a literature review which was current and comprehensive. I was pleased with this and decided that this would form a part of the final report. I was also writing up my data as I went along. My questionnaire analysis formed a major part of this writing. My results were in the form of computer-generated tables related to each question. I wrote an extensive commentary on these tables. I also wrote a separate section on my interview data, reporting in some detail what each interviewee had said. The result was that I had a major section on my data which I was satisfied would form the bulk of my report.

Meanwhile I had a meeting with Eddie to report progress. He seemed pleased that I had collected so much data. He said he was in the annual process of chasing some students who seemed to have done little, despite the fast approaching deadline for handing in. I had done a lot. But I think Eddie felt I was rather complacent about what I had done. He asked to see of a copy of my draft report. I said that a little more time was needed to get it together. We agreed that it would be with Eddie in two weeks' time.

I must admit that the deadline passed and the draft report did not arrive. I had been hit with the normal rush to finish assignments for other parts of my course. I was pleased that I had gone ahead with writing my project report because it meant that I was able to hand in all my work. I also thought there wasn't much I could do to the report since I had already hit the word limit. I sent Eddie a note to explain the problems I had experienced. I told him that I would 'polish up' what I had written and submit that for examination.'

Louise went to see Eddie to report on her meeting with Lata. This was Eddie's reaction.

To be honest I'm not surprised it turned out like this. The report is far too descriptive. It's good at the description, but that is about all. There is no attempt to link the data to the literature review and not really much connection between the data and the research questions. It reads a bit like two separate reports. One of these is a review of the literature in the field and the other a report of what Lata found out in Midshire. Both, in their own right, are quite good, but as a project report it simply doesn't come together. However, my main criticism is that it doesn't actually say anything . . . you know, it doesn't draw any conclusions. When I finished reading it I couldn't help saying: 'So what?'.

The material is there for Lata to write a decent report. But I'm afraid she has a lot more work to do.

Case-study questions

1 Where do you think Lata went wrong in her approach to the process of preparing her research report?

2 How do you think Lata could have overcome Eddie's criticism that 'it reads a bit like two separate reports"?

3 How may Lata have approached the writing of her results section?

4 How could Lata have prevented Eddie saying 'So what?' to himself after he had finished reading her report?

Answers to self-check questions

Self-check question 13.1

Easier said than done. Start by going through your results chapter continuously asking yourself: 'Did I find this out?'. You will probably weed out a lot of things which you have thought about which are related to points you found out. These belong in the conclusions (or discussion) chapter.

Now turn to the conclusions chapter and ask yourself the same question. You will probably find less results in the conclusions chapter than vice versa.

Self-check question 13.2

It shows you have thought about your research design. It demonstrates that you have insight into the various ways of pursuing research. Remember that there is no perfect research design. Look again at Section 4.4. This asked the question, 'How do you know that the answer to the research question(s) is the correct one?'. The answer, of course, is that in the literal sense of the question you can't know. All you can do is to reduce the possibility of getting the answer wrong.

Self-check question 13.3

Academic writing is often difficult to understand. This is not usually because the subject matter is complex or the thoughts profound. It is because the writer thinks it necessary to write in an 'academic' way.

Self-check question 13.4

The 'road map' you announced in the introduction may not now be correct. The previews and summaries at the beginning and end of the relevant chapters may need to be changed. A more serious potential problem is that the storyline may have been altered. This should not be the case. Nonetheless, it is important to re-read the whole report to ensure the repositioning does not alter its sense of coherence.

BIBLIOGRAPHY

Ackroyd, S. and Hughes, J. (1992) *Data Collection in Context* (2nd edn), London, Longman.

Adams, G. and Schvaneveldt, J. (1991) *Understanding Research Methods* (2nd edn), New York, Longman.

Babbie, E. and Halley, F. (1995) *Adventures in Social Research: Data Analysis using SPSS for Windows*, London, Pine Forge Press.

Barnett, V. (1991) *Sample Survey Principles and Method*, London, Edward Arnold.

Barrow, M. (1995) *The Times 1000 1996*, London, Times Books.

Becker, H. (1986) *Writing for Social Scientists*, Chicago, University of Chicago Press.

Bell, J. (1993) *Doing your Research Project* (2nd edn), Buckingham, Open University Press.

Bennett, R. (1991) 'What is Management Research', in Smith, N.C. and Dainty, P. (eds) *The Management Research Handbook*, London, Routledge, pp. 67–77.

Bloom, B. (1956) (ed.) *Taxonomy of Educational Objectives: Cognitive Domain*, New York, McKay.

Borg, W.R. and Gall, M.D. (1989) *Educational Research: An Introduction* (5th edn), New York, Longman.

Bourque, L.B. and Clark, V.A. (1994) 'Processing Data: The Survey Example', in Lewis-Beck, M.S. (ed.) *Research Practice*, London, Sage, pp. 1–88.

Bryman, A. (1988) *Quantity and Quality in Social Research*, London, Unwin Hyman.

Bryman, A. (1989) *Research Methods and Organisation Studies*, London, Unwin Hyman.

Buchanan, D., Boddy, D. and McAlman, J. (1988) 'Getting In, Getting On, Getting Out and Getting Back', in Bryman, A. (ed.) *Doing Research in Organisations*, London, Routledge, pp. 53–67.

Buzan, T. with Buzan, B. (1995) *The Mind Map Book* (revised edition), London, BBC Books.

Campbell, D. and Campbell, M. (1995) *The Students' Guide to Doing Research on the Internet*, Reading, Massachusetts, Addison-Wesley.

Carroll, L. (1989) *Alice's Adventures in Wonderland*, London, Hutchinson.

Central Statistical Office (1992) *Standard Industrial Classification of Economic Activities*, London, HMSO.

Central Statistical Office (1994) *Economic Trends Annual Supplement 1994 edition*, London, HMSO.

Church, J. (1995) (ed.) *Regional Trends 30*, London, HMSO.

Collins, D. and White, A. (1995) 'Making the next Census form more respondent-friendly', *Social Survey Methodology Bulletin*, 37, July, 8–14.

Collinson, J.A. (1995) *Ethical Principles and Guidelines for Research with Human Participants*, Cheltenham, Cheltenham and Gloucester College of Higher Education.

Craig, P.B. (1991) 'Designing and Using Mail Questionnaires', in Smith, N.C. and Dainty, P. (eds) *The Management Research Handbook*, London, Routledge, pp. 181–9.

Dale, A. (1993) 'Fieldwork and Data Processing', in Dale, A. and Marsh, C. (eds) *The 1991 Census User's Guide*, London, HMSO, pp. 84–110.

Dale, A., Arber, S. and Procter, M. (1988) *Doing Secondary Research*, London, Unwin Hyman.

Day, R. (1989) *How to Write and Publish a Scientific Paper* (3rd edn), Cambridge, Cambridge University Press.

Deci, E.L. (1972) 'The effects of contingent and non-contingent rewards and controls on intrinsic motivation', *Organisational Behaviour and Human Performance*, 8, 217–19.

Delbridge, R. and Kirkpatrick, I. (1994) 'Theory and Practice of Participant Observation', in Wass, V. and Wells, P. (eds) *Principles and Practice in Business and Management Research*, Aldershot, Dartmouth, pp. 35–62.

Dennis, G., (1995) (ed.) *Annual Abstract of Statistics 1995*, London, HMSO.

Dennis, G., Pearson, N. and Ukueku, C. (eds) (1995) *Annual Abstract of Statistics*, London, HMSO.

Denzin, N. (1970) *The Research Act: A Theoretical Introduction to Sociological Methods*, Chicago, Aldine.

deVaus, D.A. (1991) *Surveys in Social Research* (3rd edn), London, UCL Press and Allen & Unwin.

Dey, I. (1993) *Qualitative Data Analysis*, London, Routledge.

Dillman, D.A. (1978) *Mail and Telephone Surveys: The Total Design Method*, New York, Wiley.

Ditton, J. (1977) *Part-Time Crime: An Ethnography of Fiddling and Pilferage*, London, Macmillan.

Dixon, B., Bouma, G. and Atkinson, G. (1987) *A Handbook of Social Science Research: A Comprehensive and Practical Guide for Students*, Oxford, Oxford University Press.

Dunkerley, D. (1988) 'Historical Methods and Organizational Analysis', in Bryman, A. (ed.) *Doing Research in Organisations*, London, Routledge, pp. 82–95.

Easterby-Smith, M., Thorpe, R. and Lowe, A. (1991) *Management Research: An Introduction*, London, Sage.

The Economist (1993) *The Economist Numbers Guide*, London, Hamish Hamilton.

Ellsworth, J.H. and Ellsworth, M.V. (1994) *The Internet Business Book*, New York, John Wiley.

Emory, C. and Cooper, D. (1991) *Business Research Methods* (4th edn), Homewood, Illinois, Richard D. Irwin.

Erlandson, D.A., Harris, E.L., Skipper, B.L. and Allen, S.D. (1993) *Doing Naturalistic Inquiry*, Newbury Park, California and London, Sage.

ESRC Data Archive (1995a) *ESRC Data Archive Abbreviated Catalogue*, Colchester, ESRC Data Archive.

ESRC Data Archive (1995b) *The ESRC Data Archive: Sharing and Preserving Research Data*, Colchester, ESRC Data Archive.

Evans, A. (1991) *Computers and Personnel Systems: A Practical Guide*, London, Institute of Personnel Management.

Fenwick, D. and Denman, J. (1995) 'The monthly claimant unemployment count: change and consistency', *Labour Market Trends*, November, 397–400.

Fink, A. (1995a) *How to Ask Survey Questions*, Thousand Oaks, California, Sage.

Fink, A. (1995b) *The Survey Handbook*, Thousand Oaks, California, Sage.

Fink, A. (1995c) *How to Analyze Survey Data*, Thousand Oaks, California, Sage.

Foster, K., Jackson, B., Thomas, M., Hunter, P. and Bennett, N. (1995) *General Household Survey, 1993*, London, HMSO.

Fox, J. and Long, J.S. (eds) (1990) *Modern Methods of Data Analysis*, Newbury Park, California, Sage.

Ghauri, P. Grønhaug, K. and Kristianslund, I. (1995) *Research Methods in Business Studies: A Practical Guide*, London, Prentice Hall.

Gibb, F. (1995) 'Consumer group accuses lawyers of shoddy service', *The Times*, 5 October.

Gill, J. and Johnson, P. (1991) *Research Methods for Managers*, London, Paul Chapman.

Glaser, B. (1978) *Theoretical Sensitivity: Advances in the Methodology of Grounded Theory*, Mill Valley, California, Sociology Press.

Glaser, B. and Strauss, A. (1967) *The Discovery of Grounded Theory*, Chicago, Aldine.

Griffiths, M. (1993) 'Productive writing', *The New Academic*, Autumn, 29–30.

Grummitt, J. (1980) *Interviewing Skills*, London, The Industrial Society.

Gummesson, E. (1991) *Qualitative Methods in Management Research*, Newbury Park, California, Sage.

Hakim, C. (1982) *Secondary Analysis in Social Research*, London, Allen & Unwin.

Hakim, C. (1987) *Research Design: Strategies and Choices in the Design of Social Research*, London, Allen & Unwin.

Hammersley, M. and Atkinson, P. (1983) *Ethnography Principles in Practice*, London, Routledge.

Hays, W.L. (1994) *Statistics* (4th edn), London, Holt-Saunders.

Haythornthwaite, J. (ed.) (1990) *The Business Information Maze: An Essential Guide*, London, ASLIB.

Haywood, P. and Wragg, E.C. (1982) *Evaluating the Literature: Rediguide 2*, Nottingham, University of Nottingham School of Education.

Healey, M.J. (1991) 'Obtaining Information from Businesses', in Healey, M.J. (ed.) *Economic Activity and Land Use*, Harlow, Longman, pp. 193–251.

Healey, M.J. and Rawlinson, M.B. (1993) 'Interviewing Business Owners and Managers: A Review of Methods and Techniques', *Geoforum*, 24: 3, 339–55.

Healey, M.J. and Rawlinson, M.B. (1994) 'Interviewing Techniques in Business and Management Research', in Wass, V.J. and Wells, P.E. (eds) *Principles and Practice in Business and Management Research*, Aldershot, Dartmouth, pp. 123–146.

Hedrick, T.E., Bickmann, L. and Rog, D.J. (1993) *Applied Research Design*, Newbury Park California, Sage.

Henry, G.T. (1990) *Practical Sampling*, Newbury Park, California, Sage.

Hodson, R. (1991) 'The Active Worker: Compliance and Autonomy at the Workplace', *Journal of Contemporary Ethnography*, 20: 1, 47–48.

Hofstede, G. (1991) *Cultures and Organisations*, London, McGraw-Hill.

Hoinville, G., Jowell, R. and Associates (1978) *Survey Research Practice*, London, Heinemann.

Howard, K. and Sharp, J.A. (1983) *The Management of a Student Research Project*, Aldershot, Gower.

Jacob, H. (1994) 'Using Published Data: Errors and Remedies', in Lewis-Beck, M.S. (ed.) *Research Practice*, London, Sage and Toppan Publishing, pp. 339–89.

Jankowicz, A.D. (1995) *Business Research Projects for Students* (2nd edn), London, Chapman & Hall.

Johnson, G. (1996) 'The debate begins', *BAM News*, 6, 1–2.

Johnson, J.M. (1975) *Doing Field Research*, New York, Free Press.

Jowell, R., Curtice, J., Brook, L. and Ahrendt, D. (1994) *British Social Attitudes – the 11th Report*, Aldershot, Dartmouth.

Kahn, R. and Cannell, C. (1957) *The Dynamics of Interviewing*, New York and Chichester, John Wiley.

Kervin, J.B. (1992) *Methods for Business Research*, New York, HarperCollins.

King, J. (1995) (ed.) *Family Spending – A Report on the 1994–95 Family Expenditure Survey*, London, HMSO.

Krueger, R.C. (1994) *Focus Groups: A Practical Guide for Applied Research* (2nd edn), London, Sage.

Mackintosh, N. (ed.) (1995) *Cyril Burt: Fraud or Framed?*, Oxford, Oxford University Press.

Marsh, C. (1993) 'An Overview', in Dale, A. and Marsh, C. (eds) *The 1991 Census User's Guide*, London, HMSO, pp. 1–15.

Marshall, C. and Rossman, G.B. (1989) *Designing Qualitative Research*, Newbury Park, California and London, Sage.

McNeill, P. (1990) *Research Methods* (2nd edn), London, Routledge.

Meyer, H., Kay, E. and French, J. (1965) 'Split roles in performance appraisal', *Harvard Business Review*, 43: 1, 123–9.

Miles, M.B. and Huberman, A.M. (1994) *Qualitative Data Analysis* (2nd edn), Thousand Oaks, California, Sage.

Millmore, M. (1995) *HRM in C&GCHE?: Assessing the current state of play*, Unpublished MA Dissertation, Cheltenham, Cheltenham & Gloucester College of Higher Education.

Millward, N., Stevens, M., Smart, D. and Hawes, W.R. (1992) *Workplace industrial relations in transition*, Aldershot, Dartmouth.

Mintzberg, H. (1973) *The nature of Managerial Work*, New York, Harper and Row.

Mintzberg, H. and Waters, J. (1989) 'Of Strategies, Deliberate and Emergent', in Asch, D. and Bowman, C. (eds) *Readings in Strategic Management*, Basingstoke, Macmillan Education, pp. 4–19.

Moody, P.E. (1983) *Decision Making: Proven Methods for Better Decisions*, London, McGraw-Hill.

Morgan, M. (1995) 'The case of the dubious data', *The Guardian*, 4 August, Second section, 10–11.

Morris, C. (1993) *Quantitative Approaches in Business Studies* (3rd edn), London, Pitman Publishing.

Morris, T. and Wood, S. (1991) 'Testing the Survey Method: Continuity and Change in British Industrial Relations', *Work Employment and Society*, 5: 2, 259–82.

Mort, D. (1992) *UK Statistics – A Guide for Business Users*, Aldershot, Ashgate.

Moser, C.A. and Kalton, G. (1986) *Survey Methods in Social Investigation* (2nd edn), Aldershot, Gower.

Mullins, L. (1996) *Management and Organisational Behaviour* (4th edn), London, Pitman Publishing.

Naipaul, V.S. (1989) *A Turn in the South*, London, Penguin.

National Council for Education Technology (1993) *Information skills in action*, Coventry, National Council for Education Technology.

Neuman, W.L. (1991) *Social Research Methods*, London, Allyn and Bacon.

North, D.J., Leigh, R. and Gough, J. (1983) 'Monitoring industrial change at the local level: some comments on methods and data sources', in Healey, M.J. (ed.) *Urban and Regional Industrial Research: The Changing UK Data Base*, Norwich, Geo Books, pp. 111–29.

Norusis, M.J. (1992) *SPSS for Windows Base System User's Guide*, Chicago, SPSS Inc.

Office of Population Censuses and Surveys (1990a) *Standard Occupational Classification*, Volume 1, London, HMSO.

Office of Population Censuses and Surveys (1990b) *Standard Occupational Classification*, Volume 2, London, HMSO.

Office of Population Censuses and Surveys (1991) *Standard Occupational Classification*, Volume 3, London, HMSO.

Office of Population Censuses and Surveys (1994) *International Migration 1992*, London, HMSO.

Office of Population Censuses and Surveys and General Registrar's Office for Scotland (1992) *1991 Census Definitions Great Britain*, London, HMSO.

Oppenheim, A.N. (1992) *Questionnaire Design, Interviewing and Attitude Measurement* (new edition), London, Pinter.

Owen, F. and Jones, R. (1990) *Statistics* (3rd edn), London, Pitman Publishing.

Patton, M.Q. (1990) *Qualitative Evaluation and Research Methods* (2nd edn), Newbury Park, California, Sage.

Peters, T. and Waterman, R. (1982) *In Search of Excellence*, New York, Harper and Row.

Phillips, E. and Pugh, D. (1994) *How to get a PhD* (2nd edn), Buckingham, Open University Press.

Powney, J. and Watts, M. (1987) *Interviewing in Educational Research*, London, Routledge and Kegan Paul.

Pugh, D. (1988) 'The Aston Research Programme' in Bryman, A. (ed.) *Doing Research in Organisations*, London, Routledge, pp. 123–35.

Punch, M. (1993) 'Observation and the Police: The Research Experience', in Hammersley, M. (ed.) *Social Research Philosophy, Politics and Practice*, London, Sage, 181–99.

Raimond, P. (1993) *Management Projects*, London, Chapman & Hall.

Reichman, C.S. (1962) *Use and Abuse of Statistics*, New York, Oxford University Press.

Riley, J. (1990) *Getting the Most from your Data: A Handbook of Practical Ideas on How to Analyse Qualitative Data*, Bristol, Technical and Educational Services Ltd.

Robson, C. (1993) *Real World Research*, Oxford, Blackwell.

Rogers, C.R. (1961) *On Becoming a Person*, Constable, London.

Rosen, M. (1991) 'Breakfast at Spiro's: Dramaturgy and Dominance', in Frost, P., Moore, L., Louis, M., Lundberg, C. and Martin, J. (eds) *Reframing Organisational Culture*, Newbury Park, California, Sage, pp. 77–89.

Rowntree, D. (1977) *Assessing Students: How Shall We Know Them?*, London, Harper & Row.

Roy, D. (1952) 'Quota restriction and goldbricking in a machine shop', *American Journal of Sociology*, 57, 427–42.

Saris, W.E. (1994) 'Computer-Assisted Interviewing', in Lewis-Beck, M.S. (ed.) *Research Practice*, London, Sage, pp. 163–250.

Saunders, M.N.K. (1993) 'Vacancy Notification and Employee Mobility', *International Journal of Manpower*, 14: 6, 39–57.

Saunders, M.N.K. and Cooper, S.A. (1993) *Understanding Business Statistics*, London, DP Publications.

Schatzman, L. and Strauss, A. (1973) *Field Research: Strategies for a Natural Sociology*, Englewood Cliffs, New Jersey, Prentice Hall.

Sekaran, U. (1992) *Research Methods for Business: A Skill-Building Approach* (2nd edn), New York, John Wiley.

Silverman, D. (1993) *Interpreting Qualitative Data*, London, Sage.

Smith, C.B. (1991) *A Guide to Business Research*, Chicago, Nelson-Hall.

Smith, H. (1975) *Strategies of Social Research: The Methodological Imagination*, Englewood Cliffs, New Jersey, Prentice Hall.

Smith, N.C. and Dainty, P. (1991) *The Management Research Handbook*, London, Routledge.

Sparrow, J. (1989) 'Graphic displays in information systems: some data properties influencing the effectiveness of alternate forms', *Behaviour and Information Technology*, 8: 1, 43–56.

Stewart, D.W. and Kamins, M.A. (1993) *Secondary Research: Information Sources and Methods* (2nd edn), Newbury Park, California, Sage.

Strauss, A. and Corbin, J. (1990) *Basics of Qualitative Research: Grounded Theory Procedures and Techniques*, Newbury Park, California, Sage.

Sykes, W. (1991) 'Taking stock: issues from the literature in validity and reliability in qualitative research', *Journal of Market Research Society*, 33, 3–12.

Taylor, S. and Bogdan, R. (1984) *Introduction to Qualitative Research Methods: The Search for Meanings*, New York, John Wiley.

Tesch, R. (1990) *Qualitative Research: Analysis Types and Software Tools*, New York, Falmer.

Thomas, P. and Smith, K. (1995) 'Results of the 1993 Census of Employment', *Employment Gazette*, October, 369–77.

Torrington, D. (1991) *Management Face to Face*, London, Prentice-Hall.

Tukey, J.W. (1977) *Exploratory Data Analysis*, Reading, Massachusetts, Addison-Wesley.

Veroff, J. (1992) 'Writing', in Rudestam, K. and Newton R (eds) *Surviving your Dissertation*, Newbury Park, California, Sage, pp. 145–67.

Walker, R. (1985) *Doing Research: A Handbook for Teachers*, London, Methuen.

Wass, V.J. (1994) 'Minimizing and Managing Bias in a Mail Survey: A Study of Redundant Miners', in Wass, V.J. and Wells, P.E. (eds) *Principles and Practice in Business and Management Research*, Aldershot, Dartmouth, pp. 91–121.

Wass, V. and Wells, P. (1994) 'Research Methods in Action: An Introduction', in Wass, V.J. and Wells, P.E. (eds) *Principles and Practice in Business and Management Research*, Aldershot, Dartmouth, pp. 1–34.

Weitzman, E.A. and Miles, M.B. (1995) *Computer Programs for Qualitative Data Analysis*, Thousand Oaks, California and London, Sage.

Wells, P. (1994) 'Ethics in Business and Management Research', in Wass, V.J. and Wells, P.E. (eds) *Principles and Practice in Business and Management Research*, Aldershot, Dartmouth, pp. 277–97.

Whyte, W. (1955) *Street Corner Society* (2nd edn), Chicago, University of Chicago Press.

Wright Mills, C. (1970) *The Sociological Imagination*, London, Pelican.

Yin, R.K. (1994) *Case Study Research: Design and Methods* (2nd edn), Beverly Hills, California, Sage.

Youngman, M.B. (1986) *Analysing Questionnaires*, Nottingham, University of Nottingham School of Education.

Zikmund, W.G. (1994) *Business Research Methods*, Fort Worth, Dryden Press.

Example research project titles

The following titles are included to help stimulate possible research ideas. You should not take the inclusion of a title as an indication of the quality of the title or any associated research project.

Accountability of accountants

Competitor strategies in the mortgage market

Do the new direct methods of selling financial services pose a major threat to existing providers and, if so, what impact will this have in the future?

Does activity-based costing give companies a competitive edge?

FRS1: Are cash-flow statements a useful vehicle for conveying relevant and clear information about a business's liquidity and financial viability?

Has the introduction of the self-regulatory organisation (PIA) brought about better advice for the public?

How do financial services market to the 'youth' market?

In 1995 England had a total of 80 building societies. In 20 years' time, how many will still exist?

Insider dealing: the development of the criminal law and an evaluation of alternative approaches

Is the demand for pension products increasing from the female sector and, if so, how are life assurance companies reacting to this change?

An assessment of the potential of a major domestic and industrial food manufacturer within the children's confectionery market

The acquisition of mortgage books – managing change

The cashless society – imminent reality or impossible dream?

The change of banks and building societies to public companies

The changing face/future of banks and building societies with regard to products and services

The impact of developments in IT on financial services

The impact on the financial management of NHS hospitals with the granting of 'Trust' status: case study

The implications of introducing compulsory competitive tendering to white-collar services within local government: a critical evaluation

The importance of group personal pensions to individual employees at an organisation compared to company pension schemes

The use and application of purchasing within the organisation

With ever-increasing improvements in modern technology, will a career in accountancy become a thing of the past?

Commercial organisations and the green consumer phenomenon

Has the National Lottery had a detrimental impact on the fundraising of charitable bodies?

Global warming: what does it mean for commercial insurers?

Green revolution in the consumer goods market – a consumer-led phenomenon or the marketing industry's profit-making creation?

The impact of ozone depletion and the greenhouse warming effect on the marketing policies of the domestic refrigeration industry in recent years

The relationship between tobacco advertising and sport on television – can it be justified?

Why is there a need for a standard definition of 'cruelty free' and to what extent does the cosmetic and toiletry industry's definition correspond to the consumer's preferred interpretation?

A comparison of recruitment and selection procedures used in the UK and elsewhere in Europe

A study of the role of human resources today and its effectiveness – is there a real future for it?

Age discrimination in the workplace

An investigation into how skills are acquired on an outdoor management development course and transferred to the workplace

Corporate strategy and planning: the role of the personnel department in its formulation

Disability awareness training within leisure organisations: a case study

Equal opportunities: a marketing and recruitment concept or a reality?

From job interview to promoting a business – how effective is marketing yourself?

Graduates' job attribute preferences: to what extent can they be explained by Maslow's hierarchy of needs?

Internal communications – what role does it have within the organisation of the future?

Investors in People – an investigation into how IIP is introduced in organisations in order to gain staff support for IIP

Is personality testing a valid tool in the recruitment and selection process?

Honesty and integrity testing and the security industry

How important is employee communication today?

Performance appraisal: a review of the benefits

Psychometric testing – an effective way of selection

Racial discrimination in recruitment and selection

Stress – the cost to employers

The armed forces, equal opportunities and equality

The changing role of HRM

The effectiveness of middle management on a culture change

The extended interview technique and its validity as a method of selection

Human resource management and outsourcing

Workplace harassment and bullying: causes and effects and the need for organisations to protect their employees from behavioural excesses

A critical review of the prospects for interactive services to the home and the implications for marketing strategy

A study of the influence of information technology on management development – implementation of IT policy

Has modern technology destroyed customer services within the financial services sector?

How can information technology aid marketing communications?

Preparing for the worst – an investigation into the need for and methods of backing up business computer files

RSI in the workplace: a study of causation and management

The development and relationship of office automation, information technology strategies and their impact on the use of information technology: a case study

A woman's place – an investigation of the factors that facilitate the achievement of equal opportunities

Great British culture versus women in manufacturing

Women in management – the glass ceiling

Opportunity 2000: addressing the barriers to women's progress in organisations – a critical evaluation of current theories and practice

The rise in the number of female entrepreneurs: why is it happening and what problems are they facing?

A comparative study of marketing techniques adopted by body building supplement manufacturers

A consideration of the promotional strategies and tools used in achieving greater sales in retail organisations

A critical evaluation of strategic planning and marketing techniques used in public sector recreation provision

A study of global brands: what makes them and what can break them?

A study on the evolution of the use of target marketing in the media, entertainment and show business

Airline marketing – is there a difference between what business travellers want and what is promoted to them?

An analysis of the marketing methods employed by a professional football club

An investigation into branding within the new premium bottled lager market

An investigation into marketing activity aimed at children

An investigation into the market segmentation: has social group E developed from previous ideas?

An investigation into the marketing techniques employed by the motor industry in the UK

Marketing by general practitioner fundholders

Marketing in the NHS – is it an alien concept?

Marketing is an essential aspect of successful tourism. How can competitive analysis of similar companies improve one's product and maximise sales

Marketing of non-profit-making organisations

Marketing the changing face of licensed premises

Marketing tourism in urban areas – a comparison of Gloucester and Bradford

Benefits and disbenefits of press and radio advertising to small businesses

Brands marketing, positioning – launching of new brands

Can a leading retailer rely on its name to sell pensions?

Do marketers exploit customers through manipulative marketing?

Measurement of results within the marketing mix. Can public relations be accurately compared with the other marketing disciplines?

Employee rights in the event of transfers of undertakings: an examination of local government

Global advertising: a review

How can small businesses produce an effective marketing plan given the limited resources available?

How effective is billboard advertising within the UK?

How has Eurotunnel advertised and has this been successful in affecting people's perceptions of cross-Channel travel?

How marketers use sex to sell advertising

Implications of cross-national differences for personnel policies within the single European market, with particular reference to graduate recruitment

Justification for marketing in the food industry

The effectiveness of marketing and PR in the manufacturing industry and the place of PR in marketing mix

What are the problems of marketing a 'services' product such as insurance, compared with that of a tangible product?

Why do businesses sponsor sport?

Are quality assurance and total quality management a cost or a benefit for professional service firms?

Benchmarking: a critical evaluation

Is it possible to achieve total quality management and a high level of customer service within a commercial vehicle supplier?

Is there a link between benchmarking and total quality management (TQM)?

Quality initiatives within the insurance industry

Quality management and BS5750 in small to medium manufacturing enterprises

A study of the industrial branch, examining its past, its present and its future

An evaluation of the extent to which language training equips managers better to understand foreign business cultures

An investigation into how the management of technical and cultural change can have an effect on the organisation

An investigation into management buy outs/buy ins within the UK economy

A comparative analysis of offshore companies in Cyprus and the Isle of Man

Compulsory competitive tendering in local government

Could UK export capabilities in the Asian region be improved by gaining an understanding of their national cultures?

Competition in the parcel delivery industry

Funding of NHS and private healthcare

How beneficial is management consultancy to the manufacturing industry?

How have the theories of the quality gurus developed into the standards employed by a pharmaceutical printing firm?

Britain's future within the EU: Is full economic and monetary union in the national interest?

Is the British film industry beyond recovery?

Japanese investment and economic regeneration in South Wales

Selling to the Japanese: a critical evaluation of current theories and practice for successful market entry

The brewing industry – why did the investigation by the Monopolies and Mergers Committee have such a big impact on the industry?

The development of mail order/home shopping: a case study

The flexible organisation: is it a myth or reality?

The impact of charging for sport for 'fun'

Strategy for shareholder value

Survival of the fittest: a comparison between local independent and national/international music outlets

What are the consequences of the trade war in the yellow fat market?

Will a single European currency benefit British business?

APPENDIX 2

The Harvard and footnotes systems of referencing

Three points are important when referencing:

- credit must be given when quoting or citing other work;
- adequate information must be provided in the bibliography to enable a reader to locate the references;
- referencing should be as consistent as possible.

THE HARVARD SYSTEM

Referencing in the text

The Harvard system, which we have adopted in this book, uses the author's name and date of publication to identify cited documents within the text.

- For example: It has been shown that . . . (Saunders, 1993).
- When referring generally to work by different authors on the subject, place the authors in alphabetical order: (Baker, 1991; Lewis, 1991; Thornhill, 1993).
- When referring to dual authors: (Saunders and Cooper, 1993).
- When there are more than two authors: (Bryce et al., 1991).
- For corporate authors, for instance a company report: (Hanson Trust plc, 1990).
- For publications with no obvious author, for example the Employment Gazette: (Employment Gazette, 1993).
- When referring to different publications by the same author then the works should be ordered by date in ascending order: (Lewis, 1989, 1991).
- To differentiate between publications by the same author in the same year use a, b, c etc.: (Forster, 1991a). Make sure that this is consistent throughout the research project and corresponds with the bibliography.
- To reference an author referred to by another author where the original publication has not been read: (Granovetter, 1974, cited by Saunders, 1993). In this case the author who cites and the original document's author should both appear in the bibliography.

- Only use author's initials to differentiate between authors with the same surname.

- Quotations should be placed in inverted commas and the page number given, for example: the Harvard method of referencing provides a simple way of coping with the main text and also bibliographies (Bell, 1993: 28).

Referencing in the bibliography

In the bibliography the referenced publications are listed alphabetically by author's name and all authors' surnames and initials are listed in full. If there is more than one work by the same author, these are listed chronologically.

- An example of a reference to a book would be:
Saunders, M.N.K. and Cooper, S.A. (1993) *Understanding Business Statistics*, London, DP Publications.

- A reference to a book other than the first edition would be:
Morris, C. (1993) *Quantitative Approaches to Business Studies* (3rd edn), London, Pitman Publishing.

- A reference to a book with no obvious author would be:
Department of Trade and Industry (1992) *The Single Market. Europe Open for Professions UK Implementation*, London, HMSO.

- A reference to a particular chapter in a book would be:
Robson, C. (1993) *Real World Research*, Oxford, Blackwell, Chapter 3.

- A reference to a particular chapter in an edited book would be:
Craig, P.B. (1991) 'Designing and Using Mail Questionnaires', in Smith, N.C. and Dainty, P. (eds) *The Management Research Handbook*, London, Routledge, pp. 181–89.

- An example of a reference to an article in a journal (in this example volume 20, part 6) would be:
Brewster, C. and Bournois, F. (1992) 'Human Resource Management: A European Perspective', *Personnel Review*, 20: 6, 4–13.

- A reference to an article in a (trade) journal with no obvious author would be:
Local Government Chronicle (1993) 'Westminster poised for return to AMA fold', *Local Government Chronicle*, 5 November, 5.

- A reference to an item found on the Internet would also include the fact that it was accessed on-line, the date of access and the full Internet address:
Jenkins, M. and Bailey, L. (1995) 'The role of learning centre staff in supporting student learning', *Journal of Learning and Teaching*, 1: 1, Spring [online] [cited 29 Mar 1996] Available from Internet

<URL:http://www.chelt.ac.uk/cwis/pubs/jolt/issue 1.1/page 2.htm>

FOOTNOTES

Referencing in the text

When using *footnotes*, references within the research report are shown by a number.

■ For example: Recent research[1] indicates that . . .

This number refers directly to the references.

Referencing in the references

These list the referenced publications sequentially in the order they are referred to in your research report. This can be useful as it enables you to include comments and footnotes as well as the references (Jankowicz, 1995).

■ The layout of individual references in the bibliography is the same as that for the Harvard system.

■ If you find that you refer to the same item more than once you can use standard bibliographic abbreviations to save repeating in full the reference (Table A2.1).

■ The publications referred to only include those you have cited in your report. They should therefore be headed 'References' rather than 'Bibliography'.

Abbreviation	Explanation
op. cit. (*opere citato*)	Meaning in the work cited. This refers to a work previously referenced and so you must give the author and date and if necessary the page number: Robson (1993) op. cit. pp. 23–4.
loc. cit. (*loco citato*)	Meaning in the place cited. This refers to the same page of a work previously referenced and so you must give the author and date: Robson (1993) loc. cit.
ibid. (*ibidem*)	Meaning the same work given immediately before. This refers to the work referenced immediately before and replaces all details of the previous reference other than a page number if necessary: ibid.

Table A2.1 Bibliographic abbreviations

APPENDIX 3

Ethical principles and guidelines for research with human participants

Documentation concerning ethics and ethical codes produced by the British Sociological Association and the British Psychological Society is gratefully acknowledged, as is information supplied by Jonathan Elcock.

1 Introduction

These principles and guidelines relate to social research undertaken with human participants and should be followed by all researchers within the College, whether they are members of staff, postgraduate or undergraduate students. Faculties or Departments may operate their own specific guidelines or codes of practice, and researchers are advised to check with their Faculty Office.

2 Process of approval

2.1 Members of staff

The appropriate Faculty Research Committee is responsible for ensuring that staff are aware of, and agree to abide by, the guidelines.

2.2 Research students

All research students are required to signal their adherence to the College's ethical guidelines on the registration form RD1, as is the supervisory team for each research degree programme. The Faculty Research Director signs the form to confirm that student and supervisors are aware of, and agree to abide by the guidelines.

2.3 All taught students

The Course Tutor is responsible for ensuring that all taught students are aware of, and agree to abide by the guidelines.

3 General responsibilities

3.1 Towards research participants

Researchers have a responsibility to ensure as far as possible that the physical, social and psychological well-being of their research participants is not detrimentally affected by the research, and research relationships should be characterised, whenever possible, by trust.

3.2 Towards other researchers

Researchers should avoid, wherever possible, actions which may have deleterious consequences for other researchers or which might undermine the reputation of their discipline. Research directors should bear in mind their responsibilities towards members of their research teams and should aim to anticipate and guard against the possible harmful consequences of the research for team members.

4 Informed consent

4.1 Research should be based, as far as possible and practicable, on the freely given informed consent of those under study. However, it is recognised that it some cases it may be necessary to employ covert methods should these constitute the only means to obtain the required data, in which case the researcher should refer to section 5 below.

4.2 It is the responsibility of the researcher to explain as fully as possible, and in terms meaningful to the participants: the aims and nature of the research, who is undertaking it, who is funding it, its likely duration, why it is being undertaken, the possible consequences of the research, and how the results are to be disseminated.

4.3 The power imbalance between researcher and researched should be addressed. Care should be taken to ensure that as far as possible the latter are not pressurised into participation. Research participants should be aware of their right to refuse participation whenever and for whatever reason and should not be given the impression that they are required to participate. It should also be recognised that research may involve a lengthy data-gathering period and that it may be necessary to regard consent not as obtained once and for all, but subject to renegotiation over time.

4.4 The researcher should explain how far research participants will be afforded anonymity and confidentiality and participants should have the option of rejecting the use of data-gathering devices such as tape-recorders and video cameras.

4.5 If there is a likelihood of data being shared with or divulged to other researchers, the potential uses of the data should be discussed with the participants and their agreement to such use should be obtained.

4.6 Where access to a research setting is gained via a 'gatekeeper', researchers should also obtain the informed consent of research participants, while at the same time taking account of the gatekeeper's interests. It should be borne in mind that the relationship between research participant and gatekeeper may well continue long after the research has been undertaken.

4.7 Where research participants are young children or other vulnerable groups such as elderly, disabled or sick people or people with learning difficulties, whose understanding is impaired in some way so that they are unable to give full informed consent, it may be necessary to use a proxy in order to gather data. In this case great care must be taken not to intrude upon the privacy of the vulnerable participants. The researcher should consult relevant professionals, parents/guardians and relatives, as appropriate. Researchers should attempt to obtain the informed consent of children and their parents and in relation to schoolchildren those in *loco parentis*.

4.8 In addition to obtaining the informed consent of those under study, researchers should attempt to anticipate and guard against the possible harmful consequences of their research for participants.

5 Covert research

5.1 While it is recognised that there is a continuum of covert–overt research and therefore difficulty in defining research as entirely covert or overt, researchers should endeavour, wherever possible and practicable to avoid the use of deception in their research methods, as this violates the principle of informed consent and may invade the privacy of those under study, particularly in non-public spaces. If it appears that the employment of covert research methods is the only means to obtain the required data, the researcher should seek to assure her/himself that no other non-deceptive research methods could be employed to achieve the research objectives.

5.2 Covert research in non-public spaces or experimental manipulation of research participants without their knowledge should be a last resort when it is impossible to use other methods to obtain the required data. It is particularly important in such cases to safeguard the anonymity of participants.

5.3 If covert methods are employed and informed consent has not been obtained prior to the research, every attempt should be made to obtain this *post hoc*.

6 Confidentiality and anonymity

6.1 The anonymity and privacy of research participants should be respected and personal information relating to participants should be kept confidential and secure. Researchers must comply with the provisions of the Data Protection Act and should consider whether it is proper or appropriate even to record certain kinds of sensitive information.

6.2 Where possible, threats to the confidentiality and anonymity of research data should be anticipated by researchers and normally the identities and research records of participants should be kept confidential, whether or not an explicit pledge of confidentiality has been given.

6.3 Whilst the researcher should take every practicable measure to ensure the confidentiality and anonymity of research participants, s/he should also take care not to give unrealistic assurances or guarantees of confidentiality. Research participants with easily identifiable characteristics or positions within an organisation should be reminded that it may be difficult to disguise their identity totally without distorting the data.

J A Collinson

APPENDIX 4

Calculating the minimum sample size

In some situations, such as experimental research, it is necessary for you to calculate the precise *minimum sample size* you require. This calculation assumes that data will be collected from all cases in the sample and is based on:

- how confident you need to be that the estimate is accurate (the level of confidence in the estimate);
- how accurate the estimate needs to be (the margin of error that can be tolerated);
- the proportion of responses you expect to have some particular attribute.

Provided that you know the level of confidence and the margin of error, it is relatively easy to estimate the proportion of responses you expect to have a particular attribute. To do this ideally you need to collect a pilot sample of about 30 observations and from this infer the likely proportion for your main survey. It is therefore important that the pilot sample uses the same methods as your main survey. Alternatively, you might have undertaken a very similar survey and so already have a reasonable idea of the likely proportion. If you do not, then you need to either make an informed guess or assume that 50% of the sample will have the specified attribute – the worst scenario. Most surveys will involve collecting data on more than one attribute. DeVaus (1991: 72) argues that for such multi-purpose surveys you should 'play safe' and determine the sample size on the basis of those variables where there is likely to be 'greatest diversity in the sample'.

Once you have all the information you substitute it into the formula:

$$n = p\% \times q\% \times \left(\frac{z}{e\%}\right)^2$$

where n is the minimum sample size required

   $p\%$ is the proportion belonging to the specified category

   $q\%$ is the proportion not belonging to the specified category

   z is the z value corresponding to the level of confidence required (see table A4.1)

   $e\%$ is the margin of error required

Level of confidence	z value
90% certain	1.65
95% certain	1.96
99% certain	2.57

Table A4.1 Levels of confidence and associated z values

Where your population is less than 10 000 a smaller sample size can be used without affecting the accuracy. This is called the *adjusted minimum sample size*. It is calculated using the following formula:

$$n' = \frac{n}{1 + \left(\frac{n}{N}\right)}$$

where n' is the adjusted minimum sample size
n is the minimum sample size (as calculated above)
N is the total population

WORKED EXAMPLE: *Calculating the minimum sample size*

To answer a research question you need to estimate the proportion of a total population of 4000 home care clients who receive a visit from their home care assistant at least once a week. You have been told that you need to be 95% certain that the 'estimate' is accurate (the level of confidence in the estimate); this corresponds to a z score of 1.96 (Table 4.1). You have also been told that your 'estimate' needs to be accurate to within plus or minus 5% of the true percentage (the margin of error that can be tolerated).

You still need to estimate the proportion of responses who receive a visit from their home care assistant at least once a week. From your pilot survey you discover that 12 out of the 30 clients receive a visit at least once a week, in other words 40% belong to the specified category. This means that 60% do not.

These figures can then be substituted into the formula:

$$n = 40 \times 60 \times \left(\frac{1.96}{5}\right)^2$$

$$= 2400 \times (0.392)^2$$
$$= 2400 \times 0.154$$
$$= 369.6$$

Your minimum sample size is therefore 370 returns.

As the total population of home care clients is 4000 the adjusted minimum sample size can now be calculated:

$$n' = \cfrac{369.6}{1 + \left(\cfrac{369.6}{4000}\right)}$$

$$= \frac{369.6}{1 + 0.092}$$

$$= \frac{369.6}{1.092}$$

$$= 338.46$$

Due to the small total population you only need a minimum sample size of 339. However, this assumes a response rate of 100%.

Reference

deVaus, D.A. (1991) *Surveys in Social Research* (3rd edn), London, UCL Press and Allen & Unwin.

APPENDIX 5

Random sampling numbers

78 41	11 62	72 18	66 69	58 71	31 90	51 36	78 09	41 00
70 50	58 19	68 26	75 69	04 00	25 29	16 72	35 73	55 85
32 78	14 47	01 55	10 91	83 21	13 32	59 53	03 38	79 32
71 60	20 53	86 78	50 57	42 30	73 48	68 09	16 35	21 87
35 30	15 57	99 96	33 25	56 43	65 67	51 45	37 99	54 89
09 08	05 41	66 54	01 49	97 34	38 85	85 23	34 62	60 58
02 59	34 51	98 71	31 54	28 85	23 84	49 07	33 71	17 88
20 13	44 15	22 95	98 97	60 02	85 07	17 57	20 51	01 67
36 26	70 11	63 81	27 31	79 71	08 11	87 74	85 53	86 78
00 30	62 19	81 68	86 10	65 61	62 22	17 22	96 83	56 37
38 41	14 59	53 03	52 86	21 88	55 87	85 59	14 90	74 87
18 89	40 84	71 04	09 82	54 44	94 23	83 89	04 59	38 29
34 38	85 56	80 74	22 31	26 39	65 63	12 38	45 75	30 35
55 90	21 71	17 88	20 08	57 64	17 93	22 34	00 55	09 78
81 43	53 96	96 88	36 86	04 33	31 40	18 71	06 00	51 45
59 69	13 03	38 31	77 08	71 20	23 28	92 43	92 63	21 74
60 24	47 44	73 93	64 37	64 97	19 82	27 59	24 20	00 04
17 04	93 46	05 70	20 95	42 25	33 95	78 80	07 57	86 58
09 55	42 30	27 05	27 93	78 10	69 11	29 56	29 79	28 66
46 69	28 64	81 02	41 89	12 03	31 20	25 16	79 93	28 22
28 94	00 91	16 15	35 12	68 93	23 71	11 55	64 56	76 95
59 10	06 29	83 84	03 68	97 65	59 21	58 54	61 59	30 54
41 04	70 71	05 56	76 66	57 86	29 30	11 31	56 76	24 13
09 81	81 80	73 10	10 23	26 29	61 15	50 00	76 37	60 16
91 55	76 68	06 82	05 33	06 75	92 35	82 21	78 15	19 43
82 69	36 73	58 69	10 92	31 14	21 08	13 78	56 53	97 77
03 59	65 34	32 06	63 43	38 04	65 30	32 82	57 05	33 95
03 96	30 87	81 54	69 39	95 69	95 69	89 33	78 90	30 07
39 91	27 38	20 90	41 10	10 80	59 68	93 10	85 25	59 25
89 93	92 10	59 40	26 14	27 47	39 51	46 70	86 85	76 02
99 16	73 21	39 05	03 36	87 58	18 52	61 61	02 92	07 24
93 13	20 70	42 59	77 69	35 59	71 80	61 95	82 96	48 84
47 32	87 68	97 86	28 51	61 21	33 02	79 65	59 49	89 93
09 75	58 00	72 49	36 58	19 45	30 61	87 74	43 01	93 91
63 24	15 65	02 05	32 92	45 61	35 43	67 64	94 45	95 66
33 58	69 42	25 71	74 31	88 80	04 50	22 60	72 01	27 88
23 25	22 78	24 88	68 48	83 60	53 59	73 73	82 43	82 66
07 17	77 20	79 37	50 08	29 79	55 13	51 90	36 77	68 69
16 07	31 84	57 22	29 54	35 14	22 22	22 60	72 15	40 90
67 90	79 28	62 83	44 96	87 70	40 64	27 22	60 19	52 54
79 52	74 68	69 74	31 75	80 59	29 28	21 69	15 97	35 88
69 44	31 09	16 38	92 82	12 25	10 57	81 32	76 71	31 61
09 47	57 04	54 00	78 75	91 99	26 20	36 19	53 29	11 55
74 78	09 25	95 80	25 72	88 85	76 02	29 89	70 78	93 84

Source: Morris (1993), reproduced by permission

INDEX

······················

Making Sense
of the Social World
Methods of Investigation THIRD EDITION

DANIEL F. CHAMBLISS
Hamilton College

RUSSELL K. SCHUTT
University of Massachusetts, Boston

PINE FORGE PRESS
An Imprint of SAGE Publications, Inc.
Los Angeles • London • New Delhi • Singapore • Washington DC

For information:

Pine Forge Press
A SAGE Publications Company
2455 Teller Road
Thousand Oaks, California 91320
E-mail: order@sagepub.com

SAGE Publications Ltd.
1 Oliver's Yard
55 City Road
London EC1Y 1SP
United Kingdom

SAGE Publications India Pvt. Ltd.
1 Mohan Cooperative Industrial Area
Mathura Road, New Delhi 110 044
India

SAGE Publications Asia-Pacific Pte. Ltd.
33 Pekin Street #02-01
Far East Square
Singapore 048763

Printed in the United States of America.

Library of Congress Cataloging-in-Publication Data

Chambliss, Daniel F.
Making sense of the social world: Methods of investigation/Daniel F. Chambliss,
Russell K. Schutt—3rd ed.
    p. cm.
Includes bibliographical references and index.
ISBN 978-1-4129-6939-0 (pbk.)
    1. Social problems—Research. 2. Social sciences—Research. I. Schutt, Russell K. II. Title.

HN29.C468 2009
361.1072—dc22   2008041069

Printed on acid-free paper

09   10   11   12   13   10   9   8   7   6   5   4   3   2   1

Acquiring Editor:	Jerry Westby
Editorial Assistant:	Eve Oettinger
Production Editor:	Sarah K. Quesenberry
Copy Editor:	Paula L. Fleming
Proofreader:	Jenifer Kooiman
Indexer:	Sheila Bodell
Typesetter:	C&M Digitals (P) Ltd.
Cover Designer:	Edgar Abarca
Marketing Manager:	Jennifer Reed Banando

Making Sense
of the Social World

THIRD EDITION

RELATED TITLES IN RESEARCH METHODS AND STATISTICS FROM PINE FORGE PRESS

Investigating the Social World: The Process and Practice of Research, Sixth Edition, by Russell K. Schutt

Investigating the Social World: The Process and Practice of Research, Sixth Edition, With SPSS Student Version 16.0, by Russell K. Schutt

The Practice of Research in Social Work, Second Edition, by Rafael J. Engel and Russell K. Schutt

The Practice of Research in Criminology and Criminal Justice, Third Edition, by Ronet K. Bachman and Russell K. Schutt

Fundamentals of Research in Criminology and Criminal Justice, by Ronet K. Bachman and Russell K. Schutt

Designing Surveys: A Guide to Decisions and Procedures, Second Edition, by Ronald F. Czaja and Johnny Blair

A Guide to Field Research, Second Edition, by Carol A. Bailey

Adventures in Social Research, Sixth Edition, by Earl Babbie, Fred Halley, and Jeanne Zaino

Adventures in Social Research With SPSS Student Version 14.0, Sixth Edition, by Earl Babbie, Fred Halley, and Jeanne Zaino

Adventures in Criminal Justice Research, Fourth Edition, by Kim Logio, George Dowdall, Earl Babbie, and Fred Halley

Social Statistics for a Diverse Society, Fifth Edition, by Chava Frankfort-Nachmias and Anna Leon-Guerrero

Social Statistics for a Diverse Society, Fifth Edition, With SPSS Student Version 16.0, by Chava Frankfort-Nachmias and Anna Leon-Guerrero

OTHER PINE FORGE PRESS TITLES OF INTEREST

Aging, Sixth Edition, by Harry R. Moody

Diversity and Society, Second Edition, by Joseph Healey

The McDonaldization of Society, Fifth Edition, by George Ritzer

Our Social World, Second Edition, by Jeanne Ballantine and Keith Roberts

Production of Reality, Fourth Edition, by Jodi O'Brien

Race, Ethnicity, Gender, and Class, Fifth Edition, by Joseph Healey

Second Thoughts, Fourth Edition, by Janet Ruane and Karen Cerulo

Social Problems, Second Edition, by Anna Leon-Guerrero

Sociology: Architecture of Everyday Life, Seventh Edition, by David Newman

The Sociology of Religion by George Lundskow

Brief Contents

ON THE STUDY SITE

Detailed Contents

ON THE STUDY SITE

About the Authors

Daniel F. Chambliss, PhD, is the Eugene M. Tobin Distinguished Professor of Sociology at Hamilton College in Clinton, New York, where he has taught since 1981. He received his PhD from Yale University in 1982; later that year, his thesis research received the American Sociological Association's Medical Sociology Dissertation Prize. In 1988, he published the book *Champions: The Making of Olympic Swimmers,* which received the Book of the Year Prize from the U.S. Olympic Committee. In 1989, he received the American Sociology Association's Theory Prize for work on organizational excellence based on his swimming research. Recipient of both Fulbright and Rockefeller Foundation fellowships, Professor Chambliss published his second book, *Beyond Caring: Hospitals, Nurses, and the Social Organization of Ethics,* in 1996; for that work, he was awarded the ASA's Elliot Freidson Prize in Medical Sociology. His research and teaching interests include organizational analysis, higher education, social theory, and comparative research methods. He is currently Director of the Project for Assessment of Liberal Arts Education at Hamilton College, funded by the Andrew W. Mellon Foundation, and is a member of the Middle States Commission on Higher Education.

Russell K. Schutt, PhD, is Professor of Sociology at the University of Massachusetts, Boston, where he received the 2007 Chancellor's Award for Distinguished Service. Since 1990, he has also been Lecturer on Sociology in the Department of Psychiatry (Beth Israel-Deaconess Medical Center) at the Harvard Medical School. He completed his BA, MA, and PhD degrees at the University of Illinois at Chicago and was a Postdoctoral Fellow in the Sociology of Social Control Training Program at Yale University. In addition to six editions of the text on which this brief edition is based, *Investigating the Social World: The Process and Practice of Research,* and two other coauthored versions—for the fields of social work (with Ray Engel) and criminal justice (with Ronet Bachman)—he is the author of *Organization in a Changing Environment,* coeditor of *The Organizational Response to Social Problems,* and coauthor of *Responding to the Homeless: Policy and Practice.* He has authored and coauthored numerous journal articles, book chapters, and research reports on homelessness, mental health, organizations, law, and teaching research methods. He recently directed a large translational research project at the Harvard Medical School for the Women's Health Network program of the Massachusetts Department of Public Health and a project funded by the National Cancer Institute, "Educating Underserved Communities About Cancer Clinical Trials." His primary research focuses on social factors that shape the impact of housing, employment, and services for severely mentally ill persons and on the service preferences of homeless persons and service personnel. He has also studied influences on well-being, satisfaction, and cognitive functioning; processes of organizational change and the delivery of case management; decision making in juvenile justice and in union admissions; political participation; media representations of mental illness; and HIV/AIDS prevention.

Preface

If you have been eager to begin your first course in social science research methods, we are happy to affirm that you've come to the right place. We have written this book to give you just what you were hoping for—an introduction to research that is interesting, thoughtful, and thorough.

But what if you've been looking toward this course with dread, putting it off for longer than you should, wondering why all this "scientific" stuff is required of students who are really seeking something quite different in their major? Well, even if you had just some of these thoughts, we want you to know that we've had your concerns in mind, too. In *Making Sense of the Social World,* we introduce social research with a book that combines professional sophistication with unparalleled accessibility: Any college student will be able to read and understand it—even enjoy it—while experienced social science researchers, we hope, can learn from our integrated approach to the fundamentals. And whatever your predisposition to research methods, we think you'll soon realize that understanding them is critical to being an informed citizen in our complex, fast-paced social world.

▣ TEACHING AND LEARNING GOALS

Our book will introduce you to social science research methods that can be used to study diverse social processes and to improve our understanding of social issues. Each chapter illustrates important principles and techniques in research methods with interesting examples drawn from formal social science investigations and everyday experiences.

Even if you never conduct a formal social science investigation after you complete this course, you will find that improved understanding of research methods will sharpen your critical faculties. You will become a more informed consumer, and thus a better user, of the results of the many social science studies that shape social policy and popular beliefs. Throughout this book, you will learn what questions to ask when critiquing a research study and how to evaluate the answers. You can begin to sharpen your critical teeth on the illustrative studies throughout the book. Exercises at the end of each chapter will allow you to find, discuss, critique, and actually do similar research.

If you are already charting a course toward a social science career, or if you decide to do so after completing this course, we aim to give you enough "how to" instruction so that you can design your own research projects. We also offer "doing" exercises at the end of each chapter that will help you try out particular steps in the research process.

But our goal is not just to turn you into a more effective research critic or a good research technician. We do not believe that research methods can be learned by rote or applied mechanically. Thus, you will learn the benefits and liabilities of each major research approach as well as the rationale for using a combination of methods in some situations. You will also come to appreciate why the results of particular research studies must be interpreted within the context of prior research and through the lens of social theory.

ORGANIZATION OF THE BOOK

The first three chapters introduce the why and how of research in general. Chapter 1 shows how research has helped us understand how social relations have changed in recent years and the impact of these changes. Chapter 2 illustrates the basic stages of research with studies of domestic violence, Olympic swimmers, and environmental disasters. Chapter 3 introduces the ethical considerations that should guide your decisions throughout the research process. The next three chapters discuss how to evaluate the way researchers design their measures (Chapter 4), draw their samples (Chapter 5), and justify their statements about causal connections (Chapter 6).

As we present the logic of testing causal connections in Chapter 6, we also present the basics of the experimental designs that provide the strongest tests for causality. In Chapter 7, we cover the most common method of data collection in sociology—surveys—and in Chapter 8, we present the basic statistical methods that are used to analyze the results of the quantitative data that often are collected in experiments and surveys. Here we examine the results of the 2006 General Social Survey to see how these statistics are used.

Chapters 9 and 10 shift the focus from strategies for collecting and analyzing quantitative data to strategies for collecting and analyzing qualitative data. In Chapter 9, we focus on the basic methods of collecting qualitative data: participant observation, intensive interviews, and focus groups. In Chapter 10, we review the logic of qualitative data analysis and several specific approaches: ethnography, ethnomethodology, narrative analysis, conversation analysis, and grounded theory. Chapter 11 explains how you can combine different methods to evaluate social programs. Chapter 12 covers the review of prior research, the development of research proposals, and the writing and reporting of research results.

DISTINCTIVE FEATURES OF THIS EDITION

In making changes for this edition, we feel we have advanced even further in pursuit of our goal of making research methods one of your most enjoyable and engaging courses. We have incorporated valuable suggestions from many faculty reviewers and students who have used the book over the several years since it was first released. As in the previous two editions, this book has also benefited from advances in its parent volume, Russell Schutt's *Investigating the Social World: The Process and Practice of Research* (now in its sixth edition).

A New Chapter on Research Ethics—Chapter 3 provides a thorough review of ethical issues in research, including an introduction to the role of the institutional review board. Our review of controversies concerning Stanley Milgram's research on obedience to authority will make ethics issues "come alive."

A New Chapter on Evaluation Research—Chapter 11 introduces the decisions that researchers must make when designing evaluations of social programs, as well as the different types of evaluation research designs. Our placement of this chapter after the others on data collection and analysis reflects the fact that evaluation research projects often use all the other research methods.

New End-of-Chapter Material—We have revised many discussion questions to ensure that they will facilitate in-class discussion, and we have added new questions on research ethics after each chapter.

Updated Appendix on Secondary Data Resources—Appendix B on sources of secondary data has been updated.

Updated Information on the Impact of Cell Phones and the Web on Survey Response—Chapter 7 on survey research provides the latest information on the impact of increasing use of cell phones and the Web on survey practice.

   As in the first two editions, our text also offers other distinctive features:

Brief Examples of Social Research—In each chapter, these illustrate particular points and show how research techniques are used to answer important social questions. Whatever your particular substantive interests in social science, you'll find some interesting studies that will arouse your curiosity.

Integrated Treatment of Causality and Experimental Design—We have combined the discussions of causation and experimental design so we could focus on the issues that are most often encountered in research in sociology, criminal justice, education, social work, communications, and political science.

Realistic Coverage of Ethical Concerns and Ethical Decision Making—Like the parent volume, *Investigating the Social World,* this text presents ethical issues that arise in the course of using each method of data collection, as well as comprehensive coverage of research ethics in a new chapter.

Engaging End-of-Chapter Exercises—We organize the exercises under the headings of "discussing," "finding," "critiquing," and "doing" and end with questions about "ethics." New exercises have been added, and some of the old ones have been omitted. The result is a set of learning opportunities that should greatly facilitate the learning process.

Software-Based Learning Opportunities—The text's Web site (**http://www.pineforge.com/ mssw3**) includes review exercises to help you master the concepts of social research, a set of articles that provide examples of different methods, and a portion of the 2006 General Social Survey so you can try out quantitative data analysis (if your school provides access to the SPSS statistical package). Appendix C provides an introduction to SPSS.

Aids to Effective Study—Lists of main points and key terms provide quick summaries at the end of each chapter. In addition, key terms are highlighted in boldface type when first introduced and defined in the text. Definitions of key terms can also be found in the glossary/index at the end of the book. The Pine Forge Press Web site (**http://www .pineforge.com/mssw3**) offers more review questions. An instructor's manual includes more exercises that have been specially designed for collaborative group work in and outside of class. Appendix A, Finding Information, provides up-to-date information about using the Internet, and Appendix B lists secondary data sources.

Acknowledgments

First, we would like to thank Jerry Westby, senior editor at Pine Forge Press, our main managerial contact and source of encouragement as we developed our text. Other members of the Pine Forge Press and Sage team helped in multiple ways: Denise Simon provided expert assistance with the review of the reviews, Sarah Quesenberry smoothly guided the manuscript through the production process, and Paula L. Fleming did a superb job of copyediting.

The reviewers for this edition helped us to realize the potential for the revision. We are very grateful for the wisdom and critical acumen of the following:

Cristina Bodinger-deUriarte, California State University–Los Angeles

Matthew M. Caverly, University of Florida

Jin Young Choi, Sam Houston State University

Kellie J. Hagewen, University of Nebraska–Lincoln

Jerome L. Himmelstein, Amherst College

Karen McCue, University of New Mexico

Kate Peirce, Texas State University

Travis N. Ridout, Washington State University

Nick Sanyal, University of Idaho

Steve Swinford, Montana State University

Felicia P. Wiltz, Suffolk University

Reviewers of the first edition were the following:

Sandy D. Alvarez, Indiana State University

Julio Borquez, University of Michigan–Dearborn

Matthew W. Brosi, Oklahoma State University

Keith F. Durkin, Ohio Northern University

Juanita M. Firestone, University of Texas at San Antonio

Dena Hanley, University of Akron

Laura Hecht, California State University–Bakersfield

Ann Marie Kinnell, The University of Southern Mississippi

Manfred Kuechler, Hunter College

Vera Lopez, Arizona State University

Ed Nelson, California State University–Fresno

Colin Olson, University of New Mexico

Kristen Zgoba, Rutgers University

Reviewers of the first edition proposal were the following:

Diane C. Bates, Sam Houston State University

Mark Edwards, Oregon State University

David Folz, University of Tennessee–Knoxville

Ann Marie Kinnell, University of Southern Mississippi

Ronald Perry, Arizona State University

Chenyang Xiao, Washington State University

David Zehr, Plymouth State College

We are grateful to Sunshine Hillygus, Director of Harvard University's Program on Survey Research, for sharing with us the latest findings about survey response rates. Elizabeth Schneider's contributions to Appendix A draws on her comparable work with Russ Schutt (her husband) for the sixth edition of *Investigating the Social World*. We thank Megan Reynolds for reviewing the interactive exercises, many of which had been written for the first edition by Kathryn Stoeckert, and we thank VPG Integrated Media for the online programming.

We also have some personal thank-yous:

Dan Chambliss: I wish gratefully to acknowledge the assistance, in many areas, of Marcia Wilkinson, who as typist, transcriber, organizer, and administrative aide and daily conscience is simply irreplaceable. My students at Hamilton College have been a blessing throughout: Chris Takacs helped to design and create several of the new exhibits, solving intellectual problems through graphic displays; Shauna Sweet told me where the book was good and where it wasn't, clarified the regression effect, and showed me how people actually should read contingency tables; Katey Healy-Wurzburg, in one of many moments of intellectual brilliance, explained the underlying rhetorical problem of the ecological fallacy; and Erin Voyik, as a teaching assistant in my Methods class, laid out for me time and again what students do and don't actually understand, and enjoy, about social research methods. Many others, students and colleagues alike, have contributed without recognition; let's just say that all of intellectual life is communal, and we fully appreciate that fact. And finally, I hope that my wife, Susan Morgan, enjoyed, at least vicariously, the thrills I felt in working on this book as much as I enjoyed sharing them with her.

Russ Schutt: I am grateful to the many reviewers of the six editions of *Investigating the Social World,* as well as to the many staff and consultants at Pine Forge Press and Sage Publications who helped to make that text a success. My thanks to Jeff Xavicr, the outstanding graduate student who checked Web exercises and many other materials throughout the text and for the Web site. I also want to express my appreciation to my many research collaborators, with whom I have shared so many fascinating and educational experiences and from whom I have learned so much, and for the many fine students at the University of Massachusetts, Boston, who continue to renew my enthusiasm for quality teaching. Most importantly, I thank my wife, Beth Schneider, for her ongoing support and love, and my daughter, Julia, for being such a marvelous young woman.

Dan and Russ: Finally, Dan wants to say that Russ Schutt is a wonderful coauthor, with whom he is honored to work: totally responsible and respectful, hardworking, serious in his scholarship but without a trace of arrogance. His generous personality has allowed this collaboration to sail along beautifully. Russ adds that Dan is the perfect model of the gentleman and scholar, whose research savvy and keen intelligence are matched to a warm and caring persona. We both like to think that our talents are almost entirely complementary. We are immensely grateful for the chance to work together.

Dan:
To my sweetheart Susan and to the gifts she brought to me—
Sarah, Daniel, Anne, and Rebecca

Russ:
To Beth and Julia

CHAPTER 1

Science, Society, and Social Research

Are social ties weakening in modern society? It's a key question for social scientists. It was a central issue in Emile Durkheim's (1906/1956) studies of European societies around the turn of the last century. It was the focus of David Riesman's (1950, 1961/2000) *The Lonely Crowd,* a study of "organization men," at midcentury. And it's the key question for Robert Putnam's (2000) national best seller, *Bowling Alone.* As you might surmise from the title, Putnam's answer to that question is rather pessimistic; moreover, he identifies so many adverse consequences to "the collapse of American community" that we must hasten to point out that he does suggest that the "collapse" can, with effort, be reversed.

The evidence of weakening social ties in the last decades of the 20th century is substantial. During roughly the last four decades, Putnam (2000:31–32) reports that the rate of voting in U.S. presidential elections declined by 14 percentage points (to 49%), the percentage of voters who had actually done some work for a political party had dropped by almost half (to 2.5%), church attendance slid by about 10 percentage points (to 37%), and union membership plunged to half of its earlier level (to 15%). Even the frequency of having a social evening with neighbors has declined by more than 10 percentage points (to about 50% of single people).

It's the social science research presented in *Bowling Alone* that makes the book's argument so compelling. The argument is not just Robert Putnam's opinion, nor is it a collection of anecdotes obtained from quick "man-on-the-street" media interviews, nor is it what "everyone knows" or what "we've always believed." Instead, Putnam examines a great deal of evidence about social ties and reviews much of the research done by others. In the rest of this chapter, you will learn how Putnam's study and other social science investigations are helping to answer questions about social ties. By the chapter's end, you should know what is "scientific" in social science and appreciate how the methods of science can help us understand the workings of society. You may also find yourself developing new respect for the challenges that the social world presents to even careful social scientists, as you might already realize if you know that the voting rate in presidential elections, which Putnam reported as 48% in 1996, 51% in 2000, 54% in 2004, and 57% in 2008 (Bureau of the Census, 2004–2005:12, 239; Gray, 2004:1; McDonald, 2009).

▥ WHAT IS THE PROBLEM?

You may have your own interests in studying social ties; following are some possible examples:

Improve your own social connections. Perhaps you're transferring to a new school or planning to buy a home in a new community. Maybe you want to help your child develop a more supportive network of friends. Maybe you want to understand what factors create strong marriages so you can have one. Such personal motivations often stimulate social research.

Reverse the decline of social ties in your own community. Community leaders may need information for planning "get out the vote" campaigns; others may want to increase volunteering for community improvement activities—and may hire you to do research on the current state of social ties. Law enforcement agencies may need to understand the bases of social cohesion in gangs or other criminal groups. Policy motivations like these could lead to much social research about social ties.

Understand the consequences of weakening social ties. People with fewer social ties seem to have poorer health, both mental and physical. Communities with weaker social networks seem to have more crime. Organizations with poorer interpersonal relations seem to have less satisfied employees. The desire to identify and understand such consequences is an important academic motivation for research.

How to proceed? What methods should you use, and how much can you trust the conclusions of other studies? Should we turn our sociological backs to the Putnam research because the rate of voting in presidential elections has increased in the 2004 and 2008 elections, reversing the decline that Putnam (2000:35) termed "merely the most visible symptom of a broader disengagement from community life"? It is questions like these that this book will help you to answer.

Consider the topic of social trust—the belief that people can be trusted (an attitude that strengthens social ties). Responses to several surveys indicate that the fraction of the

American population that believes that "most people can be trusted" has dropped from about 55% to about 35%—and plunged to 25% among high school students (Exhibit 1.1). But it turns out that this change is not due to shifts in individual attitudes; instead, the decline in social trust among the population as a whole is due to the lower levels of trust among younger age cohorts. For example, only 50% of people born after 1960 agree that "most people are honest," compared to 75% of those born before 1930 (Putnam, 2000:140–141).

Could you have predicted the results of this survey research? Opinions about the state of social ties can be based on direct experience or on what other people have said or written. Do you see how different people, with different experiences, can come to different conclusions about social issues?

People come to different conclusions about the social world for another reason: It's easy to make errors in logic, particularly when we are analyzing the social world, in which we ourselves are conscious participants. We can call some of these errors "everyday errors,"

| EXHIBIT 1.1 | **Four Decades of Dwindling Trust: U.S. Adults and Teenagers, 1960–1999** |

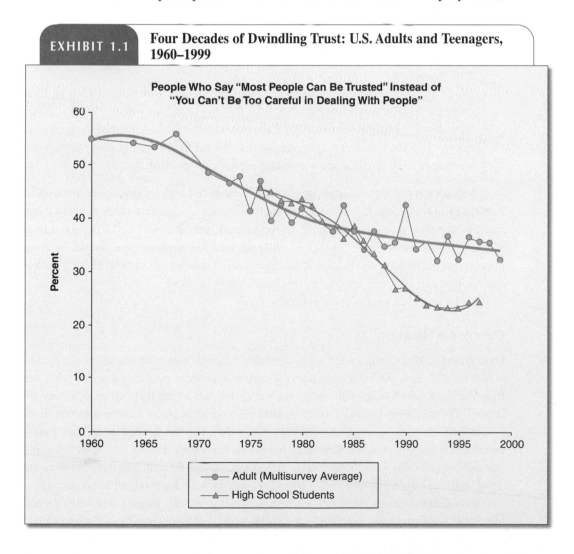

because they occur so frequently in the nonscientific, unreflective conversations that we hear on a daily basis.

Our favorite example of such errors in reasoning comes from a letter to Ann Landers, the newspaper advice columnist (sadly, now deceased). See if you can spot the problems here: The letter was written by a woman who had just moved, with her two pet cats, from an apartment in the city to a house in the country. In the city, she had not let the cats go outside, but she felt guilty about keeping them locked up. Upon arrival at the country house, she let the cats out—but they tiptoed cautiously to the door, looked outside, then went right back into the living room and lay down!

The woman concluded that people shouldn't feel guilty about keeping their cats indoors, since even when they have the chance, cats don't really want to play outside.

Did you spot this person's errors in reasoning?

- *Overgeneralization*—She observed only two cats, both of which were previously confined indoors. Maybe they aren't like most cats.
- *Selective or inaccurate observation*—She observed the cats at the outside door only once. But maybe if she let them out several times, they would become more comfortable with going out.
- *Illogical reasoning*—She assumed that other people feel guilty about keeping their cats indoors. But maybe they don't.
- *Resistance to change*—She was quick to conclude that she had no need to change her approach to the cats. But maybe she just didn't want to change her own routines and was eager to believe that she was managing her cats just fine already.

You don't have to be a scientist or use sophisticated research techniques to avoid these four errors in reasoning. If you recognize them and make a conscious effort to avoid them, you can improve your own reasoning. In the process, you also will be taking the advice of your parents (or minister, teacher, or other adviser) not to stereotype people, to avoid jumping to conclusions, and to look at the big picture. These are the same kinds of mistakes that the methods of social science are designed to help us avoid.

Let's look at each kind of error in turn.

Overgeneralization

Overgeneralization occurs when we unjustifiably conclude that what is true for *some* cases is true for *all* cases. We are always drawing conclusions about people and social processes from our own interactions with them, but sometimes we forget that our experiences are limited. The social (and natural) world is, after all, a complex place. Maybe someone made a wisecrack about the ugly shoes you're wearing today, but that doesn't mean that "everyone is talking about you." Or there may have been two drunk-driving accidents following fraternity parties this year, but by itself, this doesn't mean that all fraternity brothers are drunk drivers. Or maybe you had a boring teacher in your high school chemistry class, but that doesn't mean all chemistry teachers are boring. We can interact with only a small fraction of the individuals who inhabit the social world, especially in a limited span of time;

rarely are they completely typical people. One heavy Internet user found that his online friendships were "much deeper and have better quality" than his other friendships (Parks & Floyd, 1996). Would his experiences generalize to yours? To those of others?

Overgeneralization: Occurs when we unjustifiably conclude that what is true for *some* cases is true for *all* cases

---

Selective or Inaccurate Observation

We also have to avoid **selective** or **inaccurate observation**—choosing to look only at things that are in line with our preferences or beliefs. When we dislike individuals or institutions, it is all too easy to notice their every failing. For example, if we are convinced that heavy Internet users are antisocial, we can find many confirming instances. But what about elderly people who serve as Internet pen pals for grade school children or therapists who deliver online counseling? If we acknowledge only the instances that confirm our predispositions, we are victims of our own selective observation. Exhibit 1.2 depicts the difference between selective observation and overgeneralization.

Selective or inaccurate observation: Choosing to look only at things that are in line with our preferences or beliefs

---

| EXHIBIT 1.2 | The Difference Between Overgeneralization and Selective Observation |

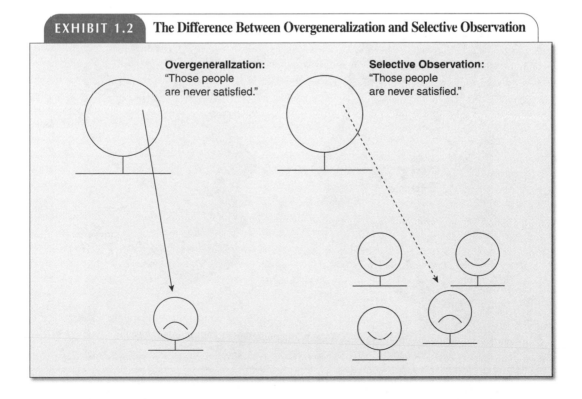

Our observations can also simply be inaccurate. When you were in high school, maybe your mother complained that you were "always staying out late with your friends." Perhaps that was inaccurate; you only stayed out late occasionally. And when you complained that she "yelled" at you, even though her voice never actually increased in volume, that, too, was an inaccurate observation. In social science, we try to be more precise than that.

Such errors often occur in casual conversation and in everyday observation of the world around us. What we think we have seen is not necessarily what we really have seen (or heard, smelled, felt, or tasted). Even when our senses are functioning fully, our minds have to interpret what we have sensed (Humphrey, 1992). The optical illusion in Exhibit 1.3, which can be viewed as either two faces or a vase, should help you realize that even simple visual perception requires interpretation.

Illogical Reasoning

When we prematurely jump to conclusions or argue on the basis of invalid assumptions, we are using **illogical reasoning**. For example, we might think that people who don't have

---

EXHIBIT 1.3   **An Optical Illusion**

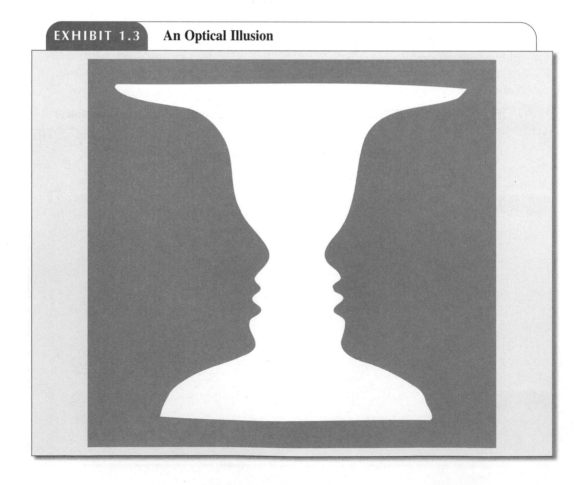

many social ties just aren't friendly, even if we know they have just moved into a community and started a new job. Obviously, that's not logical. On the other hand, an unquestioned assumption that everyone seeks social ties or benefits from them overlooks some important considerations, such as the impact of childhood difficulties on social trust and the exclusionary character of many tightly knit social groups. Logic that seems impeccable to one person can seem twisted to another—but the problem usually is caused by people having different assumptions rather than just failing to "think straight."

Illogical reasoning: The premature jumping to conclusions or arguing on the basis of invalid assumptions

Resistance to Change

Resistance to change, the reluctance to change our ideas in light of new information, is a common problem. After all, we know how tempting it is to make statements that conform to our own needs rather than to the observable facts ("I can't live on that salary!"). It can also be difficult to admit that we were wrong once we have staked out a position on an issue ("I don't want to discuss this anymore."). Excessive devotion to tradition can stifle adaptation to changing circumstances ("This is how we've always done it, that's why."). People often accept the recommendations of those in positions of authority without question ("Only the president has all the facts."). In all of these ways, we often close our eyes to what's actually happening in the world.

Resistance to change: The reluctance to change our ideas in light of new information

🔲 CAN SOCIAL SCIENTISTS SEE THE SOCIAL WORLD MORE CLEARLY?

Can social science do any better? Can we see the social world more clearly if we use the methods of social science? **Science** relies on logical and systematic methods to answer questions, and it does so in a way that allows others to inspect and evaluate its methods. So social scientists develop, refine, apply, and report their understanding of the social world more systematically, or "scientifically," than the general public does.

- **Social science** research methods reduce the likelihood of overgeneralization by using systematic procedures for selecting individuals or groups to study so that the study subjects are representative of the individuals or groups to which we wish to generalize.

- To avoid illogical reasoning, social researchers use explicit criteria for identifying causes and for determining whether these criteria are met in a particular instance.
- Social science methods can reduce the risk of selective or inaccurate observation by requiring that we measure and sample phenomena systematically.
- Scientific methods lessen the tendency to answer questions about the social world from ego-based commitments, excessive devotion to tradition, and/or unquestioning respect for authority. Social scientists insist: Show us the evidence!

Science: A set of logical, systematic, documented methods for investigating nature and natural processes; the knowledge produced by these investigations

Social science: The use of scientific methods to investigate individuals, societies, and social processes; the knowledge produced by these investigations

---

Social Research in Practice

Although all social science research seeks to minimize errors in reasoning, different projects may have different goals. The four most important goals of social research are description, exploration, explanation, and evaluation. Let's look at examples of each.

Description: How Often Do Americans "Neighbor"?

During the last quarter of the 20th century, the annual (biennial since 1996) General Social Survey (GSS) has investigated a wide range of characteristics, attitudes, and behaviors. Each year, more than 1,000 adults in the United States complete GSS phone interviews; many questions are repeated from year to year so that trends can be identified. Robert Putnam often used GSS data in his investigation of social ties in America.

Survey responses indicate that "neighboring" has been declining throughout this period. As indicated in Exhibit 1.4 (Putnam, 2000:106), the percentage of GSS respondents who reported spending "a social evening with someone who lives in your neighborhood . . . about once a month or more often" was 60% for married people in 1975 and about 65% for singles. By 1998, the comparable percentages were 45% for married people and 50% for singles. This is **descriptive research** because the findings simply *describe* differences or variations in social phenomena.

Descriptive research: Research in which social phenomena are defined and described

---

Exploration: How Do Athletic Teams Build Player Loyalty?

Organizations like combat units, surgical teams, and athletic teams must develop intense organizational loyalty among participants if they are to maximize their performance. How do they do it? This question motivated Patricia and Peter Adler (2000) to study college

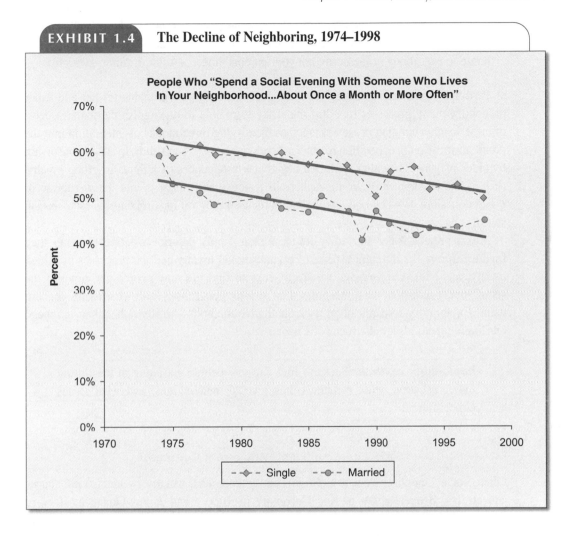

EXHIBIT 1.4 **The Decline of Neighboring, 1974–1998**

People Who "Spend a Social Evening With Someone Who Lives In Your Neighborhood...About Once a Month or More Often"

athletics. So Peter Adler joined his college basketball team as a "team sociologist," while Patti participated in some team activities as his wife and as a professor in the school. They recorded observations and comments at the end of each day for a period of 5 years. They also interviewed at length the coaches and all 38 basketball team members during that period.

Careful and systematic review of their notes led Adler and Adler to conclude that intense organizational loyalty emerged from five processes: domination, identification, commitment, integration, and goal alignment. We won't review each of these processes here, but the following quote indicates how they found the process of integration into a cohesive group to work:

By the time the three months were over [the summer before they started classes] I felt like I was there a year already, I felt so connected to the guys. You've played with them, it's been 130 degrees in the gym, you've elbowed each other, knocked each other around. Now you've felt a relationship, it's a team, a brotherhood type of thing. Everybody's got to eat the same rotten food, go through the same thing, and all you have is each other. So you've got a shared bond, a camaraderie. It's a whole houseful of brothers. And that's home to everybody in the dorm, not your parents' house. (Adler & Adler, 2000:43)

Participating in and observing the team over this long period enabled Adler and Adler to identify many processes like this one. They were able to distinguish particular aspects of these loyalty-building processes, such as identifying three modes of integration into the group: unification in opposition to others, development of group solidarity, and sponsorship by older players. They also identified negative consequences of failures in group loyalty, such as the emergence of an atmosphere of jealousy and mistrust, and the disruption of group cohesion, as when one team member focused only on maximizing his own scoring statistics.

In this project, Adler and Adler did more than simply describe what people did—they tried to *explore* the different aspects of organizational loyalty and the processes by which loyalty was built. **Exploratory research** seeks to find out how people get along in the setting under question, what meanings they give to their actions, and what issues concern them. Exploratory research often uses qualitative methods—words rather than numbers. Qualitative methods are the focus of Chapter 9.

Exploratory research: Seeks to find out how people get along in the setting under question, what meanings they give to their actions, and what issues concern them

---

Explanation: Does Social Context Influence Adolescent Outcomes?

Often, social scientists want to *explain* social phenomena, usually by identifying causes and effects. Bruce Rankin at Koc University in Turkey and James Quane at Harvard (Rankin & Quane, 2002) analyzed data collected in a large survey of African American mothers and their adolescent children to test the effect of social context on adolescent outcomes. Their source of data was a study funded by the MacArthur Foundation, *Youth Achievement and the Structure of Inner City Communities,* in which face-to-face interviews were conducted with more than 636 youth living in 62 poor and mixed-income urban Chicago neighborhoods.

Explanatory research like this seeks to identify causes and effects of social phenomena and to predict how one phenomenon will change or vary in response to variation in another phenomenon. Rankin and Quane (2002) were most concerned with determining the relative importance of three different aspects of social context—neighborhoods, families, and peers—on adolescent outcomes (both positive and negative). To make this determination, they had to conduct their analysis in a way that allowed them to separate the effects of neighborhood characteristics, like residential stability and economic disadvantage, from parental involvement in child rearing and other family features, as well as from peer influence. They found that neighborhood characteristics affect youth outcomes primarily by influencing the extent of parental monitoring and the quality of peer groups.

Explanatory research: Seeks to identify causes and effects of social phenomena and to predict how one phenomenon will change or vary in response to variation in another phenomenon

---

Evaluation: Does More Social Capital Result in More Community Participation?

The "It's Our Neighbourhood's Turn" project (Onze Burrt aan Zet, or OBAZ) in the city of Enschede, the Netherlands, was one of a series of projects initiated by the Dutch Interior and Kingdom Relations ministry to increase the quality of life and safety of individuals in the most deprived neighborhoods in the Netherlands. In the fall of 2001, residents in three of the city's poorest neighborhoods were informed that their communities had received funds to use for community improvement and that residents had to be actively involved in formulating and implementing the improvement plans (Lelieveldt 2003:1). Political scientist Herman Lelieveldt (2004:537) at the University of Twente, the Netherlands, and others then surveyed community residents to learn about their social relations and their level of local political participation; a second survey was conducted 1 year after the project began.

Lelieveldt wanted to *evaluate* the impact of the OBAZ project—to see whether the "livability and safety of the neighborhood" could be improved by taking steps like those Putnam (2000:408) recommended to increase "social capital," meaning that citizens would spend more time connecting with their neighbors

It turned out that residents who had higher levels of social capital participated more in community political processes. However, not every form of social capital made much of a difference. Neighborliness—the extent to which citizens are engaged in networks with their neighbors—was an important predictor of political participation, as was a feeling of obligation to participate. By contrast, a sense of trust in others (something that Putnam emphasizes) was not consistently important (Lelieveldt 2004:535, 547–548): Those who got more involved in the OBAZ political process tended to *distrust* their neighbors. When researchers focus their attention on social programs like the OBAZ project, they are conducting **evaluation research**—research that describes or identifies the impact of social policies and programs.

Evaluation research: Research that describes or identifies the impact of social policies and programs

---

Certainly many research studies have more than one such goal—all studies include some description, for instance. But clarifying your primary goal can often help when deciding how to do your research.

▣   HOW WELL HAVE WE DONE OUR RESEARCH?

Social scientists want **validity** in their research findings—they want to find the truth. The goal of social science is not to reach conclusions that other people will like or that suit our personal preferences. We shouldn't start our research determined to "prove" that our college's writing program is successful, or that women are portrayed unfairly in advertisements, or that the last presidential election was rigged, or that homeless people are badly treated. We may learn that all of these are true, or aren't; but our goal as social scientists should be to learn the truth, even if it's sometimes disagreeable to us. The goal is to figure out how and why some part of the social world operates as it does and to reach valid conclusions. We reach the goal of validity when our statements or conclusions about empirical reality are correct. In *Making Sense of the Social World: Methods of Investigation,* we will be concerned with three kinds of validity: measurement validity, generalizability, and causal validity (also known as internal validity). We will learn that invalid measures, invalid generalizations, or invalid causal inferences result in invalid conclusions.

Validity: The state that exists when statements or conclusions about empirical reality are correct

---

Measurement Validity

Measurement validity is our first concern, because without having measured what we *think* we've measured, we don't even know what we're talking about. So when Putnam (2000:291) introduces a measure of "social capital" that has such components as number of club meetings attended and number of times worked on a community project, we have to stop and consider the validity of this measure. Measurement validity is the focus of Chapter 4.

Measurement validity: Exists when an indicator measures what we think it measures

---

Problems with measurement validity can occur for many reasons. In studies of Internet forums, for instance, researchers have found that some participants use fictitious identities, even pretending to be a different gender (men posing as women, for instance) (Donath, 1999). Therefore, it's difficult to measure gender in these forums, and researchers could not rely on gender as disclosed in the forums when identifying differences in usage patterns between men and women. Similarly, if you ask people, "Are you an alcoholic?" they probably won't say yes, even if they are; the question elicits less valid information than would be forthcoming by asking them how many drinks they consume, on average, each day. Some college men may be hesitant to admit to watching reruns of *The Simpsons* on television 6 hours a day, so researchers use electronic monitoring devices on TV sets to measure what programs people watch and how often.

Generalizability

The **generalizability** of a study is the extent to which it can inform us about persons, places, or events that were *not* directly studied. For instance, if we ask our favorite students how much they enjoyed our Research Methods course, can we assume that other students (perhaps not as favored) would give the same answers? Maybe they would—but probably not. Generalizability is the focus of Chapter 5.

Generalizability: Exists when a conclusion holds true for the population, group, setting, or event that we say it does, given the conditions that we specify

---

Generalizability is always an important consideration when you review social science research. Even the huge, international National Geographic Society (2000) survey of Internet users had some limitations in generalizability. Only certain people were included in the sample: people who were connected to the Internet, who had heard about the survey, and who actually chose to participate. This meant that many more respondents came from wealthier countries, which had higher rates of computer and Internet use, than from poorer countries. However, the inclusion of individuals from 178 countries and territories does allow some interesting comparisons among countries.

There are two kinds of generalizability: sample and cross-population.

Sample generalizability is a key concern in survey research. Political polls, such as the Gallup Poll or Zogby International, may study a sample of 1,400 likely voters, for example, and then generalize the findings to the entire American population of 80 million likely voters. No one would be interested in the results of political polls if they represented only the tiny sample that actually was surveyed rather than the entire population.

Sample generalizability: Exists when a conclusion based on a sample, or subset, of a larger population holds true for that population

---

Cross-population generalizability occurs to the extent that the results of a study hold true for multiple populations; these populations may not all have been sampled, or they may be represented as subgroups within the sample studied. We can only wonder about the cross-population generalizability of Putnam's findings about social ties in the United States. Has the same decline occurred in Mexico, Argentina, Britain, or Thailand?

Cross-population generalizability: Exists when findings about one group, population, or setting hold true for other groups, populations, or settings (see Exhibit 1.5). Also called *external validity.*

| EXHIBIT 1.5 | Sample and Cross-Population Generalizability |

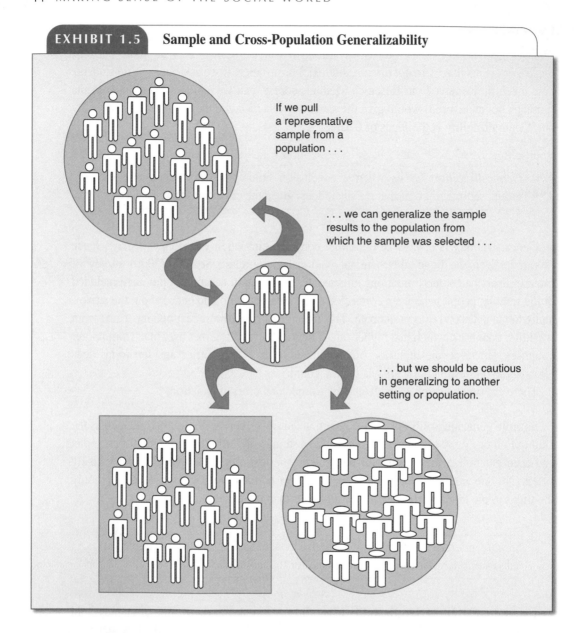

If we pull a representative sample from a population . . .

. . . we can generalize the sample results to the population from which the sample was selected . . .

. . . but we should be cautious in generalizing to another setting or population.

Causal Validity

Causal validity, also known as **internal validity,** refers to the truthfulness of an assertion that A causes B. It is the focus of Chapter 6.

Causal validity (internal validity): Exists when a conclusion that A leads to, or results in, B is correct

Most research seeks to determine what causes what, so social scientists frequently must be concerned with causal validity. For example, Gary Cohen and Barbara Kerr (1998) asked whether computer-mediated counseling could be as effective as face-to-face counseling for mental health problems—that is, whether one type of counseling leads to better results than the other. They could have compared people who had voluntarily experienced one of these types of treatment, but it's quite likely that individuals who sought out a live person for counseling would differ, in important ways, from those who sought computer-mediated counseling. Younger people tend to use computers more; so do more educated people. Or maybe less sociable people would be more drawn to computer-mediated counseling. Normally it would be hard to tell if different results from the two therapies were caused by the therapies themselves or by different kinds of people going to each.

So Cohen and Kerr designed an experiment in which students seeking counseling were assigned randomly (by a procedure somewhat like flipping a coin) to either computer-mediated or face-to-face counseling. In effect, people going to one kind of counseling were just like people going to another. The result? There was no difference in the outcomes; students in both groups benefited the same amount (see Exhibit 1.6). By using the random assignment procedure, Cohen and Kerr strengthened the causal validity of this conclusion.

EXHIBIT 1.6 **Partial Evidence of Causality**

Precounseling Anxiety Score	Type of Counseling	Postcounseling Anxiety Score
35	Computer-mediated	28
35	Face-to-face	29

Precounseling anxiety score: 35 — Computer-mediated counseling → Postcounseling anxiety score: 28

Precounseling anxiety score: 35 — Face-to-face counseling → Postcounseling anxiety score: 29

On the other hand, even in properly randomized experiments, causal findings can be mistaken because of some factor that was not recognized during planning for the study. If the computer-mediated counseling sessions were conducted in a modern building with all the latest amenities, while face-to-face counseling was delivered in a run-down building, this difference might have led to different outcomes for reasons quite apart from the type of counseling. Also, Cohen and Kerr didn't have a group that received no counseling. Maybe just a little quiet time or getting older would provide the same benefits as therapy.

So establishing causal validity can be quite difficult. In subsequent chapters, you will learn in more detail how experimental designs and statistics can help us evaluate causal propositions, but the solutions are neither easy nor perfect. We always have to consider critically the validity of causal statements that we hear or read.

🔲 CONCLUSION

This first chapter should have given you an idea of what to expect in the rest of the book. Social science provides us with a variety of methods for avoiding everyday errors in reasoning and for coming to valid conclusions about the social world. We will explore different kinds of research, using different techniques, in the chapters to come, always asking, "Is this answer likely to be correct?" The techniques are fairly simple, but they are powerful nonetheless if properly executed. You will also learn some interesting facts about social life. We have already seen, for instance, some evidence that

- social ties of many sorts have declined in the United States in the last 25 years, *but*
- social ties can be strengthened by organizational processes that build loyalty, as happens on athletic teams, *and*
- neighborhoods in which social ties are weaker may result in less effective forms of parenting, but both parenting and peer group quality have stronger effects than neighborhood social ties on adolescent outcomes, *and*
- government programs to increase social capital in neighborhoods can increase local political participation, *and*
- students may benefit as much from computer-mediated counseling as from face-to-face counseling.

Remember, you must ask a direct question of each research project you examine: How valid are its conclusions? The theme of *validity* ties the chapters in this book together. Each technique will be evaluated in terms of its ability to help us with measurement validity, generalizability, and causal validity.

To illustrate the process of doing research, in Chapter 2, we describe studies of domestic violence, community disaster, student experience of college, and other topics. We will review the types of problems that social scientists study, the role of theory, the major steps in the research process, and other sources of information that may be used in social research. We stress the importance of considering scientific standards in social research and review generally accepted ethical guidelines. In Chapter 3, we set out the general principles of ethical research that social scientists try to follow. As well, examples of ethical challenges to good research will be presented in many of the chapters that follow.

Then in Chapters 4, 5, and 6, we return to the subject of validity—the three kinds of validity and the specific techniques used to maximize the validity of our measures, our generalizations, and our causal assertions. Chapter 6 also introduces experimental studies, one of the best methods for establishing causal connections relationships.

Other methods of data collection and analysis are introduced in Chapters 7, 8, 9, and 10. Survey research is the most common method of data collection in sociology, and in Chapter 7, we devote attention to the different types of surveys. Chapter 8 is not a substitute for an entire course in statistics, but it gives you a good idea of how to use statistics honestly in reporting the results of your own studies using quantitative methods and in critically interpreting the results of research reported by others. Chapter 9 shows how qualitative methods like participant observation, intensive interviewing, and focus groups can uncover aspects of the social world that we are likely to miss in experiments and surveys, while Chapter 10, on qualitative data analysis, illustrates several approaches that researchers can take to the analysis of the data they collect in qualitative projects.

Evaluation research can use a variety of methods. Chapter 11 explains the role of evaluation research in investigating social programs and how to design evaluation research studies. Finally, Chapter 12 focuses on how to review prior research, how to propose new research, and how to report original research. We give special attention to how to formulate research proposals and how to critique, or evaluate, reports of research that you encounter.

Throughout these chapters, we will try to make the ideas interesting and useful to you, both as a consumer of research (as reported in newspapers, for instance) and as a potential producer (if, say, you do a survey in your college or neighborhood). Each chapter ends with several helpful learning tools. Lists of key terms and chapter highlights will help you to review, and exercises will help you to apply your knowledge. Social research isn't rocket science, but it does take some clear thinking, and these exercises should give you a chance to practice.

A closing thought: Vince Lombardi, legendary coach of the Green Bay Packers of the National Football League during the 1960s, used to say that championship football was basically a matter of "four yards and a cloud of dust." Nothing too fancy, no razzle-dazzle plays, no phenomenally talented players doing it all alone—just solid, hard-working, straight-ahead fundamentals. This may sound strange, but excellent social research can be done—can "win games"—in the same way. We'll show you how to design and conduct surveys that get the right answers, interviews that discover people's true feelings, and experiments that pinpoint what causes what. And we'll show you how to avoid getting bamboozled by every "Studies Show . . . We're Committing More Crimes!" article you see in the newspaper. It takes a little effort initially, but we think you will find it worthwhile— even enjoyable.

KEY TERMS

Causal validity (internal validity)
Cross-population generalizability (external validity)
Descriptive research
Evaluation research
Explanatory research
Exploratory research
Generalizability
Illogical reasoning

Inaccurate observation
Measurement validity
Overgeneralization
Resistance to change
Sample generalizability
Science
Selective (inaccurate) observation
Social science
Validity

HIGHLIGHTS

- Four common errors in everyday reasoning are overgeneralization, selective or inaccurate observation, illogical reasoning, and resistance to change. These errors result from the complexity of the social world, subjective processes that affect the reasoning of researchers and those they study, researchers' self-interestedness, and unquestioning acceptance of tradition or of those in positions of authority.

- Social science is the use of logical, systematic, documented methods to investigate individuals, societies, and social processes, as well as the knowledge produced by these investigations.

- Social research can be motivated by personal interest, policy guidance and program management needs, or academic concerns.

- Social research can be descriptive, exploratory, explanatory, or evaluative—or some combination of these.

- Valid knowledge is the central concern of scientific research. The three components of validity are measurement validity, generalizability (both from the sample to the population from which it was selected and from the sample to other populations), and causal (internal) validity.

STUDENT STUDY SITE

To assist you in completing the Web Exercises, please access the Study Site at http://www.pineforge.com/mssw3, where you'll find the Web Exercises with accompanying links. You'll find other useful study materials like self-quizzes and e-flashcards for each chapter, along with a group of carefully selected articles from research journals that illustrate the major concepts and techniques presented in the book.

EXERCISES

Discussing Research

1. Select a social issue that interests you, such as Internet use or crime. List at least four of your beliefs about this phenomenon. Try to identify the sources of each of these beliefs.

2. Does the academic motivation to do the best possible job of understanding how the social world works conflict with policy and/or personal motivations? How could personal experiences with social isolation or with Internet use shape research motivations? In what ways might the goal of influencing policy about social relations shape how a researcher approaches this issue?

3. Pick a contemporary social issue of interest to you. List a descriptive, exploratory, explanatory, and evaluative question that you could investigate about this issue.

4. Review each of the three sets of research alternatives. Which alternatives are most appealing to you? Which combination of alternatives makes the most sense to you (one possibility, for example, is quantitative research with a basic science orientation)? Discuss the possible bases of your research preferences in terms of your academic interests, personal experiences, and policy orientations.

Finding Research

1. Read the abstracts (initial summaries) of each article in a recent issue of a major social science journal. (Ask your instructor for some good journal titles.) On the basis of the abstract only, classify each research project represented in the articles as primarily descriptive, exploratory, explanatory, or evaluative. Note any indications that the research focused on other types of research questions.

2. From the news, record statements of politicians or other leaders about some social phenomenon. Which statements do you think are likely to be in error? What evidence could the speakers provide to demonstrate the validity of these statements?

3. Check out Robert Putnam's Web site (http://www.bettertogether.org) and review survey findings about social ties in several cities. Prepare a 5- to 10-minute class presentation on what you have found about social ties and the ongoing research-based efforts to understand them.

Critiquing Research

1. Scan one of the publications about the Internet and social relations at the Stanford Institute for the Quantitative Study of Society's Web site, http://www.stanford.edu/group/siqss/. Describe one of the surveys discussed: its goals, methods, and major findings. What do the researchers conclude about the impact of the Internet on social life in the United States?

2. Compare the methods used in the OBAZ project (http://www.essex.ac.uk/ecpr/events/jointsessions/paperarchive/edinburgh/ws22/Lelieveldt.pdf) with those used in a Canadian study

by Keith Hampton and Barry Wellman (http://www.chass.utoronto.ca/~wellman/publications/ neighboring/neighboring_netville.pdf) concerning the impact of Internet use on community social relations. Did these studies investigate the same issues? How did the design of these research projects differ? Did they ask similar questions of the same types of people? Which approach do you think is more likely to result in valid causal conclusions?

Doing Research

1. What topic would you focus on if you could design a social research project without any concern for costs? What are your motives for studying this topic?

2. Develop four questions that you might investigate about the topic you just selected. Each question should reflect a different research motive: description, exploration, explanation, or evaluation. Be specific. Which question most interests you? Why?

Ethics Questions

Throughout the book, we will be discussing the ethical challenges that arise in social research. At the end of each chapter, we will ask you to consider some questions about ethical issues related to that chapter's focus. We introduce this critical topic formally in Chapter 3, but we will begin here with some questions for you to ponder.

1. The chapter began with a brief description of research on social ties. What would *you* do if you were interviewing elderly persons in the community and found that one was very isolated and depressed or even suicidal, apparently as a result of the isolation? Do you believe that social researchers have an obligation to take action in a situation like this? What if you discovered a similar problem with a child? What guidelines would you suggest for researchers?

2. Would you encourage social researchers to announce their findings about problems such as social isolation in press conferences and to encourage relevant agencies to adopt policies encouraged to lessen social isolation? Should policies regarding attempts to garner publicity and shape policy depend on the strength of the research evidence? Do you think there is a fundamental conflict between academic and policy motivations? Do social researchers have an ethical obligation to recommend policies that their research suggests would help other people?

CHAPTER 2

The Process and Problems of Social Research

In Chapter 1, we introduced the reasons *why* we do social research: to describe, explore, explain, and evaluate. Each type of social research can have tremendous impact. Alfred Kinsey's descriptive studies of the sex lives of Americans, conducted in the 1940s and 1950s, were at the time a shocking exposure of the wide variety of sexual practices that apparently staid, "normal" people engaged in behind closed doors—and the studies helped introduce the unprecedented sexual openness we see 50 years later (Kinsey, Pomeroy, & Martin, 1948; Kinsey, Pomeroy, Martin, & Gebhard, 1953). At around the same time, Gunnar Myrdal's exploratory book, *An American Dilemma* (1944/1964), forced our grandparents and great-grandparents to confront the tragedy of institutional racism. Myrdal's research was an important factor in the 1954 Supreme Court decision *Brown v. Topeka Board of Education*, which ended school segregation in America. The explanatory "broken windows" theory of crime, which was developed during the 1980s, dramatically changed police practices in our cities. And evaluative social research today actively influences advertising campaigns, federal housing programs, the organization of military units (from Army fire teams to Navy submarine crews), drug treatment programs, and corporate employee benefit plans.

We now introduce the *how* of social research. In this chapter, you will learn about the process of specifying a research question, developing an appropriate research strategy and design with which to investigate that question, choosing appropriate units of analysis, and conforming to scientific and ethical guidelines during the investigation. By the chapter's end, you should be ready to formulate a question, to design a strategy for answering the question, and to begin to critique previous studies that addressed the question.

WHAT IS THE QUESTION?

A **social research question** is a question about the social world that you seek to answer through the collection and analysis of firsthand, verifiable, empirical data. Questions like this may emerge from your own experience, from research by other investigators, from social theory, or from a "request for research" issued by a government agency that needs a study of a particular problem.

Social research question: A question about the social world that is answered through the collection and analysis of firsthand, verifiable, empirical data

---

Some researchers of the health care system, for example, have had personal experiences as patients with serious diseases, as nurses or aides working in hospitals, or as family members touched directly and importantly by doctors and hospitals. They may want to learn why our health care system failed or helped them. Feminist scholars study violence against women in hopes of finding solutions to this problem as part of a broader concern with improving women's lives. One colleague of ours, Veronica Tichenor, was fascinated by a prominent theory of family relations that argues that men do less housework than women because they earn more money; Professor Tichenor did research on couples in which the woman made far more money than the man to test the theory. (She found, by the way, that the women still did more of the housework.) Some researchers working for large corporations or major polling firms conduct marketing studies simply to make money. So a wide variety of motives can push a researcher to ask research questions.

A good research question doesn't just spring effortlessly from a researcher's mind. You have to refine and evaluate possible research questions to find one that is worthwhile. It's a good idea to develop a list of possible research questions as you are thinking about a research area. At the appropriate time, you can narrow your list to the most interesting and feasible candidate questions.

What makes a research question "good"? Many social scientists evaluate their research questions in terms of three criteria: *feasibility* given the time and resources available, *social importance,* and *scientific relevance* (King, Keohane, & Verba, 1994):

- Can you start and finish an investigation of your research question with available resources and in the time allotted? If so, your research question is feasible.

- Will an answer to your research question make a difference in the social world, even if it only helps people understand a problem they consider important? If so, your research question is socially important.
- Does your research question help to resolve some contradictory research findings or a puzzling issue in social theory? If so, your research question is scientifically relevant.

Here's a good example of a question that is feasible, socially important, and scientifically relevant: Does arresting accused spouse abusers on the spot prevent repeat incidents? Beginning in 1981, the Police Foundation and the Minneapolis Police Department began an experiment to find the answer. The Minneapolis experiment was first and foremost scientifically relevant: It built on a substantial body of contradictory theory regarding the impact of punishment on criminality (Sherman & Berk, 1984). Deterrence theory predicted that arrest would deter individuals from repeat offenses, but labeling theory predicted that arrest would make repeat offenses more likely. The researchers found one prior experimental study of this issue, but it had been conducted with juveniles. Studies among adults had not yielded consistent findings. Clearly, the Minneapolis researchers had good reason for conducting a study.

As you consider research questions, you should begin the process of consulting and then reviewing the published literature. Your goal here and in subsequent stages of research should be to develop a research question and specific expectations that build on prior research and to use the experiences of prior researchers to chart the most productive directions and design the most appropriate methods. Appendix A describes how to search the literature, and Chapter 12 includes detailed advice for writing up the results of your search in a formal review of the relevant literature.

▣ WHAT IS THE THEORY?

Theories have a special place in social research because they help us make connections to general social processes and large bodies of research. Building and evaluating **theory** is, therefore, one of the most important objectives of social science. A social theory is a logically interrelated set of propositions about empirical reality (i.e., the social world as it actually exists). You may know, for instance, about conflict theory, which proposes that (1) people are basically self-interested, (2) power differences between people and groups reflect the different resources available to groups, (3) ideas (religion, political ideologies, etc.) reflect the power arrangements in a society, (4) violence is always a potential resource and the one that matters most, and so on (Collins, 1975). These statements are related to each other, and the sum of conflict theory (entire books are devoted to it) is a sizable collection of such statements. Dissonance theory in psychology, deterrence theory in criminology, and labeling theory in sociology are other examples of social theories.

Theory: A logically interrelated set of propositions about empirical reality

Social theories suggest the areas on which we should focus and the propositions that we should consider testing. For example, Sherman and Berk's (1984) domestic violence research in the Minneapolis spouse abuse experiment was actually a test of predictions that they derived from two varying theories on the impact of punishment on crime (Exhibit 2.1).

Deterrence theory expects punishment to deter crime in two ways. General deterrence occurs when people see that crime results in undesirable punishments—that "crime doesn't pay." The persons who are punished serve as examples of what awaits those who engage in proscribed acts. Specific deterrence occurs when persons who are punished decide not to commit another offense so they can avoid further punishment (Lempert & Sanders, 1986:86–87). Deterrence theory leads to the prediction that arresting spouse abusers will lessen their likelihood of reoffending.

Labeling theory distinguishes between primary deviance, the acts of individuals that lead to public sanction, and secondary deviance, the deviance that occurs in response to public sanction (Hagan, 1994:33). Arrest or some other public sanction for misdeeds labels the offender as deviant in the eyes of others. Once the offender is labeled, others will treat the offender as a deviant, and he or she is then more likely to act in a way that is consistent with

---

EXHIBIT 2.1   **Two Social Theories and Their Predictions About the Effect of Arrest on Domestic Assault**

	Rational choice theory	Symbolic interactionism
Theoretical assumption	People's behavior is shaped by calculations of the costs and benefits of their actions.	People give symbolic meanings to objects, behaviors, and other people.
	⬇	⬇
Criminological component	Deterrence theory: People break the law if the benefits of doing so outweigh the costs.	Labeling theory: People label offenders as deviant, promoting further deviance.
	⬇	⬇
Prediction (effect of arrest for domestic assault)	Abusing spouse, having seen the costs of abuse (namely, arrest), decides not to abuse again.	Abusing spouse, having been labeled as "an abuser," abuses more often.

the deviant label. Ironically, the act of punishment stimulates more of the very behavior that it was intended to eliminate. This theory suggests that persons arrested for domestic assault are more likely to reoffend than those who are not punished, which is the reverse of the deterrence theory prediction.

How do we find relevant social theory and prior research? You may already have encountered some of the relevant material in courses pertaining to research questions that interest you, but that won't be enough. The social science research community is large and active, and new research results appear continually in scholarly journals and books. The World Wide Web contains reports on some research even before it is published in journals (like some of the research reviewed in Chapter 1). Conducting a thorough literature review in library sources and checking for recent results on the Web are essential steps for evaluating scientific relevance. (See Appendix A for instructions on how to search the literature and the Web.)

▣ WHAT IS THE STRATEGY?

When conducting social research, we try to connect theory with empirical data—the evidence we obtain from the real world. Researchers may make this connection in one of two ways:

1. By starting with a social theory and then testing some of its implications with data. This is called **deductive research**; it is most often the strategy used in quantitative methods.

2. By collecting the data and then developing a theory that explains it. This inductive research process is typically used with qualitative methods.

A research project can use both deductive and inductive strategies.

Let's examine the two different strategies in more detail. We can represent both within what is called the **research circle**.

Deductive research: The type of research in which a specific expectation is deduced from a general premise and is then tested

Research circle: A diagram of the elements of the research process, including theories, hypotheses, data collection, and data analysis

---

Deductive Research

In deductive research, we start with a theory and then try to find data that will confirm or deny it. Exhibit 2.2 shows how deductive research starts with a theoretical premise and logically *deduces* a specific expectation. Let's begin with an example of a theoretical idea: When people have emotional and personal connections with coworkers, they will be more

EXHIBIT 2.2 **The Research Circle**

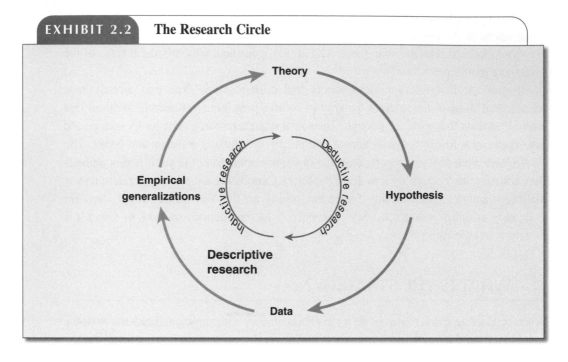

committed to their work. We could extend this idea to college life by deducing that if students know their professors well, they will be more engaged in their work. And from this, we can deduce a more specific expectation—or **hypothesis**—that smaller classes, which allow more student-faculty contact, will lead to higher levels of engagement. Now that we have a hypothesis, we can collect data on levels of engagement in small and large classes and compare them. We can't always directly test the general theory, but we can test specific hypotheses that are deduced from it.

Hypothesis: A tentative statement about empirical reality involving a relationship between two or more variables. *Example:* The higher the poverty rate in a community, the higher the percentage of community residents who are homeless.

A hypothesis states a relationship between two or more **variables**—characteristics or properties that can vary, or change. Classes can be large, like a 400-student introductory psychology course, or they can be small, like an upper-level seminar. Class size is thus a variable. And hours of homework done per week can also vary (obviously); you can do 2 hours or 20. So, too, can "engagement" vary, as measured in any number of ways. (Nominal designations like religion are variables, too, because they can vary among Protestant, Catholic, Jew, and so on.)

But a hypothesis doesn't just state that there is a connection between variables; it suggests that one variable actually influences another—that a change in the first one somehow propels (or predicts, influences, or causes) a change in the second. It says that *if* one thing happens, *then* another thing is likely: *If* you stay up too late, *then* you will be tired the next day. *If* you smoke cigarettes for many years, *then* you are more likely to develop heart disease or cancer. *If* a nation loses a major war, *then* its government is more likely to collapse. And so on.

So in a hypothesis, we suggest that one variable influences another—or that the second in some ways "depends" on the first. We may believe, again, that students' reported enthusiasm for a class "depends" on the size of the class. Hence, we call enthusiasm the **dependent variable**—the variable that *depends* on another, at least partially, for its level. If cigarettes damage your health, then health is the dependent variable; if lost wars destabilize governments, then government stability is the dependent variable; if enthusiasm for a course depends (in some degree) on class size, then enthusiasm is the dependent variable.

The predicted result in a hypothesis, then, is called the **dependent variable**. And the hypothesized cause is called the **independent variable**, because in the stated hypothesis, it doesn't depend on any other variable.

These terms—hypothesis, variable, independent variable, and dependent variable—are used repeatedly in this book and are widely used in all fields of natural and social science, so they are worth knowing well!

Variable: A characteristic or property that can vary (take on different values or attributes). *Examples:* poverty rate, percentage of community residents who are homeless.

Dependent variable: A variable that is hypothesized to vary depending on or under the influence of another variable. *Example:* percentage of community residents who are homeless.

Independent variable: A variable that is hypothesized to cause, or lead to, variation in another variable. *Example:* poverty rate.

You may have noticed that sometimes an increase in the independent variable leads to a corresponding increase in the dependent variable; in other cases, it leads to a decrease. An increase in your consumption of fatty foods will often lead to a corresponding increase in the cholesterol levels in your blood. But an increase in cigarette consumption leads to a decrease in health. In the first case, we say that the **direction of association** is positive; in the second, we say it is negative. Either way, you can clearly see that a change in one variable leads to a predictable change in the other.

Direction of association: A pattern in a relationship between two variables—that is, the value of a variable tends to change consistently in relation to change in the other variable. The direction of association can be either positive or negative.

In both explanatory and evaluative research, you should say clearly what you expect to find (your hypothesis) and design your research accordingly to test that hypothesis. Doing this strengthens the confidence we can place in the results. So the deductive researcher (to use a poker analogy) states her expectations in advance, shows her hand, and lets the chips fall where they may. The data are accepted as a fair picture of reality.

Domestic Violence and the Research Circle

The Sherman and Berk (1984) study of domestic violence is a good example of how the research circle works. Sherman and Berk's study was designed to test a hypothesis based on deterrence theory: "Arrest for spouse abuse reduces the risk of repeat offenses." In this hypothesis, arrest or release is the independent variable, and variation in the risk of repeat offenses is the dependent variable (it is hypothesized to depend on arrest).

Sherman and Berk tested their hypothesis by setting up an experiment in which the police responded to complaints of spouse abuse in one of three ways, one of which was to arrest the offender. When the researchers examined their data (police records for the persons in their experiment), they found that of those arrested for assaulting their spouse, only 13% repeated the offense, compared to a 26% recidivism rate for those who were separated from their spouse by the police but were not arrested. This pattern in the data, or empirical generalization, was consistent with the hypothesis that the researchers deduced from deterrence theory. The theory thus received support from the experiment (see Exhibit 2.3).

Inductive Research

In contrast to deductive research, **inductive research** begins with specific data, which are then used to develop ("induce") a theory to account for the data. (Hint: When you start *in* the data, you are doing *in*ductive research.)

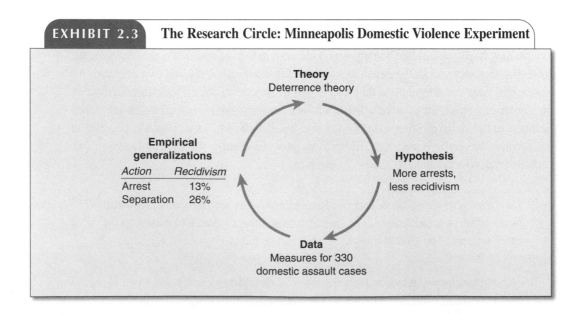

EXHIBIT 2.3   **The Research Circle: Minneapolis Domestic Violence Experiment**

Inductive research: The type of research in which general conclusions are drawn from specific data; compare to deductive research

One way to think of this process is in terms of the research circle. Rather than starting at the top of the circle with a theory, the inductive researcher starts at the bottom of the circle with data and then moves up to a theory. Some researchers committed to an inductive approach even resist formulating a research question before they begin to collect data. Their technique is to let the question emerge from the social situation itself (Brewer & Hunter, 1989:54–58). In the research for his book *Champions: The Making of Olympic Swimmers,* Dan Chambliss (1988) spent several years living and working with world-class competitive swimmers who were training for the Olympics. Chambliss entered the research with no definite hypotheses and certainly no developed theory about how athletes became successful, what their lives were like, or how they related to their coaches and teams. He simply wanted to understand who these people were, and he decided to report on whatever struck him as most interesting in his research.

As it turned out, what Chambliss learned was not how special these athletes were but actually how ordinary they were. Becoming an Olympic athlete was less about innate talent, special techniques, or inspired coaching than it was about actually paying attention to all the little things that make one perform better in one's sport. His theory was "induced" from what he learned in his studies (Chambliss, 1988) while being immersed "in" the data.

Research designed using an inductive approach, as in Chambliss's study, can result in new insights and provocative questions. **Inductive reasoning** also enters into deductive research when we find unexpected patterns in data collected for testing a hypothesis. Sometimes such patterns are **anomalous**, in that they don't seem to fit the theory being proposed, and they can be **serendipitous**, in that we may learn exciting, surprising new things from them. Even if we do learn inductively from such research, the adequacy of an explanation formulated after the fact is necessarily less certain than an explanation presented prior to the collection data. Every phenomenon can always be explained in some way. Inductive explanations are more trustworthy if they are tested subsequently with deductive research. Great insights and ideas can come from inductive studies, but verifiable proof comes from deductive research.

Inductive reasoning: The type of reasoning that moves from the specific to the general

Anomalous: Unexpected patterns in data that do not seem to fit the theory being proposed

Serendipitous: Unexpected patterns in data, which stimulate new ideas or theoretical approaches

An Inductive Study of Response to a Disaster

Qualitative research is often inductive: The researcher begins by observing social interaction or interviewing social actors in depth and then developing an explanation for what has been found. The researchers often ask questions like "What is going on here?" "How do people interpret these experiences?" or "Why do people do what they do?" Rather than testing a hypothesis, the researchers are trying to make sense of some social phenomenon.

In 1972, for example, towns along the 17-mile Buffalo Creek hollow in West Virginia were wiped out when a dam at the top of a hollow broke, sending 132 million gallons of water, mud, and garbage crashing down through the towns that bordered the creek. After the disaster, sociologist Kai Erikson went to the Buffalo Creek area and interviewed survivors. In the resulting book, *Everything in Its Path,* Erikson (1976) described the trauma suffered by those who survived the disaster. His explanation of their psychological destruction—an explanation that grew out of his interviews with the residents—was that people were traumatized not only by the violence of what had occurred but also by the "destruction of community" that ensued during the recovery efforts. Families were transplanted all over the area with no regard for placing them next to their former neighbors. Extended families were broken up in much the same way, as federal emergency housing authorities relocated people with little concern for whether they knew the people with whom they would be housed. Church congregations were scattered, lifelong friends were resettled miles apart, and entire neighborhoods simply vanished, both physically— that is, their houses were destroyed—and socially. Erikson's explanation grew out of his in-depth immersion in his data—the conversations he had with the people themselves.

Inductive explanations such as Erikson's feel authentic because we hear what people have to say "in their own words" and we see the social world "as they see it." These explanations are often richer and more finely textured than those in deductive research; on the other hand, they are probably based on fewer cases and drawn from a more limited area.

Descriptive Research: A Necessary Step

Both deductive and inductive research move halfway around the research circle, connecting theory with data. Descriptive research does not go that far, but it is still part of the research circle shown earlier in Exhibit 2.2. Descriptive research starts with data and proceeds only to the stage of making empirical generalizations; it does not generate entire theories.

Valid description is actually critical in all research. The Minneapolis Domestic Violence Experiment was motivated in part by a growing body of descriptive research indicating that spouse abuse is very common: 572,000 reported cases of women victimized by a violent partner each year; 1.5 million women (and 500,000 men) requiring medical attention each year due to a domestic assault (Buzawa & Buzawa, 1996:1–3).

Much important research for the government and private organizations is primarily descriptive: How many poor people live in this community? Is the health of the elderly improving? How frequently do convicted criminals return to crime? Description of social phenomena can stimulate more ambitious deductive and inductive research. Simply put, good description of data is the cornerstone for the scientific research process and an essential component of understanding the social world.

▣ WHAT IS THE DESIGN?

Researchers usually start with a question, although some begin with a theory or a strategy. If you're very systematic, the *question* is related to a *theory,* and an appropriate *strategy* is chosen for the research. All of these, you will notice, are critical defining issues for the researcher. If your research question is trivial (How many shoes are in my closet?), or your theory sloppy (More shoes reflect better fashion sense.), or your strategy inappropriate (I'll look at lots of shoes and see what I learn.), the project is doomed from the start.

But let's say you've settled these first three elements of a sound research study. Now we must begin a more technical phase of the research: the design of a study. From this point on, we will be introducing a number of terms and definitions that may seem arcane or difficult. In every case, though, these terms will help to clarify your thinking. Like exact formulae in an algebra problem or precisely the right word in an essay, these technical terms help, or even require, scientists to be absolutely clear about what they are thinking—and to be precise in describing their work to other people.

An overall research strategy can be implemented through several different types of research design. One important distinction between research designs is whether data are collected at one point in time—a **cross-sectional research design**—or at two or more points in time—a **longitudinal research design**. Another important distinction is between research designs that focus on individuals—the **individual unit of analysis**—and those that focus on groups, or aggregates of individuals—the **group unit of analysis**.

Cross-sectional research design: A study in which data are collected at only one point in time

Longitudinal research design: A study in which data are collected that can be ordered in time; also defined as research in which data are collected at two or more points in time

Individual unit of analysis: A unit of analysis in which individuals are the source of data and the focus of conclusions

Group unit of analysis: A unit of analysis in which groups are the source of data and the focus of conclusions

Cross-Sectional Designs

In a cross-sectional design, all of the data are collected at one point in time. In effect, you take a "cross-section"—a slice that cuts across an entire population—and use that to see all the different parts, or sections, of that population. Imagine cutting out a slice of a tree trunk, from bark to core. In looking at this cross-section, one can see all the different parts, including the rings of the tree. In social research, you might do a cross-sectional study of a college's student body, with a sample that includes freshmen through seniors. This "slice" of the population, taken at a single point in time, would allow one to compare the different groups.

But cross-sectional studies, because they use data collected at only one time, suffer from a serious weakness: They don't directly measure the impact of time. For instance, you may see that seniors at your college write more clearly than do freshmen. You might conclude, then, that the difference is because of what transpired over time; that is, what they learned in college. But in fact, it may be because this year's seniors were recruited under a policy that favored better writers. In other words, the cross-sectional study doesn't distinguish if the seniors have learned a lot in college or if they were just better than this year's freshmen when they first enrolled.

Or let's say that in 2009, you conduct a study of the American workforce and find that older workers make more money than younger workers. You may conclude (erroneously) that "as one gets older, one makes more money." But you didn't actually observe that happening because you didn't track actual people over time. It *may* be that the older generation (say, people born in 1945) have just enjoyed higher wages all along than have people born in 1975.

With a cross-sectional study, we can't be sure which explanation is correct, and that's a big weakness. Of course, we could ask workers what they made when they first started working, or we could ask college seniors what test scores they received when they were freshmen, but we are then injecting a "longitudinal" element into our cross-sectional research design. Because of the fallibility of memory and the incentives for distorting the past, taking such an approach is not a good way to study change over time.

Longitudinal Designs

In longitudinal research, data are collected over time. By measuring independent and dependent variables at each of several different times, the researcher can determine whether change in the independent variable does in fact precede change in the dependent variable—that is, whether the hypothesized cause comes before the effect, as a true cause must. In a cross-sectional study, when the data are all collected at one time, you can't really show if the hypothesized cause occurs first; in longitudinal studies, though, you can see if a cause occurs and then, later in time, an effect occurs. So if possible to do, longitudinal research is always preferable.

But collecting data more than once takes time and work. Often researchers simply cannot, or are unwilling to, delay completion of a study for even 1 year to collect follow-up data. Still, many research questions really should have a long follow-up period: What is the impact of job training on subsequent employment? How effective is a school-based program in improving parenting skills? Under what conditions do traumatic experiences in childhood result in later mental illness? The value of longitudinal data is great, so every effort should be made to develop longitudinal research designs whenever they are appropriate.

There are three basic longitudinal research designs (see Exhibit 2.4). In the first, you conduct a simple *cross-sectional* study but then *repeat* that study several times; therefore, this approach is referred to as a *repeated cross-sectional,* or *trend,* design. The frequency of follow-up measurement can vary, ranging from a simple before-and-after design with just one follow-up to studies in which various indicators are measured every month for many years. In such trend studies, the population from which the sample is selected may be defined broadly or narrowly, but members of the sample are rotated or completely replaced each time a measurement is done. In effect, you look at the population over time, drawing a new sample at each of a number of different points in time. You are looking for trends in the population.

The second major longitudinal design is called a *panel* study. A panel study uses a single group of people who are questioned or studied at multiple points across time; the same people are asked questions on multiple occasions, so how they change and develop as individuals can be studied.

Let's consider these two basic longitudinal designs first to see how they are done and their strengths and weaknesses. We'll then review the third type of longitudinal design, cohort studies, which is not used as often as the other two types.

EXHIBIT 2.4 **Three Types of Research Design**

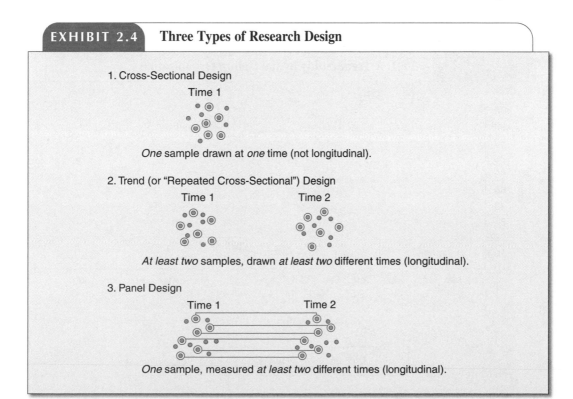

1. Cross-Sectional Design

Time 1

One sample drawn at *one* time (not longitudinal).

2. Trend (or "Repeated Cross-Sectional") Design

Time 1   Time 2

At least two samples, drawn *at least two* different times (longitudinal).

3. Panel Design

Time 1   Time 2

One sample, measured *at least two* different times (longitudinal).

Trend Designs

Trend designs, also known as **repeated cross-sectional studies**, are conducted as follows:

1. A sample is drawn from a population at Time 1, and data are collected from the sample.
2. As time passes, some people leave the population and others enter it.
3. At Time 2, a different sample is drawn from this population.

The Gallup polls, begun in the 1930s, are a well-known example of trend studies. One Gallup poll, for instance, asks people how well they believe the American president is doing his job (Exhibit 2.5). Every so often, the Gallup organization takes a sample of the American population (usually about 1,400 people) and asks them this question. Each time, they ask a different, though roughly demographically equivalent, group of people the question; they aren't talking to the same people every time. Then they use the results of a series of these questions to analyze trends in support for presidents. That is, they can see when support for presidents is high and when it is low, in general. This is a trend study.

Repeated cross-sectional design: A longitudinal study in which data are collected at two or more points in time from different samples of the same population

---

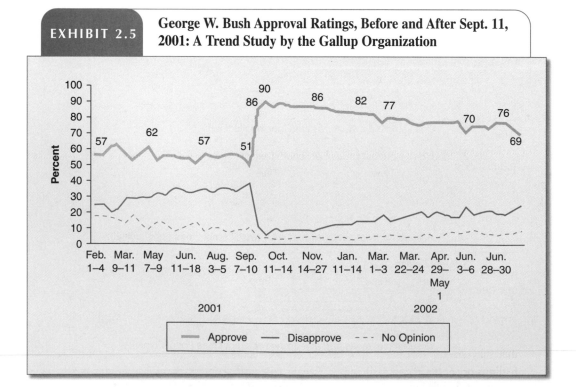

EXHIBIT 2.5   **George W. Bush Approval Ratings, Before and After Sept. 11, 2001: A Trend Study by the Gallup Organization**

When the goal is to determine whether a population has changed over time, trend (or repeated cross-sectional) designs are appropriate. Has racial tolerance increased among Americans in the past 20 years? Are employers more likely to pay maternity benefits today than they were in the 1950s? Are college students today more involved in their communities than college students were 10 years ago? These questions concern changes in populations as a whole, not changes in individuals.

Panel Designs

When we need to know whether individuals in the population changed, we must turn to a **panel design**. In the Mellon Foundation Assessment Project at Hamilton College, under way as this book is being written, a panel of 100 students just entering college was selected from the first-year class, each student to be interviewed once a year for each of their 4 years at Hamilton. The goal is to determine which experiences in their college career are valuable and which are a hindrance to their education. By following the same people over a period of time, we can see how changes happen in the lives of individual students.

Panel designs allow clear identification of changes in the units (individuals, groups, or whatever) we are studying. Here is the process for conducting fixed-sample panel studies:

1. A sample (called a panel) is drawn from a population at Time 1, and data are collected from the sample (for instance, 100 freshmen are selected and interviewed).

2. As time passes, some panel members become unavailable for follow-up, and the population changes (some students transfer to other colleges or decline to continue participating).

3. At Time 2, data are collected from the same people (the panel) as at Time 1, except for those people who cannot be located (the remaining students are reinterviewed).

Panel design: A longitudinal study in which data are collected from the same individuals—the panel—at two or more points in time

---

A panel design allows us to determine how individuals change, as well as how the population as a whole has changed; this is a great advantage. However, panel designs are difficult to implement successfully and often are not even attempted, for two reasons:

1. *Expense and attrition*—It can be difficult and expensive to keep track of individuals over a long period, and inevitably the proportion of panel members who can be located for follow-up will decline over time. Panel studies often lose more than one quarter of their members through attrition (Miller, 1991:170).

2. *Subject fatigue*—Panel members may grow weary of repeated interviews and drop out of the study, or they may become so used to answering the standard questions in the survey that they start giving stock answers rather than actually thinking about their current feelings or actions (Campbell, 1992). This is called the problem of *subject fatigue*.

Because panel studies are so useful, social researchers have developed increasingly effective techniques for keeping track of individuals and overcoming subject fatigue. But if your resources do not permit use of these techniques to maintain an adequate panel and you plan to do a cross-sectional study instead, remember that it is preferable to use a repeated cross-sectional design rather than a one-time-only cross-sectional study.

Cohort Designs

Trend and panel studies can track both the results of an event (such as World War II) or the progress of a specific historical generation (for instance, people born in 1985). In this case, the historically specific group of people being studied is known as a **cohort**, and this cohort makes up the basic population for your trend or panel study. Such a study has a **cohort design**. If you were doing a trend study, the cohort would be the population from which you draw your different samples. If you were doing a panel study, the cohort provides the population from which the panel itself is drawn. Examples of cohorts include the following:

- *Birth cohorts*—Those who share a common period of birth (those born in the 1940s, 1950s, 1960s, etc.)
- *Seniority cohorts*—Those who have worked at the same place for about 5 years, about 10 years, and so on
- *School cohorts*—Freshmen, sophomores, juniors, seniors

Cohort: Individuals or groups with a common starting point. Examples include the college class of 1997, people who graduated from high school in the 1980s, General Motors employees who started work between 1990 and 2000, and people who were born in the late 1940s or the 1950s (the "baby boom generation"). Cohorts can form the initial population for either trend or panel studies.

Cohort design: A longitudinal study in which data are collected at two or more points in time from individuals in a cohort

---

We can see the value of longitudinal research in comparing two studies that estimated the impact of public and private schooling on high school students' achievement test scores. In an initial cross-sectional (not longitudinal) study, James Coleman, Thomas Hoffer, and Sally Kilgore (1982) compared standardized achievement test scores of high school sophomores and seniors in public, Catholic, and other private schools. They found that test scores were higher in the private (including Catholic) high schools than in the public high schools.

But was this difference a causal effect of private schooling? Perhaps the parents of higher-performing children were choosing to send them to private schools rather than to public ones. So James Coleman and Thomas Hoffer (1987) went back to the high schools and studied the test scores of the former sophomores 2 years later, when they were seniors; in other words, the researchers used a panel (longitudinal) design. This time, they found that the verbal and math achievement test scores of the Catholic school students had increased more over the 2 years than the scores of the public school students had. Irrespective of students' initial achievement test scores, the Catholic schools seemed to "do more" for their students than did the public schools. The researchers' causal conclusion rested on much stronger ground because they used a longitudinal panel design.

Units and Levels of Analysis

Finally, as a social science student, you probably understand by now that groups don't act or think like individuals do. They are different units of analysis. **Units of analysis** are the things you are studying, whose behavior you want to understand. Often these are people, but they can also be, for instance, families, groups, colleges, governments, or nations. All of these could be units of analysis for your research. The unit of analysis is the entity you are studying and trying to learn about.

Units of analysis: The level of social life on which a research question is focused, such as individuals, groups, towns, or nations

---

As these examples suggest, units exist at different *levels* of analysis, from the most micro (small) to the most macro (large). Individual people are easily seen and talked to, and you can learn about them quite directly. A university, however, although you can certainly visit it and walk around it, is harder to visualize, and data regarding it may take longer to gather. Finally, a nation is not really a "thing" at all and can never be seen by human eyes; understanding such a unit may require many years of study. People, universities, and nations exist at different *levels* of social reality.

Sometimes researchers confuse levels of analysis, mistakenly using data from one level to draw conclusions about a different level. Even the best social scientists fall into this trap. In Emile Durkheim's classic (1951) study of suicide, for example, nationwide suicide rates were compared for Catholic and Protestant countries (in an early stage of his research). Obviously, the data on suicide were collected for individual people, and religion was tallied for individuals as well. Then Durkheim used aggregated numbers to characterize entire countries as being high or low suicide countries and as Protestant (England, Germany, Norway) or Catholic (Italy, France, Spain) countries. He found that Catholic countries had lower rates of suicide than Protestant countries. His accurate finding was about countries, then, not about people; the unit of analysis was the country, and he ranked countries by their suicide rates. Yes, the data were collected from individuals and were about individuals, but it had been combined (aggregated) so as to describe entire nations. Thus, Durkheim's units of analysis were countries. So far, so good.

But Durkheim then made his big mistake. He used his findings from one level of analysis to make statements about units at a different level. He used country data to draw conclusions about individuals, claiming that Catholic individuals were less likely than

Protestant individuals to commit suicide. Much of his later discussion in *Suicide* (1951) was about why Catholic individuals would be less likely to kill themselves.

Confusions about levels of analysis can take several forms (Lieberson, 1985). Durkheim's mistake was to use findings from a "higher" level (countries) to draw conclusions about a "lower" level (individuals). This is called the **ecological fallacy**, because the "ecology"—the broader surrounding setting, in this case a country—is mistakenly believed to determine what happens for individuals. The ecological fallacy occurs when group-level data are used to draw conclusions about individual-level processes. It's a mistake, and a common one.

Ecological fallacy: An error in reasoning in which incorrect conclusions about individual-level processes are drawn from group-level data

---

Try to spot the ecological fallacy in each of the following deductions. The first half of each sentence is true, but the second half doesn't logically follow from the first:

- Richer countries have higher rates of heart disease; therefore, richer people have higher rates of heart disease.
- Florida counties with the largest number of black residents have the highest rates of Ku Klux Klan membership; therefore, blacks join the Klan more than whites.
- In fall 2000, the presidential election was very close; therefore, Americans wanted a divided government.

In each case, a group-level finding from data is used to draw (erroneous) conclusions about individuals. In rich countries, yes, there is more heart disease, but actually it's among the poor individuals within those countries. Florida counties with more black people attract more white individuals to the Klan. And although America (as a whole) was certainly divided in the 2000 election, just as certainly many individual Americans, both Republican and Democratic, had no ambivalence whatsoever about who was their favorite candidate. *America* as a whole may want a divided government, but relatively few *Americans* do. A researcher who draws such hasty conclusions about individual-level processes from group-level data is committing an ecological fallacy.

So conclusions about processes at the individual level must be based on individual-level data; conclusions about group-level processes must be based on data collected about groups (see Exhibit 2.6.)

We don't want to leave you with the belief that conclusions about individual processes based on group-level data are *necessarily* wrong. We just don't know for sure. Suppose, for example, that we find that communities with higher average incomes have lower crime rates. Perhaps something about affluence improves community life such that crime is reduced; that's possible. Or it may be that the only thing special about these communities is that they have more individuals with higher incomes, who tend to commit fewer crimes. Even though we collected data at the group level and analyzed them at the group level, they

EXHIBIT 2.6

Levels of Analysis. Data from one level of analysis should lead to conclusions only about that level of analysis.

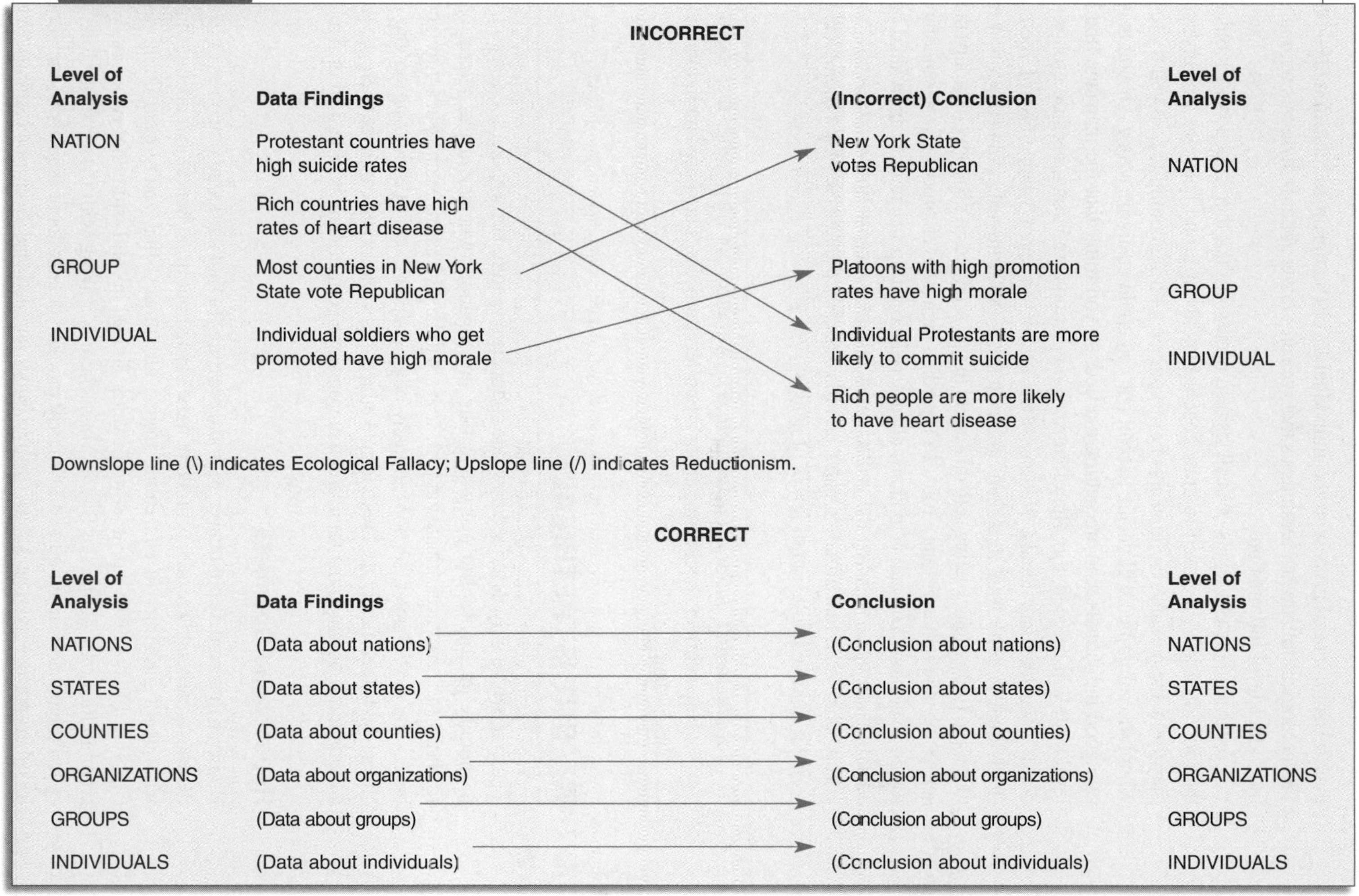

INCORRECT

Level of Analysis	Data Findings	(Incorrect) Conclusion	Level of Analysis
NATION	Protestant countries have high suicide rates	New York State votes Republican	NATION
	Rich countries have high rates of heart disease		
GROUP	Most counties in New York State vote Republican	Platoons with high promotion rates have high morale	GROUP
INDIVIDUAL	Individual soldiers who get promoted have high morale	Individual Protestants are more likely to commit suicide	INDIVIDUAL
		Rich people are more likely to have heart disease	

Downslope line (\) indicates Ecological Fallacy; Upslope line (/) indicates Reductionism.

CORRECT

Level of Analysis	Data Findings	Conclusion	Level of Analysis
NATIONS	(Data about nations)	(Conclusion about nations)	NATIONS
STATES	(Data about states)	(Conclusion about states)	STATES
COUNTIES	(Data about counties)	(Conclusion about counties)	COUNTIES
ORGANIZATIONS	(Data about organizations)	(Conclusion about organizations)	ORGANIZATIONS
GROUPS	(Data about groups)	(Conclusion about groups)	GROUPS
INDIVIDUALS	(Data about individuals)	(Conclusion about individuals)	INDIVIDUALS

39

may reflect a causal process at the individual level (Sampson & Lauritsen, 1994:80–83). The ecological fallacy just reminds us that we can't *know* about individuals without having individual-level information.

Confusion between levels of analysis also occurs in the other direction, when data from the individual level are used to draw conclusions about group behavior. For instance, you may know the personal preferences of everyone on a hiring committee, so you try to predict whom the committee will decide to hire; but you could easily be wrong. Or you may know two good individuals who are getting married, so you think that the marriage (the higher-level unit) will be good, too. But often, such predictions are wrong, because groups as units don't work like individuals. Nations often go to war even when most of their people (individually) don't want to. Adam Smith, in the 1700s, famously pointed out that millions of people (individuals) acting selfishly could in fact produce an economy (a group) that acted selflessly, helping everyone. You can't predict higher-level processes or outcomes from lower-level ones. You can't, in short, always reduce group behavior to individual behavior added up; doing so is called the **reductionist fallacy**, or **reductionism**, (since it "reduces" group behavior to that of individuals), and it's basically the reverse of the ecological fallacy. Both involve confusion of levels of analysis.

Reductionist fallacy (reductionism): An error in reasoning that occurs when incorrect conclusions about group-level processes are based on individual-level data

---

▣   BUT IS IT ETHICAL?

Thus far, we've only described how one conducts research, not whether the research project is morally justifiable. But every scientific investigation, whether in the natural or social sciences, has an ethical dimension to it, so we will be addressing such issues throughout this book. The next chapter, sections in many other chapters, and questions at the end of each chapter will specifically deal with formal ethical principles in research, but here we will give a quick introduction to the topic and mention some common areas of ethical difficulty.

Honesty and Openness

Research distorted by political or personal pressures to find particular outcomes or to achieve the most marketable results is unlikely to be carried out in an honest and open fashion. And what about the ethics of concealing from your subjects that you're even doing research? Carolyn Ellis (1986) spent several years living in and studying two small fishing communities on Chesapeake Bay in Massachusetts. Living with these "fisher folk," as she called them, she learned quite a few fairly intimate details about their lives, including their less-than-perfect hygiene habits (many simply smelled bad from not bathing). When the book was published, many townspeople were enraged that Ellis had lived among them and then, in effect, betrayed their innermost secrets without having told them that she was planning to write a book. There was enough detail in the book, in fact, that some of the fisher folk could be identified, and Ellis had never fully disclosed to the fisher folk that she was doing research. The episode stirred quite a debate among professional sociologists as well.

Here's another example of hiding one's motives from one's subjects. In the early 1980s, Professor Erich Goode spent three and a half years doing research on the National Association to Aid Fat Americans. Professor Goode was interested primarily in how overweight people managed their identity and enhanced their own self-esteem by forming support groups. Twenty years after the research, in 2002, Goode published an article in which he revealed that in doing the research, he met and engaged in romantic and sexual relationships with more than a dozen women in that organization. There was a heated discussion among the editors and board members of the journal in which the article was published, not only about the ethics of the researcher doing such a thing but also about the ethics of the journal then publishing an article that seemed to take inappropriate advantage of the unusual subject matter.

Openness about research procedures and results goes hand in hand with honesty in research design. Openness is also essential if researchers are to learn from the work of others. In the 1980s, there was a long legal battle between a U.S. researcher, Robert Gallo, and a French researcher, Luc Montagnier, about which of them first discovered the virus that causes AIDS. In 2008, Montagnier received the Nobel Prize in recognition of his work (Altman, 2008). (Scientists are like other people in their desire to be first.) Enforcing standards of honesty and encouraging openness about research is the best solution for these problems.

The Uses of Science

Scientists must also consider the uses to which their research is put. For example, during the 1980s, Murray Straus, a prominent researcher of family violence (wife battering, child abuse, corporal punishment, and the like) found in his research that in physical altercations between husband and wife, the wife was just as likely as the husband to throw the first punch. This is a startling finding when taken by itself. But Straus also learned that regardless of who actually hit first, the wife nearly always wound up being physically injured far more severely than the man. Whoever started the fight, she lost it (Straus & Gelles, 1988). In this respect (as well as in certain others), Straus's finding that "women hit first as often as men" is quite misleading when taken by itself. When Straus published his findings, a host of social scientists and feminists protested loudly on the grounds that his research was likely to be misused by those who believe that wife battering is not, in fact, a serious problem. It seemed to suggest that, really, men are no worse in their use of violence than are women. Do researchers have an obligation to try to correct what seem to be misinterpretations of their findings?

Social scientists who conduct research on behalf of organizations and agencies may face additional difficulties when the organization, not the researcher, controls the final report and the publicity it receives. If organizational leaders decide that particular research results are unwelcome, the researcher's desire to have findings used appropriately and reported fully can conflict with contractual obligations. This possibility cannot be avoided entirely, but because of it, researchers should acknowledge their funding sources in reports.

Research on People

The chapter on ethics will deal fully with the general history and topic of human subjects research, but here we suggest a couple of the problems that arise.

Maintaining **confidentiality**, for instance, is a key ethical obligation; it should be reflected in a statement in the informed consent agreement about how each subject's privacy will be protected (Sieber, 1992). Procedures, such as locking records and creating special identifying codes, must be created to minimize the risk of access by unauthorized persons. However, statements about confidentiality should be realistic. In 1993, sociologist Rik Scarce was jailed for 5 months for contempt of court after refusing to testify to a grand jury about so-called "eco-terrorists." Scarce, a PhD candidate at Washington State University at the time, was researching radical environmentalists and may have had information about a 1991 "liberation" raid on an animal research lab at Washington State. Scarce was eventually released from jail, but he never did violate the confidentiality he claimed to have promised his informants (Scarce, 2005). Laws allow research records to be subpoenaed and may require reporting child abuse. A researcher also may feel compelled to release information if a health- or life-threatening situation arises and participants need to be alerted.

Confidentiality: Provided by research in which identifying information that could be used to link respondents to their responses is available only to designated research personnel for specific research needs

---

The potential of withholding a beneficial treatment from some subjects is another cause for ethical concern. Sometimes, in an ethically debatable practice, researchers will actually withhold treatments from some subjects, knowing that those treatments would probably help the people, to accurately measure *how much* they helped. For example, in some recent studies of AIDS drugs conducted in Africa, researchers provided different levels of AIDS-combating drugs to different groups of patients with the disease. Some patients received no drug therapy at all, despite the fact that all indications were that the drug treatments would help them. From the point of view of pure science, this makes sense: You can't really know how effective the drugs are unless you try different treatments on different people who start from the same situation (e.g., having AIDS). But the research has provoked a tremendous outcry across the world because many people find the practice of deliberately not treating people—in particular, impoverished black people living in Third World countries—to be morally repugnant.

The extent to which ethical issues are a problem for researchers and their subjects varies dramatically with research design. Most survey research, in particular, creates few ethical problems (Reynolds, 1979:56–57). On the other hand, some experimental studies in the social sciences that have put people in uncomfortable or embarrassing situations have generated vociferous complaints and years of debate about ethics (Reynolds, 1979; Sjoberg,

1967). Moreover, adherence to ethical guidelines must take into account each aspect of the research procedures. For example, full disclosure of "what is really going on" in an experimental study is unnecessary if subjects are unlikely to be harmed.

What it comes down to is that the researcher must think through in advance the potential for ethical problems, must make every effort to foresee all possible risks and to weigh the possible benefits of the research against these risks, must establish clear procedures that minimize the risks and maximize the benefits, and must inform research subjects in advance about the potential risks.

Ultimately, these decisions about ethical procedures are not just up to you, as a researcher, to make. Your university's human subjects protection committee (**institutional review board**, or **IRB**) sets the human subjects protection standards for your institution and may even require that you submit your research proposal to it for review. Before submitting a project for review, you should also consult with individuals with different perspectives to develop a realistic risk/benefit assessment (Sieber, 1992:75–108).

Institutional review board (IRB): A group of organizational and community representatives required by federal law to review the ethical issues in all proposed research that is federally funded, involves human subjects, or has any potential for harm to subjects

---

▣ CONCLUSION

Social researchers can find many questions to study, but not all questions are equally worthy. The ones that warrant the expense and effort of social research are feasible, socially important, and scientifically relevant.

Selecting a worthy research question does not guarantee a worthwhile research project. The simplicity of the research circle presented in this chapter belies the complexity of the social research process. In the following chapters, we will focus on particular aspects of that process. Chapter 4 examines the interrelated processes of conceptualization and measurement, arguably the most important parts of research. Measurement validity is the foundation for the other two aspects of validity, which are discussed in Chapters 5 and 6. Chapter 5 reviews the meaning of generalizability and the sampling strategies that help us to achieve this goal. Chapter 6 introduces the third aspect of validity—causal validity—and illustrates different methods for achieving causal validity and explains basic experimental data collection. The next two chapters introduce approaches to data collection—surveys and qualitative research—that help us, in different ways, to achieve validity.

Ethical issues also should be considered in the evaluation of research proposals and completed research studies. As the preceding examples show, ethical issues in social research are no less complex than the other issues that researchers confront. And it is inexcusable to jump into research on people without any attention to ethical considerations. Chapter 3 continues our discussion of research ethics.

You are now forewarned about the difficulties that all scientists, but social scientists in particular, face in their work. We hope that you will return often to this chapter as you read the subsequent chapters, when you criticize the research literature, and when you design your own research projects. To be conscientious, thoughtful, and responsible—this is the mandate of every social scientist. If you formulate a feasible research problem, ask the right questions in advance, try to adhere to the research guidelines, and steer clear of the most common difficulties, you will be well along the road to fulfilling this mandate.

KEY TERMS

Anomalous
Cohort
Cohort design
Confidentiality
Cross-sectional research design
Deductive research
Dependent variable
Direction of association
Ecological fallacy
Group unit of analysis
Hypothesis
Independent variable
Individual unit of analysis

Inductive reasoning
Inductive research
Institutional review board (IRB)
Longitudinal research design
Panel design
Reductionist fallacy (reductionism)
Repeated cross-sectional design
Research circle
Serendipitous
Social research question
Theory
Units of analysis
Variable

HIGHLIGHTS

- Research questions should be feasible (within the time and resources available), socially important, and scientifically relevant.
- Building social theory is a major objective of social science research. Investigate relevant theories before starting social research projects and draw out the theoretical implications of research findings.
- The type of reasoning in most research can be described as primarily deductive or inductive. Research based on deductive reasoning proceeds from general ideas, deduces specific expectations from these ideas, and then tests the ideas with empirical data. Research based on inductive reasoning begins with ("in!") specific data and then develops (induces) general ideas or theories to explain patterns in the data.
- It may be possible to explain unanticipated research findings after the fact, but such explanations have less credibility than those that have been tested with data collected for the purpose of the study.
- The scientific process can be represented as circular, with connections from theory, to hypotheses, to data, and to empirical generalizations. Research investigations may begin at different points along the research circle and traverse different portions of it. Deductive research begins at the point of theory; inductive research begins with data but ends with theory. Descriptive research begins with data and ends with empirical generalizations.

- Scientific research should be conducted and reported in an honest and open fashion. Contemporary ethical standards also require that social research cause no harm to subjects, that participation be voluntary as expressed in informed consent, that researchers fully disclose their identity, that benefits to subjects outweigh any foreseeable risks, and that anonymity or confidentiality be maintained for participants unless it is voluntarily and explicitly waived.

STUDENT STUDY SITE

To assist you in completing the Web Exercises, please access the Study Site at http://www.pineforge.com/mssw3, where you'll find the Web Exercises with accompanying links. You'll find other useful study materials like self-quizzes and e-flashcards for each chapter, along with a group of carefully selected articles from research journals that illustrate the major concepts and techniques presented in the book.

EXERCISES

Discussing Research

1. Pick a social issue about which you think research is needed. Draft three research questions about this issue. Refine one of the questions and evaluate it in terms of the three criteria for good research questions.

2. Identify variables that are relevant to your three research questions. Now formulate three related hypotheses. Which are the independent and which are the dependent variables in these hypotheses?

3. If you were to design research about domestic violence, would you prefer an inductive approach or a deductive approach? Explain your preference. What would be the advantages and disadvantages of each approach? Consider in your answer the role of social theory, the value of searching the literature, and the goals of your research.

4. Sherman and Berk's study of the police response to domestic violence tested a prediction derived from deterrence theory. Propose hypotheses about the response to domestic violence that are consistent with labeling theory. Which theory seems to you to provide the best framework for understanding domestic violence and how to respond to it?

5. Review our description of the research projects in the section "Social Research in Practice" in Chapter 1. Can you identify the stages of each project corresponding to the points on the research circle? Did each project include each of the four stages? Which theory (or theories) seem applicable to each of these projects?

Finding Research

1. State a problem for research—some feature of social life that interests you. If you have not already identified a problem for study, or if you need to evaluate whether your research problem is doable, a few suggestions should help to get the ball rolling and keep you on course.

a. Jot down several questions that have puzzled you about people and social relations, perhaps questions that have come to mind while reading textbooks or research articles, talking with friends, or hearing news stories.

b. Now take stock of your interests, your opportunities, and the work of others. Which of your research questions no longer seem feasible or interesting? What additional research questions come to mind? Pick out one question that is of interest and seems feasible and that has probably been studied before.

c. Do you think your motives for doing the research would affect how the research is done? How? Imagine several different motives for doing the research. Might any of them affect the quality of your research? How?

d. Write out your research question in one sentence; then elaborate on it in one paragraph. List at least three reasons why it is a good research question for you to investigate. Then present your question to your classmates and instructor for discussion and feedback.

2. Review Appendix A: Finding Information and then search the literature (and the Internet) on the research question you identified. Copy down at least five citations to articles (with abstracts from CSA Sociological Abstracts) and two Web sites reporting research that seems highly relevant to your research question. Look up at least two of these articles and one of the Web sites. Inspect the article bibliographies and the links at the Web site and identify at least one more relevant article and Web site from each source.

Write a brief description of each article and Web site you consulted and evaluate its relevance to your research question. What additions or changes to your thoughts about the research question are suggested by the sources?

3. You can read descriptions of major social theories at this Web site: http://ryoung001.homestead .com/AssessingTheory.html Which description do you find most appealing? Can you state several of the predictions from this theory as "if-then" hypotheses? What are the independent variables? The dependent variables?

4. You've been assigned to write a paper on domestic violence and the law. To start, you would like to find out what the American Bar Association's stance is on the issue. Go to the American Bar Association Commission on Domestic Violence's Web site (http://www.abanet.org/domviol/ docs/StandardsBlackLetter.pdf) What is the American Bar Association's policy about domestic violence? How does the ABA define *domestic violence*?

Critiquing Research

1. Using recent newspapers or magazines, find three articles that report on large interview or survey research studies. Describe each study briefly. Then say (a) whether the study design was longitudinal or cross-sectional and (b) if that mattered; that is, if the study's findings would possibly have been different using the alternative design.

2. Search the journal literature for three studies concerning some social program or organizational policy after you review the procedures in Appendix A. Several possibilities are research on Head Start, on the effects of welfare payments, on boot camps for offenders, and on standardized statewide testing in the public schools. Would you

characterize the findings as largely consistent or inconsistent? How would you explain discrepant findings?

3. Criticize one of the studies described in this chapter in terms of its adherence to each of the ethics guidelines for social research. List each guideline and indicate what problem or problems might have occurred as a result of deviation from it. How would you weigh the study's contribution to knowledge and social policy against its potential risks to human subjects?

Doing Research

1. Formulate four research questions about support for capital punishment. Provide one question for each research purpose: descriptive, exploratory, explanatory, and evaluative.

2. State four hypotheses in which support for capital punishment is the dependent variable and some other variable is the independent variable.
   a. Justify each hypothesis in a sentence or two.
   b. Propose a design to test each hypothesis. Design the studies to use different longitudinal designs and different units of analysis. What difficulties can you anticipate with each design?

3. Write a statement for one of your proposed research designs that states how you will ensure adherence to each ethical guideline for the protection of human subjects. Which standards for the protection of human subjects might pose the most difficulty for researchers on your proposed topic? Explain your answers and suggest appropriate protection procedures for human subjects.

Ethics Questions

1. Sherman and Berk (1984) and those who replicated their research on the police response to domestic violence assigned persons accused of domestic violence by chance (randomly) to be arrested or not. Their goal was to ensure that the people who were arrested were similar to those who were not arrested. Based on what you now know, do you feel that this random assignment procedure was ethical? Why or why not?

2. Concern with how research results are used is one of the hallmarks of ethical researchers, but deciding what form that concern should take is often difficult. You learned in this chapter about the controversy that occurred after Sherman and Berk (1984) encouraged police departments to adopt a pro-arrest policy in domestic abuse cases, based on findings from their Minneapolis study. Do you agree with the researchers' decision, in an effort to minimize domestic abuse, to suggest policy changes to police departments based on their study? Several replication studies failed to confirm the Minneapolis findings. Does this influence your evaluation of what the researchers should have done after the Minneapolis study was completed? What about Larry Sherman's (1992) argument that failure to publicize the Omaha study's finding of the effectiveness of arrest warrants resulted in some cases of abuse that could have been prevented?

CHAPTER 3

Ethics in Research

Imagine this: One spring morning as you are drinking coffee and reading the newspaper, you notice a small ad for a psychology experiment at the local university.

WE WILL PAY YOU $45 FOR ONE HOUR OF YOUR TIME

Persons Needed for a Study of Memory

"Earn money and learn about yourself," it continues. Feeling a bit bored, you call and schedule an evening visit to the lab.

You are about to enter one of the most ethically controversial experiments in the history of social science.

You arrive at the assigned room at the university and are immediately impressed by the elegance of the building and the professional appearance of the personnel. In the waiting room, you see a man dressed in a lab technician's coat talking to another visitor, a middle-aged fellow dressed in casual attire. The man in the lab coat turns, introduces himself, and explains that, as a psychologist, he is interested in whether people learn better when they are punished for making mistakes. He quickly convinces you that this is an important question; he then explains that his experiment on punishment and learning will discover the answer. Then he announces,

> "I'm going to ask one of you to be the teacher here tonight and the other one to be the learner."

The Experimenter [as we'll refer to him from now on] says he will write either "Teacher" or "Learner" on small identical slips of paper and then asks both of you to draw one. Yours says "Teacher."

The Experimenter now says, in a matter-of-fact way,

> "All right. Now the first thing we'll have to do is to set the Learner up so that he can get some type of punishment."

He leads you both behind a curtain, sits the Learner in the chair, straps down both of his arms, and attaches an electric wire to his left wrist (Exhibit 3.1). The wire is connected to a console with 30 switches and a large dial, on the other side of the curtain. When you ask what the wire is for, the Experimenter demonstrates. He asks you to take hold of the end of

EXHIBIT 3.1	**Learner Strapped in Chair With Electrodes**

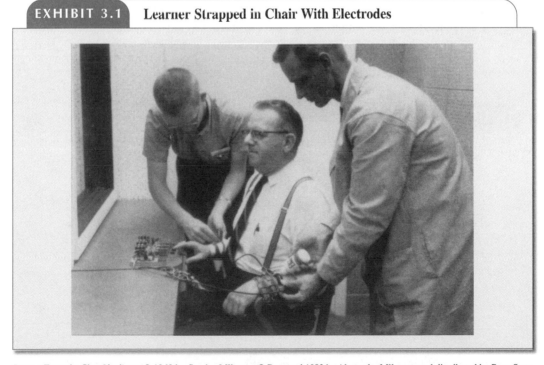

Source: From the film *Obedience* © 1968 by Stanley Milgram, © Renewed 1993 by Alexandra Milgram, and distributed by Penn State, Media Sales.

the wire, walks back to the control console, and flips several switches. You hear a clicking noise, see the dial move, and then feel an electric shock in your hand. When the experimenter flips the next switch, the shock increases.

"Ouch!" you say. "So that's the punishment. Couldn't it cause injury?" The Experimenter explains that the machine is calibrated so that it will not cause permanent injury but admits that when turned up all the way, it is very, very painful.

Now you walk back to the other side of the room (so that the Learner is behind the curtain) and sit before the console (Exhibit 3.2). The experimental procedure has four simple steps:

1. You read aloud a series of word pairs, like "blue box," "nice day," "wild duck," etc.

2. You read one of the first words from those pairs and a set of four words, one of which is the original paired word. For example, you might say, "Blue: sky-ink-box-lamp."

3. The Learner states the word that he thinks was paired with the first word you read ("blue"). If he gives a correct response, you compliment him and move on to the next word. If he makes a mistake, you flip a switch on the console. This causes the Learner to feel a shock on his wrist.

4. After each mistake, you are to flip the next switch on the console, progressing from left to right. You note that a label corresponds to every 5th mark on the dial, with the 1st mark labeled "slight shock," the 5th mark labeled "moderate shock," the 10th "strong shock," and so on through "very strong shock," "intense shock," "extreme intensity shock," and "danger: severe shock."

| EXHIBIT 3.2 | Milgram's "Shock Generator" |

Source: From the film *Obedience* © 1968 by Stanley Milgram, © Renewed 1993 by Alexandra Milgram, and distributed by Penn State, Media Sales.

You begin. The Learner at first gives some correct answers, but then he makes a few errors. Soon you are beyond the 5th mark ("slight shock") and are moving in the direction of more and more severe shocks. As you turn the dial, the Learner's reactions increase in intensity: from a grunt at the 15th mark ("strong shock") to painful groans at higher levels, to anguished cries of "Get me out of here!" at the "extreme intensity shock" levels, to a deathly silence at the highest level. When you protest at administering the stronger shocks, the Experimenter tells you, "The experiment requires that you continue." Occasionally he says, "It is absolutely essential that you continue."

This is a simplified version of the famous "obedience" experiments by Stanley Milgram (1963), begun at Yale University in 1960. Outside the laboratory, Milgram surveyed Yale undergraduates and asked them to indicate at what level they would terminate their "shocks" if they were in the study. Please mark on the console below the most severe shock that you would agree to give the Learner (Exhibit 3.3).

The average (mean) maximum shock level predicted by the Yale undergraduates was 9.35, corresponding to a "strong" shock. Only one student predicted that he would provide a stimulus above that level, at the "very strong" level. Responses were similar from nonstudent groups.

But the actual average level of shock administered by the 40 adults who volunteered for the experiment was 24.53—higher than "extreme intensity shock" and just short of "danger: severe shock." Twenty-five of Milgram's original 40 subjects complied entirely with the experimenter's demands, going all the way to the top of the scale (labeled simply as "XXX"). Judging from the subjects' visibly high stress, and from their subsequent reports, they believed that the Learner was receiving physically painful shocks.

We introduce the Milgram experiment not to discuss obedience to authority but instead to introduce research ethics. We refer to Milgram's obedience studies throughout this chapter, since they ultimately had as profound an influence on scientists' thinking about ethics as on how we understand obedience to authority.

EXHIBIT 3.3   Shock Meter

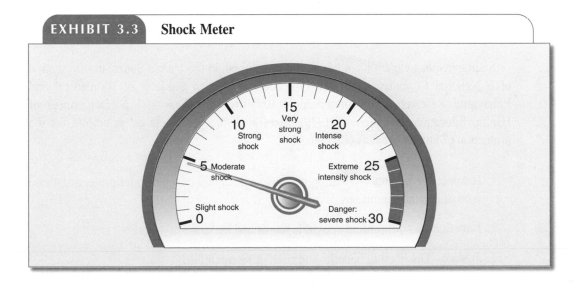

Throughout this book, we discuss ethical problems common to various research methods; in this particular chapter, we present in more detail some of the general ethical principles that professional social scientists use in monitoring their work.

▣ HISTORICAL BACKGROUND

Formal procedures for the protection of participants in research grew out of some widely publicized abuses. A defining event occurred in 1946, when the **Nuremberg war crime trials** exposed horrific medical experiments conducted during World War II by Nazi doctors in the name of "science." During the 1950s and 1960s, American military personnel and Pacific Islanders were sometimes unknowingly exposed to radiation during atomic bomb tests. And in the 1970s, Americans were shocked to learn that researchers funded by the U.S. Public Health Service had, for decades, studied 399 low-income African American men diagnosed with syphilis in the 1930s to follow the "natural" course of the illness (Exhibit 3.4). In the **Tuskegee syphilis study**, many participants were not informed of their illness and were denied treatment until 1972, even though a cure (penicillin) was developed in the 1950s (Jones, 1993).

Nuremberg war crime trials: Trials held in Nuremberg, Germany, in the years following World War II, in which the former leaders of Nazi Germany were charged with war crimes and crimes against humanity; frequently considered the first trials for people accused of genocide

Tuskegee syphilis study: Research study conducted by a branch of the U.S. government, lasting for roughly 50 years (ending in the 1970s), in which a sample of African American men diagnosed with syphilis were deliberately left untreated, without their knowledge, to learn about the lifetime course of the disease

---

Such egregious violations of human rights resulted, in the United States, in the creation of a National Commission for the Protection of Human Subjects of Biomedical and Behavioral Research. The Commission's 1979 *Belmont Report* (U.S. Department of Health, Education, and Welfare, 1979) established three basic ethical principles for the protection of human subjects (Exhibit 3.5):

1. **Respect for persons**—Treating persons as autonomous agents and protecting those with diminished autonomy

2. **Beneficence**—Minimizing possible harms and maximizing benefits

3. **Justice**—Distributing benefits and risks of research fairly

EXHIBIT 3.4 **Tuskegee Syphilis Experiment**

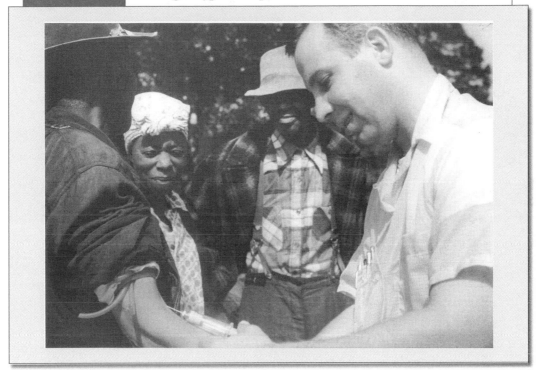

Belmont Report: Report in 1979 of the National Commission for the Protection of Human Subjects of Biomedical and Behavioral Research stipulating three basic ethical principles for the protection of human subjects: respect for persons, beneficence, and justice

Beneficence: Minimizing possible harms and maximizing benefits

Justice: As used in human research ethics discussions, distributing benefits and risks of research fairly

Respect for persons: In human subjects ethics discussions, treating persons as autonomous agents and protecting those with diminished autonomy

The Department of Health and Human Services and the Food and Drug Administration then translated these principles into specific regulations, which were adopted in 1991 as the **Federal Policy for the Protection of Human Subjects**. This policy has shaped the course of social science research ever since, and you will have to take it into account as you design your own research investigations. Some professional associations, such as the American Psychological Association, the American Political Science Association, the American Sociological Association, university review boards, and ethics committees in other

EXHIBIT 3.5   *Belmont Report* **Principles**

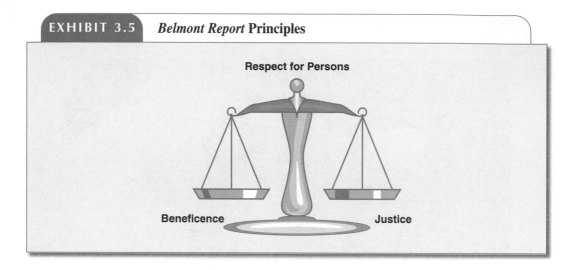

organizations, set standards for the treatment of human subjects by their members, employees, and students; these standards are designed to comply with the federal policy.

> *Federal Policy for the Protection of Human Subjects:* Federal regulations codifying basic principles for conducting research on human subjects; used as the basis for professional organizations' guidelines

Federal regulations require that every institution that seeks federal funding for biomedical or behavioral research on human subjects have an institutional review board (IRB) that reviews research proposals. IRBs at universities and other agencies apply ethics standards that are set by federal regulations but can be expanded or specified by the IRB itself (Sieber, 1992:5, 10). To promote adequate review of ethical issues, the regulations require that IRBs include members with diverse backgrounds. The **Office for Protection from Research Risks in the National Institutes of Health** monitors IRBs, with the exception of research involving drugs (which is the responsibility of the federal Food and Drug Administration).

> *Office for Protection from Research Risks, National Institutes of Health:* Federal agency that monitors institutional review boards (IRBs)

▣ ETHICAL PRINCIPLES

The American Sociological Association (ASA), like other professional social science organizations, has adopted, for practicing sociologists, ethical guidelines that are more specific than the federal regulations. Professional organizations may also review complaints of unethical practices when asked.

The *Code of Ethics* of the ASA (1997) is summarized at the ASA Web site (www.asanet.org); the complete text of the *Code* is also available at this site.

Mostly, ethical issues in research are covered by four guidelines:

1. To protect research subjects

2. To maintain honesty and openness

3. To achieve valid results

4. To encourage appropriate application

Each of these guidelines became a focus of the debate about Milgram's experiments, to which we will refer frequently. Did Stanley Milgram respect the spirit expressed in these principles? You will find that there is no simple answer to the question of what is (or isn't) ethical research practice.

Protecting Research Subjects

This guideline, our most important, can be divided into four specific directions:

1. Avoid harming research participants.

2. Obtain informed consent.

3. Avoid deception in research, except in limited circumstances.

4. Maintain privacy and confidentiality.

Avoid Harming Research Participants

This standard may seem straightforward, but can be difficult to interpret in specific cases. Does it mean that subjects should not be harmed even mentally or emotionally? That they should feel no anxiety or distress?

The most serious charge leveled against the ethics of Milgram's study was that he had harmed his subjects. A verbatim transcript of one session will give you an idea of what participants experienced as the "shock generator," which made it appear they were delivering increasingly severe shocks to the "learner" (Milgram, 1965:67):

150 volts delivered. You want me to keep going?

165 volts delivered. That guy is hollering in there. . . . He's liable to have a heart condition. You want me to go on?

180 volts delivered. He can't stand it! I'm not going to kill that man in there! You hear him hollering? He's hollering. He can't stand it. . . . I mean who is going to take responsibility if anything happens to that gentleman? *[The experimenter accepts responsibility.]* All right.

195 volts delivered. You see he's hollering. Hear that. Gee, I don't know. *[The experimenter says: "The experiment requires that you go on."]* I know it does, sir, but I mean—phew—he don't know what he's in for. He's up to 195 volts.

210 volts delivered.

225 volts delivered.

240 volts delivered.

The experimental manipulation generated "extraordinary tension" (Milgram, 1963:377):

Subjects were observed to sweat, tremble, stutter, bite their lips, groan and dig their fingernails into their flesh. . . . Full-blown, uncontrollable seizures were observed for 3 subjects. One . . . seizure so violently convulsive that it was necessary to call a halt to the experiment [for that individual]. (Milgram 1963:375)

An observer (behind a one-way mirror) reported, "I observed a mature and initially poised businessman enter the laboratory smiling and confident. Within 20 minutes he was reduced to a twitching, stuttering wreck, who was rapidly approaching a point of nervous collapse" (Milgram, 1963:377).

Milgram's "Behavioral Study of Obedience" was published in 1963 in the *Journal of Abnormal and Social Psychology*. In the next year, the *American Psychologist* published a critique of the experiment's ethics by psychologist Diana Baumrind (1964:421). From Baumrind's (422) perspective, the emotional disturbance in subjects was "potentially harmful because it could easily effect an alteration in the subject's self-image or ability to trust adult authorities in the future." Stanley Milgram (1964:849) quickly countered that

momentary excitement is not the same as harm. As the experiment progressed there was no indication of injurious effects in the subjects; and as the subjects themselves strongly endorsed the experiment, the judgment I made was to continue the experiment.

Milgram (1963:374) also attempted to minimize harm to subjects with postexperiment procedures "to assure that the subject would leave the laboratory in a state of well being." A friendly reconciliation was arranged between the subject and the victim, and an effort was made to reduce any tensions that arose as a result of the experiment.

In some cases, the "dehoaxing" (or "debriefing") discussion was extensive, and all subjects were promised (and later received) a comprehensive report (Milgram, 1964:849). But Baumrind (1964:422) was unconvinced: "It would be interesting to know what sort of procedures could dissipate the type of emotional disturbance just described."

When Milgram (1964:849) surveyed subjects in a follow-up, 83.7% endorsed the statement that they were "very glad" or "glad" "to have been in the experiment," 15.1% were "neither sorry nor glad," and just 1.3% were "sorry" or "very sorry" to have participated. Interviews by a psychiatrist a year later found no evidence "of any traumatic reactions" (Milgram, 1974:197). Subsequently, Milgram argued that "the central moral justification for allowing my experiment is that it was judged acceptable by those who took part in it" (Milgram as cited in Cave & Holm, 2003:32).

In a later article, Baumrind (1985:168) dismissed the value of the self-reported "lack of harm" of subjects who had been willing to participate in the experiment and noted that 16% did *not* endorse the statement that they were "glad" they had participated in the experiment. Many social scientists, ethicists, and others concluded that Milgram's procedures had not harmed subjects and so were justified by the knowledge they produced; others sided with Baumrind's criticisms (Miller, 1986:88–138).

Or consider the possible harm to subjects in the famous **prison simulation study** at Stanford University (Haney, Banks, & Zimbardo, 1973). The study was designed to investigate the impact of being either a guard or a prisoner in a prison, a "total institution." The researchers selected apparently stable and mature young male volunteers and asked them to sign a contract to work for 2 weeks as a guard or a prisoner in a simulated prison. Within the first 2 days after the prisoners were incarcerated in a makeshift basement prison, the prisoners began to be passive and disorganized, while the guards became "sadistic"— verbally and physically aggressive (Exhibit 3.6). Five "prisoners" were soon released for depression, uncontrollable crying, fits of rage, and, in one case, a psychosomatic rash. Instead of letting things continue for 2 weeks as planned, Zimbardo and his colleagues terminated the experiment after 6 days to avoid harming subjects.

Prison simulation study (Zimbardo's): Famous study from the early 1970s, organized by Stanford psychologist Philip Zimbardo, demonstrating the willingness of average college students quickly to become harsh disciplinarians when put in the role of (simulated) prison guards over other students; usually interpreted as demonstrating an easy human readiness to become cruel

---

Participants playing the prisoner role certainly felt some stress, but this seemed to be relieved by postexperiment discussion sessions; follow-up during the next year indicated no lasting negative effects on the participants and some benefits in the form of greater insight. And besides, Zimbardo and his colleagues had no way of predicting the bad outcome; indeed, they were themselves surprised (Haney et al., 1973).

Even well-intentioned researchers may fail to foresee potential ethical problems. Milgram (1974:27–31) reported that he and his colleagues were surprised by the subjects' willingness to administer such severe shocks. In Zimbardo's prison simulation, all the participants signed consent forms, but even the researchers did not realize that participants would fall apart so quickly, that some prisoners would have to be released within a few days, or that others would soon be begging to be released from the mock prison. Since some risks cannot be foreseen, they cannot be consented to.

Obtain Informed Consent

Just defining informed consent may also be more difficult than it first appears. To be informed, consent must be given by persons who are competent to consent, have consented

| EXHIBIT 3.6 | **Chart of Guard and Prisoner Behavior** |

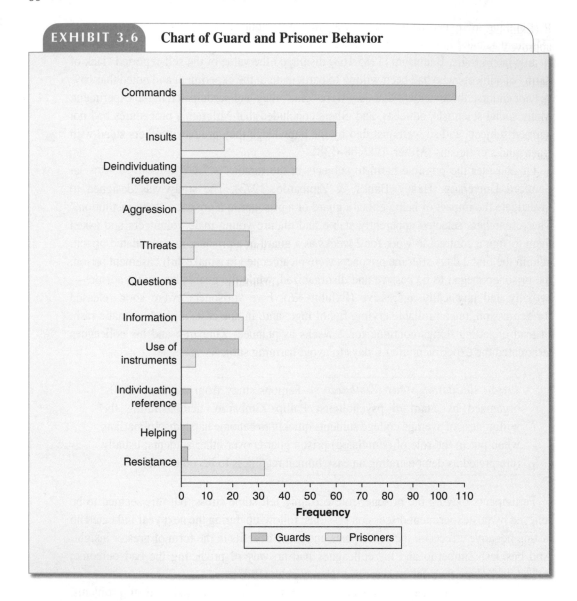

voluntarily, are fully informed about the research, and have comprehended what they have been told (Reynolds, 1979). Yet you probably realize, as did Diana Baumrind (1985:165), that due to the inability to communicate perfectly, "Full disclosure of everything that could possibly affect a given subject's decision to participate is not possible, and therefore cannot be ethically required."

Obtaining informed consent creates additional challenges for researchers. For instance, the language of the consent form must be clear and understandable yet sufficiently long and detailed to explain what will actually happen in the research. Examples A (Exhibit 3.7) and

B (Exhibit 3.8) illustrate two different approaches to these tradeoffs. Consent form A was approved by a university for a substance abuse survey with undergraduate students. It is brief and to the point but leaves quite a bit to the imagination of the prospective participants. Consent form B reflects the requirements of an academic hospital's IRB. Because the hospital is used to reviewing research proposals involving drugs and other treatment interventions with hospital patients, it requires a very detailed and lengthy explanation of procedures and related issues, even for a simple survey. Requiring prospective participants to sign such lengthy forms can reduce their willingness to participate in research and perhaps influence their responses if they do agree to participate (Larson 1993:114).

When an experimental design requires subject deception, researchers may withhold information before the experiment but then debrief subjects after the experiment ends (Milgram did this). In the **debriefing**, the researcher explains what really happened in the experiment, and why, and responds to subjects' questions. A carefully designed debriefing procedure can often help research participants deal with their anger or embarrassment at having been deceived (Sieber, 1992:39–41), thus substituting for fully informed consent prior to the experiment.

EXHIBIT 3.7   **Consent Form A**

University of Massachusetts at Boston

Department of Sociology

October 28, 1996

Dear _____:

The health of students and their use of alcohol and drugs are important concerns for every college and university. The enclosed survey is about these issues at UMass/Boston. It is sponsored by University Health Services and the PRIDE Program (Prevention, Resources, Information, and Drug Education). The questionnaire was developed by graduate students in Applied Sociology, Nursing, and Gerontology.

You were selected for the survey with a scientific, random procedure. Now it is important that you return the questionnaire so that we can obtain an unbiased description of the undergraduate student body. Health Services can then use the results to guide campus education and prevention programs.

The survey requires only about 20 minutes to complete. Participation is completely voluntary and anonymous. No one will be able to link your survey responses to you. In any case, your standing at the University will not be affected whether or not you choose to participate. Just be sure to return the enclosed postcard after you mail the questionnaire so that we know we do not have to contact you again.

Please return the survey by November 15th. If you have any questions or comments, call the PRIDE program at 287–5680 or Professor Schutt at 287–6250. Also call the PRIDE program if you would like a summary of our final report.

Thank you in advance for your assistance.

Russell K. Schutt, Ph.D.

Professor and Chair

EXHIBIT 3.8   **Consent Form B**

Research Consent Form for Social and Behavioral Research

Dana-Farber/Harvard Cancer Center

BIDMC/BWH/CH/DFCI/MGH/Partners Network Affiliates   OPRS 11-05

Protocol Title: ASSESSING COMMUNITY HEALTH WORKERS' ATTITUDES AND KNOWLEDGE ABOUT EDUCATING COMMUNITIES ABOUT CANCER CLINICAL TRIALS

DF/HCC Principal Research Investigator / Institution: Dr. Russell Schutt, Ph.D. / Beth Israel Deaconess Medical Center and Univ. of Massachusetts, Boston

DF/HCC Site-Responsible Research Investigator(s) / Institution(s):

Lidia Schapira, M.D. / Massachusetts General Hospital

Interview Consent Form

A. <u>INTRODUCTION</u>

We are inviting you to take part in a research study. Research is a way of gaining new knowledge. A person who participates in a research study is called a "subject." This research study is evaluating whether community health workers might be willing and able to educate communities about the pros and cons of participating in research studies.

It is expected that about 10 people will take part in this research study.

An institution that is supporting a research study either by giving money or supplying something that is important for the research is called the "sponsor." The sponsor of this protocol is National Cancer Institute and is providing money for the research study.

This research consent form explains why this research study is being done, what is involved in participating in the research study, the possible risks and benefits of the research study, alternatives to participation, and your rights as a research subject. The decision to participate is yours. If you decide to participate, please sign and date at the end of the form. We will give you a copy so that you can refer to it while you are involved in this research study.

If you decide to participate in this research study, certain questions will be asked of you to see if you are eligible to be in the research study. The research study has certain requirements that must be met. If the questions show that you can be in the research study, you will be able to answer the interview questions.

If the questions show that you cannot be in the research study, you will not be able to participate in this research study.

Page 1 of 6

DFCI Protocol Number:	06-085	Date DFCI IRB Approved This Consent Form:	January 16, 2007
Date Posted for Use:	January 16, 2007	Date DFCI IRB Approval Expires:	August 13, 2007

**Research Consent Form for Social and
Behavioral Research**

Dana-Farber/Harvard Cancer Center

BIDMC/BWH/CH/DFCI/MGH/Partners Network Affiliates   OPRS 11-05

We encourage you to take some time to think this over and to discuss it with other people and to ask questions now and at any time in the future.

B. WHY IS THIS RESEARCH STUDY BEING DONE?

Deaths from cancer in general and for some specific cancers are higher for black people compared to white people, for poor persons compared to nonpoor persons, and for rural residents compared to nonrural residents. There are many reasons for higher death rates between different subpopulations. One important area for changing this is to have more persons from minority groups participate in research about cancer. The process of enrolling minority populations into clinical trials is difficult and does not generally address the needs of their communities. One potential way to increase participation in research is to use community health workers to help educate communities about research and about how to make sure that researchers are ethical. We want to know whether community health workers think this is a good strategy and how to best carry it out.

C. WHAT OTHER OPTIONS ARE THERE?

Taking part in this research study is voluntary. Instead of being in this research study, you have the following option:

- Decide not to participate in this research study.

D. WHAT IS INVOLVED IN THE RESEARCH STUDY?

Before the research starts (screening): After signing this consent form, you will be asked to answer some questions about where you work and the type of community health work you do to find out if you can be in the research study.

If the answers show that you are eligible to participate in the research study, you will be eligible to participate in the research study. If you do not meet the eligibility criteria, you will not be able to participate in this research study.

After the screening procedures confirm that you are eligible to participate in the research study:
You will participate in an interview by answering questions from a questionnaire. The interview will take about 90 minutes. If there are questions you prefer not to answer we can skip those questions. The questions are about the type of work you do and your opinions about participating in research. If you agree, the interview will be taped and then transcribed. Your name and no other information about you will be associated:

. . .

Page 2 of 6

DFCI Protocol Number:	06-085	Date DFCI IRB Approved This Consent Form:	January 16, 2007
Date Posted for Use:	January 16, 2007	Date DFCI IRB Approval Expires:	August 13, 2007

(Continued)

(Continued)

Research Consent Form for Social and Behavioral Research

Dana-Farber/Harvard Cancer Center

BIDMC/BWH/CH/DFCI/MGH/Partners Network Affiliates   OPRS 11-05

with the tape or the transcript. Only the research team will be able to listen to the tapes. Immediately following the interview, you will have the opportunity to have the tape erased if you wish to withdraw your consent to taping or participation in this study. You will receive $30.00 for completing this interview.

After the interview is completed: Once you finish the interview there are no additional interventions.

. . .

N. **DOCUMENTATION OF CONSENT**

My signature below indicates my willingness to participate in this research study and my understanding that I can withdraw at any time.

_____   _____
Signature of Subject   Date
or Legally Authorized Representative

_____   _____
Person obtaining consent   Date

To be completed by person obtaining consent:

The consent discussion was initiated on _____ (date) at _____ (time).

☐ A copy of this signed consent form was given to the subject or legally authorized representative.

For Adult Subjects

☐ The subject is an adult and provided consent to participate.

☐ The subject is an adult who lacks capacity to provide consent, and his/her legally authorized representative:

    ☐ gave permission for the adult subject to participate

    ☐ did not give permission for the adult subject to participate

---

Page 6 of 6

DFCI Protocol Number: 06-085	Date DFCI IRB Approved This Consent Form: January 16, 2007
Date Posted for Use: January 16, 2007	Date DFCI IRB Approval Expires: August 13, 2007

> *Debriefing:* A researcher's informing subjects after an experiment about the experiment's purposes and methods and evaluating subjects' personal reactions to the experiment

Finally, some participants can't truly give informed consent. College students, for instance, may feel unable to refuse if their professor asks them to be in an experiment. Legally speaking, children cannot give consent to participate in research; a child's legal guardian must give written informed consent to have the child participate in research (Sieber, 1992). Then the child must in most circumstances be given the opportunity to give or withhold *assent* to participate in research, usually by a verbal response to an explanation of the research. Special protections exist for other vulnerable populations—prisoners, pregnant women, mentally disabled persons, and educationally or economically disadvantaged persons. And in a sense, anyone deliberately deceived in an experiment cannot be said to really have given "informed" consent, since the person wasn't honestly told what would happen.

Laud Humphreys (1970) decided that truly informed consent would be impossible to obtain for his study of the social background of men who engage in homosexual behavior in public facilities. Humphreys served as a lookout—a "watch queen"—for men who were entering a public bathroom in a city park with the intention of having sex. In a number of cases, he then left the bathroom and copied the license plate numbers of the cars driven by the men. One year later, he visited the homes of the men and interviewed them as part of a larger study of social issues. Humphreys changed his appearance so that the men did not recognize him. In his book *Tearoom Trade,* Humphreys concluded that the men who engaged in what were widely viewed as deviant acts were, for the most part, married, suburban men whose families were unaware of their sexual practices. But debate has continued ever since about Humphreys's failure to tell the men what he was really doing in the bathroom or why he had come to their homes for the interview. He was criticized by many, including some faculty members at the University of Washington who urged that his doctoral degree be withheld. However, many other professors and some members of the gay community praised Humphreys for helping to normalize conceptions of homosexuality (Miller, 1986:135).

> *Tearoom Trade:* Book by Laud Humphreys investigating the social background of men who engage in homosexual behavior in public facilities; controversially, he did not obtain informed consent from his subjects

If you served on your university's IRB, would you allow research such as Humphreys's to be conducted?

Avoid Deception in Research, Except in Limited Circumstances

Deception occurs when subjects are misled about research procedures. Frequently, this is done to simulate real-world conditions in the lab. The goal is to get subjects "to accept as true what is false or to give a false impression" (Korn, 1997:4). In Milgram's (1964) experiment, for example, deception seemed necessary because actually giving electric shocks to the "stooge" would be cruel. Yet to test obedience, the task had to be troubling for the subjects. Milgram (1992:187–188) insisted that the deception was absolutely essential. Many other psychological and social psychological experiments would be worthless if subjects understood what was really happening to them while the experiment was in progress. But is this sufficient justification to allow the use of deception?

Some important topics have been cleverly studied using deception. Gary Marshall and Philip Zimbardo (of prison study fame), in a 1979 study, told the student volunteers that they were being injected with a vitamin supplement to test its effect on visual acuity (Korn, 1997:2–3). But to determine the physiological basis of emotion, they actually injected them with adrenaline, so that their heart rate and sweating would increase, and then placed them in a room with a student "stooge" who acted silly. Piliavin and Piliavin, in a 1972 study, staged fake seizures on subway trains to study helpfulness (Korn:3–4). Again, would you allow such deceptive practices if you were a member of your university's IRB? Giving people stimulating drugs, apart from the physical dangers, is using their very bodies for research without their knowledge. Faking an emergency may lessen one's willingness to help in the future or may, in effect, punish the research subjects—through embarrassment— for their reaction to what is really "just an experiment."

But perhaps risk, not deception per se, is the real problem. Aronson and Mills's (1959) study of severity of initiation to groups is a good example of experimental research that does not pose greater-than-everyday risks to subjects but still uses deception. This study was conducted at an all-women's college in the 1950s. The student volunteers who were randomly assigned to the "severe initiation" experimental condition had to read a list of embarrassing words. Even in the 1950s, reading a list of potentially embarrassing words in a laboratory setting, then listening to a taped discussion, was unlikely to increase the risks to which students were exposed in their everyday lives. Moreover, the researchers informed subjects that they would be expected to talk about sex and could decline to participate in the experiment if this requirement would bother them. None dropped out. To further ensure that no psychological harm was caused, Aronson and Mills explained the true nature of the experiment to subjects after the experiment. The subjects did not seem perturbed: "None of the Ss expressed any resentment or annoyance at having been misled. In fact, the majority were intrigued by the experiment, and several returned at the end of the academic quarter to ascertain the result" (179).

Are you satisfied that this procedure caused no harm? The minimal deception in the Aronson and Mills experiment, coupled with the lack of any ascertainable risk to subjects and a debriefing, satisfies the ethical standards for research of most psychologists and IRBs, even today.

Maintain Privacy and Confidentiality

Maintaining privacy and confidentiality after a study is completed is another way to protect subjects, and the researcher's commitment to that standard should be included in the informed consent agreement (Sieber, 1992). Procedures to protect each subject's privacy, such as locking records and creating special identifying codes, must be created to minimize the risk of access by unauthorized persons. For the protection of health care data, the **Health Insurance Portability and Accountability Act (HIPAA)** passed by Congress in 1996 created much more stringent regulations. As implemented by the U.S. Department of Health and Human Services in 2000 (and revised in 2002), the HIPAA Final Privacy Rule applies to oral, written, and electronic information that "relates to the past, present, or future physical or mental health or condition of an individual" (Legal Information Institute, 2006, § 1320d[6][B]). The HIPAA Rule requires that researchers have valid authorization for any use or disclosure of "protected health information" (PHI) from a health care provider. Waivers of authorization can be granted in special circumstances (Cava, Cushman, & Goodman, 2007).

Health Insurance Portability and Accountability Act (HIPAA): A U.S. federal law passed in 1996 that guarantees, among other things, specified privacy rights for medical patients, in particular those in research settings

---

However, statements about confidentiality also need to be realistic. The law allows even confidential research records to be subpoenaed and may require reporting child abuse. A researcher may feel compelled to release information if a health- or life-threatening situation arises and participants need to be alerted. The National Institutes of Health can issue a **Certificate of Confidentiality** to protect researchers from being legally required to disclose confidential information. Researchers who are focusing on high-risk populations or behaviors or sensitive topics, such as crime, substance abuse, sexual activity, or genetic information, can request such a certificate. Suspicions of child abuse or neglect must still be reported, and in some states, researchers may still be required to report such crimes as elder abuse (Arwood & Panicker, 2007).

Certificate of Confidentiality: Document issued by the National Institutes of Health to protect researchers from being legally required to disclose confidential information

---

Maintaining Honesty and Openness

Protecting subjects, then, is the primary focus of research ethics. But researchers have obligations to other groups, including the scientific community, whose concern with validity requires that scientists be open in disclosing their methods and honest in presenting their findings. To assess the validity of a researcher's conclusions and the ethics of his or her procedures, you need to know how the research was conducted. This means that articles or other reports must include a detailed methodology section, perhaps supplemented by appendixes containing the research instruments or Web sites or other contact information where more information can be obtained. Biases or political motives should be acknowledged, since research distorted by political or personal pressures to find particular outcomes is unlikely to be carried out in an honest and open fashion.

Stanley Milgram's research exemplifies adherence to the goal of honesty and openness (Exhibit 3.9). His initial 1963 article included a description of study procedures, including details about the procedures involved in the learning task, administration of the "sample shock," the shock instructions and the preliminary practice run, the standardized feedback from the "victim" and from the experimenter, and the measures used. Many more details, including pictures, were provided in Milgram's (1974) subsequent book.

The act of publication itself is a vital element in maintaining openness and honesty, since then others can review procedures and debate with the researcher. Although Milgram disagreed sharply with Diana Baumrind's criticisms of his experiments, their mutual commitment to public discourse in journals widely available to psychologists resulted in more comprehensive presentation of study procedures and more thoughtful conversation about research ethics. Almost 50 years later, this commentary continues to inform debates about research ethics (Cave & Holm, 2003).

In spite of this need for openness, researchers may hesitate to disclose their procedures or results to prevent others from "stealing" their ideas and taking the credit. However, failure to be open about procedures can result in difficult disputes. In the 1980s, for instance, as mentioned in Chapter 2, there was a long legal battle between a U.S. researcher, Dr. Robert Gallo, and a French researcher, Dr. Luc Montagnier, both of whom claimed credit for discovering the AIDS virus. Eventually the dispute was settled at the

EXHIBIT 3.9   **Diagram of Milgram Experiment**

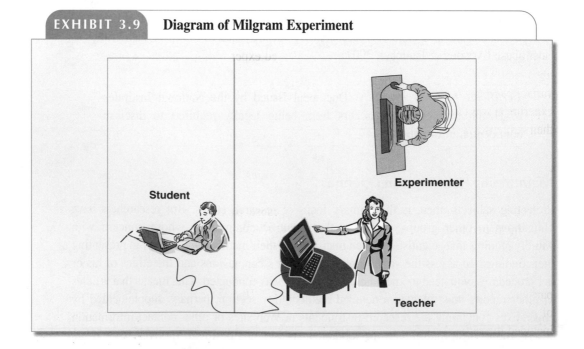

highest levels of government, through an agreement announced by American President Ronald Reagan and French Prime Minister Jacques Chirac (Altman, 1987). Gallo and Montagnier jointly developed a chronology of discovery as part of the agreement. Enforcing standards of honesty and encouraging openness about research are often the best solutions to such problems.

Achieving Valid Results

It is the pursuit of objective knowledge—the goal of validity—that justifies our investigations and our claims to the use of human subjects. We have no business asking people to answer questions, submit to observations, or participate in experiments if we are simply trying to trumpet our own prejudices or pursue our personal interests. If, on the other hand, we approach our research projects objectively, setting aside our predilections in the service of learning a bit more about human behavior, we can honestly represent our actions as potentially contributing to the advancement of knowledge.

The details in Milgram's 1963 article and 1974 book on the obedience experiments make a compelling case for his commitment to achieving valid results—to learning how obedience influences behavior. In Milgram's (1963:371) own words,

> It has been reliably established that from 1933–45 millions of innocent persons were systematically slaughtered on command. . . . Obedience is the psychological mechanism that links individual action to political purpose. It is the dispositional cement that binds men to systems of authority . . . for many persons obedience may be a deeply ingrained behavior tendency. . . . Obedience may [also] be ennobling and educative and refer to acts of charity and kindness, as well as to destruction.

Milgram (1963:372) then explains how he devised experiments to study the process of obedience in a way that would seem realistic to the subjects and still allow "important variables to be manipulated at several points in the experiment." Every step in the experiment was carefully designed to ensure that subjects received identical stimuli and that their responses were measured carefully.

Obedience experiments (Milgram's): A series of famous experiments conducted during the 1960s by Stanley Milgram, a psychologist from Yale University, testing subjects' willingness to cause pain to another person if instructed to do so

---

Milgram's (1963:377) attention to validity is also apparent in his reflections on "the particular conditions" of his experiment, for, he notes, "Understanding of the phenomenon of obedience must rest on an analysis of [these conditions]." These particular conditions included the setting for the experiment at Yale University, its purported "worthy purpose" to advance knowledge about learning and memory, and the voluntary participation of the subject as well as of the Learner—as far as the subject knew. The importance of some of these "particular conditions" (such as the location at Yale) was then tested in subsequent replications of the basic experiment (Milgram, 1965).

However, not all psychologists agreed that Milgram's approach could achieve valid results. Baumrind's (1964:423) critique begins with a rejection of the external validity—the generalizability—of the experiment. "The laboratory is unfamiliar as a setting and the rules of behavior ambiguous. . . . Therefore, the laboratory is not the place to study degree of obedience or suggestibility, as a function of a particular experimental condition." And so, "the parallel between authority-subordinate relationships in Hitler's Germany and in Milgram's laboratory is unclear."

Stanley Milgram (1964:850) quickly published a rejoinder in which he disagreed with (among other things) the notion that it is inappropriate to study obedience in a laboratory setting: "A subject's obedience is no less problematical because it occurs within a social institution called the psychological experiment."

Milgram (1974:169–178) also pointed out that his experiment had been replicated in other places and settings with the same results, that there was considerable evidence that subjects had believed that they actually were administering shocks, and that the "essence" of his experimental manipulation—the request that subjects comply with a legitimate authority—was shared with the dilemma faced by people in Nazi Germany and soldiers at the My Lai massacre in Vietnam (Miller, 1986:182–183).

But Baumrind (1985:171) was still not convinced. In a follow-up article in the *American Psychologist,* she argued that "far from illuminating real life, as he claimed, Milgram in fact appeared to have constructed a set of conditions so internally inconsistent that they could not occur in real life."

Milgram assumed that obedience could fruitfully be studied in the laboratory; Baumrind disagreed. Both, however, buttressed their ethical arguments with assertions about the external validity (or invalidity) of the experimental results. They agreed, in other words, that a research study is in part justified by its valid findings—the knowledge to be gained. If the findings aren't valid, they can't justify the research at all. It is hard to justify any risk for human subjects, or even any expenditure of time and resources, if our findings tell us nothing about human behavior.

Encouraging Appropriate Application

Finally, scientists must consider the uses to which their research is put. Although many scientists believe that personal values should be left outside the laboratory, some feel that it is proper—even necessary—for scientists to concern themselves with the way their research is used.

Stanley Milgram made it clear that he was concerned about the phenomenon of obedience precisely because of its implications for people's welfare. As you have already learned, his first article (1963) highlighted the atrocities committed under the Nazis by citizens and soldiers who were "just following orders." In his more comprehensive book on the obedience experiments (1974), he also used his findings to shed light on the atrocities committed in the Vietnam War at My Lai, slavery, the destruction of the American Indian population, and the internment of Japanese Americans during World War II. Milgram makes no explicit attempt to "tell us what to do" about this problem. In fact, as a dispassionate psychological researcher, Milgram (1974:xi) tells us, "What the present study [did was] to give the dilemma [of obedience to authority] contemporary form by treating it as subject matter for experimental inquiry, and with the aim of understanding rather than judging it from a moral standpoint."

Yet it is impossible to ignore the very practical implications of Milgram's investigations. His research highlighted the extent of obedience to authority and identified multiple factors that could be manipulated to lessen blind obedience (such as encouraging dissent by just one group member, removing the subject from direct contact with the authority figure, and increasing the contact between the subject and the victim).

A widely publicized experiment on the police response to domestic violence provides an interesting cautionary tale about the uses of science. Lawrence Sherman and Richard Berk (1984) arranged with the Minneapolis police department for the random assignment of persons accused of domestic violence to be either arrested or simply given a warning. The results of this field experiment indicated that those who were arrested were less likely subsequently to commit violent acts against their partners. Sherman (1993) explicitly cautioned police departments not to adopt mandatory arrest policies based solely on the results of the Minneapolis experiment, but the results were publicized in the mass media and encouraged many jurisdictions to change their policies (Binder & Meeker, 1993; Lempert, 1989). Although we now know that the original finding of a deterrent effect of arrest did not hold up in many other cities where the experiment was repeated, Sherman (1992:150–153) later suggested that implementing mandatory arrest policies might have prevented some subsequent cases of spouse abuse. In particular, in a follow-up study in Omaha, arrest warrants reduced repeat offenses among spouse abusers who had already left the scene when police arrived. However, this Omaha finding was not publicized, so it could not be used to improve police policies. So how much publicity is warranted, and at what point in the research should it occur?

Social scientists who conduct research on behalf of specific organizations may face additional difficulties when the organization, instead of the researcher, controls the final report and the publicity it receives. If organizational leaders decide that particular research results are unwelcome, the researcher's desire to have findings used appropriately and reported fully can conflict with contractual obligations. Researchers can anticipate such dilemmas and resolve them when the contract is negotiated—or simply decline a particular research opportunity altogether. But often such problems arise only after a report has been drafted, or the problems are ignored by a researcher who needs the job or to maintain a personal relationship. These possibilities cannot be avoided entirely, but because of them, it is always important to acknowledge the source of research funding in reports and to consider carefully the sources of funding for research reports written by others.

▣ CONCLUSION

Different kinds of research produce different kinds of ethical problems. Most survey research, for instance, creates few if any ethical problems and can even be enjoyable for participants. In fact, researchers from Michigan's Institute for Survey Research interviewed a representative national sample of adults and found that 68% of those who had participated in a survey were somewhat or very interested in participating in another; the more times respondents had been interviewed, the more willing they were to participate again (Reynolds, 1979:56–57). On the other hand, some experimental studies in the social sciences that have put people in uncomfortable or embarrassing situations have generated vociferous complaints and years of debate about ethics (Reynolds; Sjoberg, 1967).

Research ethics should be based on a realistic assessment of the overall potential for harm and benefit to research subjects. In this chapter, we have presented some basic guidelines, and examples in other chapters suggest applications, but answers aren't always obvious. For example, full disclosure of "what is really going on" in an experimental study is unnecessary if subjects are unlikely to be harmed. In one student observation study on cafeteria workers, for instance, the IRB didn't require consent forms to be signed. The legalistic forms and signatures, they felt, would be more intrusive or upsetting to workers than the very benign and confidential research itself. The committee put the feelings of subjects above the strict requirement for consent.

Ultimately, then, these decisions about ethical procedures are not just up to you, as a researcher, to make. Your university's IRB sets the human subjects protection standards for your institution and will require that researchers—even, in most cases, students—submit their research proposal to the IRB for review. So the ethical propriety of your research will be guarded by an institutional committee, following professional codes and guidelines; but still, that is an uncertain substitute for your own conscience.

KEY TERMS

Belmont Report
Beneficence
Certificate of Confidentiality
Debriefing
Federal Policy for the Protection
   of Human Subjects
Health Insurance Portability and
   Accountability Act (HIPAA)
Justice

Nuremberg war crime trials
Obedience experiments (Milgram's)
Office for Protection from Research Risks,
   National Institutes of Health
Prison simulation study
   (Zimbardo's)
Respect for persons
Tearoom Trade
Tuskegee syphilis study

HIGHLIGHTS

- Stanley Milgram's obedience experiments led to intensive debate about the extent to which deception could be tolerated in psychological research and how harm to subjects should be evaluated.

- Egregious violations of human rights by researchers, including scientists in Nazi Germany and researchers in the Tuskegee syphilis study, led to the adoption of federal ethical standards for research on human subjects.
- The 1979 *Belmont Report* developed by a national commission established three basic ethical standards for the protection of human subjects: respect for persons, beneficence, and justice.
- The Department of Health and Human Services adopted in 1991 the Federal Policy for the Protection of Human Subjects. The policy requires that every institution seeking federal funding for biomedical or behavioral research on human subjects have an institutional review board to exercise oversight.
- Standards for the protection of human subjects require avoiding harm, obtaining informed consent, avoiding deception except in limited circumstances, and maintaining privacy and confidentiality.
- Scientific research should maintain high standards for validity and be conducted and reported in an honest and open fashion.
- Effective debriefing of subjects after an experiment can help to reduce the risk of harm due to the use of deception in the experiment.

STUDENT STUDY SITE

To assist you in completing the Web Exercises, please access the Study Site at http://www.pineforge.com/mssw3, where you'll find the Web Exercises with accompanying links. You'll find other useful study materials like self-quizzes and e-flashcards for each chapter, along with a group of carefully selected articles from research journals that illustrate the major concepts and techniques presented in the book.

EXERCISES

Discussing Research

1. Should social scientists be permitted to conduct replications of Milgram's obedience experiments? Zimbardo's prison simulation? Can you justify such research as permissible within the current ASA ethical standards? If not, do you believe that these standards should be altered so as to permit Milgram-type research?

2. Why does unethical research occur? Is it inherent in science? Does it reflect "human nature"? What makes ethical research more or less likely?

3. Does debriefing solve the problem of subject deception? How much must researchers reveal after the experiment is over, as well as before it begins?

Finding Research

1. The Collaborative Institutional Training Initiative (CITI) offers an extensive online training course in the basics of human subjects protections issues. Go to the public access CITI site at https://www.citiprogram.org/rcrpage.asp?affiliation=100 and complete the course in social and behavioral research. Write a short summary of what you have learned.

2. The U.S. Department of Health and Human Services maintains extensive resources concerning the protection of human subjects in research. Read several documents that you find on its Web site at http://www.hhs.gov/ohrp/ and share your findings in a short report.

Critiquing Research

1. Pair up with one other student and select one of the research articles you have reviewed for other exercises. Criticize the research in terms of its adherence to each of the ethical principles for research on human subjects, as well as for the authors' apparent honesty, openness, and consideration of social consequences. Try to be critical but fair. The student with whom you are working should critique the article in the same way but from a generally positive standpoint, defending its adherence to the four guidelines but without ignoring the study's weak points. Together, write a summary of the study's strong and weak points or conduct a debate in class.

2. How do you evaluate the current American Sociological Association ethical code? Is it too strict, too lenient, or just about right? Are the enforcement provisions adequate? What provisions could be strengthened?

3. IRB members and the researchers who submit proposals to them must be familiar with a number of key concepts about ethical principles. The "Ethics" lesson at the text's study site will help you learn how to do this.

   To use these lessons, choose one of the four "Ethics" exercises from the opening menu for the Interactive Exercises. Follow the instructions for entering your answers and responding to the program's comments.

4. Now go to the book's Study Site at **http://www.pineforge.com/mssw3** and choose the Learning from Journal Articles option. Read one article based on research involving human subjects. What ethical issues did the research pose, and how were they resolved? Does it seem that subjects were appropriately protected?

Doing Research

1. List elements in a research plan for the project you envisioned for Chapter 2's "Doing Research" section that an IRB might consider to be relevant to the protection of human subjects. Rate each element from 1 to 5, where 1 indicates no more than a minor ethical issue and 5 indicates a major ethical problem that probably cannot be resolved.

2. Write one page for the application to the IRB that explains how you will ensure that your research adheres to each relevant standard.

Ethics Questions

1. Read the entire American Sociological Association *Code of Ethics* at the ASA Web site (http://www.asanet.org/cs/root/leftnav/ethics/code_of_ethics_table_of_contents).

2. Discuss the potential challenges in adhering to the ASA's ethical standards in research.

CHAPTER 4

Conceptualization and Measurement

Every time you begin to review or design a research study, you will have to answer two questions: (1) What do the main concepts mean in this research? and (2) How are the main concepts measured? Both questions must be answered to evaluate the validity of any research. For instance, to study a hypothesized link between religious fundamentalism and terrorism, you may conceptualize terrorism as "nongovernmental political violence" and measure incidents of terrorism by counting for a 5-year period the number of violent attacks that have explicit political aims. You will also need to define and measure "religious fundamentalism," no easy task. What counts? And how should you decide what counts? We cannot make sense of a researcher's study until we know how the concepts were *defined* and *measured*. Nor can we begin our own research until we have defined our concepts clearly and constructed valid measures of them.

In this chapter, we briefly address the issue of conceptualization, or defining your main terms. We then describe measurement sources such as available archive data; questions; observations; and less direct, or unobtrusive, measures. We then discuss the level of measurement reflected in different measures. The final topic is to assess the validity and reliability of these measures. By the chapter's end, you should have a good understanding of measurement, the first of the three legs (measurement, generalizability, and causality) on which a research project's validity rests.

▣ WHAT DO WE HAVE IN MIND?

A May 2000 *New York Times* article (Stille, 2000) announced that the "social health" of the United States had risen a bit, after a precipitous decline in the 1970s and 1980s. Should we be relieved? Concerned? What, after all, does "social health" mean? To social scientist Marc Miringoff, it has to do with social and economic inequalities. To political pundit William J. Bennett, it is more a matter of moral values. In fact, the concept of social health means different things to different people. Most agree that it has to do with "things that are not measured in the gross national product" and is supposed to be "a more subtle and more meaningful way of measuring what's important to [people]" (Stille:A19). But until we agree on a definition of social health, we can't decide whether it has to do with child poverty, trust in government, out-of-wedlock births, alcohol-related traffic deaths, or some combination of these or other phenomena.

Conceptualization

A continuing challenge for social scientists, then, rests on the fact that many of our important topics of study (social health, for instance) are not clearly defined things or objects (like trees or rocks) but are abstract concepts or ideas. A **concept** is an image or idea, not a simple object. Some concepts are relatively simple, such as a person's age or sex: Almost everyone would agree what it means to be 14 years old or female. But other concepts are more ambiguous. For instance, if you want to count the number of families in Chicago, what counts as a family? A husband and wife with two biological children living in one house— yes, that's a family. Do cousins living next door count? Cousins living in California? Or maybe the parents are divorced, the children are adopted, or the children are grown. Maybe two women live together with one adopted child and one biological child fathered by a now-absent man. So perhaps "living together" is what defines a family—or is it biology? Or is it a crossing of generations—that is, the presence of adults and children? The particular definition you develop will affect your research findings, and some people probably won't like it whatever you do, but how you define "family" obviously affects your results.

Concept: A mental image that summarizes a set of similar observations, feelings, or ideas

---

Often social concepts can be used sloppily or even misleadingly. In some years, you may hear that "the economy" is doing well, but even then, many people may be faring badly. Typically in news reports, "the economy" refers to the gross domestic product (GDP)—the total amount of economic activity (value of goods and services, precisely) in the country in a given year. When the GDP goes up, reporters say "the economy is improving." But that's very different from saying that the average working person makes more money than he or she would have 30 years ago—in fact, the average American man makes a little less, and for women it's close. We could use the concept of "the economy" to refer to the economic well-being of actual people, but that's not typically how it's used.

Defining concepts clearly can be quite difficult because many concepts have several meanings and can be measured in many ways. What is meant, for instance, by the idea of "power?" The classic definition, provided by German sociologist Max Weber (1947/1997:152), is that power is the ability to meet your goals over the objections of other people. That definition implies that unknown people can be quite powerful, whereas certain presidents of the United States, very well known, have been relatively powerless. A different definition might equate power to one's official position; in that case, the president of the United States would always be powerful. Or perhaps power is equated with prestige, so famous intellectuals like Albert Einstein would be considered powerful. Or maybe power is defined as having wealth, so that rich people are seen as powerful.

And even if we can settle on a definition, how then do we actually measure power? Should we ask a variety of people if a certain person is powerful? Should we review that person's acts over the last 10 years and see when the person exerted his or her will over others? Should we try to uncover the true extent of the individual's wealth and use that? How about power at a lower level, say, as a member of student government? The most visible and vocal people in your student assembly may be, in fact, quite unpopular and perhaps not very powerful at all—just loud. At the same time, there may be students who are members of no official body whatsoever, but somehow they always get what they want. Isn't that power? From these varied cases, you can see that power can be quite difficult to conceptualize.

Likewise, describing what causes "crime," or even what causes "theft," is inherently problematic, since the very definition of these terms is spectacularly flexible and indeed forms part of their interest for us. What counts as theft varies dramatically, depending on the thief—a next-door neighbor, a sister, or a total stranger wandering through town—and what item is taken: a bottle of water, your watch, a lawn mower, a skirt, your reputation, or $5. Indeed, part of what makes social science interesting is the debates over, for instance, what is a theft or what is crime.

So **conceptualization**—working out what your key terms will mean in your research—is a crucial part of the research process. Definitions need to be explicit. Sometimes conceptualization is easy: "Older men are more likely to suffer myocardial infarction than younger men," or "Career military officers mostly vote for Republican candidates in national elections." Most of the concepts used in those statements are easily understood and easy to measure (gender, age, military status, voting). In other cases, conceptualization is quite difficult: "As people's moral standards deteriorate, the family unit starts to die," or "Intelligence makes you more likely to succeed."

Conceptualization, then, is the process of matching up terms (family, sex, happiness, power) to clarified definitions for them—really, figuring out what are the social "things" you'll be talking about.

Conceptualization: The process of specifying what we mean by a term. In deductive research, conceptualization helps to translate portions of an abstract theory into testable hypotheses involving specific variables. In inductive research, conceptualization is an important part of the process used to make sense of related observations.

It is especially important to define clearly concepts that are abstract or unfamiliar. When we refer to concepts like "social control," "anomie," or "social status," we cannot count on others knowing exactly what we mean. Even experts may disagree about the meaning of frequently used concepts if they base their conceptualizations on different theories. That's OK. The point is not that there can be only one definition of a concept; rather, we have to specify clearly what we mean when we use a concept, and we should expect others to do the same.

Conceptualization also involves creating concepts, or thinking about how to conceive of the world: What things go together? How do we slice up reality? Cell phones, for instance, may be seen as communication devices, like telephones, radios, telegraphs, or two tin cans connected by a string. But they can also be conceived in another way: a college administrator we know, seeing students leaving class outside her building, said, "Cell phones have replaced cigarettes." She reconceptualized cell phones, seeing them not as communication tools but as something to fiddle with, like cigarettes, chewing gum wrappers, keys on a lanyard, or the split ends of long hair. In conceptualizing the world, we create the lenses through which we see it.

Our point is not that conceptualization problems are insurmountable, but that (1) you need to develop and clearly state what you *mean* by your key concepts and (2) your measurements will need to be clear and consistent with the definitions you've settled on (more on that topic shortly).

Variables and Constants

After we define the concepts for a study, we must identify variables that correspond to those concepts. For example, we might be interested in what affects students' engagement in their academic work—when they are excited about their studies, when they become eager to learn more, and so on. Our main concept, then, would be "engagement." We could use any number of variables to measure engagement: the student's reported interest in classes, a teacher's evaluation of student engagement, the number of hours spent on homework, or an index including a number of different questions. Any of these variables could show a high or low level of student engagement. If we are to study variation in engagement, we must identify variables to measure that are most pertinent to our theoretical concerns.

You should be aware that not every concept in a particular study is represented by a variable. In our student engagement study, all of the students *are* students—there is no variation in that. So "student," in this study, is a **constant** (it's always the same), not a variable.

Constant: A number that has a fixed value in a given situation; a characteristic or value that does not change

---

Many variables could measure student engagement. Which variables should we select? It's very tempting, and all too common, to simply try to "measure everything" by including in a study every variable we can think of. We could collect self-reports of engagement, teacher ratings, hours studied per week, pages of essays written for class, number of visits to the library per week, frequency of participation in discussion, times met with professors, and on and on. This haphazard approach will inevitably result in the collection of some useless data and the failure to collect some important data. Instead, we should take four steps:

1. Examine the theories that are relevant to our research question to identify those concepts that would be expected to have some bearing on the phenomenon we are investigating.

2. Review the relevant research literature and assess the utility of variables used in prior research.

3. Consider the constraints and opportunities for measurement that are associated with the specific setting(s) we will study. Distinguish constants from variables in this setting.

4. Look ahead to our analysis of the data. What role will each variable play in our analysis?

Remember: A few well-chosen variables are better than a barrel full of useless ones.

回 HOW WILL WE KNOW WHEN WE'VE FOUND IT?

Once we have defined our concepts in the abstract—that is, after conceptualizing—and we have identified the variables that we want to measure, we must develop our measurement procedures. The goal is to devise **operations** that actually measure the concepts we intend to measure—in other words, to achieve measurement validity.

Operation: A procedure for identifying or indicating the value of cases on a variable

Exhibit 4.1 represents the **operationalization** process in three studies. The first researcher defines his or her concept, binge drinking, and chooses one variable—frequency of heavy episodic drinking—to represent it. This variable is then measured with responses to a single question, or *indicator:* "How often within the last 2 weeks did you drink five or more drinks containing alcohol in a row?" Because "heavy" drinking is defined differently for men and women (relative to their different metabolisms), the question is phrased in terms of "four or more drinks" for women. The second researcher defines his or her concept—poverty—as having two aspects or dimensions, subjective poverty and absolute poverty. Subjective poverty is measured with responses to a survey question: "Would you say that you are poor?" Absolute poverty is measured by comparing family income to the poverty threshold. The third researcher decides that his or her concept—social class—is defined by a position on three measured variables: income, education, and occupational prestige.

Operationalization: The process of specifying the operations that will indicate the value of cases on a variable

Measures can be based on activities as diverse as asking people questions, reading judicial opinions, observing social interactions, coding words in books, checking census data tapes, enumerating the contents of trash receptacles, or drawing urine and blood samples. Experimental researchers may operationalize a concept by manipulating its value; for example, to operationalize the concept of exposure to antidrinking messages, some subjects may listen to a talk about binge drinking while others do not. We will focus here on the operations of using published data, asking questions, observing behavior, and using unobtrusive means of measuring people's behavior and attitudes.

The variables and measurement operations chosen for a study should be consistent with the purpose of the research question. Suppose we hypothesize that college students who go abroad for the junior year have a more valuable experience than those who remain at the college. If our purpose is *evaluation* of different junior-year options, we can operationalize "junior-year programs" by comparing (1) traditional coursework at home, (2) study in a foreign country, and (3) internships at home that are not traditional college courses. A simple question—for example, asking students in each program, "How valuable do you feel your experience was?"—would help to provide the basis for determining the relative value of these programs. But if our purpose is *explanation,* we would probably want to interview students to learn what features of the different programs made them valuable to find out the underlying dynamics of educational growth.

Time and resource limitations also must be taken into account when we select variables and devise measurement operations. For many sociohistorical questions (such as "How has the poverty rate varied since 1950?"), census data or other published counts must be used.

EXHIBIT 4.1   **Concepts, Variables, and Indicators: Operationalizing Concepts**

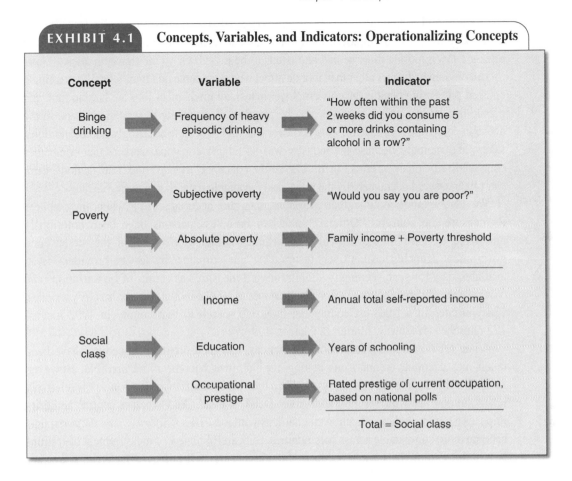

Concept	Variable	Indicator
Binge drinking	Frequency of heavy episodic drinking	"How often within the past 2 weeks did you consume 5 or more drinks containing alcohol in a row?"
Poverty	Subjective poverty	"Would you say you are poor?"
	Absolute poverty	Family income + Poverty threshold
Social class	Income	Annual total self-reported income
	Education	Years of schooling
	Occupational prestige	Rated prestige of current occupation, based on national polls
		Total = Social class

On the other hand, a historical question about the types of social bonds among combat troops in 20th-century wars probably requires retrospective interviews with surviving veterans. The validity of the data is lessened by the unavailability of many veterans from World War I and by problems of recall, but direct observation of their behavior during the war is certainly not an option.

Using Available Data

Government reports are rich, accessible sources of social science data. Organizations ranging from nonprofit service groups to private businesses also compile a wealth of figures that may be available to some social scientists for some purposes. In addition, the data collected in many social science surveys are archived and made available for researchers who were not involved in the original survey project.

Before we assume that available data will be useful, we must consider how appropriate they are for our concepts of interest, whether other measures would work better, or whether our concepts can be measured at all with these data. For example, many organizations informally (and sometimes formally) use turnover—that is, how many employees quit each year—as a measure of employee morale (or satisfaction). If turnover is high (or retention rates are low), morale must be bad and needs to be raised. Or so the thinking goes.

But obviously, factors other than morale affect whether people quit their jobs. When a single chicken-processing plant is the only employer in a small town, other jobs are hard to find, and people live on low wages, turnover may be very low even among miserable workers. In the dot-com companies of the late 1990s, turnover was high—despite amazingly good conditions, salary, and morale—because the industry was so hungry for good workers that companies competed ferociously to attract them. Maybe the concepts "morale" and "satisfaction," then, can't be measured adequately by the most easily available data; that is, turnover rates.

We also cannot assume that available data are accurate, even when they appear to measure the concept. "Official" counts of homeless persons have been notoriously unreliable because of the difficulty of locating homeless persons on the streets, and government agencies have at times resorted to "guesstimates" by service providers. Even available data for such seemingly straightforward measures as counts of organizations can contain a surprising amount of error. For example, a 1990 national church directory reported 128 churches in a Midwest county; an intensive search in that county in 1992 located 172 churches (Hadaway, Marler, & Chaves, 1993:744).

When legal standards, enforcement practices, and measurement procedures have been taken into account, comparisons among communities become more credible. However, such adjustments may be less necessary when the operationalization of a concept is relatively unambiguous, as with the homicide rate: Dead is dead. And when a central authority imposes a common data collection standard, as with the FBI's *Uniform Crime Reports*, data become more comparable across communities. But careful review of measurement operations is still important, because procedures for classifying a death as a homicide can vary between jurisdictions and over time.

Another rich source of already-collected data is survey datasets archived and made available to university researchers by the Inter-University Consortium for Political and Social Research (1996). One of its most popular survey datasets is the General Social Survey (GSS). The GSS is administered regularly by the National Opinion Research Center (NORC) at the University of Chicago to a sample of more than 1,500 Americans (annually until 1994; biennially since then). GSS questions vary from year to year, but an unchanging core of questions includes measures of political attitudes, occupation and income, social activities, substance abuse, and many other variables of interest to social scientists. This dataset can easily be used by college students to explore a wide range of interesting topics. However, when surveys are used in this way, after the fact, researchers must carefully evaluate the survey questions. Are the available measures sufficiently close to the measures needed that they can be used to answer the new research question?

Constructing Questions

Asking people questions is the most common, and probably most versatile, operation for measuring social variables. Do you play on a varsity team? What is your major? How often, in a week, do you go out with friends? How much time do you spend on schoolwork? Most concepts about individuals are measured with such questions. In this section, we'll introduce some options for writing single questions, explain why single questions can sometimes be inadequate measures, and then examine the use of multiple questions to measure a concept.

In principle, questions, asked perhaps as part of a survey, can be a straightforward and efficient means by which to measure individual characteristics, facts about events, level of knowledge, and opinions of any sort. In practice, though, survey questions can easily result in misleading or inappropriate answers. All questions proposed for a survey must be screened carefully for their adherence to basic guidelines and then tested and revised until the researcher feels some confidence that they will be clear to the intended respondents (Fowler, 1995). Some variables may prove to be inappropriate for measurement with any type of question. We have to recognize that memories and perceptions of the events about which we might like to ask can be limited.

Specific guidelines for reviewing questions are presented in Chapter 7; here, our focus is on the different types of survey questions.

Single Questions

Measuring variables with single questions is very popular. Public opinion polls based on answers to single questions are reported frequently in newspaper articles and TV newscasts: "Do you favor or oppose U.S. policy in Iraq?" "If you had to vote today, for which candidate would you vote?" Social science surveys also rely on single questions to measure many variables: "Overall, how satisfied are you with your job?" "How would you rate your current health?"

Single questions can be designed with or without explicit response choices. The question that follows is a **closed-ended**, or **fixed-choice, question**, because respondents are offered explicit responses from which to choose. It has been selected from the Core Alcohol and Drug Survey distributed by the Core Institute, Southern Illinois University, for the FIPSE Core Analysis Grantee Group (Presley, Meilman, & Lyerla, 1994).

Closed-ended (fixed-choice) question: A survey question that provides preformatted response choices for the respondent to circle or check

---

Compared with other campuses with which you are familiar, this campus's use of alcohol is . . . (Mark one)

___ *Greater than other campuses*

___ *Less than other campuses*

___ *About the same as other campuses*

Most surveys of a large number of people contain primarily fixed-choice questions, which are easy to process with computers and analyze with statistics. However, fixed-response choices can obscure what people really think, unless the choices are designed carefully to match the range of possible responses to the question.

Most important, response choices should be **mutually exclusive** and **exhaustive**, so that every respondent can find *one and only one* choice that applies to him or her (unless the question is of the "Check all that apply" variety). To make response choices exhaustive, researchers may need to offer at least one option with room for ambiguity. For example, a questionnaire asking college students to indicate their school status should not use freshman, sophomore, junior, senior, and graduate student as the only response choices. Most campuses also have students in a "special" category, so you might add "Other (please specify)" to the five fixed responses to this question. If respondents do not find a response option that corresponds to their answer to the question, they may skip the question entirely or choose a response option that does not indicate what they are really thinking.

Mutually exclusive: A variable's attributes (or values) are mutually exclusive when every case can be classified as having only one attribute (or value)

Exhaustive: Every case can be classified as having at least one attribute (or value) for the variable

---

Researchers who study small numbers of people often use **open-ended questions**, which don't have explicit response choices and allow respondents to write in their answers. The next question is an open-ended version of the earlier fixed-choice question:

How would you say alcohol use on this campus compares to that on other campuses?

An open-ended format is preferable when the full range of responses cannot be anticipated, especially when questions have not been used previously in surveys or when questions are asked of new groups. Open-ended questions also can allow clear answers when questions involve complex concepts. In the previous question, for instance, "alcohol use" may cover how many students drink, how heavily they drink, if the drinking is public or not, if it affects levels of violence on campus, and so on.

Open-ended question: A survey question to which the respondent replies in his or her own words, either by writing or by talking

---

Just like fixed-choice questions, open-ended questions should be reviewed carefully for clarity before they are used. For example, if respondents are asked, "When did you move to Boston?" they might respond with a wide range of answers: "In 1944." "After I had my first child." "When I was 10." "20 years ago." Such answers would be very hard to compile. To avoid such ambiguity, rephrase the question to clarify the form of the answer; for instance, "In what year did you move to Boston?" Or provide explicit response choices (Center for Survey Research, 1987).

Indexes and Scales

When several questions are used to measure one concept, the responses may be combined by taking the sum or average of responses. A composite measure based on this type of sum or average is termed an **index**. The idea is that idiosyncratic variation in response to particular questions will average out, so that the main influence on the combined measure will be the concept that all the questions focus on. In addition, the index can be considered a more complete measure of the concept than can any one of the component questions.

Index: A composite measure based on summing, averaging, or otherwise combining the responses to multiple questions that are intended to measure the same concept

---

Creating an index is not just a matter of writing a few questions that seem to focus on a concept. Questions that seem to you to measure a common concept might seem to respondents to concern several different issues. The only way to know that a given set of questions does, in fact, form an index is to administer the questions to people like those you plan to study. If a common concept is being measured, people's responses to the different questions should display some consistency.

Because of the popularity of survey research, indexes already have been developed to measure many concepts, and some of these indexes have proved to be reliable in a range of studies. Usually it is much better to use such an index than it is to try to form a new one. Use of a preexisting index both simplifies the work of designing a study and facilitates the comparison of findings from other studies.

The questions in Exhibit 4.2 represent a short form of an index used to measure depression; it is called the Center for Epidemiologic Studies Depression Index (CES-D). Many researchers in different studies have found that these questions form a reliable index. Note that each question concerns a symptom of depression. People may well have one particular symptom without being depressed; for example, persons who have been suffering from a physical ailment may say that they have a poor appetite. By combining the answers to questions about several symptoms, the index reduces the impact of this idiosyncratic variation. (This set of questions uses what is termed a "matrix" format, in which a series of questions that concern a common theme are presented together with the same response choices.)

Usually an index is calculated by simply averaging responses to the questions, so that every question counts equally. But sometimes, either intentionally by the researcher or by happenstance, questions on an index arrange themselves in a kind of hierarchy in which an answer to one question effectively provides answers to others. For instance, a person who supports abortion on demand almost certainly supports it in cases of rape and incest as well. Such questions form a **scale**. In a scale, we give different weights to the responses to different questions before summing or averaging the responses. Responses to one question might be counted two or three times as much as responses to another. For example, based on Christopher Mooney and Mei Hsien Lee's (1995) research on abortion law reform, a scale to indicate

| EXHIBIT 4.2 | Example of an Index: Excerpt From the Center for Epidemiologic Studies Depression Index (CES-D) | | |

At any time during the past week . . . (Circle one response on each line)	Never	Some of the time	Most of the time
a. Was your appetite so poor that you did not feel like eating?	1	2	3
b. Did you feel so tired and worn out that you could not enjoy anything?	1	2	3
c. Did you feel depressed?	1	2	3
d. Did you feel unhappy about the way your life is going?	1	2	3
e. Did you feel discouraged and worried about your future?	1	2	3
f. Did you feel lonely?	1	2	3

support for abortion might give a 1 to agreement that abortion should be allowed "when the pregnancy results from rape or incest" and a 4 to agreement with the statement that abortion should be allowed "whenever a woman decides she wants one." A 4 rating is much stronger, in that anyone who gets a 4 would probably agree to all lower-number questions as well.

Scale: A composite measure based on combining the responses to multiple questions pertaining to a common concept after these questions are differentially weighted, such that questions judged on some basis to be more important for the underlying concept contribute more to the composite score

---

Making Observations

Asking questions, then, is one way to operationalize, or measure, a variable. *Observations* can also be used to measure characteristics of individuals, events, and places. The observations may be the primary form of measurement in a study, or they may supplement measures obtained through questioning.

Direct observations can be used as indicators of some concepts. For example, Albert J. Reiss Jr. (1971) studied police interaction with the public by riding in police squad cars, observing police-citizen interactions, and recording the characteristics of the interactions on a form. Notations on the form indicated such variables as how many police-citizen contacts occurred, who initiated the contacts, how compliant citizens were with police directives, and whether or not police expressed hostility toward the citizens.

Often, observations can supplement what is initially learned from interviews or survey questions, putting flesh on the bones of what is otherwise just a verbal self-report. In Chambliss's (1996) book, *Beyond Caring,* a theory of the nature of moral problems in hospital nursing that was originally developed through interviews was expanded with lessons learned from observations. Chambliss found, for instance, that in interviews, nurses described their daily work as exciting, challenging, dramatic, and often even heroic. But when Chambliss himself sat for many hours and watched nurses work, he found that their daily lives were rather humdrum and ordinary, even to them. Occasionally there were bursts of energetic activity and even heroism—but the reality of day-to-day nursing was far less exciting than interviews would lead one to believe. Indeed, Chambliss modified his original theory to include a much broader role for routine in hospital life.

Direct observation is often the method of choice for measuring behavior in natural settings, as long as it is possible to make the requisite observations. Direct observation avoids the problems of poor recall and self-serving distortions that can occur with answers to survey questions. It also allows measurement in a context that is more natural than an interview. But observations can be distorted, too. Observers do not see or hear everything, and what they do see is filtered by their own senses and perspectives. Moreover, in some situations, the presence of an observer may cause people to act differently from the way they would otherwise (Emerson, 1983). If you set up a video camera in an obvious spot on campus to monitor traffic flows, you may well change the flow—just because people will see the camera and avoid it (or come over to make faces). We will discuss these issues in more depth in Chapter 9, but it is important to begin to consider them whenever you read about observational measures.

Content Analysis

Content analysis is a research method for systematically analyzing and making inferences from text (Weber, 1985:9). You can think of a content analysis as a survey of "documents," ranging from newspapers, books, or TV shows to persons referred to in other communications, themes expressed in government documents, or propositions made in tape-recorded debates. Words or other features of these units are then coded to measure the variables involved in the research question (Weber). As a simple example of content analysis, you might look at a variety of women's magazines over the past 25 years and count the number of articles in each year devoted to various topics, such as makeup, weight loss, relationships, sex, and so on. You might count the number of articles on different subjects as a measure of the media's emphasis on women's anxiety about these issues and see how that emphasis (i.e., the number of articles) has increased or decreased over the past quarter century. At the simplest level, you could code articles by whether key words (*fat, weight, pounds,* etc.) appeared in the titles.

Content analysis: A research method for systematically analyzing and making inferences from text

---

After coding procedures are developed, their reliability should be assessed by comparing different coders' results for the same variables. Computer programs for content analysis can be used to enhance reliability (Weitzman & Miles, 1994). The computer is programmed with certain rules for coding text so that these rules will be applied consistently.

Collecting Unobtrusive Measures

Unobtrusive measures allow us to collect data about individuals or groups without their direct knowledge or participation. In their recently revised classic book, Eugene Webb and his colleagues (Webb, Campbell, Schwartz, & Sechrest, 2000) identified four types of unobtrusive measures: physical trace evidence, archives (available data), simple observation, and contrived observation (using hidden recording hardware or manipulation to elicit a response). These measures provide valuable supplements or alternatives to more standard survey-based measures, because they are not affected by an interviewer's appearance or how he or she asks questions. We have already considered some types of archival and observational data.

Unobtrusive measure: A measurement based on physical traces or other data that are collected without the knowledge or participation of the individuals or groups that generated the data

---

Potential unobtrusive measures are everywhere. Webb and his colleagues (2000:37) suggested measuring the interest in museum exhibits by the frequency with which tiles in front of the exhibits needed to be replaced. If auto mechanics note the radio dial settings in cars brought in for repairs, they can target their advertising to those stations to which their customers listen most. A quick glance at the hands of patrons in a neighborhood bar could help you see if they do heavy manual work (calluses).

The physical traces of past behavior are one type of unobtrusive measure that provides creative opportunities; for instance, "community urinalysis." As reported in the *New York Times* "Year in Ideas" issue, "since all drug users urinate, and since the urine eventually winds up in the sewers, [Oregon State chemist Jennifer] Field and her fellow researchers figured that sewer water would contain traces of whatever drugs the citizens were using." Samples detected varying usage by city of cocaine, methamphetamine, and—most popular of all—caffeine. Cocaine use, interestingly, peaked on weekends, while methamphetamine use tended to be steady across the week (Thompson, 2007).

Unobtrusive measures can also be created from such diverse forms of media as newspaper archives, magazine articles, TV or radio talk shows, legal opinions, historical documents, personal letters, or e-mail messages. Researchers may read and evaluate the text of Internet listservs, as Fox and Roberts (1999) did in a study of British physicians. We could even learn about cities by comparing their telephone directory Yellow Pages! For example, we find that Sarasota, Florida, has many pages devoted to nursing homes and hospital appliances; Chattanooga, Tennessee, which has approximately the same number of people, rather than having pages devoted to medical care, has many pages listing churches. Admittedly, that's a rough way to compare cities, but it may alert us to key differences between them.

Combining Measurement Operations

The choice of a particular measurement method—questions, observations, archives, and the like—is often determined by available resources and opportunities, but measurement is improved if this choice also takes into account the particular concept or concepts to be measured. Responses to questions such as "How socially adept were you at the party?" or "How many days did you use sick leave last year?" are unlikely to provide valid information on shyness or illness. Direct observation or company records may work better. On the other hand, observations at cocktail parties may not fully answer our questions about why some people are shy; we may just have to ask people. Or if a company keeps no record of sick leave, we may have to ask direct questions and hope for accurate memories. Every choice of a measurement method entails some compromise between the perfect and the possible.

Triangulation—the use of two or more different measures of the same variable—can strengthen measurement considerably (Brewer & Hunter, 1989:17). When we achieve similar results with different measures of the same variable, particularly when they are based on such different methods as survey questions and field-based observations, we can be more confident of the validity of each measure. In surveys, for instance, people may say that they would return a lost wallet they found on the street. But field observation may prove that in practice, many succumb to the temptation to keep the wallet. The two methods produce different results. In a contrasting example, postcombat interviews of American soldiers in World War II found that most GIs never fired their weapons in battle, and the written, archival records of ammunition resupply patterns confirmed this interview finding (Marshall, 1947/1978). If results diverge when using different measures, it may indicate that we are sustaining more measurement error than we can tolerate.

Triangulation: The use of multiple methods to study one research question

---

Divergence between measures could also indicate that each measure actually operationalizes a different concept. An interesting example of this interpretation of divergent results comes from research on crime. Crime statistics are often inaccurate measures of actual crime; what gets reported to the police and shows up in official statistics is not at all the same thing as what happens according to victimization surveys (in which random people are asked if they have been a crime victim). Social scientists generally regard victim surveys as a more valid measure of crime than police-reported crime. We know, for instance, that rape is a dramatically underreported crime, with something like 4 to 10 times the number of rapes occurring as are reported to police. But auto theft is an *overreported* crime: More auto thefts are reported to police than actually occur. This may strike you as odd, but remember that almost everyone who owns a car also owns car insurance; if the car is stolen, the victim will definitely report it to the police to claim the insurance. Plus, some other people might report cars stolen when they haven't been because of the financial incentive. (By the way, insurance companies are quite good at discovering this scam, so it's a bad way to make money.)

Murder, however, is generally reported to police at roughly the same rate at which it actually occurs (i.e., official police reports generally match victim surveys). When someone is killed, it's very difficult to hide the fact. A body is missing, a human being doesn't show up for work, people find out. At the same time, it's very hard to pretend that someone was murdered when they weren't. There they are, still alive, in the flesh. Unlike rape or auto theft, there are no obvious incentives for either underreporting or overreporting murders. The official rate is generally valid.

So if you can, it's best to use multiple measures of the same variable; that way, each measure helps to check the validity of the others.

⊞   HOW MUCH INFORMATION DO WE REALLY HAVE?

There are many ways of collecting information, or different *operations* for gathering data: asking questions, using previously gathered data, analyzing texts, and so on. Some of this data contains mathematically detailed information; it represents a higher level of measurement. There are four **levels of measurement**: nominal, ordinal, interval, and ratio. Exhibit 4.3 depicts the differences among these four levels.

Level of measurement: The mathematical precision with which the values of a variable can be expressed. The nominal level of measurement, which is qualitative, has no mathematical interpretation; the quantitative levels of measurement—ordinal, interval, and ratio—are progressively more precise *mathematically.*

Nominal Level of Measurement

The **nominal level of measurement** identifies variables whose values have no mathematical interpretation; they vary in kind or quality but not in amount. "State" (referring to the United States) is one example. The variable has 50 attributes (or categories or qualities), but none of them is more "state" than another. They're just different. Religious affiliation is another nominal variable, measured in categories: Christian, Muslim, Hindu, Jewish, and so on. Nationality, occupation, and region of the country are also measured at the nominal level. A person may be Spanish or Portuguese, but one nationality does not represent more nationality than another—just a different nationality (see Exhibit 4.3). A person may be a doctor or a truck driver, but one does not represent three units "more occupation" than the other. Of course, more people may identify themselves as being of one nationality than of another, or one occupation may have a higher average income than another occupation, but these are comparisons involving variables other than "nationality" or "occupation" themselves.

Nominal level of measurement: Variables whose values have no mathematical interpretation; they vary in kind or quality but not in amount

---

EXHIBIT 4.3 **Levels of Measurement**

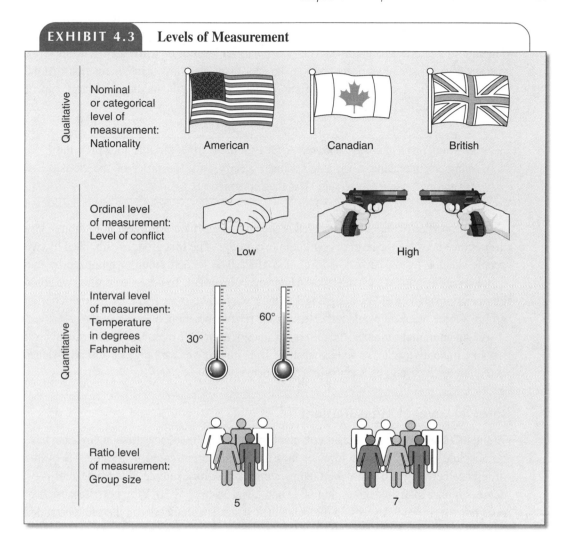

Although the attributes of nominal variables do not have a mathematical meaning, they must be assigned to cases with great care. The attributes we use to measure, or categorize, cases must be mutually exclusive and exhaustive:

- A variable's attributes or values are mutually exclusive if every case can have only one attribute.
- A variable's attributes or values are exhaustive when every case can be classified into one of the categories.

When a variable's attributes are mutually exclusive and exhaustive, every case corresponds to one—and only one—attribute.

Ordinal Level of Measurement

The first of the three quantitative levels is the **ordinal level of measurement**. At this level, you specify only the order of the cases in "greater than" and "less than" distinctions. At the coffee shop, for example, you might choose between a small, medium, or large cup of decaf—that's ordinal measurement.

Ordinal level of measurement: A measurement of a variable in which the numbers indicating a variable's values specify only the order of the cases, permitting "greater than" and "less than" distinctions

---

The properties of variables measured at the ordinal level are illustrated in Exhibit 4.3 by the contrast between the level of conflict in two groups. The first group, symbolized by two people shaking hands, has a low level of conflict. The second group, symbolized by two people pointing guns at each other, has a high level of conflict. To measure conflict, we could put the groups "in order" by assigning 1 to the low-conflict group and 2 to the high-conflict group, but the numbers would indicate only the relative position, or order, of the cases.

As with nominal variables, the different values of a variable measured at the ordinal level must be mutually exclusive and exhaustive. They must cover the range of observed values and allow each case to be assigned no more than one value.

Interval Level of Measurement

At the **interval level of measurement**, numbers represent fixed measurement units but have no absolute zero point. This level of measurement is represented in Exhibit 4.3 by the difference between two Fahrenheit temperatures. Note, for example, that 60 degrees is 30 degrees higher than 30 degrees, but 60 is not "twice as hot" as 30. Why not? Because heat does not "begin" at 0 degrees on the Fahrenheit scale. The numbers can therefore be added and subtracted, but ratios of them (2 to 1 or "twice as much") are not meaningful. There are thus few true interval-level measures in the social sciences; most are ratio-level, because they have zero points.

Interval level of measurement: A measurement of a variable in which the numbers indicating a variable's values represent fixed measurement units but have no absolute, or fixed, zero point

---

Sometimes, though, social scientists will create indexes by combining responses to a series of variables measured at the ordinal level and then treat these indexes as interval-level measures. An index of this sort could be created with responses to the Core Institute's questions about friends' disapproval of substance use (see Exhibit 4.4). The survey has 13 questions on the topic, each of which has the same three response choices. If "Don't disapprove" is valued at 1, "Disapprove" is valued at 2, and "Strongly disapprove" is valued

EXHIBIT 4.4

Ordinal Measures: Core Alcohol and Drug Survey. Responses could be combined to create an interval scale (see text).

26. **How do you think your close friends feel (or would feel) about you ...**
(mark one for each line)

	Don't disapprove	Disapprove	Strongly disapprove
a. Trying marijuana once or twice	○	○	○
b. Smoking marijuana occasionally	○	○	○
c. Smoking marijuana regularly	○	○	○
d. Trying cocaine once or twice	○	○	○
e. Taking cocaine regularly	○	○	○
f. Trying LSD once or twice	○	○	○
g. Taking LSD regularly	○	○	○
h. Trying amphetamines once or twice	○	○	○
i. Taking amphetamines regularly	○	○	○
j. Taking one or two drinks of an alcoholic beverage (beer, wine, liquor) nearly every day	○	○	○
k. Taking four or five drinks nearly every day	○	○	○
l. Having five or more drinks in one sitting	○	○	○
m. Taking steroids for bodybuilding or improved athletic performance	○	○	○

at 3, the summed index of disapproval would range from 13 to 39. A score of 20 could be treated as if it were 4 more units than a score of 16. Or the responses could be averaged to retain the original 1–3 range.

Ratio Level of Measurement

A **ratio level of measurement** represents fixed measuring units with an absolute zero point. Zero, in this situation, means absolutely no amount of whatever the variable indicates. On a ratio scale, 10 is 2 points higher than 8 and is also 2 times as great as 5. Ratio numbers can be added and subtracted, and because the numbers begin at an absolute zero point, they can also be multiplied and divided (so ratios can be formed between the numbers).

Ratio level of measurement: A measurement of a variable in which the numbers indicating the variable's values represent fixed measuring units *and* an absolute zero point

---

For example, people's ages can be represented by values ranging from 0 years (or some fraction of a year) to 120 or more. A person who is 30 years old is 15 years older than someone who is 15 years old (30 – 15 = 15) and is also twice as old as that person (30/15 = 2). Of course, the numbers also are mutually exclusive and exhaustive, so that every case can be assigned one and only one value. Age (in years) is clearly a ratio-level measure.

Exhibit 4.3 displays an example of a variable measured at the ratio level. The number of people in the first group is 5, and the number in the second group is 7. The ratio of the two groups' sizes is then 1.4, a number that mirrors the relationship between the sizes of the groups. Note that there does not actually have to be any "group" with a size of 0; what is important is that the numbering scheme begins at an absolute zero—in this case, the absence of any people.

Comparison of Levels of Measurement

Exhibit 4.5 summarizes the types of comparisons that can be made with different levels of measurement, as well as the mathematical operations that are legitimate with each. All four levels of measurement allow researchers to assign different values to different cases. All three quantitative measures allow researchers to rank cases in order.

Researchers choose levels of measurement in the process of operationalizing variables; the level of measurement is not inherent in the variable itself. Many variables can be measured at different levels with different procedures. Age can be measured as "young" or "old"; as 0–10, 11–20, 21–30, and so on; or as 1, 2, or 3 years old. We could gather the data by asking people their age, by having an observer guess ("Now *there's* an old guy!"), or by searching through hospital records for exact dates and times of birth. Any of these approaches could work, depending on our research goals.

Usually, though, it is a good idea to measure variables at the highest level of measurement possible. The more information available, the more ways we have to compare cases. We also have more possibilities for statistical analysis with quantitative than with qualitative variables. Even if your primary concern is only to compare teenagers to young adults, you should measure age in years rather than in categories; you can always combine the ages later into categories corresponding to "teenager" and "young adult."

EXHIBIT 4.5	Properties of Measurement Levels					
Examples of Comparison Statements	**Appropriate Math Operations**	**Relevant Level of Measurement**				
		Nominal	**Ordinal**	**Interval**	**Ratio**	
A is equal to (not equal to) B	= (≠)	✓	✓	✓	✓	
A is greater than (less than) B	> (<)		✓	✓	✓	
A is three more than (less than) B	+ (−)			✓	✓	
A is twice (half) as large as B	× (/)				✓	

Be aware, however, that other considerations may preclude measurement at a high level. For example, many people are very reluctant to report their exact incomes, even in anonymous questionnaires. So asking respondents to report their income in categories (such as less than $10,000, $10,000–$19,999, $20,000–$29,999, and so on) will elicit more responses, and thus more valid data, than asking respondents for their income in dollars.

▣ DID WE MEASURE WHAT WE WANTED TO MEASURE?

Do the operations developed to measure our variables actually do so—are they valid? If we have weighed our measurement options, carefully constructed our questions and observational procedures, and selected sensibly from the available data indicators, we should be on the right track. But we cannot have much confidence in a measure until we have empirically evaluated its validity. We must also evaluate the reliability of our measures. The reliability of a measure is the degree to which it produces a consistent answer; such reliability (consistency) is a prerequisite for measurement validity.

Measurement Validity

In Chapter 1, you learned that measurement validity refers to how well your indicators measure what they are intended to measure. For instance, a good measure of a person's age is the current year minus the year given on that person's birth certificate. Very probably, the resulting number accurately represents the person's age. A less valid measure would be for the researcher to ask the person (who may lie or forget) or for the researcher to simply guess. Measurement validity can be assessed with four different approaches: face validation, content validation, criterion validation, and construct validation.

Face Validity

Researchers apply the term **face validity** to the confidence gained from careful inspection of a concept to see if it is appropriate "on its face." More precisely, we can say that a measure has face validity if it obviously pertains to the meaning of the concept being measured more than to other concepts (Brewer & Hunter, 1989:131). For example, a count of the number of drinks people have consumed in the past week would be a face valid measure of their alcohol consumption.

Face validity: The type of validity that exists when an inspection of items used to measure a concept suggests that they are appropriate "on their face"

Although every measure should be inspected in this way, face validation in itself does not provide convincing evidence of measurement validity. Face validity has some plausibility but often not much. For instance, let's say that Sara is having some worries about her boyfriend, Jeremy. She wants to know if he loves her. So she asks him, "Jeremy, do you really love me?" He replies, "Sure, baby, you know I do." And yet he routinely goes out with other women, only calls Sara once every 3 weeks, and isn't particularly nice to her when they do go out. His answer that he loves her has a certain "face validity," but Sara should probably look for other validating measures. (At the least, she might ask her friends if they think his claim has validity.)

Content Validity

Content validity establishes that the measure covers the full range of the concept's meaning. To determine that range of meaning, the researcher may solicit the opinions of experts and review literature that identifies the different aspects, or dimensions, of the concept. A measure of student engagement based on how much one talks in class won't count the quiet, but attentive and hardworking, person in the front row. Or if you measure power by listing only elected government officials, you may miss the most important people altogether.

Content validity: The type of validity that exists when the full range of a concept's meaning is covered by the measure

---

Criterion Validity

Criterion validity is established when the results from one measure match those obtained with a more direct or an already validated measure of the same phenomenon (the "criterion"). A measure of blood-alcohol concentration, for instance, could be the criterion for validating a self-report measure of drinking. In other words, if Jason says he hasn't been drinking, we establish criterion validity by giving him a "breathalyzer" test. Observations of drinking by friends or relatives could also, in some limited circumstances, serve as a criterion for validating a self-report.

Criterion validity: The type of validity that is established by comparing the scores obtained on the measure being validated to those obtained with a more direct or already validated measure of the same phenomenon (the criterion)

The criterion that researchers select can be measured either at the same time as the variable to be validated or after that time. **Concurrent validity** exists when a criterion conducted at the same time yields scores that are closely related to scores on a measure. A store might validate a test of sales ability by administering the test to its current salespeople and then comparing their test scores to their actual sales performance. Or a measure of walking speed based on mental counting might be validated concurrently with a stopwatch. With **predictive validity**, a measure is validated by predicting scores on a criterion measured in the future—for instance, SAT scores are validated when they predict a student's college grades.

Concurrent validity: The type of validity that exists when scores on a measure are closely related to scores on a criterion measured at the same time

Predictive validity: The type of validity that exists when a measure predicts scores on a criterion measured in the future

---

Criterion validation greatly increases our confidence that a measure works, but for many concepts of interest to social scientists, it's difficult to find a criterion. Yes, if you and your roommate are together every evening, you can count the beers he drinks. You definitely know about his drinking. But if we are measuring feelings or beliefs or other subjective states, such as feelings of loneliness, what direct indicator could serve as a criterion? How do you know he's lonely? Even with variables for which a reasonable criterion exists, the researcher may not be able to gain access to the criterion—as would be the case with a tax return or employer document that we might wish we could use as a criterion for self-reported income.

Construct Validity

Measurement validity also can be established by relating a measure to other measures specified in a theory. This validation approach, known as **construct validity**, is commonly used in social research when no clear criterion exists for validation purposes.

Construct validity: The type of validity that is established by showing that a measure is related to other measures as specified in a theory

---

A historically famous example of construct validity is provided by the work of Theodor W. Adorno, Nevitt Sanford, Else Frenkel-Brunswik, and Daniel Levinson (1950) in their book *The Authoritarian Personality.* Adorno and his colleagues, working in the United States and Germany immediately after World War II, were interested in a question that troubled much of the world during the 1930s and 1940s: Why were so many people attracted to Nazism and to its Italian and Japanese fascist allies? Hitler was not an unpopular leader in Germany. In fact, in January 1933, he came to power by being elected chancellor (something like president) of Germany, although some details of the election were a bit suspicious. Millions of people supported him enthusiastically. Why did so many Germans during the 1930s come to nearly worship Adolf Hitler and believe strongly in his program—which proved, of course, to be so disastrous for Europe and the rest of the world? The Adorno research group proposed the existence of what they called an "authoritarian personality," a type of person who would be drawn to a dictatorial leader of the Hitler type. Their key concept, then, was "authoritarianism."

But of course there's no such "thing" as authoritarianism; it's not like a tree, something you can look at. It's a *construct,* an idea that we use to help make sense of the world. To establish construct validity of this idea, the researchers created a number of different scales made up of interview questions. One scale was called the "anti-Semitism" scale, in which hatred of Jews was measured. Another measure was a "fascism" scale, measuring a tendency toward favoring a militaristic, nationalist government. Another was the "political and economic conservatism" scale, and so on. Adorno and his colleagues interviewed lots of Germans and found that high scores on these different scales tended to correlate; a person who scored high on one tended to score high on the others. Hence, they determined that the "authoritarian personality" was a legitimate construct. The idea of authoritarianism, then, was validated through construct validity.

In short, a construct ("authoritarianism") was validated through the use of a number of other measures that all tended to be high or low at the same time. Simultaneous high scores on them validated the idea of authoritarianism.

Construct and criterion validation, then, compare scores on one measure to scores on other measures that are predicted to be related. Distinguishing the two forms (construct and criterion) matters less than thinking clearly about the comparison measures and whether they actually represent different views of the same phenomenon. For example, correspondence between scores on two different self-report measures of alcohol use is a weak indicator of measurement validity. A person just reports in two different ways how much she drinks; of course the two will be related. But the correspondence of a self-report measure with an observer-based measure of substance use is a much stronger demonstration of validity. The subject (1) reports how much she drinks, and then (2) an observer reports on the subject's drinking. If the results match up, it's strong evidence of validity.

Reliability

Reliability means that a measurement procedure yields consistent scores (or that the scores change only to reflect actual changes in the phenomenon). If a measure is *reliable,* it is affected less by random error, or chance variation, than if it is unreliable. Reliability is a prerequisite for measurement validity: We cannot really measure a phenomenon if the measure we are using gives inconsistent results. Let's say, for example, that you would like to know your weight and have decided on two different measures: the scales in the bathroom and your mother's estimate. Clearly, the scales are more reliable, in the sense that they will show pretty much the same thing from one day to the next unless your weight actually changes. But your mother, bless her, may say, "You're so skinny!" on Sunday; but on Monday, when she's not happy, she may say, "You look terrible! Have you gained weight?" Her estimates may bounce around quite a bit. The bathroom scales are not so fickle; they are *reliable.*

Reliability: A measurement procedure yields consistent scores when the phenomenon being measured is not changing

---

This doesn't mean that the scales are *valid*—in fact, if they are spring-operated and old, they may be off by quite a few pounds. But they will be off by the same amount every day— hence not being valid but *reliable* nonetheless.

There are four possible indications of unreliability. For example, a test of your knowledge of research methods would be unreliable if every time you took it, you received a different score, even though your knowledge of research methods had not changed in the interim, not even as a result of taking the test more than once. This is **test-retest reliability**. Similarly, an index composed of questions to measure knowledge of research methods would be unreliable if respondents' answers to each question were totally independent of their answers to the others. The index has **interitem reliability** if the component items are closely related. A measure also would be unreliable if slightly different versions of it resulted in markedly different responses (it would not achieve **alternate-forms reliability**). Finally, an assessment of the level of conflict in social groups would be unreliable if ratings of the level of conflict by two observers were not related to each other (it would then lack interobserver reliability).

Test-retest reliability: A measurement showing that measures of a phenomenon at two points in time are highly correlated, if the phenomenon has not changed or has changed only as much as the phenomenon itself

Interitem reliability: An approach that calculates reliability based on the correlation among multiple items used to measure a single concept. Also known as internal consistency

Alternate-forms reliability: A procedure for testing the reliability of responses to survey questions in which subjects' answers are compared after the subjects have been asked slightly different versions of the questions or when randomly selected halves of the sample have been administered slightly different versions of the questions

---

Test-Retest Reliability

When researchers measure an unchanging phenomenon at two different times, the degree to which the two measurements are related is the test-retest reliability of the measure. If you take a test of your math ability and then retake the test 2 months later, the test is reliable if you receive a similar score both times, presuming that your math ability stayed constant. Of course, if events between the test and the retest have changed the variable being measured, then the difference between the test and retest scores should reflect that change.

Interitem Reliability (Internal Consistency)

When researchers use multiple items to measure a single concept, they must be concerned with interitem reliability (or internal consistency). For example, if the questions in Exhibit 4.2

reliably measure depression, the answers to the different questions should be highly associated with one another. The stronger the association among the individual items and the more items that are included, the higher the reliability of the index.

Alternate-Forms Reliability

When researchers compare subjects' answers to slightly different versions of survey questions, they are testing alternate-forms reliability (Litwin, 1995:13–21). A researcher may reverse the order of the response choices in an index or may modify the question wording in minor ways and then readminister the index to subjects. If the two sets of responses are not too different, alternate-forms reliability is established.

A related test of reliability is the **split-halves reliability** approach. A survey sample is divided in two by flipping a coin or using some other random assignment method. The two forms of the questions are then administered to the two halves of the sample. If the responses of the two halves of the sample are about the same, the reliability of the measure is established.

Split-halves reliability: Reliability achieved when responses to the same questions by two randomly selected halves of a sample are about the same

Interobserver Reliability

When researchers use more than one observer to rate the same people, events, or places, **interobserver reliability** is their goal. If observers are using the same instrument to rate the same thing, their ratings should be very similar. If they are similar, we can have much more confidence that the ratings reflect the phenomenon being assessed rather than the orientations of the observers.

Interobserver reliability: When similar measurements are obtained by different observers rating the same persons, events, or places

Assessing interobserver reliability is most important when the rating task is complex. Consider a commonly used measure of mental health, the Global Assessment of Functioning Scale (GAFS), a bit of which is shown in Exhibit 4.6. The rating task seems straightforward, with clear descriptions of the subject characteristics that are supposed to lead to high or low GAFS scores. But in fact, the judgments that the rater must make while using this scale are very complex. They are affected by a wide range of subject characteristics, attitudes, and behaviors as well as by the rater's reactions. As a result, interobserver agreement is often low on the GAFS, unless the raters are trained carefully.

EXHIBIT 4.6 The Challenge of Interobserver Reliability: Excerpt From the Global Assessment of Functioning Scale (GAFS)

Consider psychological, social, and occupational functioning on a hypothetical continuum of mental health-illness. Do not include impairment in functioning due to physical (or environmental) limitations.

Code (Note: Use intermediate codes when appropriate, e.g., 45, 68, 72.)

100 | **Superior functioning in a wide range of activities, life's problems never seem to get out of hand, is sought by others because of his or her many positive qualities. No symptoms.**
91

90 | **Absent or minimal symptoms** (e.g., mild anxiety before an exam), **good functioning in all areas, interested and involved in a wide range of activities, socially effective, generally satisfied with life, no more than everyday problems or concerns** (e.g., an occasional argument with family members).
81

80 | **If symptoms are present, they are transient and expectable reactions to psychosocial stressors** (e.g., difficulty concentrating after family argument); **no more than slight impairment in social, occupational, or school functioning** (e.g., temporarily falling behind in schoolwork).
71

70 | **Some mild symptoms** (e.g., depressive mood and mild insomnia) **OR some difficulty in social, occupational, or school functioning** (e.g., occasional truancy or theft within the household), **but generally functioning pretty well, has some meaningful interpersonal relationships.**
61

60 | **Moderate symptoms** (e.g., flat affect and circumstantial speech, occasional panic attacks) **OR moderate difficulty in social, occupational, or school functioning** (e.g., few friends, conflicts with peers or co-workers).
51

50 | **Serious symptoms** (e.g., suicidal ideation, severe obsessional rituals, frequent shoplifting) **OR any serious impairment in social, occupational, or school functioning** (e.g., no friends, unable to keep a job).
41

40 | **Some impairment in reality testing or communication** (e.g., speech is at times illogical, obscure, or irrelevant) **OR major impairment in several areas, such as work or school, family relations, judgment, thinking, or mood** (e.g., depressed man avoids friends, neglects family, and is unable to work, child frequently beats up younger children, is defiant at home, and is failing at school).
31

30 | **Behavior is considerably influenced by delusions or hallucinations OR serious impairment in communication or judgment** (e.g., sometimes incoherent, acts grossly inappropriately, suicidal preoccupation) **OR inability to function in almost all areas** (e.g., stays in bed all day, no job, home, or friends).
21

20 | **Some danger of hurting self or others** (e.g., suicide attempts without clear expectation of death, frequently violent, manic excitement) **OR occasionally fails to maintain minimal personal hygiene** (e.g., smears feces) **OR gross impairment in communication** (e.g., largely incoherent or mute).
11

10 | **Persistent danger of severely hurting self or others** (e.g., recurrent violence) **OR persistent inability to maintain minimal personal hygiene OR serious suicidal act with clear expectation of death.**
1

0 | Inadequate information.

Can We Achieve Both Reliability and Validity?

The reliability and validity of measures in any study must be tested after the fact to assess the quality of the information obtained. But then, if it turns out that a measure cannot be considered reliable and valid, little can be done to save the study. Hence, it is supremely important to select in the first place measures that are likely to be both reliable and valid. The Dow Jones Industrials Index is a perfectly *reliable* measure of the state of the American economy—any two observers of it will see the same numbers—but its validity is shaky: There's more to the economy than the rise and fall of stock prices. In contrast, a good therapist's interview of a married couple may produce a *valid* understanding of their relationship, but such interviews are often not reliable, because another interviewer could easily reach different conclusions.

Finding measures that are both reliable and valid can be challenging. Don't just choose the first measure you find or can think of. Consider the different strengths of different measures and their appropriateness to your study. Conduct a pretest in which you use the measure with a small sample and check its reliability. Provide careful training to ensure a consistent approach if interviewers or observers will administer the measures. In most cases, however, the best strategy is to use measures that have been used before and whose reliability and validity have been established in other contexts. But even the selection of "tried and true" measures does not absolve researchers from the responsibility of testing the reliability and validity of the measure in their own studies.

Remember that a reliable measure is not necessarily a valid measure, as Exhibit 4.7 illustrates. The discrepancy shown is a common flaw of self-report measures of substance abuse. People's answers to the questions are consistent, but they are consistently misleading: A number of respondents will not admit to drinking, even though they drink a lot. The multiple questions in self-report indexes of substance abuse are answered by most respondents in a consistent way, so the indexes are reliable. As a result, some indexes based on self-report are reliable but invalid. Such indexes are not useful and should be improved or discarded.

回 CONCLUSION

Remember always that measurement validity is a necessary foundation for social research. Gathering data without careful conceptualization or conscientious efforts to operationalize key concepts often is a wasted effort.

The difficulties of achieving valid measurement vary with the concept being operationalized and the circumstances of the particular study. The examples in this chapter of difficulties in achieving valid measures should sensitize you to the need for caution.

Planning ahead is the key to achieving valid measurement in your own research; careful evaluation is the key to sound decisions about the validity of measures in others' research. Statistical tests can help to determine whether a given measure is valid after data have been collected, but if it appears after the fact that a measure is invalid, little can be done to correct the situation. If you cannot tell how key concepts were operationalized when you read a research report, don't trust the findings. And if a researcher does not indicate the results of tests used to establish the reliability and validity of key measures, remain skeptical.

EXHIBIT 4.7   **The Difference Between Reliability and Validity: Drinking Behavior**

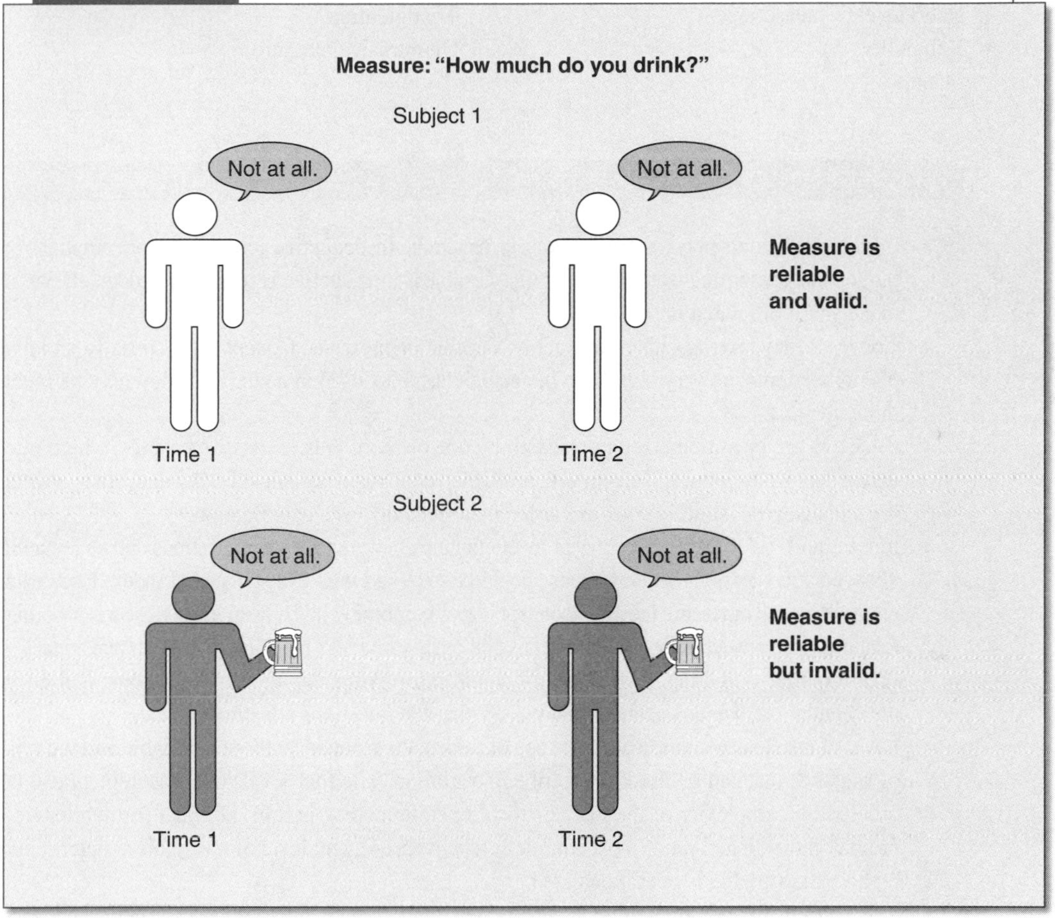

KEY TERMS

Alternate-forms reliability
Closed-ended (fixed-choice) question
Concept
Conceptualization
Concurrent validity
Constant
Construct validity
Content analysis
Content validity
Criterion validity
Exhaustive

Face validity
Index
Interitem reliability
Interobserver reliability
Interval level of measurement
Level of measurement
Mutually exclusive
Nominal level of measurement
Open-ended question
Operation
Operationalization

Ordinal level of measurement
Predictive validity
Ratio level of measurement
Reliability
Scale

Split-halves reliability
Test-retest reliability
Triangulation
Unobtrusive measure

HIGHLIGHTS

- Conceptualization plays a critical role in research. In deductive research, conceptualization guides the operationalization of specific variables; in inductive research, it guides efforts to make sense of related observations.
- Concepts may refer to either constant or variable phenomena. Concepts that refer to variable phenomena may be very similar to the actual variables used in a study, or they may be much more abstract.
- Concepts are operationalized in research by one or more indicators, or measures, which may derive from observation, self-report, available records or statistics, books and other written documents, clinical indicators, discarded materials, or some combination.
- Indexes and scales measure a concept by combining answers to several questions and so reducing idiosyncratic variation. Several issues should be explored with every intended index: Does each question actually measure the same concept? Does combining items in an index obscure important relationships between individual questions and other variables? Is the index multidimensional?
- If differential weighting, based on differential information captured by questions, is used in the calculation of index scores, then we say that the questions constitute a scale.
- Level of measurement indicates the type of information obtained about a variable and the type of statistics that can be used to describe its variation. The four levels of measurement can be ordered by complexity of the mathematical operations they permit: nominal (or qualitative), ordinal, interval, and ratio (most complex). The measurement level of a variable is determined by how the variable is operationalized.
- The validity of measures should always be tested. There are four basic approaches: face validation, content validation, criterion validation (either predictive or concurrent), and construct validation. Criterion validation provides the strongest evidence of measurement validity, but often there is no criterion to use in validating social science measures.
- Measurement reliability is a prerequisite for measurement validity, although reliable measures are not necessarily valid. Reliability can be assessed through a test-retest procedure, an interitem comparison of responses to alternate forms of the test, or the consistency of findings among observers.

STUDENT STUDY SITE

To assist you in completing the Web Exercises, please access the Study Site at **http://www.pineforge.com/mssw3,** where you'll find the Web Exercises with accompanying links. You'll find other useful study materials like self-quizzes and e-flashcards for each chapter, along with a group of carefully selected articles from research journals that illustrate the major concepts and techniques presented in the book.

EXERCISES

Discussing Research

1. What does *trust* mean to you? Identify two examples of "trust in action" and explain how they represent your concept of trust. Now develop a short definition of *trust* (without checking a dictionary). Compare your definition to those of your classmates and what you find in a dictionary. Can you improve your definition based on some feedback?

2. What questions would you ask to measure the level of trust among students? How about feelings of being "in" or "out" with regard to a group? Write five questions for an index and suggest response choices for each. How would you validate this measure using a construct validation approach? Can you think of a criterion validation procedure for your measure?

3. If you were given a questionnaire right now that asked you about your use of alcohol and illicit drugs in the past year, would you disclose the details fully? How do you think others would respond? What if the questionnaire was anonymous? What if there was a confidential ID number on the questionnaire so that the researcher could keep track of who responded? What criterion validation procedure would you suggest for assessing measurement validity?

Finding Research

1. What are some of the research questions you could attempt to answer with available statistical data? Visit your library and ask for an introduction to the government documents collection. Inspect the U.S. Bureau of the Census Web site (http://www.census.gov) and find the population figures broken down by city and state. List five questions that you could explore with such data. Identify six variables implied by these research questions that you could operationalize with the available data. What are three factors that might influence variation in these measures other than the phenomenon of interest? (Hint: Consider how the data are collected.)

2. How would you define *alcoholism*? Write a brief definition. Based on this conceptualization, describe a method of measurement that would be valid for a study of alcoholism (as you define it). Now go to the National Council on Alcohol and Drug Dependence (NCADD) Web site (http://www.ncadd.org/facts/defalc.html) and read their official *Definition of Alcoholism*. What is the definition of alcoholism used by NCADD? How is alcoholism conceptualized? How does this compare to your definition?

Critiquing Research

1. Shortly before the year 2000 national census of the United States, a heated debate arose in Congress over whether instead of a census—a total headcount—a sample should be used to estimate the number and composition of the U.S. population. As a practical matter, might a sample be more accurate in this case than a census? Why?

2. Develop a plan for evaluating the validity of a measure. Your instructor will give you a copy of a questionnaire actually used in a study. Pick out one question and define the concept that you believe it is intended to measure. Then develop a construct validation strategy involving other measures in the questionnaire that you think should be related to the question of interest—if it measures what you think it measures.

3. The questions in Exhibit 4.8 are selected from a survey of homeless shelter staff (Schutt & Fennell, 1992). First, identify the level of measurement for each question. Then rewrite each question so that it measures the same variable but at a different level. For example, you might change a question that measures age at the ratio level, in years, to one that measures age at the ordinal level, in categories. Or you might change a variable measured at the ordinal level to one

---

EXHIBIT 4.8   Selected Shelter Staff Survey Questions

1. What is your current job title?   _____

2. What is your current employment status?
   Paid, full-time 1
   Paid, part-time (less than 30 hours per week) 2

3. When did you start your current position? _____ / _____ / _____
                                              Month   Day   Year

4. In the past month, how often did you help guests deal with each of the
   following types of problems? (*Circle one response on each line.*)

	Very often						Never
Job training/placement...................	1	2	3	4	5	6	7
Lack of food or bed........................	1	2	3	4	5	6	7
Drinking problems...........................	1	2	3	4	5	6	7

5. How likely is it that you will leave this shelter within the next year?
   Very likely.. 1
   Moderately.. 2
   Not very likely... 3
   Not likely at all... 4

6. What is the highest grade in school you have completed at this time?
   First through eighth grade... 1
   Some high school.. 2
   High school diploma.. 3
   Some college.. 4
   College degree.. 5
   Some graduate work... 6
   Graduate degree... 7

7. Are you a veteran?
   Yes.. 1
   No.. 2

measured at the ratio level. For the categorical variables, those measured at the nominal level, try to identify at least two underlying quantitative dimensions of variation and write questions to measure variation along these dimensions. For example, you might change a question asking which of several factors the respondent thinks is responsible for homelessness to a series of questions that ask how important each factor is in generating homelessness.

What are the advantages and disadvantages of phrasing each question at one level of measurement rather than another? Do you see any limitations on the types of questions for which levels of measurement can be changed?

Doing Research

1. Some people have said in discussions of international politics that "democratic governments don't start wars." How could you test this hypothesis? Clearly state how you would operationalize (1) "democratic" and (2) "start."

2. Now it's time to try your hand at operationalization with survey-based measures. Formulate a few fixed-choice questions to measure variables pertaining to the concepts you researched for Exercise 1 under "Discussing Research." Arrange to interview one or two other students with the questions you have developed. Ask one fixed-choice question at a time, record your interviewee's answer, and then probe for additional comments and clarifications. Your goal is to discover what respondents take to be the meaning of the concept you used in the question and what additional issues shape their response to it.

   When you have finished the interviews, analyze your experience: Did the interviewees interpret the fixed-choice questions and response choices as you intended? Did you learn more about the concepts you were working on? Should your conceptual definition be refined? Should the questions be rewritten, or would more fixed-choice questions be necessary to capture adequately the variation among respondents?

3. Now try index construction. You might begin with some of the questions you wrote for Exercise 2. Write four or five fixed-choice questions that each measure the same concept. (For instance, you could ask questions to determine whether someone is alienated.) Write each question so it has the same response choices (a "matrix" design). Now conduct a literature search to identify an index that another researcher used to measure your concept or a similar concept. Compare your index to the published index. Which seems preferable to you? Why?

4. List three attitudinal variables.
   a. Write a conceptual definition for each variable. Whenever possible, this definition should come from the existing literature—either a book you have read for a course or the research literature that you have searched. Ask two class members for feedback on your definitions.
   b. Develop measurement procedures for each variable: Two measures should be single questions, and one should be an index used in prior research (search the Internet and the journal literature in Soc Abstracts or Psych Abstracts). Ask classmates to answer these questions and give you feedback on their clarity.
   c. Propose tests of reliability and validity for the measures.

5. Exercise your cleverness on this question: For each of the following, suggest two unobtrusive measures that might help you discover (a) how much of the required reading for this course students actually complete, (b) where are the popular spots to sit in a local park, and (c) which major U.S. cities have the highest local taxes.

Ethics Questions

1. The ethical guidelines for social research require that subjects give their "informed consent" prior to participating in an interview. How "informed" do you think subjects have to be? If you are interviewing people to learn about substance abuse and its impact on other aspects of health, is it OK just to tell respondents in advance that you are conducting a study of health issues? What if you plan to inquire about victimization experiences? Explain your reasoning.

2. Both some Homeland Security practices and inadvertent releases of Web searching records have raised new concerns about the use of unobtrusive measures of behavior and attitudes. If all identifying information is removed, do you think social scientists should be able to study the extent of prostitution in different cities by analyzing police records? How about how much alcohol different types of people use by linking credit card records to store purchases?

CHAPTER 5

Sampling

An old history professor was renowned for his ability, at semester's end, to finish grading large piles of student papers (many of them undistinguished) in a matter of a few short hours. When asked by a younger colleague how he accomplished this feat, the codger replied with a snort, "You don't have to eat the whole tub of butter to know if it's rancid." Harsh, but true.

That is the essence of sampling: A small portion, carefully chosen, can reveal the quality of a much larger whole. A survey of 1,400 Americans telephoned one Saturday afternoon can tell us very accurately how 40 million will vote for president on the following Tuesday morning.

A quick check of reports from a few selected banks can tell the Federal Reserve how strong inflation is. And when you go to the health clinic with a possible case of mononucleosis and a blood test is done, the phlebotomist needn't take all of your blood to see if you have too many atypical lymphocytes. Sampling techniques tell us how to select cases that can lead to valid generalizations about a **population**, or the entire group you wish to learn about. In this chapter, we define the key components of sampling strategy and then present the types of sampling one may use in a research study along with the strengths and weaknesses of each.

Population: The entire set of individuals or other entities to which study findings are to be generalized

▣ HOW DO WE PREPARE TO SAMPLE?

Define Sample Components and the Population

To understand how sampling works, you'll first need a few useful definitions. A **sample** is a subset of the population that we want to learn about. The individual members of this sample are called **elements,** or elementary units. These are the cases that we actually study. To select these elements, we often rely on some list of all elements in the population—a **sampling frame**.

Sample: A subset of a population used to study the population as a whole

Elements: The individual members of the population whose characteristics are to be measured

Sampling frame: A list of all elements or other units containing the elements in a population

Sometimes our sources of information are not actually the elements in our study. For example, for a survey about educational practices, a researcher might first sample schools and then, within sampled schools, interview a sample of teachers. The schools and the teachers are both termed **sampling units,** because the researcher sampled from both (Levy & Lemeshow, 1999:22). The schools are selected in the first stage of the sample, so they are the *primary sampling units* (and in this case, the elements in the study). The teachers are *secondary sampling units* (but they are not elements, because they are used to provide information about the entire school) (see Exhibit 5.1).

Sampling units: Units listed at each stage of a multistage sampling design

It is important to know exactly what population a sample can represent when you select or evaluate sample components: The population for a study is the aggregation of elements that we actually focus on and sample from, not some larger aggregation that we really wish we could have studied. If we sample students in one high school, the population for our study is the student body of that school, not all high school students in the nation.

Some populations, such as frequent moviegoers, are not identified by a simple criterion, such as a geographic boundary or an organizational membership. Clear definition of such a population is difficult but quite necessary. Anyone should be able to determine just what population was actually studied, so we would have to define clearly the concept of "frequent moviegoers" and specify how we determined their status.

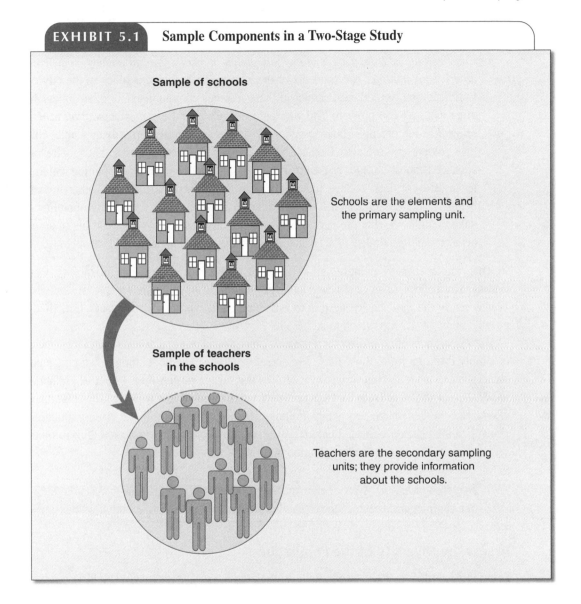

EXHIBIT 5.1 **Sample Components in a Two-Stage Study**

Sample of schools

Schools are the elements and
the primary sampling unit.

Sample of teachers
in the schools

Teachers are the secondary sampling
units; they provide information
about the schools.

Evaluate Generalizability

Once we have defined clearly the population from which we will sample, we need to determine the scope of the generalizations we will seek to make from our sample. Do you recall
the two different meanings of *generalizability* from Chapter 1?

- *Can the findings from a sample of the population be generalized to the population
  from which the sample was selected?* This issue was defined in Chapter 1. Again,
  when the Gallup polls ask some Americans for their political opinions, can those
  answers be generalized to the U.S. population? Probably so. But if Gallup's sampling

was haphazard—say, if the pollsters just talked to some people in the office—they probably couldn't make the same accurate generalizations.

- *Can the findings from a study of one population be generalized to another, somewhat different population?* Are residents of three impoverished communities in the city of Enschede, the Netherlands, similar to those in other communities? In other cities? In other nations? The problem here was defined in Chapter 1 as *cross-population generalizability.* For example, many psychology studies are run using (easily available) college students as subjects. Because such research is often on tasks that require no advanced education, such as memorizing lists of nonsense syllables or spotting patterns in an array of dots, college students may in this respect be like most other human beings, so the generalization seems legitimate. But when psychoanalyst Sigmund Freud talked with a very narrow sample of Viennese housewives in 1900, could his findings be accurately generalized (as he attempted) to the entire human race? Probably not.

This chapter focuses attention primarily on the problem of sample generalizability: Can findings from a sample be generalized to the population from which the sample was drawn? This is really the most basic question to ask about a sample, and social research methods provide many tools with which to address it.

But researchers often project their theories onto groups or populations much larger than, or simply different from, those they have actually studied. The population to which generalizations are made in this way can be termed the **target population**—a set of elements larger than or different from the population that was sampled and to which the researcher would like to generalize any study findings. Because the validity of cross-population generalizations cannot be tested empirically, except by conducting more research in other settings, we will not focus much attention on this problem here.

Target population: A set of elements larger than or different from the population sampled and to which the researcher would like to generalize study findings

---

Assess the Diversity of the Population

Sampling is unnecessary if all the units in the population are identical. The blood in one person is constantly being mixed and stirred, so it's very homogeneous—any pint is the same as any other. Physicists don't need to select a representative sample of all atomic particles to learn about basic physical processes. They can study a single atomic particle, because it is identical to every other particle of its type.

What about people? Certainly all people are not identical, but if we are studying physical or psychological processes that are the same among all people, sampling is not needed to achieve generalizable findings. Psychologists and social psychologists often conduct experiments on college students to learn about processes that they think are identical across individuals. Field researchers who observe group processes in a small community sometimes make the same assumption. But we must always bear in mind that we don't really know how generalizable our findings are to populations that we haven't actually studied.

So we usually conclude that we must study the larger population in which we are interested, if we want to be able to make generalizations about it. For this purpose, we must obtain a **representative sample** of the population to which generalizations are sought (see Exhibit 5.2).

Representative sample: A sample that "looks like" the population from which it was selected in all respects that are potentially relevant to the study. The distribution of characteristics among the elements of a representative sample is the same as the distribution of those characteristics among the total population. In an unrepresentative sample, some characteristics are overrepresented or underrepresented.

EXHIBIT 5.2 **Representative and Unrepresentative Samples**

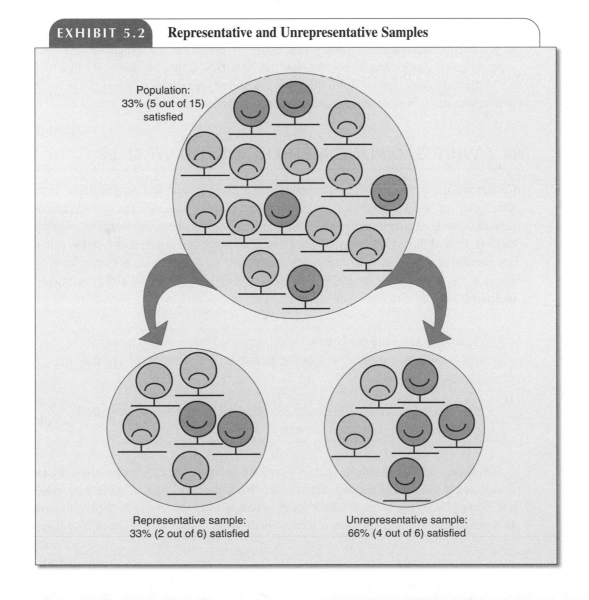

Population:
33% (5 out of 15)
satisfied

Representative sample:
33% (2 out of 6) satisfied

Unrepresentative sample:
66% (4 out of 6) satisfied

Consider a Census

In some circumstances, it may be feasible to skirt the issue of generalizability by conducting a **census**—studying the entire population of interest—rather than drawing a sample. This is what the federal government tries to do every 10 years with the U.S. Census. Censuses also include studies of all the employees (or students) in small organizations, studies comparing all 50 states, and studies of the entire population of a particular type of organization in some area.

Census: Research in which information is obtained through the responses that all available members of an entire population give to questions

---

The reason that social scientists don't often attempt to collect data from all the members of some large population is simply that doing so would be too expensive and time consuming—it was known in advance that the 2000 U.S. Census would cost more than $2.7 billion (Holmes, 1994)! But fortunately, a well-designed sampling strategy can result in a representative sample of the same population at far less cost.

▣ WHAT SAMPLING METHOD SHOULD WE USE?

Certain features of samples make them more or less likely to represent the population from which they are selected; the more representative the sample, the better. The crucial distinction about samples is whether they are based on a probability or a nonprobability sampling method. **Probability sampling methods** allow us to know in advance how likely it is that any element of a population will be selected. Sampling methods that do not let us know in advance the likelihood of selecting each element are termed **nonprobability sampling methods**.

Probability sampling method: A sampling method that relies on a random, or chance, selection method so that the probability of selection of population elements is known

Nonprobability sampling methods: Sampling methods in which the probability of selection of population elements is unknown

---

Probability sampling methods rely on a random, or chance, selection procedure, which is in principle the same as flipping a coin to decide which of two people "wins" and which one "loses." Heads and tails are equally likely to turn up in a coin toss, so both persons have an equal chance to win. That chance, their **probability of selection**, is 1 out of 2, or 0.5.

> *Probability of selection:* The likelihood that an element will be selected from the population for inclusion in the sample. In a census of all the elements of a population, the probability that any particular element will be selected is 1.0. If half the elements in the population are sampled on the basis of chance (say, by tossing a coin), the probability of selection for each element is one-half, or 0.5. As the size of the sample as a proportion of the population decreases, so does the probability of selection.

There is a natural tendency to confuse the concept of **random sampling**, in which cases are selected only on the basis of chance, with a haphazard method of sampling. On first impression, "leaving things up to chance" seems to imply not exerting any control over the sampling method. But to ensure that nothing but chance influences the selection of cases, the researcher must proceed very methodically. The researcher must follow carefully controlled procedures if a purely random process is to occur.

> *Random sampling:* A method of sampling that relies on a random, or chance, selection method so that every element of the sampling frame has a known probability of being selected

Two problems are often cause for concern when drawing random samples:

1. If the sampling frame is incomplete, a sample selected randomly from that list will not really be a random sample of the population. You should always consider the adequacy of the sampling frame. Even for a simple population like a university's student body, the registrar's list is likely to be at least somewhat out-of-date at any given time.

2. Nonresponse is a major hazard in survey research, because nonrespondents are likely to differ systematically from those who take the time to participate. If the response rate is low (say, below 65%), you should not assume that findings from even a random sample will be generalizable to the population.

Probability Sampling Methods

Probability sampling methods are those in which the probability of selection is known and is not zero (so there is some chance of selecting each element). These methods randomly select elements and therefore have no systematic **bias**; nothing but chance determines which elements are included in the sample. This feature of probability samples makes them much more desirable than nonprobability samples when the goal is to generalize to a larger population.

Bias: Sampling bias occurs when some population characteristics are over- or underrepresented in the sample because of particular features of the method of selecting the sample

---

However, even a randomly selected sample will have some degree of sampling error—some deviation from the characteristics of the population. In general, both the size of the sample and the homogeneity (sameness) of the population affect the degree of error due to chance. In spite of what you might think, the *proportion* of the population that the sample represents does not affect sample representativeness, unless that proportion is very large—it is the number of cases in the sample that is important. To elaborate:

The larger the sample, the more confidence we can have in the sample's representativeness. If we randomly pick 5 people to represent the entire population of our city, our sample is unlikely to be very representative of the entire population in terms of age, gender, race, attitudes, and so on. But if we randomly pick 100 people, the odds of having a representative sample are much better; with a random sample of 1,000, the odds become very good indeed.

The more homogeneous the population, the more confidence we can have in the representativeness of a sample of any particular size. That's why blood testing works—blood is homogeneous in any specific individual's body. Or let's say we plan to draw samples of 50 people from each of two communities to estimate mean family income. One community is very diverse, with family incomes varying from $12,000 to $85,000. In the other, more homogeneous community, family incomes are concentrated in a narrow range, from $41,000 to $64,000. The estimated mean family income based on the sample from the homogeneous community is more likely to be representative than is the estimate based on the sample from the more heterogeneous community. With less variation to represent, fewer cases are needed to represent the homogeneous community.

The fraction of the total population that a sample contains does not affect the sample's representativeness, unless that fraction is large. This isn't obvious, but it is mathematically true. The raw number of cases matters more than the proportion of the population. Other things being equal, a sample of 1,000 from a population of 1 million (with a sampling fraction of 0.001, or 0.1%) is much better than a sample of 100 from a population of 10,000 (although the sampling fraction in this case is 0.01, or 1%, which is 10 times higher). The larger size of the sample makes representativeness more likely, not the proportion of the whole that the sample represents. We can regard any sampling fraction under 2% with about the same degree of confidence (Sudman, 1976:184). In fact, sample representativeness is not likely to increase much until the sampling fraction is quite a bit higher.

Polls to predict presidential election outcomes illustrate both the value of random sampling and the problems that it cannot overcome. In most presidential elections, pollsters have predicted fairly accurately the outcomes of the actual votes by using random sampling and, these days, phone interviewing to learn for whom likely voters intend to vote. Exhibit 5.3

shows how close these sample-based predictions have been in the last 11 contests. The exceptions were the 1980 and 1992 elections, when third-party candidates had an unpredicted effect. Otherwise, the small discrepancies between the votes predicted through random sampling and the actual votes can be attributed to random error.

The Gallup poll did quite well in predicting the result of the remarkable 2000 presidential election. The final Gallup prediction was that George W. Bush would win with 48% (Al Gore was predicted to receive only 46%, and Green Party candidate Ralph Nader was predicted to secure 4%). Although the race turned out to be much closer, with Gore actually winning the popular vote (before losing in the electoral college), Gallup accurately noted that there appeared to have been a late-breaking trend in favor of Gore (Newport, 2000).

But election polls have produced some major errors in prediction. In 1948, pollsters mistakenly predicted that Thomas E. Dewey would beat Harry S. Truman, based on the random sampling method that George Gallup had used successfully since 1934. The problem? Pollsters stopped collecting data several weeks before the election, and in those weeks, many people changed their minds (Kenney, 1987). So the sample was systematically biased by underrepresenting shifts in voter sentiment just before the election.

Now that we have sung the praises of probability-based samples in general, we need to introduce the different types of random samples. The four most common types of random sample are simple random sampling, systematic random sampling, cluster sampling, and stratified random sampling.

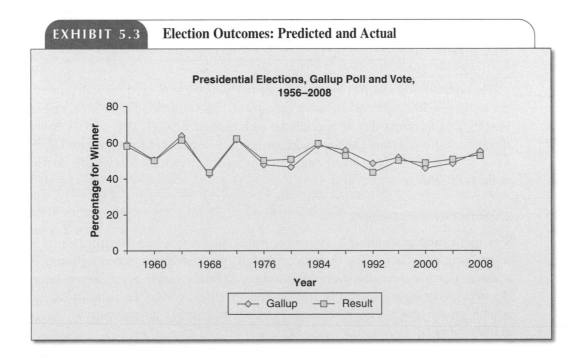

EXHIBIT 5.3 **Election Outcomes: Predicted and Actual**

Simple Random Sampling

Simple random sampling identifies cases strictly on the basis of chance. Both flipping a coin and rolling a die can be used to identify cases strictly on the basis of chance, but these procedures are not very efficient tools for drawing a sample. A **random number table** simplifies the process considerably. The researcher numbers all the elements in the sampling frame and then uses a systematic procedure for picking corresponding numbers from the random number table. (Exercise 1 under "Doing Research" at the end of this chapter explains the process step-by-step.) Alternatively, a researcher may use a lottery procedure. Each case number is written on a small card, and then the cards are mixed up and the sample selected from the cards. A computer program can also easily generate a random sample of any size.

Phone surveys often use a technique called **random digit dialing** to draw a random sample. A machine dials random numbers within the phone prefixes corresponding to the area in which the survey is to be conducted. Random digit dialing is particularly useful when a sampling frame (list of elements) is unavailable, because the dialing machine can just skip ahead if a phone number is not in service.

Simple random sampling: A method of sampling in which every sample element is selected only on the basis of chance through a random process

Random number table: A table containing lists of numbers that are ordered solely on the basis of chance; it is used for drawing a random sample

Random digit dialing: The random dialing by a machine of numbers within designated phone prefixes, which creates a random sample for phone surveys

---

The probability of selection in a true simple random sample is equal for each element. If a sample of 500 is selected from a population of 17,000 (that is, a sampling frame of 17,000), then the probability of selection for each element is 500/17,000, or 0.03. Every element has an equal chance of being selected, just like the odds in a toss of a coin (1/2) or a roll of a die (1/6). Thus, simple random sampling is an *equal probability of selection method (EPSEM)*.

Systematic Random Sampling

Systematic random sampling is a variant of simple random sampling. The first element is selected randomly from a list or from sequential files, and then every nth element is selected. This is a convenient method for drawing a random sample when the population elements are arranged sequentially. It is particularly efficient when the elements are not actually printed (that is, there is no sampling frame) but instead are represented by folders in filing cabinets.

> *Systematic random sampling:* A method of sampling in which sample elements are selected from a list or from sequential files, with every *n*th element being selected after the first element is selected randomly within the first interval

In almost all sampling situations, systematic random sampling yields what is essentially a simple random sample. The exception is a situation in which the sequence of elements is affected by **periodicity**—that is, the sequence varies in some regular, periodic pattern. For example, the houses in a new development with the same number of houses on each block (8, for example) may be listed by block, starting with the house in the northwest corner of each block and continuing clockwise. If the **sampling interval** is 8, the same as the periodic pattern, all the cases selected will be in the same position (see Exhibit 5.4). But in reality, periodicity and the sampling interval are rarely the same, so this usually isn't a problem.

> *Periodicity:* A sequence of elements (in a list to be sampled) that varies in some regular, periodic pattern
>
> *Sampling interval:* The number of cases between one sampled case and another in a systematic random sample

Cluster Sampling

Cluster sampling is useful when a sampling frame—a definite list—of elements is not available, as often is the case for large populations spread out across a wide geographic area or among many different organizations. We don't have a good list of all the Catholics in America, all the businesspeople in Arizona, or all the waiters in New York. A **cluster** is a naturally occurring, mixed aggregate of elements of the population, with each element (person, for instance) appearing in one and only one cluster. Schools could serve as clusters for sampling students, city blocks could serve as clusters for sampling residents, counties could serve as clusters for sampling the general population, and restaurants could serve as clusters for sampling waiters.

> *Cluster sampling:* Sampling in which elements are selected in two or more stages, with the first stage being the random selection of naturally occurring clusters and the last stage being the random selection of elements within clusters
>
> *Cluster:* A naturally occurring, mixed aggregate of elements of the population

Cluster sampling is at least a two-stage procedure. First, the researcher draws a random sample of clusters. (A list of clusters should be much easier to obtain than a list of all the individuals in each cluster in the population.) Next, the researcher draws a random sample

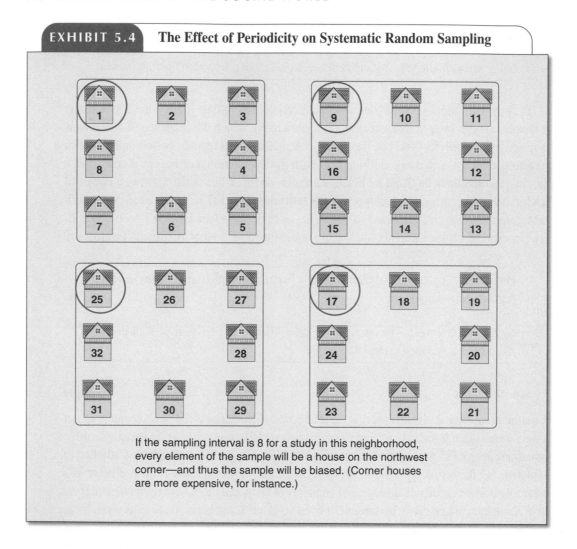

EXHIBIT 5.4   **The Effect of Periodicity on Systematic Random Sampling**

If the sampling interval is 8 for a study in this neighborhood, every element of the sample will be a house on the northwest corner—and thus the sample will be biased. (Corner houses are more expensive, for instance.)

of elements within each selected cluster. Because only a fraction of the total clusters is involved, obtaining the sampling frame at this stage should be much easier.

Cluster samples often involve multiple stages, with clusters within clusters, as when a national study of middle school students might involve first sampling states, then counties, then schools, and finally students within each selected school (see Exhibit 5.5).

How many clusters and how many individuals within clusters should be selected? As a general rule, the more clusters you select, with the fewest individuals in each, the more representative your sampling will be. Unfortunately, this strategy also maximizes the cost of the sample. The more clusters selected, the higher the travel costs. Remember, too, that the more internally homogeneous the clusters, the fewer cases needed per cluster. Homogeneity within a cluster is good.

EXHIBIT 5.5 **Multistage Cluster Sampling**

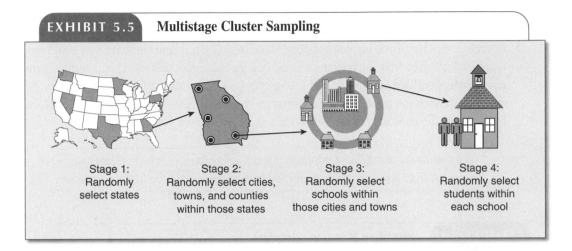

Stage 1: Randomly select states

Stage 2: Randomly select cities, towns, and counties within those states

Stage 3: Randomly select schools within those cities and towns

Stage 4: Randomly select students within each school

Cluster sampling is a very popular method among survey researchers, but it has one general drawback: Sampling error is greater in a cluster sample than in a simple random sample, because there are two steps involving random selection rather than just one. This sampling error increases as the number of clusters decreases, and it decreases as the homogeneity of cases per cluster increases. This is another way of restating the points above: It's better to include as many clusters as possible in a sample, and it's more likely that a cluster sample will be representative of the population if cases are relatively similar within clusters.

Stratified Random Sampling

Suppose you want to survey soldiers of an army to determine their morale. Simple random sampling would produce large numbers of enlisted personnel—that is, of lower ranks—but very few, if any, generals. But you want generals in your sample. **Stratified random sampling** ensures that various groups will be included.

Stratified random sampling: A method of sampling in which sample elements are selected separately from population strata that are identified in advance by the researcher

---

First, all elements in the population (that is, in the sampling frame) are distinguished according to their value on some relevant characteristic (army rank, for instance: generals, captains, privates, etc.). That characteristic determines the sampling strata. Next, elements are sampled randomly from within these strata: so many generals, so many captains, and so on. Of course, to use this method, more information is required prior to sampling than is the case with simple random sampling. Each element must belong to one and only one stratum.

For "proportionate to size" sampling, the size of each stratum in the population must be known. This method efficiently draws an appropriate representation of elements across strata. Imagine that you plan to draw a sample of 500 from an ethnically diverse neighborhood.

The neighborhood population is 15% black, 10% Hispanic, 5% Asian, and 70% white. If you drew a simple random sample, you might end up with somewhat disproportionate numbers of each group. But if you created sampling strata based on race and ethnicity, you could randomly select cases from each stratum in exactly the same proportions. This is termed **proportionate stratified sampling**, and it eliminates any possibility of sampling error in the sample's distribution of ethnicity. Each stratum would be represented exactly in proportion to its size in the population from which the sample was drawn (see Exhibit 5.6).

Proportionate stratified sampling: Sampling method in which elements are selected from strata in exact proportion to their representation in the population

---

EXHIBIT 5.6   **Stratified Random Sampling**

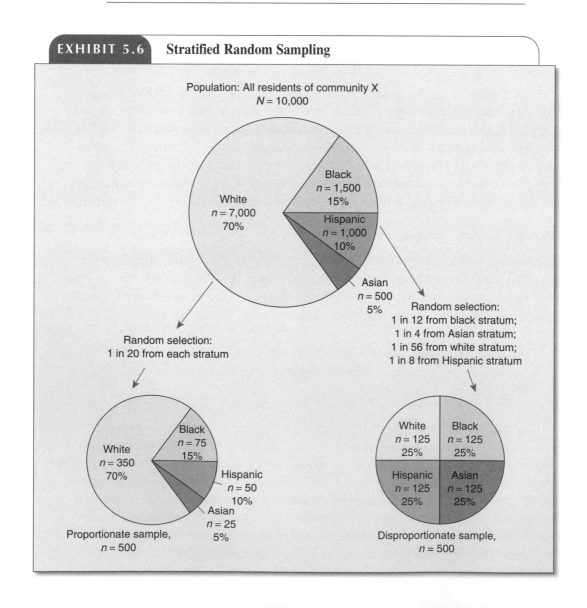

In **disproportionate stratified sampling**, the proportion of each stratum that is included in the sample is intentionally varied from what it is in the population. In the case of the sample stratified by ethnicity, you might select equal numbers of cases from each racial or ethnic group: 125 blacks (25% of the sample), 125 Hispanics (25%), 125 Asians (25%), and 125 whites (25%). In this type of sample, the probability of selection of every case is known but unequal between strata. You know what the proportions are in the population, so you can easily adjust your combined sample statistics to reflect these true proportions. For instance, if you want to combine the ethnic groups and estimate the average income of the total population, you would have to "weight" each case in the sample to reflect its representation in the population.

Disproportionate stratified sampling: Sampling in which elements are selected from strata in proportions different from those that appear in the population

---

Why would anyone select a sample that is so unrepresentative in the first place? The most common reason is to ensure that cases from smaller strata are included in the sample in sufficient numbers to allow separate statistical estimates and to facilitate comparisons between strata. Remember that one of the determinants of sample quality is sample size. The same is true for subgroups within samples. If a key concern in a research project is to describe and compare the incomes of people from different racial and ethnic groups, then it is important that the researchers base the mean income of each group on enough cases to be a valid representation. If few members of a particular minority group are in the population, they need to be oversampled.

Nonprobability Sampling Methods

Nonprobability sampling methods are often used in qualitative research; they also are used in quantitative studies when researchers are unable to use probability selection methods. There are four common nonprobability sampling methods: availability sampling, quota sampling, purposive sampling, and snowball sampling. Because they do not use a random selection procedure, we cannot expect a sample selected with any of these methods to yield a representative sample. Nonetheless, these methods are useful when random sampling is not possible; with a research question that calls for an intensive investigation of a small population; or for a preliminary, exploratory study.

Availability Sampling

Elements are selected for **availability sampling** (sometimes called "convenience" sampling) because they're available or easy to find. For example, sometimes people stand outside stores in a shopping mall asking passersby to answer a few questions about their shopping habits. That may make sense, but asking the same people for their views on the economy doesn't. In certain respects, regular mall shoppers are not representative people.

Availability sampling: Sampling in which elements are selected on the basis of convenience

---

An availability sample is often appropriate at key points in social research—for example, when a field researcher is exploring a new setting and trying to get some sense of prevailing attitudes or when a survey researcher conducts a preliminary test of a new set of questions. Intensive qualitative research efforts also often rely on availability samples. Howard Becker's classic work on jazz musicians, for instance, was based on groups Becker himself played in (Becker, 1963).

Availability sampling often masquerades as a more rigorous form of research. Popular magazines periodically survey their readers by printing a questionnaire for readers to fill out and mail in. For many years, *Playboy* magazine has conducted a sex survey among its readers using this technique. But usually only a small fraction of readers return the questionnaire, and these respondents might—how to say it?—have more interesting sex lives than other readers of *Playboy,* not to mention the rest of us (or so they claim).

Quota Sampling

Quota sampling is intended to overcome the most obvious flaw of availability sampling—that the sample will just consist of whoever or whatever is available, whether or not it represents the population. In this approach, quotas are set to ensure that the sample represents certain characteristics in proportion to their prevalence in the population.

Quota sampling: A nonprobability sampling method in which elements are selected to ensure that the sample represents certain characteristics in proportion to their prevalence in the population

---

Suppose that you want to sample 500 adult residents of a town. You know from the town's annual report what the proportions of town residents are in terms of gender, employment status, and age. To draw a quota sample of a certain size, you then specify that interviews must be conducted with 500 residents who match the town population in terms of gender, employment status, and age.

The problem is that even when we know that a quota sample is representative of the particular characteristics for which quotas have been set, we have no way of knowing if the sample is representative in terms of any other characteristics. In Exhibit 5.7, for example, quotas have been set for gender only. Under the circumstances, it's no surprise that the sample is representative of the population only in terms of gender, not in terms of race.

Of course, you must know the relevant characteristics of the entire population to set the right quotas. In most cases, researchers know what the population looks like in terms of no

EXHIBIT 5.7 **Quota Sampling**

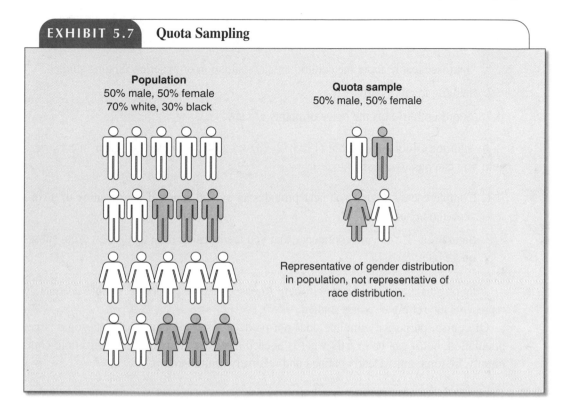

Population
50% male, 50% female
70% white, 30% black

Quota sample
50% male, 50% female

Representative of gender distribution
in population, not representative of
race distribution.

more than a few of the characteristics relevant to their concerns. And in some cases, they have no such information on the entire population.

If you're now feeling skeptical of quota sampling, you've gotten the drift of our remarks. Nonetheless, in situations in which you can't draw a random sample, it may be better to establish quotas than to have no parameters at all.

Purposive Sampling

In **purposive sampling**, each sample element is selected for a purpose, usually because of the unique position of the sample elements. Purposive sampling may involve studying the entire population of some limited group (directors of shelters for homeless adults) or a subset of a population (midlevel managers with a reputation for efficiency). Or a purposive sample may be a "key informant survey," which targets individuals who are particularly knowledgeable about the issues under investigation.

Purposive sampling: A nonprobability sampling method in which elements are selected for a purpose, usually because of their unique position

Herbert Rubin and Irene Rubin (1995:66) suggest three guidelines for selecting informants when designing any purposive sampling strategy. Informants should be

1. "knowledgeable about the cultural arena or situation or experience being studied,"

2. "willing to talk," and

3. "represent[ative of] the range of points of view."

In addition, Rubin and Rubin (1995:72–73) suggest continuing to select interviewees until you can pass two tests:

1. Completeness—"What you hear provides an overall sense of the meaning of a concept, theme, or process."

2. Saturation—"You gain confidence that you are learning little that is new from subsequent interview[s]."

Adhering to these guidelines will help to ensure that a purposive sample adequately represents the setting or issues studied.

Of course, purposive sampling does not produce a sample that represents some larger population, but it can be exactly what is needed in a case study of an organization, community, or some other clearly defined and relatively limited group.

Snowball Sampling

For **snowball sampling**, you identify one member of the population and speak to him or her, then ask that person to identify others in the population and speak to them, then ask them to identify others, and so on. The sample thus "snowballs" in size. This technique is useful for hard-to-reach or hard-to-identify, interconnected populations (at least some members of the population know each other). An example of a study using snowball sampling is Patricia Adler's (1993) study of Southern California drug dealers. Wealthy philanthropists, top business executives, or Olympic athletes, all of whom may have reason to refuse a "cold call" from an unknown researcher, might be sampled effectively using the snowball technique. However, researchers using snowball sampling normally cannot be confident that their sample represents the total population of interest, so generalizations must be tentative.

Snowball sampling: A method of sampling in which sample elements are selected as they are identified by successive informants or interviewees

---

回 CONCLUSION

Sampling is a powerful tool for social science research. Probability sampling methods allow a researcher to use the laws of chance, or probability, to draw samples from which population parameters can be estimated with a high degree of confidence. A sample of just 1,000 or 1,500 individuals can be used to estimate reliably the characteristics of the population of a nation comprising millions of individuals.

But researchers do not come by representative samples easily. Well-designed samples require careful planning, some advance knowledge about the population to be sampled, and adherence to systematic selection procedures—all so that the selection procedures are not biased. And even after the sample data are collected, the researcher's ability to generalize from the sample findings to the population is not completely certain.

The alternatives to random, or probability-based, sampling methods are almost always much less palatable for quantitative studies, even though they are typically much cheaper. Without a method of selecting cases likely to represent the population in which the researcher is interested, research findings must be carefully qualified. Qualitative researchers whose goal is to understand a small group or setting in depth may necessarily have to use unrepresentative samples, but they must keep in mind that the generalizability of their findings will not be known. Additional procedures for sampling in qualitative studies will be introduced in Chapter 9.

Social scientists often seek to generalize their conclusions from the population that they studied to some larger target population. Careful design of appropriate sampling strategies makes such generalizations possible.

KEY TERMS

Availability sampling	Random digit dialing
Bias	Random number table
Census	Random sampling
Cluster	Representative sample
Cluster sampling	Sample
Disproportionate stratified sampling	Sampling frame
Elements	Sampling interval
Periodicity	Sampling units
Population	Simple random sampling
Probability of selection	Snowball sampling
Probability sampling method	Stratified random sampling
Proportionate stratified sampling	Systematic random sampling
Purposive sampling	Target population
Quota sampling	

HIGHLIGHTS

- Sampling theory focuses on the generalizability of descriptive findings to the population from which the sample was drawn. It also considers whether statements can be generalized from one population to another.
- Sampling is unnecessary when the elements that would be sampled are identical, but the complexity of the social world often makes it difficult to argue that different elements are identical.

Conducting a complete census of a population also eliminates the need for sampling, but the resources required for a complete census of a large population are usually prohibitive.

- Nonresponse undermines sample quality: The obtained sample, not the desired sample, determines sample quality.

- Probability sampling methods rely on a random selection procedure to ensure no systematic bias in the selection of elements. In a probability sample, the odds of selecting elements are known, and the method of selection is carefully controlled.

- A sampling frame (a list of elements in the population) is required in most probability sampling methods. The adequacy of the sampling frame is an important determinant of sample quality.

- Simple random sampling and systematic random sampling are equivalent probability sampling methods in most situations. However, systematic random sampling is inappropriate for sampling from lists of elements that have a regular, periodic structure.

- Stratified random sampling uses prior information about a population to make sampling more efficient. Stratified sampling may be either proportionate or disproportionate. Disproportionate stratified sampling is useful when a research question focuses on a stratum or on strata that make up a small proportion of the population.

- Cluster sampling is less efficient than simple random sampling but is useful when a sampling frame is unavailable. It is also useful for large populations spread out across a wide area or among many organizations.

- Nonprobability sampling methods can be useful when random sampling is not possible, when a research question does not concern a larger population, and when a preliminary exploratory study is appropriate. However, the representativeness of nonprobability samples cannot be determined.

STUDENT STUDY SITE

To assist you in completing the Web Exercises, please access the Study Site at **http://www.pineforge.com/mssw3,** where you'll find the Web Exercises with accompanying links. You'll find other useful study materials like self-quizzes and e-flashcards for each chapter, along with a group of carefully selected articles from research journals that illustrate the major concepts and techniques presented in the book.

EXERCISES

Discussing Research

1. When (if ever) is it reasonable to assume that a sample is not needed because "everyone is the same"—that is, the population is homogeneous? Does this apply to research such as Stanley Milgram's on obedience to authority? What about investigations of student substance abuse? How about investigations of how people (or their bodies) react to alcohol? What about research on likelihood of voting (the focus of Chapter 8)?

2. All adult U.S. citizens are required to participate in the decennial census, but some do not. Some social scientists have argued for putting more resources into getting a large representative sample so that census takers can secure higher rates of response from hard-to-include

groups. Do you think that the U.S. census should shift to a probability-based sampling design? Why or why not?

3. What increases sampling error in probability-based sampling designs? Stratified rather than simple random sampling? Disproportionate (rather than proportionate) stratified random sampling? Stratified rather than cluster random sampling? Why do researchers select disproportionate (rather than proportionate) stratified samples? Why do they select cluster rather than simple random samples?

4. What are the advantages and disadvantages of probability-based sampling designs compared with nonprobability-based designs? Could any of the researches that are described in this chapter with a nonprobability-based design have been conducted instead with a probability-based design? What difficulties might have been encountered in an attempt to use random selection? How would you discuss the degree of confidence you can place in the results obtained from research using a nonprobability-based sampling design?

Finding Research

1. Locate one or more newspaper articles reporting the results of an opinion poll. What information does the article provide on the sample that was selected? What additional information do you need to determine whether the sample was a representative one?

2. From professional journals, select five articles that describe research using a sample drawn from some population. Identify the type of sample used in each study and note any strong and weak points in how the sample was actually drawn. Did the researchers have a problem due to nonresponse? Considering the sample, how confident are you in the validity of generalizations about the population based on the sample? Do you need any additional information to evaluate the sample? Do you think a different sampling strategy would have been preferable? To what larger population were the findings generalized? Do you think these generalizations were warranted? Why or why not?

3. Research on time use has been flourishing all over the world in recent years. Search the Web for sites that include the words "time use" and see what you find. Choose one site and write a paragraph about what you learned from it.

4. Check out the "people" section of the U.S. Bureau of the Census Web site (http://www.census .gov) Based on some of the data you find there, write a brief summary of some aspect of the current characteristics of the American population.

Critiquing Research

1. Shere Hite's popular book *Women and Love* (1987) is a good example of the claims that are often made based on an availability sample. In this case, however, the sample didn't necessarily appear to be an availability sample because it consisted of so many people. Hite distributed 100,000 questionnaires to church groups and many other organizations and received back 4.5%; 4,500 women took the time to answer some or all of her 127 essay questions regarding love and sex. Is Hite's sample likely to represent American women in general?

Why or why not? You might take a look at the book's empirical generalizations and consider whether they are justified.

2. In newspapers or magazines, find three examples of poor sampling, where someone's conclusions—either in formal research or in everyday reasoning—are weakened by the selection of cases he or she has looked at. How is the author's sampling flawed, and how might that systematically distort the findings? Don't just say "the cases might not be typical"—try to guess, for instance, the direction of error. For example, did the person pick unusually friendly or accessible people? The most well-known examples? And how might their approach affect the findings?

Doing Research

1. Select a random sample using a table of random numbers (either one provided by your instructor or one from a Web site, such as http://www.bmra.com/extras/man-rand.htm). Compute a statistic based on your sample and compare it to the corresponding figure for the entire population. Here's how to proceed:

   a. First select a very small population for which you have a reasonably complete sampling frame. One possibility would be the listing of some characteristic of states in a U.S. Census Bureau publication, such as average income or population size. Another possible population would be the list of asking prices for houses advertised in your local paper.

   b. Next, create a sampling frame, a numbered list of all the available elements in the population. If you are using a complete listing of all elements, as from a U.S. Census Bureau publication, the sampling frame is the same as the list. Just number the elements (states). If your population is composed of housing ads in the local paper, your sampling frame will be those ads that contain a housing price. Identify these ads, then number them sequentially, starting with 1.

   c. Decide on a method of picking numbers out of the random number table, such as taking every number in each row, row by row, or moving down or diagonally across the columns. Use only the first (or last) digit in each number if you need to select 1 to 9 cases or only the first (or last) two digits if you want 10 to 99 cases.

   d. Pick a starting location in the random number table. It's important to pick a starting point in an unbiased way, perhaps by closing your eyes and then pointing to some part of the page.

   e. Record the numbers you encounter as you move from the starting location in the direction you decided on in advance, until you have recorded as many random numbers as the number of cases you need in the sample. If you are selecting states, 10 might be a good number. Ignore numbers that are too large (or small) for the range of numbers used to identify the elements in the population. Discard duplicate numbers.

   f. Calculate the average value in your sample for some variable that was measured (for example, population size in a sample of states or housing price for the housing ads). Calculate the average by adding up the values of all the elements in the sample and dividing by the number of elements in the sample.

   g. Go back to the sampling frame and calculate this same average for all the elements in the list. How close is the sample average to the population average?

h. Estimate the range of sample averages that would be likely to include 90% of the possible samples.

Ethics Questions

1. How much pressure is too much pressure to participate in a probability-based sample survey? Is it OK for the U.S. government to mandate legally that all citizens participate in the decennial census? Should companies be able to require employees to participate in survey research about work-related issues? Should students be required to participate in surveys about teacher performance? Should parents be required to consent to the participation of their high school-age students in a survey about substance abuse and health issues? Is it OK to give monetary incentives for participation in a survey of homeless shelter clients? Can monetary incentives be coercive? Explain your decisions.

2. Federal regulations require special safeguards for research on persons with impaired cognitive capacity. Special safeguards are also required for research on prisoners and on children. Do you think special safeguards are necessary? Why or why not? Do you think it is possible for individuals in any of these groups to give "voluntary consent" to research participation? What procedures might help make consent to research truly voluntary in these situations? How could these procedures influence sampling plans and results?

CHAPTER 6

Causation and Experimental Design

Identifying causes—figuring out why things happen—is the goal of most social science research. Unfortunately, valid explanations of the causes of social phenomena do not come easily. Why did the homicide rate in the United States drop for 15 years and then start to rise in 1999 (Butterfield, 2000:12)? Was it because of changes in the style of policing (Radin, 1997) or because of changing attitudes among young people (Butterfield, 1996a)? Was it due to variation in patterns of drug use (Krauss, 1996), or to more stringent handgun regulations (Butterfield, 1996b)? Did better emergency medical procedures result in higher survival rates for victims (Ramirez, 2002)? If we are to evaluate these alternative explanations, we must design our research strategies carefully.

This chapter considers the meaning of causation, the criteria for achieving causally valid explanations, the ways in which experimental and quasi-experimental research designs seek to meet these criteria, and the difficulties that can sometimes result in invalid conclusions. By the end of the chapter, you should have a good grasp of the meaning of causation and the logic of experimental design. Most social research, both academic and applied, uses data collection methods other than experiments. But because experimental designs are the best way to evaluate causal hypotheses, a better understanding of them will help you to be aware of the strengths and weaknesses of other research designs, which we will consider in subsequent chapters.

回 CAUSAL EXPLANATION

A cause is an explanation of some characteristic, attitude, or behavior of groups, individuals, or other entities (such as families, organizations, or cities) or of events. For example, Sherman and Berk (1984) conducted a study to determine whether adults who were accused of a domestic violence offense would be less likely to repeat the offense if police arrested them rather than just warned them. Their conclusion that this hypothesis was correct meant that they believed police response had a **causal effect** on the likelihood of committing another domestic violence offense.

Causal effect: The finding that change in one variable leads to change in another variable, *ceteris paribus* (other things being equal). *Example:* Individuals arrested for domestic assault tend to commit fewer subsequent assaults than similar individuals who are accused in the same circumstances but are not arrested.

More specifically, a causal effect is said to occur if variation in the independent variable is followed by variation in the dependent variable, when all other things are equal (*ceteris paribus*). For instance, we know that for the most part, men earn more income than women do. But is this because they are men—or could it be due to higher levels of education or to longer tenure in their jobs (with no pregnancy breaks), or is it due to the kinds of jobs men go into as compared to those that women choose? We want to know if men earn more than women, *ceteris paribus*—other things (job, tenure, education, etc.) being equal.

Ceteris paribus: Latin phrase meaning "other things being equal"

We admit that you can legitimately argue that "all" other things can't literally be equal: We can't compare the same people at the same time in exactly the same circumstances except for the variation in the independent variable (King et al., 1994). However, you will see that we can design research to create conditions that are very comparable so that we can isolate the impact of the independent variable on the dependent variable.

▣ WHAT CAUSES WHAT?

Five criteria should be considered in trying to establish a causal relationship. The first three criteria are generally considered as requirements for identifying a causal effect: (1) empirical association, (2) temporal priority of the independent variable, and (3) nonspuriousness. You must establish these three to claim a causal relationship. Evidence that meets the other two criteria—(4) identifying a causal mechanism and (5) specifying the context in which the effect occurs—can considerably strengthen causal explanations.

Research designs that allow us to establish these criteria require careful planning, implementation, and analysis. Many times, researchers have to leave one or more of the criteria unmet and are left with some important doubts about the validity of their causal conclusions, or they may even avoid making any causal assertions.

Association

The first criterion for establishing a causal effect is an empirical (or observed) **association** (sometimes called a *correlation*) between the independent and dependent variables. They must vary together such that when one goes up (or down), the other goes up (or down) at the same time. Here are some examples: When cigarette smoking goes up, so does lung cancer. The longer you stay in school, the more money you will make later in life. Single women are more likely to live in poverty than married women. When income goes up, so does overall health. In all of these cases, a change in an independent variable correlates, or is associated with, a change in a dependent variable. If there is no association, there cannot be a causal relationship. For instance, empirically there seems to be no correlation between the use of the death penalty and a reduction in the rate of serious crime. That may seem unlikely to you, but empirically it is the case: There is no correlation. So there cannot be a causal relationship.

Association: A criterion for establishing a nomothetic causal relationship between two variables: Variation in one variable is related to variation in another variable

---

Time Order

Association is necessary for establishing a causal effect, but it is not sufficient. We must also ensure that the variation in the independent variable came before variation in the dependent variable—the cause must come before its presumed effect. This is the criterion of **time order**, or the temporal priority of the independent variable. Motivational speakers sometimes say that to achieve success (the dependent variable in our terms), you really need to believe in yourself (the independent variable). And it is true that many very successful politicians, actors, and businesspeople seem remarkably confident—there is an association. But it may well be that their confidence is the result of their success, not its cause. Until you know which came first, you can't establish a causal connection.

Time order: A criterion for establishing a causal relationship between two variables. The variation in the presumed cause (the independent variable) must occur before the variation in the presumed effect (the dependent variable).

Nonspuriousness

The third criterion for establishing a causal effect is **nonspuriousness**. *Spurious* means false or not genuine. We say that a relationship between two variables is **spurious** when it is actually due to changes in a third variable, so what appears to be a direct connection is in fact not one. Have you heard the old adage "Correlation does not prove causation"? It is meant to remind us that an association between two variables might be caused by something else. If we measure children's shoe sizes and their academic knowledge, for example, we will find a positive association. However, the association results from the fact that older children have larger feet as well as more academic knowledge. A third variable (age) is affecting both shoe size and knowledge so that they correlate, but one doesn't cause the other. Shoe size does not cause knowledge, or vice versa. The association between the two is, we say, spurious.

Nonspuriousness: A criterion for establishing a causal relation between two variables; when a relationship between two variables is not due to variation in a third variable

Spurious: Nature of a presumed relationship between two variables that is actually due to variation in a third variable

If this point seems obvious, consider a social science example. Do schools with better resources produce better students? There is certainly a correlation, but consider the fact that parents with more education and higher income tend to live in neighborhoods that spend more on their schools. These parents are also more likely to have books in the home and to provide other advantages for their children (see Exhibit 6.1). Maybe parents' income causes variation in both school resources and student performance. If so, there would be an association between school resources and student performance, but it would be at least partially spurious. What we want, then, is *non*spuriousness.

Mechanism

A causal **mechanism** is the process that creates the connection between the variation in an independent variable and the variation in the dependent variable that it is hypothesized to cause (Cook & Campbell, 1979:35; Marini & Singer, 1988). Many social scientists (and scientists in other fields) argue that no causal explanation is adequate until a mechanism is identified.

Mechanism: A discernible process that creates a causal connection between two variables

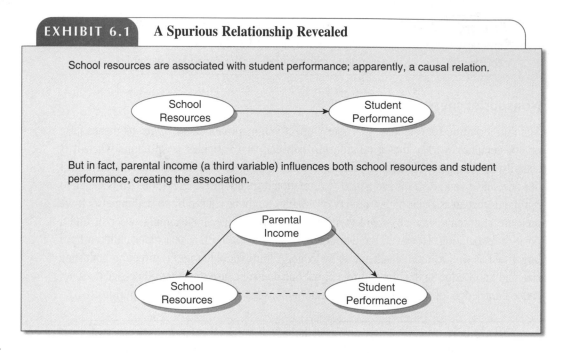

EXHIBIT 6.1 **A Spurious Relationship Revealed**

School resources are associated with student performance; apparently, a causal relation.

But in fact, parental income (a third variable) influences both school resources and student performance, creating the association.

For instance, there seems to be an empirical association at the individual level between poverty and delinquency: Children who live in impoverished homes seem more likely to be involved in petty crime. But why? Some researchers have argued for a *mechanism* of low parent/child attachment, inadequate supervision of children, and erratic discipline as the means by which poverty and delinquency are connected (Sampson & Laub, 1994). In this way, figuring out some aspects of the process by which the independent variable influenced the variation in the dependent variable can increase confidence in our conclusion that a causal effect was at work (Costner, 1989).

Context

No cause has its effect apart from some larger **context** involving other variables. When, for whom, and in what conditions does this effect occur? A cause is really one among a set of interrelated factors required for the effect (Hage & Meeker, 1988; Papineau, 1978). Identification of the context in which a causal effect occurs is not itself a criterion for a valid causal conclusion, and it is not always attempted; but it does help us to understand the causal relationship.

Context: A focus of idiographic causal explanation; a particular outcome is understood as part of a larger set of interrelated circumstances

You may hypothesize, for example, that if you offer employees higher wages to work harder, they will indeed work harder. In the context of America, this seems indeed to be the case; incentive pay causes harder work. But in noncapitalist societies, workers often want only enough money to meet their basic needs and would rather work less than drive themselves hard just to have more money. In America, the correlation of incentive pay with greater effort seems to work; in medieval Europe, for instance, it did not (Weber, 1930/1992).

As another example, in America in the 1960s, children of divorced parents ("from a broken home") were more likely to suffer from a variety of problems; they lived in a context of mostly intact families. In recent years, though, many parents are divorced, and the causal link between divorced parents and social pathology no longer seems to hold (Coontz, 1997).

回 WHY EXPERIMENT?

Experimental research provides the most powerful design for testing causal hypotheses, because it allows us to establish confidently the first three criteria for causality—association, time order, and nonspuriousness. **True experiments** have at least three features that help us meet these criteria:

1. Two comparison groups (in the simplest case, an experimental group and a control group), which establish association

2. Variation in the independent variable before assessment of change in the dependent variable, which establishes time order

3. Random assignment to the two (or more) comparison groups, which establishes nonspuriousness

---

True experiment: Experiment in which subjects are assigned randomly to an experimental group that receives a treatment or other manipulation of the independent variable and a comparison group that does not receive the treatment or receives some other manipulation. Outcomes are measured in a posttest.

We can determine whether an association exists between the independent and dependent variables in a true experiment, because two or more groups, the **comparison groups**, differ in terms of their value on the independent variable. One group receives some "treatment," which is a manipulation of the value of the independent variable. This group is termed the **experimental group**. In a simple experiment, there may be one other group that does not receive the treatment; it is termed the **control group**.

Comparison groups: In an experiment, groups that have been exposed to different treatments, or values of the independent variable (e.g., a control group and an experimental group)

Experimental group: In an experiment, the group of subjects that receives the treatment or experimental manipulation

Control group: A comparison group that receives no treatment

Consider an example in detail (see the simple diagram in Exhibit 6.2). Does drinking coffee improve one's writing of an essay? Imagine a simple experiment. Suppose you believe that drinking 2 cups of strong coffee before class will help you in writing an in-class essay. But other people think that coffee makes them too nervous and "wired" and so doesn't help in writing the essay. To test your hypothesis ("Coffee drinking causes improved performance."), you need to compare two groups of subjects, a control group and an experimental group. First, the two groups will sit and write an in-class essay. Then, the control group will drink no coffee, while the experimental group will drink 2 cups of strong coffee. Next, both groups will sit and write another in-class essay. At the end, all of the essays will be graded, and you will see which group improved more. Thus, you may establish *association.*

You may find an association outside the experimental setting, of course, but it won't establish time order. Perhaps good writers hang out in cafés and coffeehouses and then start drinking lots of coffee. So there would be an association, but not the causal relation we're looking for. By controlling who gets the coffee, and when, we establish *time order.*

All true experiments have a **posttest**—that is, a measurement of the outcome in both groups after the experimental group has received the treatment. In our example, you grade the papers. Many true experiments also have **pretests**, which measure the dependent variable before the experimental intervention. A pretest is exactly the same as a posttest, just administered at a different time. Strictly speaking, though, a true experiment does not require a pretest. When researchers use random assignment, the groups' initial scores on the dependent variable and on all other variables are very likely to be similar. Any difference

---

EXHIBIT 6.2 **A True Experiment**

Experimental Group:	R	O_1	X	O_2
Comparison Group:	R	O_1		O_2

Key: R = Random assignment
       O = Observation (pretest [O_1] or posttest [O_2])
       X = Experimental treatment

	O_1	X	O_2
Experimental Group	Pretest Essay	Coffee	Posttest Essay
Comparison Group	Pretest Essay		Posttest Essay

in outcome between the experimental and comparison groups is therefore likely to be due to the intervention (or to other processes occurring during the experiment), and the likelihood of a difference just on the basis of chance can be calculated.

Posttest: In experimental research, the measurement of an outcome (dependent) variable after an experimental intervention or after a presumed independent variable has changed for some other reason. The posttest is exactly the same "test" as the pretest, but it is administered at a different time.

Pretest: In experimental research, the measurement of an outcome (dependent) variable prior to an experimental intervention or change in a presumed independent variable for some other reason. The pretest is exactly the same "test" as the posttest, but it is administered at a different time.

Finally, it is crucial that the two groups be more or less equal at the beginning of the study. If you let students choose which group to be in, the more ambitious students may pick the coffee group, hoping to stay awake and do better on the paper. Or people who simply don't like the taste of coffee may choose the noncoffee group. Either way, your two groups won't be equivalent at the beginning of the study, and any difference in their writing may be the result of that initial difference (a source of spuriousness), not the drinking of coffee.

So you randomly sort the students into the two different groups. You can do this by flipping a coin for each student, by pulling names out of a hat, or by using a random number table as described in the previous chapter. In any case, the subjects themselves should not be free to choose, nor should you (the experimenter) be free to put them into whatever group you want. (If you did that, you might unconsciously put the better students into the coffee group, hoping to get the results you're looking for.) Thus, we hope to achieve nonspuriousness.

Note that the random assignment of subjects to experimental and comparison groups is not the same as random sampling of individuals from some larger population (see Exhibit 6.3). In fact, **random assignment (randomization)** does not help at all to ensure that the research subjects are representative of some larger population; instead, representativeness is the goal of random sampling. What random assignment does— create two (or more) equivalent groups—is useful for ensuring internal validity, not generalizability.

Random assignment: A procedure by which each experimental subject is placed in a group randomly

---

Matching is another procedure sometimes used to equate experimental and comparison groups, but by itself, it is a poor substitute for randomization. Matching of individuals in a treatment group with those in a comparison group might involve pairing persons on the

EXHIBIT 6.3 Random Sampling Versus Random Assignment

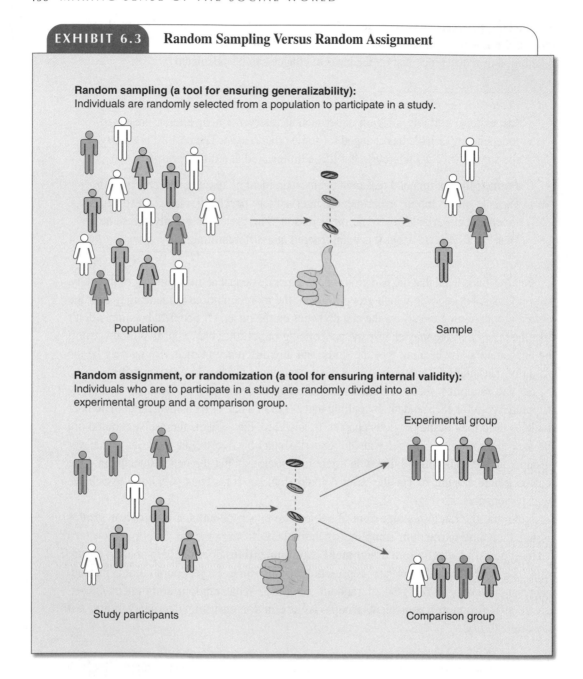

Random sampling (a tool for ensuring generalizability):
Individuals are randomly selected from a population to participate in a study.

Population

Sample

Random assignment, or randomization (a tool for ensuring internal validity):
Individuals who are to participate in a study are randomly divided into an
experimental group and a comparison group.

Experimental group

Study participants

Comparison group

basis of similarity of gender, age, year in school, or some other characteristic. The
basic problem is that, as a practical matter, individuals can be matched on only a few
characteristics; unmatched differences between the experimental and comparison groups
may still influence outcomes.

> *Matching:* A procedure for equating the characteristics of individuals in different comparison groups in an experiment. Matching can be done on either an individual or an aggregate basis. For individual matching, individuals who are similar in terms of key characteristics are paired prior to assignment, and then the two members of each pair are assigned to the two groups. For aggregate matching, groups are chosen for comparison that are similar in terms of the distribution of key characteristics.

These defining features of true experimental designs give us a great deal of confidence that we can meet the three basic criteria for identifying causes: association, time order, and nonspuriousness. However, we can strengthen our understanding of causal connections, and increase the likelihood of drawing causally valid conclusions, by also investigating causal mechanism and causal context.

▣ WHAT IF A TRUE EXPERIMENT ISN'T POSSIBLE?

Often, testing a hypothesis with a true experimental design is not feasible. A true experiment may be too costly or take too long to carry out, it may not be ethical to randomly assign subjects to the different conditions, or it may be too late to do so. Researchers may instead use "quasi-experimental" designs that retain several components of experimental design but differ in important details.

In **quasi-experimental design**, a comparison group is predetermined to be comparable to the treatment group in critical ways, such as being eligible for the same services or being in the same school cohort (Rossi & Freeman, 1989:313). These research designs are only *quasi*-experimental, because subjects are not randomly assigned to the comparison and experimental groups. As a result, we cannot be as confident in the comparability of the groups as in true experimental designs. Nonetheless, to term a research design quasi-experimental, we have to be sure that the comparison groups meet specific criteria.

We will discuss here the two major types of quasi-experimental designs, as well as one type—ex post facto (after the fact) control group design—that is often mistakenly termed quasi-experimental (other types can be found in Cook & Campbell, 1979; Mohr, 1992):

- *Nonequivalent control group designs*—**Nonequivalent control group designs** have experimental and comparison groups that are designated before the treatment occurs but are not created by random assignment.
- *Before-and-after designs*—**Before-and-after designs** have a pretest and posttest but no comparison group. In other words, the subjects exposed to the treatment serve, at an earlier time, as their own control group.
- *Ex post facto control group designs*—**Ex post facto control group designs** use nonrandomized control groups designated after the fact.

> *Quasi-experimental design:* A research design in which there is a comparison group that is comparable to the experimental group in critical ways but subjects are not randomly assigned to the comparison and experimental groups
>
> *Nonequivalent control group design:* A quasi-experimental design in which there are experimental and comparison groups that are designated before the treatment occurs but are not created by random assignment
>
> *Before-and-after design:* A quasi-experimental design consisting of several before-and-after comparisons involving the same variables but different groups
>
> *Ex post facto control group design:* A nonexperimental design in which comparison groups are selected after the treatment, program, or other variation in the independent variable has occurred

Exhibit 6.4 diagrams one study using the ex post facto control group design and another study using the multiple group before-and-after design, one type of before-and-after design. (The diagram for an ex post facto control group design is the same as for a nonequivalent control group design, but the two types of experiment differ in how people are able to join the groups.)

If quasi-experimental designs are longitudinal, they can establish time order. Where these designs are weaker than true experiments is in establishing the nonspuriousness of an observed association—that it does not result from the influence of some third, uncontrolled variable. On the other hand, because these quasi-experiments do not require the high degree of control necessary to achieve random assignment, quasi-experimental designs can be conducted using more natural procedures in more natural settings, so we may be able to achieve a more complete understanding of causal context. In identifying the mechanism of a causal effect, though, quasi-experiments are neither better nor worse than experiments.

Nonequivalent Control Group Designs

In this type of quasi-experimental design, a comparison group is selected so as to be as comparable as possible to the treatment group. Two selection methods can be used:

1. *Individual matching*—Individual cases in the treatment group are matched with similar individuals in the comparison group. This can sometimes create a comparison group that is very similar to the experimental group, such as when Head Start participants were matched with their siblings to estimate the effect of participation in Head Start. However, in many studies, it may not be possible to match on the most important variables.

2. *Aggregate matching*—In most situations when random assignment is not possible, the second method of matching makes more sense: identifying a comparison group that matches the treatment group in the aggregate rather than trying to match individual

EXHIBIT 6.4	**Quasi-Experimental Designs**

Nonequivalent control group design:

		Pretest	Treatment	Posttest
Experimental group:		O_1	X_a	O_2
Comparison group 1:		O_1	X_b	O_2
Comparison group 2:		O_1	X_c	O_2
		Pretest	*Treatment*	*Posttest*
Team Interdependence	Group	Team performance	Independent tasks	Team performance
	Hybrid	Team performance	Mixed tasks	Team performance
	Individual	Team performance	Individual tasks	Team performance

Before-and-after design:
Soap opera suicide and actual suicide (Phillips, 1982)

	Pretest	Treatment	Posttest
Experimental group:	O_{11}	X_1	O_{21}
	O_{12}	X_2	O_{22}
	O_{13}	X_3	O_{23}
	O_{14}	X_4	O_{24}
	Pretest	*Treatment*	*Posttest*
	Suicide rate	Soap-opera suicides	Suicide rate

Key: O = Observation (pretest or posttest)
  X = Experimental treatment

cases. This means finding a comparison group that has similar distributions on key variables: the same average age, the same percentage female, and so on. For this design to be considered quasi-experimental, however, it is important that individuals themselves have chosen to be in the treatment group or the control group.

Nonequivalent control group designs allow you to determine whether an association exists between the presumed cause and effect.

Before-and-After Designs

The common feature of before-and-after designs is the absence of a comparison group: All cases are exposed to the experimental treatment. The basis for comparison is instead provided by the pretreatment measures in the experimental group. These designs are thus useful for studies of interventions that are experienced by virtually every case in some population, such as total coverage programs like Social Security or single-organization studies of the effect of a new management strategy.

The simplest type of before-and-after design is the fixed-sample panel design. As you may recall from Chapter 2, in a panel design, the same individuals are studied over time; the research may entail one pretest and one posttest. However, this type of before-and-after design does not qualify as a quasi-experimental design, because comparing subjects to themselves at just one earlier point in time does not provide an adequate comparison group. Many influences other than the experimental treatment may affect a subject following the pretest—for instance, basic life experiences for a young subject.

David P. Phillips's (1982) study of the effect of TV soap opera suicides on the number of actual suicides in the United States illustrates a more powerful **multiple group before-and-after design.** In this design, before-and-after comparisons are made of the same variables between different groups. Phillips identified 13 soap opera suicides in 1977 and then recorded the U.S. suicide rate in the weeks prior to and following each TV story. In effect, the researcher had 13 different before-and-after studies, 1 for each suicide story. In 12 of these 13 comparisons, deaths due to suicide increased from the week before each soap opera suicide to the week after (see Exhibit 6.5). Phillips also found similar increases in motor vehicle deaths and crashes during the same period, some portion of which reflects covert suicide attempts.

Multiple group before-and-after design: A type of quasi-experimental design in which several before-and-after comparisons are made involving the same independent and dependent variables but different groups

---

Another type of before-and-after design involves multiple pretest and posttest observations of the same group. **Repeated measures panel designs** include several pretest and posttest observations, allowing the researcher to study the process by which an intervention or treatment has an impact over time; hence, they are better than simple before-and-after studies.

Repeated measures panel design: A quasi-experimental design consisting of several pretest and posttest observations of the same group

---

Time series designs include many (preferably 30 or more) such observations in both pretest and posttest periods. They are particularly useful for studying the impact of new laws or social programs that affect large numbers of people and that are readily assessed by some ongoing measurement. For example, we might use a time series design to study the impact of a new seat belt law on the severity of injuries in automobile accidents, using a monthly state government report on insurance claims. Special statistics are required to analyze time series data, but the basic idea is simple: Identify a trend in the dependent variable up to

EXHIBIT 6.5 **Real Suicides and Soap Opera Suicides**

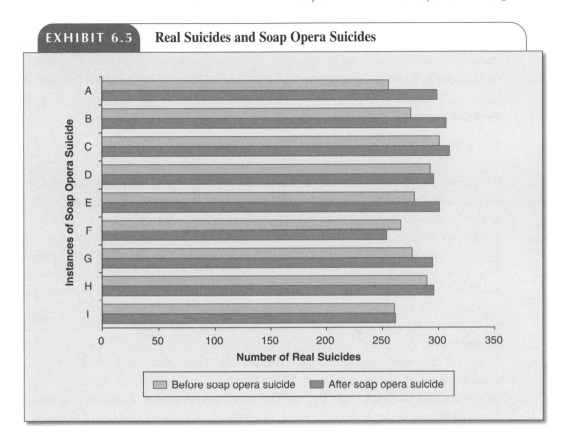

the date of the intervention, then project the trend into the postintervention period. This *projected* trend is then compared to the *actual* trend of the dependent variable after the intervention. A substantial disparity between the actual and projected trends is evidence that the intervention or event had an impact (Rossi & Freeman, 1989:260–261, 358–363).

Time series design: A quasi-experimental design consisting of many pretest and posttest observations of the same group

---

How well do these before-and-after designs meet the five criteria for establishing causality? The before-and-after comparison enables us to determine whether an *association* exists between the intervention and the dependent variable (because we can determine whether a change occurred after the intervention). They also clarify whether the change in the dependent variable occurred after the intervention, so *time order* is not a problem. However, there is no control group, so we cannot rule out the influence of extraneous factors as the actual cause of the change we observed; *spuriousness* may be a problem.

Some other event may have occurred during the study that resulted in a change in posttest scores. Overall, the longitudinal nature of before-and-after designs can help to identify causal mechanisms, while the loosening of randomization requirements makes it easier to conduct studies in natural settings, where we learn about the influence of contextual factors.

Ex Post Facto Control Group Designs

The ex post facto control group design appears to be very similar to the nonequivalent control group design and is often confused with it, but it does not meet as well the criteria for quasi-experimental designs. Like nonequivalent control group designs, this design has experimental and comparison groups that are not created by random assignment. But unlike the groups in nonequivalent control group designs, the groups in ex post facto designs are designated after the treatment has occurred. The problem with this is that if the treatment takes any time at all, people with particular characteristics may select themselves for the treatment or avoid it. Of course, this makes it difficult to determine whether an association between group membership and outcome is spurious. However, the particulars will vary from study to study; in some circumstances, we may conclude that the treatment and control groups are so similar that causal effects can be tested (Rossi & Freeman, 1989:343–344).

Susan Cohen and Gerald Ledford Jr.'s (1994) study of the effectiveness of self-managing teams used a well-constructed ex post facto design. They studied a telecommunications company with some work teams that were self-managing and some that were traditionally managed (meaning that a manager was responsible for the team's decisions). Cohen and Ledford found the self-reported quality of work life to be higher in the self-managing groups than in the traditionally managed groups.

▣ WHAT ARE THE THREATS TO VALIDITY IN EXPERIMENTS?

Experimental designs, like any research design, must be evaluated for their ability to yield valid conclusions. Remember, there are three kinds of validity: internal (or causal), external (or generalizability), and measurement. True experiments are good at producing internal validity, but they fare less well in achieving external validity (generalizability). Quasi-experiments may provide more generalizable results than true experiments but are more prone to problems of internal invalidity. Measurement validity is a central concern for both kinds of research, but even true experimental design offers no special advantages or disadvantages in measurement.

In general, nonexperimental designs, such as those used in survey research and field research, offer less certainty of internal validity, a greater likelihood of generalizability, and no particular advantage or disadvantage in terms of measurement validity. We will introduce survey and field research designs in the following chapters; in this section, we focus on the ways in which experiments help (or don't help) to resolve potential problems of internal validity and generalizability.

Threats to Internal (Causal) Validity

The following sections discuss 10 threats to validity (also referred to as "sources of invalidity") that occur frequently in social science research (see Exhibit 6.6). These "threats" exemplify five major types of problems that arise in research design.

EXHIBIT 6.6   **Threats to Internal Validity**

Problem	Example	Type
Selection	Girls who choose to see a therapist are not representative of population.	Noncomparable Groups
Mortality	Students who most dislike college drop out, so aren't surveyed.	Noncomparable Groups
Instrument Decay	Interviewer tires, losing interest In later interviews, so poor answers result.	Noncomparable Groups
Testing	If someone has taken the SAT before, they are familiar with the format, so do better.	Endogenous Change
Maturation	Everyone gets older in high school; it's not the school's doing.	Endogenous Change
Regression	The lowest-ranking students on IQ must improve their rank; they can't do worse.	Endogenous Change
History	The O. J. Simpson trial affects members of diversity workshops.	History
Contamination	"John Henry" effect; people in study compete with one another.	Contamination
Experimenter Expectation	Researchers unconsciously help their subjects, distorting results.	Treatment Misidentification
Placebo Effect	Fake pills in medical studies produce improved health.	Treatment Misidentification
Hawthorne Effect	Workers enjoy being subjects and work harder.	Treatment Misidentification

Noncomparable Groups

The problem of noncomparable groups occurs when the experimental group and the control group are not really comparable—that is, when something interferes with the two groups being essentially the same at the beginning (or end) of a study.

- *Selection bias*—Occurs when the subjects in your groups are initially different. If the ambitious students decide to be in the "coffee" group, you'll think their performance was helped by coffee—but it could have been their ambition.

Everyday examples of **selection bias** are everywhere. Harvard graduates are very successful people, but Harvard *admits* students who are likely to be successful anyway. Maybe Harvard itself had no effect on them. A few years ago, a psychotherapist named Mary Pipher wrote a best seller called *Reviving Ophelia* (1994) in which she described the difficult lives of—as she saw it—typical adolescent girls. Pipher painted a stark picture of depression, rampant eating disorders, low self-esteem, academic failure, suicidal thoughts, and even suicide itself. Where did she get this picture? From her patients—that is, from adolescent girls who were in deep despair, or at least were unhappy enough to seek help. If Pipher had talked with a comparison sample of girls who hadn't sought help, perhaps the story would not have been so bleak.

Selection bias: A source of internal (causal) invalidity that occurs when characteristics of experimental and comparison group subjects differ in any way that influences the outcome

---

In the Sherman and Berk (1984) domestic violence experiment in Minneapolis, some police officers sometimes violated the random assignment plan when they thought the circumstances warranted arresting a suspect who had been randomly assigned to receive just a warning; thus, they created a selection bias in the experimental group.

- *Mortality*—Even when random assignment works as planned, the groups can become different over time because of **mortality**, or **differential attrition**; this can also be called "deselection." That is, the groups become different because subjects in one group are more likely to drop out for various reasons compared to subjects in the other group(s). At some colleges, satisfaction surveys show that seniors are more likely to rate their colleges positively than are freshmen. But remember that the freshmen who really hated the place may have transferred out, so their ratings aren't included with senior ratings. In effect, the lowest scores are removed; that's a mortality problem. This is not a likely problem in a laboratory experiment that occurs in one session, but some laboratory experiments occur over time, so differential attrition can become a problem. Subjects who experience the experimental condition may become more motivated to continue in the experiment than comparison subjects.

Differential attrition (mortality): A problem that occurs in experiments when comparison groups become different because subjects in one group are more likely to drop out for various reasons compared to subjects in the other group(s)

Note that whenever subjects are not assigned randomly to treatment and comparison groups, the threat of selection bias or mortality is very great. Even if the comparison group matches the treatment group on important variables, there is no guarantee that the groups were similar initially in terms of either the dependent variable or some other characteristic. However, a pretest helps the researchers to determine and control for selection bias.

- *Instrument decay*—Measurement instruments of all sorts wear out, producing different results for cases studied later in the research. An ordinary spring-operated bathroom scale, for instance, becomes "soggy" after some years, showing slightly heavier weights than would be correct. Or a college teacher—a kind of instrument for measuring student performance—gets tired after reading too many papers one weekend and starts giving everyone a B. Research interviewers can get tired or bored, too, leading perhaps to shorter or less thoughtful answers from subjects. In all these cases, the measurement instrument has "decayed," or worn out.

Endogenous Change

The next three problems, subsumed under the label **endogenous change**, occur when natural developments in the subjects, independent of the experimental treatment itself, account for some or all of the observed change between pretest and posttest.

- *Testing*—Taking the pretest can itself influence posttest scores. As the Kaplan SAT prep courses attest, there is some benefit just to getting used to the test format. Having taken the test beforehand can be an advantage. Subjects may learn something or may be sensitized to an issue by the pretest and, as a result, respond differently the next time they are asked the same questions on the posttest.
- *Maturation*—Changes in outcome scores during experiments that involve a lengthy treatment period may be due to maturation. Subjects may age, gain experience, or grow in knowledge—all as part of a natural maturational experience—and thus respond differently on the posttest than on the pretest. In many high school yearbooks, seniors are quoted as saying, for instance, "I started at West Geneva High as a boy and leave as a man. WGHS made me grow up." Well, he probably would have grown up anyway, high school or not. WGHS wasn't the cause.
- *Regression*—Subjects who are chosen for a study because they received very low scores on a test may show improvement in the posttest, on average, simply because some of the low scorers were having a bad day. Whenever subjects are selected for study

because of extreme scores (either very high or very low), the next time you take their scores, they will likely "regress," or move toward the average. For instance, suppose you give an IQ test to third graders and then pull the bottom 20% of the class out for special attention. The next time that group (the 20%) take the test, they'll almost certainly do better—and not just because of testing practice. In effect, they *can't* do worse—they were at the bottom already. On average, they must do better. A football team that goes 0–12 one season almost has to improve. A first-time novelist writes a wonderful book and gains worldwide acclaim and a host of prizes. The next book is not so good, and critics say, "The praise went to her head." But it didn't; she *couldn't* have done better. Whenever you pick people for being on an extreme end of a scale, odds are that next time, they'll be more average. This is called the **regression effect.**

Endogenous change: A source of causal invalidity that occurs when natural developments or changes in the subjects (independent of the experimental treatment itself) account for some or all of the observed change from the pretest to the posttest

Regression effect: A source of causal invalidity that occurs when subjects who are chosen for a study because of their extreme scores on the dependent variable become less extreme on the posttest due to natural cyclical or episodic change in the variable

---

Testing, maturation, and regression effects are generally not a problem in experiments that have a control group, because they would affect the experimental group and the comparison group equally. However, these effects could explain any change over time in most before-and-after designs, because these designs do not have a comparison group. Repeated measures, panel studies, and time series designs are better in this regard, because they allow the researcher to trace the pattern of change or stability in the dependent variable up to and after the treatment. Ongoing effects of maturation and regression can thus be identified and taken into account.

History

History, or **external events** during the experiment (things that happen outside the experiment), could change subjects' outcome scores. Examples are newsworthy events that concern the focus of an experiment and major disasters to which subjects are exposed. If you were running a series of diversity workshops for some insurance company employees while the notorious 1995 O. J. Simpson murder trial was taking place, for instance, participants' thoughts on race relations at the end of the workshops may say less about you than about O. J. Simpson or about their own relationship with the judicial system. This problem is often referred to as a **history effect**—history during the experiment, that is. It is a particular concern in before-and-after designs.

> *External events:* Events external to the study that influence posttest scores, resulting in causal invalidity
>
> *History effect:* A source of causal invalidity that occurs when something other than the treatment influences outcome scores; also called an effect of external events

Causal conclusions can be invalid in some true experiments because of the influence of external events. For example, in an experiment in which subjects go to a special location for the treatment, something at that location unrelated to the treatment could influence these subjects. External events are a major concern in studies that compare the effects of programs in different cities or states (Hunt, 1985:276–277).

Contamination

Contamination occurs in an experiment when the comparison and treatment groups somehow affect each other. When comparison group members know they are being compared, they may increase their efforts just to be more competitive. This has been termed **compensatory rivalry**, or the **John Henry effect**, named after the "steel-driving man" of the folk song, who raced against a steam drill in driving railroad spikes and killed himself in the process. Knowing that they are being denied some advantage, comparison group subjects may as a result increase their efforts to compensate. On the other hand, comparison group members may become demoralized if they feel that they have been left out of some valuable treatment, performing worse than expected as a result. Both compensatory rivalry and demoralization thus distort the impact of the experimental treatment.

> *Contamination:* A source of causal invalidity that occurs when either the experimental and/or the comparison group is aware of the other group and is influenced in the posttest as a result
>
> *Compensatory rivalry:* A type of contamination in experimental and quasi-experimental designs that occurs when control group members are aware that they are being denied some advantage and increase their efforts by way of compensation. This problem has also been referred to as the *John Henry effect*.

The danger of contamination can be minimized if the experiment is conducted in a laboratory, if members of the experimental group and the comparison group have no contact while the study is in progress, and if the treatment is relatively brief. Whenever these conditions are not met, the likelihood of contamination increases.

Treatment Misidentification

Sometimes the subjects experience a "treatment" that wasn't intended by the researcher. The following are three possible sources of **treatment misidentification**:

1. *Expectancies of experiment staff*—Change among experimental subjects may be due to the positive **expectancies of experiment staff** who are delivering the treatment rather than to the treatment itself. Even well-trained staff may convey their enthusiasm for an experimental program to the subjects in subtle ways. This is a special concern in evaluation research, when program staff and researchers may be biased in favor of the program for which they work and are eager to believe that their work is helping clients. Such positive staff expectations thus create a **self-fulfilling prophecy**. However, in experiments on the effects of treatments such as medical drugs, **double-blind procedures** can be used: Staff delivering the treatments do not know which subjects are getting the treatment and which are receiving a placebo—something that looks like the treatment but has no effect.

Treatment misidentification: A problem that occurs in an experiment when the treatment itself is not what causes the outcome but rather the outcome is caused by some intervening process that the researcher has not identified and is not aware of

Expectancies of experiment staff: A source of treatment misidentification in experiments and quasi-experiments that occurs when change among experimental subjects is due to the positive expectancies of the staff who are delivering the treatment, rather than to the treatment itself; also called a *self-fulfilling prophecy*

Double-blind procedure: An experimental method in which neither the subjects nor the staff delivering experimental treatments know which subjects are getting the treatment and which are receiving a placebo

---

2. *Placebo effect*—In medicine, a *placebo* is a chemically inert substance (a sugar pill, for instance) that looks like a drug but actually has no direct physical effect. Research shows that such a pill can actually produce positive health effects in two thirds of patients suffering from relatively mild medical problems (Goleman, 1993:C3). In other words, if you wish that a pill will help, it often actually does. In social science research, such **placebo effects** occur when subjects think their behavior should improve through an experimental treatment and then it does—not from the treatment, but from their own belief. Researchers might then misidentify the treatment as having produced the effect.

Placebo effect: A source of treatment misidentification that can occur when subjects receive a treatment that they consider likely to be beneficial and improve as a result of that expectation rather than the treatment itself

---

3. *Hawthorne effect*—Members of the treatment group may change in terms of the dependent variable because their participation in the study makes them feel special. This problem could occur when treatment group members compare their situation to

that of members of the control group who are not receiving the treatment, in which case it would be a type of contamination effect. But experimental group members could feel special simply because they are in the experiment. This is termed a **Hawthorne effect** after a classic worker productivity experiment conducted at the Hawthorne electric plant outside Chicago in the 1920s. No matter what conditions the researchers changed to improve or diminish productivity (for instance, increasing or decreasing the lighting in the plant), the workers seemed to work harder simply because they were part of a special experiment. Oddly enough, some later scholars suggested that in the original Hawthorne studies, there was actually a selection bias, not a true Hawthorne effect—but the term has stuck (see Bramel & Friend, 1981). Hawthorne effects are also a concern in evaluation research, particularly when program clients know that the research findings may affect the chances for further program funding.

Hawthorne effect: Λ type of contamination in experimental and quasi-experimental designs that occurs when members of the treatment group change in terms of the dependent variable because their participation in the study makes them feel special

---

Process analysis is a technique for avoiding treatment misidentification (Hunt, 1985:272–274). Periodic measures are taken throughout an experiment to assess whether the treatment is being delivered as planned. For example, Drake and his colleagues (Drake, McHugo, Becker, Anthony, & Clark, 1996) collected process data to monitor the implementation of two employment service models that they tested. One site did a poorer job of implementing the individual placement and support model than the other site, although the required differences between the experimental conditions were still achieved. Process analysis is often a special focus in evaluation research because of the possibility of improper implementation of the experimental program.

Process analysis: A research design in which periodic measures are taken to determine whether a treatment is being delivered as planned, usually in a field experiment

---

Generalizability

The need for generalizable findings can be thought of as the Achilles' heel of true experimental design. The design components that are essential for a true experiment and that minimize the threats to causal validity make it more difficult to achieve sample generalizability—being able to apply the findings to some clearly defined larger population—and cross-population generalizability—generalizing across subgroups and to other populations and settings.

Sample Generalizability

Subjects who can be recruited for a laboratory experiment, randomly assigned to a group, and kept under carefully controlled conditions for the duration of the study are unlikely to be a representative sample of any large population of interest to social scientists. Can they be expected to react to the experimental treatment in the same way as members of the larger population? The generalizability of the treatment and of the setting for the experiment also must be considered (Cook & Campbell, 1979:73–74). The more artificial the experimental arrangements, the greater the problem (Campbell & Stanley, 1966:20–21).

In some limited circumstances, a researcher may be able to sample subjects randomly for participation in an experiment and thus select a generalizable sample—one that is representative of the population from which it is selected. This approach is occasionally possible in **field experiments**. For example, some studies of the effects of income supports on the work behavior of poor persons have randomly sampled persons within particular states before randomly assigning them to experimental and comparison groups. Sherman and Berk's (1984) field experiment about the impact of arrest in actual domestic violence incidents (see Chapter 2) used a slightly different approach. In this study, all eligible cases were treated as subjects in the experiment during the data collection periods. As a result, we can place a good deal of confidence in the generalizability of the results to the population of domestic violence arrest cases in Minneapolis.

Field experiment: An experimental study conducted in a real-world setting

---

Cross-Population Generalizability

Researchers often are interested in determining whether treatment effects identified in an experiment hold true across different populations, times, or settings. When random selection is not feasible, the researchers may be able to increase the cross-population generalizability of their findings by selecting several different experimental sites that offer marked contrasts on key variables (Cook & Campbell, 1979:76–77).

Within a single experiment, researchers also may be concerned with whether the relationship between the treatment and the outcome variable holds true for certain subgroups. This demonstration of "external validity" is important evidence about the conditions that are required for the independent variable(s) to have an effect. Price, Van Ryn, and Vinokur (1992) found that intensive job search assistance reduced depression among individuals who were at high risk for it because of other psychosocial characteristics; however, the intervention did not influence the rate of depression among individuals at low risk for depression. This is an important limitation on the generalizability of the findings, even if the sample taken by Price et al. were representative of the population of unemployed persons.

Finding that effects are consistent across subgroups does not establish that the relationship also holds true for these subgroups in the larger population, but it does provide supportive evidence. We have already seen examples of how the existence of treatment effects in particular subgroups of experimental subjects can help us predict the cross-population generalizability of the findings. For example, Sherman and Berk's research (1984; see Chapter 2) found that arrest did not deter subsequent domestic violence for unemployed individuals; arrest also failed to deter subsequent violence in communities with high levels of unemployment.

There is always an implicit tradeoff in experimental design between maximizing causal validity and generalizability. The more that assignment to treatments is randomized and all experimental conditions are controlled, the less likely it is that the research subjects and setting will be representative of the larger population. College students are easy to recruit and to assign to artificial but controlled manipulations, but both practical and ethical concerns preclude this approach with many groups and with respect to many treatments. However, although we need to be skeptical about the generalizability of the results of a single experimental test of a hypothesis, the body of findings accumulated from many experimental tests with different people in different settings can provide a very solid basis for generalization (Campbell & Russo, 1999:143).

Interaction of Testing and Treatment

A variant on the problem of external validity occurs when the experimental treatment has an effect only when particular conditions created by the experiment occur. One such problem occurs when the treatment has an effect only if subjects have had the pretest. The pretest sensitizes the subjects to some issue so that when they are exposed to the treatment, they react in a way they would not have reacted if they had not taken the pretest. In other words, testing and treatment interact to produce the outcome. For example, answering questions in a pretest about racial prejudice may sensitize subjects so that when they are exposed to the experimental treatment, seeing a film about prejudice, their attitudes are different from what they would have been. In this situation, the treatment truly had an effect, but it would not have had an effect if it were repeated without the sensitizing pretest. This possibility can be evaluated by using the Solomon Four-Group Design to compare groups with and without a pretest (see Exhibit 6.7). If testing and treatment do interact, the difference in outcome scores between the experimental and comparison groups will be different for subjects who took the pretest and those who did not.

As you can see, no single procedure establishes the external validity of experimental results. Ultimately, we must base our evaluation of external validity on the success of replications taking place at different times and places and using different forms of the treatment.

EXHIBIT 6.7	Solomon Four-Group Design Testing the Interaction of Pretesting and Treatment			
Experimental group:	R	O_1	X	O_2
Comparison group:	R	O_1		O_2
Experimental group:	R		X	O_2
Comparison group:	R			O_2

Key:　R = Random assignment
　　　O = Observation (pretest or posttest)
　　　X = Experimental treatment

▣ HOW DO EXPERIMENTERS PROTECT THEIR SUBJECTS?

Social science experiments often involve subject deception. Primarily because of this feature, some experiments have prompted contentious debates about research ethics. Experimental evaluations of social programs also pose ethical dilemmas, because they require researchers to withhold possibly beneficial treatment from some of the subjects just on the basis of chance. Such research may also yield sensitive information about program compliance, personal habits, and even illegal activity—information that is protected from legal subpoenas only in some research concerning mental illness or criminal activity (Boruch, 1997). In this section, we will give special attention to the problems of deception and the distribution of benefits in experimental research.

Deception

Deception occurs when subjects are misled about research procedures to determine how they would react to the treatment if they were not research subjects. Deception is a critical component of many social experiments, in part because of the difficulty of simulating real-world stresses and dilemmas in a laboratory setting. Stanley Milgram's (1963) classic study of obedience to authority provides a good example. (If you have read Chapter 3 already, you'll be familiar with this example.) Volunteers were recruited for what they were told was a study of the learning process. The experimenter told the volunteers they were to play the role of "teacher" and to administer an electric shock to a "student" in the next room when the student failed a memory test. The shocks were phony (and the students were actors), but the real subjects, the volunteers, didn't know this. They were told to increase the intensity of the shocks, even beyond what they were told was a lethal level. Many subjects continued to obey the authority in the study (the experimenter), even when their obedience involved administering what they thought were potentially lethal shocks to another person.

But did the experimental subjects actually believe that they were harming someone? Observational data suggest they did: "Persons were observed to sweat, tremble, stutter, bite their lips, and groan as they found themselves increasingly implicated in the experimental conflict" (Milgram, 1965:66).

Verbatim transcripts of the sessions also indicated that participants were in much psychological agony about administering the "shocks." So it seems that Milgram's deception "worked." Moreover, it seemed "necessary," since Milgram could not have administered real electric shocks to the students, nor would it have made sense for him to order the students to do something that wasn't so troubling, nor could he have explained what he was really interested in before conducting the experiment. The real question: Is this sufficient justification to allow the use of deception?

Aronson and Mills's study (1959) of severity of initiation (at an all-women's college in the 1950s), also mentioned in Chapter 3, provides a very different example of the use of deception in experimental research—one that does not pose greater-than-everyday risks to subjects. The students who were randomly assigned to the "severe initiation" experimental condition had to read a list of embarrassing words. Even in the 1950s, reading a list of potentially embarrassing words in a laboratory setting and listening to a taped discussion were unlikely to increase the risks to which students were exposed in their everyday lives. Moreover, the researchers informed subjects that they would be expected to talk about sex and could decline to participate in the experiment if this requirement would bother them. No one dropped out.

To further ensure that no psychological harm was caused, Aronson and Mills (1959) explained the true nature of the experiment to the subjects after the experiment, in what is called **debriefing**. The subjects' reactions were typical: "None of the Ss expressed any resentment or annoyance at having been misled. In fact, the majority were intrigued by the experiment, and several returned at the end of the academic quarter to ascertain the result" (179).

Debriefing: A researcher's informing subjects after an experiment about the experiment's purposes and methods and evaluating subjects' personal reactions to the experiment

---

Although the American Sociological Association's *Code of Ethics* does not discuss experimentation explicitly, one of its principles highlights the ethical dilemma posed by deceptive research:

(a) Sociologists do not use deceptive techniques (1) unless they have determined that their use will not be harmful to research participants; is justified by the study's prospective scientific, educational, or applied value; and that equally effective alternative procedures that do not use deception are not feasible, and (2) unless they have obtained the approval of institutional review boards or, in the absence of such boards, with another authoritative body with expertise on the ethics of research.

(b) Sociologists never deceive research participants about significant aspects of the research that would affect their willingness to participate, such as physical risks, discomfort, or unpleasant emotional experiences. (ASA, 1997:3)

Selective Distribution of Benefits

Field experiments conducted to evaluate social programs also can involve issues of informed consent (Hunt, 1985:275–276). One ethical issue that is somewhat unique to field experiments is the **distribution of benefits**: How much are subjects harmed by the way treatments are distributed in the experiment? For example, Sherman and Berk's (1984) experiment, and its successors, required police to make arrests in domestic violence cases largely on the basis of a random process. When arrests were not made, did the subjects' abused spouses suffer? Price et al. (1992) randomly assigned unemployed individuals who had volunteered for job search help to an intensive program. Were the unemployed volunteers who were assigned to the comparison group at a big disadvantage?

Distribution of benefits: An ethical issue about how much researchers can influence the benefits subjects receive as part of the treatment being studied in a field experiment

Is it ethical to give some potentially advantageous or disadvantageous treatment to people on a random basis? Random distribution of benefits is justified when the researchers do not know whether some treatment actually is beneficial or not—and, of course, it is the goal of the experiment to find out. Chance is as reasonable a basis for distributing the treatment as any other. Also, if insufficient resources are available to fund fully a benefit for every eligible person, distribution of the benefit on the basis of chance to equally needy persons is ethically defensible (Boruch, 1997:66–67).

回 CONCLUSION

Causation and the means for achieving causally valid conclusions in research is the last of the three legs on which the validity of research rests. In this chapter, you have learned about the five criteria used to evaluate the extent to which particular research designs may achieve causally valid findings. You have been exposed to the problem of spuriousness and the way that randomization deals with it. You also have learned why we must take into account the units of analysis in a research design to come to appropriate causal conclusions.

True experiments help greatly to achieve more valid causal conclusions—they are the "gold standard" for testing causal hypotheses. Even when conditions preclude use of a true experimental design, many research designs can be improved by adding some experimental components. However, although it may be possible to test a hypothesis with an experiment, it is not always desirable to do so. Laboratory experiments may be inadvisable when they do not test the real hypothesis of interest but test instead a limited version that is amenable to laboratory manipulation. It also does not make sense to test the impact of social programs that cannot actually be implemented because of financial or political problems (Rossi & Freeman, 1989:304–307). Yet the virtues of experimental designs mean that they should always be considered when explanatory research is planned.

We emphasize that understandings of causal relationships are always partial. Researchers must always wonder whether they have omitted some relevant variables from their controls or whether their experimental results would differ if the experiment were conducted in another setting or at another time in history. But the tentative nature of causal conclusions means that we must give more—not less—attention to evaluating the causal validity of social science research whenever we need to ask the simple question "What caused variation in this social phenomenon?"

KEY TERMS

Association	Matching
Before-and-after design	Mechanism
Causal effect	Multiple group before-and-after design
Ceteris paribus	Nonequivalent control group design
Comparison groups	Nonspuriousness
Compensatory rivalry (John Henry effect)	Placebo effect
Contamination	Posttest
Context	Pretest
Control group	Process analysis
Debriefing	Quasi-experimental design
Differential attrition (mortality)	Random assignment
Distribution of benefits	Randomization
Double-blind procedure	Regression effect
Endogenous change	Repeated measures panel design
Expectancies of experiment staff	Selection bias
Experimental group	Self-fulfilling prophecy
Ex post facto control group design	Spurious
External events	Time order
Field experiment	Time series design
Hawthorne effect	Treatment misidentification
History effect	True experiment

HIGHLIGHTS

- Three criteria generally are viewed as necessary for identifying a causal relationship: association between the variables, proper time order, and nonspuriousness of the association. In addition, the basis for concluding that a causal relationship exists is strengthened by identification of a causal mechanism and the context.

- Association between two variables by itself is insufficient evidence of a causal relationship. This point is commonly made by the expression "Correlation does not prove causation."
- The independent variable in an experiment is represented by a treatment or other intervention. Some subjects receive one type of treatment; others may receive a different treatment or no treatment. In true experiments, subjects are assigned randomly to comparison groups.
- Experimental research designs have three essential components: use of at least two groups of subjects for comparison, measurement of the change that occurs as a result of the experimental treatment, and use of random assignment. In addition, experiments may include identification of a causal mechanism and control over experimental conditions.
- Random assignment of subjects to experimental and comparison groups eliminates systematic bias in group assignment. The odds of there being a difference between the experimental and comparison groups on the basis of chance can be calculated. They become very small for experiments with at least 30 subjects per group.
- Random assignment and random sampling both rely on a chance selection procedure, but their purposes differ. Random assignment involves placing predesignated subjects into two or more groups on the basis of chance; random sampling involves selecting subjects out of a larger population on the basis of chance. Matching of cases in the experimental and comparison groups is a poor substitute for randomization, because identifying in advance all important variables on which to make the match is not possible. However, matching can improve the comparability of groups when it is used to supplement randomization.
- Ethical and practical constraints often preclude the use of experimental designs.
- A quasi-experimental design can be either a nonequivalent control group design or a before-and-after design. Nonequivalent control groups can be created through either individual matching of subjects or matching of group characteristics. In either case, these designs can allow us to establish the existence of an association and the time order of effects, but they do not ensure that some unidentified extraneous variable did not cause what we think of as the effect of the independent variable. Before-and-after designs can involve one or more pretests and posttests. Although multiple pretests and posttests make it unlikely that another, extraneous influence caused the experimental effect, they do not guarantee it.
- Ex post facto control group designs involve a comparison group that individuals could decide to join precisely because they prefer this experience rather than what the experimental group offers. This creates differences in subject characteristics between the experimental and control groups, which might very well result in a difference in the dependent variable. Because of this possibility, this type of design is not considered a quasi-experimental design.
- Invalid conclusions about causality may occur when relationships between variables measured at the group level are assumed to apply at the individual level (the ecological fallacy) and when relationships between variables measured at the level of individuals are assumed to apply at the group level (the reductionist fallacy). Nonetheless, many research questions point to relationships at multiple levels and may profitably be answered by studying different units of analysis.
- Causal conclusions derived from experiments can be invalid because of selection bias, endogenous change, the effects of external events, cross-group contamination, or treatment misidentification. In true experiments, randomization should eliminate selection bias and bias due to endogenous change. External events, cross-group contamination, and treatment misidentification can threaten the validity of causal conclusions in both true experiments and quasi-experiments.

- Process analysis can be used in experiments to identify how the treatment had (or didn't have) an effect—a matter of particular concern in field experiments. Treatment misidentification is less likely when process analysis is used.
- The generalizability of experimental results declines if the study conditions are artificial and the experimental subjects are unique. Field experiments are likely to produce more generalizable results than experiments conducted in the laboratory.
- The external validity of causal conclusions is determined by the extent to which they apply to different types of individuals and settings. When causal conclusions do not apply to all the subgroups in a study, they are not generalizable to corresponding subgroups in the population; consequently, they are not externally valid with respect to those subgroups. Causal conclusions can also be considered externally invalid when they occur only under the experimental conditions.
- Subject deception is common in laboratory experiments and poses unique ethical issues. Researchers must weigh the potential harm to subjects and debrief subjects who have been deceived. In field experiments, a common ethical problem is selective distribution of benefits. Random assignment may be the fairest way of allocating treatment when treatment openings are insufficient for all eligible individuals and when the efficacy of the treatment is unknown.

STUDENT STUDY SITE

To assist you in completing the Web Exercises, please access the Study Site at http://www.pineforge.com/mssw3, where you'll find the Web Exercises with accompanying links. You'll find other useful study materials like self-quizzes and e-flashcards for each chapter, along with a group of carefully selected articles from research journals that illustrate the major concepts and techniques presented in the book.

EXERCISES

Discussing Research

1. There's a lot of "sound and fury" in the social science literature about units of analysis and levels of explanation. Some social researchers may call another a "reductionist" if the researcher explains a problem, such as substance abuse, as due to "lack of self-control." The idea is that the behavior requires consideration of social structure—a group level of analysis rather than an individual level of analysis. Another researcher may be said to commit an "ecological fallacy" if he or she assumes that group-level characteristics explain behavior at the individual level (such as saying that "immigrants are more likely to commit crime" because the neighborhoods with higher proportions of immigrants have higher crime rates). Do you favor causal explanations at the individual or the group (or social structural) level? If you were forced to mark on a scale from 0 to 100 the percentage of crime that is due to problems with individuals rather than to problems with the settings in which they live and other aspects of social structure, where would you make your mark? Explain your decision.

2. Researchers often try to figure out how people have changed over time by conducting a cross-sectional survey of people of different ages. The idea is that if people who are in their 60s tend

to be happier than people who are in their 20s, it is because people tend to "become happier" as they age. But maybe people who are in their 60s now were just as happy when they were in their 20s and people in their 20s now will be just as unhappy when they are in their 60s. (That's called a "cohort effect.") We can't be sure unless we conduct a panel study (survey the same people at different ages). What, in your experience, are the major differences between the generations today in social attitudes and behaviors? Which would you attribute to changes as people age and which to differences between cohorts in what they have experienced (such as common orientations among "baby boomers")? Explain your reasoning.

3. The chapter begins with some alternative explanations for recent changes in the homicide rate. Which of the explanations make the most sense to you? Why? How could you learn more about the effect on crime of one of the "causes" you have identified in a laboratory experiment? What type of study could you conduct in the community to assess its causal impact?

4. This chapter discusses both experimental and quasi-experimental approaches to identifying causes. What are the advantages and disadvantages of both approaches for achieving each of the five criteria identified for causal explanations?

Finding Research

1. Read an original article describing a social experiment. (Social psychology "readers," collections of such articles for undergraduates, are a good place to find interesting studies.) Critique the article, using as your guide the article review questions presented in Exhibit 12.2. Focus on the extent to which experimental conditions were controlled and the causal mechanism was identified. Did inadequate control over conditions or inadequate identification of the causal mechanism make you feel uncertain about the causal conclusions?

2. Go to the Web site of the Community Policing Consortium at http://www.policing.com/links/index.html. What causal assertions are made? Pick one of these assertions and propose a research design with which to test this assertion. Be specific.

3. Go to Sociosite at http://www.pscw.uva.nl/sociosite/. Choose "Subject Areas." Choose a sociological subject area you are interested in. Find an example of research that has been done using experimental methods in this subject. Explain the experiment. Choose at least five of the Key Terms listed at the end of this chapter that are relevant to and incorporated in the research experiment you have located on the Internet. Explain how each of the five Key Terms you have chosen plays a role in the research example you found on the Web.

Critiquing Research

1. From newspapers or magazines, find two recent studies of education (reading, testing, etc.). For each study, list in order what you see as the most likely sources of internal invalidity (selection, mortality, etc.).

2. Select a true experiment, perhaps from the *Journal of Experimental and Social Psychology,* the *Journal of Personality and Social Psychology,* or sources suggested in class. Diagram the

experiment using the exhibits in this chapter as a model. Discuss the extent to which experimental conditions were controlled and the causal mechanism was identified. How confident can you be in the causal conclusions from the study, based on review of the threats to internal validity discussed in this chapter: selection bias, endogenous change, external events, contamination, and treatment misidentification? How generalizable do you think the study's results are to the population from which the cases were selected? To specific subgroups in the study? How thoroughly do the researchers discuss these issues?

3. Repeat the previous exercise with a quasi-experiment.

4. Critique the ethics of one of the experiments presented in this chapter or some other experiment you have read about. What specific rules do you think should guide researchers' decisions about subject deception and the selective distribution of benefits?

Doing Research

1. Try out the process of randomization. Go to the Web site http://www.randomizer.org. Now just type numbers into the randomizer for an experiment with two groups and 20 individuals per group. Repeat the process for an experiment with four groups and 10 individuals per group. Plot the numbers corresponding to each individual in each group. Does the distribution of numbers within each group truly seem to be random?

2. Participate in a social psychology experiment on the Internet. Go to http://www.socialpsychology .org/expts.htm. Pick an experiment in which to participate and follow the instructions. After you finish, write a description of the experiment and evaluate it using the criteria discussed in the chapter.

3. Volunteer for an experiment. Contact the psychology department and ask about opportunities for participating in laboratory experiments. Discuss the experience with your classmates.

Ethics Questions

1. Randomization is a key feature of experimental designs that are often used to investigate the efficacy of new treatments for serious and often incurable terminal diseases. What ethical issues do these techniques raise in studies of experimental treatments for incurable, terminal diseases? Would you make an ethical argument that in some situations, it is more ethical to use random assignment than the usual procedures for deciding whether patients receive a new treatment?

2. In their study of "neighborhood effects" on crime, sociologists Sampson and Raudenbush had observers drive down neighborhood streets in Chicago and record the level of disorder they observed. What should have been the observers' response if they observed a crime in progress? What if they just suspected that a crime was going to occur? What if the crime was a drug dealer interacting with a driver at the curb? What if it was a prostitute soliciting a customer? What, if any, ethical obligation does a researcher studying a neighborhood have to residents in that neighborhood? Should research results be shared at a neighborhood forum?

Survey Research

Some 6 months after the September 11, 2001, attacks on the World Trade Center and the Pentagon, a small group of students at Hamilton College and their professor, Dennis Gilbert (2002), conducted a nationwide survey of American Muslims. The survey found that nearly 75% of the respondents either knew someone who had, or had themselves, experienced anti-Muslim discrimination since the attacks. "You are demons," "Pig religion," "You guys did it," some were told. Respondents described actions such as "He spit in my face," "He pulled off my daughter's hajib [her head covering]"—the list of abuses went on. In all, 517 American Muslims were contacted, through a careful sampling procedure, and were interviewed via telephone by Gilbert's students and by employees of the Zogby International polling firm. This survey provided a snapshot of the views of an important segment of American society.

In this chapter, we will use the "Muslim America" project, a "youth and guns" survey also done by Gilbert, and other surveys to illustrate some key features of survey research. We explain the major steps in questionnaire design and then consider the features of four types of surveys, highlighting the unique problems attending each one and suggesting some possible solutions. (For instance, how do we develop an initial list—a sampling frame—of American Muslims?) We discuss ethics issues in the final section. By the chapter's end, you should be well on your way to becoming an informed consumer of survey reports and a knowledgeable developer of survey designs.

🔲 WHY IS SURVEY RESEARCH SO POPULAR?

Survey research collects information from a *sample of individuals* through their responses to *standardized questions*. As you probably have observed, a great many social scientists rely on surveys as their primary method of data collection. In fact, surveys have become so common that we cannot evaluate much of what we read in the newspaper or see on TV without having some understanding of this method of data collection (Converse, 1984).

> *Survey research:* Research in which information is collected from a sample of individuals through their responses to a set of standardized questions

Survey research owes its popularity to three advantages: versatility, efficiency, and generalizability. The *versatility* of surveys is apparent in the wide range of uses to which they are put, including opinion polls, election campaigns, marketing surveys, community needs assessments, and program evaluations. Surveys are *efficient* because they are a relatively fast means of collecting data on a wide range of issues at relatively little cost—ranging from about $10 to $15 per respondent in mailed surveys of the general population to $30 for a telephone survey and then as much as $300 for in-person interview surveys (from January 7, 1998, personal communication with Floyd J. Fowler of the Center for Survey Research, University of Massachusetts, Boston; see also Dillman, 1982/1991; Groves & Kahn, 1979/1991). Because they can be widely distributed to representative samples (see Chapter 5), surveys also help in achieving *generalizable* results.

Perhaps the most efficient type of survey is an **omnibus survey**, which includes a range of topics of interest to different social scientists or to other sponsors. The General Social Survey (GSS) of the National Opinion Research Center at the University of Chicago is a prime example of an omnibus survey. It is a 90-minute interview administered biennially to a probability sample of almost 3,000 Americans, with a wide range of questions and topic areas chosen by a board of overseers. The resulting datasets are made available to many universities, instructors, and students (Davis & Smith, 1992; National Opinion Research Center, 1992).

> *Omnibus survey:* A survey that covers a range of topics of interest to different social scientists

▣ HOW SHOULD WE WRITE SURVEY QUESTIONS?

Questions are the centerpiece of survey research, so selecting good questions is the single most important concern for survey researchers. All hope for achieving measurement validity is lost unless the questions in a survey are clear and convey the intended meaning to respondents.

Question writing for a particular survey might begin with a brainstorming session or a review of previous surveys. The Muslim America survey began with students formulating questions with help from Muslim students and professors. Most professionally prepared surveys contain previously used questions as well as some new ones, but every question that is considered for inclusion must be reviewed carefully for clarity and for its ability to convey the intended meaning to the respondents.

Adherence to the following basic principles will go a long way toward ensuring clear and meaningful questions.

Be Clear; Avoid Confusing Phrasing

In most cases, a *simple, direct approach* to asking a question minimizes confusion ("Overall, do you enjoy living in Ohio?"). Use shorter rather than longer words and sentences: *brave* rather than *courageous*; *job concerns* rather than *work-related employment issues* (Dillman, 2000:52). On the other hand, questions shouldn't be abbreviated so much that the results are ambiguous. The simple statement,

Residential location: _____

is *too* simple. Does it ask for town? Country? Street address? In contrast, asking, "In what city or town do you live?" focuses attention clearly on a specific geographic unit, a specific time, and a specific person.

Avoid *negative phrases or words,* especially **double negatives**: "Do you disagree that there should not be a tax increase?" Respondents have a hard time figuring out which response matches their sentiments. Such errors can easily be avoided with minor wording changes, but even experienced survey researchers can make this mistake.

Double negative: A question or statement that contains two negatives, which can muddy the meaning of the question

---

Avoid **double-barreled questions**; these actually ask two questions but allow only one answer. For instance, "Our business uses reviews and incentive plans to drive employee behavior. Do you agree or disagree?" What if the business uses only reviews? How should respondents answer? Double-barreled questions can lead to dramatically misleading results. For example, during the Watergate scandal in the 1970s, the Gallup poll asked, "Do you think President Nixon should be impeached and compelled to leave the presidency, or not?" Only about a third of Americans said yes. But when the wording was changed to ask whether President Nixon should be brought to trial before the Senate, more than half answered yes. The first version combined impeachment—trial—with conviction and may have confused people (Kagay, 1992:E5).

Double-barreled question: A single survey question that actually asks two questions but allows only one answer

---

It is also important to identify clearly what kind of information each question is to obtain. Some questions focus on attitudes, or on what people say they want or how they feel. Some questions focus on beliefs, or what people think is true. Some questions focus on behavior, or on what people do. And some questions focus on attributes, or on what people are like or have experienced (Dillman, 1978:79–118; Gordon, 1992). Rarely can a single question effectively address more than one of these dimensions at a time.

Minimize Bias

The words used in survey questions should not trigger biases, unless doing so is the researcher's conscious intent. Biased words and phrases tend to produce misleading answers. Some polls ask obviously loaded questions, such as "Isn't it time for Americans to stand up for morality and stop the shameless degradation of the airwaves?" Especially when describing abstract ideas (e.g., "freedom," "justice," "fairness"), your choice of words can dramatically affect how respondents answer. Take the difference between "welfare" and "assistance for the poor." On average, surveys have found that public support for "more assistance for the poor" is about *39 percentage points higher* than for "welfare" (Smith, 1987). Most people favor helping the poor; most people oppose welfare. The "truly needy" gain our sympathy, but "loafers and bums" do not.

Sometimes responses can be distorted through the lack of good alternative answers. For example, the Detroit Area Study (Turner & Martin, 1984:252) asked the following question: "People feel differently about making changes in the way our country is run. In order to keep America great, which of these statements do you think is best?" When the only two response choices were "We should be very cautious of making changes," or "We should be free to make changes," only 37% said that we should be free to make changes. However, when a stronger response choice was added suggesting that we should "constantly" make changes, 24% chose that response and another 32% still chose the "free to make changes" response. So instead of 37%, we now had a total of 56% who seemed open to making changes in the way our country is run (Turner & Martin:252). Including the more extreme positive alternative ("constantly" make changes) made the less extreme positive alternative more attractive.

To minimize biased responses, researchers have to test reactions to the phrasing of a question.

Allow for Disagreement

Some respondents tend to "agree" with a statement just to avoid disagreeing. In a sense, they want to be helpful. You can see the impact of this human tendency in a 1974 Michigan Survey Research Center survey about crime and lawlessness in the United States (Schuman & Presser, 1981). When one question stated that individuals were more to blame for crime than were social conditions, 60% of the respondents agreed. But when the question was rephrased so respondents were asked, "In general, do you believe that individuals or social conditions are more to blame for crime and lawlessness in the United States?" only 46% chose individuals.

As a rule, you should present both sides of attitude scales in the question itself (Dillman, 2000:61–62). The response choices themselves should be phrased to make each one seem as socially approved, as "agreeable," as the others.

Most people, for instance, won't openly admit to having committed a crime or other disreputable activities. In this situation, you should write questions that make agreement seem more acceptable. Rather than ask, "Have you ever shoplifted something from a store?" Dillman (2000:75) suggests "Have you ever taken anything from a store without paying for it?" Asking about a range of behaviors or attitudes can also facilitate agreeing with those that are socially unacceptable.

Don't Ask Questions They Can't Answer

Respondents should be *competent* to answer questions. Too many surveys expect accurate answers from people who couldn't reasonably know the answers. One campus survey we've seen asked professors to agree or disagree with statements such as the following:

"Minority students are made to feel they are second-class citizens."

"The Campus Center does a good job of meeting the informal needs of students."

"The Campus Center is where students go to meet one another and socialize informally."

"Alcohol contributes to casual scx among students."

But of course, most professors are in no position to know the answers to these questions about students' lives. To know what students do or feel, one should ask students, not professors. You should also realize that memory isn't a perfect tool—most of us, for instance, cannot accurately report what we ate for lunch on a Tuesday 2 weeks ago. To get accurate lunch information, ask about today's meal.

Sometimes your survey itself can sort people by competence so that they answer the appropriate questions. For instance, if you include a question about job satisfaction in a survey of the general population, first ask respondents whether they have a job. These **filter questions** create **skip patterns**. For example, respondents who answer no to one question are directed to skip ahead to another question, but respondents who answer yes go on to the **contingent question**. Skip patterns should be indicated clearly, as demonstrated in Exhibit 7.1.

Filter question: A survey question used to identify a subset of respondents who then are asked other questions

Skip pattern: The unique combination of questions created in a survey by filter questions and contingent questions

Contingent question: A question that is asked of only a subset of survey respondents

Allow for Uncertainty

Some respondents just don't know—about your topic, about their own feelings, about what they think. Or they like to be neutral and won't take a stand on anything. Or they don't have any information. All of these choices are OK, but you should recognize and allow for them.

Many people, for instance, are **floaters**: respondents who choose a substantive answer even when they really don't know. Asked for their opinion on a law of which they're completely ignorant, a third of the public will give an opinion anyway, if "Don't know" isn't an option. But if it *is* an option, 90% of that group will pick that answer. You should give them the chance to say that they don't know (Schuman & Presser, 1981:113–160).

Floaters: Survey respondents who provide an opinion on a topic in response to a closed-ended question that does not include a "Don't know" option but who will choose "Don't know" if it is available

Because there are so many floaters in the typical survey sample, the decision to include an explicit "Don't know" option for a question is important, especially with surveys of less

---

EXHIBIT 7.1 **Filter Questions and Skip Patterns**

9. (GUNSHOT) Not including military combat, have you or anyone close to you ever been shot by a gun?

   1. Yes   2. No (**skip to 11**)   3. Not sure (**do not read**)

10. (OPENSHOT) Could you explain the circumstances? _____

11. (GUNLAWS) In general, do you feel that laws covering the sale of firearms should be made more strict, less strict, or kept as they are now?

    1. More strict
    2. Less strict
    3. Kept as are
    4. Not sure (**do not read**)

educated populations. "Don't know" responses are chosen more often by those with less education (Schuman & Presser, 1981:113–146). Unfortunately, the inclusion of an explicit "Don't know" response choice also allows some people who *do* have a preference to take the easy way out and choose "Don't know."

Fence-sitters, people who see themselves as being neutral, may skew the results if you force them to choose between opposites. In most cases, about 10% to 20% of respondents—those who do not have strong feelings on an issue—will choose an explicit middle, neutral alternative (Schuman & Presser, 1981:161–178). Adding an explicit neutral response option is appropriate when you want to find out who is a fence-sitter.

Fence-sitters: Survey respondents who see themselves as being neutral on an issue and choose a middle (neutral) response that is offered

---

Fence-sitting and floating can be managed by including an explicit "no opinion" category after all the substantive responses. If neutral sentiment is a possibility, also include a neutral category in the middle of the substantive responses (such as "neither agree nor disagree") (Dillman, 2000:58–60). Finally, adding an open-ended question in which respondents are asked to discuss their opinions (or reasons for having no opinion) can help by shedding some light on why some persons choose "Don't know" in response to a particular question (Smith, 1984).

Make Response Categories Exhaustive and Mutually Exclusive

Questions with fixed response choices must provide one and only one possible response for everyone who is asked the question. First, all of the possibilities should be offered (choices should be "exhaustive"). In one survey of employees who were quitting their jobs at a telecommunications company, respondents were given these choices for "Why are you leaving [the company]?": (a) poor pay, (b) poor working environment, (c) poor benefits, or (d) poor relations with my boss. Clearly, there may be other reasons (e.g., family or health reasons, geographical preferences) to leave an employer. The response categories were not exhaustive. Or when asking college students their class (senior, junior, etc.), you should probably consider having an "other" category for nontraditional matriculants who may be on an unusual track.

Second, response choices shouldn't overlap—they should be mutually exclusive so that picking one rules out picking another. If I say, for instance, that I'm 25 years old, I cannot also be 50 years old; but I may claim to be both "young" and "mature." Those two choices aren't mutually exclusive, so they shouldn't be used as response categories for a question about age.

There are two exceptions to these principles: Filter questions may tell some respondents to skip over a question (the response choices do not have to be exhaustive), and respondents may be asked to "check all that apply" (the response choices are not mutually exclusive). Even these exceptions should be kept to a minimum. Respondents to a self-administered questionnaire should not have to do a lot of "skipping around," or else they may lose interest in completing carefully all the applicable questions. And some survey respondents react to a "check all that apply" request by just checking enough responses so that they feel they have "done enough" for that question and then ignoring the rest of the choices (Dillman, 2000:63).

▣ HOW SHOULD QUESTIONNAIRES BE DESIGNED?

Survey questions are asked as part of a **questionnaire** (or **interview schedule**, in interview-based studies); they are not isolated from other questions. The context created by the questionnaire as a whole has a major impact on how individual questions are interpreted and answered. Therefore, survey researchers must carefully design the questionnaire itself, not just each individual question. Several steps, explained in the following sections, will help you design a good questionnaire.

Questionnaire: A survey instrument containing the questions in a self-administered survey

Interview schedule: A survey instrument containing the questions asked by the interviewer in an in-person or phone survey

---

Build on Existing Instruments

If another researcher has already designed a set of questions to measure a key concept and previous surveys indicate that this measure is reliable and valid, then by all means use that instrument. Resources such as the *Handbook of Research Design and Social Measurement, 6th edition* (Miller & Salkind, 2002), can give you many ideas about existing questionnaires; your literature review at the start of a research project should be an even better source.

But there is a tradeoff here. Questions used previously may not concern quite the right concept or may not be appropriate in some ways for your population. A good rule of thumb is to use a previously designed instrument if it measures the concept of concern to you and it seems appropriate for your survey population.

Refine and Test Questions

The only good question is a pretested question. Before you rely on a question in your research, you need evidence that your respondents will understand what it means. So try it out on a few people (Dillman, 2000:140–147).

One important form of pretesting is discussing the questionnaire with colleagues. You can also review prior research in which your key questions or indexes have been used. Another increasingly popular form of pretesting comes from guided discussions among potential respondents. Such "focus groups" let you check for consistent understanding of terms and identify the range of events or experiences about which people will be asked to report (Fowler, 1995). (See Chapter 9 for more about this technique.)

Professional survey researchers have also developed a technique for evaluating questions called the **cognitive interview** (Fowler, 1995). Although the specifics vary, the basic approach is to ask people to "think aloud" as they answer questions. The researcher asks a test question and then probes with follow-up questions to learn how the question was understood and whether its meaning varied for different respondents. This method can identify many potential problems.

Cognitive interview: A technique for evaluating questions in which researchers ask people test questions, then probe with follow-up questions to learn how they understood the question and what their answers mean

---

Conducting a pilot study is the final stage of questionnaire preparation. For the Muslim America study, students placed 550 telephone calls and in the process learned (a) the extent of fear that many respondents felt about such a poll; (b) that females were, for cultural reasons, less likely to respond in surveys of the Muslim population; and (c) that some of their questions were worded ambiguously.

To do a pilot study, draw a small sample of individuals from the population you are studying or one very similar to it (it is best to draw a sample of at least 100 respondents) and carry out the survey procedures with them. You may include in the pretest version of a written questionnaire some space for individuals to add comments on each key question or, with in-person interviews, audiotape the test interviews for later review. Review the distribution of responses to each question and revise any that respondents do not seem to understand.

A survey researcher also can try to understand what respondents mean by their responses after the fact—that is, by including additional questions in the survey itself. Adding such **interpretive questions** after key survey questions is always a good idea, but it is of utmost importance when the questions in a survey have not been thoroughly pretested (Labaw, 1980).

Interpretive questions: Questions included in a questionnaire or interview schedule to help explain answers to other important questions

---

Maintain Consistent Focus

A survey (with the exception of an omnibus survey) should be guided by a clear conception of the research problem under investigation and the population to be sampled. Remember to have measures of all of the independent and dependent variables you plan to use. Of course, not even the best researcher can anticipate the relevance of every question. Researchers tend to try to avoid "missing something" by erring on the side of extraneous questions (Labaw, 1980:40).

At the same time, respondents are dismayed by long lists of redundant or unimportant questions, so respect their time and make sure that each question counts. Surveys too often include too many irrelevant questions.

Order the Questions

The sequence of questions on a survey matters. As a first step, the individual questions should be sorted into broad thematic categories, which then become separate sections in the questionnaire. Both the sections and the questions within the sections must then be organized in a logical order that would make sense in a conversation.

The first question deserves special attention, particularly if the questionnaire is to be self-administered. This question signals to the respondent what the survey is about, whether it will be interesting, and how easy it will be to complete ("Overall, would you say your physical health right now is excellent, good, fair, or poor?") The first question should be connected to the primary purpose of the survey, it should be interesting, it should be easy, and it should apply to everyone in the sample (Dillman, 2000:92–94). Don't try to jump right into sensitive issues ("In general, how well do you think your marriage is working?"); respondents have to "warm up" before they will be ready for such questions. As a standard practice, for instance, most researchers ask any questions about income or finances near the end of a survey, because many people are cautious about discussing such matters.

Question order can lead to **context effects** when one or more questions influence how subsequent questions are interpreted (Schober, 1999:89–98). The potential for context effects is greatest when two or more questions concern the same issue or closely related issues. For example, if an early question asks respondents to state for whom they plan to vote in an election, they may hesitate in later questions to support views that are clearly not those of that candidate. In general, people try to appear consistent (even if they are not); be sensitive to this and realize that earlier questions may "commit" respondents to answers on later questions.

Context effects: In survey research, refers to the influence that earlier questions may have on how subsequent questions are answered

---

Make the Questionnaire Attractive

An attractive questionnaire—neat, clear, clean, and spacious—is more likely to be completed and less likely to confuse either the respondent or, in an interview, the interviewer.

An attractive questionnaire does not look cramped; plenty of "white space"—more between questions than within question components—makes the questionnaire appear easy to complete. Response choices are listed vertically and are distinguished clearly and consistently, perhaps by formatting them in all capital letters and keeping them in the middle of the page. Skip patterns are indicated with arrows or other graphics. Some distinctive type of formatting should be used to identify instructions. Printing a multipage questionnaire in booklet form usually results in the most attractive and simple-to-use questionnaire (Dillman, 2000:80–86).

Exhibit 7.2 contains portions of a telephone interview questionnaire that illustrates these features, making it easy for the interviewer to use.

EXHIBIT 7.2 **Sample Interview Guide**

Hi, my name is _____. I am calling on behalf of (I am a student at) Hamilton College in New York. We are conducting a national opinion poll of high school students.

SCREENER: Is there a sophomore, junior, or senior in high school in your household with whom I may speak?

    1. Yes   2. No/not sure/refuse **(End)**

(If student not on phone, ask:) Could he or she come to the phone?

(When student is on the phone) Hi, my name is _____. I am calling on behalf of (I am a student at) Hamilton College in New York. We are conducting a national opinion poll of high school students about gun control. Your answers will be completely anonymous. Would you be willing to participate in the poll?

    1. Yes   2. No/not sure/refuse **(End)**

1. (SKOLYR) What year are you in school?
    1. Sophomore
    2. Junior
    3. Senior
    4. Not sure/refuse **(do not read) (End)**

Now some questions about your school:

2. (SKOL) Is it a public, Catholic, or private school?
    1. Public   2. Catholic   3. Private   4. Not sure **(do not read)**

▣ WHAT ARE THE ALTERNATIVES FOR ADMINISTERING SURVEYS?

Surveys can be administered in at least five different ways. They can be *mailed* or *group-administered* or conducted *by telephone, in person,* or *electronically.* (Exhibit 7.3 summarizes the typical features of each.) Each approach differs from the others in one or more important features:

- *Manner of administration*—Mailed, group, and electronic surveys are completed by the respondents themselves. During phone and in-person interviews, however, the researcher or a staff person asks the questions and records the respondent's answers.
- *Questionnaire structure*—Most mailed, group, phone, and electronic surveys are highly structured, fixing in advance the content and order of questions and response choices. In-person interviews may be highly structured, but they also may include many questions without fixed response choices.

EXHIBIT 7.3	Typical Features of the Five Survey Designs

Design	Manner of Administration	Setting	Questionnaire Structure	Cost
Mailed survey	Self	Individual	Mostly structured	Low
Group survey	Self	Group	Mostly structured	Very low
Phone survey	Professional	Individual	Structured	Moderate
In-person interview	Professional	Individual or unstructured	Structured	High
Electronic survey	Self	Individual	Mostly structured	Very low

- *Setting*—Mailed, electronic, and phone interviews are usually intended for only one respondent. The same is usually true of in-person interviews, although sometimes researchers interview several family members at once. On the other hand, some surveys are distributed simultaneously to a group of respondents, who complete the survey while the researcher (or assistant) waits.
- *Cost*—As mentioned earlier, in-person interviews are clearly the most expensive type of survey. Phone interviews are much less expensive, and surveying by mail is cheaper yet. Electronic surveys are now the least expensive method, because there are no interviewer costs; no mailing costs; and, for many designs, almost no costs for data entry. (Of course, extra staff time and expertise are required to prepare an electronic questionnaire.)

Because of their different features, the five administrative options vary in the types of error to which they are most prone and the situations in which they are most appropriate. The rest of this section focuses on each format's unique advantages and disadvantages.

Mailed, Self-Administered Surveys

A **mailed (self-administered) survey** is conducted by mailing a questionnaire to respondents, who then take the survey by themselves. The central problem for a mailed survey is maximizing the response rate. Even an attractive questionnaire with clear questions will probably be returned by no more than 30% of a sample unless extra steps are taken. A response rate of 30%, of course, is a disaster, destroying any hope of a representative sample. That's because people who *do* respond are often systematically different from people who *don't* respond—women respond more often, for instance, to most surveys; people with very strong opinions respond more than those who are indifferent; very wealthy and very poor people, for different reasons, are less likely to respond.

> *Mailed (self-administered) survey:* A survey involving a mailed questionnaire to be completed by the respondent

Fortunately, the conscientious use of systematic techniques can push the response rate to 70% or higher for most mailed surveys (Dillman, 2000:27), which is acceptable. Sending follow-up mailings to nonrespondents is the single most important technique for obtaining an adequate response rate. The follow-up mailings explicitly encourage initial nonrespondents to return a completed questionnaire; implicitly, they convey the importance of the effort. Dillman (155–158, 177–188) has demonstrated the effectiveness of a standard procedure for the mailing process: a preliminary introductory letter, a well-packaged survey mailing with a personalized cover letter, a reminder postcard 2 weeks after the initial mailing, and then new cover letters and replacement questionnaires 2 to 4 weeks and 6 to 8 weeks after that mailing.

The **cover letter**, actually, is critical to the success of a mailed survey. This statement to respondents sets the tone for the entire questionnaire. The cover letter or introductory statement must establish the credibility of the research and the researcher, it must be personalized (including a personal salutation and an original signature), it should be interesting to read, and it must explain issues about voluntary participation and maintaining subject confidentiality (Dillman, 1978:165–172). A carefully prepared cover letter should increase the response rate and result in more honest and complete answers to the survey questions; a poorly prepared cover letter can have the reverse effects. Exhibit 7.4 is an example of a cover letter for a questionnaire.

> *Cover letter:* The letter sent with a mailed questionnaire. It explains the survey's purpose and auspices and encourages the respondent to participate.

Other steps that help to maximize the response rate include clear and understandable questions, not many open-ended questions, a credible research sponsor, a token incentive (such as a $1 coupon), and presurvey advertising (Fowler, 1988:99–106; Mangione, 1995:79–82).

Group-Administered Surveys

A **group-administered survey** is completed by individual respondents assembled in a group. The response rate is usually high because most group members will participate. Unfortunately, this method is seldom feasible because it requires a captive audience. With the exception of students, employees, members of the armed forces, and some institutionalized populations, most people cannot be sampled in such a setting.

> *Group-administered survey:* A survey that is completed by individual respondents who are assembled in a group

EXHIBIT 7.4 **Sample Questionnaire Cover Letter**

University of Massachusetts at Boston
Department of Sociology
May 24, 2009

Jane Doe
AIDS Coordinator
Shattuck Shelter

Dear Jane:

AIDS is an increasing concern for homeless people and for homeless shelters. The enclosed survey is about the AIDS problem and related issues confronting shelters. It is sponsored by the Life Lines AIDS Prevention Project for the Homeless—a program of the U.S. Centers for Disease Control and the Massachusetts Department of Public Health.

As an AIDS coordinator/shelter director, you have learned about homeless persons' problems and about implementing programs in response to those problems. The Life Lines Project needs to learn from your experience. Your answers to the questions in the enclosed survey will improve substantially the base of information for improving AIDS prevention programs.

Questions in the survey focus on AIDS prevention activities and on related aspects of shelter operations. It should take about 30 minutes to answer all the questions.

Every shelter AIDS coordinator (or shelter director) in Massachusetts is being asked to complete the survey. And every response is vital to the success of the survey: The survey report must represent the full range of experiences.

You may be assured of complete confidentiality. No one outside of the university will have access to the questionnaire you return. (The ID number on the survey will permit us to check with nonrespondents to see if they need a replacement survey or other information.) All information presented in the report to Life Lines will be in aggregate form, with the exception of a list of the number, gender, and family status of each shelter's guests.

Please mail the survey back to us by Monday, June 4, and feel free to call if you have any questions.

Thank you for your assistance.

Yours sincerely,

Russell K. Schutt

Russell K. Schutt, Ph.D.
Project Director

Whoever is responsible for administering the survey to the group must be careful to minimize comments that might bias answers or that could vary between different groups in the same survey (Dillman, 2000:253–256). A standard introductory statement should be read to the group that expresses appreciation for their participation, describes the steps of the survey, and emphasizes (in classroom surveys) that the survey is not the same as a test. A cover letter like that used in mailed surveys also should be distributed with the question-naires. To emphasize confidentiality, respondents should be given envelopes in which to seal their questionnaires after they are completed.

Another issue of special concern with group-administered surveys is the possibility that respondents will feel coerced to participate and, therefore, will be less likely to answer questions honestly. Also, because administering group surveys requires approval of the authorities—and this sponsorship is made quite obvious, because the survey is conducted on the organization's premises—respondents may infer that the researcher is in league with the sponsor. No complete solution to this problem exists, but it helps to make an introductory statement emphasizing the researcher's independence and giving participants a chance to ask questions about the survey. The sponsor should keep a low profile and allow the researcher both control over the data and autonomy in report writing.

Telephone Surveys

In a **phone survey**, interviewers question respondents over the phone and then record respondents' answers. Phone interviewing is traditionally a very popular method of conducting surveys in the United States because almost all families have phones. But two problems often threaten the validity of a phone survey: not reaching the proper sampling units (or "coverage error") and not getting enough successfully completed responses to make the results generalizable.

Phone survey: A survey in which interviewers question respondents over the phone and record their answers

---

Reaching Sample Units

The first big problem lies in the difficulty of actually contacting the sample units (typically households). Most telephone surveys use random digit dialing (RDD) at some point in the sampling process (Lavrakas, 1987) to contact a random sample of households. A machine calls random phone numbers within the designated exchanges, whether or not the numbers are published. RDD is a good way to "capture" unlisted numbers, whose owners are systematically different (often they are wealthier than the general population). When the machine reaches an inappropriate household (such as a business, in a survey of individuals), the phone number is simply replaced with another.

But the tremendous recent (since 2000) popularity of cellular, or mobile, telephones has made accurate coverage of random samples almost impossible, for several reasons (Tourangeau, 2004:781–792): (1) Cell phones are typically not listed in telephone directories, so they can't be included in prepared calling lists; (2) laws generally forbid the use of automated (RDD) dialers to contact cell phones; (3) close to 20% of the U.S. population now has only a cell phone (no landline) and therefore can't be reached by either RDD or many directory lists; and (4) for 18- to 24-year-olds, some 30% have cell phones only, and cell phone-only households are also more common among non–English speakers.

The net effect, then, of widespread cell phone usage is to underrepresent young people in particular from inclusion in most large telephone surveys, obviously damaging the results.

Maximizing Response to Phone Surveys

Even if an appropriate (for sampling) number is dialed, responses may not be completed. First, because people often are not home, multiple callbacks will be needed for many sample members. With large numbers of single-person households, dual-earner families, and out-of-home activities, survey research organizations have had to increase the usual number of phone contact attempts from just 4–8 to 20—a lot of attempts just to reach one person. Caller ID and call waiting allow potential respondents to avoid answering calls from strangers, including researchers. The growth of telemarketing has accustomed individuals nowadays to refuse calls from unknown individuals and organizations or to use their answering machines to screen calls (Dillman, 2000:8, 28). In the Muslim America study, many people were afraid to talk with the researchers or were actively hostile; after all, respondents don't really know who is calling and may have good reason to be suspicious. And since a huge number of cell phone users are children, and so legally unavailable for surveys, calls made to them are all wasted efforts for researchers.

Such problems mean that careful training and direction of interviewers is essential in phone surveys. The instructions shown in Exhibit 7.5 were developed to clarify procedures for asking and coding a series of questions in the phone interviews conducted for the youth and guns survey.

EXHIBIT 7.5 **Sample Interviewer Instructions**

Sample Interviewer Instructions, Youth and Guns Survey, 2000

22. (CONSTIT) To your knowledge, does the U.S. Constitution guarantee citizens the right to own firearms?
    1. Yes   2. No **(skip to 24)**   3. Not sure **(do not read)**

23. (CONLAW) Do you believe that laws regulating the sale and use of handguns violate the constitutional rights of gun owners?
    1. Yes   2. No   3. Not sure **(do not read)**

24. (PETITION) In some localities, high school students have joined campaigns to change the gun laws, and sometimes they have been successful. Earlier you said that you thought that the current gun control laws were (**if Q11 = 1, insert "not strict enough"; if Q11 = 2, insert "too strict"**). Suppose a friend who thinks like you do about this asked you to sign a petition calling for (**if Q11 = 1, insert "stronger gun control laws"; if Q11 = 2, insert "less restrictive gun control laws"**). On a scale from 1 to 5, with 1 being very unlikely and 5 being very likely, how likely is it that you would sign the petition?
    1. (Very unlikely)
    2.
    3.
    4.
    5. (Very likely)
    6. Not sure **(do not read)**

Phone surveying is the method of choice for relatively short surveys of the general population. Response rates in phone surveys traditionally have tended to be very high—often above 80%—because few individuals would hang up on a polite caller or refuse to stop answering questions (at least within the first 30 minutes or so). But the problems we have noted, especially those connected with cell phone usage, makes this method of surveying populations increasingly difficult.

In-Person Interviews

What is unique to the **in-person interview**, compared to the other survey designs, is the face-to-face social interaction between interviewer and respondent. If money is no object, in-person interviewing is often the best survey design.

In-person interview: A survey in which an interviewer questions respondents face-to-face and records their answers

---

In-person interviewing has several advantages: Response rates are higher than with any other survey design; questionnaires can be much longer than with mailed or phone surveys; the questionnaire can be complex, with both open-ended and closed-ended questions and frequent branching patterns; the order in which questions are read and answered can be controlled by the interviewer; the physical and social circumstances of the interview can be monitored; and respondents' interpretations of questions can be probed and clarified. The interviewer, therefore, is well placed to gain a full understanding of what the respondent really wants to say.

However, researchers must be alert to some special hazards due to the presence of an interviewer. Ideally, every respondent should have the same interview experience—that is, each respondent should be asked the same questions in the same way by the same type of person, who reacts similarly to the answers. Suppose one interviewer is smiling and pleasant while another is gruff and rude; the two interviewers will likely elicit very different results in their surveys, if only in the length of responses. Careful training and supervision are essential (Groves, 1989:404–406).

Maximizing Response to Interviews

Several factors affect the response rate in interview studies. Contact rates tend to be lower in central cities, in part because of difficulties in finding people at home and gaining access to high-rise apartments, and, in part, because of interviewer reluctance to visit some areas at night, when people are more likely to be home (Fowler, 1988:45–60). Households with young children or elderly adults tend to be easier to contact, whereas single-person households are more difficult to reach (Groves & Couper, 1998:119–154).

Refusal rates vary with some respondent characteristics. People with less education participate somewhat less in surveys of political issues (perhaps because they are less aware of current political issues). Less education is also associated with higher rates of "Don't know" responses (Groves, 1989). On the other hand, wealthy people often refuse to be surveyed about their income or buying habits, perhaps to avoid being plagued by sales calls. Such problems can be lessened with an advance letter introducing the survey project and by multiple contact attempts throughout the day and evening, but they cannot be entirely avoided (Fowler, 1988:52–53).

Electronic Surveys

The widespread use of personal computers and the growth of the Internet have created new possibilities for survey research. **Electronic surveys** can be prepared in two ways (Dillman, 2000:352–354). **E-mail surveys** can be sent as messages to respondent e-mail addresses. Respondents then mark their answers in the message and send them back to the researcher. This approach is easy for researchers to develop and for respondents to use. However, this approach is cumbersome for surveys that are more than four or five pages long. **Web surveys** are stored on a server that is controlled by the researcher; respondents are then asked to visit the Web site (often by just clicking an e-mailed link) and respond to the questionnaire by checking answers. Web surveys require more programming by the researcher, but a well-designed Web survey can tailor its questions to a given respondent and thus seem shorter, more interesting, and more attractive.

Electronic survey: A survey that is sent and answered by computer, either through e-mail or on the Web

E-mail survey: A survey that is sent and answered through e-mail

Web survey: A survey that is accessed and responded to on the World Wide Web

---

Web surveys are becoming a popular form of electronic survey in part because they are so flexible and inexpensive (see Exhibit 7.6). The questionnaire design can feature appealing graphic and typographic elements. By clicking on linked terms, respondents can view definitions of words or instructions for answering questions. Lengthy sets of response choices can be presented with pull-down menus. Pictures and audio segments can be added. Because answers are recorded directly in the researcher's database, data entry errors are virtually eliminated, and results can be reported quickly.

The most important drawback to either electronic survey approach is the large number of households that are not yet connected to the Internet—about 40% of U.S. households are not connected to the Internet. Households without Internet access also tend to be older and poorer than those that are connected (Tourangeau, 2004:792–793). Remember, regardless of your sampling work, there's zero chance of a non–computer user responding to an electronic survey. But there's another, almost opposite problem with Web surveys: Because they are so easy and cheap to set up, you can find hundreds of Web surveys on a wide range of topics and for many different purposes. Among Internet users, almost anyone can participate in many of these Web surveys. The large number of respondents such an

EXHIBIT 7.6   Survey.Net—Year 2000 Presidential Election Survey

Your source for information, opinions & demographics from the Net Community!

Year 2000 Presidential Election Survey

Take the year 2000 presidential election survey!

1. What is your age?
   No Answer ⬍

2. Your Sex:
   No Answer ⬍

3. Your highest level of education completed:
   No Answer ⬍

4. Your political affiliation:
   No Answer ⬍

5. Who did you vote for in 1996?
   No Answer ⬍

6. Even though not all of these candidates are necessarily running, if the presidential election were held today, who would you vote for?
   No Answer ⬍

7. Of the following TWO potential presidential candidates, who would you vote for?
   No Answer ⬍

8. Of the following presidential candidates, who would you vote for?
   No Answer ⬍

9. Do you consider yourself...
   No Answer ⬍

10. What political concepts do you agree with? *(check all that apply)*

☐ - We need less government regulation in general
☐ - We need more responsible government regulation
☐ - States should have more responsibility than the Federal Gov.

☐ - The government should NOT mandate moral standards
☐ - The government SHOULD mandate moral standards

☐ - Tax breaks are more important than reducing the deficit
☐ - Reducing the deficit is more important than tax breaks

☐ - Unions are destroying American productivity
☐ - Unions protect the worker

☐ - The economy is more important than the environment
☐ - The environment is more important than the economy

11. In your opinion, what is the worst problem with our society?
[No Answer ⬍]

12. Of those items listed, what should be our next President's highest priority?
[No Answer ⬍]

13. Without turning this into a partisan/rhetorical argument, who do you want to see for president in 2000 and why? (*Limit this to one or two sentences*)
[⬍]

Thanks very much for participating in the survey!

To submit your survey choices, select:
[SUBMIT SURVEY]

or [Reset survey settings]

You can view the latest survey results after you submit your answers.

We hope you will also participate in other surveys online as well. Please note that you should only complete each survey <u>once</u>.

uncontrolled method can generate should not cause you to forget the importance of a representative sample. Uncontrolled Web surveys are guaranteed to produce, instead, a very biased sample (Dillman, 2000:355).

When the population to be surveyed has a high rate of Internet use and access is controlled, however, the Web makes possible fast and effective surveys (Dillman, 2000:354–355). For example, Titus K. L. Schleyer and Jane L. Forrest (2000:420) achieved a 74% response rate in a survey of dental professionals who were already Internet users. Many corporations use Web surveys for gathering information and attitude profiles of their own employees and get response rates of 80% or more. A skilled Web programmer can generate a survey layout with many attractive features that make it more likely that respondents will give their answers—and have a clear understanding of the question (Smyth, Dillman, Christian, & Stern 2004:4–5). Under proper conditions, electronic surveys are an excellent tool.

▣ A COMPARISON OF SURVEY DESIGNS

Which survey design should you use for a study? Let's compare the four major survey designs: mailed surveys, phone surveys, in-person surveys, and electronic surveys. (Group-administered surveys are similar in most respects to mailed surveys except that they require the unusual circumstance of having access to the sample in a group setting.) Exhibit 7.7 summarizes these strong and weak points.

The most important difference among these four methods is their varying response rates. Because of the low response rates of *mailed surveys,* they are weakest from a sampling standpoint. However, researchers with limited time, money, and staff may still prefer a mailed survey. Mailed surveys can be useful in asking sensitive questions (e.g., questions about marital difficulties or financial situation), because respondents won't be embarrassed by answering in front of an interviewer.

Contracting with an established survey research organization for a *phone survey* is often the best alternative to a mailed survey. The persistent follow-up attempts that are necessary to secure an adequate response rate are much easier over the phone than in person, although you must be careful about the cell phone sampling and response problem. A phone survey limits the length and complexity of the questionnaire but offers the possibility of very carefully monitoring interviewers (Fowler, 1988:61–73).

In-person surveys can be long and complex, and the interviewer can easily monitor the conditions (the room, noise and other distractions, etc.). Although interviewers may themselves distort results, either by changing the wording of questions or failing to record answers properly, this problem can be lessened by careful training and monitoring of interviewers and by tape-recording the answers.

The advantages and disadvantages of *electronic surveys* depend on the populations to be surveyed. Too many people do not have Internet connections for general use of Internet surveying. But when your entire sample has access and ability (e.g., college students, corporate employees), Web-based surveys can be very effective.

EXHIBIT 7.7	Advantages and Disadvantages of Four Survey Designs

Characteristics of Design	Mail Survey	Phone Survey	In-Person Survey	Web Survey
Representative sample				
Opportunity for inclusion is known				
For completely listed populations	High	High	High	Medium
For incompletely listed populations	Medium	Medium	High	Low
Selection within sampling units is controlled	Medium	High	High	Low
(e.g., specific family members must respond)				
Respondents are likely to be located				
If samples are heterogeneous	Medium	High	High	Low
If samples are homogeneous and specialized	High	High	High	High
Questionnaire construction and question design				
Allowable length of questionnaire	Medium	Medium	High	Medium
Ability to include				
Complex questions	Medium	Low	High	High
Open questions	Low	High	High	Medium
Screening questions	Low	High	High	High
Tedious, boring questions	Low	High	High	Low
Ability to control question sequence	Low	High	High	High
Ability to ensure questionnaire completion	Medium	High	High	Low
Distortion of answers				
Odds of avoiding social desirability bias	High	Medium	Low	High
Odds of avoiding interviewer distortion	High	Medium	Low	High
Odds of avoiding contamination by others	Medium	High	Medium	Medium
Administrative goals				
Odds of meeting personnel requirements	High	High	Low	Medium
Odds of implementing quickly	Low	High	Low	High
Odds of keeping costs low	High	Medium	Low	High

So overall, in-person interviews are the strongest design and are generally preferable when sufficient resources and a trained interview staff are available; telephone surveys have many of the advantages of in-person interviews at much less cost, but coverage response rates are an increasing problem. Any decision about the best survey design for a particular study must take into account the particular features and goals of the study.

🔲 ETHICAL ISSUES IN SURVEY RESEARCH

Survey research designs usually pose fewer ethical dilemmas than do experimental or field research designs. Potential respondents to a survey can easily refuse to participate, and a cover letter or introductory statement that identifies the sponsors of and motivations for the survey gives them the information required to make this decision. Little is concealed from the respondents, and the methods of data collection are quite obvious. Only in group-administered survey designs might the respondents (such as students or employees) be, in effect, a captive audience, so they require special attention to ensure that participation is truly voluntary. (Those who do not wish to participate may be told they can just hand in a blank form.)

Sometimes, political or marketing surveys are used unscrupulously to sway opinion under the guise of asking for it. So-called "push polls" are sometimes employed in political campaigns to distort an opponent's image ("If you knew Congressman Jones was cheating on his wife, would you consider him fit for high office?"). Advertisers can use surveys that pretend to collect opinions or "register" a purchase for warranty purposes, but often they are really trying to collate information about where you live, your phone numbers, your buying habits, and the like.

Confidentiality is most often the primary focus of ethical concern in survey research. Many surveys include questions that might prove damaging to the subjects if their answers were disclosed. When a survey of employees asks, "Do you think management here, especially your boss, is doing a good job?" or when student course evaluations ask, "On a scale of 1 to 5, how fair would you say the professor is?" respondents may well hesitate; if the boss or professor saw the results, workers or students could be hurt.

To prevent any disclosure of such information, it is critical to preserve subject confidentiality. Only research personnel should have access to information that could be used to link respondents to their responses, and even that access should be limited to what is necessary for specific research purposes. Only numbers should be used to identify respondents on their questionnaires, and the researcher should keep the names that correspond to these numbers in a safe, private location, unavailable to staff and others who might come across them. Follow-up mailings or contact attempts that require linking the ID numbers with names and addresses should be carried out by trustworthy assistants under close supervision. If an electronic survey is used, encryption technology should be used to make information that is provided over the Internet secure from unauthorized people. Usually confidentiality can be protected readily; the key is to be aware of the issue. Don't allow bosses to collect workers' surveys or professors to pick up course evaluations. Be aware of your respondents' concerns and be even a little more careful than you need to be.

Few surveys can provide true **anonymity**, where no identifying information is ever recorded to link respondents with their responses. The main problem with anonymous surveys is that they preclude follow-up attempts to contact nonrespondents and they prevent panel designs, which measure change through repeated surveys of the same individuals. In-person surveys rarely can be anonymous, because an interviewer must, in almost all cases, know the name and address of the interviewee. However, phone surveys that are meant only to sample opinion at one point in time, as in political polls, can safely be completely anonymous. When no future follow-up is desired, group-administered surveys also can be anonymous. To provide anonymity in a mail survey, the researcher should omit identifying codes from the questionnaire but may include a self-addressed, stamped postcard, so the respondent can notify the researcher that the questionnaire has been returned without creating any linkage to the questionnaire itself (Mangione, 1995:69).

Anonymity: Provided by research in which no identifying information is recorded that could be used to link respondents to their responses

---

回 CONCLUSION

Survey research is an exceptionally efficient and productive method for investigating a wide array of social research questions. In addition to the potential benefits for social science, considerations of time and expense frequently make a survey the preferred data collection method. One or more of the five survey designs reviewed in this chapter can be applied to almost any research question. It is no wonder that surveys have become the most popular research method in sociology and that they frequently inform discussion and planning about important social and political questions. As use of the Internet increases, survey research should become even more efficient and popular.

The relative ease of conducting at least some types of survey research leads many people to imagine that no particular training or systematic procedures are required. Nothing could be further from the truth. But as a result of this widespread misconception, you will encounter a great many nearly worthless survey results. You must be prepared to examine carefully the procedures used in any survey before accepting its findings as credible. And if you decide to conduct a survey, you must be prepared to invest the time and effort required by proper procedures.

KEY TERMS

Anonymity
Cognitive interview
Context effects
Contingent question
Cover letter
Double-barreled question
Double negative
Electronic survey
E-mail survey
Fence-sitters
Filter question
Floaters

Group-administered survey
In-person interview
Interpretive questions
Interview schedule
Mailed (self-administered)
  survey
Omnibus survey
Phone survey
Questionnaire
Skip pattern
Survey research
Web survey

HIGHLIGHTS

- Surveys are the most popular form of social research because of their versatility, efficiency, and generalizability. Many survey datasets, like the General Social Survey, are available for social scientists to use in teaching and research.
- Omnibus surveys cover a range of topics of interest and generate data useful to multiple sponsors.
- Questions must be worded carefully to avoid confusing respondents, encouraging less-than-honest responses, or triggering biases. Inclusion of "Don't know" choices and neutral responses may help, but the presence of such options also affects the distribution of answers. Open-ended questions can be used to determine the meaning that respondents attach to their answers. Answers to any survey questions may be affected by the questions that precede them in a questionnaire or interview schedule.
- Questions can be tested and improved through review by experts, focus group discussions, cognitive interviews, and/or pilot testing. Every questionnaire and interview schedule should be pretested on a small sample that is like the sample to be surveyed.
- The cover letter for a mailed questionnaire should be credible, personalized, interesting, and responsible.
- Response rates in mailed surveys are typically well below 70%, unless multiple mailings are made to nonrespondents and the questionnaire and cover letter are attractive, interesting, and carefully planned. Response rates for group-administered surveys are usually much higher than for mailed surveys.
- Phone interviews using random digit dialing allow fast turnaround and efficient sampling. Multiple callbacks are often required, and the rate of nonresponse to phone interviews is rising. Phone interviews should be limited in length to about 30 to 45 minutes.
- In-person interviews have several advantages over other types of surveys: They allow longer and more complex interview schedules, monitoring of the conditions when the questions are answered, probing for respondents' understanding of the questions, and high response rates. However, the interviewer must balance the need to establish rapport with the respondent with the need to adhere to a standardized format.
- Electronic surveys may be e-mailed or posted on the Web. Interactive voice response systems using the telephone are another option. At this time, use of the Internet is not sufficiently widespread to allow e-mail or Web surveys of the general population, but these approaches can be fast and efficient for populations with high rates of computer use.
- The decision to use a particular survey design must take into account the unique features and goals of the study. In general, in-person interviews are the strongest but most expensive survey design.
- Most survey research poses few ethical problems because respondents can decline to participate—an option that should be stated clearly in the cover letter or introductory statement. Special care must be taken when questionnaires are administered in group settings (to "captive audiences") and when sensitive personal questions are to be asked; subject confidentiality should always be preserved.

EXERCISES

Discussing Research

1. Response rates to phone surveys are declining, even as phone usage increases. Part of the problem is that lists of cell phone numbers are not available and wireless service providers do not allow outside access to their networks. Cell phone users may also have to pay for incoming calls. Do you think regulations should be passed to increase the ability of survey researchers to include cell phones in their random digit dialing surveys? How would you feel about receiving survey calls on your cell phone? What problems might result from "improving" phone survey capabilities in this way?

2. In-person interviews have for many years been the "gold standard" in survey research, because the presence of an interviewer increases the response rate, allows better rapport with the interviewee, facilitates clarification of questions and instructions, and provides feedback about the interviewee's situation. However, researchers who design in-person interviewing projects are now making increasing use of technology to ensure consistent questioning of respondents and to provide greater privacy while answering questions. But having a respondent answer questions on a laptop while the interviewer waits is a very different social process than asking the questions verbally. Which approach would you favor in survey research? What tradeoffs can you suggest there might be in terms of quality of information collected, rapport building, and interviewee satisfaction?

Finding Research

1. What resources are available for survey researchers? This question can be answered in part through careful inspection of a Web site maintained by the Survey Research Laboratory at the University of Illinois at Chicago: http://www.srl.uic.edu/srllink/srllink.htm#Organizations. Spend some time reviewing these resources and write a brief summary of them.

2. Go to the Research Triangle Institute (RTI) site and browse the work it does and the resources it offers in survey design: http://www.rti.org/page.cfm/Capabilities/. What steps in the survey process can be improved through use of these resources? Give specific examples.

Critiquing Research

1. Read one of the original articles that reported one of the surveys described in this chapter. Critique the article using the questions presented in Exhibit 12.2 as your guide but focus particular attention on sampling, measurement, and survey design.

2. Each of the following questions was used in a survey that we received at some time in the past. Evaluate each question and its response choices using the guidelines for question writing presented in this chapter. What errors do you find? Try to rewrite each question to avoid such errors and improve question wording.

   a. The first question in an *Info World* (computer publication) "product evaluation survey":

   ```
   How interested are you in PostScript Level 2 printers?

   _____ Very _____ Somewhat _____ Not at all
   ```

   b. From the Greenpeace National Marine Mammal Survey:

   ```
   Do you support Greenpeace's nonviolent direct action to inter-
   cept whaling ships, tuna fleets and other commercial fisher-
   men in order to stop their wanton destruction of thousands of
   magnificent marine mammals?

   _____ Yes _____ No _____ Undecided
   ```

   c. From a U.S. Department of Education survey of college faculty:

   ```
   How satisfied or dissatisfied are you with each of the follow-
   ing aspects of your instructional duties at this institution?
   ```

	Very dissatisfied	Somewhat dissatisfied	Somewhat satisfied	Very satisfied
a. The authority I have to make decisions about what courses I teach........	1	2	3	4
b. Time available for working with students as advisor, mentor..	1	2	3	4

   d. From a survey about affordable housing in a Massachusetts community:

   ```
   Higher than single-family density is acceptable in order
   to make housing affordable.
   ```

Strongly Agree	Agree	Undecided	Disagree	Strongly Disagree
1	2	3	4	5

e. From a survey of faculty experience with ethical problems in research:

Are you reasonably familiar with the codes of ethics of any
of the following professional associations?

	Very Familiar	Familiar	Not too Familiar
American Sociological Association	1	2	0
Society for the Study of Social Problems	1	2	0
American Society of Criminology	1	2	0

If you are familiar with any of the above codes of ethics,
to what extent do you agree with them?

Strongly Agree_____ Agree_____ No Opinion_____
Disagree_____ Disagree Strongly_____

Some researchers have avoided using a *professional code
of ethics* as a guide for the following reasons. Which
responses, if any, best describe your reasons for not using
all or any of the parts of the codes?

	Yes	No
1. Vagueness	1	0
2. Political pressures	1	0
3. Codes protect only individuals, not groups	1	0

f. From a survey of faculty perceptions:

Of the students you have observed while teaching college
courses, please indicate the percentage who significantly
improved their performance in the following areas:

Reading _____ %

Organization _____ %

Abstraction _____ %

g. From a University of Massachusetts, Boston student survey:

A person has a responsibility to stop a friend or relative
from driving when drunk.

Strongly Agree _____ Agree _____ Disagree _____
Strongly Disagree _____

Even if I wanted to, I would probably not be able to stop
most people from driving drunk.

Strongly Agree _____ Agree _____ Disagree _____
Strongly Disagree _____

3. We received in a university mailbox some years ago a two-page questionnaire that began with the following "cover letter" at the top of the first page:

Faculty Questionnaire

This survey seeks information on faculty perception of the learning process and student performance in their undergraduate careers. Surveys have been distributed in nine universities in the Northeast, through random deposit in mailboxes of selected departments. This survey is being conducted by graduate students affiliated with the School of Education and the Sociology Department. We greatly appreciate your time and effort in helping us with our study.

Critique this cover letter and then draft a more persuasive one.

4. Go to the Centre for Applied Social Surveys Question Bank at http://qb.soc.surrey.ac.uk. Click on the link for one of the listed surveys. Review 10 questions used in the survey and critique them in terms of the principles for question writing that you have learned. Do you find any question features that might be attributed to the use of British English?

Doing Research

1. Write 10 questions for a one-page questionnaire that concerns your proposed research question. Your questions should operationalize at least three of the variables on which you have focused, including at least one independent and one dependent variable. (You may have multiple questions to measure some variables.) Make all but one of your questions closed-ended. If you completed the "research proposal" exercises in Chapter 2, "Doing Research," you can select your questions from the ones you developed for those exercises.

2. Conduct a preliminary pretest of the questionnaire by conducting cognitive interviews with two students or other persons like those to whom the survey is directed. Follow up the closed-ended questions with open-ended probes that ask the respondents what they meant by each response or what came to mind when they were asked each question. Take account of the feedback you receive when you revise your questions.

3. Polish up the organization and layout of the questionnaire, following the guidelines in this chapter. Prepare a rationale for the order of questions in your questionnaire. Write a cover letter directed to the appropriate population that contains appropriate statements about research ethics (human subject issues).

Ethics Questions

1. Group-administered surveys are easier to conduct than other types of surveys, but they always raise an ethical dilemma. If a teacher allows a social research survey to be distributed in his or her class, or if an employer allows employees to complete a survey on company time, is the survey truly voluntary? Is it sufficient to read a statement to the group stating that their participation is entirely up to them? How would you react to a survey in your class? What general guidelines should be followed in such situations?

2. Tjaden and Thoennes (2000) sampled adults with random digit dialing to study violent victimization from a nationally representative sample of adults. What ethical dilemmas do you see in reporting victimizations that are identified in a survey? What about when the survey respondents are under the age of 18? What about children under the age of 12?

CHAPTER 8

Elementary Quantitative Data Analysis

*"S*how me the data," says your boss. Presented with a research conclusion, most people—not just bosses—want evidence to support it; presented with piles of data, you the researcher need to uncover what it all means. To handle the data gathered by your research, you need to use straightforward methods of data analysis.

In this chapter, we will introduce several common statistics used in social research and explain how they can be used to make sense of the "raw" data gathered in your research. Such **quantitative data analysis,** using numbers to discover and describe patterns in your data, is the most elementary use of social statistics.

Quantitative data analysis: Statistical techniques used to describe and analyze variation in quantitative measures

---

▣ WHY DO STATISTICS?

A **statistic**, in ordinary language usage, is a numerical description of a population, usually based on a sample of that population. (In the technical language of mathematics, a *parameter* describes a population, and a *statistic* specifically describes a sample.) Some statistics are useful for describing the results of measuring single variables or for constructing and evaluating multi-item scales. These statistics include frequency distributions, graphs, measures of central tendency and variation, and reliability tests. Other statistics are used primarily to describe the association among variables and to control for other variables and, thus, to enhance the causal validity of our conclusions. Cross-tabulation, for example, is one simple technique for measuring association and controlling other variables; it is introduced in this chapter. All of these statistics are termed **descriptive statistics**, because they describe the distribution of and relationship among variables. Statisticians also use **inferential statistics** to estimate the degree of confidence that can be placed in generalizations from a sample to the population from which the sample was selected.

Statistic: A numerical description of some feature of a variable or variables in a sample from a larger population

Descriptive statistics: Statistics used to describe the distribution of and relationship among variables

Inferential statistics: Statistics used to estimate how likely it is that a statistical result based on data from a random sample is representative of the population from which the sample is assumed to have been selected

---

Case Study: The Likelihood of Voting

In this chapter, we use for examples some data from the General Social Survey (GSS) on voting and other forms of political participation (NORC, 1996). What influences the likelihood of voting? Prior research on voting in both national and local settings provides a great deal of support for one hypothesis: The likelihood of voting increases with social status (Milbrath & Goel, 1977:92–95; Salisbury, 1975:326; Verba & Nie, 1972:126). We will find out whether this hypothesis was supported in the 2006 GSS and examine some related issues.

The variables we will use from the 2006 GSS are listed in Exhibit 8.1. We will use these variables to illustrate particular statistics throughout this chapter.

▣ HOW TO PREPARE DATA FOR ANALYSIS

Our analysis of voting in this chapter is an example of what is called **secondary data analysis**. It is secondary because we received the data secondhand. A great many high-quality

EXHIBIT 8.1	List of GSS 2006 Variables for Analysis of Voting

Variable[a]	SPSS Variable Name	Description
Social status		
Family income	INCOME4R	Family income in 2006 (categories)
Education	EDUCR3	Years of education completed (categories)
Age	AGE4	Years old (categories)
Gender	SEX	Sex
Marital status	MARITAL	Married, never married, widowed, divorced
Race	RACED	White, minority
Politics		
Party	PARTYID3	Political party affiliation
Voting	VOTE04D	Voted in 2004 presidential election (yes/no)
Political views	POLVIEWS3	Liberal, moderate, conservative
Interpersonal trust	TRUSTD	Believe others can be trusted

a. Some variables recoded.

datasets are available for reanalysis from the Inter-University Consortium for Political and Social Research at the University of Michigan (1996), and many others can be obtained from the government, individual researchers, and other research organizations (see Appendix B).

Secondary data analysis: Analysis of data collected by someone other than the researcher or the researcher's assistants

---

If you have conducted your own survey or experiment, your quantitative data must be prepared in a format suitable for computer entry. Questionnaires or other data entry forms can be designed to facilitate this process (see Exhibit 8.2). Data from such a form can be entered online, directly into a database, or first on a paper form and then typed or even scanned into a computer database. Whatever data entry method is used, the data must be checked carefully for errors—a process called **data cleaning**. Most survey research organizations now use a database management program to monitor data entry so that invalid codes can be corrected immediately. After data are entered, a computer program must be written to "define the data." A data definition program identifies the variables that are coded in each column or range of columns, attaches meaningful labels to the codes, and distinguishes values representing missing data. The procedures vary depending on the specific statistical package used.

Data cleaning: The process of checking data for errors after the data have been entered in a computer file

---

EXHIBIT 8.2 Data Entry Procedures

OMB Control No: 6691-0001
Expiration Date: 04/30/07

Bureau of Economic Analysis
Customer Satisfaction Survey

1. Which data products do you use?	Frequently (every week)	Often (every month)	Infrequently	Rarely	Never	Don't know or not applicable
GENERAL DATA PRODUCTS	(On a scale of 1-5, please circle the appropriate answer.)					
Survey of Current Business...............	5	4	3	2	1	N/A
CD-ROMs	5	4	3	2	1	N/A
BEA Web site (www.bea.gov)	5	4	3	2	1	N/A
STAT-USA Web site (www.stat-usa.gov)..	5	4	3	2	1	N/A
Telephone access to staff.................	5	4	3	2	1	N/A
E-mail access to staff	5	4	3	2	1	N/A
INDUSTRY DATA PRODUCTS						
Gross Product by Industry	5	4	3	2	1	N/A
Input-Output Tables	5	4	3	2	1	N/A
Satellite Accounts	5	4	3	2	1	N/A
INTERNATIONAL DATA PRODUCTS						
U.S. International Transactions .... (Balance of Payments)	5	4	3	2	1	N/A
U.S. Exports and Imports of .... Private Services	5	4	3	2	1	N/A
U.S. Direct Investment Abroad	5	4	3	2	1	N/A
Foreign Direct Investment in .... the United States	5	4	3	2	1	N/A
U.S. International Investment Position	5	4	3	2	1	N/A
NATIONAL DATA PRODUCTS						
National Income and Product .... Accounts (GDP)	5	4	3	2	1	N/A
NIPA Underlying Detail Data	5	4	3	2	1	N/A
Capital Stock (Wealth) and .... Investment by Industry	5	4	3	2	1	N/A
REGIONAL DATA PRODUCTS						
State Personal Income	5	4	3	2	1	N/A
Local Area Personal Income	5	4	3	2	1	N/A
Gross State Product by Industry	5	4	3	2	1	N/A
RIMS II Regional Multipliers	5	4	3	2	1	N/A

▣ WHAT ARE THE OPTIONS FOR DISPLAYING DISTRIBUTIONS?

The first step in data analysis is usually to discover the variation in each variable of interest. How many people in the sample are married? What is their typical income? Did most of them complete high school? Graphs and frequency distributions are the two most popular display formats. Whatever format is used, the primary concern of the analyst is to display accurately the distribution's shape; that is, to show how cases are distributed across the values of the variable.

Three features are important in describing the shape of the distribution: **central tendency**, **variability**, and **skewness** (lack of symmetry). All three features can be represented in a graph or in a frequency distribution.

Central tendency: The most common value (for variables measured at the nominal level) or the value around which cases tend to center (for a quantitative variable)

Variability: The extent to which cases are spread out through the distribution or clustered around just one value

Skewness: The extent to which cases are clustered more at one or the other end of the distribution of a quantitative variable rather than in a symmetric pattern around its center. Skew can be positive (a right skew), with the number of cases tapering off in the positive direction, or negative (a left skew), with the number of cases tapering off in the negative direction.

We will now examine graphs and frequency distributions that illustrate the three features of shape. Several summary statistics used to measure specific aspects of central tendency and variability will be presented in a separate section.

Graphs

There are many types of graphs, but the most common and most useful for the statistician are bar charts, histograms, and frequency polygons. Each has two axes, the vertical axis (the *y*-axis) and the horizontal axis (the *x*-axis), and labels to identify the variables and the values, with tick marks showing where each indicated value falls along each axis.

A **bar chart** contains solid bars separated by spaces. It is a good tool for displaying the distribution of variables measured in discrete categories (e.g., nominal variables such as religion or marital status), because such categories don't blend into each other. The bar chart of marital status in Exhibit 8.3 indicates that about half of adult Americans were married at the time of the survey. Smaller percentages were divorced, separated, widowed, or never married. The most common value in the distribution is "married." There is a moderate amount of variability in the distribution, because the half who are not married are spread across the categories of widowed, divorced, separated, and never married. Because marital status is not a quantitative variable, the order in which the categories are presented is arbitrary, and there is no need to discuss skewness.

Bar chart: A graphic for qualitative variables in which the variable's distribution is displayed with solid bars separated by spaces

Histograms, in which the bars are adjacent, are used to display the distribution of quantitative variables that vary along a continuum that has no necessary gaps. Exhibit 8.4 shows a histogram of years of education from the 2006 GSS data. The distribution has a clump of cases centered at 12 years. The distribution is skewed because there are more cases just above the central point than below it.

Histogram: A graphic for quantitative variables in which the variable's distribution is displayed with adjacent bars

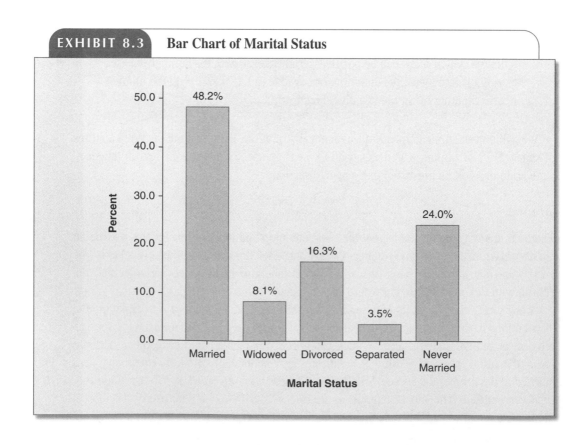

EXHIBIT 8.3 **Bar Chart of Marital Status**

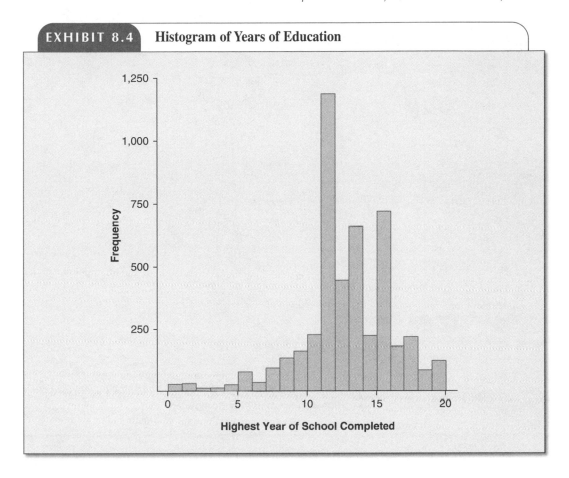

EXHIBIT 8.4 | **Histogram of Years of Education**

In a **frequency polygon**, a continuous line connects the points representing the number or percentage of cases with each value. It is easy to see in the frequency polygon of years of education in Exhibit 8.5 that the most common value is 12 years (high school completion) and that this value also seems to be the center of the distribution. There is moderate variability in the distribution, with many cases having more than 12 years of education and almost one third having completed at least 4 years of college (16 years). The distribution is highly skewed in the negative direction, with few respondents reporting less than 10 years of education.

Frequency polygon: A graphic for quantitative variables in which a continuous line connects data points representing the variable's distribution

---

If graphs are misused, they can distort rather than display the shape of a distribution. Compare, for example, the two graphs in Exhibit 8.6. The first graph shows that high school

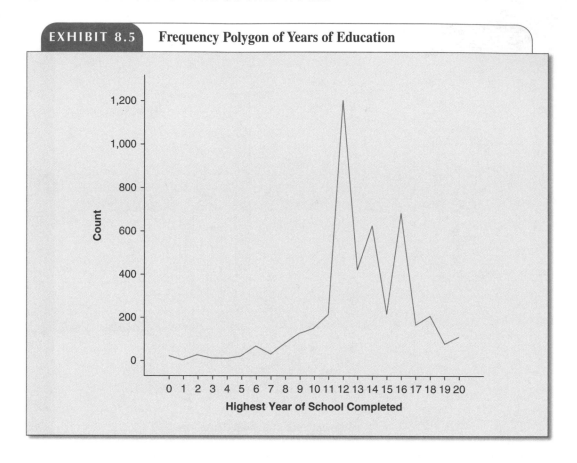

EXHIBIT 8.5 Frequency Polygon of Years of Education

seniors reported relatively stable rates of lifetime use of cocaine between 1980 and 1985. The second graph, using exactly the same numbers, appeared in a 1986 *Newsweek* article on "the coke plague" (Orcutt & Turner, 1993). To look at this graph, you would think that the rate of cocaine usage among high school seniors had increased dramatically during this period. But, in fact, the difference between the two graphs is due simply to changes in how the graphs were drawn. In the *Newsweek* graph, the percentage scale on the vertical axis begins at 15 rather than at 0, making what was about a 1 percentage point increase look very big indeed. In addition, omission from this graph of the more rapid increase in reported usage between 1975 and 1980 makes it look as if the tiny increase in 1985 were a new, and thus more newsworthy, crisis. Finally, these numbers report "lifetime use," not current or recent use; such numbers can drop only when anyone who has used cocaine dies. The graph is, in total, grossly misleading.

Adherence to several guidelines (Tufte, 1983; Wallgren, Wallgren, Persson, Jorner, & Haaland, 1996) will help you to spot such problems and to avoid them in your own work:

- Begin the graph of a quantitative variable at 0 on both axes. The difference between bars can be misleadingly exaggerated by cutting off the bottom of the vertical axis

EXHIBIT 8.6 Two Graphs of Cocaine Usage

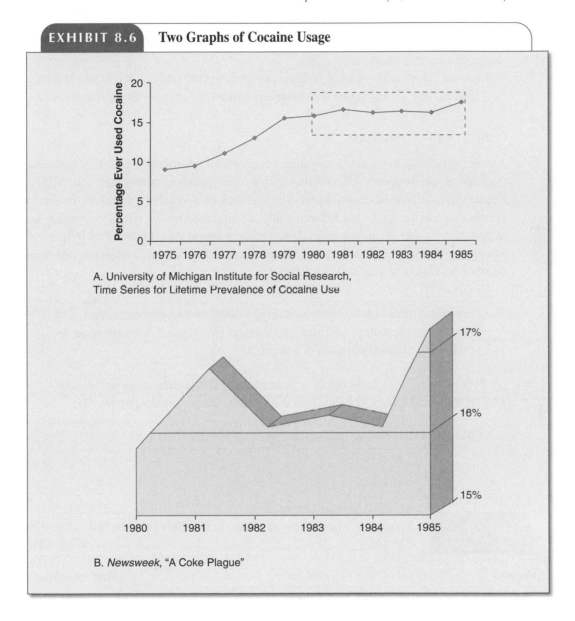

A. University of Michigan Institute for Social Research,
Time Series for Lifetime Prevalence of Cocaine Use

B. *Newsweek*, "A Coke Plague"

and displaying less than the full height of the bars. It may at times be reasonable to violate this guideline, as when an age distribution is presented for a sample of adults; but in this case, be sure to mark the break clearly on the axis.

• Always use bars of equal width. Bars of unequal width, including pictures instead of bars, can make particular values look as if they carry more weight than their frequency warrants.

- The two axes usually should be of approximately equal length. Either shortening or lengthening the vertical axis will obscure or accentuate the differences in the number of cases between values.
- Avoid "chart junk"—a lot of verbiage or excessive marks, lines, lots of cross-hatching, and the like. It can confuse the reader and obscure the shape of the distribution.

Frequency Distributions

Another good way to present a univariate (one-variable) distribution is with a frequency distribution. A **frequency distribution** displays the number, **percentage** (the relative frequencies), or both of cases corresponding to each of a variable's values. A frequency distribution will usually be labeled with a title, a stub (labels for the values), a caption, and perhaps the number of missing cases. If percentages are presented rather than frequencies (sometimes both are included), the total number of cases in the distribution (the **base number** N) should be indicated (see Exhibit 8.7).

Frequency distribution: Numerical display showing the number of cases, and usually the percentage of cases (the relative frequencies), corresponding to each value or group of values of a variable

Percentage: The relative frequency, computed by dividing the frequency of cases in a particular category by the total number of cases and multiplying by 100

Base number (N): The total number of cases in a distribution

EXHIBIT 8.7	**Frequency Distribution of Voting in the 2004 Presidential Election**	
Value	*Frequency*	*Valid Percentage*
Voted	3,037	73.6%
Did not vote	1,089	26.4
Ineligible	335	—
Don't know	34	—
No answer	15	—
Total	4,510	100.0% (4,126)

Constructing and reading frequency distributions for variables with few values is not difficult. The frequency distribution of voting in Exhibit 8.7, for example, shows that 73.6% of the respondents eligible to vote said they voted and that 26.4% reported they did not vote. The total number of respondents to this question was 4,126, although 4,510 actually were interviewed. The rest were ineligible to vote, just refused to answer the question, said they did not know whether they had voted, or gave no answer.

When the distributions of variables with many values (for instance, age) are to be presented, the values must first be grouped. Exhibit 8.8 shows both an ungrouped and a grouped frequency distribution of age. You can see why it is so important to group the values, but we have to be sure that in doing so, we do not distort the distribution. Follow these two rules, and you'll avoid problems:

1. Categories should be logically defensible and should preserve the shape of the distribution.

2. Categories should be mutually exclusive and exhaustive so that every case is classifiable in one and only one category.

⊡ WHAT ARE THE OPTIONS FOR SUMMARIZING DISTRIBUTIONS?

Summary statistics describe particular features of a distribution and facilitate comparison among distributions. We can, for instance, show that average income is higher in Connecticut than in Mississippi and higher in New York than in Louisiana. But if we just use one number to represent a distribution, we lose information about other aspects of the distribution's shape. For example, a measure of central tendency (such as the mean or average) would miss the point entirely for an analysis about differences in income inequality among states. A high average income could as easily be found in a state with little income inequality as in one with much income inequality; the average says nothing about the distribution of incomes. For this reason, analysts who report summary measures of central tendency usually also report a summary measure of variability or present the distributions themselves to indicate skewness.

Measures of Central Tendency

Central tendency is usually summarized with one of three statistics: the mode, the median, or the mean. For any particular application, one of these statistics may be preferable, but each has a role to play in data analysis. To choose an appropriate measure of central tendency, the analyst must consider a variable's level of measurement, the skewness of a quantitative variable's distribution, and the purpose for which the statistic is used.

EXHIBIT 8.8	Grouped Versus Ungrouped Frequency Distributions

Ungrouped		Grouped	
Age	Percentage	Age	Percentage
18	0.4%	18–19	1.5%
19	1.0	20–29	15.6
20	1.1	30–39	19.8
21	1.2	40–49	21.5
22	1.6	50–59	17.9
23	1.4	60–69	11.8
24	1.4	70–79	7.7
25	1.6	80–89	4.3
26	1.8		100.0%
27	1.9		(4,492)
28	1.8		
29	1.8		
30	1.9		
31	1.5		
32	2.2		
33	2.0		
34	2.0		
35	1.8		
36	2.3		
37	2.0		
38	2.1		
39	2.1		
40	2.1		
41	2.1		
42	2.2		
43	2.1		
44	2.2		
45	1.8		
46	2.0		

Mode

The **mode** is the most frequent value in a distribution. In a distribution of Americans' religious affiliations, Protestant Christian is the most frequently occurring value—the largest single group. In an age distribution of college students, 18- to 22-year-olds are by far the largest group and, therefore, the mode. One silly, but easy, way to remember the definition of the *mode* is to think of apple pie "á la mode," which means pie with a big blob of vanilla ice cream on top. Just remember, the mode is where the big blob is—the largest collection of cases.

Mode: The most frequent value in a distribution; also termed the probability average

The mode is also sometimes termed the probability average, because being the most frequent value, it is the most probable. For example, if you were to pick a case at random from the distribution of age (refer to Exhibit 8.8), the probability of the case being in his or her 30s would be 0.199 out of 1, or 19.9%—the most probable value in the distribution.

The mode is used much less often than the other two measures of central tendency, because it can so easily give a misleading impression of a distribution's central tendency. One problem with the mode occurs when a distribution is **bimodal**, in contrast to being **unimodal**. A bimodal distribution has two categories with a roughly equal number of cases and clearly more cases than the other categories. In this situation, there is no single mode.

Bimodal: A distribution in which two nonadjacent categories have about the same number of cases and these categories have more cases than any others

Unimodal: A distribution of a variable in which only one value is the most frequent

Nevertheless, there are occasions when the mode is very appropriate. The mode is the only measure of central tendency that can be used to characterize the central tendency of variables measured at the nominal level. In addition, because it is the most probable value, it can be used to answer questions such as which ethnic group is most common in a given school.

Median

The **median** is the position average, or the point that divides the distribution in half (the 50th percentile). Think of the median of a highway—it divides the road exactly in two parts. To determine the median, we simply array a distribution's values in numerical order and find the value of the case that has an equal number of cases above and below it. If the median point falls between two cases (which happens if the distribution has an even number of cases), the median is defined as the average of the two middle values and is computed by adding the values of the two middle cases and dividing by 2. The median is not appropriate for variables that are measured at the nominal level; their values cannot be put in order, so there is no meaningful middle position.

Median: The position average, or the point, that divides a distribution in half (the 50th percentile)

The median in a frequency distribution is determined by identifying the value corresponding to a cumulative percentage of 50. Starting at the top of the years of education distribution in Exhibit 8.9, for example, and adding up the percentages, we find that we reach 44% in the 12 years category and then 72% in the 13–15 years category. The median is therefore 13–15.

EXHIBIT 8.9	Years of Education Completed

Years of Education	Percentage
Less than 8	4.5%
8–11	12.8
12	26.7
13–15	28.0
16	15.2
17 or more	12.8
	100.0%
	(4,510)

Mean

The **mean** is just the arithmetic average. (Many people, you'll notice, use the word *average* a bit more generally to designate everything we've called "central tendency.") In calculating a mean, any higher numbers pull it up, and any lower numbers pull it down. Therefore, it takes into account the values of each case in a distribution—it is a weighted average. (The median, by contrast, only depends on whether the numbers are higher or lower compared to the middle, not *how* high or low.)

Mean: The arithmetic, or weighted, average computed by adding up the value of all the cases and dividing by the total number of cases

---

The mean is computed by adding up the values of all the cases and dividing the result by the total number of cases, thereby taking into account the value of each case in the distribution:

$$\text{Mean} = \text{Sum of value of cases} / \text{Number of cases}$$

In algebraic notation, the equation is: $X = \Sigma Xi / N$. For example, to calculate the mean value of 8 cases, we add the values of all the cases (ΣXi) and divide by the number of cases (N):

$$(28 + 117 + 42 + 10 + 77 + 51 + 64 + 55) / 8 + 444 / 8 + 55.5$$

Computing the mean obviously requires adding up the values of the cases. So it makes sense to compute a mean only if the values of the cases can be treated as actual quantities—that is, if they reflect an interval or ratio level of measurement—or if we assume that an ordinal measure can be treated as an interval (which is a fairly common practice). It makes no sense to calculate the mean of a qualitative (nominal) variable such as religion, for example. Imagine a group of four people in which there were 2 Protestants, 1 Catholic, and 1 Jew. To calculate the mean, you would need to solve the equation (Protestant + Protestant + Catholic + Jew) / 4 = ?. Even if you decide that Protestant = 1, Catholic = 2, and Jew = 3 for data entry purposes, it still doesn't make sense to add these numbers because they don't represent quantities of religion. In general, certain statistics (such as the mean) can apply only if there is a high enough level of measurement.

Median or Mean?

Because the mean is based on adding the value of all the cases, it will be pulled in the direction of exceptionally high (or low) values. In a positively skewed distribution, the value of the mean is larger than the median—more so the more extreme the skew. For instance, in Seattle, the presence of Microsoft owner Bill Gates possibly the world's richest person—probably pulls the mean wealth number up quite a bit. One extreme case can have a disproportionate effect on the mean.

This differential impact of skewness on the median and mean is illustrated in Exhibit 8.10. On the first balance beam, the cases (bags) are spread out equally, and the median and mean are in the same location. On the second balance beam, the median corresponds to the value of the middle case, but the mean is pulled slightly upward toward the value of the one case with an unusually high value. On the third beam, the mean is clearly pulled up toward an unusual value. For a similar reason, the mean age (47.14) for the 4,492 cases represented partially in the detailed age distribution in Exhibit 8.8 is higher than the median age (46.0). Although in this instance the difference is small, in some distributions the two measures will have markedly different values, and in such instances usually the median is preferred. (Income is a very common variable that is best measured by the median, for instance.)

Measures of Variation

Central tendency is only one aspect of the shape of a distribution—the most important aspect for many purposes but still just a piece of the total picture. The distribution, we have seen, also matters. It is important to know that the median household income in the United States is a bit over $50,000 a year, but if the variation in income isn't known—the fact that incomes range from zero up to hundreds of millions of dollars—we haven't really learned much. Measures of variation capture how widely and densely spread income (for instance) is. Four popular measures of variation for quantitative variables are the range, the interquartile range, the variance, and the standard deviation (which is the single most popular measure of variability). Each conveys a certain kind of information, with strengths and weaknesses. Statistical measures of variation are used infrequently with qualitative variables and are not presented here.

EXHIBIT 8.10 The Mean as a Balance Point

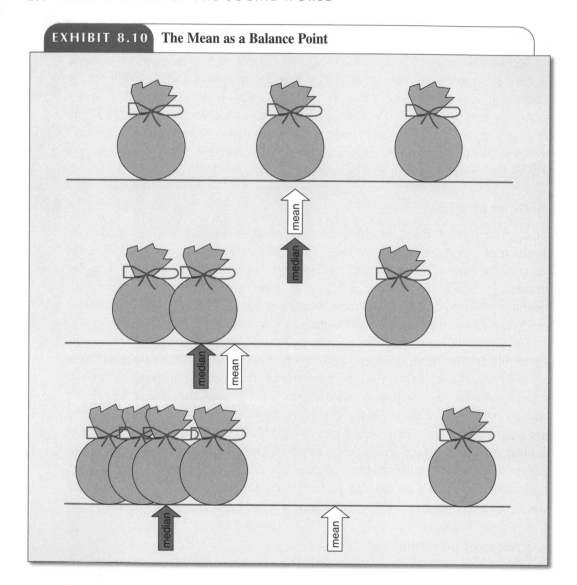

Range

The **range** is the simplest measure of variation, calculated as the highest value in a distribution minus the lowest value, plus 1:

$$\text{Range} = \text{Highest value} - \text{Lowest value} + 1$$

It often is important to report the range of a distribution—to identify the whole range of possible values that might be encountered. However, because the range can be altered drastically by just one exceptionally high or low value (termed an **outlier**), it's not a good summary measure for most purposes.

Range: The true upper limit in a distribution minus the true lower limit (or the highest rounded value minus the lowest rounded value, plus 1)

Outlier: An exceptionally high or low value in a distribution

Interquartile Range

The **interquartile range** avoids the problem created by outliers by showing the range where most cases lie. **Quartiles** are the points in a distribution that correspond to the first 25% of the cases, the first 50% of the cases, and the first 75% of the cases. You already know how to determine the 2nd quartile, corresponding to the point in the distribution covering half of the cases—it is another name for the median. The interquartile range is the difference between the 1st quartile and the 3rd quartile (plus 1).

Interquartile range: The range in a distribution between the end of the 1st quartile and the beginning of the 3rd quartile

Quartiles: The points in a distribution corresponding to the first 25% of the cases, the first 50% of the cases, and the last 25% of the cases

Variance

The **variance**, in its statistical definition, is the average squared deviation of each case from the mean; you take each case's distance from the mean, square that number, and take the average of all such numbers. Thus, variance takes into account the amount by which each case differs from the mean. The variance is mainly useful for computing the standard deviation, which comes next in our list here. An example of how to calculate the variance, using the following formula, appears in Exhibit 8.11:

$$\sigma^2 = \frac{\sum (X_i - \overline{X})^2}{N}$$

Symbol key: $\overline{X}$ = mean; N = number of cases; Σ = sum over all cases; X_i = value of case i on variable X.

The variance is used in many other statistics, although it is more conventional to measure variability with the closely related standard deviation than with the variance.

Variance: A statistic that measures the variability of a distribution as the average squared deviation of each case from the mean

EXHIBIT 8.11 **Calculation of the Variance**

Case #	Score (X$_i$)	X$_i$ – X̄	(X$_i$ – X̄)^2
1	21	−3.27	10.69
2	30	5.73	32.83
3	15	−9.27	85.93
4	18	−6.27	39.31
5	25	0.73	0.53
6	32	7.73	59.75
7	19	−5.27	27.77
8	21	−3.27	10.69
9	23	−1.27	1.61
10	37	12.73	162.05
11	26	1.73	2.99
	267		434.15

Mean: $\overline{X} = 267/11 = 24.27$
Sum of squared deviations = 434.15
Variance: $\sigma^2 = 434.15/11 = 39.47$

Standard Deviation

Very roughly, the standard deviation is the distance from the mean that covers a clear majority of cases (about two thirds). More precisely, the **standard deviation** is simply the square root of the variance. It is the square root of the average squared deviation of each case from the mean:

$$\sigma = \sqrt{\frac{\sum (X_i - \overline{X})^2}{N}}$$

Symbol key: $\overline{X}$ = mean; N = number of cases; Σ = sum over all cases; Xi = value of case i on variable X; $\sqrt{}$ = square root.

Standard deviation: The square root of the average squared deviation of each case from the mean

The standard deviation has mathematical properties that make it the preferred measure of variability in many cases, particularly when a variable is normally distributed. A graph of a **normal distribution** looks like a bell, with one "hump" in the middle, centered around the population mean, and the number of cases tapering off on both sides of the mean (see

Exhibit 8.12). A normal distribution is symmetric: If you were to fold the distribution in half at its center (at the population mean), the two halves would match perfectly. If a variable is normally distributed, 68% of the cases (almost exactly two thirds) will lie between ±1 standard deviation from the distribution's mean, and 95% of the cases will lie between 1.96 standard deviations above and below the mean.

Normal distribution: A symmetric distribution shaped like a bell and centered around the population mean, with the number of cases tapering off in a predictable pattern on both sides of the mean

---

So the standard deviation, in a single number, tells you quickly about how wide the variation is of any set of cases, or the range in which most cases will fall. It's very useful.

▣ HOW CAN WE TELL WHETHER TWO VARIABLES ARE RELATED?

Univariate distributions are nice, but they don't say how variables relate to each other—for instance, if religion affects education or if marital status is related to income. To establish cause, of course, one's first task is to show an association between independent and dependent variables (cause and effect). **Cross-tabulation** is a simple, easily understandable first step in such quantitative data analysis. Cross-tabulation displays the distribution of one variable

EXHIBIT 8.12 **The Normal Distribution**

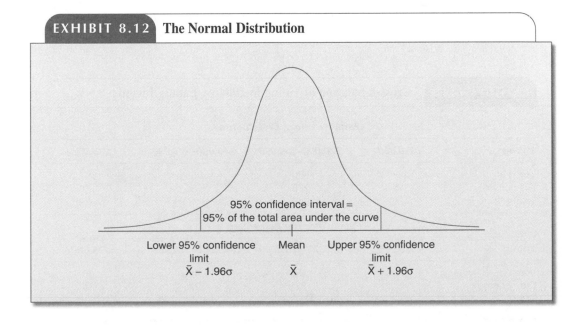

within each category of another variable; it can also be termed a *bivariate distribution*, since it shows two variables at the same time. Exhibit 8.13 displays the cross-tabulation of voting by income so that we can see if the likelihood of voting increases as income goes up.

Cross-tabulation (crosstab): In the simplest case, a bivariate (two-variable) distribution showing the distribution of one variable for each category of another variable; can also be elaborated using three or more variables

---

The "crosstab" table is presented first (the upper part) with frequencies and then again (the lower part) with percentages. The *cells* of the table are where row and column values intersect; for instance, the first cell is where <$20,000 meets Voted; 447 is the value. Each cell represents cases with a unique combination of values of the two variables. The independent variable is usually the column variable, listed across the top; the dependent variable, then, is usually the row variable. This format isn't necessary, but social scientists typically use it.

Reading the Table

The first (upper) table in Exhibit 8.13 shows the raw number of cases with each combination of values of voting and family income. It is hard to look at the table in this form and determine whether there is a relationship between the two variables. What we really want to know is the likelihood, for any level of income, that someone voted. So we need to convert the cell frequencies into percentages. Percentages show the likelihood per 100 ("per cent," in Latin) that something occurs. The second table, then, presents the data as percentages within the categories of the independent variable (the column variable, in this case). In other words, the cell frequencies have been converted into percentages of the column totals (the *n* in each column). For example, in Exhibit 8.13, the number of people

EXHIBIT 8.13	**Cross-tabulation of Voting in 2004 by Family Income**

Family Income: Cell Counts				
Voting	*<$20,000*	*$20,000–$39,999*	*$40,000–$74,999*	*$75,000+*
Voted	447	580	805	807
Did not vote	313	268	230	126
Total (*n*)	(760)	(848)	(1035)	(933)

Family Income: Percentages				
Voting	*<$20,000*	*$20,000–$39,999*	*$40,000–$74,999*	*$75,000+*
Voted	59%	68%	78%	86%
Did not vote	41	32	22	14
Total	100%	100%	100%	100%

earning less than $20,000 who voted is 447 out of 760, or 59%. Because the cell frequencies have been converted to percentages of the column totals, the numbers add up to 100 in each column but not across the rows.

Note carefully: You must *always* calculate percentages within levels of the independent variable—adding numbers down the columns in our standard format. In this example, we want to know the chance that a person with an income of less than $20,000 voted, so we calculate what percentage of those people voted. Then we *compare* that to the chance that people of other income levels voted. Calculating percentages across the table, by contrast, will not show the effect of the independent variable on voting. To repeat: *Always* calculate percentages within levels of the independent variable (think: with*in* the *in*dependent variable).

To read the percentage table, compare the percentage distribution of voting/not voting across the columns. Start with the lowest income category (in the left column). Move slowly from left to right, looking at each distribution down the columns. As income increases, you will see that the percentage who voted also increases, from 59% of those with annual incomes under $20,000 (in the first cell in the first column) up to 86% of those with incomes of $75,000 or more (the last cell in the body of the table in the first row). This result is consistent with the hypothesis: It seems that higher income is moderately associated with a greater likelihood of voting.

Now look at Exhibit 8.14, which relates gender (as the independent variable) to voting (the dependent variable). The independent variable is listed across the top, and the percentages have been calculated, correctly, down the columns with values of the independent variable. Does gender affect voting? As you look down the first column, you see that 73% of men voted; then, in the second column, 74% of women voted. The difference is so small that it's probably negligible. Gender does not, in this table, have an effect on voting.

Some standard practices should be followed in formatting percentage tables (crosstabs): When a table is converted to percentages, usually just the percentages in each cell should be presented, not the number of cases in each cell. Include 100% at the bottom of each column (if the independent variable is the column variable) to indicate that the percentages add up to 100, as well as the base number (*N*) for each column (in parentheses). If the

| EXHIBIT 8.14 | Voting in 2004 by Gender |

	Gender	
Voting	*Male*	*Female*
Voted	73%	74%
Did not vote	27	26
Total	100%	100%
(*n*)	(1,815)	(2,311)

percentages add up to 99 or 101 due to rounding error, just indicate so in a footnote. As noted already, there is no requirement that the independent variable always be the column variable, although consistency within a report or paper is a must. If the independent variable is the row variable, we calculate percentages in the cells of the table on the row totals (the *n* in each row), and the percentages add up to 100 across the rows.

Try your hand at table reading with the larger table in Exhibit 8.15. This table describes the relationship between education and income. Examine the distribution of income for those with only a grade school education (first column). Almost half (46%) reported an income under $20,000, whereas just 6% reported an income of $75,000 or more. Then examine the distribution of income for the respondents who have finished high school but gone no further. Here, the distribution of income has shifted upward, with just 26% reporting an income under $20,000 and 17% reporting incomes of $75,000 or more—that's twice the percentage in that category than we saw for those with a grade school education. You can see there are also more respondents in the $40,000–$74,999 category than there were for the grade schoolers. Now examine the column representing those who have completed at least some college. The percentage with incomes under $20,000 has dropped again, to 20%, whereas the percentage in the highest income category has risen to 23%. If you step back and compare the income distributions across the three categories of education, you see that incomes increase markedly and consistently. The relationship is positive (fortunately for those of you attending college).

When you read research reports and journal articles, you will find that social scientists usually judge the strength of association on the basis of more statistics than just a cross-tabulation table. A **measure of association** is a descriptive statistic used to summarize the strength of an association. One measure of association in cross-tabular analyses with ordinal variables is called **gamma**. The value of gamma ranges from –1 to +1. The closer a gamma value is to –1 or +1, the stronger the relationship between the two variables; a gamma of zero indicates that there is no relationship between the variables. Inferential

| EXHIBIT 8.15 | Income by Education | | | |

| Family Income | Education | | | |
	Grade School	High School	Some College	College Graduate
<$20,000	46%	26%	20%	8%
$20,000–$39,999	34	28	26	14
$40,000–$74,999	14	29	31	32
$75,000+	6	17	23	46
Total	100%	100%	100%	100%
(*n*)	(641)	(1,029)	(1,082)	(1,114)

statistics go further, addressing whether an association exists in the larger population from which the (random) sample was drawn. Even when the empirical association between two variables supports the researcher's hypothesis, it is possible that the association was just due to the vagaries of random sampling. In a crosstab, estimation of this probability can be based on the inferential statistic, **chi-square**. The probability is customarily reported in a summary form such as "$p < .05$," which can be translated as "The probability that the association was due to chance is less than 5 out of 100 (5%)."

Measure of association: A type of descriptive statistic that summarizes the strength of an association

Gamma: A measure of association that is sometimes used in cross-tabular analysis

Chi-square: An inferential statistic used to test hypotheses about relationships between two or more variables in a cross-tabulation

---

When the analyst feels reasonably confident (at least 95% confident, or $p < .05$) that an association was not due to chance, it is said that the association is statistically significant. **Statistical significance** basically means we conclude that the relationship is actually there; it's not a chance occurrence. Convention (and the desire to avoid concluding that an association exists in the population when it doesn't) dictates that the criterion be a probability of less than 5%. Statistical significance, though, doesn't equal substantive significance. That is, while the relationship is really occurring, not just happening accidentally, it may still not matter very much. It may be a minor part of what's happening.

Statistical significance: The mathematical likelihood that an association is not due to chance, judged by a criterion set by the analyst (often that the probability is less than 5 out of 100, or $p < .05$)

Controlling for a Third Variable

Cross-tabulation also can be used to study the relationship between three or more variables. The single most important reason for introducing a third variable into a bivariate relationship is to see whether that relationship is spurious. A third, **extraneous variable**, for instance, may influence both the independent and dependent variables, creating an association between them that disappears when the extraneous variable is controlled. Ruling out possible extraneous variables helps to strengthen considerably the conclusion that the relationship between the independent and dependent variables is causal—that it is nonspurious. In general, adding variables is termed **elaboration analysis**: the process of introducing control or intervening variables into a bivariate relationship to better understand the relationship (Davis, 1985; Rosenberg, 1968).

Extraneous variable: A variable that influences both the independent and dependent variables so as to create a spurious association between them that disappears when the extraneous variable is controlled

Elaboration analysis: The process of introducing a third variable into an analysis to better understand—to elaborate—the bivariate (two-variable) relationship under consideration. Additional control variables also can be introduced.

For example, we have seen a positive association between incomes and the likelihood of voting. But perhaps that association only exists because both income and likelihood of voting are influenced by education; maybe when we control for education—that is, when we hold the value of education constant—we will find that there is no longer an association between income and voting. This possibility is represented by the hypothetical three-variable causal model in Exhibit 8.16 in which the arrows show that education influences both income and voting, thereby creating a relationship between the two. To test whether there is such an effect of education, we create the trivariate table in Exhibit 8.17, showing the bivariate crosstabs for various levels of education separately. This allows us to see if the income/voting relationship still exists after we hold education constant.

The trivariate cross-tabulation in Exhibit 8.17 shows that the relationship between voting and income is *not* spurious due to the effect of education. The association between voting and income occurs in all three subtables. So our original hypothesis—that income as a social status indicator has an effect on voting—is not weakened.

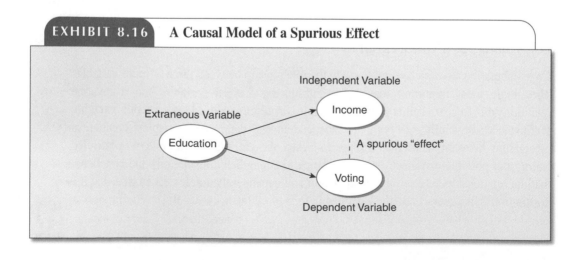

EXHIBIT 8.16   A Causal Model of a Spurious Effect

Independent Variable

Extraneous Variable

Income

Education

A spurious "effect"

Voting

Dependent Variable

EXHIBIT 8.17	Voting in 2004 by Income by Education

Education = Grade School

Voting	Family Income			
	<$20,000	$20,000–$39,999	$40,000–$74,999	$75,000+
Voted	43%	39%	50%	59%
Did not vote	57	61	50	41
Total	100%	100%	100%	100%
(n)	(244)	(166)	(82)	(29)

Education = High School

Voting	Family Income			
	<$20,000	$20,000–$39,999	$40,000–$74,999	$75,000+
Voted	58%	71%	69%	74%
Did not vote	42	29	31	26
Total	100%	100%	100%	100%
(n)	(238)	(261)	(284)	(171)

Education = Some College

Voting	Family Income			
	<$20,000	$20,000–$39,999	$40,000–$74,999	$75,000+
Voted	71%	76%	78%	88%
Did not vote	29	24	22	12
Total	100%	100%	100%	100%
(n)	(194)	(267)	(321)	(240)

Education = College Graduate

Voting	Family Income			
	<$20,000	$20,000–$39,999	$40,000–$74,999	$75,000+
Voted	78%	84%	91%	92%
Did not vote	22	16	9	8
Total	100%	100%	100%	100%
(n)	(78)	(152)	(347)	(493)

Our goal in introducing you to cross-tabulation has been to help you think about the association among variables and to give you a relatively easy tool for describing association. To read most statistical reports and to conduct more sophisticated analyses of social data, you will have to extend your statistical knowledge, at least to include the technique of *regression* or *correlation analysis*. These statistics have many advantages over cross-tabulation—as well as some disadvantages. You will need to take a course in social statistics to become proficient in the use of statistics based on regression and correlation.

▣ ANALYZING DATA ETHICALLY: HOW NOT TO LIE WITH STATISTICS

Using statistics ethically means first and foremost being honest and open. Findings should be reported honestly, and the researcher should be open about the thinking that guided the decision to use particular statistics. Although this section has a mildly humorous title (after Darrell Huff's 1954 little classic, *How to Lie With Statistics*), make no mistake about the intent: It is possible to distort social reality with statistics, and it is unethical to do so knowingly, even when the error is due more to carelessness than to deceptive intent.

There are a few basic rules to keep in mind:

- Inspect the shape of any distribution for which you report summary statistics to ensure that the statistics do not mislead your readers because of an unusual degree of skewness.
- When you create graphs, be sure to consider how the axes you choose may change the distribution's apparent shape; don't deceive your readers. You have already seen that it is possible to distort the shape of a distribution by manipulating the scale of axes, clustering categories inappropriately, and the like.
- Whenever you need to group data in a frequency distribution or graph, inspect the ungrouped distribution and then use a grouping procedure that does not distort the distribution's basic shape.
- Hypotheses formulated in advance of data collection must be tested as they were originally stated. When evaluating associations between variables, it becomes very tempting to search around in the data until something interesting emerges. Social scientists sometimes call this a "fishing expedition." Although it's not wrong to examine data for unanticipated relationships, inevitably some relationships between variables will appear just on the basis of chance association alone. Exploratory analyses must be labeled in research reports as such.
- Be honest about the limitations of using survey data to test causal hypotheses. Finding that a hypothesized relationship is not altered by controlling for some other variables does not establish that the relationship is causal. There is always a possibility that some other variable that we did not think to control, or that was not even measured in the survey, has produced a spurious relationship between the independent and dependent variables in our hypothesis (Lieberson, 1985). We have to think about the possibilities and be cautious in our causal conclusions.

▣ CONCLUSION

With some simple statistics (means, standard deviations, and the like), a researcher can describe social phenomena, identify relationships among them, explore the reasons for these relationships (especially through elaboration), and test hypotheses about them. Statistics—carefully constructed numbers that describe an entire population of data—are amazingly helpful in giving a simple summation of complex situations. Statistics provide a remarkably useful tool for developing our understanding of the social world, a tool that we can use both to test our ideas and to generate new ones.

Unfortunately, to the uninitiated, the use of statistics can seem to end debate right there—one can't argue with the numbers. But you now know better. Numbers are worthless if the methods used to generate the data are not valid, and numbers can be misleading if they are not used appropriately, taking into account the type of data to which they are applied. In a very poor town with one wealthy family, the mean income may be fairly high—but grossly misleading. And even assuming valid methods and proper use of statistics, there's one more critical step, because the numbers do not speak for themselves. Ultimately, how we interpret and report statistics determines their usefulness.

KEY TERMS

Bar chart	Measure of association
Base number (*N*)	Median
Bimodal	Mode (probability average)
Central tendency	Normal distribution
Chi-square	Outlier
Cross-tabulation (crosstab)	Percentage
Data cleaning	Quantitative data analysis
Descriptive statistics	Quartiles
Elaboration analysis	Range
Extraneous variable	Secondary data analysis
Frequency distribution	Skewness
Frequency polygon	Standard deviation
Gamma	Statistic
Histogram	Statistical significance
Inferential statistics	Unimodal
Interquartile range	Variability
Mean	Variance

HIGHLIGHTS

- Data entry options include direct collection of data through a computer, use of scannable data entry forms, and use of data entry software. All data should be cleaned during the data entry process.
- Use of secondary data can save considerable time and resources but may limit data analysis possibilities.
- Bar charts, histograms, and frequency polygons are useful for describing the shape of distributions. Care must be taken with graphic displays to avoid distorting a distribution's apparent shape.
- Frequency distributions display variation in a form that can be easily inspected and described. Values should be grouped in frequency distributions in a way that does not alter the shape of the distribution. Following several guidelines can reduce the risk of problems.

- Summary statistics are often used to describe the central tendency and variability of distributions. The appropriateness of the mode, mean, and median vary with a variable's level of measurement, the distribution's shape, and the purpose of the summary.

- The variance and standard deviation summarize variability around the mean. The interquartile range is usually preferable to the range to indicate the interval spanned by cases due to the effect of outliers on the range. The degree of skewness of a distribution is usually described in words rather than with a summary statistic.

- Cell frequencies in cross-tabulation should normally be converted to percentages within the categories of the independent variable. A cross-tabulation can be used to determine the existence, strength, direction, and pattern of an association.

- Elaboration analysis can be used in cross-tabular analysis to test for spurious relationships.

- Inferential statistics are used with sample-based data to estimate the confidence that can be placed in a statistical estimate of a population parameter. Estimates of the probability that an association between variables may have occurred on the basis of chance are also based on inferential statistics.

- Honesty and openness are the key ethical principles that should guide data summaries.

STUDENT STUDY SITE

To assist you in completing the Web Exercises, please access the Study Site at **http://www.pineforge.com/mssw3**, where you'll find the Web Exercises with accompanying links. You'll find other useful study materials like self-quizzes and e-flashcards for each chapter, along with a group of carefully selected articles from research journals that illustrate the major concepts and techniques presented in the book.

EXERCISES

Discussing Research

1. We presented in this chapter several examples of bivariate and trivariate cross-tabulations involving voting in the 2004 presidential election. What additional influences would you recommend examining to explain voting in elections? Suggest some additional independent variables for bivariate analyses with voting, as well as several additional control variables to be used in three-variable crosstabs.

2. When should we control just to be honest? Should social researchers be expected to investigate alternative explanations for their findings? Should they be expected to check to see if the associations they find occur for different subgroups in their samples? Justify your answers.

Finding Research

1. Do a Web search for information on a social science subject in which you are interested. How much of the information you find relies on statistics as a tool for understanding the subject? How do statistics allow researchers to test their ideas about the subject and generate new ideas? Write your findings in a brief report, referring to the Web sites on which you relied.

2. The U.S. Bureau of the Census provides many graphs and numeric tables about current economic conditions. Review some of these presentations at http://www.census.gov/cgi-bin/briefroom/

BriefRm/. Which displays are most effective in conveying information? Summarize what you can learn from this site about economic conditions in just one of the "briefing rooms."

Critiquing Research

1. Become a media critic. For the next week, scan a newspaper or some magazines for statistics. How many articles can you find that use frequency distributions, graphs, and the summary statistics introduced in this chapter? Are these statistics used appropriately and interpreted correctly? Would any other statistics have been preferable or useful in addition to those presented?

Doing Research

1. Create frequency distributions from lists in U.S. Bureau of the Census reports on the characteristics of cities or counties or any similar listing of data for at least 100 cases. You will have to decide on a grouping scheme for the distribution of variables, such as average age and population size; how to deal with outliers in the frequency distribution; and how to categorize qualitative variables, such as the predominant occupation. Decide what summary statistics to use for each variable. How well were the features of each distribution represented by the summary statistics? Describe the shape of each distribution. Propose a hypothesis involving two of these variables and develop a crosstab to evaluate the support for this hypothesis. Describe each relationship in terms of the four aspects of an association after converting cell frequencies to percentages in each table within the categories of the independent variable. Does the hypothesis appear to have been supported?

2. Exhibit 8.18 is a three-variable table created with survey data from 355 employees hired during the previous year at a large telecommunications company. Employees were asked if the presence of on-site child care at the company's offices was important in their decision to join the company.

   Reading the table:

   a. Does gender affect attitudes?
   b. Does marital status affect attitudes?
   c. Which of the preceding two variables matters more?
   d. Does being married affect men's attitudes more than women's?

EXHIBIT 8.18	Is Child Care Important? by Gender and Marital Status			
	MEN		**WOMEN**	
	Single	*Married*	*Single*	*Married*
Not important	54%	48%	33%	12%
Somewhat important	24%	30%	45%	31%
Very important	22%	22%	22%	57%
	100%	100%	100%	100%
n =	(125)	(218)	(51)	(161)

3. If you have access to the SPSS statistical program, you can analyze data contained in the 2006 General Social Survey (GSS) file on the Study Site for this text. See Appendix C for instructions on using SPSS.

Call up the GSS 2006chap8 file in SPSS, after you have saved it on your own drive, and use it to describe basic social and demographic characteristics of the U.S. population in 2006.

a. From the menu, select

Graphs → Bar

From the Bar Graph window, select

Simple Define [Marital—Category Axis]

Bars represent % of cases. Select Options (do not display groups defined by missing values). Repeat this process with the variable SEX.

Describe the distribution of both variables.

b. Select

Histogram [EDUC, CHILDS, PRESTG80]

Describe the distributions.

c. Generate frequency distributions and descriptive statistics for these variables. From the menu, select

Analyze → Descriptive Statistics → Frequencies
From the Frequencies window, set MARITAL, EDUC, INCOME06M, ATTEND

Statistics [mean, median, range, std deviation]

d. Which statistics are appropriate to summarize the central tendency and variation of each variable? Do the values of any of these statistics surprise you?

4. Does confidence in organized labor vary with political party affiliation? Generate a cross-tabulation of CONLABOR by PARTYID3 to answer this question.

a. From the menu, select

Analyze → Descriptive Statistics → Crosstabs.

From the Crosstabs box, click CONLABOR into Rows and click PARTYID3 into Columns.

Click on CELLS and select Column Percentages.

b. Describe how the percentage that has confidence in organized labor varies by party identification.

Ethics Questions

1. Review the frequency distributions and graphs in this chapter. Change one of these data displays so that you are "lying with statistics." (You might consider using the graphic technique discussed by Orcutt & Turner, 1993.)

2. Consider the relationship between voting and income that is presented in Exhibit 8.13. What third variables do you think should be controlled in the analysis to understand better the basis for this relationship? How might social policies be affected by finding out that this relationship was due to differences in neighborhood of residence rather than to income itself?

CHAPTER 9

Qualitative Methods

Observing, Participating, Listening

Q ualitative research goes straight to where people live—and die:

> We see what those poor bastards go through. Seriously, when [a dying medical patient has] been resuscitated nine or ten times and their chest looks like raw meat, they've been fried from being defibrillated, they've had their chest pumped on, they've got a flat chest because their ribs are no more connected to their sternum . . . You know this guy doesn't have a chance in hell. I mean, he's already blown out, squash, herniated his brain, he doesn't have any spontaneous respirations, he's flat EEGs. You take care of him for eight hours, you know that this person is not viable, and you feel for him and you feel for the family . . . When you're resuscitating somebody and they get no response going into the code for an hour, and now has no EKG, no heart tracing, pupils are blown, fixed, no spontaneous respiration, blood gases are out in the ozone . . . you are the one that's going to turn to the resident and say, "Don't you think this is about it, don't you think we should call this?" (interview, quoted in Chambliss, 1996:164)

Throughout this chapter, you will learn that some of our greatest insights into social processes can result from what appear to be very ordinary activities: observing, participating, listening, and talking. But you will also learn that qualitative research is much more than just doing what comes naturally: Qualitative researchers must observe keenly, take notes systematically, question respondents strategically, and prepare to spend more time and invest more of their whole selves than often occurs with experiments or surveys.

We begin with an overview of the major features of qualitative research. The next section discusses participant observation research, which is the most distinctive qualitative method. We then discuss intensive interviewing—a type of interviewing that qualifies as qualitative rather than quantitative research—and focus groups, an increasingly popular qualitative method. The last two sections discuss how to analyze qualitative data and make ethical decisions in qualitative research.

▣ WHAT ARE "QUALITATIVE" METHODS?

Qualitative methods refer to several distinct research activities: participant observation, intensive interviewing, and focus groups.

> *Qualitative methods:* Methods, such as participant observation, intensive interviewing, and focus groups, that are designed to capture social life as participants experience it rather than in categories predetermined by the researcher. These methods typically involve exploratory research questions, inductive reasoning, an orientation to social context, and a focus on human subjectivity and the meanings attached by participants to events and to their lives.

Although these three qualitative designs differ in many respects, they share several features, in addition to the collection of qualitative data itself, that distinguish them from experimental and survey research designs (Denzin & Lincoln, 1994; Maxwell, 1996; Wolcott, 1995):

- Qualitative researchers typically begin with *an exploratory research question* about what people think and how they act, and why, in some social setting. Their research approach is primarily inductive.
- The designs *focus on previously unstudied processes and unanticipated phenomena,* because previously unstudied attitudes and actions can't adequately be understood with a structured set of questions or within a highly controlled experiment.
- They have an *orientation to social context,* to the interconnections between social phenomena rather than to their discrete features.
- They *focus on human subjectivity,* on the meanings that participants attach to events and that people give to their lives.

- They have a *sensitivity to the subjective role of the researcher.* The researcher considers himself or herself as necessarily part of the social process being studied and, therefore, keeps track of his or her own actions in, and reactions to, that social process.

Case Study: Beyond Caring

In preparing to write his 1996 book *Beyond Caring: Hospitals, Nurses, and the Social Organization of Ethics,* Dan Chambliss spent many months, spread over 12 years, studying hospital nurses at work. Observing in several different hospitals, in different regions of the United States, Chambliss watched countless operations and emergency room crises, but he also sat up nights chatting with nurses on geriatric floors (specializing in the care of old people) and quietly watched for hours at a time while nurses did postoperative care; bathed patients; helped patients walk down the hall; or just met with each other and with doctors, technicians, and aides to discuss the day's work. He also conducted more than 100 formal interviews, averaging 1.5 hours or more each; he attended birthday parties and softball games and saw nurses in social situations as well as at professional conferences. This project exemplifies **field research**, which combines various forms of qualitative research.

Field research: Research in which natural social processes are studied as they happen and left relatively undisturbed

---

The resulting data are nothing like the clean list of responses given to a survey questionnaire. Instead, Chambliss wrote his book from boxes full of notes on his observations, such as these:

[Today I witnessed] the needle injection of local anesthetic into a newborn (3 weeks) baby's skull, so they could remove a shunt. The two residents doing it discussed whether a local anesthetic would be sufficient; a general [anesthetic] would be dangerous. One said, "I can do it if you can." This exchange was carried out a couple of times. A nurse (man) stroked the infant's hand, talked softly to it, and calmed it immediately as they were setting up, putting in the IVs—hard to do, the veins are so small.

The resident injected the local anesthetic. Everyone around was affected by the immediate widening of the baby's eyes as the needle first went in, and then the screaming. The resident doing it, though, was absolutely concentrated on the task. At one point the female resident mentioned her concern, saying something about the whole point of anesthetic is to lessen pain, not to increase it. The baby was put in pain, couldn't have known any reason for it, was helpless to resist. [Field Notes] (Chambliss, 1996:135–136)

So fieldwork involves, at its simplest, spending time with people in their own settings, watching them do what they do. Gary Allen Fine, a prominent field researcher, has studied Little League baseball, restaurant kitchens, high school debate teams, and people who hunt for mushrooms, to name a few settings. Chambliss had complete access to the working (and sometimes personal) lives of the nurses he studied.

Such research obviously requires a huge investment of time. Chambliss moved his residence several times during his research, living in apartments near the medical centers that he studied. He built his entire schedule, for months on end, around the opportunities for seeing often unseen things—emergency resuscitations, hidden malpractice, even the boredom of some nursing work.

But the investment can be worth the cost. Chambliss's early research on nurses primarily relied on tape-recorded interviews:

These [interviews] produced many dramatic stories and often confirmed theories I already held, but as I began to spend more time in hospitals I began to doubt the veracity of interviews. I began to see how the interviews were a reflection of my interests as much as of my subjects' lives. The stories told were more exciting than the ordinary drudgery I saw; the nurses described in stories seemed more committed and courageous than some of those I actually watched. Interviewees told what they noticed and remembered, which I discovered to be a highly selective version of what actually occurred. Much of life, I found, consists precisely in not noticing what one does all the time. "There aren't any ethical problems here I can think of," said a pediatric research nurse mentioned earlier; "You should talk with people on the ethics committee," said nurses gathered outside the room of an AIDS patient. (Chambliss, 1996:194)

Chambliss wanted to learn about nurses, so in a sense he did the obvious: He worked and talked with nurses, many of them, over a long period of time. But he also took care to study a variety of hospitals and different services within hospitals; he also "sampled" different times of the day and night and different kinds of patients. True, such research is inductive, and the researcher is open to surprises; Chambliss couldn't run controlled experiments or easily isolate independent and dependent variables. But even the most unstructured kind of research still adheres to the basic discipline of scientific method.

▣ HOW DOES PARTICIPANT OBSERVATION BECOME A RESEARCH METHOD?

Dan Chambliss used **participant observation** (or "fieldwork" or "field research") to study nurses because it leaves natural social processes, in their natural setting, relatively undisturbed. It is a means for seeing the social world as the research subjects see it, in its totality, and for understanding subjects' interpretations of that world (Wolcott, 1995:66). Participant observers seek to avoid the artificiality of experimental designs and the unnatural structured questioning of survey research (Koegel, 1987:8). This method encourages consideration of the context in which social interaction occurs, of the complex and interconnected nature of social relations, and of the sequencing of events (Bogdewic, 1999:49). Through it, we can understand the *mechanisms* (one of the criteria for establishing cause) of social life.

Participant observation: A qualitative method for gathering data that involves developing a sustained relationship with people while they go about their normal activities

---

In his study of nursing homes, Timothy Diamond (1992:5) explained how his exploratory research question led him to adopt the method of participant observation:

> How does the work of caretaking become defined and get reproduced day in and day out as a business? . . . The everyday world of Ina and Aileen and their co-workers, and that of the people they tend . . . I wanted to collect stories and to experience situations like those Ina and Aileen had begun to describe. I decided that . . . I would go inside to experience the work myself.

The term *participant observer* actually represents a continuum of roles (see Exhibit 9.1), ranging from being a complete observer who does not participate in group activities and is publicly defined as a researcher to being a covert participant who acts just like other group members and does not disclose his or her research role. Many field researchers develop a role between these extremes, publicly acknowledging being a researcher but nonetheless participating in group activities.

Choosing a Role

The first concern of all participant observers is deciding what balance to strike between observing and participating and whether to reveal their roles as researchers. These decisions must take into account the specifics of the social situation being studied, the researcher's own background and personality, the larger sociopolitical context, and ethical concerns. Which balance of participating and observing is most appropriate also changes during most projects—often many times.

Complete Observation

In **complete observation**, researchers try to see things as they happen, without actively participating in these events. Chambliss watched nurses closely, but he never bathed a patient, changed a dressing, started an intravenous line, or told a family that their loved one had died. Once during an emergency surgery for a ruptured ectopic pregnancy—a drastic, immediately life-threatening event—a surgeon ordered him to "put in a Foley" (a urinary catheter), but a nurse quickly said, "He's a researcher, I'll do it." Of course, at the same time as observing a setting, researchers must take into account the ways in which their presence

| EXHIBIT 9.1 | The Observational Continuum |

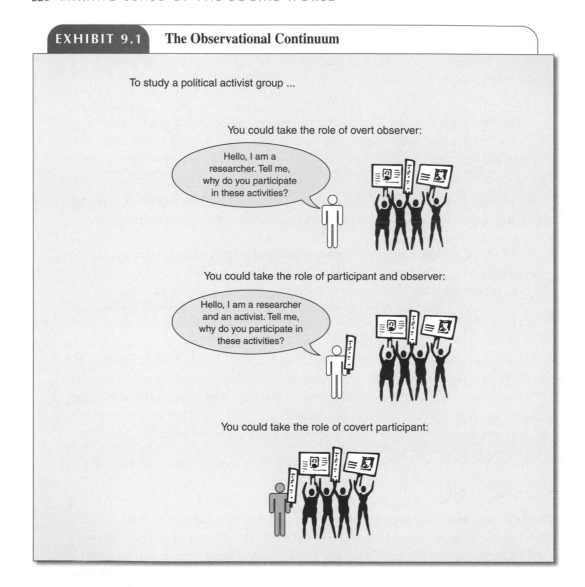

as observers itself alters the social situation being observed. Such **reactive effects** occur because it is not "natural" for someone to be present, recording observations for research and publication purposes (Thorne, 1993:20).

Complete observation: A role in participant observation in which the researcher does not participate in group activities and is publicly defined as a researcher

Reactive effects: The changes in an individual or group behavior that are due to being observed or otherwise studied

---

Mixed Participation/Observation

Most field researchers adopt a role that involves some active participation in the setting. Usually they inform at least some group members of their research interests, but then they participate in enough group activities to develop rapport with members and to gain a direct sense of what group members experience. This is not an easy balancing act. In his massive, 10-year study of gangs in urban America, Martin Sanchez Jankowski (1991:13)

> participated in nearly all the things they did. I ate where they ate, I slept where they slept, I stayed with their families, I traveled where they went, and . . . I fought with them. The only things that I did not participate in were those activities that were illegal . . . (including taking drugs).

And Jankowski (1991:12) says that although, for instance, the fights he was in "often left bruises, I was never seriously hurt. Quite remarkably, in the more than 10 years during which I conducted this research, I was only seriously injured twice."

A strategy of mixed participation and observation has two clear ethical advantages. Because group members know the researcher's real role in the group, they can choose to keep some information or attitudes hidden. By the same token, a researcher such as Jankowski can decline to participate in unethical or dangerous activities. Most field researchers get the feeling that, after they have become known and at least somewhat trusted figures in the group, their presence does not have any palpable effect on members' actions.

One especially interesting example of a "mixed" strategy is Chambliss's work on Olympic-level competitive swimmers. While working as a pure observer with a large number of world-class swimmers and teams, Chambliss himself coached, for 6 years, a small, local team in New York State. Here he tried to apply what he had learned through his years of research about what produces Olympic athletes. If his theories were correct, he reasoned, he should be able to make his *own* team much better. And, in fact, his swimmers improved dramatically, from being a rather poor local team to producing some state champions and even a few national-class athletes (Chambliss, 1989). His written reports thus include a very unusual mix of observations, theorizing, and practical field experimentation to test his theory.

Complete Participation

Some field researchers adopt a **complete participation** role in which one operates as a fully functioning member of the setting. Most often, such research is also covert, or secret— other members don't know that the researcher is doing research. In one famous covert study, Laud Humphreys (1970) served as a "watch queen" so that he could learn about men engaging in homosexual acts in a public restroom. In another case, Randall Alfred (1976) joined a group of Satanists to investigate group members and their interaction. And Erving Goffman (1961) worked as a state mental hospital attendant while studying the treatment of psychiatric patients.

> *Complete participation:* A role in field research in which the researcher does not reveal his or her identity as a researcher to those who are observed. Also called *covert participation.*

Covert participants don't disrupt their settings, but they do face other problems. They must write up notes from memory and must do so when it would be natural for them to be away from group members. Researchers often run to the bathroom to scribble their notes, jot "reminders" on napkins to expand on later, or whisper into hand-held recorders when they are out of the room. Researchers' spontaneous reactions to every event are unlikely to be consistent with those of the regular participants (Mitchell, 1993), because they are not "really" interested in washroom sex, Satanists, or psychiatric ward attendants. When Timothy Diamond (1992:47–48) did covert research as an aide in a nursing home, his economic resources showed:

> "There's one thing I learned when I came to the States," [said a Haitian nursing assistant]. "Here you can't make it on just one job." She tilted her head, looked at me curiously, then asked, "You know, Tim, there's just one thing I don't understand about you. How do you make it on just one job?"

Ethical issues have been at the forefront of the debate over the strategy of covert participation. Some covert observers may become so wrapped up in the role they are playing that they adopt not just the mannerisms but also the perspectives and goals of the regular participants—they "go native"—and so may end up "going along to get along" with group activities that are themselves unethical. Kai Erikson (1967) argues that covert participation is, therefore, by its very nature unethical and should not be allowed except in public settings. If others suspect the researcher's identity or if the researcher contributes to, or impedes, group action, these consequences can be adverse. Covert researchers cannot anticipate the unintended consequences of their actions for research subjects or even for other researchers; covert research may, for instance, increase public distrust of all social scientists.

Entering the Field

Entering the field, the setting under investigation, is a critical stage in a participant observation project. Chambliss (1996) used a very "soft" technique for gaining access to hospitals. Rather than preparing a formal proposal to present to top administrators, he began quite informally:

> I use an informal series of contacts with lower level members of the organization. In the present study, I would try first to meet some staff nurses who worked at the target hospitals, see them socially—for instance, by inviting them to lunch—and tell them I was interested in learning about nursing, hospitals, and ethical problems therein. This gave me a chance, first, to learn a lot about nursing in a comfortable setting. More

important, it gave the people I met a chance to see that I was easy to talk to, trustworthy, and a decent human being who was not out to do an exposé.

Typically, such conversations ended with my new acquaintance suggesting that I talk with still another nurse or administrator and providing a phone number. I would immediately follow up on this suggestion. A series of such meetings and introductions typically concluded in my being invited by suitably authorized administrators to visit the hospital, observe various units, and talk with whomever I pleased. At that point, as needed, I would present a formal proposal for research, get necessary permission, and so on. Basically, my assumption is that once potential subjects get to know me, they won't be afraid of my doing research on them. (190–191)

When participant observing involves public figures who are used to reporters and researchers, a more direct approach may secure entry into the field. Richard Fenno (1978:257) simply wrote a letter to most of the members of Congress whom he sought to study, asking for their permission to observe them at work. He received only two refusals and attributed this high rate of subject cooperation to such reasons as interest in a change in the daily routine, commitment to making themselves available, a desire for more publicity, the flattery of scholarly attention, and interest in helping to teach others about politics. Other groups have other motivations, but in every case, some consideration of these potential motives in advance should help smooth entry into the field.

In short, field researchers must be very sensitive to the impression they make and the ties they establish when entering the field. This stage lays the groundwork for collecting data from people who have different perspectives and for developing relationships that the researcher can use to surmount the problems in data collection that inevitably arise in the field. The researcher should be ready to explain to participants why he or she is involved in the field and how they might benefit from that involvement. Discussion about these issues with key participants, or **gatekeepers**, should be honest and should identify what the participants can expect from the research, without necessarily going into detail about the researcher's hypotheses or research questions (Rossman & Rallis, 1998:51–53, 105–108).

Gatekeeper: A person in a field setting who can grant researchers access to the setting

---

Developing and Maintaining Relationships

Researchers must be careful to manage their relationships in the research setting so that they can continue to observe and interview diverse members of the setting throughout the long period typical of participant observation (Maxwell, 1996:66). Interaction early in the research process is particularly sensitive, because participants don't know the researcher and the researcher doesn't know the group norms.

In his classic study *Street Corner Society,* William F. Whyte (1955) used what in retrospect was a sophisticated two-part strategy to develop and maintain relationships with poor men whose informal relationships he studied in "Cornerville" (an Italian American slum neighborhood in Boston). The first part of Whyte's strategy was to maintain good relations with a group leader known as Doc and, through Doc, to stay on good terms with the others. Doc became a **key informant** in the research setting—a knowledgeable insider who knew the group's culture and was willing to share access and insights with the researcher (Gilchrist & Williams, 1999). The less obvious part of Whyte's strategy was a consequence of his decision to move into Cornerville, a move he decided was necessary to understand and be accepted in the community fully. The room he rented in a local family's home became his base of operations. In some respects, this family became an important dimension of Whyte's immersion in the community: He tried to learn Italian by speaking with family members, and they conversed late at night as if Whyte were a real family member. But Whyte recognized that he needed a place to unwind after his days of constant alertness in the field, so he made a conscious decision not to include the family as an object of study. Living in this family's home became a means for Whyte to maintain standing as a community insider without becoming totally immersed in the demands of research (Whyte:294–297).

Key informant: An insider who is willing and able to provide a field researcher with superior access and information, including answers to questions that arise in the course of the research

---

Experienced participant observers recommend developing a plausible (and honest) explanation for yourself and your study and keeping the support of key individuals to maintain relationships in the field. They also suggest being somewhat "laid-back," neither showing off your expertise nor being too aggressive in questioning others. Another good bit of advice is not faking social similarity with those you are observing and not offering monetary rewards for participation (Bogdewic, 1999:53–54; Rossman & Rallis, 1998:105–108; Whyte, 1955:300–306; Wolcott, 1995:91–95).

Sampling People and Events

Qualitative researchers intensively study people, places, or other phenomena of interest, so they tend to limit their focus to just one or a few sites or programs. Still, the sample must be appropriate and adequate for the study, even if it is not representative. The qualitative researcher may select a "critical case" that is unusually rich in information pertaining to the research question; a "typical case," precisely because it is judged to be typical; and/or a "deviant case," which provides a useful contrast (Kuzel, 1999). Within a research site, plans may be made to sample different settings, people, events, and artifacts (see Exhibit 9.2).

Studying more than one case or setting almost always strengthens the causal conclusions and makes the findings more generalizable (King, Keohane, & Verba, 1994). For example,

EXHIBIT 9.2	Sampling Plan for a Participant Observation Project in Schools

	Type of Information to Be Obtained				
Information Source*	*Collegiality*	*Goals & Community*	*Action Expectations*	*Knowledge Orientation*	*Base*
SETTINGS					
Public places (halls, main offices)					
Teacher's lounge	X	X		X	X
Classrooms		X	X	X	X
Meeting rooms	X		X	X	
Gymnasium or locker room		X			
EVENTS					
Faculty meetings	X		X		X
Lunch hour	X				X
Teaching		X	X	X	X
PEOPLE					
Principal		X	X	X	X
Teachers	X	X	X	X	X
Students		X	X	X	
ARTIFACTS					
Newspapers		X	X		X
Decorations		X			

* Selected examples in each category.

Diamond (1992:5) worked in three different Chicago nursing homes "in widely different neighborhoods" and with different percentages of residents supported by Medicaid. He then "visited many homes across the United States to validate my observations."

Other approaches to sampling in field research are more systematic. Researchers use **theoretical sampling** when they focus their investigation on particular processes that seem to be important and select instances to allow comparisons or checks with which they can test these perceptions (Ragin, 1994:98–101) (see Exhibit 9.3). Jankowski (1991:6–7), again, provides an impressive example of conscientious theoretical sampling in field research:

It was first essential to investigate *gangs in different cities* in order to control for the different socioeconomic and political environments that they operate in. Second, in order to determine if there were any differences associated with ethnicity, it was critical to

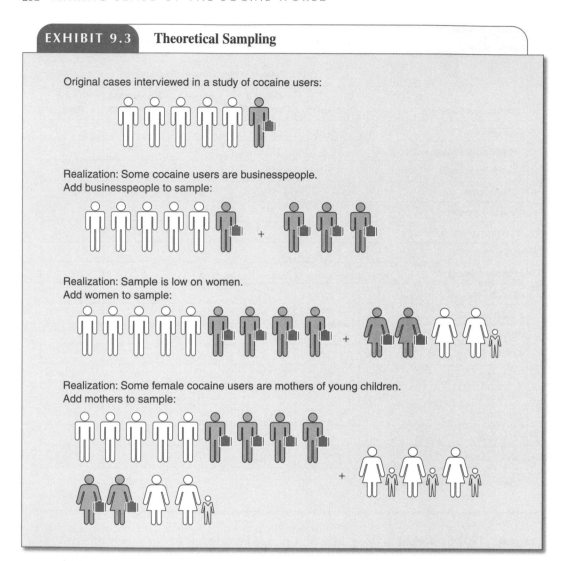

EXHIBIT 9.3   **Theoretical Sampling**

Original cases interviewed in a study of cocaine users:

Realization: Some cocaine users are businesspeople.
Add businesspeople to sample:

Realization: Sample is low on women.
Add women to sample:

Realization: Some female cocaine users are mothers of young children.
Add mothers to sample:

compare gangs composed of different ethnic groups. Three metropolitan areas were therefore chosen for the study: the greater Los Angeles area, various boroughs of New York City, and the greater Boston area.

Two were eastern cities with certain weather patterns; the other was western with a completely different weather pattern. (Weather has often been thought to have an impact on gang activity, with colder weather restricting activity and warmer weather encouraging it.)

Of the thirty-seven gangs studied, thirteen were in the Los Angeles area, twenty were in the New York City area, and four were in the Boston area. Various ethnic groups are represented in the sample, which includes gangs composed of Irish, African-American, Puerto Rican, Chicano, Dominican, Jamaican, and Central American members. The sample also involves gangs of varying size. The smallest had thirty-four members; the largest had more than one thousand. . . . Within this sample, stratified by ethnicity, I randomly selected ten in each city. It was my intention to study African-American gangs, Latino gangs, Asian gangs, and white gangs, and so gangs representing each of these ethnic groups were chosen. Because I wanted to include gangs of varying membership sizes, I randomly selected gangs from my ethnically stratified list until I obtained a sample representing gangs of different sizes. Since my overall strategy was to study five gangs in Los Angeles and five in New York for two years, then add more, and finally add several Boston gangs, I selected five of the original ten chosen and began my effort to secure their participation.

Theoretical sampling: A sampling method recommended for field researchers by Glaser and Strauss (1967). A theoretical sample is drawn in a sequential fashion, with settings or individuals selected for study as earlier observations or interviews indicate that these settings or individuals are influential

---

Taking Notes

Notes are the primary means of recording participant observation data (Emerson, Fretz, & Shaw, 1995). It is almost always a mistake to try to take comprehensive notes while engaged in the field—the process of writing extensively is just too disruptive. The usual procedure is to jot down brief notes about highlights of the observation period. These brief notes then serve as memory joggers when writing the actual **field notes** later. It also helps to maintain a daily log in which each day's activities are recorded (Bogdewic, 1999:58–67). With the aid of the **jottings** and some practice, researchers usually remember a great deal of what happened—as long as the comprehensive field notes are written immediately afterward or at least within the next 24 hours, and before they have been discussed with anyone else.

Field notes: Notes that describe what has been observed, heard, or otherwise experienced in a participant observation study. These notes usually are written after the observational session

Jottings: Brief notes written in the field about highlights of an observation period

---

Usually writing up notes takes much longer—at least three times longer—than the observing did. Field notes must be as complete, detailed, and true to what was observed and heard as possible. Direct quotes should be distinguished clearly from paraphrased quotes, and both should be set off from the researcher's observations and reflections. The surrounding context should receive as much attention as possible, and a map of the setting should be included, with indications of where individuals were at different times.

Careful note taking yields a big payoff. On page after page, field notes will suggest new concepts, causal connections, and theoretical propositions. Notes also should include descriptions of the methodology and a record of the researcher's feelings and thoughts while observing. Exhibit 9.4 illustrates these techniques with notes from the Chambliss study.

EXHIBIT 9.4 **Sample Field Notes From the Chambliss Nursing Study**

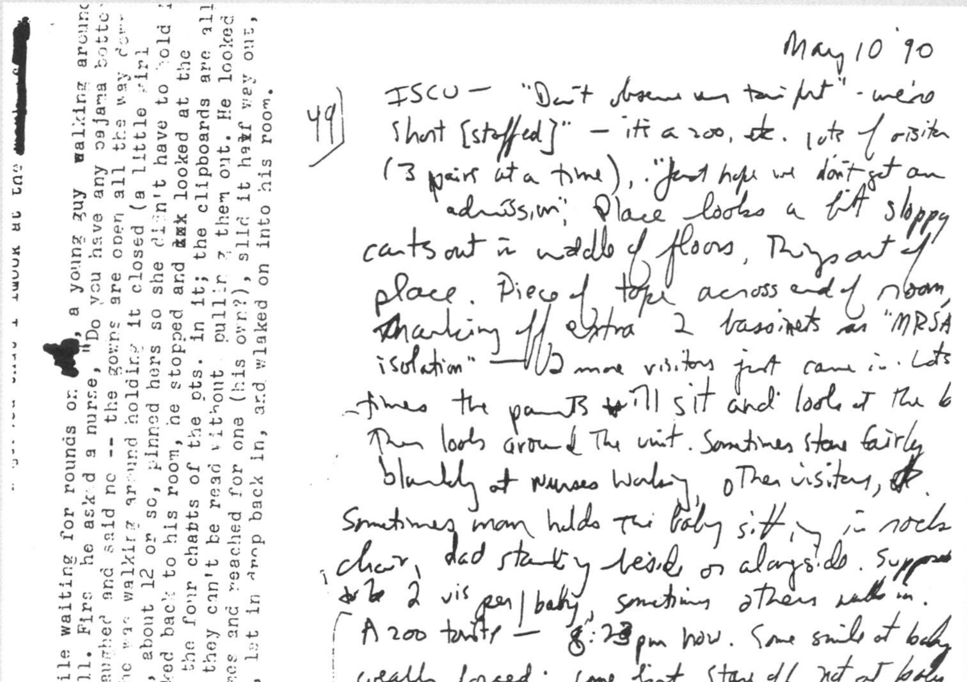

Note: Original field notes, either written on site or typed later that day. Identifying information has been blacked out. "ISCU" stands for "Infant Special Care Unit," where premature infants are cared for. The first sentence reads, "Don't observe us tonight," "we're short [staffed]," a quotation from a nurse in the unit.

Managing the Personal Dimensions

Field researchers cannot help but be affected on a personal, emotional level by social processes in the social situation they are studying. At the same time, those being studied react to researchers not just as researchers but as personal acquaintances—and often as friends. Managing and learning from this personal side of field research is an important part of any project.

> The researcher, like his informants, is a social animal. He has a role to play, and he has his own personality needs that must be met in some degree if he is to function successfully. Where the researcher operates out of a university, just going into the field for a few hours at a time, he can keep his personal social life separate from field activity. His problem of role is not quite so complicated. If, on the other hand, the researcher is living for an extended period in the community he is studying, his personal life is inextricably mixed with his research. (Whyte, 1955:279)

Barrie Thorne (1993:26), a sociologist known for her research on gender roles among children, wondered whether "my moments of remembering, the times when I felt like a ten-year-old girl, [were] a source of distortion or insight?" She concluded they were both: "Memory, like observing, is a way of knowing and can be a rich resource." But "when my own responses . . . were driven by emotions like envy or aversion, they clearly obscured my ability to grasp the full social situation."

There is no formula for successfully managing the personal dimension of field research. It is much more art than science and flows more from the researcher's own personality and natural approach to other people than from formal training. But novice field researchers often neglect to consider how they will manage personal relationships when they plan and carry out their projects. Attention to a few guidelines based on our personal experience with field research, provided in Exhibit 9.5, should maximize the likelihood of a project's success.

▣ HOW DO YOU CONDUCT INTENSIVE INTERVIEWS?

Participant observation can provide a wonderfully rich view, then, of the social world. But it remains a *view,* seen by the observer. Often we wonder what individuals think or feel or how they see their world. For this purpose, one can use **intensive interviews**.

Unlike the more structured interviewing that may be used in survey research (discussed in Chapter 7), intensive or *depth* interviewing relies on open-ended questions to develop a comprehensive picture of the interviewee's background, attitudes, and actions—to "listen to people as they describe how they understand the worlds in which they live and work" (Rubin & Rubin, 1995:3).

EXHIBIT 9.5	Nine Steps to Successful Field Research

1. *Have a simple, one-sentence explanation of your project.* "I want to learn about the problems nurses face in their work," or "I want to learn what makes a great swimming team." People will ask what you're doing, but no one cares to hear all your theories.

2. *Be yourself.* Don't lie about who you are. First, it's wrong. Second, you'll get caught and ruin the trust you're trying to build. (Yes, there are exceptions, but very few.)

3. *Don't interfere.* They got along just fine before you came along, and they can do it again. Don't be a pest.

4. *Listen, actively.* Be genuinely interested in what they say. Movie stars, politicians, and other celebrities are used to having other people listen to what they say, but that's not true for most people. If you really care to listen, they'll tell you everything.

5. *Show up,* at every opportunity—3:00 in the morning, or if you have to walk 5 miles. Go to their parties and their funerals. Make a 5-hour trip for a 15-minute interview, and they'll notice—and give you everything you want.

6. *Pay attention to everything,* especially when you're bored. That's when the important stuff is happening, the stuff *no one else* notices.

7. *Protect your sources,* more than is necessary. When word gets around that you can be trusted, you won't believe what people will tell you.

8. *Write everything down, that day.* By tomorrow, you'll forget 90% of the best material, and then it's gone forever.

9. Always remember: *It's not about you, it's about them.* Don't try to be smart, or savvy, or hip; don't try to be the center of attention. Stop thinking about yourself all the time. Pay attention to other people.

Intensive interviewing: A qualitative method that involves open-ended, relatively unstructured questioning in which the interviewer seeks in-depth information on the interviewee's feelings, experiences, and perceptions. Also called *depth interviewing.*

For instance:

We had two or three patients, and they were terminally ill with cancer. We would give the patients, every two or three hours around the clock toward the end, morphine sulphate, intramuscular.

I was really worried about giving them a morphine injection because the morphine depresses the respiration. I thought, well, is this injection going to do them in?

If I don't give the injection, they will linger on longer, but they might also have more pain. If I do give the injection, the end result of death is going to occur faster. Am I playing God?" [Interview] (Chambliss, 1996:171)

The key to eliciting such a response is *active listening*—which is not the same as just being quiet. Instead, you must actively question, ask for explanations, and show a genuine deep curiosity about the subject's views and feelings. The researcher's own opinions are not important here; you must suspend all judgment of what the respondent is saying, even if you regard the person's opinions as obnoxious or even immoral. Remember, the goal is to learn what the *respondent* thinks, not to express what *you* think.

Therefore, depth interviews may be highly unstructured. Rather than asking standard questions in a fixed order, a researcher conducting intensive interviews may allow the specific content and order of questions to vary from one interviewee to another. Like participant observation studies, intensive interviewing engages researchers actively with subjects. The researchers must listen to lengthy explanations, ask follow-up questions tailored to the preceding answers, and seek to learn about interrelated belief systems or personal approaches to things rather than measure a limited set of variables. As a result, intensive interviews are often much longer than standardized interviews, sometimes as long as 15 hours, conducted in several different sessions.

The intensive interview can become more like a conversation between partners than between a researcher and a subject (Kaufman, 1986:22–23). Some call it "a conversation with a purpose" (Rossman & Rallis, 1998:126). Robert Bellah, Richard Madsen, William Sullivan, Ann Swidler, and Steven Tipton elaborate on this aspect of intensive interviewing in a methodological appendix to their national best seller about American individualism, *Habits of the Heart* (1985:304):

> We did not, as in some scientific version of "Candid Camera," seek to capture their beliefs and actions without our subjects being aware of us. Rather, we sought to bring our preconceptions and questions into the conversation and to understand the answers we were receiving not only in terms of the language but also, so far as we could discover, in the lives of those we were talking with. Though we did not seek to impose our ideas on those with whom we talked . . . , we did attempt to uncover assumptions, to make explicit what the person we were talking to might rather have left implicit. The interview as we employed it was active, Socratic.

Random selection is rarely used to select respondents for intensive interviews, but the selection method still must be considered carefully. Researchers should try to select interviewees who are knowledgeable about the subject of the interview, who are open to talking, and who represent a range of perspectives (Rubin & Rubin, 1995:65–92). Selection of new interviewees should continue, if possible, at least until the **saturation point** is reached, the point when new interviews seem to yield little additional information (see Exhibit 9.6).

Saturation point: The point at which subject selection is ended in intensive interviewing because new interviews seem to yield little additional information

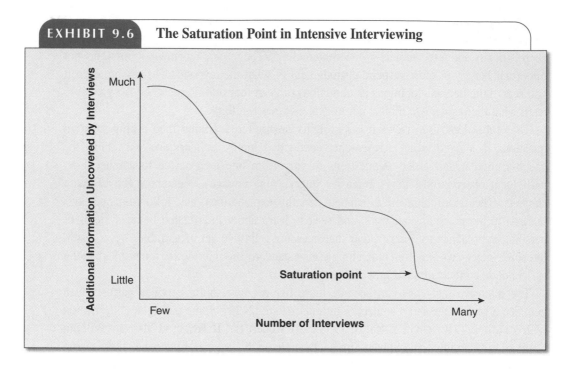

EXHIBIT 9.6   The Saturation Point in Intensive Interviewing

Establishing and Maintaining a Partnership

Because intensive interviewing does not engage researchers as participants in subjects' daily affairs, the problems of entering the field are much reduced. However, the logistics of arranging long periods for personal interviews can still be pretty complicated. It also is important to establish rapport with subjects by considering in advance how they will react to the interview arrangements and by developing an approach that does not violate their standards for social behavior. Interviewees should be treated with respect, as knowledgeable partners whose time is valued (in other words, don't be late for your appointments). A commitment to confidentiality should be stated and honored (Rubin & Rubin, 1995).

Asking Questions and Recording Answers

Intensive interviewers must plan their main questions around an outline of the interview topic. The questions generally should be short and to the point. More details can then be elicited through nondirective probes (such as "Can you tell me more about that?" or "Uh-huh," echoing the respondent's comment, or just maintaining a moment of silence). Follow-up questions can then be tailored to answers to the main questions.

Interviewers should strategize throughout an interview about how best to achieve their objectives while taking into account interviewees' answers. *Habits of the Heart* (Bellah et al., 1985:304) again provides a useful illustration:

[Coinvestigator Steven] Tipton, in interviewing Margaret Oldham [a pseudonym], tried to discover at what point she would take responsibility for another human being:

Q: So what are you responsible for?

A: I'm responsible for my acts and for what I do.

Q: Does that mean you're responsible for others, too?

A: No.

Q: Are you your sister's keeper?

A: No.

Q: Your brother's keeper?

A: No.

Q: Are you responsible for your husband?

A: I'm not. He makes his own decisions. He is his own person. He acts his own acts. I can agree with them, or I can disagree with them. If I ever find them nauseous enough, I have a responsibility to leave and not deal with it any more.

Q: What about children?

A: I . . . I would say I have a legal responsibility for them, but in a sense I think they in turn are responsible for their own acts.

Do you see how the interviewer actively encouraged the subject to *explain* what she meant by "responsibility"? This sort of active questioning undoubtedly did a better job of clarifying the interviewee's concept of responsibility than a fixed set of questions would have.

Tape recorders commonly are used for recording intensive interviews and focus group interviews. They do not inhibit most interviewees and, in fact, are routinely ignored. Occasionally a respondent is very concerned with his or her public image and may therefore speak "for the tape recorder," but such individuals are unlikely to speak frankly in any research interview. In any case, constant note taking during an interview prevents adequate displays of interest and is distracting. Sometimes, though, the very act of visibly turning off the recorder may free a respondent to tell that one great secret he or she has been keeping— and interviewers often use that very technique.

▣ HOW DO YOU RUN FOCUS GROUPS?

Finally, for quick, emotionally resonant answers, **focus groups** can be the qualitative researcher's best friend. Long favored by advertisers, marketing researchers, and political consultants who want to see "what message pushes their buttons," focus groups are collections of unrelated individuals, convened by a researcher and then led in group discussion of a topic for 1 to 2 hours. The researcher asks specific questions and guides the discussion, but the resulting information is qualitative and relatively unstructured. Focus groups need not involve representative samples; instead, a few individuals are recruited for the group who have the time to participate, have some knowledge pertinent to the focus group topic, and share key characteristics with the target population. Throughout the Mellon Project on liberal arts education at Hamilton College, focus groups—of dean's list students, minority students, or study abroad participants, for instance—have been used to assess major problem areas in various programs rapidly and to develop areas for more systematic investigation.

Focus groups: A qualitative method that involves unstructured group interviews in which the focus group leader actively encourages discussion among participants on the topics of interest

---

Focus group research typically proceeds like this: The researcher convenes a series of groups, each including 7–10 people, for the discussions. Sometimes the groups are heterogeneous, with many dissimilar people (old and young, boss and employees, Democrats and Republicans); this can stimulate a broader array of opinions. But usually groups are, by design, homogeneous by categories one wishes to compare. For instance, a business might run eight focus groups, four from the sales offices and four from service offices, to learn how these different functions see their customers. Or a college could run focus groups of freshmen and sophomores to learn about the different ways these groups approach course registration. It's generally best (though not always possible) to have group members be strangers so that personal relationships don't affect their answers, and it's crucial to avoid power differentials—no bosses with subordinates, teachers with students, or parents with their children. Such combinations will prevent open and honest opinion from emerging.

Once completed, focus group discussions are relatively easy to analyze: Just compare the responses, on each question, from one kind of group (say, salespeople) to responses for the same question by another kind of group (say, service representatives).

Richard Krueger (1988:33–37) provides a good example of a situation in which focus groups were used effectively:

[A] University recently launched a $100 million fund drive. The key aspect of the drive was a film depicting science and research efforts. The film was shown in over two dozen focus groups of alumni, with surprising results to University officials. Alumni simply did not like the film and instead were more attracted to supporting undergraduate humanistic education.

Focus group methods share with other field research techniques an emphasis on discovering unanticipated findings and exploring hidden meanings. Although weak in developing reliable, generalizable results (the strength of survey research), focus groups can be indispensable for developing hypotheses and survey questions, for investigating the meaning of survey results, and for quickly assessing the range of opinion about an issue. Exhibit 9.7 presents guidelines for running focus groups.

EXHIBIT 9.7   **Keys to Running Focus Groups**

- A great moderator—Is neutral and genuinely respects the participants and is a great listener who can draw people out.
- Main questions—These ask what you really want to know, can be answered by participants, are clear and understandable to the participants, and provide useful answers.
- Participants—Are homogeneous by relevant category for comparisons, with no power differentials within the group.
- Sampling—Is purposeful, representing the entire range of responses, and is random within the pools meeting criteria. Ideally, participants in any group should be strangers to each other. Use reminders to attend with incentives.
- Recording—Audio recording, with an assistant taking notes, is best.
- Analysis—Compare answers of different groups to different questions (groups on differently colored paper, sorted by question, etc.).
- Reporting—You are speaking for the participants. Lead with the big insights and answer the questions that were asked of the study. Interesting quotations get attention!
- When in doubt—Ask the potential participants about food, setting, issues, moderator, etc.

Basically, good focus groups get honest answers, on important topics, from people who know.

ANALYZING QUALITATIVE DATA

The data for a qualitative study most often are notes jotted down in the field or during an interview—from which the original comments, observations, and feelings are reconstructed—or text transcribed from audiotapes. What to do with all this material? Chapter 10 is a full discussion of this topic, but a few comments here provide an introduction.

Many field research projects have slowed to a halt because a novice researcher becomes overwhelmed by the quantity of information that has been collected. (A 1-hour interview can generate 20 to 25 pages of single-spaced text [Kvale, 1996:169].) Boxes filled with those scribbled notes—old napkins with some words, flyers for events attended, e-mails from informants—can seem daunting, but a few simple steps can clarify the whole mess rather quickly.

The Phases of Analysis

Basically, there are two approaches to analyzing qualitative data: the *deductive,* or hypothesis-testing approach, and the *inductive,* or exploratory approach. Jankowski (1991:16), in his study of gangs, used a deductive method:

I began the analysis by establishing topics that would need to be covered in a book about gangs, such as gang recruitment, gang organization, violence, and so on. I then proceeded to read each of my notes (daily notes, daily summaries, weekly summaries) and place them in stacks having to do with each topic I wanted to cover.

When notes pertained to more than one topic, I photocopied them and placed each under the additional topics.

My analysis began by taking a topic and reviewing what other researchers had found concerning gangs. Their findings would be written down in hypothesis form and then I would read my notes to determine what my evidence suggested.

Jankowski created a series of topics and sorted his notes into those categories, which were created in advance. He then used the material in each category to test hypotheses from the literature on gangs.

An *inductive* approach, by contrast, allows themes and topics to emerge from the data themselves. In his nursing study, Chambliss first spent several weeks reading through all of his notes and skimming transcripts, taking notes on the topics covered; then he read through the notes themselves, organizing them into a handful of topics (e.g., routines of work, ethical problems, the role of the nurse) that seemed to arise repeatedly; and finally he re-sorted all of his "notes and quotes" into huge piles, one for each of those main topics. (As he did this work, his notes covered the entire living room floor of his apartment.)

As observation, interviewing, and reflection continue, researchers refine their definitions of problems, concepts, and select indicators. They can then check the frequency and distribution of phenomena. How many people made a particular type of comment? How often did social interaction lead to arguments? Hypotheses are modified as researchers gain experience in the setting. For the final analysis, the researchers check their models carefully against their notes and make a concerted attempt to discover negative evidence that might suggest the model is incorrect. Such an approach combines the inductive with the deductive.

回 ETHICAL ISSUES IN QUALITATIVE RESEARCH

Qualitative research can raise some complex ethical issues. No matter how hard the field researcher strives to study the social world naturally, leaving no traces, the very act of research itself imposes something "unnatural" on the situation. It is up to the researcher to identify and take responsibility for the consequences of her or his involvement. Five main ethical issues arise:

1. *Voluntary participation*—Ensuring that subjects are participating in a study voluntarily is not often a problem with intensive interviewing and focus group research, but it is often a point of contention in participant observation studies. Few researchers or institutional review boards are willing to condone covert participation, because it does not offer any way to ensure that participation by the subjects is voluntary. Even when the researcher's role is more open, interpreting the standard of voluntary participation still can be difficult. Should the requirement of voluntary participation apply equally to every member of an organization being observed? What if the manager consents, the workers are ambivalent, and the union says no?

2. *Subject well-being*—Before beginning a project, every field researcher should consider carefully how to avoid harm to subjects. It is not possible to avoid every theoretical possibility of harm or to be sure that a project will cause no adverse consequences whatsoever to any individual, but direct harm to the reputations or feelings of particular individuals should be avoided at all costs. The risk of such harm can be minimized by maintaining the confidentiality of research subjects and by not adversely affecting the course of events while engaged in a setting. Whyte (1955:335–337) found himself regretting having recommended that a particular politician be allowed to speak to a social club he was observing, because the speech led to serious dissension in the club and strains between Whyte and some club members.

3. *Identity disclosure*—Current ethical standards require informed consent of research subjects, and most would argue that this standard cannot be met in any meaningful way if researchers do not disclose fully their identity. But how much disclosure about the study is necessary, and how hard should researchers try to make sure that their research purposes are understood? In field research on Codependents Anonymous, Leslie Irvine (1998) found that the emphasis on anonymity and the expectations for group discussion made it difficult for her to disclose her identity. Can a balance be struck between the disclosure of critical facts and a coherent research strategy?

4. *Confidentiality*—Field researchers normally use fictitious names for the characters in their reports, but doing so does not always guarantee confidentiality to their research subjects. In Chambliss's nursing book, reference to "the director of the medical center" might have identified that person, at least to other employees of the center who knew Chambliss did his research there. And anyone studying public figures or national leaders in a social movement must exercise special care, because such people can be privately recognized by their own followers or enemies. Researchers should thus make every effort to expunge any possible identifying material from published information and to alter unimportant aspects of a description when necessary to prevent identity disclosure. In any case, no field research project should begin if some participants clearly will suffer serious harm by being identified in project publications.

5. *Online research*—The large number of discussion groups and bulletin boards on the Internet has stimulated much interest in conducting research like that of Fox and Roberts (1999), who observed physicians' listservs in the United Kingdom. Such research can violate the principles of voluntary participation and identity disclosure when researchers participate in discussions and record and analyze text but do not identify themselves as researchers (Associated Press, 2000).

These ethical issues cannot be evaluated independently. The final decision to proceed must be made after weighing the relative benefits and risks to participants. Few qualitative research projects will be barred by consideration of these ethical issues, however, except for those involving covert participation. The more important concern for researchers is to identify the ethically troublesome aspects of their proposed research and resolve them before the project begins, as well as to act on new ethical issues as they come up during the project.

▣ CONCLUSION

Qualitative research has both immediate and lasting attractions. Many of the classic works of social science, from Sigmund Freud's *Interpretation of Dreams* (1900/1999) and Margaret Mead's *Coming of Age in Samoa* (1928/2001) to Erving Goffman's *Presentation of Self in Everyday Life* (1959) and Kristin Luker's *Abortion and the Politics of Motherhood* (1985), rest on qualitative forms of social research. Telling true stories of real people, laying out their feelings and emotions, is qualitative research—interviews, fieldwork, and focus groups cut through the dry numbers and correlations, the abstract variables, and the hypotheses of contemporary quantitative social science. Qualitative research aims to go, as we said at the beginning of this chapter, where real people live. It thereby can become, at its best, a form of literature, beautifully teaching its readers the deeper truths of the human condition. More modestly, many students simply find reading reports of qualitative research to be far more interesting than the statistics used in survey analysis.

But "interesting" is not always the same as accurate, correct, or even representative. The juiciest stories that Dan Chambliss heard from his nurses were not, as it happens, what typically happened in their lives. Researchers love a "good quote," but it may not represent the truth of a setting; fieldworkers love finding a key informant whose views may not be those of the average subject. Like journalists, even the best qualitative researchers may be drawn to the odd, the unusual, or the available—and all of those may be poor substitutes for representative sampling, standardized questions, and other more sober approaches to learning about social life. The statistics of survey analysis and the control groups of experiments force us to face reality with self-discipline; they make it harder to fool ourselves about what we see.

In the end, qualitative methods are one—and only one—excellent set of tools, complementary in purpose to the tools of surveys, experiments, and other methods. Each has its strengths and its weaknesses. When surveys find that college students complain about "social life" but also rejoice that they "made my best friends ever here," interviews can explain the (apparent) contradiction. When police statistics and crime surveys can't fathom the logic of gang life, Martin Sanchez Jankowski steps in and tells us the story in all its richness. And remember: No experiment, however carefully designed with an eye to protecting internal validity, could ever have uncovered what Sigmund Freud found by just sitting quietly next to a patient on a couch—and listening.

KEY TERMS

Complete observation
Complete (covert) participation
Field notes
Field research
Focus groups
Gatekeeper
Intensive (depth) interviewing

Jottings
Key informant
Participant observation
Qualitative methods
Reactive effects
Saturation point
Theoretical sampling

HIGHLIGHTS

- Qualitative methods are most useful in exploring new issues, in investigating hard-to-study groups, and in determining the meaning people give to their lives and actions. In addition, most social research projects can be improved in some respects by taking advantage of qualitative techniques.
- Qualitative researchers tend to develop ideas inductively; they try to understand the social context and sequential nature of attitudes and actions and explore the subjective meanings that participants attach to events. They rely primarily on participant observation, intensive interviewing, and, in recent years, focus groups.
- Participant observers may adopt one of several roles for a particular research project. Each role represents a different balance between observing and participating. Many field researchers prefer a moderate role, participating as well as observing in a group but acknowledging publicly the researcher role. Such a role avoids the ethical issues posed by covert participation while still allowing the insights into the social world derived from participating directly in it. The role that the participant observer chooses should be based on an evaluation of the problems likely to arise from reactive effects and the ethical dilemmas of covert participation.
- Field researchers must develop strategies for entering the field, developing and maintaining relations in the field, sampling, and recording and analyzing data. Selection of sites or other units to study may reflect an emphasis on typical cases, deviant cases, and/or critical cases that can provide more information than others. Sampling techniques commonly used within sites or in selecting interviewees in field research include theoretical sampling.
- Recording and analyzing notes is a crucial step in field research. Jottings are used as brief reminders about events in the field, whereas daily logs are useful to chronicle the researcher's activities. Detailed field notes should be recorded daily. Periodic analysis of the notes can guide refinement of methods used in the field and of the concepts, indicators, and models developed to explain what has been observed.
- Intensive interviews involve open-ended questions and follow-up probes, with the specific question content and order varying from one interview to another.
- Focus groups combine elements of participant observation and intensive interviewing. They can increase the validity of attitude measurement by revealing what people say when presenting their opinions in a group context instead of the artificial one-on-one interview setting.
- Computer software is used increasingly for the analysis of qualitative, textual, and pictorial data. Users can record their notes, categorize observations, specify links between categories, and count occurrences.
- The four main ethical issues in field research concern voluntary participation, subject well-being, identity disclosure, and confidentiality.

STUDENT STUDY SITE

To assist you in completing the Web Exercises, please access the Study Site at **http://www.pineforge.com/mssw3**, where you'll find the Web Exercises with accompanying links. You'll find other useful study materials like self-quizzes and e-flashcards for each chapter, along with a group of carefully selected articles from research journals that illustrate the major concepts and techniques presented in the book.

EXERCISES

Discussing Research

1. Maurice Punch (1994:91) once opined that "the crux of the matter is that some deception, passive or active, enables you to get at data not obtainable by other means." What aspects of the social world would be difficult for participant observers to study without being covert? Might any situations require the use of covert observation to gain access? What might you do as a participant observer to lessen access problems while still acknowledging your role as a researcher?

2. Review the experiments and surveys described in previous chapters. Pick one and propose a field research design that would focus on the same research question but use participant observation techniques in a local setting. Propose the role that you would play in the setting, along the participant observation continuum, and explain why you would favor this role. Describe the stages of your field research study, including your plans for entering the field, developing and maintaining relationships, sampling, and recording and analyzing data. Then discuss what you would expect your study to add to the findings resulting from the study described in the book.

3. Intensive interviews are the core of many qualitative research designs. How do they differ from the structured survey procedures that you studied in the last chapter? What are their advantages and disadvantages over standardized interviewing? How does intensive interviewing differ from the qualitative method of participant observation? What are the advantages and disadvantages of these two methods?

Finding Research

1. Go to the *Annual Review of Sociology*'s Web site by following the publications link at http://annualreviews.org. Search for articles that use qualitative methods as the primary method of gathering data on any one of the following subjects: child development/socialization, gender/sex roles, or aging/gerontology. Enter "Qualitative AND Methods" in the subject field to begin this search. Review at least five articles and report on the specific method of field research used in each.

2. Go to Intute's database of social sciences Internet resources at http://www.intute.ac.uk/socialsciences/. Choose "Research Tools and Methods" and then "Qualitative Methods." Now choose three or four interesting sites to find out more about field research—either professional organizations of field researchers or journals that publish their work. Explore the sites to find out what information they provide regarding field research, what kinds of projects are being done that involve field research, and the purposes for which specific field research methods are being used.

3. You have been asked to do field research on the World Wide Web's impact on the socialization of children in today's world. The first part of the project involves your writing a compare-and-contrast report on the differences between how you and your generation were socialized as

children and the way children today are being socialized. Collect your data by surfing the Web "as if you were a kid." The Web is your field, and you are the field researcher.

Using any of the major search engines, explore the Web within the "Kids" or "Children" subject heading, keeping field notes on what you observe.

Write a brief report based on the data you have collected. How has the Web impacted child socialization in comparison to when you were a child?

Critiquing Research

1. Read and summarize one of the qualitative studies discussed in this chapter or another classic study recommended by your instructor. Review and critique the study using the article review questions presented in Exhibit 12.2. What questions are answered by the study? What questions are raised for further investigation?

2. Write a short critique of the ethics of Ellis's (1986) study (discussed in Chapter 2). Read the book ahead of time to clarify the details and then focus on each of the ethical guidelines presented in this chapter: voluntary participation, subject well-being, identity disclosure, and confidentiality. Conclude with a statement about the extent to which field researchers should be required to disclose their identities and the circumstances in which they should not be permitted to participate actively in the social life they study.

Doing Research

1. Conduct a brief observational study in a public location on campus where students congregate. A cafeteria, a building lobby, or a lounge would be ideal. You can sit and observe, taking occasional notes unobtrusively and without violating any expectations of privacy. Observe for 30 minutes. Write up field notes, being sure to include a description of the setting and a commentary on your own behavior and your reactions to what you observed.

2. Review the experiments and surveys described in previous chapters. Pick one and propose a field research design that would focus on the same research question but with participant observation techniques in a local setting. Propose the role along the participant observation continuum that you would play in the setting and explain why you would favor this role. Describe the stages of your field research study, including your plans for entering the field, developing and maintaining relationships, sampling, and recording and analyzing data. Then discuss what you would expect your study to add to the findings resulting from the study described in the book.

3. Develop an interview guide that focuses on a research question addressed in one of the studies in this book. Using this guide, conduct an intensive interview with one person who is involved with the topic in some way. Take only brief notes during the interview; then write up as complete a record of the interview as you can immediately afterward. Turn in an evaluation of your performance as an interviewer and note taker together with your notes.

Ethics Questions

1. Should covert observation ever be allowed in social science research? Do you believe that social scientists should simply avoid conducting research on groups or individuals who refuse to admit researchers into their lives? Some have argued that members of privileged groups do not need to be protected from covert research by social scientists—that this restriction should only apply to disadvantaged groups and individuals. Do you agree? Why or why not?

2. Should any requirements be imposed on researchers who seek to study other cultures to ensure that procedures are appropriate and interpretations are culturally sensitive? What practices would you suggest for cross-cultural researchers to ensure that ethical guidelines are followed? (Consider the wording of consent forms and the procedures for gaining voluntary cooperation.)

CHAPTER 10

Qualitative Data Analysis

What Is Distinctive About Qualitative Data Analysis?

Qualitative Data Analysis as an Art
Qualitative Compared to Quantitative Data Analysis

What Techniques Do Qualitative Data Analysts Use?

Documentation
Conceptualization, Coding, and Categorizing
Examining Relationships and Displaying Data
Authenticating Conclusions
Reflexivity

What Are Some Alternatives in Qualitative Data Analysis?

Ethnography
Ethnomethodology
Narrative Analysis
Conversation Analysis
Grounded Theory

Visual Sociology

How Can Computers Assist Qualitative Data Analysis?

What Ethical Issues Arise in Doing Qualitative Data Analysis?

Conclusion

I was at lunch standing in line and he [another male student] came up to my face and started saying stuff and then he pushed me. I said . . . I'm cool with you, I'm your friend and then he push me again and calling me names. I told him to stop pushing me and then he push me hard and said something about my mom. And then he hit me, and I hit him back. After he fell I started kicking him.

—Morrill, Yalda, Adelman, Musheno, and Bejarano (2000:521)

This statement was made by a real student writing an in-class essay about conflicts in which he had participated. It was written for a team of social scientists who were studying conflicts in high schools to better understand their origins and to inform prevention policies.

In qualitative data analysis, the raw data to be analyzed are text—words—rather than numbers. In the high school conflict study by Morrill et al. (2000), there were initially no variables or hypotheses. The use of text, not numbers, and the (initial) absence of variables are just two of the ways in which qualitative analysis differs from quantitative.

In this chapter, we present and illustrate the features that most qualitative analyses share. There is no one correct way to analyze textual data. To quote Michael Quinn Patton (2002:432), "Qualitative analysis transforms data into findings. No formula exists for that transformation. Guidance, yes. But no recipe. Direction can and will be offered, but the final destination remains unique for each inquirer, known only when—and if—arrived at."

We first discuss different types of qualitative analyses and then describe computer programs for qualitative data analysis. You will see that these increasingly popular programs are blurring the distinctions between quantitative and qualitative approaches to textual analysis.

🔲 WHAT IS DISTINCTIVE ABOUT QUALITATIVE DATA ANALYSIS?

The focus on text—on qualitative data rather than on numbers—is the most important feature of **qualitative data analysis**. The "text" that qualitative researchers analyze is most often transcripts of interviews or notes from participant observation sessions, but the term can also refer to pictures or other images that the researcher examines.

Qualitative data analysis: Techniques used to search and code textual, aural, and pictorial data and to explore relationships among the resulting categories

---

What can one learn from a text? There are two kinds of answers to this question. Some researchers view textual analysis as a way to understand what participants "really" thought or felt or did in some situation or at some point in time. The text becomes a way to get "behind the numbers" that are recorded in a quantitative analysis to see the richness of real social experience. In this approach, interviews or field studies can, for instance, illuminate what survey respondents really meant by their answers.

Other qualitative researchers, however, have adopted a "hermeneutic" perspective on texts, viewing interpretations as never totally true or false. The text has many possible interpretations (Patton, 2002:114). The meaning of a text, then, is negotiated among a community of interpreters, and to the extent that some agreement is reached about meaning at a particular time and place, that meaning can only be based on consensual community validation. From the hermeneutic perspective, a researcher is constructing a "reality" with his or her interpretations of a text provided by the subjects of research; other researchers with different backgrounds could come to markedly different conclusions.

Qualitative and quantitative data analyses, then, differ in the priority given to the views of the subjects of the research versus those of the researcher. Qualitative data analysts seek to capture the setting or people who produced this text on their own terms rather than in terms of predefined (by researchers) measures and hypotheses. So qualitative data analysis tends typically to be inductive—the analyst identifies important categories in the data, as well as patterns and relationships, through a process of discovery. There are often no predefined measures or hypotheses. Anthropologists term this an **emic focus**, which means representing the setting in terms of the participants, rather than an **etic focus**, in which the setting and its participants are represented in terms that the researcher brings to the study.

Emic focus: Representing a setting with the participants' terms

Etic focus: Representing a setting with the researcher's terms

---

Good qualitative data analyses focus on the interrelated aspects of the setting or group, or person, under investigation—the case—rather than breaking the whole up into separate parts. The whole is always understood to be greater than the sum of its parts, so the social context of events, thoughts, and actions becomes essential for interpretation. Within this framework, it doesn't really make sense to focus on two variables out of an interacting set of influences and test the relationship between just those two.

Qualitative data analysis is an iterative and reflexive process that begins as data are being collected rather than after data collection has ceased (Stake, 1995). Next to his or her field notes or interview transcripts, the qualitative analyst jots down ideas about the meaning of the text and how it might relate to other issues. This process of reading through the data and interpreting it continues throughout the project. When it appears that additional concepts need to be investigated or new relationships explored, the analyst adjusts the data collection. This process is termed **progressive focusing** (Parlett & Hamilton, 1976).

We emphasize placing an interpreter in the field to observe the workings of the case, one who records objectively what is happening but simultaneously examines its meaning and redirects observation to refine or substantiate those meanings. Initial research questions may be modified or even replaced in mid-study by the case researcher. The aim is to thoroughly understand [the case]. If early questions are not working, if new issues become apparent, the design is changed. (Stake, 1995:9)

Progressive focusing: The process by which a qualitative analyst interacts with the data and gradually refines his or her focus

---

Elijah Anderson (2003:235–236) describes the progressive focusing process in his memoir about his study of Jelly's Bar:

I also wrote conceptual memos to myself to help me sort out my findings. Usually not more than a page long, they represented theoretical insights that emerged from my engagement with the data in my field notes. As I gained tenable hypotheses and propositions, I began to listen and observe selectively, focusing in on those events that I thought might bring me alive to my research interests and concerns. This method of dealing with the information I was receiving amounted to a kind of dialogue with the data, sifting out ideas, weighing new notions against the reality with which I [was] faced there on the streets and back at my desk.

Following a few guidelines will help when a researcher starts analyzing qualitative data (Miller & Crabtree, 1999:142–143):

- Know yourself—your biases and preconceptions.
- Know your question.
- Seek creative abundance. Consult others and keep looking for alternative interpretations.
- Be flexible.
- Exhaust the data. Try to account for all the data in the texts, then publicly acknowledge the unexplained and remember the next principle.
- Celebrate anomalies. They are the windows to insight.
- Get critical feedback. The solo analyst is a great danger to self and others.
- Be explicit. Share the details with yourself, your team members, and your audiences.

Qualitative Data Analysis as an Art

If you miss the certainty of predefined measures and deductively derived hypotheses, you are beginning to understand the difference between quantitative and qualitative data analyses. Qualitative data analysis is even described by some as involving as much "art" as science—as a "dance." In the words of William Miller and Benjamin Crabtree (1999:138–139),

Interpretation is a complex and dynamic craft, with as much creative artistry as technical exactitude, and it requires an abundance of patient plodding, fortitude, and discipline. There are many changing rhythms; multiple steps; moments of jubilation, revelation, and exasperation. . . . The dance of interpretation is a dance for two, but those two are often multiple and frequently changing, and there is always an audience, even if it is not always visible. Two dancers are the interpreters and the texts.

The "dance" of qualitative data analysis captures the alternation between immersion in the text to identify meanings and editing the text to create categories and codes. The process involves three steps in reading the text:

1. When the researcher reads the text *literally,* he or she is focused on its literal content and form; the text "leads" the dance.

2. Then the researcher reads the text *reflexively*, focusing on how his or her own orientation shapes interpretations and focus. Now, the researcher leads the dance.

3. Finally, the researcher reads the text *interpretively*; the researcher tries to construct his or her own interpretation of what the text means.

In this artful way, analyzing text involves both inductive and deductive processes: The researcher generates concepts and linkages between them based on reading the text and also checks the text to see whether his or her concepts and interpretations are reflected in it.

Qualitative Compared to Quantitative Data Analysis

With these points in mind, let's review the differences of the logic behind qualitative versus quantitative analysis (Denzin & Lincoln, 2000:8–10; Patton, 2002:13–14):

- A focus on meanings rather than on quantifiable phenomena
- Collection of much data on a few cases rather than little data on many cases
- Study in depth and detail, without predetermined categories or directions, rather than emphasis on analyses and categories determined in advance
- Conception of the researcher as an "instrument" rather than as the designer of objective instruments to measure particular variables
- Sensitivity to context, rather than seeking universal generalizations
- Attention to the impact of the researcher's and others' values on the course of the analysis, rather than presuming the possibility of value-free inquiry
- A goal of rich descriptions of the world rather than measurement of specific variables

Of course, even the most qualitative textual data can also be transposed to quantitative data through a process of categorization and counting. Some qualitative analysts also share with quantitative researchers a positivist goal of describing the world as it "really" is, but others have adopted a postmodern "hermeneutic" goal of trying to understand how different people see and make sense of the world, without believing that there is one uniquely correct description.

▣ WHAT TECHNIQUES DO QUALITATIVE DATA ANALYSTS USE?

Most approaches to qualitative data analysis take five steps:

1. Documentation of the data and data collection

2. Conceptualization and coding

3. Examining relationships to show how one concept may influence another

4. Authenticating conclusions by evaluating alternative explanations, disconfirming evidence, and searching for negative cases

5. Reflexivity

The analysis of qualitative research notes begins in the field at the time of observation and/or interviewing, as the researcher identifies problems and concepts that appear likely to help in understanding the situation. Simply reading the notes or transcripts is an important step in the analytic process. Researchers should make frequent notes in the margins to identify important statements and to propose ways of coding the data: "husband/wife conflict," perhaps, or "tension reduction strategy."

An interim stage may consist of listing the concepts developed in the notes and perhaps diagramming the relationships among concepts (Maxwell, 1996:78–81). In large projects, regular team meetings are an important part of this process. In her study of neighborhood police officers, Susan Miller's (1999:233) research team met to go over their field notes and to resolve points of confusion, as well as to talk with other skilled researchers who helped to identify emerging concepts:

> The fieldwork team met weekly to talk about situations that were unclear and to troubleshoot any problems. We also made use of peer-debriefing techniques. Here, multiple colleagues, who were familiar with qualitative data analysis but not involved in our research, participated in preliminary analysis of our findings.

The back-and-forth of refining concepts usually continues throughout the entire qualitative research project.

Let's examine each of the steps of qualitative analysis in more detail.

Documentation

The data for a qualitative study most often are notes jotted down in the field or during an interview or text transcribed from audiotapes. "The basic data are these observations and conversations, the actual words of people reproduced to the best of my ability from the field notes" (Diamond, 1992:7). What to do with all this material? As mentioned in Chapter 9, many novice researchers have become overwhelmed by the quantity of information, and their research projects have ground to a halt as a result.

Analysis is less daunting, however, if the researcher maintains a disciplined transcription schedule:

> Usually, I wrote these notes immediately after spending time in the setting or the next day. Through the exercise of writing up my field notes, with attention to "who" the speakers and actors were, I became aware of the nature of certain social relationships and their positional arrangements within the peer group. (Anderson, 2003:235)

You can see Anderson's analysis already emerging from the simple process of taking notes.

The first formal analytical step is documentation. The various contacts, interviews, written documents, and notes all need to be saved and catalogued in some fashion. Documentation is critical to qualitative research for several reasons: It is essential for keeping track of what will be a rapidly growing volume of notes, tapes, and documents; it provides a way of developing an outline for the analytic process; and it encourages ongoing conceptualizing and strategizing about the text.

Miles and Huberman (1994:53) provide a good example of a contact summary form that was used to keep track of observational sessions in a qualitative study of a new school curriculum (Exhibit 10.1).

EXHIBIT 10.1	**Example of a Contact Summary Form**

Contact type: Site: Tindale

Visit   X   Contact date: 11/28-29/79

Phone   Today's date: 12/28/79

       (with whom)   Written by: BLT

1. What were the main issues or themes that struck you in this contact?

    Interplay between highly prescriptive, "teacher-proof" curriculum that is top-down imposed and the actual writing of the curriculum by the teachers themselves.

    Split between the "watchdogs" (administrators) and the "house masters" (dept. chairs & teachers) vis a vis job foci.

    District curric, coord'r as decision maker re school's acceptance of research relationship.

2. Summarize the information you got (or failed to get) on each of the target questions you had for this contact.

Question	Information
History of dev. of innov'n	Conceptualized by Curric., Coord'r, English Chairman & Assoc. Chairman; written by teachers in summer; revised by teachers following summer with field testing data
School's org'l structure	Principal & admin'rs responsible for discipline; dept chairs are educ'l leaders
Demographics	Racial conflicts in late 60's; 60% black stud. pop.; heavy emphasis on discipline & on keeping out non-district students slipping in from Chicago
Teachers' response to innov'n	Rigid, structured, etc. at first; now, they say they like it/NEEDS EXPLORATION
Research access	Very good; only restriction: teachers not required to cooperate

3. Anything else that struck you as salient, interesting, illuminating or important in this contact?
    Thoroughness of the innov'n's development and training.

    Its embeddedness in the district's curriculum, as planned and executed by the district curriculum coordinator.

    The initial resistance to its high prescriptiveness (as reported by users) as contrasted with their current acceptance and approval of it (again, as reported by users).

4. What new (or remaining) target questions do you have in considering the next contact with this site?

    How do users really perceive the innov'n? If they do indeed embrace it, what accounts for the change from early resistance?

    Nature and amount of networking among users of innov'n.

    Information on "stubborn" math teachers whose ideas weren't heard initially – who are they? Situation particulars? Resolution?

    Follow-up on English teacher Reilly's "fall from the chairmanship."

    Follow a team through a day of rotation, planning, etc.

    CONCERN: The consequences of eating school cafeteria food two days per week for the next four or five months . . .

    Stop

Conceptualization, Coding, and Categorizing

Identifying and refining important concepts is a key part of the iterative process of qualitative research. Sometimes conceptualization begins with a simple observation that is interpreted directly, "pulled apart," and then put back together more meaningfully. Robert Stake provides an example (1995:74):

> When Adam ran a pushbroom into the feet of the children nearby, I jumped to conclusions about his interactions with other children: aggressive, teasing, arresting. Of course, just a few minutes earlier I had seen him block the children climbing the steps in a similar moment of smiling bombast. So I was aggregating, and testing my unrealized hypotheses about what kind of kid he was, not postponing my interpreting. . . . My disposition was to keep my eyes on him.

The focus in this conceptualization "on the fly" is to provide a detailed description of what was observed and a sense of why it was important.

More often, analytic insights are tested against new observations; the initial statement of problems and concepts is refined; and the researcher then collects more data, interacts with it again, and the process continues. Elijah Anderson (2003:18–19) recounts how his conceptualization of social stratification at Jelly's Bar developed over a long period of time:

> I could see the social pyramid, how certain guys would group themselves and say in effect, "I'm here and you're there." I made sense of these crowds [initially] as the "respectables," the "non-respectables," and the "near-respectables." . . . Inside, such non-respectables might sit on the crates, but if a respectable came along and wanted to sit there, the lower status person would have to move.

But this initial conceptualization changed with experience as Anderson (2003:28) realized that the participants themselves used other terms to differentiate social status: "winehead," "hoodlum," and "regular." What did they mean by these terms? "The 'regulars' basically valued 'decency.' They associated decency with conventionality but also with 'working for a living,' or having a 'visible means of support'" (29). In this way, Anderson progressively refined his concept as he gained experience in the setting.

Howard S. Becker (1958:658) provides another excellent illustration of this iterative process of conceptualization in his study of medical students:

> When we first heard medical students apply the term "crock" to patients, we made an effort to learn precisely what they meant by it. We found, through interviewing students about cases both they and the observer had seen, that the term referred in a derogatory way to patients with many subjective symptoms but no discernible physical pathology. Subsequent observations indicated that this usage was a regular feature of student behavior and thus that we should attempt to incorporate this fact into our model of student-patient behavior. The derogatory character of the term suggested in particular

that we investigate the reasons students disliked these patients. We found that this dislike was related to what we discovered to be the students' perspective on medical school: the view that they were in school to get experience in recognizing and treating those common diseases most likely to be encountered in general practice. "Crocks," presumably having no disease, could furnish no such experience. We were thus led to specify connections between the student-patient relationship and the student's view of the purpose of his professional education. Questions concerning the genesis of this perspective led to discoveries about the organization of the student body and communication among students, phenomena which we had been assigning to another [segment of the larger theoretical model being developed]. Since "crocks" were also disliked because they gave the student no opportunity to assume medical responsibility, we were able to connect this aspect of the student-patient relationship with still another tentative model of the value system and hierarchical organization of the school, in which medical responsibility plays an important role.

In this excerpt, the researcher was first alerted to a concept by observations in the field, then refined his understanding of this concept by investigating its meaning. By observing the concept's frequency of use, he came to realize its importance. Finally, he incorporated the concept into an explanatory model of student-patient relationships.

A well-designed chart, or **matrix**, can facilitate the coding and categorization process. Exhibit 10.2 shows an example of a coding form designed by Miles and Huberman (1994:93–95) to represent the extent to which teachers and teachers' aides ("users") and administrators at a school gave evidence of various supporting conditions that indicated preparedness for a new reading program. The matrix condenses data into simple categories, reflects further analysis of the data to identify "degree" of support, and provides a multidimensional summary that will facilitate subsequent, more intensive analysis. Direct quotes still impart some of the flavor of the original text.

Matrix: A chart used to condense qualitative data into simple categories and provide a multidimensional summary that will facilitate subsequent, more intensive analysis

---

Examining Relationships and Displaying Data

Examining relationships is the centerpiece of the analytic process, because it allows the researcher to move from simple description of the people and settings to explanations of why things happened as they did with those people in that setting. A matrix can show how different concepts are related or, perhaps, what causes are linked with what effects.

In Exhibit 10.3, a matrix relates stakeholders' stake in a new program with the researcher's estimate of their attitude toward the program. Each cell of the matrix was to be filled in with a summary of an illustrative case study. In other matrix analyses, quotes might be included in the cells to represent the opinions of these different stakeholders, or the

EXHIBIT 10.2	Example of Checklist Matrix

Presence of Supporting Conditions

Condition	For Users	For Administrators
Commitment	*Strong*—"wanted to make it work."	*Weak* at building level. Prime movers in central office committed; others not.
Understanding	*Basic* ("felt I could do it, but I just wasn't sure how") for teacher. *Absent* for aide ("didn't understand how we were going to get all this.")	*Absent* at building level and among staff. *Basic* for 2 prime movers ("got all the help we needed from developer"). *Absent* for other central office staff.
Materials	*Inadequate*: ordered late, puzzling ("different from anything I ever used"), discarded.	N.A.
Front-end training	*Sketchy* for teacher ("it all happened so quickly"); no demo class. *None* for aide: ("totally unprepared. I had to learn along with the children")	Prime movers in central office had training at developer site; none for others.
Skills	*Weak-adequate* for teacher. *None* for aide.	One prime mover (Robeson) skilled in substance; others unskilled.
Ongoing inservice	*None*, except for monthly committee meeting; no substitute funds.	*None*
Planning, coordination time	*None*: both users on other tasks during day; lab tightly scheduled, no free time.	*None*
Provisions for debugging	*None* systematized; spontaneous work done by users during summer.	*None*
School admin. support	*Adequate*	N.A.
Central admin. support	*Very Strong* on part of prime movers.	Building admin. only acting on basis of central office commitment.
Relevant prior experience	*Strong* and useful in both cases: had done individualized instruction, worked with low achievers. But [the] aide [had] no diagnostic experience.	*Present* and useful in central office, esp. Robeson (specialist).

number of cases of each type might appear in the cells. The possibilities are almost endless. Keeping this approach in mind will generate many fruitful ideas for structuring a qualitative data analysis.

| EXHIBIT 10.3 | **Coding Form for Relationships: Stakeholders' Stakes** |

| *Estimate of Various Stakeholders' Inclination Toward the Program* | | |
How high are the stakes for various primary stakeholders?	Favorable	Neutral or Unknown	Antagonistic
High			
Moderate			
Low			

Note: Construct illustrative case studies for each cell based on fieldwork.

The simple relationships that are identified with a matrix like that shown in Exhibit 10.3 can be examined and then extended to create a more complex causal model. Such a model can represent the multiple relationships among the important explanatory constructs. A great deal of analysis must precede the construction of such a model with careful attention to identification of important variables and the evidence that suggests connections between them. Exhibit 10.4 provides an example from a study of the implementation of a school program.

Authenticating Conclusions

No set standards exist for evaluating the validity or "authenticity" of conclusions in a qualitative study, but the need to consider carefully the evidence and methods on which conclusions are based is just as great as with other types of research. Individual items of information can be assessed in terms of at least three criteria (Becker, 1958):

1. *How credible was the informant?* Were statements made by someone with whom the researcher had a relationship of trust or by someone the researcher had just met? Did the informant have reason to lie? If the statements do not seem to be trustworthy as indicators of actual events, can they at least be used to help understand the informant's perspective?

2. *Were statements made in response to the researcher's questions, or were they spontaneous?* Spontaneous statements are more likely to indicate what would have been said had the researcher not been present.

3. *How does the presence or absence of the researcher or the researcher's informant influence the actions and statements of other group members?* Reactivity to being observed can never be ruled out as a possible explanation for some directly observed

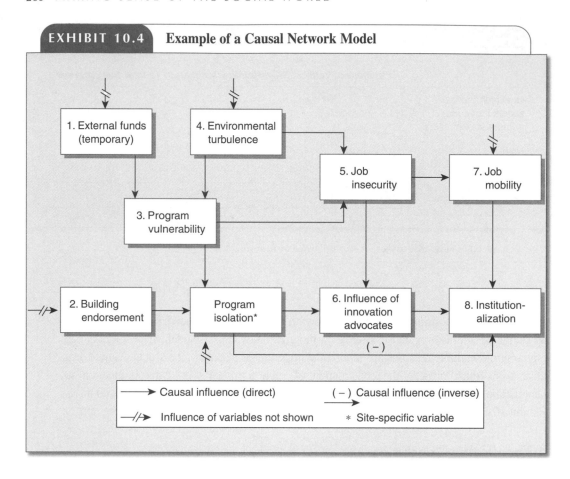

EXHIBIT 10.4 **Example of a Causal Network Model**

1. External funds (temporary)

4. Environmental turbulence

5. Job insecurity

7. Job mobility

3. Program vulnerability

2. Building endorsement

Program isolation*

6. Influence of innovation advocates

8. Institution-alization

(–)

—→ Causal influence (direct)   (–) Causal influence (inverse)

—//→ Influence of variables not shown   * Site-specific variable

social phenomenon. However, if the researcher carefully compares what the informant says goes on when the researcher is not present, what the researcher observes directly, and what other group members say about their normal practices, the extent of reactivity can be assessed to some extent.

A qualitative researcher's conclusions should also be judged by their ability to explain credibly some aspect of social life. Explanations should capture group members' **tacit knowledge** of the social processes that were observed, not just their verbal statements about these processes. Tacit knowledge—"the largely unarticulated, contextual understanding that is often manifested in nods, silences, humor, and naughty nuances"—is reflected in participants' actions as well as their words and in what they fail to state but nonetheless feel deeply and even take for granted (Altheide & Johnson, 1994:492–493). These features are evident in Whyte's (1955:255–257) analysis of Cornerville social patterns:

The corner-gang structure arises out of the habitual association of the members over a long period of time. The nuclei of most gangs can be traced back to early boyhood. . . . Home plays a very small role in the group activities of the corner boy.

. . . The life of the corner boy proceeds along regular and narrowly circumscribed channels. . . . Out of [social interaction within the group] arises a system of mutual obligations which is fundamental to group cohesion. . . . The code of the corner boy requires him to help his friends when he can and to refrain from doing anything to harm them. When life in the group runs smoothly, the obligations binding members to one another are not explicitly recognized.

Tacit knowledge: In field research, a credible sense of understanding of social processes that reflects the researcher's awareness of participants' actions, as well as their words, and of what they fail to state, feel deeply, and take for granted

---

Comparing conclusions from a qualitative research project to those obtained by other researchers conducting similar projects can also increase confidence in their authenticity. Miller's 1999 study of neighborhood police officers (NPOs) found striking parallels in the ways they defined their masculinity to processes reported in research about males in nursing and other traditionally female jobs (as cited in Bachman & Schutt, 2007:307):

In part, male NPOs construct an exaggerated masculinity so that they are not seen as feminine as they carry out the social-work functions of policing. Related to this is the almost defiant expression of heterosexuality, so that the men's sexual orientation can never truly be doubted even if their gender roles are contested. Male patrol officers' language—such as their use of terms like "pansy police" to connote neighborhood police officers—served to affirm their own heterosexuality. . . . In addition, the male officers, but not the women, deliberately wove their heterosexual status into conversations, explicitly mentioning their female domestic partner or spouse and their children. This finding is consistent with research conducted in the occupational field. The studies reveal that men in female-dominated occupations, such as teachers, librarians, and pediatricians, over-reference their heterosexual status to ensure that others will not think they are gay.

Reflexivity

Confidence in the conclusions from a field research study is also strengthened by an honest and informative account about how the researcher interacted with subjects in the field, what problems he or she encountered, and how these problems were or were not resolved. Such a "natural history" of the development of the evidence enables others to evaluate the findings. Such an account is important first and foremost because of the evolving and variable nature of field research: To an important extent, the researcher "makes up" the method in the context of a particular investigation rather than applying standard procedures that are specified before the investigation begins.

Barrie Thorne (1993:8–9) provides a good example of this final element of the analysis:

> Many of my observations concern the workings of gender categories in social life. For example, I trace the evocation of gender in the organization of everyday interactions, and the shift from boys and girls as loose aggregations to "the boys" and "the girls" as self-aware, gender-based groups. In writing about these processes, I discovered that different angles of vision lurk within seemingly simple choices of language. How, for example, should one describe a group of children? A phrase like "six girls and three boys were chasing by the tires" already assumes the relevance of gender. An alternative description of the same event—"nine fourth-graders were chasing by the tires"—emphasizes age and downplays gender. Although I found no tidy solutions, I have tried to be thoughtful about such choices. . . . After several months of observing at Oceanside, I realized that my field notes were peppered with the words "child" and "children," but that the children themselves rarely used the term. "What do they call themselves?" I badgered in an entry in my field notes. The answer it turned out, is that children use the same practices as adults. They refer to one another by using given names ("Sally," "Jack") or language specific to a given context ("that guy on first base"). They rarely have occasion to use age-generic terms. But when pressed to locate themselves in an age-based way, my informants used "kids" rather than "children."

Qualitative data analysts, more often than quantitative researchers, display real sensitivity to how a social situation or process is interpreted from a particular background and set of values and not simply based on the situation itself (Altheide & Johnson, 1994). Researchers are only human, after all, and must rely on their own senses and process all information through their own minds. By reporting how and why they think they did what they did, they can help others determine whether, or how, the researchers' perspectives influenced their conclusions.

Elijah Anderson's (2003) memoir about the Jelly's Bar research illustrates the type of "tracks" that an ethnographer makes, as well as how he or she can describe those tracks. He acknowledges that his tracks began as a child (1–2):

> While growing up in the segregated black community of South Bend, from an early age, I was curious about the goings on in the neighborhood, but particularly streets, and more particularly, the corner taverns that my uncles and my dad would go to hang out and drink in. . . . Hence, my selection of Jelly's as a field setting was a matter of my background, intuition, reason, and with a little bit of luck.

After starting to observe at Jelly's, Anderson's (2003:4) "tracks" led to Herman:

> After spending a couple of weeks at Jelly's, I met Herman and I felt that our meeting marked a big achievement. We would come to know each other well. . . . [He was]

something of an informal leader at Jelly's. . . . We were becoming friends. . . . He seemed to genuinely like me, and he was one person I could feel comfortable with.

Anderson's observations were shaped in part by Herman's perspective, but we also learn here that Anderson maintained some engagement with fellow students. This contact outside the bar helped to shape his analysis: "By relating my experiences to my fellow students, I began to develop a coherent perspective or a 'story' of the place which complemented the accounts that I had detailed in my accumulating field notes" (2003:6).

So Anderson's analysis came in part from the way in which he "played his role" as a researcher and participant, not just from the setting itself.

⬚ WHAT ARE SOME ALTERNATIVES IN QUALITATIVE DATA ANALYSIS?

The qualitative data analyst can choose from many interesting alternative approaches. Of course, the research question should determine the approach, but a researcher's preferences will also inevitably play a role as well. The alternative approaches we present here (ethnography, narrative analysis, conversation analysis, and grounded theory) will give you a good sense of the possibilities (Patton, 2002).

Ethnography

Ethnography is the study of a culture or cultures that some group of people share (Van Maanen, 1995:4). As a method, it usually refers to participant observation by a single investigator who immerses himself or herself in the group for a long period of time (often 1 or more years). Ethnographic research can also be termed "naturalistic," because it seeks to describe and understand the natural social world as it really is, in all its richness and detail. As you learned in Chapter 9, anthropological field research has traditionally been ethnographic, and much sociological fieldwork shares these same characteristics. But there are no particular methodological techniques associated with ethnography other than just "being there." The analytic process relies on the thoroughness and insight of the researcher to "tell us like it is" in the setting, as he or she experienced it.

Ethnography: The study and systematic recording of human cultures

---

Code of the Street, Elijah Anderson's (2000:11) award-winning study of Philadelphia's inner city, captures the flavor of this approach:

My primary aim in this work is to render ethnographically the social and cultural dynamics of the interpersonal violence that is currently undermining the quality of life of too many urban neighborhoods. . . . How do the people of the setting perceive their situation? What assumptions do they bring to their decision making?

Anderson's methods are described in the book's preface: participant observation, including direct observation and in-depth interviews; impressionistic materials drawn from various social settings around the city; and interviews with a wide variety of people. Like most traditional ethnographers, Anderson (2000:11) describes his concern with being "as objective as possible" and using his training, as other ethnographers do, "to look for and to recognize underlying assumptions, their own and those of their subjects, and to try to override the former and uncover the latter."

From analysis of the data obtained in these ways, a rich description emerges of life in the inner city. Although we often do not "hear" the residents speak, we feel the community's pain in Anderson's (2000:138) description of "the aftermath of death":

When a young life is cut down, almost everyone goes into mourning. The first thing that happens is that a crowd gathers about the site of the shooting or the incident. The police then arrive, drawing more of a crowd. Since such a death often occurs close to the victim's house, his mother or his close relatives and friends may be on the scene of the killing. When they arrive, the women and girls often wail and moan, crying out their grief for all to hear, while the young men simply look on, in studied silence. . . . Soon the ambulance arrives.

Anderson (2000:326) uses these descriptions as a foundation on which he develops the key concepts in his analysis, such as "code of the street":

The "code of the street" is not the goal or product of any individual's actions but is the fabric of everyday life, a vivid and pressing milieu within which all local residents must shape their personal routines, income strategies, and orientations to schooling, as well as their mating, parenting, and neighbor relations.

Anderson's (2003) report on his Jelly's Bar study illustrates how an ethnographic analysis deepened as he became more socially integrated into the Jelly's Bar group. He thus became more successful at "blending the local knowledge one has learned with what we already know sociologically about such settings" (39).

I engaged the denizens of the corner and wrote detailed field notes about my experiences, and from time to time looked for patterns and relationships in my notes. In this way, an understanding of the setting came to me in time, especially as I participated more fully in the life of the corner and wrote my field notes about my experiences; as my notes accumulated, and as I reviewed them occasionally and supplemented them with conceptual memos to myself, their meanings became more clear, while even more questions emerged. (15)

This rich ethnographic tradition is being abandoned by some qualitative data analysts, however. Many doubt that social scientists can perceive the social world objectively or receive impressions from people that are unaffected by their being studied (Van Maanen,

2002). As a result, alternative techniques and approaches to qualitative data analysis have proliferated. The next sections introduce several of these alternative approaches.

Ethnomethodology

Ethnomethodology studies the way that participants construct the social world in which they live—how they "create reality"—rather than trying to describe the social world objectively. In fact, ethnomethodologists do not necessarily believe that we can find an objective reality; instead, how participants come to create and sustain a sense of "reality" is the focus of study. In the words of Jaber F. Gubrium and James A. Holstein (1997:41), in ethnomethodology, as compared to the naturalistic orientation of ethnography,

> The focus shifts from the scenic features of everyday life onto the ways through which the world comes to be experienced as real, concrete, factual, and "out there." An interest in members' methods of constituting their worlds supersedes the naturalistic project of describing members' worlds as they know them.

Unlike the ethnographic analyst, who seeks to describe the social world as the participants see it, the ethnomethodological analyst seeks to maintain some distance from that world. The ethnomethodologist views a "code" of conduct, like that described by Elijah Anderson (2003), not as a description of a real normative force that constrains social action but as the way that people in the setting create a sense of order and social structure (Gubrium & Holstein, 1997:44–45). The ethnomethodologist focuses on how reality is *constructed,* not on what it *is.*

> *Ethnomethodology:* A qualitative research method focused on the way that participants in a social setting create and sustain a sense of reality

Narrative Analysis

Narrative "displays the goals and intentions of human actors; it makes individuals, cultures, societies, and historical epochs comprehensible as wholes" (Richardson, 1995:200). **Narrative analysis** focuses on "the story itself" and seeks to preserve the integrity of personal biographies or a series of events that cannot adequately be understood in terms of their discrete elements (Riessman, 2002:218). The coding for a narrative analysis is typically of the narratives as a whole rather than of the different elements within them. The coding strategy revolves around reading the stories and classifying them into general patterns.

> *Narrative analysis:* A form of qualitative analysis in which the analyst focuses on how respondents impose order on the flow of experience in their lives and so make sense of events and actions in which they have participated

For example, Calvin Morrill and his colleagues (2000:534) read through 254 conflict narratives written by ninth graders (mentioned at the beginning of this chapter) and found four different types of stories:

1. *Action tales,* in which the author represents himself or herself and others as acting within the parameters of taken-for-granted assumptions about what is expected for particular roles among peers

2. *Expressive tales,* in which the author focuses on strong, negative emotional responses to someone who has wronged him or her

3. *Moral tales,* in which the author recounts explicit norms that shaped his or her behavior in the story and influenced the behavior of others

4. *Rational tales,* in which the author represents himself or herself as a rational decision maker navigating through the events of the story

Morrill et al. (2000:534–535) also classified the stories along four stylistic dimensions: plot structure (such as whether the story unfolds sequentially), dramatic tension (how the central conflict is represented), dramatic resolution (how the central conflict is resolved), and predominant outcomes (how the story ends). Coding reliability was checked through a discussion by the two primary coders, who found that their classifications agreed for a large percentage of the stories.

The excerpt that begins this chapter exemplifies what Morrill et al. (2000:536) termed an "action tale." Such tales

unfold in matter-of-fact tones kindled by dramatic tensions that begin with a disruption of the quotidian order of everyday routines. A shove, a bump, a look . . . triggers a response. . . . Authors of action tales typically organize their plots as linear streams of events as they move briskly through the story's scenes. . . . This story's dramatic tension finally resolves through physical fighting, but . . . only after an attempted conciliation.

You can contrast that "action tale" with the following narrative, which Morrill et al. (2000:545–546) classify as a "moral tale," in which the student authors "explicitly tell about their moral reasoning, often referring to how normative commitments shape their decision making":

I . . . got into a fight because I wasn't allowed into the basketball game. I was being harassed by the captains that wouldn't pick me and also many of the players. The same type of things had happened almost every day where they called me bad words so I decided to teach the ring leader a lesson. I've never been in a fight before but I realized that sometimes you have to make a stand against the people that constantly hurt you, especially emotionally. I hit him in the face a couple of times and I got respect I finally deserved.

Morrill et al. (2000:553) summarize their classification of the youth narratives in a simple table that highlights the frequency of each type of narrative and the characteristics associated with each of them (Exhibit 10.5). How does such an analysis contribute to our understanding of youth violence? Morrill et al. first emphasize that their narratives "suggest that consciousness of conflict among youths—like that among adults—is not a singular entity but comprises a rich and diverse range of perspectives" (551).

Theorizing inductively, Morrill et al. (2000:553–554) then attempt to explain why action tales were much more common than the more adult-oriented normative, rational, or emotionally expressive tales. They say that one possibility is to be found in Gilligan's theory of moral development, which suggests that younger students are likely to limit themselves to the simpler action tales that "concentrate on taken-for-granted assumptions of their peer and wider cultures, rather than on more self-consciously reflective interpretation and evaluation." More generally, Morrill et al. argue, "We can begin to think of the building blocks of cultures as different narrative styles in which various aspects of reality are accentuated, constituted, or challenged, just as others are deemphasized or silenced" (556).

In this way, Morrill et al.'s narrative analysis allowed an understanding of youth conflict to emerge from the youths' own stories while also informing our understanding of broader social theories and processes.

EXHIBIT 10.5   Summary Comparison of Youth Narratives*

Representation of	Action Tales (N = 144)	Moral Tales (N = 51)	Expressive Tales (N = 35)	Rational Tales (N = 24)
Bases of everyday conflict	disruption of everyday routines & expectations	normative violation	emotional provocation	goal obstruction
Decision making	intuitive	principled stand	sensual	calculative choice
Conflict handling	confrontational	ritualistic	cathartic	deliberative
Physical violence[†]	in 44% (N = 67)	in 27% (N = 16)	in 49% (N = 20)	in 29% (N = 7)
Adults in youth conflict control	invisible or background	sources of rules	agents of repression	institutions of social control

*Total N = 254.

[†]Percentages based on the number of stories in each category.

Conversation Analysis

Conversation analysis is a specific qualitative method for analyzing ordinary conversation. Unlike narrative analysis, it focuses on the sequence and details of conversational interaction rather than on the "stories" that people are telling. Like ethnomethodology, from which it developed, conversation analysis focuses on how reality is constructed rather than on what it "is."

Three premises guide conversation analysis (Gubrium & Holstein, 2000:492):

1. Interaction is sequentially organized, and talk can be analyzed in terms of the process of social interaction rather than in terms of motives or social status.

2. Talk, as a process of social interaction, is contextually oriented—it is both shaped by interaction and creates the social context of that interaction.

3. These processes are involved in all social interaction, so no interactive details are irrelevant to understanding it.

Consider these premises as you read the following dialogue between British researcher Ann Phoenix (2003:235) and a boy she called "Thomas" in her study of notions of masculinity, bullying, and academic performance among 11- to 14-year-old boys in 12 London schools.

Thomas: It's your attitude, but some people are bullied for no reason whatsoever just because other people are jealous of them. . . .

Q: How do they get bullied?

Thomas: There's a boy in our year called James, and he's really clever and he's basically got no friends, and that's really sad because . . . he gets top marks in every test and everyone hates him. I mean, I like him. . . .

Ann Phoenix (2003:235) notes that here,

Thomas dealt with the dilemma that arose from attempting to present himself as both a boy and sympathetic to school achievement. He . . . distanced himself from . . . being one of those who bullies a boy just because they are jealous of his academic attainments . . . constructed for himself the position of being kind and morally responsible.

Note that Thomas was a boy talking to a woman. Do you imagine that his talk would have been quite different if his conversation had been with other boys?

An example of the very detailed data recorded in a formal conversation analysis appears in Exhibit 10.6. It is from David R. Gibson's (2005:1566) study of the effects of superior-subordinate and friendship interaction on the transitions that occur in the course of conversation—in this case, in meetings of managers. Every type of "participation-shift" (P-shift) is recorded and distinguished from every other type. Some shifts involve "turn claiming," in which one person (X) begins to talk after the first person (A) has addressed the group as a whole (0), without being prompted by the first speaker. Some shifts involve "turn receiving," in which the first person (A) addresses the second (B), who then responds. In "turn usurping," by contrast, the second person (X) speaks after the first person (A) has addressed a comment to a third person (B), who is thus prevented from responding. Examining this type of data can help us to see how authority is maintained or challenged in social groups.

| **EXHIBIT 10.6** | **Inventory of P-Shifts With Examples** |

Type of Information to Be Obtained

Information Source*	Collegiality	Goals & Community	Action Expectations	Knowledge Orientation	Base
SETTINGS					
Public places (halls, main offices)	X	X	X	X	X
Teacher's lounge	X	X		X	X
Classrooms		X	X	X	X
Meeting rooms	X		X	X	
Gymnasium or locker room		X			
EVENTS					
Faculty meetings	X		X		X
Lunch hour	X				X
Teaching		X	X	X	X
PEOPLE					
Principal		X	X	X	X
Teachers	X	X	X	X	X
Students		X	X	X	
ARTIFACTS					
Newspapers		X	X		X
Decorations		X			

Note: The initial speaker is denoted A and the initial target B, unless the group is addressed (or the target was ambiguous), in which case the target is 0. Then, the P-shift is summarized in the form (speaker$_1$)(target$_1$)-(speaker$_2$)(target$_2$), with A or B appearing after the hyphen only if the initial speaker or target serves in one of these two positions in the second turn. When the speaker in the second turn is someone other than A or B, X is used; and when the target in the second turn is someone other than A, B, or the group 0, Y is used.

Grounded Theory

Theory development occurs continually in qualitative data analysis (Coffey & Atkinson, 1996:23). The goal of many qualitative researchers is to create **grounded theory**—that is, to build up inductively a systematic theory that is "grounded" in, or based on, the observations. The observations are summarized into conceptual categories, which are tested directly in the research setting with more observations. Over time, as the conceptual categories are refined and linked, a theory evolves (Glaser & Strauss, 1967; Huberman & Miles, 1994:436).

> *Grounded theory:* Systematic theory developed inductively, based on observations that are summarized into conceptual categories, re-evaluated in the research setting, and gradually refined and linked to other conceptual categories

As observation, interviewing, and reflection continue, researchers refine their definitions of problems and concepts and select indicators. They can then check the frequency and distribution of phenomena: How many people made a particular type of comment? How often did social interaction lead to arguments? Social system models may then be developed, which specify the relationships among different phenomena. These models are modified as researchers gain experience in the setting. For the final analysis, the researchers check their models carefully against their notes and make a concerted attempt to discover negative evidence that might suggest the model is incorrect.

🔲 VISUAL SOCIOLOGY

The analysis of the "text" of social life, then, can be conducted in a variety of ways. But words are not the only form of qualitative data. For about 150 years, people have been recording the social world with photography. This creates the possibility of "observing" the social world through photographs and films and of interpreting the resulting images as a "text." Visual sociology is a method both to learn how others "see" the social world and to create images of it for further study. As with written text, however, the visual sociologist must be sensitive to the way in which a photograph or film "constructs" the reality that it depicts.

An analysis by Eric Margolis (2004) of photographic representations of American Indian boarding schools gives you an idea of the value of analysis of photographs. On the left is a picture taken in 1886 of Chiricahua Apaches who had just arrived at the Carlisle Indian School in Carlisle, Pennsylvania (see Exhibit 10.7). The school was run by a Captain Richard Pratt, who, like many Americans in that period, felt that tribal societies were communistic, indolent, dirty, and ignorant, while Western civilization was industrious and individualistic. So Captain Pratt set out to acculturate American Indians to the dominant culture. The second picture shows the result: the same group of Apaches looking like European, not Native, Americans, dressed in "standard" (per the dominant culture) uniforms with standard haircuts and with more standard posture.

Many other pictures display the same type of transformation. Are these pictures each "worth a thousand words"? They capture the ideology of the school management, but we

EXHIBIT 10.7	Pictures of Chiricahua Apache Children Before and After Starting Carlisle Indian School, Carlisle, Pennsylvania, 1886

can be less certain that they document accurately the "before and after" status of the students. Captain Pratt "consciously used photography to represent the boarding school mission as successful" (Margolis, 2004:79). While he clearly tried to ensure a high degree of conformity, there were accusations that the contrasting images were exaggerated to overemphasize the change (Margolis:78). In these photographs, reality was being constructed, not just depicted.

With the widespread use of cell phone cameras and video recorders, visual sociology will certainly become an increasingly important aspect of qualitative analyses of social settings and the people in them. The result will be richer descriptions of the social world, but remember Darren Newbury's (2005:1) reminder to readers of his journal, *Visual Studies:* "Images cannot be simply taken of the world, but have to be made within it."

▣   HOW CAN COMPUTERS ASSIST QUALITATIVE DATA ANALYSIS?

Computer-assisted qualitative data analysis can dramatically accelerate the techniques used traditionally to analyze such text as notes, documents, or interview transcripts: preparation, coding, analysis, and reporting (Coffey & Atkinson, 1996; Richards & Richards, 1994). Two of the most popular programs can illustrate these steps: HyperRESEARCH and QSR NVivo. (You can link to a trial copy of HyperRESEARCH and tutorials about it on the book's Study Site at **http://www.pineforge.com/mssw3**.)

Computer-assisted qualitative data analysis: Analysis of textual, aural, or pictorial data using a special computer program that facilitates searching and coding text

---

Text preparation begins with typing or scanning text in a word processor or, with NVivo, directly into the program's rich text editor. NVivo will create or import a rich text file (*.rtf). HyperRESEARCH requires that your text be saved as a text file (as "ASCII" in most word processors, or *.txt) before you transfer it into the analysis program. HyperRESEARCH expects your text data to be stored in separate files corresponding to each unique case, such as an interview with one subject.

Coding the text involves categorizing particular text segments. This is the foundation of much qualitative analysis. Either program allows you to assign a code to any segment of text (in NVivo, you drag through the characters to select them; in HyperRESEARCH, you click on the first and last words to select text). You can either make up codes as you go through a document or assign codes that you have already developed to text segments. Exhibits 10.8a and 10.8b show the screens that appear in the two programs at the coding stage, when a particular text segment is being labeled. You can also have the programs "autocode" text by identifying a word or phrase that should always receive the same code, or, in NVivo, by coding each section identified by the style of the rich text document—for example, each question or speaker. (Of course, you should check carefully the results of autocoding.) Both programs also let you examine the coded text "in context"—embedded in its place in the original document.

EXHIBIT 10.8a   **HyperRESEARCH Coding Stage**

HyperRESEARCH™ 1.56

Untitled

CASE NAME: Untitled

✓	Type	Reference	Code Name
✓	TEXT	char 2 to 181 of page 1 of Interview 1	non trad field

Interview 1   <- 1 ->

The year is 2010. I am 40 years old. What is my life like? That's a pretty difficult question to answer. For starters, I am the president of Copley and Mini Advertising Agency. I love my job, probably because I face a new challenge every day. I also like having power, and knowing that many people work below me. All kidding aside, the best part of my job is my six figure salary. Everything is just so expensive, and any extra money helps.

My husband, Michael, also has an excellent job. He works for an engineering company, where he is very happy. With both of our salaries combined we live very comfortably, but not extravagantly. We both set aside portions of our pay every week and put it in an account that will one day pay for our children's college education. I knew what it was like to

EXHIBIT 10.8b NVivo Coding Stage

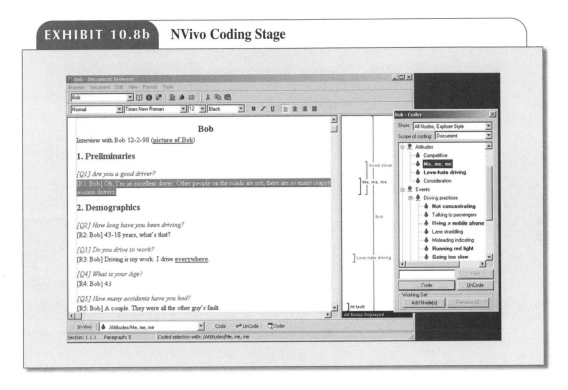

In qualitative data analysis, coding is not a one-time-only or one-code-only procedure. Both HyperRESEARCH and NVivo allow you to be inductive and holistic in your coding: You can revise codes as you go along, assign multiple codes to text segments, and link your own comments ("memos") to text segments. In NVivo you can work "live" with the coded text to alter coding or create new, more subtle categories. You can also place hyperlinks to other documents in the project or any multimedia files outside it.

Analysis focuses on reviewing cases or text segments with similar codes and examining relationships among different codes. You may decide to combine codes into larger concepts. You may specify additional codes to capture more fully the variation among cases. You can test hypotheses about relationships among codes. NVivo allows development of an indexing system to facilitate thinking about the relationships among concepts and the overarching structure of these relationships. It also allows you to draw more free-form models (see Exhibit 10.9). In HyperRESEARCH, you can specify combinations of codes that identify cases that you want to examine.

Reports from both programs can include text to illustrate the cases, codes, and relationships that you specify. You can also generate counts of code frequencies and then import these counts into a statistical program for quantitative analysis. However, the many types of analyses and reports that can be developed with qualitative analysis software do not lessen the need for a careful evaluation of the quality of the data on which conclusions are based.

EXHIBIT 10.9   A Free-Form Model in NVivo

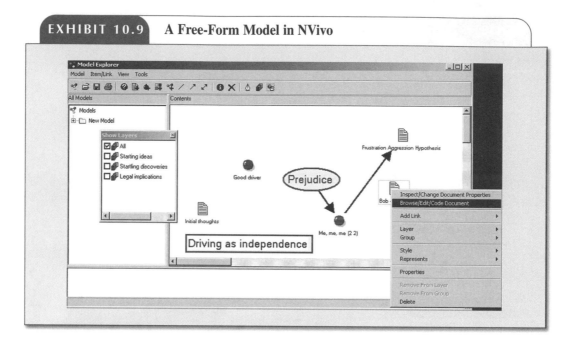

In practice, using these programs is not always as time saving as it may first appear (Bachman & Schutt, 2007:319). Scott Decker and Barrik Van Winkle (1996:53–54) described the difficulty they faced in using a computer program to identify instances of "drug sales":

> The software we used is essentially a text retrieval package. . . . One of the dilemmas faced in the use of such software is whether to employ a coding scheme within the interviews or simply to leave them as unmarked text. We chose the first alternative, embedding conceptual tags at the appropriate points in the text. An example illustrates this process. One of the activities we were concerned with was drug sales. Our first chore (after a thorough reading of all the transcripts) was to use the software to "isolate" all of the transcript sections dealing with drug sales. One way to do this would be to search the transcripts for every instance in which the word "drugs" was used. However, such a strategy would have the disadvantages of providing information of too general a character while often missing important statements about drugs. Searching on the word "drugs" would have produced a file including every time the word was used, whether it was in reference to drug sales, drug use, or drug availability, clearly more information than we were interested [in]. However, such a search would have failed to find all of the slang used to refer to drugs ("boy" for heroin, "Casper" for crack cocaine) as well as the more common descriptions of drugs, especially rock or crack cocaine.

Decker and Van Winkle (1996) solved this problem by parenthetically inserting conceptual tags in the text whenever talk of drug sales was found. This process allowed them to examine all of the statements made by gang members about a single concept (drug sales). As you can imagine, however, this still left the researchers with many pages of transcript material to analyze.

▣ WHAT ETHICAL ISSUES ARISE IN QUALITATIVE DATA ANALYSIS?

The qualitative data analyst is never far from ethical issues and dilemmas. Throughout the analytic process, the analyst must consider how the findings will be used and how participants in the setting will react. Miles and Huberman (1994:204–205) suggest several specific questions that should be kept in mind:

Research integrity and quality. Is my study being conducted carefully, thoughtfully, and correctly in terms of some reasonable set of standards? Real analyses have real consequences, so you owe it to yourself and those you study to adhere strictly to the analysis methods that you believe will produce authentic, valid conclusions.

Ownership of data and conclusions. Who owns my field notes and analyses: I, my organization, my funders? And once my reports are written, who controls their dissemination? Of course, these concerns arise in any social research project, but the intimate involvement of the qualitative researcher with participants in the setting studied makes conflicts of interest between different stakeholders much more difficult to resolve. Working through the issues as they arise is essential.

Use and misuse of results. Do I have an obligation to help my findings be used appropriately? What if they are used harmfully or wrongly? It is prudent to develop understandings early in the project with all major stakeholders that specify what actions will be taken to encourage the appropriate use of project results and to respond to what is considered misuse of these results.

▣ CONCLUSION

The success of qualitative analyses may be difficult to judge, but Norman Denzin (2002:362–363) suggests that the following "interpretive criteria" questions could be asked:

- *Does it illuminate the phenomenon as lived experience?* In other words, do the materials bring the setting alive in terms of the people in that setting?
- *Is it based on thickly contextualized materials?* We should expect **thick descriptions** that encompass the social setting studied.
- *Is it historically and relationally grounded?* There must be a sense of the passage of time between events and the presence of relationships between social actors.
- *Is the research processual and interactional?* The researcher must have described the research process and his or her interactions within the setting.
- *Does it engulf what is known about the phenomenon?* This includes situating the analysis in the context of prior research and acknowledging the researcher's own orientation upon first starting the investigation.

If the answers are yes, a study has achieved much of the promise of qualitative research.

Thick description: A rich description that conveys a sense of what social reality is like from the standpoint of the natural actors in that setting

KEY TERMS

Computer-assisted qualitative data analysis
Emic focus
Ethnography
Ethnomethodology
Etic focus
Grounded theory

Matrix
Narrative analysis
Progressive focusing
Qualitative data analysis
Tacit knowledge
Thick description

HIGHLIGHTS

- Qualitative data analysts are guided by an emic focus of representing persons in the setting on their own terms rather than by an etic focus on the researcher's terms.
- Ethnographers attempt to understand the culture of a group.
- Narrative analysis attempts to understand a life or a series of events as they unfolded in a meaningful progression.
- Grounded theory connotes a general explanation that develops in interaction with the data and is continually tested and refined as data collection continues.
- Special computer software can be used for the analysis of qualitative, textual, and pictorial data. Users can record their notes, categorize observations, specify links between categories, and count occurrences.

STUDENT STUDY SITE

To assist you in completing the Web Exercises, please access the Study Site at **http://www.pineforge.com/mssw3**, where you'll find the Web Exercises with accompanying links. You'll find other useful study materials like self-quizzes and e-flashcards for each chapter, along with a group of carefully selected articles from research journals that illustrate the major concepts and techniques presented in the book.

EXERCISES

Discussing Research

1. List the primary components of qualitative data analysis strategies. Compare and contrast each of these components with those relevant to quantitative data analysis. What are the similarities and differences? What differences do these make?

2. Does qualitative data analysis result in trustworthy results—in findings that achieve the goal of "authenticity"? Why would anyone question its use? What would you reply to the doubters?

3. Narrative analysis provides the "large picture" of how a life or event has unfolded, while conversation analysis focuses on the details of verbal interchange. When is each method most appropriate? How could one method add to the other?

4. Ethnography and grounded theory both refer to aspects of data analysis that are an inherent part of the qualitative approach. What do these approaches have in common? How do they differ? Can you identify elements of these two approaches in this chapter's examples of ethnomethodology, conversation analysis, and narrative analysis?

Finding Research

1. The *Qualitative Report* is an online journal about qualitative research. Inspect the table of contents for a recent issue at http://www.nova.edu/ssss/QR/index.html. Read one of the articles and write a brief article review.

2. Be a qualitative explorer! Go to this list of qualitative research Web sites and see what you can find that enriches your understanding of qualitative research (http://www.qualitativeresearch .uga.edu/QualPage/). Be careful to avoid textual data overload.

Critiquing Research

1. Read the complete text of one of the qualitative studies presented in this chapter and evaluate its analysis and conclusions for authenticity, using the criteria in this chapter.

Doing Research

1. Attend a sports game as an ethnographer. Write up your analysis and circulate it for criticism.

2. Write a narrative in class about your first date, car, college course, or something else you and your classmates agree on. Then collect all the narratives and analyze them in a "committee of the whole." Follow the general procedures discussed in the example of narrative analysis in this chapter.

3. Try out the HyperRESEARCH tutorials that you can link to on the book Study Site. How might qualitative analysis software facilitate the analysis process? Might it might hinder the analysis process in some ways? Explain your answers.

Ethics Questions

1. Pictures are worth a thousand words, so to speak, but is that 1,000 words too many? Should qualitative researchers (like yourself) feel free to take pictures of social interaction or other behaviors anytime, anywhere? What limits should an institutional review board place on researchers' ability to take pictures of others? What if the "after" picture of the Apache children in this chapter (Exhibit 10.7) also included Captain Pratt in a military uniform?

2. Participants in social settings often "forget" that an ethnographer is in their midst, planning to record what they say and do, even when the ethnographer has announced his or her role. New participants may not have heard the announcement, and everyone may simply get used to the ethnographer as if he or she was just "one of us." What efforts should an ethnographer take to keep people informed about his or her work in the setting under study? Consider settings such as a sports team, a political group, and a book group.

CHAPTER 11

Evaluation Research

What Is the History of Evaluation Research?

What Is Evaluation Research?

What Are the Alternatives in Evaluation Designs?

Black Box or Program Theory
Researcher or Stakeholder Orientation
Quantitative or Qualitative Methods
Simple or Complex Outcomes

What Can an Evaluation Study Focus On?

Needs Assessment
Evaluability Assessment
Process Evaluation
Impact Analysis
Efficiency Analysis

Ethical Issues in Evaluation Research

Conclusion

Drug Abuse Resistance Education (D.A.R.E.), as you probably know, is offered in elementary schools across America. For parents worried about drug abuse among youth and for any concerned citizens, the program has immediate appeal. It brings a special police officer into the schools once a week to talk to students about the hazards of drug abuse and to establish a direct link between local law enforcement and young people. You only have to check out bumper stickers or attend a few PTO meetings to learn that it's a popular program. It is one way many local governments have implemented antidrug policies.

And it is appealing. D.A.R.E. seems to improve relations between the schools and law enforcement and to create a positive image of the police in the eyes of students.

> It's a very positive program for kids . . . a way for law enforcement to interact with children in a nonthreatening fashion . . . DARE sponsored a basketball game. The middle school jazz band played. . . . We had families there. . . . DARE officers lead activities at the [middle school]. . . . Kids do woodworking and produce a play. (Taylor, 1999:1, 11)

For some, the positive police-community relationships created by the program are enough to justify its continuation (Birkeland, Murphy-Graham, & Weiss, 2005:248), but most communities are concerned with its value in implementing antidrug policies. Does

D.A.R.E. lessen the use of illicit drugs among D.A.R.E. students? Does it do so while they are enrolled in the program or, more important, after they enter middle or high school? Evaluations of D.A.R.E. using social science methods led to the conclusion that students who participated in D.A.R.E. were no less likely to use illicit drugs than comparable students who did not participate in D.A.R.E. (Ringwalt et al., 1994).

If, like us, you have a child who enjoyed D.A.R.E., or if you were yourself a D.A.R.E. student, this may seem like a depressing way to begin a chapter on evaluation research. Nonetheless, it drives home an important point: To know whether social programs work, or how they work, we have to evaluate them systematically and fairly, whether we personally like the programs or not. And there's actually an optimistic conclusion to this introductory story: Evaluation research can make a difference. A "new" D.A.R.E. program has now been implemented, building in part on the problems identified by early evaluation researchers (Toppo, 2002).

> Gone is the old-style approach to prevention in which an officer stands behind a podium and lectures students in straight rows. . . . New DARE officers are trained as "coaches" to support students using research-based refusal strategies in high-stakes peer-pressure environments. (McConnell, 2006:33)

And so, of course, this approach is now being evaluated, too.

In this chapter, you will read about a variety of social program evaluations, alternative approaches to evaluation, and the different types of evaluation research and review ethical concerns. You should finish the chapter with a much better understanding of how the methods of applied social research can help improve society.

▣ WHAT IS THE HISTORY OF EVALUATION RESEARCH?

Evaluation research is not a method of data collection, like survey research or experiments; nor is it a unique component of research designs, like sampling or measurement. Instead, **evaluation research** is conducted for a distinctive purpose: to investigate social programs (such as substance abuse treatment programs, welfare programs, criminal justice programs, or employment and training programs). For each project, an evaluation researcher must select a research design and method of data collection that are useful for answering the particular research questions posed and appropriate for the particular program investigated.

Evaluation research: Research that describes or identifies the impact of social policies and programs

---

So you can see why we placed this chapter after most of the others in the text. When you review or plan evaluation research, you have to think about the research process as a whole and how different parts of that process can best be combined.

The development of evaluation research as a major enterprise followed on the heels of the expansion of the federal government during the Great Depression and World War II. Large Depression-era government outlays for social programs stimulated interest in monitoring program output, and the military effort in World War II led to some of the necessary review and contracting procedures for sponsoring evaluation research. However, not until the Great Society programs of the 1960s did evaluation begin to be required when new social programs were funded (Rossi & Freeman, 1989:34). The World Bank and International Monetary Fund (IMF) began to require evaluation of the programs they fund in other countries (Dentler, 2002:147). More than 100 contract research and development firms began in the United States between 1965 and 1975, and many federal agencies developed their own research units. The RAND Corporation expanded from its role as a U.S. Air Force planning unit into a major social research firm; SRI International spun off from Stanford University as a private firm; and Abt Associates in Cambridge, Massachusetts, which began in a garage in 1965, grew to employ more than 1,000 employees in five offices in the United States, Canada, and Europe.

With the decline of many Great Society programs in the early 1980s, many such evaluation research firms closed down. But recently, with more calls for government "accountability," the evaluation research enterprise has been growing again. The Community Mental Health Act Amendments of 1975 (Public Law 94–63) required quality assurance (QA) reviews, which often involve evaluation-like activities (Patton, 2002: 147–151). The Government Performance and Results Act of 1993 required some type of evaluation of all government programs (Office of Management and Budget, n.d.). At century's end, the federal government was spending about $200 million annually on evaluating $400 billion in domestic programs, and the 30 major federal agencies had between them 200 distinct evaluation units (Boruch, 1997). Recently, the new Governmental Accounting Standards Board urged that more attention be given to service efforts and accomplishments in standard government fiscal reports (GASB, 2008).

The growth of evaluation research is also reflected in the social science community. The American Evaluation Association was founded in 1986 as a professional organization for evaluation researchers (merging two previous associations) and is the publisher of an evaluation research journal. In 1999, evaluation researchers founded the Campbell Collaboration to publicize and encourage systematic review of evaluation research studies. Their online archive contains 10,449 reports on randomized evaluation studies (Davies, Petrosino, & Chalmers, 1999).

▣ WHAT IS EVALUATION RESEARCH?

Exhibit 11.1 illustrates the process of evaluation research as a simple systems model. First, clients, customers, students, or some other persons or units—cases—enter the program as **inputs.** (Notice that this model regards programs as machines, with clients—people—seen as raw materials to be processed.) Students may begin a new school program, welfare

EXHIBIT 11.1 **A Model of Evaluation**

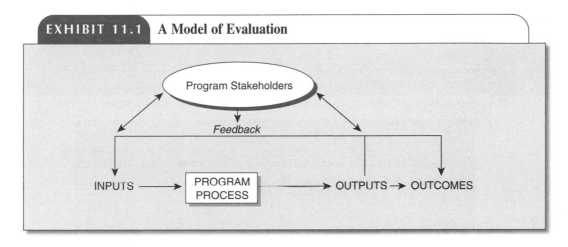

recipients may enroll in a new job-training program, or crime victims may be sent to a victim advocate. Resources and staff required by a program are also program inputs.

Inputs: Resources, raw materials, clients, and staff that go into a program

---

Next, some service or treatment is provided to the cases. This may be attendance in a class, assistance with a health problem, residence in new housing, or receipt of special cash benefits. This process of service delivery—the **program process**—may be simple or complicated, short or long, but it is designed to have some impact on the cases as inputs are consumed and outputs are produced.

Program process: The complete treatment or service delivered by the program

---

Program **outputs** are the direct product of the program's service delivery process. They could include clients served, case managers trained, food parcels delivered, or arrests made. The program outputs may be desirable in themselves, but primarily they indicate that the program is operating.

Outputs: The services delivered or new products produced by the program process

---

Program **outcomes** indicate the impact of the program on the cases that have been processed. Outcomes can range from improved test scores or higher rates of job retention to fewer criminal offenses and lower rates of poverty. There are likely to be multiple outcomes of any social program, some intended and some unintended, some viewed as positive and others viewed as negative.

Outcomes: The impact of the program process on the cases processed

---

Through a **feedback** process, variation in outputs and outcomes can influence the inputs to the program. If not enough clients are being served, recruitment of new clients may increase. If too many negative side effects result from a trial medication, the trials may be limited or terminated. If a program does not lead to improved outcomes, clients may be sent elsewhere.

Feedback: Information about service delivery system outputs, outcomes, or operations that is available to any program inputs

---

Evaluation research itself is really just a systematic approach to feedback; it strengthens the feedback loop through credible analyses of program operations and outcomes. Evaluation research also broadens this loop to include connections to parties outside of the program itself. A funding agency or political authority may mandate the research; outside experts may be brought in to conduct the research; and the evaluation research findings may be released to the public, or at least to funders, in a formal report.

The evaluation process as a whole, and the feedback in particular, can be understood only in relation to the interests and perspectives of program stakeholders. **Stakeholders** are those individuals and groups who have some basis of concern for the program. They might be clients, staff, managers, funders, or the public. The board of a program or agency, the parents or spouses of clients, the foundations that award program grants, the auditors who monitor program spending, the members of Congress—each is a potential program stakeholder, and each has an interest in the outcome of any program evaluation. Some may fund the evaluation, some may provide research data, and some may review—or even approve—the research report (Martin & Kettner, 1996:3). Who the program stakeholders are, and what role they play in the program evaluation, can have tremendous consequences for the research.

Stakeholders: Individuals and groups who have some basis of concern with the program

---

Thus, there are real differences between traditional social science and evaluation research (Posavac & Carey, 1997). Social science is motivated by theoretical concerns and is guided by the standards of research methods without consideration (ideally) for political factors. It examines specific organizations for what, in general, we can learn from them, not for improving that one organization. Practical ramifications, for particular programs, are not usually of any import. For evaluation research, on the other hand, the particular program and its impact are paramount. How the program works also matters—not to advance a theory but to improve the program. Finally, stakeholders of all sorts—not an abstract "scientific community"—have a legitimate role in setting the research agenda and may well intervene, even when they aren't supposed to. But overall, there is no sharp boundary between the two approaches: In their attempt to explain how and why the program has an impact and whether the program is needed, evaluation researchers often bring social theories into their projects—but for immediately practical aims.

回 WHAT ARE THE ALTERNATIVES IN EVALUATION DESIGNS?

Evaluation research tries to learn if, and how, real-world programs produce results. But that simple statement covers a number of important alternatives in research design, including the following:

- *Black box or program theory*—Do we care how the program gets results?
- *Researcher or stakeholders orientation*—Whose goals matter most?
- *Quantitative or qualitative methods*—Which methods provide the best answers?
- *Simple or complex outcomes*—How complicated should the findings be?

Black Box or Program Theory

Most evaluation research tries to determine whether a program has the intended effect. If the effect occurred, the program "worked"; if the effect didn't occur, then, some would say, the program should be abandoned or redesigned. In this simple approach, the process by which a program produces outcomes is often treated as a "black box" in which the "inside" of the program is unknown. The focus of such research is whether cases have changed as a result of their exposure to the program between the time they entered as inputs and when they exited as outputs (Chen, 1990). The assumption is that program evaluation requires only the test of a simple input/output model, like that in Exhibit 11.1. There may be no attempt to "open the black box" of the program process.

But there are good reasons to open the black box and investigate how the process works (or doesn't work). Consider recent research on welfare-to-work programs. The Manpower Demonstration Research Corporation reviewed findings from research on these programs in Florida, Minnesota, and Canada (Lewin, 2001a). In each location, adolescents with parents in a welfare-to-work program were compared to a control group of teenagers whose parents were also on welfare but were *not* enrolled in welfare-to-work. In all three locations, teenagers in the welfare-to-work program families did *worse* in school than those in the control group.

But why did requiring welfare mothers to get jobs hurt their children's schoolwork? Unfortunately, because the researchers had not investigated program process—had not opened the black box—we can't know for sure. Martha Zaslow, an author of the resulting research report, speculated (in Lewin, 2001a:A16) that

> parents in the programs might have less time and energy to monitor their adolescents' behavior once they were employed. . . . Under the stress of working, they might adopt harsher parenting styles . . . The adolescents' assuming more responsibilities at home when parents got jobs was creating too great a burden.

Unfortunately, as Ms. Zaslow (in Lewin, 2001a:A16) admitted, "We don't know exactly what's causing these effects, so it's really hard to say, at this point, what will be the long-term effects on these kids."

If an investigation of program process had been conducted, though, a **program theory** could have been developed. A program theory describes what has been learned about how the program has its effect. When a researcher has sufficient knowledge before the investigation begins, outlining a program theory can help to guide the investigation of program process in the most productive directions. This is termed a **theory-driven evaluation**.

Program theory: A descriptive or prescriptive model of how a program operates and produces effects

Theory-driven evaluation: A program evaluation guided by a theory that specifies the process by which the program has an effect

---

A program theory specifies how the program is expected to operate and identifies which program elements are operational (Chen, 1990:32). In addition, a program theory specifies how a program is to produce its effects, thus improving the understanding of the relationship between the independent variable (the program) and the dependent variable (the outcome or outcomes). For example, Exhibit 11.2 illustrates the theory for an alcoholism treatment program. It shows that persons entering the program are expected to respond to the combination of motivational interviewing and peer support. A program theory also can decrease the risk of failure when the program is transported to other settings, because it will help to identify the conditions required for the program to have its intended effect.

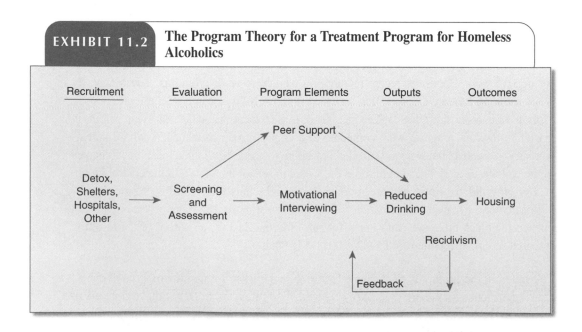

EXHIBIT 11.2 **The Program Theory for a Treatment Program for Homeless Alcoholics**

Program theory can be either descriptive or prescriptive (Chen, 1990). *Descriptive theory* specifies impacts that are generated and how this occurs. It suggests a causal mechanism, including intervening factors and the necessary context for the effects. Descriptive theories are generally empirically based. On the other hand, *prescriptive theory* specifies what *ought* to be done by the program and is not actually tested. Prescriptive theory specifies how to design or implement the treatment, what outcomes should be expected, and how performance should be judged. Comparison of the program's descriptive and prescriptive theories can help to identify implementation difficulties and incorrect understandings that can be fixed (Patton, 2002:162–164).

Researcher or Stakeholder Orientation

Whose prescriptions direct the program? What outcomes it should achieve? Whom it should serve? Most social science assumes that the researcher decides. Research results are usually reported in professional journals or conferences, where scientific standards determine how it is judged. In program evaluation, however, the research question is often set by the program sponsors or a government agency; in consulting projects for businesses, the client—a manager, perhaps, or a division president—decides what question researchers will study. Research findings are reported to these authorities, who most often also specify the outcomes to be investigated. The primary evaluator of evaluation research, then, is the funding agency, not the professional social science community. Evaluation research is research for a client, and its results may directly affect the services, treatments, or even punishments (in the case of prison studies, for example) that program users receive. Who pays the piper, picks the tune.

Should the evaluation researcher insist on designing the project and specifying its goals? Or should he or she accept the suggestions and goals of the funding agency? What role should program staff and clients play? What responsibility does the researcher have to politicians and taxpayers when evaluating government-funded programs?

Various evaluation researchers have answered these questions through different—stakeholders, social science, and integrative—approaches. (Chen, 1990:66–68). **Stakeholder approaches** encourage researchers to be responsive to program stakeholders. Issues for study are to be based on the views of people involved with the program, and reports are to be made to program participants (Stake, 1975). The program theory is developed by the researcher to clarify and develop the key stakeholders' theory of the program (Wholey, 1987). In one stakeholder approach, termed *utilization-focused evaluation,* the evaluator forms a task force of program stakeholders, who help to shape the evaluation project so that they are most likely to use its results (Patton, 2002:171–175). In evaluation research termed *action research* or *participatory research,* program participants are engaged with the researchers as coresearchers and help to design, conduct, and report the research. One research approach, termed *appreciative inquiry,* eliminates the professional researcher altogether in favor of a structured dialogue about needed changes among program participants themselves (Patton:177–185).

Stakeholder approaches (to evaluation): An orientation to evaluation research that expects researchers to be responsive primarily to the people involved with the program

---

Egon Guba and Yvonna Lincoln (1989:11) argue for a stakeholder approach in their book, *Fourth Generation Evaluation:*

The stakeholders and others who may be drawn into the evaluation are welcomed as equal partners in every aspect of design, implementation, interpretation, and resulting action of an evaluation—that is, they are accorded a full measure of political parity and control. . . . determining what questions are to be asked and what information is to be collected on the basis of stakeholder inputs.

Social science approaches, in contrast, emphasize researcher expertise autonomy to develop the most trustworthy, unbiased program evaluation. They assume that "evaluators cannot passively accept the values and views of the other stakeholders" (Chen, 1990:78). Instead, the researcher derives a program theory from information on how the program operates and current social science theory, not from the views of stakeholders. In one somewhat extreme form of this approach, *goal-free evaluation,* researchers do not even permit themselves to learn what goals the program stakeholders have for the program. Instead, the researcher assesses and then compares the needs of participants to a wide array of program outcomes (Scriven, 1972). The goal-free evaluator wants to see the unanticipated outcomes and to remove any biases caused by knowing the program goals in advance.

Social science approaches (to evaluation): An orientation to evaluation research that expects researchers to emphasize the importance of researcher expertise and maintenance of autonomy from program stakeholders

---

Of course, there are disadvantages to both stakeholder and social science approaches to program evaluation. If stakeholders are ignored, researchers may find that participants are uncooperative, that their reports are unused, and that the next project remains unfunded. On the other hand, if social science procedures are neglected, standards of evidence will be compromised, conclusions about program effects will likely be invalid, and results are unlikely to be generalizable to other settings. These equally undesirable possibilities have led to several attempts to develop more integrated approaches to evaluation research.

Integrative approaches attempt to cover issues of concern to both stakeholders and evaluators (Chen & Rossi, 1987:101–102). The emphasis given to either stakeholder or scientific concerns varies with the specific circumstances. Integrative approaches seek to balance responsiveness to stakeholders with objectivity and scientific validity. Evaluators negotiate regularly with key stakeholders during the planning of the research; preliminary findings are reported back to decision makers so they can make improvements; and when the final evaluation is conducted, the research team may operate more autonomously, minimizing intrusions from program stakeholders. Evaluators and clients thus work together.

Integrative approaches (to evaluation): An orientation to evaluation research that expects researchers to respond to the concerns of people involved with the program stakeholders, as well as to the standards and goals of the social scientific community

---

Quantitative or Qualitative Methods

Quantitative and qualitative approaches to evaluation each have their strengths and appropriate uses. Quantitative research, with its clear percentages and numerical scores, allows quick comparisons over time and categories and, thus, is typically used in attempts to identify the effects of a social program. With numbers, you can systematically track change over time or compare outcomes between an experimental and a control group. Did the response times of emergency personnel tend to decrease? Did the students' test scores increase more in the experimental group than in the control group? Did housing retention improve for all subjects or just for those who were not substance abusers? Quantified results also can prevent distraction by the powerful anecdote, forcing you to see what happens in most cases, not just in the dramatic cases; they "force you to face reality," as a friend of ours puts it.

Qualitative methods, on the other hand, can add depth, detail, and nuance; they can clarify the meaning of survey responses and reveal more complex emotions and judgments people may have (Patton, 2002). Perhaps the greatest contribution qualitative methods can make is in investigating program process—finding out what is "inside the black box." Quantitative measures, like staff contact hours or frequency of complaints, can track items such as service delivery, but finding out how clients experience the program is best accomplished by directly observing program activities and interviewing staff and clients intensively.

For example, Tim Diamond's (1992:17) observational study of work in a nursing home shows how the somewhat cool professionalism of new program aides was softened to include a greater sensitivity to interpersonal relations:

> The tensions generated by the introductory lecture and . . . ideas of career professionalism were reflected in our conversations as we waited for the second class to get under way. Yet within the next half hour they seemed to dissolve. Mrs. Bonderoid, our teacher, saw to that. . . . "What this [work] is going to take," she instructed, "is a lot of mother's wit." "Mother's wit," she said, not "mother wit," which connotes native intelligence irrespective of gender. She was talking about maternal feelings and skills.

Surveys could have asked the aides how satisfied they were with their training but would not have revealed the subtler side of "mother's wit."

Qualitative methods also can uncover how different individuals react to the treatment. For example, a quantitative evaluation of student reactions to an adult basic skills program for new immigrants relied heavily on the students' initial statements of their goals. However, qualitative interviews revealed that most new immigrants lacked sufficient experience in America to set meaningful goals; their initial goal statements simply reflected their eagerness to agree with their counselors' suggestions (Patton, 2002:177–181).

Qualitative methods can, in general, help in understanding how social programs actually operate. In complex social programs, it is not always clear whether any particular features are responsible for the program's effect (or noneffect). Lisbeth B. Schorr, director of the Harvard Project on Effective Interventions, and Daniel Yankelovich, president of Public Agenda, put it this way (2000:A14): "Social programs are sprawling efforts with multiple components requiring constant mid-course corrections, the involvement of committed human beings, and flexible adaptation to local circumstances." Schorr and Yankelovich pointed to the Ten Point Coalition, an alliance of black ministers that helped to reduce gang warfare in Boston through multiple initiatives, "ranging from neighborhood probation patrols to safe havens for recreation" (A14). Qualitative methods would help to describe a complex, multifaceted program like this. In general, the more complex the social program, the more value that qualitative methods can add to the evaluation process.

Simple or Complex Outcomes

Few programs have only one outcome. Colleges provide not only academic education, for instance, but also—importantly—an amazingly efficient marketplace for potential spouses and lifetime friends. D.A.R.E. programs may not reduce drug use, but they often seem to improve student-police relations. Some outcomes are direct and intended; others happen only over time, are uncertain, and may well not be desired. A decision to focus exclusively on a single outcome—probably the officially intended one—can easily cause a researcher to ignore even more important results.

Sometimes a single policy outcome is sought but is found not to be sufficient, either methodologically or substantively. When Sherman and Berk (1984) evaluated the impact of an immediate arrest policy in cases of domestic violence in Minneapolis, they focused on recidivism—repeating the offense—as the key outcome. Similarly, the reduction of recidivism was the single desired outcome of the prison boot camps that began opening in the 1990s. Boot camps were military-style programs for prison inmates that provided tough, highly regimented activities and harsh punishment for disciplinary infractions with the goal of scaring inmates "straight." But these single-purpose programs, both designed to reduce recidivism, turned out not to be quite so simple to evaluate. The Minneapolis researchers found that there were no adequate single sources for recidivism in domestic violence cases, so they had to hunt for evidence from court and police records, perform follow-up interviews with victims, and review family member reports. More easily measured variables, such as partners' ratings of the accused's subsequent behavior, received more attention. Boot camp research soon concluded that the experience did not reduce recidivism, but some participants felt that boot camps did have some beneficial effects (Latour, 2002:B7):

[A staff member] saw things unfold that he had never witnessed among inmates and their caretakers. . . . Profoundly affected the drill instructors and their charges . . . Graduation ceremonies routinely reduced inmates . . . sometimes even supervisors to tears. . . . Here, it was a totally different experience.

Some now argue that the failure of boot camps to reduce recidivism was due to the lack of postprison support rather than to failure of the camps to promote positive change in inmates. Looking at recidivism rates alone would ignore some important positive results.

So in spite of the difficulties, most evaluation researchers attempt to measure multiple outcomes (Mohr, 1992). One such evaluation appears in Exhibit 11.3. Project New Hope was an ambitious experimental evaluation of the impact of guaranteeing jobs to poor people (DeParle, 1999). It was designed to answer the following question: If low-income adults are given a job at a sufficient wage, above the poverty level, with child care and health care assured, how many would ultimately prosper?

In Project New Hope, 677 low-income adults in Milwaukee, Wisconsin, were offered a job involving work for 30 hours a week, as well as child care and health care benefits. A control group did not receive the guaranteed jobs. The outcome? Only 27% of the 677 stuck with the job long enough to lift themselves out of poverty, and their earnings as a whole were only slightly higher than those of the control group. Levels of depression were not

EXHIBIT 11.3 **Multiple Outcomes in Evaluation of Project New Hope**		
Income and Employment (2nd program year)	*New Hope*	*Control Group*
Earnings	$6,602	$6,129
Wage subsidies	1,477	862
Welfare income	1,716	1,690
Food stamp income	1,418	1,242
Total income	11,213	9,915
% above poverty level	27%	19%
% continuously unemployed for 2 years	6%	13%
Hardships and Stress	*New Hope*	*Control Group*
% reporting:		
Unmet medical needs	17%	23%
Unmet dental needs	27%	34%
Periods without health insurance	49%	61%
Living in overcrowded conditions	14%	15%
Stressed much or all of the time	45%	50%
Satisfied or very satisfied with standard of living	65%	67%

decreased, nor was self-esteem increased by the job guarantee. But there were some positive effects: The number of people who never worked at all declined, and rates of health insurance and use of formal child care increased. Perhaps most importantly, the classroom performance and educational hopes of participants' male children increased, with the boys' test scores rising by the equivalent of 100 points on the SAT and their teachers ranking them as better behaved.

So did the New Hope program "work"? Clearly it didn't live up to initial expectations, but it certainly showed that social interventions can have some benefits. Would the boys' gains continue through adolescence? Longer-term outcomes would be needed. Why didn't girls (who were already performing better than the boys) benefit from their parents' enrollment in New Hope just as the boys did? A process analysis would add a great deal to the evaluation design. Collection of multiple outcomes, then, gives a better picture of program impact.

▣ WHAT CAN AN EVALUATION STUDY FOCUS ON?

Evaluation projects can focus on a variety of different questions related to social programs and their impact:

- What is the level of need for the program?
- Can the program be evaluated?
- How does the program operate?
- What is the program's impact?
- How efficient is the program?

The question asked will determine what research methods are used.

Needs Assessment

A **needs assessment** attempts, with systematic, credible evidence, to evaluate what needs exist in a population. Need may be assessed by social indicators, such as the poverty rate or the level of home ownership; interviews with local experts, such as school board members or team captains; surveys of populations potentially in need; or focus groups with community residents (Rossi & Freeman, 1989).

Needs assessment: A type of evaluation research that attempts to determine the needs of some population that might be met with a social program

---

It is not as easy as it sounds (Posavac & Carey, 1997). Whose definitions of need should be used? How will we deal with ignorance of need? How can we understand the level of need without understanding the social context? (Short answer to that one: We can't!) What, after all, does "need" mean in the abstract?

Consider what kind of housing people need. The Boston McKinney Project, in which Russell Schutt (one of your authors) was a co-investigator, experimentally evaluated whether formerly homeless mentally ill people would do better in group housing or in individual housing (Goldfinger et al., 1997). We first asked two clinicians to estimate which of the two housing alternatives would be best for each project participant and separately asked each participant which type of housing he or she wanted (Schutt & Goldfinger, 1996).

Exhibit 11.4 displays the findings. The clinicians recommended group housing for most participants, but most participants themselves wanted individual housing. So which perspective reveals the real "need" for group versus individual housing? Of course, there's no objective answer. Policymakers' values, and their understanding of mental illness and homelessness, will influence which answer they prefer.

In general, it is a good idea to use multiple indicators of need. There is no absolute definition of need in this situation, nor is there in most projects. A good evaluation researcher will try to capture different perspectives on need and then help others make sense of the results.

Evaluability Assessment

Evaluation research is pointless if the program cannot be evaluated. Yes, some type of study is always possible, but to identify specifically the effects of a program may not be possible within the available time and resources. So researchers may conduct an **evaluability assessment** to learn this in advance, rather than expend time and effort on a fruitless project (Patton, 2002:164).

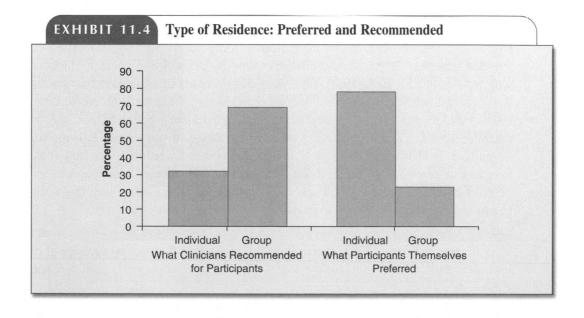

EXHIBIT 11.4 **Type of Residence: Preferred and Recommended**

Evaluability assessment: A type of evaluation research conducted to determine whether it is feasible to evaluate a program's effects within the available time and resources

---

Why might a social program not be evaluable?

- Management only wants to have its superior performance confirmed and does not really care whether the program is having its intended effects. This is a very common problem.
- Staff are so alienated from the agency that they don't trust any attempt sponsored by management to check on their performance.
- Program personnel are just "helping people" or "putting in time" without any clear sense of what the program is trying to achieve.
- The program is not clearly distinct from other services delivered by the agency and so can't be evaluated by itself.

Because they are preliminary studies to "check things out," evaluability assessments often rely on qualitative methods. Program managers and key staff may be interviewed, or program sponsors may be asked about the importance they attach to different goals.

Sometimes an evaluability assessment can actually help to solve problems. Discussion with program managers and staff can result in changes in program operations. The evaluators may use the evaluability assessment to sensitize participants to the importance of clarifying their goals and objectives. The knowledge gained can be used to refine evaluation plans.

Process Evaluation

What actually happens in a social program? In the New Jersey Income Maintenance Experiment, some welfare recipients received higher payments than others (Kershaw & Fair, 1976): simple enough, and not too difficult to verify that the right people received the intended treatment. In the Minneapolis experiment on the police response to domestic violence (Sherman & Berk, 1984), some individuals accused of assaulting their spouses were arrested, whereas others were just warned. This is a little bit more complicated, because the severity of the warning might have varied among police officers and, to minimize the risk of repeat harm, police officers were allowed to override the experimental assignment. To identify this deviation from the experimental design, the researchers would have had to keep track of the treatments delivered to each accused spouse and collect information on what officers actually *did* when they warned an accused spouse. This would be **process evaluation**—research to investigate the process of service delivery.

Process evaluation: Evaluation research that investigates the process of service delivery

---

Process evaluation is more important when more complex programs are evaluated. Many social programs comprise multiple elements and are delivered over an extended period of time, often by different providers in different areas. Due to this complexity, it is quite possible that the program as delivered is neither the same for all program recipients nor consistent with the formal program design.

The evaluation of D.A.R.E. by Research Triangle Institute researchers Christopher Ringwalt and others (1994) included a process evaluation designed to address these issues:

- Assess the organizational structure and operation of representative D.A.R.E. programs nationwide
- Review and assess the factors that contribute to the effective implementation of D.A.R.E. programs nationwide
- Assess how D.A.R.E. and other school-based drug prevention programs are tailored to meet the needs of specific populations

The process evaluation (they called it an "implementation assessment") was an ambitious research project with site visits and informal interviews, discussions, and surveys of D.A.R.E. program coordinators and advisers. These data indicated that D.A.R.E. was operating as designed and was running relatively smoothly. Drug prevention coordinators in D.A.R.E. school districts rated the program more highly than coordinators in districts with other alcohol and drug prevention programs rated theirs.

Process evaluation can also identify which specific part of the service delivery has the greatest impact. This, in turn, helps to explain why the program has an effect and which conditions are required for the effect. (In Chapter 6, we described this as identifying the causal "mechanism.") In the D.A.R.E. research, site visits revealed an insufficient number of officers and a lack of Spanish-language D.A.R.E. books in a largely Hispanic school. At the same time, classroom observations indicated engaging presentations and active student participation (Ringwalt et al., 1994:69, 70).

Process analysis of this sort can also help to show how apparently clear findings may be incorrect. The apparently disappointing results of the Transitional Aid Research Project (TARP) provide an instructive lesson. TARP was a social experiment designed to determine whether financial aid during the transition from prison to the community would help released prisoners find employment and avoid returning to crime. Two thousand participants in Georgia and Texas were randomized to receive either a particular level of benefits over a particular period of time or no benefits (the control group). Initially, it seemed that the payments had no effect: The rate of subsequent arrests for property or nonproperty crimes was not altered by the TARP treatment condition.

But this wasn't all there was to it. Peter Rossi tested a more elaborate causal model of TARP's effects, which is summarized in Exhibit 11.5. Participants who received TARP payments had more income to begin with and so had more to lose if they were arrested; therefore, they were less likely to commit crimes. However, TARP payments also created a disincentive to work and, therefore, increased the time available in which to commit crimes.

EXHIBIT 11.5 Model of TARP Effects

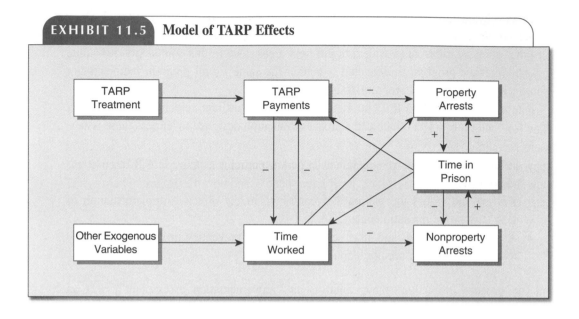

Thus, the positive direct effect of TARP (more to lose) was canceled out by its negative indirect effect (more free time).

Formative evaluation occurs when the evaluation findings are used to help shape and refine the program (Rossi & Freeman, 1989), for instance by being incorporated into the initial development of the service program. Evaluation may then lead to changes in recruitment procedures, program delivery, or measurement tools (Patton, 2002:220).

Formative evaluation: Process evaluation that is used to shape and refine program operations

---

You can see the "formative" element in the following government report on the performance of the Health Care Finance Administration (HCFA):

While HCFA's performance report and plan indicate that it is making some progress toward achieving its Medicare program integrity outcome, progress is difficult to measure because of continual goal changes that are sometimes hard to track or that are made with insufficient explanation. Of the five fiscal year 2000 program integrity goals it discussed, HCFA reported that three were met, a fourth unmet goal was revised to reflect a new focus, and performance data for the fifth will not be available until mid-2001. HCFA plans to discontinue three of these goals. Although the federal share of Medicaid is projected to be $124 billion in fiscal year 2001, HCFA had no program integrity goal for Medicaid for fiscal year 2000. HCFA has since added a developmental goal concerning Medicaid payment accuracy. (U.S. Government Accounting Office, 2001:7)

Process evaluation can employ a wide range of indicators. Program coverage can be monitored through program records, participant surveys, community surveys, and analysis of utilizers versus dropouts and ineligibles. Service delivery may be monitored through service records completed by program staff, a management information system maintained by program administrators, and reports by program recipients (Rossi & Freeman, 1989).

Qualitative methods are often a key component of process evaluation studies, because they can be used to elucidate and understand internal program dynamics—even those that were not anticipated (Patton, 2002:159; Posavac & Carey, 1997). Qualitative researchers may develop detailed descriptions of how program participants engage with each other, how the program experience varies for different people, and how the program changes and evolves over time.

Impact Analysis

The core questions of evaluation research are these: Did the program work? Did it have the intended result? This kind of research is variously called **impact analysis**, **impact evaluation**, or **summative evaluation**. Formally speaking, impact analysis compares what happened after a program was implemented with what *would* have happened had there been no program at all.

Impact analysis: Evaluation research that answers these questions: Did the program work? Did it have the intended result? Also called *impact evaluation* and *summative evaluation.*

Think of the program—such as a new strategy for combating domestic violence or an income supplement—as an independent variable and the result it seeks as a dependent variable. The D.A.R.E. program (independent variable), for instance, tries to reduce drug use (dependent variable). If the program is present, we should expect less drug use. In a more elaborate study, we might have multiple values of the independent variable, for instance, comparing conditions of "no program," "D.A.R.E. program," and "other drug/alcohol education."

As in other areas of research, an experimental design is the preferred method for maximizing internal validity—that is, for making sure your causal claims about program impact are justified. Cases are assigned randomly to one or more experimental treatment groups and to a control group so that there is no systematic difference between the groups at the outset (see Chapter 6). The goal is to achieve a fair, unbiased test of the program itself so that the judgment about the program's impact is not influenced by differences between the types of people who are in the different groups. It can be a difficult goal to achieve, because the usual practice in social programs is to let people decide for themselves whether they want to enter a program, as well as to establish eligibility criteria that ensure that people who enter the program are different from those who do not (Boruch, 1997). In either case, a selection bias is introduced.

But sometimes researchers are able to conduct well-controlled experiments. Robert Drake et al. (1996) evaluated the impact of two different approaches to providing employment services for people diagnosed with severe mental disorders, using a randomized experimental design. One approach, group skills training (GST), emphasized pre-employment skills training and used separate agencies to provide vocational and mental health services. The other approach, individual placement and support (IPS), provided vocational and mental health services in a single program and placed people directly into jobs without pre-employment skills training. The researchers hypothesized that GST participants would be more likely to obtain jobs during the 18-month study period than would IPS participants.

Their experimental design is depicted in Exhibit 11.6. Cases were assigned randomly to the two groups, and then

1. both groups received a pretest;

2. one group received the experimental intervention (GST), and the other received the IPS approach; and

3. both groups received three posttests, at 6, 12, and 18 months.

Contrary to the researchers' hypothesis, the IPS participants were twice as likely to obtain a competitive job as the GST participants. The IPS participants also worked more hours and earned more total wages. Although this was not the outcome Drake et al. had anticipated, it was valuable information for policy makers and program planners—and the study was rigorously experimental.

Program impact also can be evaluated with quasi-experimental designs (see Chapter 6), nonexperimental designs, or field research methods without a randomized experimental design. If program participants can be compared to nonparticipants who are reasonably

EXHIBIT 11.6	Randomized Comparative Change Design: Employment Services for People With Severe Mental Disorders

Key: R = Random assignment
O = Observation (employment status at pretest or posttest)
X = Experimental treatment

	O1	X	O2	O3	O4
Experimental Group	Pretest	Preemployment skills training	Posttest at 6 months	Posttest at 12 months	Posttest at 18 months
Comparison Group	Pretest		Posttest at 6 months	Posttest at 12 months	Posttest at 18 months

R

comparable except for their program participation, causal conclusions about program impact can still be made. However, researchers must evaluate carefully the likelihood that factors other than program participation might have resulted in the appearance of a program effect. For example, when a study at New York's maximum-security prison for women found that "education [i.e., classes] is found to lower risk of new arrest," the conclusions were immediately suspect: The research design did not ensure that the women who enrolled in the prison classes were the same as those who were not, "leaving open the possibility that the results were due, at least in part, to self-selection, with the women most motivated to avoid reincarceration being the ones who took the college classes" (Lewin, 2001b:A18). Such nonequivalent control groups are often our only option, but you should be alert to their weaknesses.

Impact analysis is an important undertaking that fully deserves the attention it has been given in government program funding requirements. However, you should realize that more rigorous evaluation designs are less likely to conclude that a program has the desired effect; as the standard of proof goes up, success is harder to demonstrate. The prevalence of "null findings" (or "we can't be sure it works") has led to a bit of gallows humor among evaluation researchers.

The Output/Outcome/Downstream Impact Blues

Donors often say,

And this is a fact,

Get out there and show us,

Your impact.

You must change people's lives,

And help us take the credit,

Or next time you want funding,

You just might not get it.

So donors wake up,

From your impossible dream.

You drop in your funding,

A long way upstream.

The waters they flow,

They mingle, they blend,

So how can you take credit,

For what comes out in the end?

—Terry Smutylo, Director, Evaluation
International Development Research Centre
Ottawa, Canada (excerpt reprinted in Patton, 2002:154; used by permission)

Efficiency Analysis

Finally, a program may be evaluated for how efficiently it provides its benefit; typically, financial measures are used. Are the program's financial benefits sufficient to offset the program's costs? The answer is provided by a **cost-benefit analysis.** How much does it cost to achieve a given effect? This answer is provided by a **cost-effectiveness analysis.** Program funders often require one or both of these types of **efficiency analysis.**

Cost-benefit analysis: A summary statistic that varies from 0 to 1 or -1, with 0 indicating the absence of a linear relationship between two quantitative variables and 1 or -1 indicating that the relationship is completely described by the line representing the regression of the dependent variable on the independent variable

Cost-effectiveness analysis: A type of evaluation research that compares program costs with actual program outcomes

Efficiency analysis: A type of evaluation research that compares program costs with program effects. It can be either a cost-benefit analysis or a cost-effectiveness analysis.

A cost-benefit analysis must (obviously) identify the specific costs and benefits to be studied, but my "benefit" may easily be your "cost." Program clients, for instance, will certainly have a different perspective on these issues than do taxpayers or program staff. Exhibit 11.7 lists factors that can be considered costs or benefits in a supported employment

---

EXHIBIT 11.7 **Potential Costs and Benefits of a Social Program, by Beneficiary**

Costs/Benefits	Perspective of Program Participants	Perspective of Rest of Society	Perspective of Entire Society*
Costs			
Operational costs of the program	0	–	–
Forgone leisure and home production	–	0	–
Benefits			
Earnings gains	+	0	+
Reduced costs of nonexperimental services	0	+	+
Transfers			
Reduced welfare benefits	–	+	0
Wage subsidies	+	–	0
Net benefits	±	±	±

Note: – = program costs; + = program benefits; ± = program costs and benefits; 0 = no program costs or benefits.

*Entire society = program participants + rest of society.

program from the standpoint of participants and taxpayers (Schalock & Butterworth, 2000). Note that some anticipated impacts of the program (e.g., taxes and subsidies) are a cost to one group but a benefit to the other, and some impacts are not relevant to either.

After potential costs and benefits have been identified, they must be measured. This need is highlighted in recent government programs (Campbell, 2001:1):

> The Governmental Accounting Standards Board's (GASB) mission is to establish and improve standards of accounting and financial reporting for state and local governments in the United States. In June 1999, the GASB issued a major revision to current reporting requirements ("Statement 34"), which aims to provide information so citizens and other users can understand the financial position and cost of programs.

In addition to measuring services and their associated costs, a cost-benefit analysis must be able to make some type of estimation of how clients benefited from the program and what the economic value of this benefit was. A recent study of therapeutic communities provides a clear illustration. A *therapeutic community* is a method for treating substance abuse in which abusers participate in an intensive, structured living experience with other addicts who are attempting to stay sober. Because the treatment involves residential support as well as other types of services, it can be quite costly. Are those costs worth it?

Sacks, McKendrick, DeLeon, French, and McCollister (2002) conducted a cost-benefit analysis of a modified therapeutic community (TC) in which 342 homeless, mentally ill chemical abusers were randomly assigned to either a TC or a "treatment-as-usual" comparison group. Employment status, criminal activity, and utilization of health care services were each measured for the 3 months prior to entering treatment and the 3 months after treatment. Earnings from employment in each period were adjusted for costs incurred by criminal activity and utilization of health care services.

Was it worth it? The average cost of TC treatment for a client was $20,361. In comparison, the economic benefit (based on earnings) to the average TC client was $305,273, which declined to $273,698 after comparing post- to preprogram earnings. After adjusting for the cost of the program, the benefit was still $253,337. The resulting benefit-cost ratio was 13:1, although this ratio declined to only 5.2:1 after further adjustments (for cases with extreme values). Nonetheless, the TC program studied seems to have had a substantial benefit relative to its costs.

▣ ETHICAL ISSUES IN EVALUATION RESEARCH

Whenever you evaluate the needs of clients or analyze the impact of a program, you directly affect people's lives. Social workers want to believe their efforts matter; drug educators think they're preventing drug abuse. Homeless people have problems and may really appreciate the services an agency provides. Program administrators have bosses to please;

foundations need big programs to fund; and domestic violence, for instance, is a real problem—and finding solutions to it matters. Participants and clients in social programs, then, are not just subjects eager to take part in your research; they care about your findings, deeply. This produces serious ethical as well as political challenges for the evaluation researcher (Boruch, 1997:13; Dentler, 2002:166).

There are many specific ethical challenges in evaluation research:

- How can confidentiality be preserved when the data are owned by a government agency or are subject to discovery in a legal proceeding?
- Who decides what burden an evaluation project can impose upon participants?
- Can a research decision legitimately be shaped by political considerations?
- Must findings be shared with all stakeholders or only with policy makers?
- Will a randomized experiment yield more defensible evidence than the alternatives?
- Will the results actually be used?

Is it fair to assign persons randomly to receive some social program or benefit? What fairer way to distribute scarce benefits than through a lottery? The State of Oregon has recently begun doing exactly this with some health care benefits. (Yardley, 2008) This is exactly the process that is involved in a randomized experimental design.

The Health Research Extension Act of 1985 (Public Law 99–158) mandated that the Department of Health and Human Services require all research organizations receiving federal funds to have an institutional review board (IRB) to assess all research for adherence to ethical practice guidelines. There are six federally mandated criteria (Boruch, 1997:29–33):

- Are risks minimized?
- Are risks reasonable in relation to benefits?
- Is the selection of individuals equitable? (Randomization implies this.)
- Is informed consent given?
- Are the data monitored?
- Are privacy and confidentiality ensured?

Evaluation researchers must consider these criteria before they even design a study. Subject confidentiality is particularly thorny because researchers, in general, are not usually exempted from providing evidence sought in legal proceedings. However, several federal statutes have been passed specifically to protect research data about certain vulnerable populations from legal disclosure requirements. For example, the Crime Control and Safe Streets Act (28CFR Part 11) includes the following stipulation (Boruch, 1997:60):

Copies of [research] information [about persons receiving services under the act or the subject of inquiries into criminal behavior] shall be immune from legal process and shall not, without the consent of the persons furnishing such information, be admitted as evidence or used for any purpose in any action, suit, or other judicial or administrative proceedings.

When ethical standards can't be met, modifications may be made in the study design. Several steps can be taken (Boruch, 1997:67–68):

- Alter the group allocation ratios to minimize the number in the untreated control group.
- Use the minimum sample size required to be able to test the results adequately.
- Test just parts of new programs rather than entire programs.
- Compare treatments that vary in intensity (rather than presence or absence).
- Vary treatments between settings rather than among individuals within a setting.

▣ CONCLUSION

In social policy circles, hopes for evaluation research are high: Society would benefit from the programs that work well, that accomplish their goals, and that serve people who genuinely need them. At least that is the hope. Unfortunately, there are many obstacles to realizing this hope. Because social programs and the people who use them are complex, evaluation research designs can easily miss important outcomes or aspects of the program process. Because the many program stakeholders all have an interest in particular results from the evaluation, researchers can be subjected to an unusual level of cross-pressures and demands. Because the need to include program stakeholders in research decisions may undermine adherence to scientific standards, research designs can be weakened. Because program administrators may want to believe their programs really work well, researchers may be pressured to avoid null findings or, if they are not responsive, find their research reports ignored. Because the primary audience for evaluation research reports is program administrators, politicians, or members of the public, evaluation findings may need to be overly simplified, distorting the findings (Posavac & Carey, 1997). Plenty of well-done evaluation research studies wind up in a recycling bin or hidden away in a file cabinet.

The rewards of evaluation research are often worth the risks, however. Evaluation research can provide social scientists with rare opportunities to study complex social processes, with real consequences, and to contribute to the public good. Although they may face unusual constraints on their research designs, most evaluation projects can also result in high-quality analyses and publications in reputable social science journals. In many respects, evaluation research is an idea whose time has come. We may never achieve Donald Campbell's vision of an "experimenting society" (Campbell & Russo, 1999) in which research is consistently used to evaluate new programs and to suggest constructive changes, but we are close enough to continue trying.

KEY TERMS

Cost-benefit analysis
Cost-effectiveness analysis
Efficiency analysis
Evaluability assessment
Evaluation research
Feedback
Formative evaluation
Impact analysis
Inputs
Integrative approaches (to evaluation)
Needs assessment

Outcomes
Outputs
Process evaluation
Program process
Program theory
Social science approaches (to evaluation)
Stakeholder approaches (to evaluation)
Stakeholders
Summative evaluation
Theory-driven evaluation

HIGHLIGHTS

- Evaluation research is social research that is conducted for a distinctive purpose: to investigate social programs.
- The development of evaluation research as a major enterprise followed on the heels of the expansion of the federal government during the Great Depression and World War II.
- The evaluation process can be modeled as a feedback system, with inputs entering the program, which generate outputs and then outcomes, which feed back to program stakeholders and affect program inputs.
- The evaluation process as a whole, and the feedback process in particular, can only be understood in relation to the interests and perspectives of program stakeholders.
- The process by which a program has an effect on outcomes is often treated as a "black box," but there is good reason to open the black box and investigate the process by which the program operates and produces, or fails to produce, an effect.
- A program theory may be developed before or after an investigation of the program process is completed. The theory can be either descriptive or prescriptive.
- Evaluation research is research for a client, and its results may directly affect the services, treatments, or punishments that program users receive. Evaluation researchers differ in the extent to which they attempt to orient their evaluations to program stakeholders.
- Qualitative methods are useful in describing the process of program delivery.
- Multiple outcomes are often necessary to understand program effects.
- There are five primary types of program evaluation: needs assessment, evaluability assessment, process evaluation (including formative evaluation), impact analysis (also termed summative evaluation), and efficiency (cost-benefit) analysis.
- Evaluation research raises complex ethical issues because it may involve withholding desired social benefits.

EXERCISES

Discussing Research

1. Would you prefer that evaluation researchers use a stakeholder or a social science approach? Compare and contrast these perspectives and list at least four arguments for the one you favor.

2. Propose a randomized experimental evaluation of a social program with which you are familiar. Include in your proposal a description of the program and its intended outcomes. Discuss the strengths and weaknesses of your proposed design. Think of your primary health care provider as providing a "program" that should be evaluated. (If that makes you squeamish, you can focus on your college as the "program" instead.)

3. How would you describe the contents of the "black box" of program operations? What "program theory" would specify how the program operates?

4. What would be the advantages and disadvantages of using qualitative methods to evaluate this program? What would be the advantages and disadvantages of using quantitative methods? Which approach would you prefer and why?

Finding Research

1. Inspect the Web site maintained by the Governmental Accounting Standards Board: http://www.seagov.org. Read and report on performance measurement in government as described in one of the case studies.

2. Describe the resources available for evaluation researchers at one of the following three Web sites: http://www.wmich.edu/evalctr/, http://www.stanford.edu/~davidf/empowermentevaluation .html, or http://www.worldbank.org/oed/.

Critiquing Research

1. Read and summarize an evaluation research report published in the *Evaluation and Program Planning* journal. Be sure to identify the type of evaluation research that is described.

2. Select one of the evaluation research studies described in this chapter, read the original report (book or article) about it, and review its adherence to the ethical guidelines for evaluation research. Which guidelines do you feel are most important? Which are most difficult to adhere to?

Doing Research

1. Propose a randomized experimental evaluation of a social program with which you are familiar. Include in your proposal a description of the program and its intended outcomes. Discuss the strengths and weaknesses of your proposed design.

2. Identify the key stakeholders in a local social or educational program. Interview several stakeholders to determine their goals for the program and what tools they use to assess goal achievement. Compare and contrast the views of each stakeholder and try to account for any differences you find.

Ethics Questions

1. What if you learned that a student in the school where you were observing was talking seriously about cutting himself? If you were the ethnographer, would you have immediately informed school personnel about this? Would you have told anyone? What if the student asked you not to tell anyone? In what circumstances would you feel it is ethical to take action to prevent the likelihood of a subject's harming himself or herself or others?

2. Is it ethical to assign people to receive some social benefit on a random basis? Form two teams and debate the ethics of the TARP randomized evaluation of welfare payments described in this chapter.

CHAPTER 12

Reviewing, Proposing, and Reporting Research

In a sense, we end this book where we began. As you begin writing up your findings, you can see the gaps in the research. While reviewing the literature—and finding where your own work fits in—you may discover more interesting possibilities or more exciting studies to be started. In the process of concluding each study, we almost naturally begin the next.

The primary goals of this chapter are to guide you in evaluating the research of other scholars, developing research proposals, and writing worthwhile reports of your own. We first discuss how to evaluate prior research—a necessary step before writing a research report or proposal. We then focus on writing research proposals and reports.

🔲 COMPARING RESEARCH DESIGNS

From different methods, we learn different things. Even when used to study the same social processes, the central features of experiments, surveys, qualitative methods, and evaluation research provide distinct perspectives. Comparing subjects randomly assigned to a treatment group and to a comparison group, asking standard questions of the members of a random sample, observing while participating in a natural social setting, or studying program impact involve markedly different decisions about measurement, causality, and generalizability. As you can see in Exhibit 12.1, not one of these methods can reasonably be graded as superior to the others in all respects, and each varies in its suitability to different research questions and goals. Choosing among them for a particular investigation requires consideration of the research problem, opportunities and resources, prior research, philosophical commitments, and research goals.

Experimental designs are strongest for testing nomothetic causal hypotheses (lawlike explanations that identify a common influence on a number of cases or events). These designs are most appropriate for studies of treatment effects (see Chapter 6). Research questions that are believed to involve basic social psychological processes are most appealing for laboratory studies, because the problem of generalizability is reduced. Random assignment reduces the possibility of pre-existing differences between treatment and comparison groups to small, specifiable, chance levels, so many of the variables that might create a spurious association are controlled. Laboratory experiments permit unsurpassed control over conditions and are excellent for establishing internal validity (causality).

But experimental designs have weaknesses. For most laboratory experiments, people volunteer as subjects; since volunteers aren't like other people, generalizability is not good. Ethical and practical constraints limit your treatments (for instance, you can't randomly assign race or social class). Although some processes may be the same for all people, so that generalizing from volunteer subjects will work, it's difficult to know in advance which processes are really invariant. Field experiments, although apparently more generalizable studies, allow for less control than lab experiments; hence, treatments may not be delivered as intended, or other influences may intrude (see Chapter 9). Also, field experiments typically require unusual access (e.g., permission to revise a school curriculum or change police department policy) and can be very expensive.

Surveys, because of their probability sampling and standardized questions, are excellent for generalizable descriptive studies of large populations (see Chapter 7). They can include a large number of variables, unlike experiments, so that potential spuriousness can be statistically controlled; therefore, surveys can be used readily to test hypothesized causal relationships. And because many closed-ended questions are available that have been used in previous studies, it's easy to find reliable measures of commonly used variables.

EXHIBIT 12.1   **Comparison of Research Methods[a]**

Design	Measurement Validity	Generalizability	Causal Validity
Experiments	+	−	+
Surveys	+	+	−/+[b]
Participant Observation	−/+[c]	−	−

a. A plus (+) sign indicates where a method is strong; a minus (−) sign indicates where a method is weak.

b. Surveys are a weaker design for identifying causal effects than true experiments, but use of statistical controls can strengthen causal arguments.

c. Reliability is low compared to surveys, and systematic evaluation of measurement validity is often not possible. However, direct observations may lead to great confidence in the validity of measures.

But surveys, too, have weaknesses. Survey questionnaires can measure only what respondents are willing to say; they may not uncover behavior or attitudes that are socially unacceptable. Survey questions, being standardized, may miss the nuances of a respondent's feelings or the complexities of an attitude; they lump together what may be interestingly different responses. They rely on the truthfulness of respondents and on their accuracy in reporting (for instance, students are asked how many hours a week they study—Do they know? Is study time constant?).

Qualitative methods allow intensive measurement of new or developing concepts, subjective meanings, and causal mechanisms (see Chapter 9). In field research, a "grounded theory" approach helps you create and refine concepts and theories based on direct observation or in-depth interviewing. Interviewing reveals what people really mean by their ideas and allows you to explore their feelings at great length. How, exactly, social processes unfold over time can be explored using interviews and fieldwork. Qualitative methods can identify the multiple successive events that might have led to some outcome, thus identifying idiographic causal processes; they are excellent for studying new or poorly understood settings and populations that seek to remain hidden. When exploratory questions are posed or new groups studied, qualitative methods are preferred.

But such intensive study is time consuming, so fewer cases can be examined. Single or a few cases or unique settings are interesting but don't produce generalizable results. Also, most researchers can't spend 6 months away from home doing a project. Open-ended interviews take time—not just the 1 or 2 hours of the interview itself but time in scheduling, in missed appointments, in travel to reach your subjects, and so on.

When qualitative methods can find real differences in an independent variable—for example, several different management styles in a manufacturing company—you can test nomothetic causal hypotheses. But the impossibility of controlling numerous possible extraneous influences makes qualitative methods a weak approach to hypothesis testing.

▣ REVIEWING RESEARCH

A good literature review is the foundation for a research proposal, both in identifying gaps in current knowledge and in considering how to design a research project. It is also important to review the literature prior to writing an article about the research findings—the latest findings on your topic should be checked, and prior research on new issues should be consulted. This section helps you learn how to review the research that you locate. First, we focus on the process of reviewing single articles; then, we explain how to combine reviews of single articles into an overall literature review.

Exhibit 12.2 lists the questions you should ask when critiquing a social research study, and the following paragraphs provide an example. This particular critique does not answer all of the review questions, nor does it provide complete answers to all these questions, but it gives you the basic idea. In any case, remember that your goal is to evaluate research projects as integrated wholes. In addition to considering how valid the measures were and whether the causal conclusions were justified, you must consider how the *measurement*

EXHIBIT 12.2   **Questions to Ask About a Research Article**

In reading a research article, you want to know (a) What is the author's conclusion? and (b) Does the research presented adequately support that conclusion? The questions below will help you determine the answers.

I. *Overall assessment of the article*
    1. What is the basic question being posed?
    2. Is the theoretical approach appropriate?
    3. Is the literature review adequate?
    4. Does the research design suit the question?
    5. Is the study scientific in its fundamentals?
    6. Are the ethical issues adequately addressed?
    7. What are the key findings?

II. *Detailed assessment*
    1. What are the key concepts? Are they clearly defined?
    2. What are the main hypotheses?
    3. What are the main independent and dependent variables?
    4. Are the measurements valid?
    5. What are the units of analysis? Are they appropriate?
    6. Are any causal relationships successfully established?
    7. Is the effective sample (sampling plus response rate) representative?
    8. Does context matter to the causal relationship?

---

approach might have affected the causal validity of the researcher's conclusions and how the *sampling strategy* might have altered the quality of measures. In other words, all the parts of a study affect each other. Our goal here is just to illustrate the process of critically thinking about a piece of research.

Case Study: "Night as Frontier"

A minor classic in sociological literature, Murray Melbin's 1978 article "Night as Frontier" compares 20th-century extension of human activity into nighttime hours with 19th-century geographic expansion into the American West. Melbin argues that just as there was a "frontier lifestyle" in the Old West of cowboys, a similar style of behavior, particularly toward strangers, prevails among late-night inhabitants of contemporary American cities. In developing this comparison of spatial frontiers with temporal frontiers, Melbin accomplished an insightful reconceptualization of how human beings live on a sparsely populated "frontier" of a different kind.

Suppose that you are a student of urban life and curious as to whether city dwellers, such as New Yorkers, are really as unfriendly and brusque as stereotypes portray them. Melbin's article describes a number of field experiments, conducted entirely in Boston, to discover whether people were more or less helpful to others at nighttime than during the day. Perhaps you could use his findings. But was his research properly conducted?

The Research Design

Melbin and his assistants conducted four different experiments, all designed to measure if time of day affected people's willingness to be "helpful or friendly" to strangers. He drew in part on a sizable literature in this area conducted by social psychologists, but his studies were simpler in design than most psychology experiments. In most cases, he had one independent variable—time of day—and one dependent variable—how likely people were to be helpful or friendly. Melbin's assistants, using a detailed sampling procedure (sampling both times of the day and subjects), approached random people on (also sampled) streets in Boston. In one study, the researchers asked for directions; in another, they requested that subjects answer several interview questions. In a third study, they observed customers' interactions with cashiers at grocery stores. Finally, they left keys, tagged with "Please return" and an address, in various locations. In each case, the independent variable was time of day (for instance, when subjects were approached or the key was dropped on the street); the dependent variable was whether people were cooperative (directions, interviews), helpful (returning key), or friendly (smiling, conversational). A clear, simple coding scheme was used for all of these measures.

Analysis of the Design

Melbin's study was exploratory, designed to propose a new idea of how to understand nighttime in contemporary America. His experiments, therefore, were more in the manner of demonstrations—a first test of a new idea—than of continuing an established line of scientific research. Indeed, Melbin (1978) himself claimed to be advancing "the hypothesis that night is a frontier"; yet his experiments only test the idea that people at night are more "helpful and friendly" to strangers, which he argues is one of about a dozen characteristics of frontier communities.

But we can narrow our view to his specific question about helpfulness. His measures certainly have face validity, and in fact, in three of his four studies, people were indeed more friendly at night. And he didn't simply ask people if they would be helpful; he tested them in real situations in which they didn't know that it was an experiment. He also was open to surprises: In the "lost key" study, people were in fact *less* likely to return the key at night. Melbin realized that he had unintentionally slipped in another variable—whether the act of helpfulness was anonymous (the key study) or not (all the others). Only the community of face-to-face contact, he suggests, exists at night; help is not generally extended to those not part of the nighttime community. So the different trials also lend plausibility to his argument. He only studied city residents and only in Boston; it may be that the "nighttime community" exists only in urban settings, but an urban setting was a constant, not a variable, here.

There are at least two important problems in Melbin's design, despite its conscientious use of sampling, reliable coding procedures, and multiple measures. First, the studies don't really show that nighttime makes particular people more helpful and friendly; they show that people who are up at night—a self-selected group—are more helpful and friendly.

Perhaps the kind of people who prefer nightlife, not nighttime itself, is the true causal agent. And second, again, the studies were all conducted in a Northeastern city. Rural or suburban settings—a different context—could very well reveal different patterns.

An Overall Assessment

"Night as Frontier" certainly makes a persuasive argument with far more historical and theoretical detail than we've mentioned here. It tends to be research of the "exploratory" type, so its experiments are somewhat crude; neither the measures nor the studies themselves have been widely replicated. Ethically, the work is benign. Its main value may lie in the persuasiveness of the argument that nighttime is different than daytime and that the difference is much like the difference between densely settled areas and the old frontier West. For its conceptual insights, "Night as Frontier" deserves a respected place in the social science literature. In a detailed study of urban life and community, it may be helpful, but perhaps it is not fundamental.

Case Study: When Does Arrest Matter?

The goal of the literature review process is to integrate the results of your separate article reviews and develop an overall assessment of the implications of prior research. The integrated literature review should accomplish three goals (Hart, 1998:186–187):

1. Summarize prior research.

2. Critique prior research.

3. Present pertinent conclusions.

We'll discuss each of these goals in turn.

Summarize Prior Research

Your summary of prior research must focus on the particular research questions that you will address, but you may need also to provide some more general background. Carolyn Hoyle and Andrew Sanders (2000:14) begin their *British Journal of Criminology* research article about mandatory arrest policies in domestic violence cases with what they term a "provocative" question: What is the point of making it a crime for men to assault their female partners and ex-partners? They then review the different theories and supporting research that has justified different police policies: the "victim choice" position, the "pro-arrest" position, and the "victim empowerment" position. Finally, they review the research on the "controlling behaviors" of men that frames the specific research question on which they focus: how victims view the value of criminal justice interventions in their own cases (15).

Ask yourself three questions about your summary of the literature (Pyrczak, 2005: 51–59):

1. *Have you been selective?* If there have been more than a few prior investigations of your research question, you will need to narrow your focus to the most relevant and highest-quality studies. Don't cite a large number of prior articles "just because they are there."

2. *Is the research up-to-date?* Be sure to include the latest research, not just the "classic" studies.

3. *Have you used direct quotes sparingly?* To focus your literature review, you need to express the key points from prior research in your own words. Use direct quotes only when they are essential for making an important point.

Critique Prior Research

Evaluate the strengths and weaknesses of the prior research. In addition to all the points you develop as you answer the "article review questions" in Appendix B, you should also select articles for review that reflect the work of credible authors in peer-reviewed journals who have been funded by reputable sources. Consider the following questions as you decide how much weight to give each article (Locke, Silverman, & Spirduso, 1998:37–44):

1. *How was the report reviewed prior to its publication or release?* Articles published in academic journals go through a very rigorous review process, usually involving careful criticism and revision. Top "refereed" journals may accept only 10% of submitted articles, so they can be very selective. Dissertations go through a lengthy process of criticism and revision by a few members of the dissertation writer's home institution. A report released directly by a research organization is likely to have had only a limited review, although some research organizations maintain a rigorous internal review process. Papers presented at professional meetings may have had little prior review. Needless to say, more confidence can be placed in research results that have been subject to a more rigorous review.

2. *What is the author's reputation?* Reports by an author or team of authors who have published other work on the research question should be given somewhat greater credibility at the outset.

3. *Who funded and sponsored the research?* Major federal funding agencies and private foundations fund only research proposals that have been evaluated carefully and ranked highly by a panel of experts. They also often monitor closely the progress of the research. This does not guarantee that every such project report is good, but it goes a long way toward ensuring some worthwhile products. On the other hand, research

that is funded by organizations that have a preference for a particular outcome should be given particularly close scrutiny.

Present Pertinent Conclusions

Don't leave the reader guessing about the implications of the prior research for your own investigation. Present the conclusions you draw from the research you have reviewed. As you do so, follow several simple guidelines (Pyrczak, 2005:53–56):

- Distinguish clearly your own opinion of prior research from conclusions of the authors of the articles you have reviewed.
- Make it clear when your own approach is based on the theoretical framework you are using rather than on the results of prior research.
- Acknowledge the potential limitations of any empirical research project. Don't emphasize problems in prior research that you can't avoid either.

Explain how the unanswered questions raised by prior research or the limitations of methods used in prior research make it important for you to conduct your own investigation (Fink, 2005:190–192).

A good example of how to conclude an integrated literature review is provided by an article based on the replication in Milwaukee of the Minneapolis Domestic Violence Experiment. For this article, Ray Paternoster, Robert Brame, Ronet Bachman, and Lawrence Sherman (1997) sought to determine whether police officers' use of fair procedures when arresting assault suspects would lessen the rate of subsequent domestic violence. Paternoster et al. (164) concluded that there has been a major gap in the prior literature: "Even at the end of some seven experiments and millions of dollars, then, there is a great deal of ambiguity surrounding the question of how arrest impacts future spouse assault."

Specifically, they noted that each of the seven experiments focused on the effect of arrest itself but ignored the possibility that "particular kinds of police *procedure* might inhibit the recurrence of spouse assault" (Paternoster et al., 1997:165).

So Paternoster and his colleagues (1997:172) grounded their new analysis in additional literature on procedural justice and concluded that their new analysis would be "the first study to examine the effect of fairness judgments regarding a punitive criminal sanction (arrest) on serious criminal behavior (assaulting one's partner)."

▣ PROPOSING NEW RESEARCH

Be grateful for people who require you to write a formal research proposal—and even more for those who give you constructive feedback. Whether your proposal is written for a professor, a thesis committee, an organization seeking practical advice, or a government agency that funds basic research, the proposal will force you to set out a problem statement and a research plan. Too many research projects begin without a clear problem statement or with only the barest of notions about which variables must be measured or what the analysis should look like. Such projects often wander along, lurching from side to side, and then collapse entirely or just peter out with a report that is ignored—and should be. Even in circumstances when a proposal is not required, you should prepare one and present it to others for feedback. Just writing your ideas down will help you to see how they can be improved, and feedback in almost any form will help you to refine your plans.

A well-designed proposal can go a long way toward shaping the final research report and will make it easier to progress at later research stages (Locke, Spirduso, & Silverman, 2000). Every research proposal should have at least six sections:

1. *An introductory statement of the research problem,* in which you clarify what it is that you are interested in studying

2. *A literature review,* in which you explain how your problem and plans build on what has already been reported in the literature on this topic

3. *A methodological plan,* detailing just how you will respond to the particular mix of opportunities and constraints you face

4. *A budget,* presenting a careful listing of the anticipated costs

5. *An ethics statement,* identifying human subjects issues in the research and how you will respond to them in an ethical fashion

6. *A statement of limitations,* reviewing weaknesses of the proposed research and presenting plans for minimizing their consequences

A research proposal also can be strengthened considerably by presenting a result of a pilot study of the research question. This might involve administering the proposed questionnaire to a small sample, conducting a preliminary version of the proposed experiment with a group of available subjects, or making observations over a limited period of time in a setting like that proposed for a qualitative study. Careful presentation of the methods used in the pilot study and the problems that were encountered will impress anyone who reviews the proposal.

If your research proposal will be reviewed competitively, it must present a compelling rationale for funding. The research problem that you propose to study is crucial; its importance cannot be overstated (see Chapter 2). If you propose to test a hypothesis, be sure that it is one for which there are plausible alternatives, so your study isn't just a boring report of the obvious (Dawes, 1995:93).

Case Study: Treating Substance Abuse

Particular academic departments, grant committees, and funding agencies will have specific proposal requirements. As an example, Exhibit 12.3 lists the primary required sections of the "Research Plan" for proposals to the National Institutes of Health (NIH), together with excerpts from a proposal Russell Schutt submitted in this format to the National Institute of Mental Health (NIMH) with colleagues from the University of

EXHIBIT 12.3 | A Grant Proposal to the National Institute of Mental Health

Relapse Prevention for Homeless Dually Diagnosed

Abstract

This project will test the efficacy of shelter-based treatment that integrates Psychosocial Rehabilitation with Relapse Prevention techniques adapted for homeless mentally ill persons who abuse substances. Two hundred and fifty homeless persons, meeting . . . criteria for substance abuse and severe and persistent mental disorder, will be recruited from two shelters and then randomly assigned to either an experimental treatment condition . . . or to a control condition.

For one year, at the rate of three 2-hour sessions per week, the treatment group ($n = 125$) will participate for the first 6 months in "enhanced" Psychosocial Rehabilitation . . . , followed by 6 months of Relapse Prevention training. . . . The control group will participate in a Standard Treatment condition (currently comprised of a 12-step peer-help program along with counseling offered at all shelters). . . .

Outcome measures include substance abuse, housing placement and residential stability, social support, service utilization, level of distress. . . . The integrity of the experimental design will be monitored through a process analysis. Tests for the hypothesized treatment effects . . . will be supplemented with analyses to evaluate the direct and indirect effects of subject characteristics and to identify interactions between subject characteristics and treatment condition. . . .

Research Plan

1. Specific Aims

The research demonstration project will determine whether an integrated clinical shelter-based treatment intervention can improve health and well-being among homeless persons who abuse alcohol and/or drugs and who are seriously and persistently ill—the so-called "dually diagnosed." . . . We aim to identify the specific attitudes and behaviors that are most affected by the integrated psychosocial rehabilitation/relapse prevention treatment, and thus to help guide future service interventions.

2. Background and Significance

Relapse is the most common outcome in treating the chronically mentally ill, including the homeless. . . . Reviews of the clinical and empirical literature published to date indicate that treatment interventions based on social learning experiences are associated with more favorable outcomes than treatment interventions based on more traditional forms of psychotherapy and/or chemotherapy. . . . However, few tests of the efficacy of such interventions have been reported for homeless samples.

3. Progress Report/Preliminary Studies

Four areas of Dr. Schutt's research help to lay the foundation for the research demonstration project here proposed. . . . The 1990 survey in Boston shelters measured substance abuse with selected ASI [Addiction Severity Index] questions. . . . About half of the respondents evidenced a substance abuse problem. Just over one quarter of respondents had ever been treated for a mental health problem. . . . At least three quarters were interested in help with each of the problems mentioned other than substance abuse. Since help with benefits, housing, and AIDS prevention will each be provided to all study participants in the proposed research demonstration project, we project that this should increase the rate of participation and retention in the study. . . . Results [from co-investigator Dr. Walter Penk's research] . . . indicate that trainers were more successful in engaging the dually diagnosed in Relapse Prevention techniques. . . .

4. Research Design and Methods

Study Sample.
Recruitment. The study will recruit 350 clients beginning in month 4 of the study and running through month 28 for study entry. The span of treatment is 12 months and is followed by 12 months of follow-up. . . .

Study Criteria.
Those volunteering to participate will be screened and declared eligible for the study based upon the following characteristics:
1. Determination that subject is homeless using criteria operationally defined by one of the accepted definitions summarized by . . .

Attrition.
Subject enrollment, treatment engagement, and subject retention each represent potentially significant challenges to study integrity and have been given special attention in all phases of the project. Techniques have been developed to address engagement and retention and are described in detail below. . . .

Research Procedures.
All clients referred to the participating shelters will be screened for basic study criteria. . . . Once assessment is completed, subjects who volunteer are then randomly assigned to one of two treatment conditions—RPST or Standard Treatment. . . .

Research Variables and Measures.
Measures for this study . . . are of three kinds: subject selection measures, process measures, and outcome measures. . . .

5. Human Subjects
Potential risks to subjects are minor. . . . Acute problems identified . . . can be quickly referred to appropriate interventions. Participation in the project is voluntary, and all subjects retain the option to withdraw . . . at any time, without any impact on their access to shelter care or services regularly offered by the shelters. Confidentiality of subjects is guaranteed. . . . [They have] . . . an opportunity to learn new ways of dealing with symptoms of substance abuse and mental illness.

Massachusetts Medical School. The research plan is limited by NIH guidelines to 25 pages. It must be preceded by an abstract (which is excerpted), a proposed budget, biographical sketches of project personnel, and a discussion of the available resources for the project. Appendixes may include research instruments, prior publications by the authors, and findings from related work.

As you can see from the excerpts, the proposal was to study the efficacy of a particular treatment approach for homeless, mentally ill persons who abuse substances. The proposal included a procedure for recruiting subjects in two cities, randomly assigning half of the subjects to a recently developed treatment program, and measuring a range of outcomes. The NIMH review committee (composed of social scientists who were experts in these issues) approved the project for funding but did not rate it highly enough that it actually was awarded funds. (It often takes several resubmissions before even a worthwhile proposal is funded.) The committee members recognized the proposal's strengths but also identified several problems that they believed had to be overcome before the proposal could be funded. The problems were primarily methodological, stemming from the difficulties associated with providing services to and conducting research on this particular segment of the homeless population.

The proposal has many strengths, including the specially tailored intervention derived from psychiatric rehabilitation technology developed by Liberman and his associates and relapse prevention methods adapted from Marlatt.

> This fully documented treatment ... greatly facilitates the generalizability and transportability of study findings. . . . The investigative team is excellent . . . also attuned to the difficulties entailed in studying this target group. . . . While these strengths recommend the proposal . . . eligibility criteria for inclusion of subjects in the study are somewhat ambiguous. . . . This volunteer procedure could substantially underrepresent important components of the shelter population. . . . The projected time frame for recruiting subjects . . . also seems unrealistic for a three-year effort. . . . Several factors in the research design seem to mitigate against maximum participation and retention.

If you get the impression that researchers cannot afford to leave any stone unturned in working through procedures in an NIMH proposal, you are right. It is very difficult to convince a government agency that a research project is worth spending a lot of money on (we requested about $2 million). And that is as it should be: Your tax dollars should be used only for research that has a high likelihood of yielding findings that are valid and useful. But even when you are proposing a smaller project to a more generous funding source—or even presenting a proposal to your professor—you should scrutinize the proposal carefully before submission and ask others to comment on it. Other people will often think of issues you neglected to consider, and you should allow yourself time to think about these issues and to reread and redraft the proposal. Besides, you will get no credit for having thrown together a proposal as best you could in the face of an impossible submission deadline.

When you develop a research proposal, it will help to work through each of the issues in Exhibit 12.4 (also see Herek, 1995). It is too easy to omit important details and to avoid being self-critical while rushing to put a proposal together. However, it is painful to have a proposal rejected (or to receive a low grade). Better to make sure the proposal covers what it should and confronts the tough issues that reviewers (or your professor) will be sure to spot.

The points in Exhibit 12.4 can serve as a map to preceding chapters in this book and as a checklist of decisions that must be made throughout any research project. The points are organized in five sections, each concluding with a *checkpoint* at which you should consider whether to proceed with the research as planned, modify the plans, or stop the project altogether. The sequential ordering of these questions obscures a bit the way in which they should be answered: not as single questions, one at a time, but as a unit—first as five separate stages and then as a whole. Feel free to change your answers to earlier questions on the basis of your answers to later questions.

A brief review of how the questions in Exhibit 12.4 might be answered with respect to Schutt's NIMH relapse prevention proposal (with Walter E. Penk and others) should help you to review your own work. The research question concerned the effectiveness of a particular type of substance abuse treatment in a shelter for homeless persons, an evaluation research question (Question 1). This problem certainly was suitable for social research, and it could have been handled for the money we requested (Question 2). Prior research

EXHIBIT 12.4   **Decisions in Research Design**

PROBLEM FORMULATION (Chapters 1–2)
1. Developing a research question
2. Assessing researchability of the problem
3. Consulting prior research
4. Relating to social theory
5. Choosing an approach: Deductive? Inductive? Descriptive?
6. Reviewing research guidelines

   CHECKPOINT 1

   Alternatives: • Continue as planned.
   • Modify the plan.
   • STOP. Abandon the plan.

RESEARCH VALIDITY (Chapters 3–5)
7. Establishing measurement validity
8. Establishing generalizability
9. Establishing causality
10. Data required: Longitudinal or cross-sectional?
11. Units of analysis: Individuals or groups?
12. What are major possible sources of causal invalidity?

   CHECKPOINT 2

   Alternatives: • Continue as planned.
   • Modify the plan.
   • STOP. Abandon the plan.

RESEARCH DESIGN (Chapters 6–8)
13. Choosing a research design, such as survey or participant observation
14. Specifying the research plan: Types of experiments, surveys, observations, etc.
15. Assessing ethical concerns

   CHECKPOINT 3

   Alternatives: • Continue as planned.
   • Modify the plan.
   • STOP. Abandon the plan.

DATA ANALYSIS (Chapter 9)
16. Choosing statistics, such as frequencies, cross-tabulation, etc.

   CHECKPOINT 4

   Alternatives: • Continue as planned.
   • Modify the plan.
   • STOP. Abandon the plan.

REVIEWING, PROPOSING, AND REPORTING RESEARCH (Chapter 10)
17. Organizing the text
18. Reviewing ethical and practical constraints

   CHECKPOINT 5

   Alternatives: • Continue as planned.
   • Modify the plan.
   • STOP. Abandon the plan.

demonstrated clearly that our proposed treatment had potential and also that it had not previously been tried with homeless persons (3). The treatment approach was connected to psychosocial rehabilitation theory (4) and, given prior work in this area, a deductive, hypothesis-testing stance was called for (5). Our review of research guidelines continued up to the point of submission, and we felt that our proposal took each into account (6). So it seemed reasonable to continue to develop the proposal (Checkpoint 1).

Measures would include direct questions, observations by field researchers, and laboratory tests (of substance abuse) (7). The proposal's primary weakness was in the area of generalizability (8). We proposed to sample persons in only two homeless shelters in two cities, and we could offer only weak incentives to encourage potential participants to start the study and stay in it. The review committee believed that these procedures might result in an unrepresentative group of initial volunteers beginning the treatment and perhaps an even less representative group continuing through the entire program. The problem was well suited to a randomized, experimental design (9) and was best addressed with longitudinal data (10) involving individuals (11). Our randomized design controlled for selection bias and endogenous change, but external events, treatment contamination, and treatment misidentification were potential sources of causal invalidity (12). Clearly we should have modified the proposal with some additional recruitment and retention strategies—although it may be that the research could not actually be carried out without some major modification of the research question (Checkpoint 2).

A randomized experimental design was preferable because this was to be a treatment-outcome study, but we did include a field research component so that we could evaluate treatment implementation (13, 14). Because the effectiveness of our proposed treatment strategy had not been studied before among homeless persons, we could not propose doing a secondary data analysis or meta-analysis (15). We sought only to investigate causation from a nomothetic perspective, without attempting to show how the particular experiences of each participant may have led to that person's outcome (16). Because participation in the study was to be voluntary and everyone received *something* for participation, the research design seemed ethical (and it was approved by the University of Massachusetts Medical School's Institutional Review Board and by the state mental health agency's human subjects committee) (17). We planned several statistical tests, but here the review committee remarked that we should have been more specific (18). Our goal was to use our research as the basis for several academic articles, and we expected that the funding agency would also require us to prepare a report for general distribution (19, 20). We had reviewed the research literature carefully (21), but as is typical in most research proposals, we did not develop our research reporting plans any further (22, 23).

🔲 REPORTING RESEARCH

The goal of research is not just to discover something but to communicate that discovery to a larger audience: other social scientists, government officials, your teachers, the general public—perhaps several of these audiences. Whatever the study's particular outcome, if the research report enables the intended audience to comprehend the results and learn from them, the research can be judged a success. If the intended audience is not able to learn about the study's results, the research should be judged a failure—no matter how expensive the research, how sophisticated its design, or how much of yourself you invested in it.

You began writing your research report when you worked on the research proposal, and you will find that the final report is much easier to write, and more adequate, if you write more material for it as you work out issues during the project. It is very disappointing to discover that something important was left out when it is too late to do anything about it. And we don't need to point out that students (and professional researchers) often leave final papers (and reports) until the last possible minute (often for understandable reasons, including other coursework and job or family responsibilities). But be forewarned: *The last-minute approach does not work for research reports.*

Writing and Organizing

A successful report must be well organized and clearly written. Getting to such a product is a difficult but not impossible goal. Consider the following principles formulated by experienced writers (Booth, Colomb, & Williams, 1995:150–151):

- Respect the complexity of the task and don't expect to write a polished draft in a linear fashion. Your thinking will develop as you write, causing you to reorganize and rewrite.
- Leave enough time for dead ends, restarts, revisions, and so on and accept the fact that you will discard much of what you write.
- Write as fast as you comfortably can. Don't worry about spelling, grammar, and so on until you are polishing things up.
- Ask anyone you trust for reactions to what you have written.
- Write as you go along, so you have notes and report segments drafted even before you focus on writing the report.

It is important to outline a report before writing it, but neither the organization of the report nor the first written draft should be considered fixed. As you write, you will get new ideas about how to organize the report. Try them out. As you review the first draft, you will see many ways to improve your writing. Focus particularly on how to shorten and clarify your statements. Make sure that each paragraph concerns only one topic. Remember the golden rule of good writing: Writing is revising!

You can ease the burden of writing in several ways:

- Draw on the research proposal and on project notes. You aren't starting from scratch; you have all the material you've written during the course of the project.
- Refine your word processing skills on the computer so that you can use the most efficient techniques when reorganizing and editing.
- Seek criticism from friends, teachers, or other research consumers before you turn in the final product. They will alert you to problems in the research or the writing.

We often find it helpful to use *reverse outlining*. After you have written a first draft, read through the draft, noting down the key ideas as they come up. Do those notes reflect your original outline, or did you go astray? Are the paragraphs clean? How could your organization be improved?

Most important, leave yourself enough time so that you *can* revise, several times if possible, before turning in the final draft.

You can find more detailed reviews of writing techniques in Becker (1986), Booth et al. (1995), Mullins (1977), Strunk and White (1979), and Turabian (1967).

Your report should be clearly organized into sections, probably following a standard format that readers will immediately understand. Any research report should include an *introductory statement of the research problem,* a *literature review,* and a *methodology section.* These are the same three sections that should begin a research proposal. In addition, a research report must include a *findings section* with pertinent data displays. A *discussion section* may be used to interpret the findings and review the support for the study's hypotheses. A *conclusions section* should summarize the findings and draw implications for the theoretical framework used. Any weaknesses in the research design and ways to improve future research should be identified in this section. Compelling foci for additional research on the research question also should be noted. Most journals require a short abstract at the beginning that summarizes the research question and findings. A *bibliography* is also necessary. Depending on how the report is being published, *appendixes* containing the instruments used and specific information on the measures also may be included.

Exhibit 12.5 presents an outline of the sections in an academic journal article with some illustrative quotes. The article's introduction highlights the importance of the problem selected—the relation between marital disruption (divorce) and depression. The introduction also states clearly the gap in the research literature that the article is meant to fill—the untested possibility that depression might cause marital disruption rather than, or in addition to, marital disruption causing depression. The findings section (labeled "Results") begins by presenting the basic association between marital disruption and depression. Then it elaborates on this association by examining sex differences, the impact of prior marital quality, and various mediating and modifying effects. As indicated in the combined discussion and conclusions section, the analysis shows that marital disruption does indeed increase depression and specifies the time frame (3 years) during which this effect occurs.

These basic report sections present research results well, but many research reports include subsections tailored to the issues and stages in the specific study being reported. Lengthy applied reports on elaborate research projects may, in fact, be organized around the research project's different stages or foci.

The material that can be termed the *front matter* and the *back matter* of an applied report also is important. Applied reports usually begin with an executive summary: a summary list of the study's main findings, often with bullet points. Appendixes, the "back matter," may present tables containing supporting data that were not discussed in the body of the report. Applied research reports also often append a copy of the research instrument(s).

EXHIBIT 12.5   Sections in a Journal Article

INTRODUCTION
Despite 20 years of empirical research, the extent to which marital disruption causes poor mental health remains uncertain. The reason for this uncertainty is that previous research has consistently overlooked the potentially important problems of selection into and out of marriage on the basis of prior mental health. (p. 237)

SAMPLE AND MEASURES
Sample
Measures

RESULTS
The Basic Association Between Marital Disruption and Depression
Sex Differences
The Impact of Prior Marital Quality
The Mediating Effects of Secondary Changes
The Modifying Effects of Transitions to Secondary Roles

DISCUSSION [includes conclusions]
. . . According to the results, marital disruption does in fact cause a significant increase in depression compared to pre-divorce levels within a period of three years after the divorce. (p. 245)

For instance, Exhibit 12.6 outlines the sections in an applied research report. This particular report was mandated by the California State Legislature to review a state-funded program for the homeless mentally disabled. The goals of the report are described as both description and evaluation. The body of the report presents findings on the number and characteristics of homeless persons and on the operations of the state-funded program in each of 17 counties. The discussion section highlights service needs that are not being met. Nine appendixes then provide details on the study methodology and the counties studied.

An important principle for the researcher writing for a nonacademic audience is to make the findings and conclusions engaging and clear. You can see how Schutt did this in a report from a class research project designed with his graduate methods students (and in collaboration with several faculty knowledgeable about substance abuse) (Exhibit 12.7). These report excerpts indicate how he summarized key findings in an executive summary (Schutt et al., 1996:iv), emphasized the importance of the research in the introduction (Schutt et al.:1), used formatting and graphing to draw attention to particular findings in the body of the text (Schutt et al.:5), and tailored recommendations to his own university context (Schutt et al.:26).

A well-written research report requires (to be just a bit melodramatic) blood, sweat, and tears—and more time than you may at first anticipate. But writing one report will help you write the next report. And the issues you consider, if you approach your writing critically, will be sure to improve your subsequent research projects and sharpen your evaluations of other investigators' research projects.

EXHIBIT 12.6 **Sections in an Applied Report**

SUMMARY

In 1986, the California State Legislature mandated an independent review of the HMD programs that the counties had established with the state funds. The review was to determine the accountability of funds; describe the demographic and mental disorder characteristics of persons served; and assess the effectiveness of the program. This report describes the results of that review. (p. v)

INTRODUCTION

Background

California's Mental Health Services Act of 1985 . . . allocated $20 million annually to the state's 58 counties to support a wide range of services, from basic needs to rehabilitation. (pp. 1–2)

Study Objectives

Organization of the Report

HMD PROGRAM DESCRIPTION AND STUDY METHODOLOGY

The HMD Program

Study Design and Methods

Study Limitations

COUNTING AND CHARACTERIZING THE HOMELESS

Estimating the Number of Homeless People

Characteristics of the Homeless Population

THE HMD PROGRAM IN 17 COUNTIES

Service Priorities

Delivery of Services

Implementation Progress

Selected Outcomes

Effects on the Community and on County Service Agencies

Service Gaps

DISCUSSION

Underserved Groups of HMD

Gaps in Continuity of Care

A particularly large gap in the continuum of care is the lack of specialized housing alternatives for the mentally disabled. The nature of chronic mental illness limits the ability of these individuals to live completely independently. But their housing needs may change, and board-and-care facilities that are acceptable during some periods of their lives may become unacceptable at other times. (p. 57)

Improved Service Delivery

Issues for Further Research

Appendixes

A. SELECTION OF 17 SAMPLED COUNTIES

B. QUESTIONNAIRE FOR SURVEY OF THE HOMELESS

C. GUIDELINES FOR CASE STUDIES

D. INTERVIEW INSTRUMENTS FOR TELEPHONE SURVEY

E. HOMELESS STUDY SAMPLING DESIGN, ENUMERATION, AND SURVEY WEIGHTS

F. HOMELESS SURVEY FIELD PROCEDURES

G. SHORT SCREENER FOR MENTAL AND SUBSTANCE USE DISORDERS

H. CHARACTERISTICS OF THE COUNTIES AND THEIR HMD-FUNDED PROGRAMS

I. CASE STUDIES FOR FOUR COUNTIES' HMD PROGRAMS

EXHIBIT 12.7   **Student Substance Abuse, Report Excerpts**

Executive Summary

- Rates of substance abuse were somewhat lower at UMass–Boston than among nationally selected samples of college students.
- Two-thirds of the respondents reported at least one close family member whose drinking or drug use had ever been of concern to them—one-third reported a high level of concern.
- Most students perceived substantial risk of harm due to illicit drug use, but just one-quarter thought alcohol use posed a great risk of harm.

Introduction

Binge drinking, other forms of alcohol abuse, and illicit drug use create numerous problems on college campuses. Deaths from binge drinking are too common and substance abuse is a factor in as many as two-thirds of on-campus sexual assaults (Finn, 1997; National Institute of Alcohol Abuse and Alcoholism, 1995). College presidents now rate alcohol abuse as the number one campus problem (Wechsler, Davenport, Dowdall, Moeykens, & Castillo, 1994) and many schools have been devising new substance abuse prevention policies and programs. However, in spite of increasing recognition of and knowledge about substance abuse problems at colleges as a whole, little attention has been focused on substance abuse at commuter schools.

Findings

The composite index identifies 27% of respondents as at risk of substance abuse (an index score of 2 or higher).[1] One-quarter reported having smoked or used smokeless tobacco in the past two weeks.

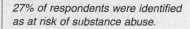

27% of respondents were identified as at risk of substance abuse.

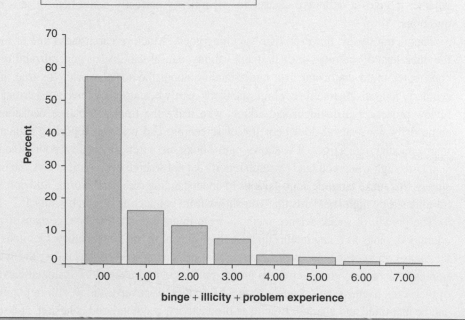

(Continued)

(Continued)

Recommendations

1. Enforce campus rules and regulations about substance use. When possible and where appropriate, communications from campus officials to students should heighten awareness of the UMass–Boston commitment to an alcohol- and drug-free environment.

2. Encourage those students involved in campus alcohol or drug-related problems or crises to connect with the PRIDE program.

3. Take advantage of widespread student interest in prevention by forming a university-wide council to monitor and stimulate interest in prevention activities.

🔲 CONCLUSION

Good critical skills are essential in evaluating research reports, whether your own or those produced by others. And it is really not just a question of sharpening your knives and going for the jugular. There are *always* weak points in any research, even published research. Being aware of the weaknesses, both in others' studies and in your own, is a major strength in itself. You need to be able to weigh the results of any particular research and to evaluate a study in terms of its contribution to understanding the social world—not in terms of whether it gives a definitive answer for all time, is perfectly controlled, or answers all questions.

This is not to say, however, that "anything goes." Much research lacks one or more of the three legs of validity—measurement validity, causal validity, or generalizability—and contributes more confusion than understanding about the social world. It's true that top scholarly journals maintain very high standards, partly because they have good critics in the review process and distinguished editors who make the final acceptance decisions. But some daily newspapers do a poor job of screening, and research reporting standards in many popular magazines, TV shows, and books are often abysmally poor. Keep your standards high when you read research reports but not so high or so critical that you dismiss studies that make tangible contributions to understanding the social world. And don't be so intimidated by high standards that you shrink from conducting research yourself.

The growth of social science methods from infancy to adolescence, perhaps to young adulthood, ranks as a key intellectual accomplishment of the 20th century. Opinions about the causes and consequences of homelessness no longer need to depend on the scattered impressions of individuals, criminal justice policies can be shaped by systematic evidence of their effectiveness, and changes in the distribution of poverty and wealth in populations can be identified and charted. Employee productivity, neighborhood cohesion, and societal conflict can each be linked to individual psychological processes and to international economic strains. Systematic researchers looking at truly representative data can make connections and see patterns that no casual observer would ever discern.

Of course, social research methods are only helpful when the researchers are committed and honest. Research methods, like all knowledge, can be used poorly or well, for good purposes or bad, when appropriate or not. A claim that "We're basing this on research!" or "Our statistics prove it!" in itself provides no extra credibility. As you have learned throughout this book, we must first learn which methods were used, how they were applied, and whether final interpretations square with the evidence. But having done all that in good faith, we do emerge from confusion into clarity in our continuing effort to make sense of the social world.

HIGHLIGHTS

- Research reports should be evaluated systematically, using the review guide in Exhibit 12.2 and taking account of the interrelations among the design elements.
- Proposal writing should be a time for clarifying the research problem, reviewing the literature, and thinking ahead about the report that will be required. Tradeoffs between different design elements should be considered and the potential for mixing methods evaluated.
- Different types of reports typically pose different problems. Authors of student papers must be guided in part by the expectations of their professors. Thesis writers have to meet the requirements of different committee members but can benefit greatly from the areas of expertise represented on a typical thesis committee. Applied researchers are constrained by the expectations of the research sponsor; an advisory committee from the applied setting can help to avoid problems. Journal articles must pass a peer review by other social scientists and often are much improved in the process.
- Research reports should include an introductory statement of the research problem, a literature review, a methodology section, a findings section with pertinent data displays, and a conclusions section that identifies any weaknesses in the research design and points out implications for future research and theorizing. This basic report format should be modified according to the needs of a particular audience.
- All reports should be revised several times and critiqued by others before being presented in final form.

STUDENT STUDY SITE

To assist you in completing the Web Exercises, please access the Study Site at **http://www.pineforge.com/mssw3**, where you'll find the Web Exercises with accompanying links. You'll find other useful study materials like self-quizzes and e-flashcards for each chapter, along with a group of carefully selected articles from research journals that illustrate the major concepts and techniques presented in the book.

EXERCISES

Discussing Research

1. A good place to start developing your critical skills would be with one of the articles reviewed in this chapter. Try reading one and fill in the answers to the article review questions that we did not cover (Appendix B). Do you agree with our answers to the other questions? Could you add some points to our critique or to the lessons on research design that we drew from these critiques?

2. How firm a foundation do social research methods provide for understanding the social world? Discuss the pro and con arguments, focusing on the variability of social research findings across different social contexts and the difficulty of understanding human subjectivity.

3. Rate four journal articles for the overall quality of the research and for the effectiveness of the writing and data displays. Discuss how each could have been improved.

Finding Research

1. Go to the National Science Foundation's Sociology Program Web site at http://www.nsf.gov/funding/pgm_summ.jsp?pims_id=5369. What components does the National Science Foundation's Sociology Program look for in a proposed piece of research? Outline a research proposal to study a subject of your choice to be submitted to the National Science Foundation for funding.

2. The National Academy of Sciences wrote a lengthy report on ethics issues in scientific research. Visit the site and read the free executive summary you can obtain at http://www.nap.edu/catalog.php?record_id=10430. Summarize the information and guidelines in the report.

3. Search a social science journal to find five examples of social science research projects. Briefly describe each. How does each differ in its approach to reporting the research results? To whom do you think the author(s) of each is "reporting" (i.e., who is the "audience")? How do you think the predicted audience has helped to shape the author's approach to reporting the results? Be sure to note the source in which you located your five examples.

Critiquing Research

1. A good place to start developing your critical skills would be with Murray Melbin's article that is reviewed in this chapter. Try reading it and fill in the answers to the article review questions that we did not cover (Exhibit 12.2). Do you agree with our answers to the other questions? Could you add some points to our critique or to the lessons about research designs that we drew from these critiques?

2. Read the journal article "Marital Disruption and Depression in a Community Sample" by Aseltine and Kessler in the September 1993 issue of *Journal of Health and Social Behavior.*

How effective is the article in conveying the design and findings of the research? Could the article's organization be improved at all? Are there bases for disagreement about the interpretation of the findings?

3. Rate four journal articles for overall quality of the research and for effectiveness of the writing and data displays. Discuss how each could have been improved.

Doing Research

1. Call a local social or health service administrator or a criminal justice official and arrange for an interview. Ask the official about his or her experience with applied research reports and conclusions about the value of social research and the best techniques for reporting to practitioners.

2. Interview a student who has written an independent paper or thesis based on collecting original data. Ask the student to describe her or his experiences while writing the thesis. Review the decisions she or he made in designing the research and ask about the stages of research design, data collection and analysis, and report writing that proved to be difficult.

3. Design a research proposal, following the outline and guidelines presented in this chapter. Focus on a research question that you could study on campus or in your local community.

Ethics Questions

1. Plagiarism is no joke. What are the regulations on plagiarism in class papers at your school? What do you think the ideal policy would be? Should this policy take into account cultural differences in teaching practices and learning styles? Do you think this ideal policy is likely to be implemented? Why or why not? Based on your experiences, do you believe that most student plagiarism is the result of misunderstanding about proper citation practices, or is it the result of dishonesty? Do you think that students who plagiarize while in school are less likely to be honest as social researchers?

2. Full disclosure of funding sources, as well as paid consulting and other business relationships, is now required by most journals. Should researchers publishing in social science journals also be required to fully disclose all sources of funding, including receipt of payment for research done as a consultant? Should full disclosure of all previous funding sources be required in each published article? Write a short justification of the regulations you propose.

APPENDIX A

Finding Information

ELIZABETH SCHNEIDER, MLS

RUSSELL K. SCHUTT, PhD

All research is conducted in order to "find information" in some sense, but the focus of this section is more specifically about finding information to inform a central research project. This has often been termed "searching the literature," but the popularity of the World Wide Web for finding information requires that we broaden our focus beyond the traditional search of the published literature. It may sound trite, but we do indeed live in an "information age," with an unprecedented amount of information of many types available to us with relatively little effort. Learning how to locate and use that information efficiently has become a prerequisite for social science.

▣ SEARCHING THE LITERATURE

It is most important to search the literature before we begin a research study. A good literature review may reveal that the research problem already has been adequately investigated; it may highlight particular aspects of the research problem most in need of further investigation; or it may suggest that the planned research design is not appropriate for the problem chosen. It can highlight the strong and weak points of related theories. When we review previous research about our research question, we may learn about weaknesses in our measures, complexities in our research problem, and possible difficulties in data collection. The more of these problems that can be taken into account before, rather than after, data are collected, the better the final research product will be. Even when the rush to "find out" what people think or are doing creates pressure to just go out and ask or observe, it is important to take the time to search the literature and try to reap the benefit of prior investigations.

But the social science literature is not just a source for guidance at the start of an investigation. During a study, questions will arise that can be answered by careful reading of earlier research. After data collection has ceased, reviewing the literature can help to develop new insights into patterns in the data. Research articles published since a project began may suggest new hypotheses or questions to explore.

The best way of searching the literature will be determined in part by what library and bibliographic resources are available to you, but a brief review of some basic procedures and alternative strategies will help you get started on a productive search.

Preparing the Search

You should formulate a research question before you begin the search, although the question may change after you begin. Identify the question's parts and subparts and any related issues that you think might play an important role in the research. List the authors of relevant studies you are aware of, possible keywords that might specify the subject for your search, and perhaps the most important journals that you are concerned with checking. For example, if your research question is "What is the effect of informal social control on crime?" you might consider searching the literature electronically for studies that mentioned "informal social control" and "crime" or "crime rate" or "violence" and "arrest." If you are concerned with more specific aspects of this question, you should also include the relevant words in your list, such as "family" or "community policing" or even "Northeast."

Conducting the Search

Now you are ready to begin searching the literature. You should check for relevant books in your library and perhaps in the other college libraries in your area. This usually means conducting a search of an online catalog using a list of subject terms. But most scientific research is published in journal articles so that research results can quickly be disseminated to other scientists. The primary focus of your search must therefore be the journal literature. Fortunately, much of the journal literature can be identified online, without leaving your personal computer, and an increasing number of published journal articles can be downloaded directly to your own computer (depending on your particular access privileges). But just because there's a lot available online doesn't mean that you need to find it all. Keep in mind that your goal is to find reports of prior research investigations; this means that you should focus on scholarly journals that choose articles for publication after they have been reviewed by other social scientists—"refereed journals." Newspaper and magazine articles just won't do, although you may find some that raise important issues or even that summarize social science research investigations.

The social science literature should be consulted at both the beginning and the end of an investigation. Even while an investigation is in progress, consultations with the literature may help to resolve methodological problems or facilitate supplementary explorations. As with any part of the research process, the method you use will affect the quality of your results. You should try to ensure that your search method includes each of the following steps:

Specify your research question. Your research question should not be so broad that hundreds of articles are judged relevant, or so narrow that you miss important literature. "Is informal social control effective?" is probably too broad. "Does informal social control reduce rates of burglary in large cities?" is probably too narrow. "Is informal social control more effective in reducing crime rates than policing?" provides about the right level of specificity.

Identify appropriate bibliographic databases to search. Sociological Abstracts (Sociofile) may meet many of your needs, but if you are studying a question about social factors in illness you should also search in Medline, the database for searching the medical literature. If your focus is on mental health, you'll also want to include a search in psychological abstracts (Psyc*INFO*). In order to find articles across the social sciences that have referred to a previous publication, like Sherman and Berk's study of the police response to domestic violence, the Social Science Citation Index (SSCI) will be helpful. SSCI has a unique "citation searching" feature that allows you to look up articles or books and see who else has cited them in their work. This is an excellent and efficient way to assemble a number of references that are highly relevant to your research and to find out which articles and books have had the biggest impact in a field. Unfortunately, some college libraries do not subscribe to SSCI, either in its print, CD-ROM, or online version, due to its expense, but if you have access to SSCI, you should consider using it whenever you want to make sure that you develop the strongest possible literature review for your topic. In addition, the search engine Google now offers anyone with Web access "Google Scholar" (which indexes and searches the full text of selected journals) and "Google Print" (which digitizes and searches the full text of the books that are owned by selected research libraries). (When this book went to press the Google Print project was on hold due to copyright concerns raised by some publishers, while the search engine and directory Yahoo was starting a similar venture that focused only on older books that are no longer covered by copyright law.) (Hafner, 2005:C1).

Choose a search technology. For most purposes, an online bibliographic database that references the published journal literature will be all you need to find the relevant social science research literature. However, searches for more obscure topics or very recent literature may require that you also search Web sites or bibliographies of relevant books. You will also need to search Web sites when you need to learn about current debate about particular social issues or you are investigating current social programs.

Create a tentative list of search terms. List the parts and subparts of your research question and any related issues that you think are important: "informal social control," "policing," "influences on crime rates," and perhaps "community cohesion and crime." List the authors of relevant studies. Specify the most important journals that deal with your topic.

Narrow your search. The sheer number of references you find can be a problem. For example, searching for "social capital" resulted in 4,635 citations in *Sociological Abstracts*. Depending on the database you are working with and the purposes of your search, you may want to limit your search to English language publications, to journal articles rather than conference papers or dissertations (both of which are more difficult to acquire), and to materials published in recent years. You should give most attention to articles published in the leading journals in the field. Your professor can help you identify them.

Refine your search. Learn as you go. If your search yields too many citations, try specifying the search terms more precisely. If you have not found much literature, try using more general terms. Whatever terms you search on first, don't consider your search complete until you have tried several different approaches and have seen how many articles you find. A search for "domestic violence" in *Sociological Abstracts* on September 7, 2008, yielded 2,836 hits; by adding "effects" OR "influences" as required search terms the number of hits dropped to 744. A good rule is to cast a net with your search terms that is wide enough to catch most of the relevant articles but not so wide that it identifies many useless citations. In any case, if you are searching a popular topic, you will need to spend a fair amount of time whittling down the list of citations.

Use Boolean search logic. It's often a good idea to narrow your search by requiring that abstracts contain combinations of words or phrases that include more of the specifics of your research question. Using the Boolean connector AND allows you to do this, while using the connector OR allows you to find abstracts containing different words that mean the same thing. Exhibit A.1 provides an example.

Use appropriate subject descriptors. Once you have found an article that you consider to be appropriate, take a look at the "descriptors" field in the citation (see Exhibit A.2). You can then redo your search after requiring that the articles be classified with some or all of these descriptor terms.

Check the results. Read the titles and abstracts you have found and identify the articles that appear to be most relevant. If possible, click on these article titles and generate a list of their references. See if you find more articles that are relevant to your research question but that you have missed so far. You will be surprised (we always are) at how many important articles your initial online search missed.

Read the articles. Now it is time to find the full text of the articles of interest. If you're lucky, many of the articles you need will be available to patrons of your library in online versions, and you'll be

---

EXHIBIT A.1 **Use of Boolean Connectors in a Literature Search**

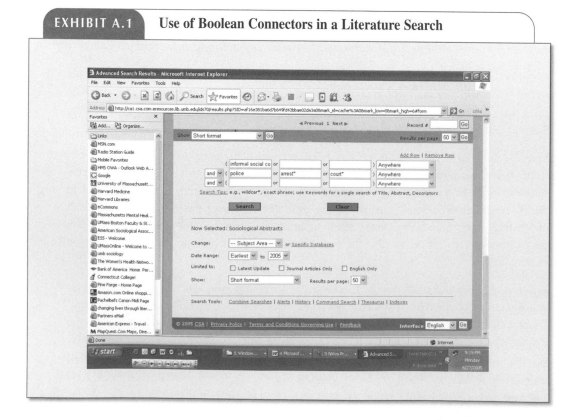

| EXHIBIT A.2 | **Checking Standard Subject Matter Descriptors** |

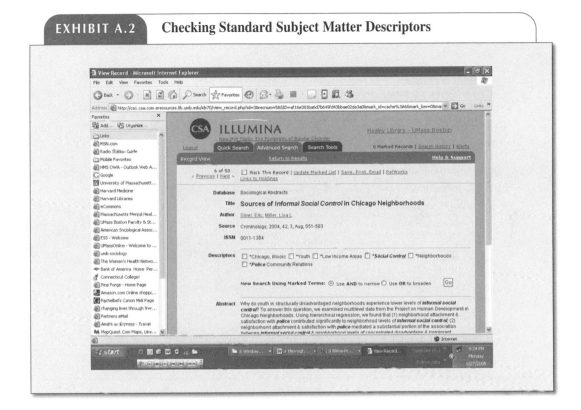

able to link to the full text just by clicking on a "full text" link. But many journals and/or specific issues of some journals will only be available in print, so you'll have to find them in your library (or order a copy through interlibrary loan). You may be tempted to write a "review" of the literature based on reading the abstracts or using only those articles available online, but you will be selling yourself short. Many crucial details about methods, findings, and theoretical implications will be found only in the body of the article and some important articles will not be available online. To understand, critique, and really learn from previous research studies, you must read the important articles, no matter how you have to retrieve them. But if you can't obtain the full text of an article, you'll just have to leave it out of your literature review and bibliography—reading the abstract just isn't enough.

Write the review. If you have done your job well, you will now have more than enough literature as background for your own research unless it is on a very obscure topic (see Exhibit A.3). (Of course, ultimately your search will be limited by the library holdings you have access to and by the time you have to order or find copies of journal articles, conference papers, and perhaps dissertations that you can't obtain online.) At this point, your main concern is to construct a coherent framework in which to develop your research question, drawing as many lessons as you can from previous research. You can use the literature to identify a useful theory and hypotheses to be reexamined, to find inadequately studied specific research questions, to explicate the disputes about your research question, to summarize the major findings of prior research, and to suggest appropriate methods of investigation.

EXHIBIT A.3   **A Search in *Sociological Abstracts* on "Informal Social Control"**

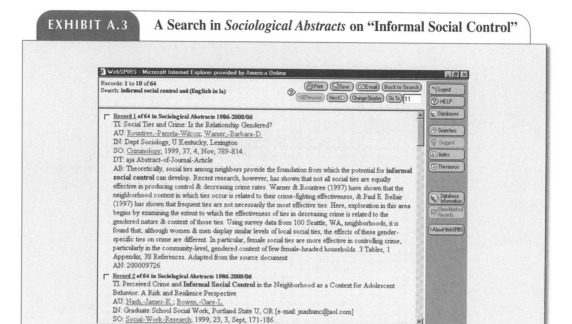

Be sure to take notes on each article you read, organizing your notes into standard sections: theory, methods, findings, conclusions. In any case, write the literature review so that it contributes to your study in some concrete way; don't feel compelled to discuss an article just because you have read it. Be judicious. You are conducting only one study of one issue; it will only obscure the value of your study if you try to relate it to every tangential point in related research.

Continue to search. Don't think of searching the literature as a one-time-only venture—something that you leave behind as you move on to your *real* research. You may encounter new questions or unanticipated problems as you conduct your research or as you burrow deeper into the literature. Searching the literature again to determine what others have found in response to these questions or what steps they have taken to resolve these problems can yield substantial improvements in your own research. There is so much literature on so many topics that it often is not possible to figure out in advance every subject you should search the literature for or what type of search will be most beneficial.

Another reason to make searching the literature an ongoing project is that the literature is always growing. During the course of one research study, whether it takes only one semester or several years, new findings will be published and relevant questions will be debated. Staying attuned to the literature and checking it at least when you are writing up your findings may save your study from being outdated. Of course, this does not make life any easier for researchers. For example, one of your authors was registered for a time with a service that every week sent citations of new journal articles on homelessness to his electronic mailbox. Most were not very important, and even looking over the abstracts for between 5 and 15 new articles each week is quite a chore—that's part of the price we pay for living in the information age!

Refer to a good book for even more specific guidance about literature searching. Arlene Fink's (2005) *Conducting Research Literature Reviews: From the Internet to Paper,* Sage Publications, is an excellent guide.

▣ SEARCHING THE WEB

The World Wide Web provides access to vast amounts of information of many different sorts (O'Dochartaigh, 2002). You can search the holdings of other libraries and download the complete text of government reports, some conference papers, and newspaper articles. You can find policies of local governments, descriptions of individual social scientists and particular research projects, and postings of advocacy groups. It's also hard to avoid finding a lot of information in which you have no interest, such as commercial advertisements, third-grade homework assignments, or college course syllabi. In 1999, there were already about 800 million publicly available pages of information on the Web (Davis, 1999). Today there may be as many as 15 billion pages on the Web (Novak, 2003).

After you are connected to the Web with a browser like Microsoft Internet Explorer or Netscape Navigator, you can use three basic strategies for finding information: direct addressing—typing in the address, or URL, of a specific site; browsing—reviewing online lists of Web sites; and searching—the most common approach. "Google" is currently the most popular search engine for searching the Web. For some purposes, you will need to use only one strategy; for other purposes, you will want to use all three. End-of-chapter Web exercises and the Pine Forge Press Study Site for this text both provide many URLs relevant to social science research.

Exhibit A.4 illustrates the first problem that you may encounter when searching the Web: the sheer quantity of resources that are available. It is a much bigger problem than when searching bibliographic databases. On the Web, less is usually more. Limit your inspection of Web sites to the first few pages that turn up in your list (they're ranked by relevance). See what those first pages contain and then try to narrow your search by including some additional terms. Putting quotation marks around a phrase that you want to search will also help to limit your search—searching for "informal social control" on Google (on September 11, 2005) produced 31,100 sites, compared to the 15,500,000 sites retrieved when we omitted the quotes, so Google searched "informal" *and* "social" *and* "control."

Remember the following warnings when you conduct searches on the Web:

- *Clarify your goals.* Before you begin the search, jot down the terms that you think you need to search for as well as a statement of what you want to accomplish with your search. This will help to ensure that you have a sense of what to look for and what to ignore.
- *Quality is not guaranteed.* Anyone can post almost anything, so the accuracy and adequacy of the information you find are always suspect. There's no journal editor or librarian to evaluate quality and relevance. You need to anticipate the different sources of information available on the Web and to decide whether it is appropriate to use each of them for specific purposes. The sources you will find include:

EXHIBIT A.4	Google Search Results for "Informal Social Control"

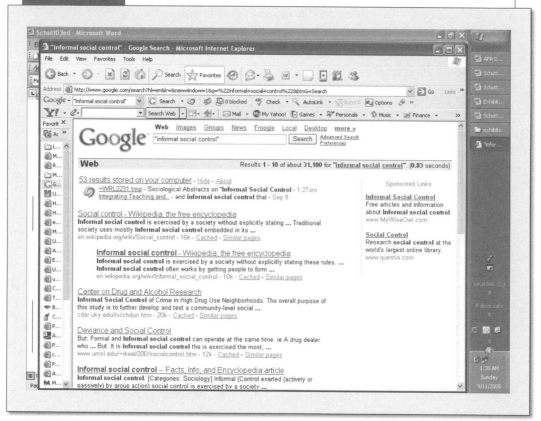

- *Newspaper articles*—These can range from local newspapers like the *Chicago Tribune* to national newspapers like the *New York Times*. Access to articles in these newspapers may be limited to subscribers.

- *Government policies*—You can find government policies and publications ranging from those done at the city or town level to those written by foreign governments.

- *Presented papers*—You may find the complete text of a formal presentation that was given at a meeting or conference.

- *Classroom lecture notes and outlines; listings from college catalogs*—These are pretty straightforward.

- *Commercial advertisements*—Advertising abounds on the Web and it is especially prolific on search engine pages. Your search engine will even retrieve ads from the Web and list them as results of your search! The boundaries between academic, nonprofit, and commercial information have become very porous, so you can't let your guard down.

- *Anticipate change.* Web sites that are not maintained by stable organizations can come and go very quickly. Any search will result in attempts to link to some URLs that no longer exist.
- *One size does not fit all.* Different search engines use different procedures for indexing Web sites. Some attempt to be all-inclusive whereas others aim to be selective. As a result, you can get different results from different search engines (such as Google or Yahoo) even though you are searching for exactly the same terms.
- *Be concerned about generalizability.* You might be tempted to characterize police department policies by summarizing the documents you find at police department Web sites. But how many police departments are there? How many have posted their policies on the Web? Are these policies representative of all police departments? In order to answer all these questions, you would have to conduct a research project just on the Web sites themselves.
- *Evaluate the sites.* There's a lot of stuff out there; so how do you know what's good? Some Web sites contain excellent advice and pointers on how to differentiate the good from the bad. You can find one example at http:// www.library.cornell.edu/olinuris/ref/research/webeval.html.
- *Avoid Web addiction.* Another danger of the extraordinary quantity of information available on the Web is that one search will lead to another and to another and. . . . There are always more possibilities to explore and one more interesting source to check. Establish boundaries of time and effort to avoid the risk of losing all sense of proportion.
- *Cite your sources.* Using text or images from Web sources without attribution is plagiarism. It is the same as copying someone else's work from a book or article and pretending that it is your own. Record the Web address (URL), the name of the information provider, and the date on which you obtain material from the site. Include this information in a footnote to the material that you use in a paper.

Secondary Data Sources

Many quantitative studies and some qualitative investigations use data available from previous research or government agencies. In the United States, the U.S. Bureau of the Census and many other government agencies make data available for general use. Data are also available for research purposes from many other countries as well as from world bodies like the United Nations and the World Bank. Academic researchers and students can draw on a very large data archive at the Inter-university Consortium for Political and Social Research (ICPSR). Qualitative researchers can also use information in published histories or other secondary sources, such as documents found in archival collections. This appendix identifies important sources of such "secondary data."

U.S. Bureau of the Census

The U.S. government has conducted a census of the population every 10 years since 1790; since 1940, this census also has included a census of housing (see also Chapter 4). This decennial Census of Population and Housing is a rich source of social science data (Lavin, 1994). The Census Bureau's monthly *Current Population Survey (CPS)* provides basic data on labor force activity that is then used in Bureau of Labor Statistics reports. The Census Bureau also collects data on agriculture, manufacturers, construction and other business, foreign countries, and foreign trade.

The U.S. Census of Population and Housing aims to survey an adult in every household in the United States. The basic "complete-count" census contains questions about household composition as well as ethnicity and income. More questions are asked in a longer form of the census that is administered to a sample of the households. A separate census of housing characteristics is conducted at the same time (Rives & Serow, 1988:15). Participation in the census is required by law, and confidentiality of the information obtained is mandated by law for 72 years after collection. Census data are reported for geographic units, including states, metropolitan areas, counties, census tracts (small, relatively permanent areas within counties), and even blocks (see Exhibit B.1). These different units allow units of analysis to be tailored to research questions.

Census data are used to apportion seats in the U.S. House of Representatives and to determine federal and state legislative district boundaries, as well as to inform other decisions by government agencies. An interactive data retrieval system, *American FactFinder,* is the primary means for distributing results from the 2000 Census: You can review it at http://factfinder.census.gov/home/saff/main.html?_ lang=en.

The catalog of the ICPSR (www.icpsr.umich.edu) also lists many census reports. Many census files containing microdata—records from persons, households, or housing units—are available online, while others can be purchased on CD-ROM or DVD from the Customer Services Center at (301) 763-INFO (4636); census data can also be inspected online or downloaded for various geographic levels, including counties, cities, census tracts, and even blocks using the DataFerrett application (Federated Electronic Research, Review, Extract, and Tabulation Tool). You can download, install, and use this tool at http://dataferrett.census.gov. This tool also provides access to data sets collected by other federal agencies.

States also maintain census bureaus and may have additional resources. Some contain the original census data collected in the state 100 or more years ago. The ambitious historical researcher can use these returns to conduct detailed comparative studies at the county or state level (Lathrop, 1968:79).

Integrated Public Use Microdata Series

Individual-level samples from U.S. Census data for the years 1850 to 1990, as well as historical census files from several other countries, are available through the Integrated Public Use Microdata Series (IPUMS) at the University of Minnesota's Minnesota Population Center (MPC). These data are prepared in an easy-to-use format that provides consistent codes and names for all the different samples.

This exceptional resource offers 25 samples of the American population selected from 13 federal censuses, with at least 100,000 persons in each sample; in recent years the samples contained more

EXHIBIT B.1   **Census Small-Area Geography**

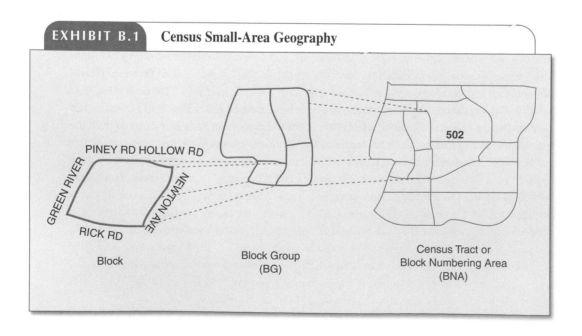

than 1 million persons. Each sample is independently selected, so that individuals are not linked between samples. In addition to basic demographic measures, variables in the U.S. samples include educational, occupational, and work indicators; respondent income; disability status; immigration status; veteran status; and various household characteristics, including family composition and dwelling characteristics. The international samples include detailed characteristics from hundreds of thousands of individuals in countries ranging from France and Mexico to Kenya and Vietnam. You can view these resources at www.ipums.umn.edu.

Many other government agencies provide data for social scientists.

Bureau of Labor Statistics (BLS)

Another good source of data is the Bureau of Labor Statistics of the U.S. Department of Labor, which collects and analyzes data on employment, earnings, prices, living conditions, industrial relations, productivity and technology, and occupational safety and health (U.S. Bureau of Labor Statistics 1991, 1997b). Some of these data are collected by the Bureau of the Census in the monthly *Current Population Survey (CPS)*; other data are collected through surveys of establishments (U.S. Bureau of Labor Statistics 1997a).

The *CPS* provides a monthly employment and unemployment record for the United States, classified by age, sex, race, and other characteristics. The *CPS* uses a stratified random sample of about 60,000 households (with separate forms for about 120,000 individuals). Detailed questions are included to determine the precise labor force status (whether they are currently working or not) of each household member over the age of 16. Statistical reports are published each month in the BLS's *Monthly Labor Review* and can also be inspected at its Web site (http://stats.bls.gov). Datasets are available on computer tapes and disks from the BLS and services like the Inter-University Consortium for Political and Social Research (ICPSR).

Other U.S. Government Sources

Many more datasets useful for historical and comparative research have been collected by federal agencies and other organizations. The National Technical Information Service (NTIS) of the U.S. Department of Commerce maintains a Federal Computer Products Center that collects and catalogs many of these datasets and related software.

By 2008, more than 2,000,000 datasets and reports were described in the NTIS *Directory*. The *Directory* is the essential source of information about the datasets and can be purchased from the U.S. Department of Commerce (National Technical Information Service, 1993). Dataset summaries can be searched in the *Directory* by either subject or agency. Government research reports cataloged by NTIS can be searched online at the NTIS Web site (http://www. fedworld.gov) and in a CD-ROM catalog available in some libraries.

International Data Sources

Comparative researchers can find datasets on population characteristics, economic and political features, and political events in many nations. Some of these are available from U.S. government agencies. For example, the Social Security Administration reports on the characteristics of social security throughout the world (Wheeler, 1995). This comprehensive report classifies nations in terms of their type of social security program and provides detailed summaries of the characteristics of each nation's programs. The 1999 volume is available on the Internet at http://www.ssa.gov/policy/docs/progdesc/ssptw/1999/index.html#toc. More recent data are organized by region. A broader range of data is available in the *World Handbook of Political and Social Indicators,* with political events and political, economic, and social data coded from 1948 to 1982 (http://www.icpsr.umich. edu, study no. 7761) (Taylor & Jodice, 1986).

The European Commission administers the Eurobarometer Survey Series at least twice yearly across all the member states of the European Union. The survey monitors social and political attitudes and reports are published regularly online:
http://www.gesis.org/en/data_service/eurobarometer/index.htm.

Case level Eurobarometer survey data are stored at the ICPSR.

ICPSR

The University of Michigan's Inter-University Consortium for Political and Social Research (ICPSR) is the premier source of secondary data useful to social science researchers. ICPSR was founded in 1962 and now includes more than 640 colleges and universities in North America and hundreds of institutions on other continents. ICPSR archives the most extensive collection of social science datasets in the United States outside of the federal government: More than 7,243 studies are represented in 450,000 files from 130 countries and from sources that range from U.S. government agencies such as the Census Bureau to international organizations like the United Nations, social research organizations like the National Opinion Research Organization, and individual social scientists who have completed funded research projects.

The datasets archived by ICPSR are available for downloading directly from the ICPSR Web site, www.icpsr.umich.edu/ICPSR/help/datausers. ICPSR makes datasets obtained from government sources available directly to the general public, but many other datasets are available only to individuals at the more than 500 colleges and universities around the world that have paid the fees required to join ICPSR. The availability of some datasets is restricted due to confidentiality issues; in order to use them, researchers must sign a contract and agree to certain conditions. http://www.icpsr.umich.edu/help/newuser.html, 7/15/2005.

Survey datasets obtained in the United States and in many other countries that are stored at the ICPSR provide data on topics ranging from elite attitudes to consumer expectations. For example, data collected in the British Social Attitudes Survey in 1998, designed by the University of Chicago's National Opinion Research Center, are available through the ICPSR (go to the ICPSR Web site, http://www.icpsr.umich.edu, and search for study no. 3101). Data collected in a monthly survey of Spaniards' attitudes, by the Center for Research on Social Reality [Spain] Survey, are also available (study no. 17). Survey data from Russia, Germany, and other countries can also be found in the ICPSR collection.

Do you have an interest in events and interactions between nations, such as threats of military force? A dataset collected by Charles McClelland includes characteristics of 91,240 such events (study no. 5211). The history of military interventions in nations around the world between 1946 and 1988 is coded in a dataset developed by Frederic Pearson and Robert Baumann (study no. 6035).

This dataset identifies the intervener and target countries, the starting and ending dates of military intervention, and a range of potential motives (such as foreign policies, related domestic disputes, and pursuit of rebels across borders).

Census data from other nations are also available through the ICPSR, as well as directly through the Internet. In the ICPSR archives, you can find a dataset from the Statistical Office of the United Nations on the 1966–1974 population of 220 nations throughout the world (study no. 7623). More current international population data are provided by the Center for International Research and the U.S. Census Bureau (study no. 8490). See also the preceding description of the Eurobarometer Survey Series.

Obtaining Data From ICPSR

You begin a search for data in the ICPSR archives at http://www.icpsr.umich. edu/access/index.html.

Exhibit B.2 shows the search screen as I began a search for data from studies involving the subject domestic violence. You can also see in this screen that you can search the data archives for specific studies, identified by study number or title, as well as for studies by specific investigators (this would be a quick way to find the dataset contributed by Lawrence Sherman from his research, discussed in Chapter 2, on the police response to domestic violence).

EXHIBIT B.2   **Search Screen: Domestic Violence**

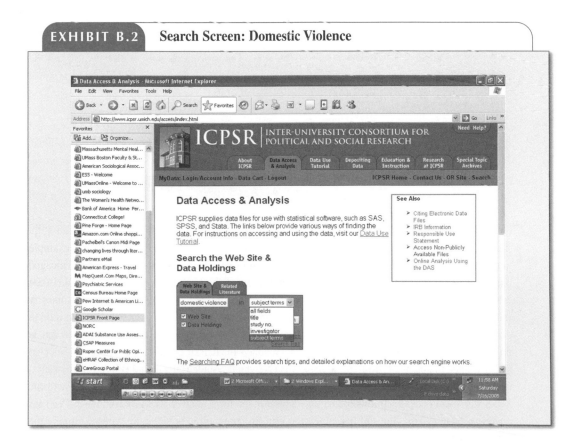

Exhibit B.3 displays the results of my search: a list of 63 datasets that involved research on domestic violence and that are available through ICPSR. For most datasets, you can obtain a description, the files that are available for downloading, and a list of "related literature"—that is, reports and articles that use the listed dataset. Some datasets are made available in collections on a CD-ROM; the CD-ROM's contents are described in detail on the ICPSR site, but you have to place an order to receive the CD-ROM itself.

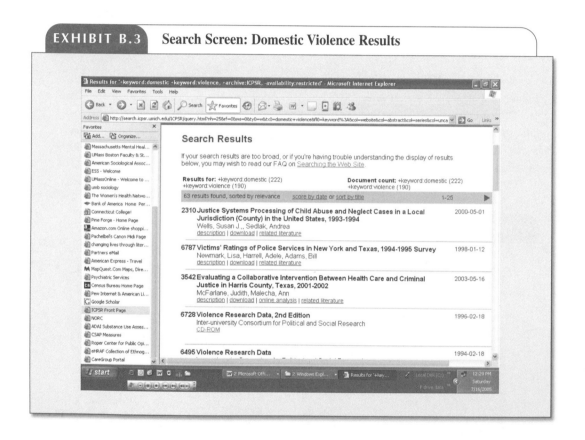

EXHIBIT B.3   Search Screen: Domestic Violence Results

When you click on the "Download" option, you are first asked to enter your e-mail address and password. What you enter will determine which datasets you can access; if you are not at an ICPSR member institution, you will be able to download only a limited portion of the datasets—mostly those from government sources. If you are a student at a member institution, you will be able to download most of the datasets directly, although you may have to be using a computer that is physically on your campus to do so. Exhibit B.4 displays the ICPSR download screen after I selected files I wanted to download from the study by Lisa Newmark, Adele Harrell, and Bill Adams of victim ratings of police response in New York and Texas. Because I wanted to analyze the data with the SPSS statistical package, I downloaded the dataset in the form of an "SPSS Portable File." The files downloaded in a "zip" file, so I had to use the WinZip© program to unzip them. After unzipping the SPSS portable file, I was able to start my data analysis with the SPSS program. If you'd like to learn how to analyze data with the SPSS statistical program, review Appendix C.

If you prepare your own paper based on an analysis of ICPSR data, be sure to include a proper citation. Here's an example from the ICPSR itself (http://www .icpsr.umich.edu/org/citation.html):

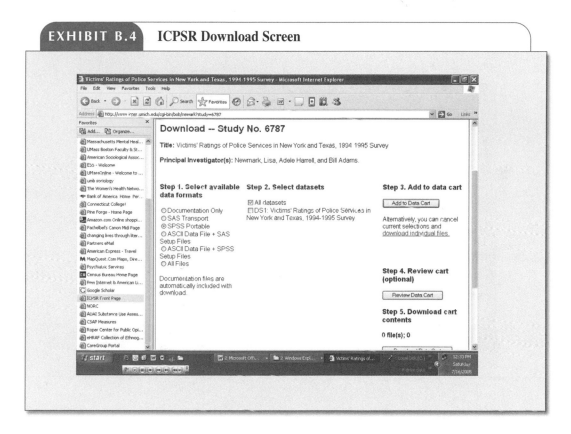

EXHIBIT B.4   **ICPSR Download Screen**

Reif, Karlheinz, and Anna Melich. *Euro-Barometer 39.0: European Community Policies and Family Life, March-April 1993* [Computer file]. Conducted by INRA (Europe), Brussels. ICPSR06195-v4. Ann Arbor, MI: Inter-University Consortium for Political and Social Research [producer], 1995. Koeln, Germany: Zentralarchiv fuer Empirische Sozialforschung/Ann Arbor, MI: Inter-University Consortium for Political and Social Research [distributors], 1997.

Some of the datasets are also offered with the option of "online analysis." If you have this option, you can immediately inspect the distributions of responses to each question in a survey and examine the relation between variables, without having any special statistical programs of your own. At the bottom of Exhibit B.5, you'll find the wording reported in the study "codebook" for a question used in the study of a collaborative health care and criminal justice intervention in Texas, as well as, in the top portion, the available statistical options. After choosing one or more variables from the codebook, you can request the analysis.

My analysis began with a chart of the distribution of victims' responses to a question about their current relationship with the abuser. As you can see in Exhibit B.6, about half had left the relationship, but half were still married or living as married with the abuser. This approach to analysis with secondary data can get you jump-started in your work. An online analysis option is also starting to appear at other Web sites that offer secondary data.

EXHIBIT B.5 ICPSR Online Analysis: Codebook Information and Statistical Options

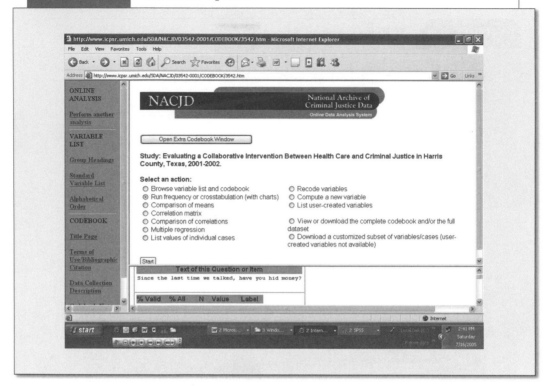

ICPSR also catalogs reports and publications containing analyses that have used ICPSR datasets since 1962—more than 45,000 citations were in this archive in September 2008. This superb resource provides an excellent starting point for the literature search that should precede a secondary data analysis. In most cases, you can learn from detailed study reports a great deal about the study methodology, including the rate of response in a sample survey and the reliability of any indexes constructed. Published articles provide examples of how others have described the study methodology, let you know what research questions have already been studied with the dataset, and outline what issues remain to be resolved. You can search this literature at the ICPSR site simply by entering the same search terms that you used to find datasets, or else by entering the specific study number of the dataset on which you have focused (see Exhibit B.7). Don't start a secondary analysis without reviewing such reports and publications.

Qualitative Data Sources

Far fewer qualitative datasets are available for secondary analysis. By far the richest source, if you are interested in cross-cultural research, is the Human Relations Area Files at Yale University. The HRAF has made anthropological field data available for international cross-cultural research since 1949 and currently contains over 800,000 pages of information on more than 365 different groups

EXHIBIT B.6 **ICPSR Online Analysis Bar Chart**

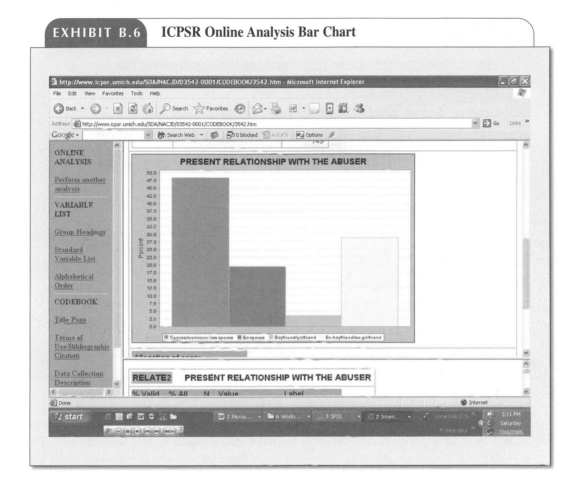

(HRAF 2005). The Human Relations Area Files (HRAF) Collection of Ethnography provides an extraordinary resource for qualitative comparative cross-sectional research (39 such studies as of September 2008) (Ember & Ember, 2005). The HRAF was founded in 1949 as a corporation designed to facilitate cross-cultural research. The HRAF ethnography collection now contains over 800,000 pages of material about 370 different cultural, ethnic, religious, and national groups all over the world. The information is indexed by topic, in 710 categories, and now made available electronically (if your school pays to maintain access to the HRAF). Exhibit B.8 is an example of a page from an HRAF document that has been indexed for easy retrieval.

The ICPSR collection includes a limited number of studies containing at least some qualitative data (19 as of July 2005), but these include some very rich data. Studies range from transcriptions of original handwritten and published materials relating to infant and child care, from the turn of the century to World War II (LaRossa, 1995) to Daniel Lockwood's (1996) transcripts of open-ended interviews with high school students involved in violent incidents.

Several other university-based centers have developed qualitative archive projects, although access is often limited. The Murray Research Center at Harvard's Radcliffe Institute for Advanced Study (http://murraydata.hmdc.harvard.edu/VDC/) focuses on studies of lives over time, with special interest

EXHIBIT B.7   ICPSR Search of "Related Literature" on Domestic Violence

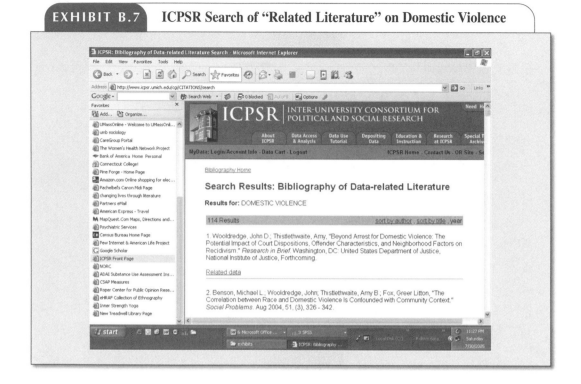

in issues of concern to women. Although the Murray Center's collection of about 300 studies contains both quantitative and qualitative datasets, it has had a special interest in qualitative data, including videotape and audiotape collections, case study data, and transcripts from intensive interview studies and data from surveys that included many open-ended questions. The Murray Research Center has now been merged with the larger Harvard-MIT Data Center, which makes available a much larger set of datasets from quantitative studies, although only to members of Harvard-Radcliffe. Access to archived datasets requires submission of an online application.

Holdings of the Economic and Social Data Service of the Universities of Sussex and Manchester in England (www.esds.ac.uk/qualitdata/online/), ESDS Qualidata, include interview transcripts and other materials from several qualitative studies, including Paul Thompson's "100 Families: Families, Social Mobility and Aging, an Intergenerational Approach." Subsets of the interviews can be browsed or searched directly online, but access is restricted to those at member institutions. Although a great many universities in Britain and throughout the world have joined the ESDS, they include very few colleges and universities in the United States.

The University of Southern Maine's Center for the Study of Lives (www.usm.maine .edu/cehd/csl) collects interview transcripts that record the life stories of people of diverse ages and backgrounds. As of October 2008, their collection included transcripts from almost 400 life stories, representing 328 different ethnic groups, telling of experiences of historical events ranging from the Great Depression to the Vietnam War, and including reports on dealing with health problems like HIV/AIDS. These qualitative data are available directly online without any registration or fee.

EXHIBIT B.8   **HRAF Indexed Document**

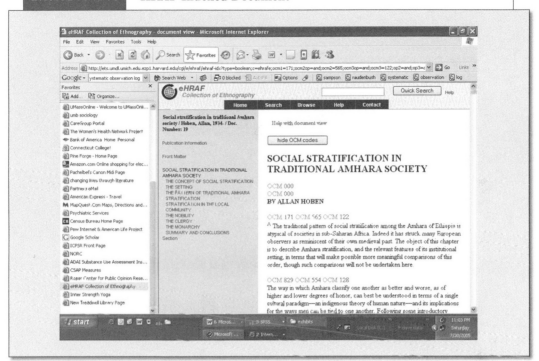

References

Adler, Patricia A. 1993. *Wheeling and dealing: An ethnography of an upper-level drug dealing and smuggling community,* 2nd ed., New York: Columbia University Press.

Adler, Patricia A. and Peter Adler. 2000. Intense loyalty in organizations: A case study of college athletics. In *Qualitative studies of organizations,* ed. John Van Maanen, 31–50. Thousand Oaks, CA: Sage.

Adorno, Theodor W., Nevitt Sanford, Else Frenkel-Brunswik, and Daniel Levinson. 1950. *The authoritarian personality.* New York: Harper.

Alfred, Randall. 1976. The church of Satan. In *The new religious consciousness,* ed. Charles Glock and Robert Bellah, 180–202. Berkeley: University of California Press.

Altheide, David L. and John M. Johnson. 1994. Criteria for assessing interpretive validity in qualitative research. In *Handbook of qualitative research,* ed. Norman K. Denzin and Yvonna S. Lincoln, 485–499. Thousand Oaks, CA: Sage.

Altman, Lawrence K. 1987. U.S. and France end rift on AIDS. *New York Times,* April 1. From http://www.nytimes.com (accessed May 28, 2007).

Altman, Lawrence K. 2008. Discoverers of AIDS and cancer viruses win Nobel. *New York Times,* October 7, 2008. From http://www.nytimes.com/2008/10/07/health/07nobel.htm (accessed October 23, 2008).

American Psychiatric Association (APA). 1994. *Diagnostic and statistical manual of mental disorders,* 4th ed. Washington, DC: American Psychiatric Association.

American Sociological Association (ASA). 1997. *Code of ethics.* Washington, DC: American Sociological Association.

Anderson, Elijah. 2000. *Code of the street: Decency, violence, and the moral life of the inner city,* reprint ed. New York: W. W. Norton.

Anderson, Elijah. 2003. Jelly's place: An ethnographic memoir (distinguished lecture). *Symbolic Interaction* 26(2): 217–237.

Aronson, Elliot and Judson Mills. 1959. The effect of severity of initiation on liking for a group. *Journal of Abnormal and Social Psychology* 59 (September): 177–181.

Arwood, Tracy and Sangeeta Panicker. 2007. Assessing risk in social and behavioral sciences. From Collaborative Institutional Training Initiative Web site: https://www.citiprogram.org/members/learners/ (accessed June 5, 2008).

Aseltine, Robert H., Jr., and Ronald C. Kessler. 1993. Marital disruption and depression in a community sample. *Journal of Health and Social Behavior* 34 (September): 237–251.

Associated Press. 2000. Researchers fear privacy breaches with online research. From http://www.wpi.edu/News/TechNews/000919/onlineresearch.html (accessed September 28, 2008).

Bachman, Ronet and Russell K. Schutt. 2007. *The practice of research in criminology and criminal justice,* 3rd ed. Thousand Oaks, CA: Sage.

Baumrind, Diana. 1964. Some thoughts on ethics of research: After reading Milgram's "Behavioral study of obedience." *American Psychologist* 19:421–423.

Baumrind, Diana. 1985. Research using intentional deception: Ethical issues revisited. *American Psychologist* 40:165–174.

Becker, Howard S. 1958. Problems of inference and proof in participant observation. *American Sociological Review* 23:652–660.

Becker, Howard S. 1963. *Outsiders: Studies in the sociology of deviance.* New York: Free Press.

Becker, Howard S. 1986. *Writing for social scientists.* Chicago: University of Chicago Press. [This can be ordered directly from the American Sociological Association, 1722 N St. NW, Washington, DC 20036, (202) 833-3410.]

Bellah, Robert N., Richard Madsen, William M. Sullivan, Ann Swidler, and Steven M. Tipton. 1985. *Habits of the heart: Individualism and commitment in American life.* New York: Harper & Row.

Binder, Arnold and James W. Meeker. 1993. Implications of the failure to replicate the Minneapolis experimental findings. *American Sociological Review* 58:886–888.

Birkeland, Sarah, Erin Murphy-Graham, and Carol Weiss. 2005. Good reasons for ignoring good evaluation: The case of the Drug Abuse Resistance Education (D.A.R.E.) program. *Evaluation and Program Planning* 28:247–256.

Bogdewic, Stephan P. 1999. Participant observation. In *Doing qualitative research,* 2nd ed., ed. Benjamin F. Crabtree and William L. Miller, 47–70. Thousand Oaks, CA: Sage.

Booth, Wayne C., Gregory G. Colomb, and Joseph M. Williams. 1995. *The craft of research.* Chicago: University of Chicago Press.

Boruch, Robert F. 1997. *Randomized experiments for planning and evaluation: A practical guide.* Thousand Oaks, CA: Sage.

Bramel, Dana and Ronal Friend. 1981. Hawthorne, the myth of the docile worker, and class bias in psychology. *American Psychologist* 38 (September): 867–878.

Brewer, John and Albert Hunter. 1989. *Multimethod research: A synthesis of styles.* Newbury Park, CA: Sage.

Brown v. Board of Education (Brown I), 347 U.S. 483 (1954).

Bureau of the Census. 2004–2005. *Statistical abstract of the United States.* Washington, DC: U.S. Department of Commerce, Bureau of the Census. From http://www.census.gov/prod/www/statistical-abstract-2001_2005.html (accessed September 28, 2008).

Butterfield, Fox. 1996a. After 10 years, juvenile crime begins to drop. *New York Times,* August 9, A1, A25.

Butterfield, Fox. 1996b. Gun violence may be subsiding, studies find. *New York Times,* October 14, A10.

Butterfield, Fox. 2000. As murder rates edge up, concern, but few answers. *New York Times,* June 18, A12.

Buzawa, Eve S. and Carl G. Buzawa, eds. 1996. *Do arrests and restraining orders work?* Thousand Oaks, CA: Sage.

Campbell, Donald T. and M. Jean Russo. 1999. *Social experimentation.* Thousand Oaks, CA: Sage.

Campbell, Donald T. and Julian C. Stanley. 1966. *Experimental and quasi-experimental designs for research.* Chicago: Rand McNally.

Campbell, Richard T. 1992. Longitudinal research. In *Encyclopedia of sociology,* ed. Edgar F. Borgatta and Marie L. Borgatta, 1146–1158. New York: Macmillan.

Cava, Anita, Reid Cushman, and Kenneth Goodman. 2007. HIPAA and human subjects research. From the University of Miami Web site: http://researchedu.med.miami.edu/x36.xml (accessed September 28, 2008).

Cave, Emma and Soren Holm. 2003. Milgram and Tuskegee: Paradigm research projects in bioethics. *Health Care Analysis* 11:27–40.

Center for Survey Research, University of Massachusetts at Boston. 1987. Methodology: Designing good survey questions. *Newsletter,* April, 3.

Chambliss, Daniel F. 1988. *Champions: The making of Olympic swimmers.* New York: Morrow.

Chambliss, Daniel F. 1989. The mundanity of excellence: An ethnographic report on stratification and Olympic swimmers. *Sociological Theory* 7(1):70–86.

Chambliss, Daniel F. 1996. *Beyond caring: Hospitals, nurses, and the social organization of ethics.* Chicago: University of Chicago Press.

Chen, Huey-Tsyh. 1990. *Theory-driven evaluations.* Newbury Park, CA: Sage.

Chen, Huey-Tsyh and Peter H. Rossi. 1987. The theory-driven approach to validity. *Evaluation and Program Planning* 10:95–103.

Coffey, Amanda and Paul Atkinson. 1996. *Making sense of qualitative data: Complementary research strategies.* Thousand Oaks, CA: Sage.

Cohen, Gary E. and Barbara A. Kerr. 1998. Computer-mediated counseling: An empirical study of a new mental health treatment. *Computers in Human Services* 15:13–26.

Cohen, Susan G. and Gerald E. Ledford Jr. 1994. The effectiveness of self-managing teams: A quasi-experiment. *Human Relations* 47:13–43.

Coleman, James S. and Thomas Hoffer. 1987. *Public and private high schools: The impact of communities.* New York: Basic Books.

Coleman, James S., Thomas Hoffer, and Sally Kilgore. 1982. *High school achievement: Public, Catholic, and private schools compared.* New York: Basic Books.

Collins, Randall. 1975. *Conflict sociology: Toward an explanatory science.* New York: Academic Press.

Converse, Jean M. 1984. Attitude measurement in psychology and sociology: The early years. In *Surveying subjective phenomena,* vol. 2, ed. Charles F. Turner and Elizabeth Martin, 3–40. New York: Russell Sage Foundation.

Cook, Thomas D. and Donald T. Campbell. 1979. *Quasi-experimentation: Design and analysis issues for field settings.* Chicago: Rand McNally.

Coontz, Stephanie. 1997. *The way we really are: Coming to terms with America's changing families.* New York: Basic Books.

Core Institute. 1994. *Core alcohol and drug survey: Long form.* Carbondale, IL: Fund for the Improvement of Postsecondary Education (FIPSE) Core Analysis Grantee Group, Core Institute, Student Health Programs, Southern Illinois University.

Costner, Herbert L. 1989. The validity of conclusions in evaluation research: A further development of Chen and Rossi's theory-driven approach. *Evaluation and Program Planning* 12:345–353.

Davies, Philip, Anthony Petrosino, and Iain Chalmers. 1999. *Report and papers from the exploratory meeting for the Campbell Collaboration.* London: School of Public Policy, University College.

Davis, James A. 1985. *The logic of causal order.* Sage University Paper Series on Quantitative Applications in the Social Sciences (series no. 07–055). Beverly Hills, CA: Sage.

Davis, James A. and Tom W. Smith. 1992. *The NORC General Social Survey: A user's guide.* Newbury Park, CA: Sage.

Davis, Ryan. 1999. "Study: Search engines can't keep up with expanding Net." *Boston Globe*, July 8, C1, C3.

Dawes, Robyn. 1995. How do you formulate a testable exciting hypothesis? In *How to write a successful research grant application: A guide for social and behavioral scientists,* ed. Willo Pequegnat and Ellen Stover, 93–96. New York: Plenum Press.

Decker, Scott H. and Barrik Van Winkle. 1996. *Life in the gang: Family, friends, and violence.* New York: Cambridge University Press.

Dentler, Robert A. 2002. *Practicing sociology: Selected fields.* Westport, CT: Praeger.

Denzin, Norman K. 2002. The interpretive process. In *The qualitative researcher's companion,* ed. A. Michael Huberman and Matthew B. Miles, 349–368. Thousand Oaks, CA: Sage.

Denzin, Norman K. and Yvonna S. Lincoln. 1994. Introduction: Entering the field of qualitative research. In *Handbook of qualitative research,* ed. Norman K. Denzin and Yvonna S. Lincoln, 1–17. Thousand Oaks, CA: Sage.

Denzin, Norman K. and Yvonna S. Lincoln. 2000. Introduction: The discipline and practice of qualitative research. *Handbook of qualitative research*, 2nd ed., ed. Norman Denzin and Yvonna S. Lincoln, 1–28. Thousand Oaks, CA: Sage.

DeParle, Jason. 1999. Project to rescue needy stumbles against the persistence of poverty. *New York Times,* May 15, A1, A10.

Diamond, Timothy. 1992. *Making gray gold: Narratives of nursing home care.* Chicago: University of Chicago Press.

Dillman, Don A. 1978. *Mail and telephone surveys: The total design method.* New York: Wiley.

Dillman, Don A. 1982/1991. Mail and other self-administered questionnaires. In *Handbook of research design and social measurement,* 5th ed., ed. Delbert C. Miller, 637–638. Repr. Newbury Park, CA: Sage.

Dillman, Don A. 2000. *Mail and Internet surveys: The tailored design method,* 2nd ed. New York: John Wiley & Sons.

Donath, Judith S. 1999. Identity and deception in the virtual community. In *Communities in cyberspace,* ed. Peter Kollock and Marc A. Smith, 29–59. New York: Routledge.

Drake, Robert E., Gregory J. McHugo, Deborah R. Becker, William A. Anthony, and Robin E. Clark. 1996. The New Hampshire study of supported employment for people with severe mental illness. *Journal of Consulting and Clinical Psychology* 64:391–399.

Durkheim, Emile. 1951. *Suicide.* New York: Free Press.

Durkheim, Emile. 1906/1956. The evolution and the role of secondary education in France. *Education and Sociology,* trans. Sherwood D. Fox, 135–154. Repr. New York: Free Press.

Ellis, Carolyn. 1986. *Fisher folk: Two communities on Chesapeake Bay.* Lexington: University Press of Kentucky.

Ember, Carol R. and Melvin Ember. 2005. *User's guide: HRAF collection of ethnography.* New Haven, CT: Yale University Human Relations Area Files. Retrieved July 4, 2005, from www.yale.edu/hraf/basiccc.htm

Emerson, Robert M., ed. 1983. *Contemporary field research.* Prospect Heights, IL: Waveland Press.

Emerson, Robert M., Rachel I. Fretz, and Linda L. Shaw. 1995. *Writing ethnographic fieldnotes.* Chicago: University of Chicago Press.

Erikson, Kai T. 1967. A comment on disguised observation in sociology. *Social Problems* 12:366–373.

Erikson, Kai T. 1976. *Everything in its path: Destruction of community in the Buffalo Creek flood.* New York: Simon & Schuster.

Fenno, Richard F., Jr. 1978. *Home style: House members in their districts.* Boston: Little, Brown.

Fink, Arlene. 2005. *Conducting research literature reviews: From the Internet to paper,* 2nd ed. Thousand Oaks, CA: Sage.

Fowler, Floyd J. 1988. *Survey research methods,* rev. ed. Newbury Park, CA: Sage.

Fowler, Floyd J. 1995. *Improving survey questions: Design and evaluation.* Thousand Oaks, CA: Sage.

Fowler, Floyd J. 1998. Personal communication, January 7. Center for Survey Research, University of Massachusetts, Boston.

Fox, Nick and Chris Roberts. 1999. GPs in cyberspace: The sociology of a "virtual community." *The Sociological Review* 47:643–669.

Freud, Sigmund. 1900/1999. *The interpretation of dreams,* 1st ed., ed. Ritchie Robertson, trans. Joyce Crick. Repr. Oxford, England: Oxford University Press.

Gallup Inc. (2008). *Election polls—Accuracy record in presidential elections.* From http://www.gallup.com/poll/9442/Election-Polls-Accuracy-Record-Presidential-Elections.aspx (accessed May 23, 2008).

Gallup Organization. 2002, August 20. *Poll analyses, July 29, 2002: Bush job approval update.* From http://media.washingtonpost.com/wp-srv/politics/ssi/polls/postpoll_072307.html (accessed September 28, 2008).

Gibson, David R. 2005. Taking turns and talking ties: Networks and conversational interaction. *American Journal of Sociology* 110(6): 1561–1597.

Gilbert, Dennis (with Zogby International). 2002. *Hamilton College Muslim America poll.* Unpublished research report.

Gilchrist, Valerie J. and Robert L. Williams. 1999. Key informant interviews. In *Doing qualitative research,* 2nd ed., ed. Benjamin F. Crabtree and William L. Miller, 71–88. Thousand Oaks, CA: Sage.

Glaser, Barney G. and Anselm L. Strauss. 1967. *The discovery of grounded theory: Strategies for qualitative research.* London: Weidenfeld and Nicholson.

Goffman, Erving. 1959. *Presentation of self in everyday life.* New York: Doubleday Anchor.

Goffman, Erving. 1961. *Asylums: Essays on the social situation of mental patients and other inmates.* Garden City, NY: Doubleday.

Goldfinger, Stephen M. and Russell K. Schutt. 1996. Comparisons of clinicians' housing recommendations of homeless mentally ill persons. *Psychiatric Services* 47(4): 413–415.

Goldfinger, Stephen M., Russell K. Schutt, George S. Tolomiczenko, Winston M. Turner, Norma Ware, Walter E. Penk, et al. 1997. Housing persons who are homeless and mentally ill: Independent living or evolving consumer households? In *Mentally ill and homeless: Special programs for special needs,* ed. William R. Breakey and James W. Thompson, 29–49. Amsterdam, the Netherlands: Harwood Academic.

Goleman, Daniel. 1993. Placebo effect is shown to be twice as powerful as expected. *New York Times,* August 17, C3.

Goode, Erich. 2002. Sexual involvement and social research in a fat civil rights organization. *Qualitative Sociology* 25(4): 501–504.

Gordon, Raymond. 1992. *Basic interviewing skills.* Itasca, IL: Peacock.

Governmental Accounting Standards Board (GASB). 2008, October 2. *Basic facts about service efforts and accomplishments reporting.* From http://www.gasb.org/SEA_fact_sheet_FINAL.pdf (accessed October 23, 2008).

Gray, Mark M. 2004. Sixty-three percent of Catholics voted in the 2004 presidential election. Washington, DC: Center for Applied Research in the Apostolate, Georgetown University. From http://cara.georgetown.edu/Press112204.pdf (accessed August 8, 2005).

Groves, Robert M. 1989. *Survey errors and survey costs.* New York: Wiley.

Groves, Robert M. and Mick P. Couper. 1998. *Nonresponse in household interview surveys.* New York: Wiley.

Groves, Robert M. and Robert L. Kahn. 1979/1991. *Surveys by telephone: A national comparison with personal interviews,* as adapted in Delbert C. Miller's *Handbook of research design and social measurement,* 5th ed. Newbury Park, CA: Sage.

Guba, Egon G. and Yvonna S. Lincoln. 1989. *Fourth generation evaluation.* Newbury Park, CA: Sage.

Gubrium, Jaber F. and James A. Holstein. 1997. *The new language of qualitative method.* New York: Oxford University Press.

Gubrium, Jaber F. and James A. Holstein. 2000. "Analyzing Interpretive Practice." In *The handbook of qualitative research*, 2nd ed., ed. Norman Denzin and Yvonna S. Lincoln, pp. 487–508. Thousand Oaks, CA: Sage.

Hadaway, C. Kirk, Penny Long Marler, and Mark Chaves. 1993. What the polls don't show: A closer look at U.S. church attendance. *American Sociological Review* 58 (December): 741–752.

Hafner, Katie. 2005. In challenge to Google, Yahoo will scan books. *New York Times*, October 3, C1, C4.

Hagan, John. 1994. *Crime and disrepute.* Thousand Oaks, CA: Pine Forge Press.

Hage, Jerald and Barbara Foley Meeker. 1988. *Social causality.* Boston: Unwin Hyman.

Haney, C., C. Banks, and Philip G. Zimbardo. 1973. Interpersonal dynamics in a simulated prison. *International Journal of Criminology and Penology* 1:69–97.

Hart, Chris. 1998. *Doing a literature review: Releasing the social science research imagination.* London: Sage.

Herek, Gregory. 1995. Developing a theoretical framework and rationale for a research proposal. In *How to write a successful research grant application: A guide for social and behavioral scientists,* ed. Willo Pequegnat and Ellen Stover, 85–91. New York: Plenum Press.

Hite, Shere. 1987. *Women and love: A cultural revolution in progress.* New York: Alfred A. Knopf.

Holmes, Steven A. 1994. Census officials plan big changes in gathering data. *New York Times,* May 16, A1, A13.

Hoyle, Carolyn and Andrew Sanders. 2000. Police response to domestic violence: From victim choice to victim empowerment. *British Journal of Criminology* 40:14–26.

HRAF. 2005. eHRAF collection of ethnography: Web. New Haven, CT: Yale University. Retrieved July 3, 2005, from www.yale.edu/hraf/collections_body_ethnoweb.htm

Huberman, A. Michael and Matthew B. Miles. 1994. Data management and analysis methods. In *Handbook of qualitative research,* ed. Norman K. Denzin and Yvonna S. Lincoln, 428–444. Thousand Oaks, CA: Sage.

Huff, Darrell. 1954. *How to lie with statistics.* New York: W. W. Norton.

Humphrey, Nicholas. 1992. *A history of the mind: Evolution and the birth of consciousness.* New York: Simon & Schuster.

Humphreys, Laud. 1970. *Tearoom trade: Impersonal sex in public places.* Chicago: Aldine.

Hunt, Morton. 1985. *Profiles of social research: The scientific study of human interactions.* New York: Russell Sage Foundation.

Inter-University Consortium for Political and Social Research. 1996. *Guide to resources and services 1995–1996.* Ann Arbor, MI: ICPSR.

Irvine, Leslie. 1998. Organizational ethics and fieldwork realities: Negotiating ethical boundaries in codependents anonymous. In *Doing ethnographic research: Fieldwork settings,* ed. Scott Grills, 167–183. Thousand Oaks, CA: Sage.

Jankowski, Martin Sanchez. 1991. *Islands in the street: Gangs and American urban society.* Berkeley: University of California Press.

Jones, James H. 1993. *Bad blood: The Tuskegee syphilis experiment,* new and expanded ed. New York: Free Press.

Kagay, Michael R. (with Janet Elder). 1992. Numbers are no problem for pollsters. Words are. *New York Times,* October 9, E5.

Kaufman, Sharon R. 1986. *The ageless self: Sources of meaning in late life.* Madison: University of Wisconsin Press.

Kenney, Charles. 1987. They've got your number. *Boston Globe Magazine,* August 30, 12, 46–56, 60.

Kershaw, David and Jerilyn Fair, eds. 1976. *Operations, surveys, and administration,* vol. 2 of *The New Jersey income-maintenance experiment.* New York: Academic Press.

King, Gary, Robert O. Keohane, and Sidney Verba. 1994. *Scientific inference in qualitative research.* Princeton, NJ: Princeton University Press.

Kinsey, Alfred C., Wardell B. Pomeroy, and Clyde E. Martin. 1948. *Sexual behavior in the human male.* Philadelphia: W. B. Saunders.

Kinsey, Alfred, C., Wardell B. Pomeroy, Clyde E. Martin, and Paul H. Gebhard. 1953. *Sexual behavior in the human female.* Philadelphia: W. B. Saunders.

Koegel, Paul. 1987. *Ethnographic perspectives on homeless and homeless mentally ill women.* Washington, DC: Alcohol, Drug Abuse, and Mental Health Administration, Public Health Service, U.S. Department of Health and Human Services.

Korn, James H. (1997). *Illusions of reality: A history of deception in social psychology.* Albany: State University of New York Press.

Krauss, Clifford. 1996. New York crime rate plummets to levels not seen in 30 years. *New York Times,* December 20, A1, B4.

Krueger, Richard A. 1988. *Focus groups: A practical guide for applied research.* Newbury Park, CA: Sage.

Krueger, Richard A. and Mary Anne Casey. 2000. *Focus groups: A practical guide for applied research,* 3rd ed. Thousand Oaks, CA: Sage.

Kuzel, Anton J. 1999. Sampling in qualitative inquiry. In *Doing qualitative research,* 2nd ed., ed. Benjamin F. Crabtree and William L. Miller, 33–45. Thousand Oaks, CA: Sage.

Kvale, Steinar. 1996. *Interviews: An introduction to qualitative research interviewing.* Thousand Oaks, CA: Sage.

Labaw, Patricia J. 1980. *Advanced questionnaire design.* Cambridge, MA: ABT Books.

LaRossa, Ralph. Parenthood in Early Twentieth-Century America Project (PETCAP), 1900–1944 [Computer file]. Atlanta, GA: Georgia State University [producer], 1995. Ann Arbor, MI: Inter-University Consortium for Political and Social Research [distributor], 1997.

Larson, Calvin J. 1993. *Pure and applied sociological theory: Problems and issues.* New York: Harcourt Brace Jovanovich.

Lathrop, Barnes F. 1968. History from the census returns. In *Sociology and history: Methods*, ed. Seymour Martin Lipset and Richard Hofstadter, pp. 79–101. New York: Basic Books.

Latour, Francie. 2002. Marching orders: After 10 years, state closes prison boot camp. *Boston Sunday Globe,* June 16, B1, B7.

Lavin, Michael R. 1994. *Understanding the 1990 census: A guide for marketers, planners, grant writers and other data users.* Kenmore, NY: Epoch Books.

Lavrakas, Paul J. 1987. *Telephone survey methods: Sampling, selection, and supervision.* Newbury Park, CA: Sage.

Legal Information Institute. 2006. *U.S. Code Collection: Title 42, Chapter 7, Subchapter XI, Part C, §1320d.* From the Cornell University Law School Web site: http://www4.law.cornell.edu/uscode/html/uscode42/usc_sec_42_00001320----d000-.html (accessed September 28, 2008).

Lelieveldt, Herman. 2003. March-April. Increasing social capital through direct democracy? A case study of the "It's Our Neighbourhood's Turn" project. Paper presented at the ECPR-Joint Sessions (Workshop 22: Bringing citizens back in: participatory democracy and political participation), Edinburgh, Scotland. From http://www.paltin.ro/biblioteca/Lelieveldt.pdf (accessed September 28, 2008).

Lelieveldt, Herman. 2004. Helping citizens help themselves: Neighborhood improvement programs and the impact of social networks, trust, and norms on neighborhood-oriented forms of participation. *Urban Affairs Review* 39:531–551.

Lempert, Richard. 1989. Humility is a virtue: On the publicization of policy-relevant research. *Law & Society Review* 23(1): 145–161.

Lempert, Richard and Joseph Sanders. 1986. *An invitation to law and social science: Desert, disputes, and distribution.* New York: Longman.

Levy, Paul S. and Stanley Lemeshow. 1999. *Sampling of populations: Methods and applications,* 3rd ed. New York: Wiley.

Lewin, Tamar. 2001a. Surprising result in welfare-to-work studies. *New York Times,* July 31, A16.

Lewin, Tamar. 2001b. Income education is found to lower risk of new arrest. *New York Times,* November 16, A18.

Lieberson, Stanley. 1985. *Making it count: The improvement of social research and theory.* Berkeley: University of California Press.

Litwin, Mark S. 1995. *How to measure survey reliability and validity.* Thousand Oaks, CA: Sage.

Locke, Lawrence F., Stephen J. Silverman, and Waneen Wyrick Spirduso. 1998. *Reading and understanding research.* Thousand Oaks, CA: Sage.

Locke, Lawrence F., Waneen Wyrick Spirduso, and Stephen J. Silverman. 2000. *Proposals that work: A guide for planning dissertations and grant proposals,* 4th ed. Thousand Oaks, CA: Sage.

Lockwood, Daniel. Violent incidents among selected public school students in two large cities of the South and the Southern Midwest, 1995: [United States] [Computer file]. ICPSR version. Atlanta, GA: Clark Atlantic University [producer], 1996. Ann Arbor, MI: Inter-university Consortium for Political and Social Research [distributor], 1998.

Lofland, John and Lyn H. Lofland. 1984. *Analyzing social settings: A guide to qualitative observation and analysis,* 2nd ed. Belmont, CA: Wadsworth.

Luker, Kristin. 1985. *Abortion & the politics of motherhood.* Berkeley and Los Angeles: University of California Press.

Mangione, Thomas W. 1995. *Mail surveys: Improving the quality.* Thousand Oaks, CA: Sage.

Margolis, Eric. 2004. Looking at discipline, looking at labour: Photographic representations of Indian boarding schools. *Visual Studies* 19:72–96.

Marini, Margaret Mooney and Burton Singer. 1988. Causality in the social sciences. In *Sociological methodology,* vol. 18, ed. Clifford C. Clogg, 347–409. Washington, DC: American Sociological Association.

Marshall, S. L. A. 1947/1978. *Men against fire.* Repr. Gloucester, MA: Peter Smith.

Martin, Lawrence L. and Peter M. Kettner. 1996. *Measuring the performance of human service programs.* Thousand Oaks, CA: Sage.

Maxwell, Joseph A. 1996. *Qualitative research design: An interactive approach.* Thousand Oaks, CA: Sage.

McConnell, Elizabeth S. 2006. DARE: Middle school program revamped. Middle Ground 9(3): 33–34. (ERIC Document Reproduction Service No ED497083)

McDonald, Michael M. 2009. *2008 General Election turnout rates.* Fairfax, VA: George Mason University. Retrieved January 26, 2009 from http://elections.gmu.edu/Turnout_2008G.html

Mead, Margaret. 1928/2001. *Coming of age in Samoa.* Repr. New York: HarperCollins Perennial.

Melbin, Murray. 1978. Night as frontier. *American Sociological Review* 43(1): 3–22.

Milbrath, Lester and M. L. Goel. 1977. *Political participation,* 2nd ed. Chicago: Rand McNally.

Miles, Matthew B. and A. Michael Huberman. 1994. *Qualitative data analysis,* 2nd ed. Thousand Oaks, CA: Sage.

Milgram, Stanley. 1963. Behavioral study of obedience. *Journal of Abnormal and Social Psychology* 67:371–478.

Milgram, Stanley. 1964. Issues in the study of obedience: A reply to Baumrind. *American Psychologist* 19:848–852.

Milgram, Stanley. 1965. Some conditions of obedience and disobedience to authority. *Human Relations* 18:57–76.

Milgram, Stanley, 1968. *Obedience.* Film. University Park, PA: Penn State Media Sales.

Milgram, Stanley. 1974. *Obedience to authority: An experimental view.* New York: Harper & Row.

Milgram, Stanley. 1992. *The individual in a social world: Essays and experiments,* 2nd ed. New York: McGraw-Hill.

Miller, Arthur G. 1986. *The obedience experiments: A case study of controversy in social science.* New York: Praeger.

Miller, Delbert C. 1991. *Handbook of research design and social measurement,* 5th ed. Newbury Park, CA: Sage.

Miller, Delbert C. and Nell J. Salkind. 2002. *Handbook of research design and social measurement,* 6th ed. Newbury Park, CA: Sage.

Miller, William L. and Benjamin F. Crabtree. 1999. The dance of interpretation. In *Doing qualitative research,* ed. Benjamin F. Crabtree and William L. Miller, 127–143. Thousand Oaks, CA: Sage.

Miller, Susan. 1999. *Gender and community policing: Walking the talk.* Boston: Northeastern University Press.

Mitchell, Richard G., Jr. 1993. *Secrecy and fieldwork.* Newbury Park, CA: Sage.

Mohr, Lawrence B. 1992. *Impact analysis for program evaluation.* Newbury Park, CA: Sage.

Mooney, Christopher Z. and Mei Hsien Lee. 1995. Legislating morality in the American states: The case of abortion regulation reform. *American Journal of Political Science* 39:599–627.

Morrill, Calvin, Christine Yalda, Madeleine Adelman, Michael Musheno, and Cindy Bejarano. 2000. Telling tales in school: Youth culture and conflict narratives. *Law & Society Review* 34:521–565.

Mullins, Carolyn J. 1977. *A guide to writing and publishing in the social and behavioral sciences.* New York: Wiley.

Myrdal, Gunnar. 1944/1964. *An American dilemma.* Repr. New York: McGraw-Hill.

National Geographic Society. 2000. *Survey 2000.* From http://business.clemson.edu/socio/s2k data211.html (accessed September 28, 2008).

National Opinion Research Center (NORC). 1992. *National data program for the social sciences: The NORC General Social Survey; Questions and answers* (mimeographed). Chicago: NORC.

National Opinion Research Center (NORC). 2006. *General social survey.* Chicago: National Opinion Research Center, University of Chicago.

National Technical Information Service, U.S. Department of Commerce. 1993. *Directory of U.S. government data files for mainframes and microcomputers.* Washington, DC: Federal Computer Products Center, National Technical Information Service, U.S. Department of Commerce.

Newbury, Darren. 2005. Editorial: The challenge of visual studies. *Visual Studies* 20:1–3.

Newport, Frank. 2000. *Popular vote in presidential race too close to call.* Princeton: The Gallup Organization. From the Gallup Web site: www.gallup.com/poll/releases/pr001107.asp (accessed December 13, 2000).

Northeastern University Division of Research Integrity. (n.d.). *Scales* (image). From http://www .research.neu.edu/research_integrity/images/scales.jpg.

Novak, David. 2003. The evolution of internet research: Shifting allegiances. *Online* 27:21.

Ó'Dochartaigh, Niall. 2002. *The Internet research handbook: A practical guide for students and researchers in the social sciences.* Thousand Oaks, CA: Sage.

Office of Management and Budget. (n.d.). *Government Performance Results Act of 1993.* From www.whitehouse.gov/omb/mgmt-gpra/gplaw2m.html (accessed September 28, 2008).

Orcutt, James D. and J. Blake Turner. 1993. Shocking numbers and graphic accounts: Quantified images of drug problems in the print media. *Social Problems* 49 (May): 190–206.

Orr, Larry L. 1999. *Social experiments: Evaluating public programs with experimental methods.* Thousand Oaks, CA: Sage.

Papineau, David. 1978. *For science in the social sciences.* London: Macmillan.

Parks, Malcolm R. and Kory Floyd. 1996. Making friends in cyberspace. *Journal of Communication* 46(1): 80–97.

Parlett, Malcolm and David Hamilton. 1976. Evaluation as illumination: A new approach to the study of innovative programmes. In *Evaluation studies review annual,* vol. 1, ed. G. Glass, 140–157. Beverly Hills, CA: Sage.

Paternoster, Raymond, Robert Brame, Ronet Bachman, and Lawrence W. Sherman. 1997. Do fair procedures matter? The effect of procedural justice on spouse assault. *Law & Society Review* 31(1): 163–204.

Patton, Michael Quinn. 2002. *Qualitative research & evaluation methods,* 3rd ed. Thousand Oaks, CA: Sage.

Phillips, David P. 1982. The impact of fictional television stories on U.S. adult fatalities: New evidence on the effect of the mass media on violence. *American Journal of Sociology* 87 (May): 1340–1359.

Phoenix, Ann. 2003. Neoliberalism and masculinity: Racialization and the contradictions of schooling for 11- to 14-year-olds. *Youth & Society* 36:227–246.

Pipher, Mary. 1994. *Reviving Ophelia: Saving the selves of adolescent girls.* New York: Ballantine Books.

Posavac, Emil J. and Raymond G. Carey. 1997. *Program evaluation: Methods and case studies,* 5th ed. Upper Saddle River, NJ: Prentice Hall.

Presley, Cheryl A., Philip W. Meilman, and Rob Lyerla. 1994. Development of the core alcohol and drug survey: Initial findings and future directions. *Journal of American College Health* 42:248–255.

Price, Richard H., Michelle Van Ryn, and Amiram D. Vinokur. 1992. Impact of a preventive job search intervention on the likelihood of depression among the unemployed. *Journal of Health and Social Behavior* 33 (June): 158–167.

Punch, Maurice. 1994. Politics and ethics in qualitative research. In *Handbook of qualitative research,* ed. Norman K. Denzin and Yvonna S. Lincoln, 83–97. Thousand Oaks, CA: Sage.

Putnam, Robert D. 2000. *Bowling alone: The collapse and revival of American community.* New York: Touchstone.

Pyrczak, Fred. 2005. *Evaluating research in academic journals: A practical guide to realistic evaluation,* 3rd ed. Glendale, CA: Pyrczak.

Radin, Charles A. 1997. Partnerships, awareness behind Boston's success. *Boston Globe,* February 19, A2, B7.

Ragin, Charles C. 1994. *Constructing social research.* Thousand Oaks, CA: Pine Forge Press.

Ramirez, Anthony. 2002. One more reason you're less likely to be murdered. *New York Times,* August 25, WK3.

Rankin, Bruce H. and James M. Quane. 2002. Social contexts and urban adolescent outcomes: The interrelated effects of neighborhoods, families, and peers on African-American youth. *Social Problems* 49:79–100.

Riesman, David. 1950. *The lonely crowd: A study of the changing American character.* New Haven, CT: Yale University Press.

Riesman, David (with Nathan Glazer and Reuel Denney). 1961/2001. *The lonely crowd: A study of the changing American character,* rev. ed. Repr. New Haven, CT: Yale University Press.

Reiss, Albert J., Jr. 1971. *The police and the public.* New Haven, CT: Yale University Press.

Riessman, Catherine Kohler. 2002. Narrative analysis. In *The qualitative researcher's companion,* ed. A. Michael Huberman and Matthew B. Miles, 217–270. Thousand Oaks, CA: Sage.

Reynolds, Paul Davidson. 1979. *Ethical dilemmas and social science research.* San Francisco: Jossey-Bass.

Richards, Thomas J. and Lyn Richards. 1994. Using computers in qualitative research. In *Handbook of qualitative research,* ed. Norman K. Denzin and Yvonna S. Lincoln, 445–462. Thousand Oaks, CA: Sage.

Richardson, Laurel. 1995. Narrative and sociology. In *Representation in ethnography,* ed. John Van Maanen, 198–221. Thousand Oaks, CA: Sage.

Ringwalt, Christopher L., Jody M. Greene, Susan T. Ennett, Ronaldo Iachan, Richard R. Clayton, and Carl G. Leukefeld. 1994. *Past and future directions of the D.A.R.E. program: An evaluation review.* Research Triangle Park, NC: Research Triangle Institute.

Rives, Norfleet W., Jr., and William J. Serow. 1988. *Introduction to applied demography: Data sources and estimation techniques.* Sage University Paper Series on Quantitative Applications in the Social Sciences, series No. 07-039. Thousand Oaks, CA: Sage.

Rosenberg, Morris. 1968. *The logic of survey analysis.* New York: Basic Books.

Rossi, Peter H. and Howard E. Freeman. 1989. *Evaluation: A systematic approach,* 4th ed. Newbury Park, CA: Sage.

Rossman, Gretchen B. and Sharon F. Rallis. 1998. *Learning in the field: An introduction to qualitative research.* Thousand Oaks, CA: Sage.

Rubin, Herbert J. and Irene S. Rubin. 1995. *Qualitative interviewing: The art of hearing data.* Thousand Oaks, CA: Sage.

Sacks, Stanley, Karen McKendrick, George DeLeon, Michael T. French, and Kathryn E. McCollister. 2002. Benefit-cost analysis of a modified therapeutic community for mentally ill chemical abusers. *Evaluation & Program Planning* 25:137–148.

Salisbury, Robert H. 1975. Research on political participation. *American Journal of Political Science* 19 (May): 323–341.

Sampson, Robert J. and John H. Laub. 1994. Urban poverty and the family context of delinquency: A new look at structure and process in a classic study. *Child Development* 65:523–540.

Sampson, Robert J. and Janet L. Lauritsen. 1994. Violent victimization and offending: individual-, situational-, and community-level risk factors. In *Social Influences,* vol. 3 of *Understanding and preventing violence,* ed. Albert J. Reiss, Jr. and Jeffrey A. Roth, 1–114. Washington, DC: National Academy Press.

Schalock, Robert and John Butterworth. 2000. *A benefit-cost analysis model for social service agencies.* Boston: Institute for Community Inclusion.

Scarce, Rik. 2005. *Eco-warriors: Understanding the radical environmental movement,* 2nd ed. Walnut Creek, CA: Left Coast Press.

Schleyer, Titus K. L. and Jane L. Forrest. 2000. Methods for the design and administration of Web-based surveys. *Journal of the American Medical Informatics Association* 7(4): 416–425.

Schober, Michael F. 1999. Making sense of survey questions. In *Cognition and survey research,* ed. Monroe G. Sirken, Douglas J. Herrmann, Susan Schechter, Norbert Schwartz, Judith M. Tanur, and Roger Tourangeau, 77–94. New York: Wiley.

Schorr, Lisbeth B. and Daniel Yankelovich. 2000. In search of a gold standard for social programs. *Boston Globe,* February 18, A19.

Schuman, Howard and Stanley Presser. 1981. *Questions and answers in attitude surveys: Experiments on question form, wording, and context.* New York: Academic Press.

Schutt, Russell K., Xiaogang Deng, Gerald R. Garrett, Stephanie Hartwell, Sylvia Mignon, Joseph Bebo, Matthew O'Neill, Mary Aruda, Pat Duynstee, Pam DiNapoli, and Helen Reiskin. 1996. Substance use and abuse among UMass Boston students. Unpublished report, Department of Sociology, University of Massachusetts, Boston.

Schutt, Russell K. and M. L. Fennell. 1992. Shelter staff satisfaction with services, the service network and their jobs. *Current Research on Occupations and Professions* 7:177–200.

Schutt, Russell K. and Stephen M. Goldfinger. 1996. Housing preferences and perceptions of health and functioning among mentally ill persons. *Psychiatric Services* 47(4): 381–386.

Scriven, Michael. 1972. Prose and cons about goal-free evaluation. *Evaluation Comment* 3:1–7.

Sherman, Lawrence W. 1992. *Policing domestic violence: Experiments and dilemmas.* New York: Free Press.

Sherman, Lawrence. W. 1993. Implications of a failure to read the literature. *American Sociological Review* 58:888–889.

Sherman, Lawrence W. and Richard A. Berk. 1984. The specific deterrent effects of arrest for domestic assault. *American Sociological Review* 49:261–272.

Sieber, Joan E. 1992. *Planning ethically responsible research: A guide for students and internal review boards.* Thousand Oaks, CA: Sage.

Sjoberg, Gideon, ed. 1967. *Ethics, politics, and social research.* Cambridge, MA: Schenkman.

Smith, Tom W. 1984. Nonattitudes: A review and evaluation. In *Surveying subjective phenomena,* vol. 2, ed. Charles F. Turner and Elizabeth Martin, 215–255. New York: Russell Sage Foundation.

Smith, Tom. 1987. That which we call welfare by any other name would smell sweeter: An analysis of the impact of question wording on response patterns. *Public Opinion Quarterly* 51(1): 75–83.

Smyth, Jolene D., Don A. Dillman, Leah Melani Christian, and Michael J. Stern. 2004. *How visual grouping influences answers to Internet surveys* (Technical Report #04-023). From Washington State University Social & Economic Sciences Research Center Web site: http://survey.sesrc.wsu .edu/dillman/papers.htm (accessed July 5, 2005). An extended version of paper presented at the 59th Annual Conference of the American Association for Public Opinion Research, Phoenix, AZ, May 13, 2004.

Stake, Robert E., ed. 1975. *Evaluating the arts in education: A responsible approach.* Columbus, OH: Merrill.

Stake, Robert E. 1995. *The art of case study research.* Thousand Oaks, CA: Sage.

Stille, Alexander. 2000. A happiness index with a long reach: Beyond G.N.P. to subtler measures. *New York Times,* May 20, A17, A19.

Straus, Murray and Richard Gelles. 1988. *Intimate violence.* New York: Simon & Schuster.

Strunk, William, Jr. and E. B. White. 1979. *The elements of style,* 3rd ed. New York: Macmillan.

Sudman, Seymour. 1976. *Applied sampling.* New York: Academic Press.

Survey.net. 2000. *Year 2000 presidential election survey.* From http://www.survey.net/sv-pres0.htm.

Taylor, Charles Lewis and David A. Jodice. 1986. *World handbook of political and social indicators III: 1948–1982.* File available from the Inter-University Consortium for Political and Social Research (ICPSR), Study #7761.

Taylor, Jerry. 1999. DARE gets updated in some area schools, others drop program. *Boston Sunday Globe,* May 16, 1, 11.

Thompson, Clive. 2007. Community urinalysis. *New York Times Magazine,* December 9. From http://www.nytimes.com/2007/12/09/magazine/09_11_urinalysis.html?ref=magazine (accessed September 28, 2008).

Thorne, Barrie. 1993. *Gender play: Girls and boys in school.* New Brunswick, NJ: Rutgers University Press.

Tjaden, Patricia and Nancy Thoennes. 2000. *Extent, nature, and consequences of intimate partner violence: Findings from the National Violence Against Women Survey* (NCJ 181867). Washington, DC: Office of Justice Programs, National Institute of Justice and the Centers for Disease Control and Prevention.

Toppo, Greg. 2002. Antidrug program backed by study. *Boston Globe,* October 29, A10.

Tourangeau, Roger, 2004. Survey research and societal change. *Annual Review of Psychology* 55:775–801.

Tufte, Edward R. 1983. *The visual display of quantitative information.* Cheshire, CT: Graphics Press.

Turabian, Kate L. 1967. *A manual for writers of term papers, theses, and dissertations,* 3rd rev. ed. Chicago: University of Chicago Press.

Turner, Charles F. and Elizabeth Martin, eds. 1984. *Surveying subjective phenomena.* 2 vols. New York: Russell Sage Foundation.

Tuskegee Syphilis Study administrative records. 1929–1972. Atlanta, GA: Records of the Centers for Disease Control and Prevention, National Archives—Southeast Region.

U.S. Bureau of the Census. 1994. *Census catalog and guide, 1994.* Washington, DC: Department of Commerce, U.S. Bureau of the Census.

U.S. Bureau of the Census. 1999. *United States census 2000, updated summary: Census 2000 Operational Plan.* Washington, DC: U.S. Department of Commerce, Bureau of the Census, February.

U.S. Bureau of Economic Analysis, Communications Division. 2004. *Customer satisfaction survey report, FY 2004.* Washington, DC: U.S. Department of Commerce. From http://www.bea.gov/ bea/about/cssr_2004_complete.pdf (accessed September 28, 2008).

U.S. Bureau of Labor Statistics, Department of Labor. 1991. *Major programs of the bureau of labor statistics.* Washington, DC: U.S. Bureau of Labor Statistics, Department of Labor.

U.S. Bureau of Labor Statistics, Department of Labor. 1997a. *Employment and earnings.* Washington, DC: U.S. Bureau of Labor Statistics, Department of Labor.

U.S. Bureau of Labor Statistics, Department of Labor. 1997b. *Handbook of methods.* Washington, DC: U.S. Bureau of Labor Statistics, Department of Labor.

U.S. Department of Health, Education, and Welfare. 1979. *The Belmont report: Ethical principles and guidelines for the protection of human subjects of research.* Washington, DC: Superintendent of Documents, U.S. Government Printing Office. (ERIC Document Reproduction Service No. ED183582)

U.S. Government Accounting Office. 2001. *Health and human services: Status of achieving key outcomes and addressing major management challenges* (GAO-01-748). From http://www .gao.gov/new.items/d01748.pdf (accessed September 28, 2008).

Van Maanen, John. 1995. An end to innocence: The ethnography of ethnography. In *Representation in ethnography*, ed. John Van Maanen, 1–35. Thousand Oaks, CA: Sage.

Van Maanen, John. 2002. The fact of fiction in organizational ethnography. In *The qualitative researcher's companion,* ed. A. Michael Huberman and Matthew B. Miles, 101–117. Thousand Oaks, CA: Sage.

Verba, Sidney and Norman Nie. 1972. *Political participation: Political democracy and social equality.* New York: Harper & Row.

Vernez, Georges M., Audrey Burnam, Elizabeth A. McGlynn, Sally Trude, and Brian S. Mirttman. 1988. *Review of California's program for the homeless mentally disabled* (R-3631-CDMH). Santa Monica, CA: RAND.

Wageman, Ruth. 1995. Interdependence and group effectiveness. *Administrative Science Quarterly* 40:145–180.

Wallgren, Anders, Britt Wallgren, Rolf Persson, Ulf Jorner, and Jan-Aage Haaland. 1996. *Graphing statistics and data: Creating better charts.* Thousand Oaks, CA: Sage.

Webb, Eugene J., Donald T. Campbell, Richard D. Schwartz, and Lee Sechrest. 2000. *Unobtrusive measures,* rev. ed. Thousand Oaks, CA: Sage.

Weber, Max. 1930/1992. *The Protestant ethic and the spirit of capitalism,* trans. Talcott Parsons. Repr. London: Routledge.

Weber, Max. 1947/1997. *The theory of social and economic organization,* trans. A. M. Henderson and Talcott Parsons. Repr. New York: Free Press.

Weber, Robert Philip. 1985. *Basic content analysis.* Thousand Oaks, CA: Sage.

Weitzman, Eben and M. B. Miles. 1994. *Computer programs for qualitative data analysis.* Thousand Oaks, CA: Sage.

Wheeler, Peter M. 1995. *Social security programs throughout the world—1995.* Research Report #64, SSA Publication No. 13–11805. Washington, DC: Office of Research and Statistics, Social Security Administration.

Wholey, J. S. 1987. Evaluability assessment: Developing program theory. In *Using program theory in evaluation: New directions for program evaluation* (no. 33), ed. Leonard Bickman, 77–92. San Francisco: Jossey-Bass.

Whyte, William Foote. 1955. *Street corner society.* Chicago: University of Chicago Press.

Wolcott, Harry F. 1995. *The art of fieldwork.* Walnut Creek, CA: AltaMira Press.

Yardley, William. 2008. Drawing lots for health care. *New York Times,* March 13. From http://www.nytimes.com/2008/03/13/us/13bend.html (accessed September 28, 2008).

Zimbardo, Philip G. 2007. *The Lucifer effect.* New York: Random House.

Credits

Chapter 1

Exhibit 1.1 From *Bowling Alone: The Collapse and Revival of American Community* by Robert D. Putnam. Copyright © 2000 by Robert D. Putnam. All rights reserved. Reprinted with the permission of Simon & Schuster, Inc.

Exhibit 1.4 From *Bowling Alone. The Collapse and Revival of American Community* by Robert D. Putnam. Copyright © 2000 by Robert D. Putnam. All rights reserved. Reprinted with the permission of Simon & Schuster, Inc.

Chapter 2

Exhibit 2.1 Data from Sherman & Berk, 1984:267.

Exhibit 2.5 The Gallup Organization. August 20, 2002. Poll Analyses, July 29, 2002. Bush Job Approval Update. http://www.gallup.com/poll/6478/Bush-Job-Approval-Update.aspx

Chapter 3

Exhibits 3.1, 3.2 From the film *Obedience* © 1968 by Stanley Milgram, © Renewed 1993 by Alexandra Milgram and distributed by Penn State, Media Sales.

Exhibit 3.4 Tuskegee Syphilis Study Administrative Records. Records of the Centers for Disease Control and Prevention. National Archives—Southeast Region (Atlanta).

Exhibit 3.5 Northeastern University Division of Research Integrity. http://www.research.neu.edu/research_integrity/images/scales.jpg

Exhibit 3.6 From *The Lucifer Effect* by Philip G. Zimbardo, copyright © 2007 by Phillip G. Zimbardo Inc. Used by permission of Random House, Inc.

Chapter 4

Exhibit 4.2 Lenore Radloff, 1977. "The CED-D Scale: A Self-Report Depression Scale for Research in the General Population." *Applied Psychological Measurement,* 1: 385-401. Reprinted by permission of Sage Publications, Inc.

Exhibit 4.4 Core Institute, Core Alcohol and Drug Survey, 1994. Carbondale, IL: Core Institute.

Exhibit 4.6 From the *Diagnostic and Statistical Manual of Mental Disorders, Text Revision,* 4th ed. Copyright © 2000. American Psychiatric Association. Reprinted with permission.

Chapter 5

Exhibit 5.3 Election Outcomes: Predicted and Actual 1960-1992 Poll Data: The Gallup Poll (Loth, 1992), 1996 poll data: The Gallup Poll http://www.gallup.com/poll/110548/Gallup-Presidential-Election-TrialHeat-Trends-19362004.aspx

Chapter 6

Exhibit 6.4 Ruth Wageman, 1995. "Interdependence and Group Effectiveness." *Administrative Science Quarterly* 40:145–180.

Exhibit 6.5 David P. Phillips, 1982. "The Impact of Fictional Television Stories on U.S. Adult Fatalities: New Evidence on the Effect of the Mass Media on Violence." *American Journal of Sociology* 87:1340. Copyright © 1982 by the University of Chicago Press.

Chapter 7

Exhibit 7.1 Filter Questions and Skip Patterns, Youth and Guns Survey, 2000.

Exhibit 7.2 Sample Interview Guide, Youth and Guns Survey, 2000.

Exhibit 7.5 Sample Interviewer Instructions, Youth and Guns Survey, 2000.

Exhibit 7.6 Survey.Net. Courtesy Otterbein College.

Exhibit 7.7 Adapted from Don A. Dillman, *Mail and Telephone Surveys: The Total Design Method* (New York: Wiley, 1978), 74–75. Copyright © 1978 Don A. Dillman.

Chapter 8

Exhibit 8.1 General Social Survey, National Opinion Research Center, 2006.

Exhibit 8.2 U.S. Bureau of Economic Analysis, 2004:14.

Exhibit 8.3 General Social Survey, National Opinion Research Center, 2006.

Exhibit 8.4 General Social Survey, National Opinion Research Center, 2006.

Exhibit 8.5 General Social Survey, National Opinion Research Center, 2006.

Exhibit 8.6 Adapted from Orcutt & Turner, 1993. Copyright 1993 by the Society for the Study of Social Problems. Reprinted by permission.

Exhibit 8.7 General Social Survey, National Opinion Research Center 2006.

Exhibit 8.8 General Social Survey, National Opinion Research Center 2006.

Exhibit 8.9 General Social Survey, National Opinion Research Center 2006.

Exhibit 8.13 General Social Survey, National Opinion Research Center 2006.

Exhibit 8.14 General Social Survey, National Opinion Research Center 2006.

Exhibit 8.15 General Social Survey, National Opinion Research Center 2006.

Exhibit 8.17 General Social Survey, National Opinion Research Center 2006.

Chapter 9

Exhibit 9.7 Adapted from Richard A. Krueger and Mary Anne Casey, 2000. *Focus Groups: A Practical Guide for Applied Research,* 3rd ed. Copyright SAGE Publications. Used with permission.

Chapter 10

Exhibit 10.1 Miles & Huberman, 1994:95, Table 5.2. Copyright SAGE Publications. Used with permission.

Exhibit 10.2 Miles & Huberman, 1994:95, Table 5.2. Copyright SAGE Publications. Used with permission.

Exhibit 10.3 Patton, 2002:472.

Exhibit 10.4 Miles & Huberman, 1994:159, Figure 6.5. Copyright SAGE Publications. Used with permission.

Exhibit 10.5 Morrill et al., 2000:553, Table 1. Copyright 2000. Reprinted with permission of Blackwell Publishing Ltd.

Exhibit 10.6 Gibson, 2005:1566. Reprinted with permission from the *American Journal of Sociology.*

Exhibit 10.7 Margolis, 2004:78.

Chapter 11

Exhibit 11.1 Adapted from Martin and Kettner, 1996. Reprinted with permission from Sage Publications Inc.

Exhibit 11.3 From DeParle, Jason, 1999. "Project to Rescue Needy Stumbles Against the Persistence of Poverty." *The New York Times*, May 15:A1, A10. Reprinted with permission.

Exhibit 11.4 Based on Goldfinger and Schutt, 1996.

Exhibit 11.5 Chen, 1990:210. Reprinted with permission from SAGE Publications.

Exhibit 11.6 Drake et al., 1996:391–399. From the New Hampshire Study of Supported Employment for People With Severe Mental Illness in the *Journal of Consulting and Clinical Psychology* 64:391-399. Used with permission.

Exhibit 11.7 Orr, 1999:224. Reprinted with permission of SAGE Publications.

Chapter 12

Exhibit 12.5 Robert H. Aseltine Jr. and Ronald C. Kessler, 1993. "Marital Disruption and Depression in a Community Sample." *Journal of Health and Social Behavior*, 34 (September):237–251.

Exhibit 12.6 Georges M. Vernez, Audrey Burnam, Elizabeth A. McGlynn, Sally Trude, and Brian S. Mirttman, 1988. *Review of California's Program for the Homeless Mentally Disabled.* Santa Monica, CA: RAND, R-3631-CDMH.

Exhibit 12.7 Schutt et al., 1996.

Glossary/Index